Applied Optimization in Automatic Control and Systems Engineering

Applied Optimization in Automatic Control and Systems Engineering

Guest Editor

Guillermo Valencia-Palomo

MDPI

Basel • Beijing • Wuhan • Barcelona • Belgrade • Novi Sad • Cluj • Manchester

Guest Editor
Guillermo Valencia-Palomo
Tecnológico Nacional de
México
Instituto Tecnológico de
Hermosillo
Hermosillo
Mexico

Editorial Office
MDPI AG
Grosspeteranlage 5
4052 Basel, Switzerland

This is a reprint of the Special Issue, published open access by the journal *Mathematical and Computational Applications* (ISSN 2297-8747), freely accessible at: https://www.mdpi.com/journal/mca/special_issues/O70J996J9R.

For citation purposes, cite each article independently as indicated on the article page online and as indicated below:

Lastname, A.A.; Lastname, B.B. Article Title. *Journal Name* **Year**, *Volume Number*, Page Range.

ISBN 978-3-7258-7885-7 (Hbk)
ISBN 978-3-7258-7886-4 (PDF)
https://doi.org/10.3390/books978-3-7258-7886-4

Contents

About the Editor

Guillermo Valencia-Palomo

Guillermo Valencia-Palomo was born in Mérida, Mexico, in 1980. He received his Engineering degree in Electronics from the TecNM-IT Mérida in 2003, his M.Sc. degree in Automatic Control from CENIDET in 2006, and his Ph.D. degree in Automatic Control and Systems Engineering from the University of Sheffield, U.K. in 2010. Since 2010, he has been a Full-time (Tenured) Professor at the Tecnológico Nacional de México-IT Hermosillo. He is the author/co-author of over 90 research papers published in JCR-indexed journals and several international conferences. He has led numerous funded research projects, including sole-investigator grants and industry-funded collaborative grants. His research interests focus on predictive control, linear parameter varying systems, fault detection, fault-tolerant control, and their applications to various physical systems. He is a member of the Editorial Board of *Mathematical and Computational Applications*. He is an Associate Editor of *IEEE Access*, *International Journal of Aerospace Engineering*, and *IEEE Latin America Transactions*.

Mathematical and Computational Applications

Editorial

Advances in Applied Optimization in Automatic Control and Systems Engineering

Guillermo Valencia-Palomo

Tecnológico Nacional de México, Instituto Tecnológico de Hermosillo, Av. Tecnológico 115, Hermosillo 83170, Mexico; gvalencia@hermosillo.tecnm.mx

Applied optimization in automatic control and systems engineering involves developing and implementing mathematical methods to improve the performance and efficiency of automated systems. This interdisciplinary field combines principles from control theory and computational algorithms to design and fine-tune systems for optimal operation. Techniques such as linear programming, nonlinear optimization, and dynamic programming are used to solve complex problems in real time, ensuring that systems respond effectively to changing conditions and constraints. Applications range from industrial automation and robotics to aerospace and energy systems, where optimizing parameters such as speed, accuracy, and resource use is crucial for achieving desired outcomes. Through continuous advancements, applied optimization in automatic control and systems engineering drives innovation and enhances the capabilities of modern automated systems.

This Special Issue aims to highlight the importance of optimization techniques in automatic control and engineering systems. To this end, it brings together fifteen high-quality articles that address diverse problems, including tuning fractional-order and proportional–integral–derivative controllers, sliding-mode strategies, and deep-learning-based supervisory systems. All of these articles share the goal to apply optimization methods to improve system stability, robustness, responsiveness, and efficiency.

Meena et al. [1] provide an overview of algorithms for analyzing power flows and short-circuit modes in microgrids across two operating modes: network and isolated. The results of a comparative analysis of various methods, such as Newton–Raphson and backward/forward sweeps, for analyzing power flows and short-circuit modes, as well as approaches to modeling various components of microgrids. The article's content is of interest, as the mass development of microgrids requires the use of the most technically effective methods with minimal financial costs for implementation.

Zambou et al. [2] introduce a hybrid algorithm for maximum power point tracking (MPPT) of a photovoltaic system under partial shading conditions, achieving fast convergence and low oscillation. This is done by integrating a nonlinear discrete proportional–derivative (PID) controller with the classical perturbation–observation algorithm. The PID controller parameters are optimized using particle swarm optimization (PSO). The result is a scheme that improves response speed, reduces oscillations around the operating point, and increases efficiency under various environmental conditions.

Mansouri et al. [3] present a fault-tolerant control (FTC) strategy for Linear Parameter Varying (LPV) systems with variable delays combining an observer and a sliding-mode controller. The proposed scheme formulates the FTC design problem using Lyapunov–Krasovskii functionals and multi-objective Linear Matrix Inequality (LMI) conditions to balance robustness, performance, and stability. The adaptability of the FTC approach effectively handles uncertainties, nonlinearities, and delay variations, demonstrating effective integration with optimization tools.

Clempner [4] addresses the long-standing challenge of incomplete information in security games by using a Bayesian Markov game model and an associated reinforcement learning (RL) technique. This research problem is indeed important in security game research and has caught wide attention from the security community. The main contribution of the manuscript is a systematic method that combines stochastic modeling, a proximal gradient approach for equilibrium computation, a Bayesian RL technique, and a random-walk approach for implementation.

Montoya et al. [5] present a work on the formulation and solution of the power flow problem for bipolar direct current networks with unbalanced constant power loads. An integrated nonlinear model is proposed that represents monopolar and bipolar load configurations, as well as voltage coupling between conductors. Different iterative algorithms based on Newtonian and quasi-Newtonian methods with constant Jacobian approximations are developed and compared. The proposed approach provides key elements for efficiently resolving operational and planning problems in modern electrical networks.

Gu and Xi [6] introduce an integral strategy for the optimal design of the diagnosticability of unmanned aerial vehicles, combining structural analysis with a quantitative metric based on the mean and covariance discrepancy and an optimization scheme using the Grey-Wolf algorithm. Starting with the generation of residuals using structurally overdetermined sets, a framework is established that enables the evaluation and improvement of fault detection and isolation capabilities, while accounting for the system's causal relationships. The proposal is validated in simulation, demonstrating significant improvements with respect to other methods in the literature.

Phan Thi et al. [7] tackle the problem of secure control and communication of electric drive systems in wireless environments. It combines a neural network-based controller with fuzzy emotional learning and a disturbance observer to enhance robustness against uncertainties and attacks. The approach is implemented on an embedded ESP32 microcontroller to conduct experimental tests validating secure real-time transmission.

Ahmed et al. [8] have developed an energy management system for electric vehicles. This system optimally manages batteries and ultracapacitors using control strategies to distribute power dynamics and recover energy through regenerative braking. The system improves overall efficiency, dynamic performance, and the lifespan of the energy storage system. The proposal is validated in numerical simulations and experimentally.

Barroso-García et al. [9] present a comprehensive evaluation of the energy performance of a compressed air system based on a screw compressor operating under real-world, variable-load conditions. It combines experimental measurements and thermodynamic modeling to identify significant deviations from nominal efficiency. Based on this analysis, operational limitations associated with low-demand regimes are identified, and techno-economic strategies, such as reactive power compensation and the adoption of more flexible operating schemes, are proposed to improve overall system performance.

Ben Alaia et al. [10] propose an adaptive observer with fixed-time convergence for perturbed systems with varying parameters, incorporating an online perturbation learning mechanism that eliminates the need for prior bounds and significantly improves noise rejection through a non-diagonal gain structure. Using a formulation based on parameter-dependent Lyapunov functions and less conservative LMI conditions, the method enables a systematic design that balances performance, robustness, and computational feasibility, as demonstrated in power system applications with substantial improvements in convergence speed and steady-state error.

Obeidat et al. [11] present a systematic literature review on the Preference Selection Index (PSI) within the framework of multi-criteria decision-making. The review consists of a detailed critical analysis of over 100 studies, identifying the strengths and weaknesses

https://doi.org/10.3390/mca31020061

of PSIs. The review includes the methodological background, areas of application, and integration with other techniques and ends with proposed future research directions to improve robustness and adaptability.

Du and Mao [12] propose a controller design approach for active suspensions based on modal-structure optimization, integrating partial self-structure allocation with a dynamic-response optimization scheme. By formulating a minimization problem that simultaneously considers vibration performance and energy consumption, the method enables the redistribution of dominant modes and the adjustment of system dynamics to improve vehicle comfort and stability. Numerical results demonstrate significant reductions in acceleration and body roll, as well as adequate robustness to uncertainties.

Sullivan et al. [13] introduce a novel framework for analyzing the behavior of convolutional neural networks from a data-centric perspective through the programmatic generation of synthetic sets that allow for the isolation and quantification of the contribution of specific features. Based on a theoretical formulation that links CNN learning with apriori-type pattern counting principles, the authors demonstrate that feature overlap across datasets can accurately predict model performance, eliminating the need for extensive training. The results show that intrinsic object characteristics dominate generalization capacity and validate a similarity algorithm that acts as a performance estimator.

Kumar and Shaik [14] present a reformulation of a mixed-integer programming model for medium- and long-term planning and scheduling in multi-stage biopharmaceutical processes. The representation of product life cycles and inventory management is modified using new binary variables and linear constraints. This modification helps to reduce computational complexity and to increase the cost-effectiveness and quality of solutions compared to previous approaches. Results obtained from case studies demonstrate greater efficiency in resource allocation and in meeting demands under realistic operational constraints.

Liu et al. [15] address the problem of emergency facility location and layout, which are critical to the efficiency of emergency rescue and resource allocation. For this, they formulate an optimization model that maximizes satisfaction with respect to response time. The problem addressed considers facility failures caused by uncertain factors and complex polygonal barriers that hinder transportation. The Artificial Ecosystem Optimization (AEO) algorithm is employed to obtain the solution. Numerical experiments and a practical case study are used to validate the method's effectiveness.

The papers in this Special Issue show how applied optimization continues to evolve and improve the field of automatic control and systems engineering. We thank all authors for their valuable contributions and the reviewers for their careful and constructive evaluations. We hope this Special Issue inspires further innovation and collaboration.

Funding: This research has been supported by Tecnológico Nacional de México under the program Proyectos de Investigación Científica y Desarrollo Tecnológico e Innovación and the international network Red Internacional de Control y Cómputo Aplicado.

Conflicts of Interest: The author declares no conflicts of interest.

References

1. Meena, G.; Meena, V.; Mathur, A.; Singh, V.P.; Azar, A.T.; Hameed, I.A. Optimizing Power Flow and Stability in Hybrid AC/DC Microgrids: AC, DC, and Combined Analysis. *Math. Comput. Appl.* **2024**, *29*, 108. [CrossRef]
2. Zambou, M.C.Z.; Kammogne, A.S.T.; Siewe, M.S.; Azar, A.T.; Ahmed, S.; Hameed, I.A. Optimized Nonlinear PID Control for Maximum Power Point Tracking in PV Systems Using Particle Swarm Optimization. *Math. Comput. Appl.* **2024**, *29*, 88. Erratum in *Math. Comput. Appl.* **2025**, *30*, 32. [CrossRef]
3. Mansouri, O.; Ben Brahim, A.; Ben Hmida, F.; Sellami, A. Sliding Mode Fault-Tolerant Control for Nonlinear LPV Systems with Variable Time-Delay. *Math. Comput. Appl.* **2024**, *29*, 96. [CrossRef]

https://doi.org/10.3390/mca31020061

4. Clempner, J.B. Learning Deceptive Tactics for Defense and Attack in Bayesian–Markov Stackelberg Security Games. *Math. Comput. Appl.* **2025**, *30*, 29. [CrossRef]
5. Montoya, O.D.; Pulgarín Rivera, J.D.; Grisales-Noreña, L.F.; Gil-González, W.; Andrade-Rengifo, F. A Family of Newton and Quasi-Newton Methods for Power Flow Analysis in Bipolar Direct Current Networks with Constant Power Loads. *Math. Comput. Appl.* **2025**, *30*, 50. [CrossRef]
6. Gu, X.; Shi, X. Causal Diagnosability Optimization Design for UAVs Based on Maximum Mean Covariance Difference and the Gray Wolf Optimization Algorithm. *Math. Comput. Appl.* **2025**, *30*, 55. [CrossRef]
7. Phan Thi, H.C.; Dang, N.Q.; Giap, V.N. Secure Communication of Electric Drive System Using Chaotic Systems Base on Disturbance Observer and Fuzzy Brain Emotional Learning Neural Network. *Math. Comput. Appl.* **2025**, *30*, 73. Erratum in *Math. Comput. Appl.* **2025**, *30*, 118. [CrossRef]
8. Ahmed, A.A.; Lee, Y.I.; Al Dawsari, S.; Diab, A.A.Z.; Ezzat, A.A. Energy Management and Power Distribution for Battery/Ultracapacitor Hybrid Energy Storage System in Electric Vehicles with Regenerative Braking Control. *Math. Comput. Appl.* **2025**, *30*, 82. [CrossRef]
9. Barrosso-García, G.J.; Monteagudo-Yanes, J.P.; Iturralde-Carera, L.A.; Constantino-Robles, C.D.; Juárez-Santiago, B.; Olivares-Ramírez, J.M.; Rodríguez-Abreo, O.; Rodríguez-Reséndiz, J. Energy Optimization of Compressed Air Systems with Screw Compressors Under Variable Load Conditions. *Math. Comput. Appl.* **2025**, *30*, 107. [CrossRef]
10. Alaia, E.B.; Dhahri, S.; Naifar, O. Adaptive Observer Design with Fixed-Time Convergence, Online Disturbance Learning, and Low-Conservatism Linear Matrix Inequalities for Time-Varying Perturbed Systems. *Math. Comput. Appl.* **2025**, *30*, 112. [CrossRef]
11. Obeidat, M.S.; Al Sliti, H.; Obeidat, A. The Preference Selection Index (PSI) in Multi-Criteria Decision-Making: A Systematic and Critical Review of Applications, Integrations, and Future Directions. *Math. Comput. Appl.* **2025**, *30*, 124. [CrossRef]
12. Du, Y.; Mao, H. Eigenstructure-Oriented Optimization Design of Active Suspension Controllers. *Math. Comput. Appl.* **2026**, *31*, 5. [CrossRef]
13. O'Sullivan, E.; Kennedy, K.; Mohammadi-Aragh, J. Gaining Understanding of Neural Networks with Programmatically Generated Data. *Math. Comput. Appl.* **2026**, *31*, 16. [CrossRef]
14. Kumar, V.; Shaik, M.A. Revised Long-Term Scheduling Model for Multi-Stage Biopharmaceutical Processes. *Math. Comput. Appl.* **2026**, *31*, 32. [CrossRef]
15. Liu, M.; Liu, L.; Yu, Z.; Liang, F.; Wang, G. Reliable Emergency Facility Location Planning Under Complex Polygonal Barriers and Facility Failure Risks. *Math. Comput. Appl.* **2026**, *31*, 50. [CrossRef]

https://doi.org/10.3390/mca31020061

Mathematical and Computational Applications

MDPI

Review

Optimizing Power Flow and Stability in Hybrid AC/DC Microgrids: AC, DC, and Combined Analysis

Ghanshyam Meena [1], Veerpratap Meena [2,*], Akhilesh Mathur [1], Vinay Pratap Singh [1], Ahmad Taher Azar [3,4,5,*] and Ibrahim A. Hameed [6,*]

[1] Department of Electrical Engineering, Malaviya National Institute of Technology, Jaipur 302017, Rajasthan, India; 2021ree9526@mnit.ac.in (G.M.); akhilesh.ee@mnit.ac.in (A.M.); vinay.ee@mnit.ac.in (V.P.S.)
[2] Department of Electrical Engineering, National Institute of Technology Jamshedpur, Jamshedpur 831014, Jharkhand, India
[3] College of Computer and Information Sciences, Prince Sultan University, Riyadh 11586, Saudi Arabia
[4] Automated Systems and Soft Computing Lab (ASSCL), Prince Sultan University, Riyadh 11586, Saudi Arabia
[5] Faculty of Computers and Artificial Intelligence, Benha University, Benha 13518, Egypt
[6] Department of ICT and Natural Sciences, Norwegian University of Science and Technology, Larsgårdsvegen 2, 6009 Ålesund, Norway
* Correspondence: vmeena1@ee.iitr.ac.in (V.M.); aazar@psu.edu.sa (A.T.A.); ibib@ntnu.no (I.A.H.)

Abstract: A microgrid (MG) is a unique area of a power distribution network that combines distributed generators (conventional as well as renewable power sources) and energy storage systems. Due to the integration of renewable generation sources, microgrids have become more unpredictable. MGs can operate in two different modes, namely, grid-connected and islanded modes. MGs face various challenges of voltage variations, frequency deviations, harmonics, unbalances, etc., due to the uncertain behavior of renewable sources. To study the impact of these issues, it is necessary to analyze the behavior of the MG system under normal and abnormal operating conditions. Two different tools are used for the analysis of microgrids under normal and abnormal conditions, namely, power flow and short-circuit analysis, respectively. Power flow analysis is used to determine the voltages, currents, and real and reactive power flow in the MG system under normal operating conditions. Short-circuit analysis is carried out to analyze the behavior of MGs under faulty conditions. In this paper, a review of power flow and short-circuit analysis algorithms for MG systems under two different modes of operation, grid-connected and islanded, is presented. This paper also presents a comparison of various power flow as well as short-circuit analysis techniques for MGs in tabular form. The modeling of different components of MGs is also discussed in this paper.

Keywords: distributed generation (DG); islanded microgrid; droop control; AC microgrids; DC microgrids; hybrid AC/DC microgrids

1. Introduction

Recently, the penetration of distributed energy resources (DERs) has expanded, and renewable energy resources are the forefront of these. The combination of distributed generation (DG) penetration and the development of active distribution networks (ADNs) has led to a growing interest in microgrids (MGs). MGs can effectively integrate DGs, energy storage, and advanced control systems to create localized and resilient energy systems. In comparison to traditional AC networks, DC MGs have many advantages:

- System efficiency is high because fewer conversion stages are necessary to connect electronic and nonlinear loads.
- More cost-effective energy storage and DG units based on DC, such as solar and fuel cells.
- More appropriate and efficient methods for DC loads, like LED lighting and electric vehicles (EVs).

- Small connecting interface with AC grids because of no synchronization and also has a more flexible energy paradigm for future expansion.

A small network made from these DGs is called an MG. An MG consists of DGs, distribution lines (AC and DC), distributed loads, energy storage systems (ESSs), etc. A hybrid MG is a promising solution for smart grid implementation in conventional distribution networks. It brings together the benefits of both AC and DC MG distribution systems, enabling direct integration of energy resources, loads, and ESSs [1,2]. A comparison of different existing review papers is presented in Table 1. This table focuses on a comparison of the existing review papers regarding the various architectures (AC, DC, and hybrid AC/DC) of microgrids. The table uses a check mark (✓) to indicate that a particular aspect is covered in a specific reference, and a cross mark (×) indicates that part is not covered in that reference regarding the microgrid architectures, interlinking converters (ILCs), power flow analysis (PFA), and short-circuit analysis (SCA). ILCs are essential to integrating AC and DC microgrid systems. Table 1 includes every aspect (AC, DC, AC/DC structures, ILC, PFA, and SCA), providing a more comprehensive review than most previous reviews, which frequently overlooked one or more components.

Table 1. Comparison of existing review papers.

Ref.	Year	Architecture			ILC	PFA	SCA
		AC	DC	AC/DC			
[3]	2007	✓	×	×	×	✓	×
[4]	2008	✓	×	×	×	✓	×
[5]	2012	✓	×	×	×	✓	×
[6]	2017	✓	✓	×	×	✓	×
[7]	2017	✓	×	✓	×	✓	×
[8]	2018	✓	×	×	×	✓	×
[9]	2020	✓	×	×	×	×	×
[10]	2020	✓	✓	×	×	×	×
[11]	2021	×	×	✓	✓	×	×
[12]	2023	×	×	✓	✓	✓	×
This review	2024	✓	✓	✓	✓	✓	✓

Note: ILC—interlinking converter; PFA—power flow analysis; SCA—short-circuit analysis.

Power flow studies are critical in the planning and design of future power system growth. Deregulation in the system has increased interest in rising DG penetration, which can meet the requirements of local loads on its own. It is a vital technique for studying the system's functioning. For optimal system reliability and efficiency, operators should conduct power flow assessments of MGs [13]. MGs can operate in islanded mode or be connected to a grid. The main grid maintains the system's voltage and frequency in grid-linked mode; however, in islanded mode, the system's voltage and frequency are not constant due to the absence of a slack bus [14,15].

Since the 1950s, conventional algorithms of power flow such as backward/forward sweep (BFS), Newton–Raphson, and Gauss–Seidel have been extensively used in AC systems. In the islanded mode of operation, droop-controlled DGs increase the computational difficulty of power flow for voltage and frequency regulation, and most of the conventional approaches are invalid. Analysis of islanded MGs' power flow is shown to have been achieved by various modified or latest-load flow techniques in the literature review section. In [16], load flows for an island MG are solved using the usual approach, where the DG of greatest rating is selected as the slack node, and the rest of the DGs are represented as PQ or PV buses. The approach assumes that an islanded MG's frequency is constant.

In a power system, different types of faults exist; these faults can be symmetrical or unsymmetrical. Symmetrical faults are usually considered three-phase faults. Unsymmetrical faults include line-to-ground (L-G), line-to-line (L-L), and double line-to-ground (LL-G) faults [17]. In the case of MG systems, the probability of a symmetrical fault occurring is very low, and unsymmetrical faults occur in most cases. The L-G fault is the most probable kind of fault in the electrical system. All probable faults must be tested for potential breaches of relay sensitivity, fuse breaking capability, and earth fault current levels. Therefore, online SCA methods should ideally meet two fundamental requirements: rapidity and precision. Modeling of the components used for SCA is described in reference [18].

The online process of fault analysis is typically performed periodically, either automatically or in response to a request for topology adjustment. Many approaches based on the concept of short-circuit calculation have been presented in [19]. These approaches take a slack node into account with a set voltage that feeds large fault currents. Due to the absence of slack nodes and the use of modest current-limiting IBDGs, islanded MGs have significantly lower levels of fault currents. In the case of islanded MGs, the author proposed a mathematical formulation in [20] for short-circuit current calculation based on a concept that cancels out slack bus influence. Short-circuit calculations for many probable fault locations are presented in [21–25].

The uniqueness of this survey includes having an in-depth investigation of short-circuit evaluation for both DC and AC MG networks under faulty circumstances, employing the concept of bidirectional ILCs. This paper also stands out by providing a full comparison with other previous MG assessments, which address topics such as issues of power distribution, sharing control, and protection mechanisms. As a result, it stands out as a complete resource, providing scholars with important information to expand their research boundaries in the field of MGs.

This work provides an extensive review of existing papers on power flow studies and short-circuit analysis methodologies for MGs. The proposed survey demonstrates the need for a good solution to tackle power flow and control problems in islanded and grid-supplied MG operations. An analysis of an electric system's power flow typically entails computing the voltage of nodes and the quantity of power flowing through the lines of a particular load. An exhaustive survey for short-circuit analysis of MGs is also carried out for both AC and DC MG systems by considering faulty conditions. The major highlights of the contribution are as follows:

- The study includes an extensive review of existing research on power flow investigations and short-circuit analysis approaches for different architectures of microgrids (MGs).
- The paper addresses the importance of solving power flow and control issues using the droop control techniques of DGs.
- Mathematical modeling of the various components used in AC, DC, and hybrid AC/DC MGs is incorporated for both islanded and grid-connected modes of operation.
- The investigation addresses a thorough analysis of short-circuit situations in both AC and DC MG systems, taking into consideration different types of faults.

The organization of this paper is as follows: Section 2 illustrates different MG architectures. Section 3 explains the modeling of different components used in AC, DC, and AC/DC coupled hybrid MG systems. Section 4 provides an exhaustive literature survey on power flow and short-circuit techniques used in MG distribution systems. Methodologies for power flow analysis and short-circuit analysis are described in Section 5. Section 6 highlights the key areas of promising scientific research discussed in this paper. Section 7 provides the conclusion of the whole paper on the basis of both parts: power flow and short-circuit analysis.

2. Different Architectures of Microgrids

Normally, an MG is a combination of distributed energy resources, lines, different types of controllers, and loads. Different MGs, e.g., DC, AC, and AC/DC coupled MGs, have been discussed in [12]. Methods of interlinking converter control have been discussed for the hybrid AC/DC coupled architecture of MGs. Issues related to power flow, short-circuit, and stability improvement methods in MGs are discussed, which depend on different factors such as voltage (v) and frequency (f). An MG's basic configuration and classification are shown in Figure 1. This explains the types of MGs, the modes in which

MGs operate, and the different sources (hydro, diesel, wind, solar, etc.) used in MG distribution systems.

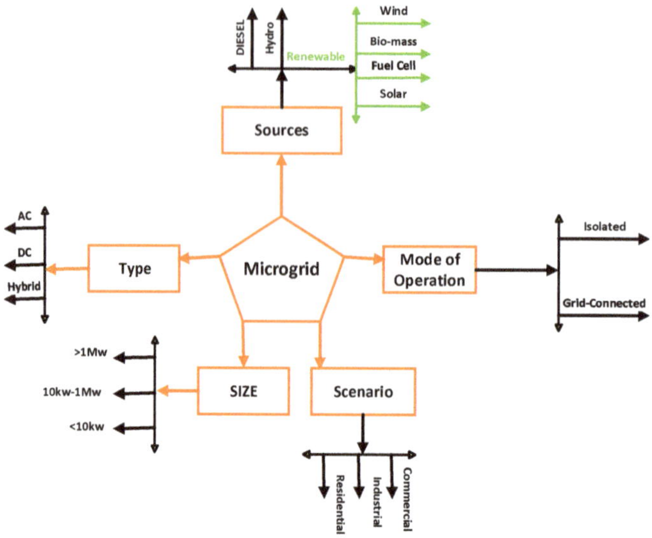

Figure 1. Configurations and classification of MGs.

2.1. DC Microgrid

In the case of a DC MG, loads are directly connected to the DC node. All energy storage elements and DERs are attached to the DC bus with the help of the converter topology, shown in Figure 2. A DC subgrid can be unipolar or bipolar. A unipolar DC subgrid is a two-wire network with just one voltage level, whereas a bipolar DC subgrid is a three-wire network (positive, neutral, or negative) with two voltage levels. Energy storage elements are connected to the bus using a bidirectional converter, according to Figure 2.

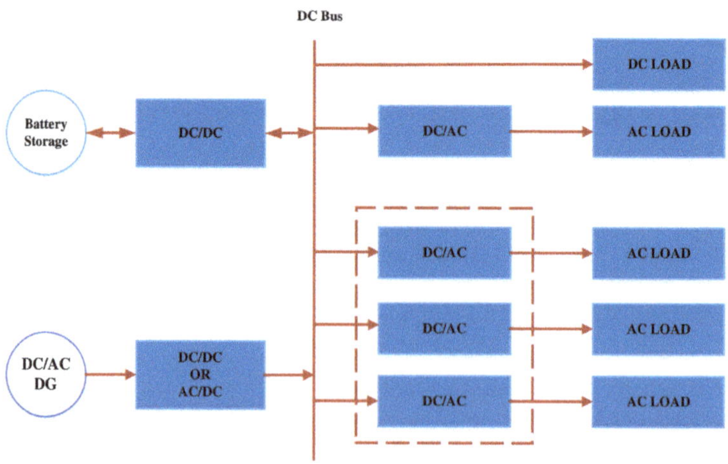

Figure 2. Architecture of DC MG.

2.2. AC Microgrid

In the AC MG structure, loads are directly connected to the AC bus. The connections between storage elements and DGs are explained in Figure 3. Energy storage elements are coupled with an AC bus with the help of a bidirectional converter interface. The voltage (V) and frequency (f) of the AC bus are maintained with the help of the grid in cases where it is grid-connected. In the case of islanded mode, an optimal control technique with supply and demand balance is used to maintain the AC bus voltage and frequency.

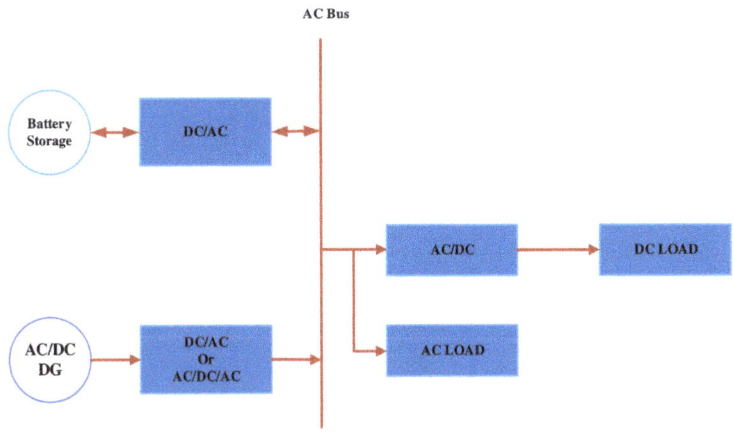

Figure 3. Architecture of AC MG.

2.3. Hybrid AC/DC Coupled Microgrid

The architecture of a hybrid AC/DC MG is depicted in Figure 4; it includes both AC and DC sections of the MG system. A hybrid MG is a combination of DC and AC subgrids linked with interlinking converters (ILCs) that can operate in various modes. DGs with AC generation are connected to the AC bus. DC-generated DGs are connected to the DC bus. The ILC used in the system acts as a bidirectional converter that can transfer power from the DC to the AC bus and vice versa. It can reduce power conversion losses and lower costs by reducing the number of converters used in MG systems. Various energy conversion topologies for hybrid AC/DC microgrids, including both DC and AC systems, are discussed in [26,27]. These references offer a more comprehensive view of the different configurations used in energy conversion chains within hybrid microgrids.

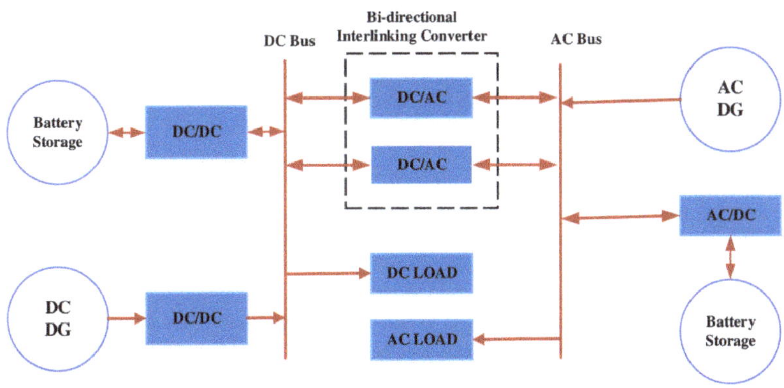

Figure 4. Architecture of AC/DC hybrid MG.

3. Modeling of Hybrid AC/DC Microgrid

The basic architecture of an AC/DC hybrid MG is given in Figure 4, which consists of DGs, loads, distribution lines, and interlinking converters.

3.1. Modeling of AC DERs

Power electronic components can be divided into voltage-controlled voltage source inverters (VCVSIs) and current-controlled voltage source inverters (CCVSIs), which are typically used to integrate DGs into MGs. The frequency and voltages of DGs can be changed or adjusted by VCVSIs. By using VCVSIs, voltage and frequency can be separately controlled within given ranges, especially in the case of islanded mode. Consider a model in which frequency and voltage are used for the function of real and reactive power, as provided in (1) and (2), respectively, for a DG connected to an AC bus *i*. The droop control characteristics of DG are explained in Figure 5, which shows the P-V and Q-V relationship [28].

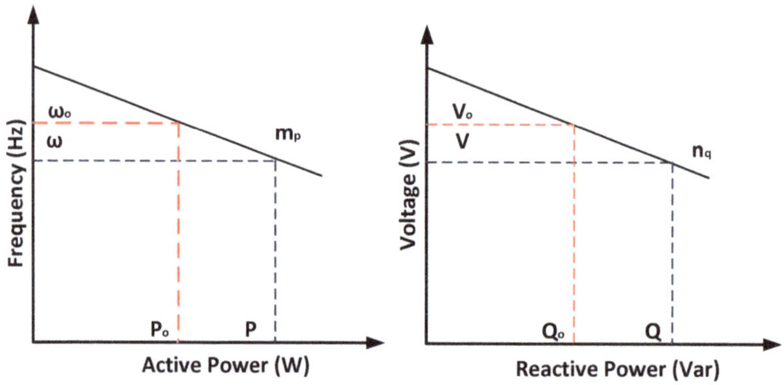

Figure 5. Droop control characteristics.

$$\omega = \omega_0 - m_p P_i, \tag{1}$$

$$V_i = V_0 - n_q Q_i, \tag{2}$$

where $i = 1, 2, 3, \cdots, N_{dg}$.

$$m_p = \frac{\omega_{max} - \omega_{min}}{P_{max,i}}, \tag{3}$$

$$n_q = \frac{|V|_{max} - |V|_{min}}{Q_{max,i}}, \tag{4}$$

Droop gains of DG units are represented in the form of active (m_p) and reactive (n_q) power gains. N_{dg} is the number of DG units.

ω_{max} and ω_{min} are the highest and lowest allowable frequencies. V_{max} and V_{min} are the AC subgrid's maximum and minimum allowable voltages.

3.2. Modeling of IBDGs

An islanded mode of operation is considered a case of a virtual slack bus, including IBDGs. IBDG sequence components are given in Figure 6. According to Figure 6, modeling of the positive sequence component is achieved with the help of virtual impedance (Z_{DG_virt1}) and a voltage source (V_{virt_pos}). With the assistance of the component's virtual impedances, the modeling of zero-sequence and negative-sequence components was completed.

$$V_{pos} = V_{virt\_pos} - I_{pos}.Z_{DG\_virt1} \tag{5}$$

$$V_{neg} = -I_{neg}.Z_{DG\_virt2} \tag{6}$$

$$V_{zero} = -I_{zero}.Z_{DG\_virt0} \tag{7}$$

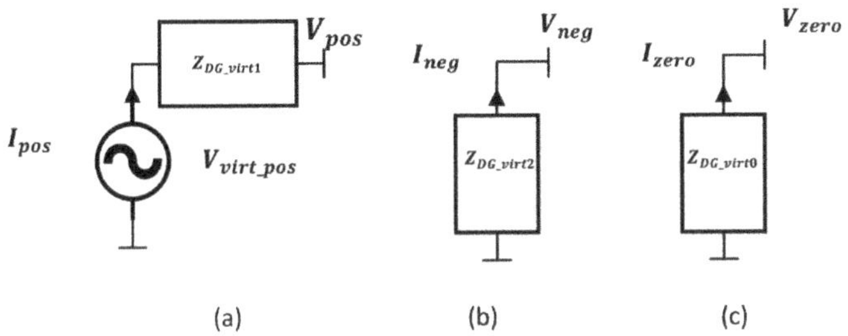

Figure 6. (**a**) Positive-sequence, (**b**) negative-sequence, and (**c**) zero-sequence components of IBDG.

3.3. Modeling of DC DERs

DC subgrid DGs are likewise subject to droop control. In contrast to an AC DG, a DC DG's active power depends entirely on voltage, which is stated as

$$V_i = V_0 - m_{p,dc}P_i, \tag{8}$$

The droop constant of DGs can be given as

$$m_{p,dc} = \frac{V_{dc}^{max} - V_{dc}^{min}}{P_{dc}^{max}}, \tag{9}$$

P_{dc}^{max} is the maximum power of a DC DG, V_{dc}^{max} is the maximum allowable voltage of the DC subgrid, and V_{dc}^{min} is the minimum allowable voltage of the DC subgrid [28].

3.4. AC Line Modeling

The modeling of an AC line considers both resistive and reactive parts; the reactance normally depends upon the frequency of the system.

$$\mathbf{Y}_{ij}(\omega) = \begin{cases} \sum_{j \neq i} Z_{ij}^{-1}(\omega) & \forall i = j \\ -Z_{ij}^{-1}(\omega) & \forall i \neq j \end{cases} \tag{10}$$

where $Z_{ij}(\omega) = R_{ij} + jX_{ij}(\omega)$ is the impedance of the line between the ith and jth bus [28].

3.5. DC Line Modeling

DC lines are entirely resistive in nature. G_{ij} is conductance for any feeder linking to DC loads between the ith and jth nodes. The overall resistance of the branch is r_{ij}, as follows:

$$G_{ij} = (r_{ij})^{-1} \tag{11}$$

The nodal supplied power of a DC bus i can be expressed as [29]

$$P_{dc,i} = \sum_{j \epsilon N_{dc}} V_{dc,i}.(r_{ij})^{-1}.V_{dc,j} \tag{12}$$

3.6. AC Load Modeling

An AC load model can represent a composite load model; these kinds of models have dynamic as well as static features. The real and imaginary parts of power are expressed using a static load model as a function of the frequency and magnitude of the bus voltage. By allocating ZIP coefficients appropriately, AC loads are modeled using ZIP and the polynomial model as a combination of constant power, constant current, and constant impedance. For each load bus, the sum of the coefficients I_p, Z_p, and P_p has to be 1, and the same is true for the coefficients of reactive power Z_q, I_q, and P_q. The constants k_{pw} and k_{qw} have ranges of 0 to 2 and −2 to 0, respectively. These are constants that show the load's dependency on frequency.

$$\left. \begin{array}{l} P_{Lac,i} = P^0_{Lac,i} \left[Z_{p,i} \left(\frac{V_{ac,i}}{V^0_{ac,i}} \right)^2 + I_{p,i} \left(\frac{V_{ac,i}}{V^0_{ac,i}} \right) + P_{p,i} \right] \\ \qquad [1 + k_{pw,i}(\omega - \omega^0)] \end{array} \right\} \tag{13}$$

$$\left. \begin{array}{l} Q_{Lac,i} = Q^0_{Lac,i} \left[Z_{q,i} \left(\frac{V_{ac,i}}{V^0_{ac,i}} \right)^2 + I_{q,i} \left(\frac{V_{ac,i}}{V^0_{ac,i}} \right) + P_{q,i} \right] \\ \qquad [1 + k_{qw,i}(\omega - \omega^0)] \end{array} \right\} \tag{14}$$

where $P_{Lac,i}$ and $Q_{Lac,i}$ are the real and reactive power consumed by the AC load at bus i, respectively. $P^0_{Lac,i}$ and $Q^0_{Lac,i}$ are the nominal real and reactive power of the AC subgrid, respectively. $V^0_{ac,i}$ is the AC subgrid's nominal voltage at the ith bus. Z_p, I_p, and P_p are the ZIP coefficients of real power, representing constant values of impedance, current, and power in AC load models. Z_q, I_q, P_q are the coefficients of reactive power of ZIP AC load models, which represent constant numeric values of impedance, current, and power according to the sequence. k_{qw} and k_{pw} are frequency-based constants of AC load reactive and real power, respectively [28].

3.7. DC Load Modeling

For DC loads, loads are similarly designed with constant values of resistance, constant current, or constant power [29]. The static voltage characteristic is also considered and given as

$$P_{Lac,i} = P^0_{Lac,i} \left[Z_{p,i} \left(\frac{V_{ac,i}}{V^0_{ac,i}} \right)^2 + I_{p,i} \left(\frac{V_{ac,i}}{V^0_{ac,i}} \right) + P_{p,i} \right] \tag{15}$$

$$Q_{Lac,i} = Q^0_{Lac,i} \left[Z_{q,i} \left(\frac{V_{ac,i}}{V^0_{ac,i}} \right)^2 + I_{q,i} \left(\frac{V_{ac,i}}{V^0_{ac,i}} \right) + P_{q,i} \right] \tag{16}$$

3.8. EV Loads

A polynomial or ZIP model of load can be used for EV loads, which consist of real and imaginary parts of apparent power, as given in (17) and (18). The mathematical expression obtained from the modeling of the battery and fast charging station is used to derive both formats of power for the EV load model.

$$P_L = P_{L,0} \left(b + a \left(\frac{|V|}{|V_0|} \right)^{\alpha} \right), \tag{17}$$

$$Q_L = P_L \times tan(\theta) \tag{18}$$

where b is the power constant, a is the voltage-dependent power, α is the exponent of active power, and θ is the power factor of the connected load [30].

3.9. Interlinking Converter Modeling

Only real power can be exchanged between the AC-side subgrid and DC subgrid. DC real power is a function of voltage. The real power of the AC side depends on frequency. The normalized data can be used to compare the AC-side subgrid's frequency and the DC-side subgrid's voltage of the bus at various scales. The governing equations are given below:

$$\hat{\omega} = \frac{\omega - 0.5\left(\omega_{ac}^{max} + \omega_{ac}^{min}\right)}{0.5\left(\omega_{ac}^{max} - \omega_{ac}^{min}\right)}, \tag{19}$$

$$\hat{V}_{DC} = \frac{V - 0.5\left(V_{DC}^{max} + V_{DC}^{min}\right)}{0.5\left(V_{DC}^{max} - V_{DC}^{min}\right)}, \tag{20}$$

Difference result of normalized voltage and current is $\Delta e = \hat{\omega} - \hat{V}_{DC}$.

When the normalized voltages of the DC-side buses are comparable to the AC subgrid's normalized frequency, proportional sharing of power between both subgrids can be accomplished. AC frequencies and DC voltage limits are standardized to $[-1, 1]$.

The process for converting power between AC and DC MGs is calculated based on the disparity between normalized voltage and frequency [29].

$$P_{ICdc} = \frac{1}{k_{IC}}\left(\hat{\omega} - \hat{V}_{DC}\right) \tag{21}$$

When the result is that $\Delta e > 0$, it is decided that AC-side MGs are more dominant than DC-side MGs, indicating that power flows from AC MGs to DC MGs, and conversely for $\Delta e < 0$.

4. Literature Review

In this research work, the main focus will be on the two most crucial challenges of hybrid AC/DC MGs, namely, (1) power flow analysis and (2) short-circuit/fault analysis. The literature on both problems is explained in a sequential flow to understand power flow and short-circuit analysis.

4.1. Power Flow Analysis

Power flow computations calculate voltages for certain load and source situations. Once all bus voltages are determined, slack node power, losses, and line power flow may be computed. We present different techniques for power flow analysis in this section. These techniques are mostly based on AC, DC, and hybrid AC/DC MGs. The power flow evaluation model, commonly referred to as the steady-state analysis framework, is used in the island situation of MGs. DGs may be linked to MGs through power electronic devices, and it is necessary to design an effective strategy for controlling electronic devices [3–5,31,32]. In [7], the author presents a review of power flow analysis using several techniques in the islanded mode of operation. The modeling of distinct operational modes of DGs is explained.

Building on the findings of the research in [28], the authors proposed algorithms related to the concept of the absence of a slack bus that solves the power flow of both AC and DC parts simultaneously. The results of this algorithm are compared with the study of already-existing algorithms of power flow that consider only one part, whether AC or DC subgrids. Furthermore, the author considers all of the distinguishing features of an islanded AC/DC MG, such as bidirectional power flow, droop-controlled DGs, and the absence of a slack bus. Finally, the technique is based on renowned N-R technology, which is efficient and straightforward to implement. When opposed to traditional networks, the power flow of islanded HMGs creates additional obstacles for the following reasons: (1) There is no such huge source to act as a slack bus, as is common in large networks. (2) Lines have a high ratio of R/X quantities. (3) The majority of the time, DGs operate in droop control mode with distinct voltage profiles. (4) Consideration should also be given to IC operation.

A power flow technique based on the Newton–Raphson (N-R) method is modeled for standalone MGs. Frequency variability is introduced to the composition in the model, and the slack bus is removed. Two types of buses are proposed for DG buses, which are PV and

QV. However, their study does not take into account how line impedances and loads are affected by changes in frequency. In addition to that research, the authors have presented another variation of the usual N-R approach in [33].

A summarization of various types of power flow techniques is given in Figure 7. In this figure, evolutionary, deterministic, and probabilistic methods of power flow analysis are explained. These methods are used for the analysis of radial and meshed network power flow, and with the use of evolutionary methods, optimizing power flow can also be analyzed.

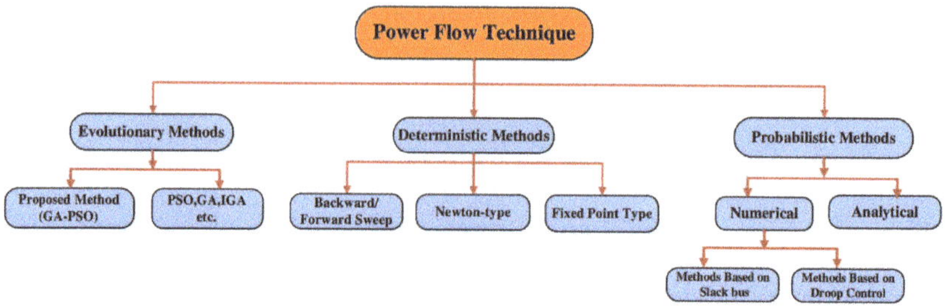

Figure 7. Summarization of power flow techniques.

The modified Newton–Raphson (MNR) technique is offered to tackle load flow problems for autonomous MGs. The MNR approach considers frequency variability and its impact on additional system variables. Other load flow strategies, like BFS presented in [34–41], are tailored to the distribution network. However, only radial and weakly meshed distribution systems can use the BFS technique and its variations.

The authors developed an elaborate power flow approach for AC-islanded and grid-connected MGs based on a survey in [42,43]. The developed method is applied to balanced and unbalanced distribution systems. The methodology is based on an implicit Z_{bus} mechanism, which ensures rapid convergence and is independent of the R/X ratio. It should be noted that islanded MGs that use a master/slave strategy can also use the standard N-R methodology [44]. The authors of [45] separated the system into two zones based on the type of DGs used, namely, renewable and conventional. Islanded MGs cannot be divided into parts because they are not connected to a traditional grid.

In [46,47], the authors discussed important issues concerning the efficient management of DC and AC MGs. Variability in energy resources based on renewables, feeder placement, and cost-effective control approaches are also discussed. Power flow equations are nonlinear. Nonlinearity of equations causes complexity in optimization and control algorithms, which leads to non-convergence problems and high computation burdens. Therefore, the process of linearization of power flow equations is adopted in the literature to simplify the complexity of algorithms [48–51].

Power flow calculations are required during the design stage of HMGs to investigate a variety of topics such as IC and DG allocation and sizing, VAR planning, voltage stability, droop parameter regulation, contingency analysis, and so on [52]. Load flow can serve as a crucial tool in the real-time simulation of HMGs. It helps to reduce losses, optimize costs, and monitor voltage and frequency, as well as several other variables like the thermal limits of lines, operational DG limits, and IC limits during anticipated isolating.

In [53], an optimization model is used to show a new supervisory control strategy based on the model predictive control (MPC) mechanism. The purpose of this study is to determine how changing real and reactive power affects system frequency. Furthermore, variations in wind and PV output power are used to calculate variations in frequency. In [54], a universally reliable and computationally viable load flow approach is created by integrating numerous DG varieties and features of unbalanced droop-controlled MGs.

A summary of power flow analysis methods is given in Tables 2 and 3. Tables 2 and 3 consider criteria based on AC, DC, and AC/DC MGs, and radial, weakly meshed, islanded, and grid-connected modes of operation, and also include unbalanced systems and loads.

Table 2. Summary of power flow analysis methods for MGs.

Ref.	Technique	Architecture			R/WM/ Is/GC	Unbalanced
		AC	DC	AC/DC		
[28]	Newton–Raphson (N-R)	×	×	✓	Is	✓
[29]	N-R	×	×	✓	Is	✓
[30]	Power system analysis toolbox (PSAT)	✓	×	×	R	×
[33]	Modified Newton–Raphson (MNR)	✓	×	×	Is	✓
[34]	Compensation-based method	✓	×	×	R/WM	✓
[36]	Tree-based load flow	✓	×	×	WM	×
[38]	Improved backward–forward sweep (IBFS)	✓	×	×	R	✓
[41]	Backward–forward sweep (BFS)	✓	×	×	R/WM	✓
[42]	Implicit Z-Bus	✓	×	×	Is/GC	✓
[43]	Modified implicit Z-Bus	×	×	✓	Is/GC	✓
[44]	Conventional PF using DR	✓	×	×	Is/GC	×
[45]	Clustering-based method	✓	×	×	R/Is	✓
[46]	Newton trust region (NTR)	×	×	✓	R/Is	✓
[47]	Modified backward–forward sweep	✓	×	×	R/Is	×
[48]	Fault identification	×	✓	×	R	×
[49]	Blockchain technology	✓	×	×	R	×
[51]	Fault current limiter	✓	×	×	R	×
[52]	Mixed-integer linear programming	✓	×	×	R/Is	×
[53]	Model predictive control	×	×	✓	Is	✓
[54]	Sequence component-based PF	✓	×	×	GC	✓
[55]	Modified branch-based approach	×	×	✓	Is	×
[56]	BFS	✓	×	×	R/Is	✓
[57]	Modified Newton–Raphson	✓	×	×	Is	✓
[58]	Controlling and power sharing	×	×	✓	Is/GC	×
[59]	Angle droop control	×	×	✓	GC	×
[60]	Droop-based power sharing	✓	×	×	Is	×
[61]	Adaptive energy calculation	×	✓	×	GC	×
[62]	Global sensitivity analysis (GSA)	✓	×	×	Is/GC	✓
[63]	MBFS PF	✓	×	×	R	✓
[64]	Newton trust region (NTR)	✓	×	×	Is	✓
[65]	Virtual impedance-based power flow	✓	✓	×	GC	×
[66]	NTR	×	×	✓	Is	✓
[67]	Unified power flow model	×	×	✓	Is	✓
[68]	Impedance based	✓	×	×	GC	×

Note: R—radial network; WM—weakly meshed network; Is—islanded MG network; GC—grid-connected MG network.

Table 3. Summary of power flow analysis methods for MGs.

Ref.	Technique	Architecture			R/WM/ Is/GC	Unbalanced
		AC	DC	AC/DC		
[69]	Local controller impedance features	✓	×	×	GC	×
[70]	Holomorphic embedding	×	×	✓	Is	✓
[71]	Sequence component-based PF	×	×	✓	Is	✓
[72]	Modified current injection method (MCIM)	✓	×	×	R	✓
[73]	Current injection method (CIM)	✓	×	×	R	✓
[74]	Multiple-input multiple-output model	×	×	✓	Is/GC	✓
[75]	Hybrid optimization model	✓	×	×	R	×
[76]	Virtual synchronous machine (VISMA)	✓	×	×	R	×
[77]	VSM-based control	✓	×	×	Is/GC	×
[78]	Virtual synchronous machine (VSM)	✓	×	×	Is	×
[79]	Current injection method (CIM)	×	✓	×	GC	✓
[80]	Bus-sectionalized method	×	×	✓	Is/GC	×
[81]	Droop control and virtual impedance	×	×	✓	GC	×
[82]	Genetic algorithm	✓	×	×	R	×
[83]	Adaptable energy management	✓	×	×	Is/GC	×
[84]	VSC control	✓	×	×	R	×
[85]	Power control	✓	×	×	R	×
[86]	Power management	×	×	✓	Is	×
[87]	Droop based	✓	×	×	GC	×

Note: R—radial network; WM—weakly meshed network; Is—islanded MG network; GC—grid-connected MG network.

The MBFS algorithm for solving load flow was considered in [30,55,56]. Droop-controlled DGs have been placed into consideration for this strategy. $Q - V$ and $P - f$ modes of operation have been appropriately taken into consideration using DG droop criteria in conjunction with regular BFS strategies.

A robust modified decoupled NR method of power flow analysis was presented in [57] for solving abnormalities that occur in the islanded operational mode of MG. To share the load among numerous DGs for voltage and frequency management, the concept of a slack bus was offered. DGs are used in power flow analysis for distributing power. When all DGs are connected to an MG converter, a frequency droop controller is less efficient and less quick to react than an angle droop controller. It was shown that by changing the voltage's amplitude and angle, the reactive and actual power that DGs share may be controlled in [58,59]. A lead–lag compensator is used for maintaining the stability of the system for power control in [60], using a high droop gain to improve load sharing. It is better to have a low gain at significant power output and a high gain at minimal output power to maintain stable situations during power sharing. An adaptive droop control is also included, which may modify the gain value in response to changes in load demand and supply provided by DGs [61].

In the literature, an N-R-based technology of power flow is considered, which relates to a modified current injection method (MCIM) [72]. PQ and PV bus representations for several electric vehicle (EV) loads have emerged. Based on National Household Travel Survey (NHTS) 2017 data, an EV load profile is created using a Monte Carlo simulation (MCS) while accounting for uncertainty in the driving patterns of plug-in hybrid electric cars (PHEVs). In [73], for unbalanced multiple-grounded four-wire distribution systems, an asymmetrical three-phase (with neutral) power flow problem based on rectification current injection methods was suggested. The proposed method was based on the formulation of the system's admittance matrix.

In [74], the author suggested a model for regularly evaluating the flow of electricity into AC/DC mixed MGs under various conditions of production and use. The suggested application was created utilizing more than one input–output model composed of blocks, including basic representations of PV arrays, wind turbines (WTs), and battery arrays. A high degree of renewable penetration can cause stability issues and have an impact on system dynamics [76–78]. VSCs have emerged as a feasible solution to provide an interface with sources of energy that are differentiated by either varying frequency or DC, such as fuel cells, wind, and P-V, because of their many advantages and improved performance. A DC MG power flow is presented in [79], in which Newton–Raphson power flow based on a technique of current injection for a bipolar DC MG is created using network static models.

The authors of [80] demonstrated the power flow of a hybrid AC/DC MG utilizing a bus-sectionalized hybrid microgrid (BSHMG). The bus-sectionalized structure improves the reliability and flexibility of the hybrid MG without changing the design of the controller. The suggested control paradigm ensures seamless mode transition and continuous power output. In [81], the authors provided harmonic compensation using interfaces and ICs, in which harmonic control was handled by a converter with various power ratings, filter designs, and frequencies. Bidirectional converters in hybrid MG systems can provide reactive power and smart commutation by themselves and act as a voltage source.

A study was attempted in [82] to fully understand the impact of incorporating internal combustion engines (ICEs) and gas turbines into an AC/DC MG outfitted with PVs. A multi-objective genetic algorithm was used to optimize the system in terms of energy costs and efficiency in general. A basic discussion on an operational energy management system was carried out in Ref. [83]. The authors investigated three scenarios involving poor, perfect, and exact predictions. They evaluated their optimization approach on standalone and grid-connected systems despite large generation–load imbalances. MGs are often regarded as weak systems because they are prone to changes in loading circumstances and generation, which can result in subsequent instability problems and huge frequency deviations [84].

Researchers proved that raising the load on an AC MG shifts the dominant system poles to an unstable zone. As a result of power exchange through IC, the stability of a hybrid MG is dependent not only on the AC sub-system but also on the DC sub-system. The concept of a hybrid MG involves additional research into control operation, stability, and power sharing. The authors investigated and proposed an independent power-sharing operation based on droop control of HMGs, ICs, and DGs [85–88].

Papers related to the power flow of hybrid AC/DC MGs have presented studies on different techniques used in MG systems for AC as well as DC systems. The literature on load flow analysis for AC, DC, and hybrid AC/DC MGs is presented using various techniques in this section. The analysis of power flow techniques focused on the study of AC/DC HMGs. It is differentiated from others based on comparisons of types, modes of operation, and methods of MG systems.

4.2. Short-Circuit Analysis

A short-circuit analysis is a study performed to analyze the behavior of an electrical system during a fault condition. A fault occurs when an abnormal current path is created due to a breakdown or failure in insulation or other components of the system. A short-circuit analysis helps in understanding the magnitude and distribution of fault currents [17,89]. It also helps in finding the consequences of faults in components and devices used for the protection of the system.

- A short circuit is defined as an electrical circuit in which the flow of current goes through an unintentional channel with very low impedance.
- When a wire's insulation cracks or another conducting substance is introduced, the charge might flow down an alternative route than it was intended to.
- Current in a short-circuit analysis is limited only by the resistance of the rest of the circuit, and it can cause severe harm, such as fire and tiny explosions. The probability of fault occurrence due to short circuits may be in between a phase and ground, a phase and neutral, or two phases.

The basic short-circuit analysis strategies for MGs can be classified into two categories. (1) Symmetrical component-based approaches; (2) phase component-based approaches. Since symmetrical component-based approaches are assumed, there is equal mutual coupling between phases. Analysis of distribution system faults is explained in [90–99].

In [97], the author proposed a method for calculating short-circuit currents in a multi-IIDG distribution network using short-circuit features of three-phase IIDGs. These DGs are controlled by current under a grid fault. The sequence network's mutual coupling for an unbalanced distribution system can be efficiently handled by the proposed method.

An IBDG was modeled in the format of a sequence component circuit to illustrate the operation of an inverter in a mode of current control for use in fault analysis. The main concept of the current-controlled inverter is based on the technique of dq-0 control. In this approach, phase factors of IBDG inverter current are first transformed into dq-0 sequence components, and a control mechanism for manipulating these converted dq-0 components is supplied. In [100], an experimental setup for fault analysis with a dq-0 control scheme for the inverter was implemented. However, these dq-0 component-based fault analysis methods were only carried out in time-domain simulation studies and were only tested on small-size distribution systems.

A conventional fault analysis method based on a system admittance matrix was proposed in [101], which includes inverter-interfaced distributed generators (IIDGs). In this scheme, it was assumed that the IIDG is operating in its voltage control mode during faults. The contribution of IIDGs during sub-transient and transient periods of the fault was also analyzed.

A $[Y_{bus}]$ matrix-based method of short-circuit analysis and transformer models based on voltage and current equations are employed in [102]. In this method, for short-circuit calculations, the network's description of the admittance matrix is constructed, and connection matrices for various transformer configurations are developed.

In the symmetrical component method, elements in the distribution system are presented by their circuits of positive-, negative-, and zero-sequence components. The fault analysis method using symmetrical components [103] uses an approach of modeling for 1-phase and 2-phase lines in the fault calculation. The three-phase impedance or admittance matrices that correspond to the distribution system's components represent them in the phase domain. The method of triangular factorization of the $[Y_{bus}]$ matrix to simulate different faults is presented in [104].

Models of co-generators (induction or synchronous generators) and three-phase transformers are also included in the test system. The method was applied to balanced, unbalanced, radial, and meshed-type distribution networks. A linear graph-based network modeling approach to forming the admittance matrix was proposed in [105]. A hybrid compensation-based short-circuit analysis method was proposed in [106]. In this method, two algorithms, namely, distribution power flow (DISFLO) and distribution short-circuit analysis (DISCA), were utilized. Two different lateral- and load-equivalent compensation-based approaches [107] were proposed for fault analysis of radial networks. For the investigation of short-circuit issues in this paper, the initial condition boundary matching (ICBM) method was utilized. Short-circuit analysis based on a technique that gives a relationship between two matrices **[BIBC]** and **[BCBV]** for radial and mesh distribution systems was presented in [108]. The correlation between the current of an injected bus and branch currents is presented by the **[BIBC]** matrix, whereas the relationship between the current of a particular branch and the voltages of each bus is shown by the **[BCBV]** matrix. The DG model used in this work is similar to the synchronous generator model used in the short-circuit study in [109]. The technique has undergone testing on several systems with various fault circumstances. The fault impedance effect on a faulted, unbalanced distribution system was described in [110]. This method is based on the bus impedance matrix $[Z_{bus}]$ of the network, which includes the effect of fault impedances in calculations of fault analysis.

An algorithm of fault analysis is proposed in [111], in which the fault resistance effect for both weakly meshed as well as radial distribution networks is taken into account for fault current calculations. In this method, fault resistance is calculated, and then a modified bus impedance matrix is obtained, which includes the effect of the calculated fault resistance. A model-based fault diagnosis scheme was designed in [112]; it was capable of real-time detection of all types of faults in the distribution network. In this paper, a linear dynamical-fault-dependent state-space model of a single-machine infinite-bus (SMIB) power system was derived. This model is capable of capturing the dynamics of a complete system over a full-time scale and is therefore suitable for fault studies of any kind of fault. A multi-phase short-circuit analysis method based on the concept of a selected inversion algorithm called Sellnv was proposed in [113].

Various methods of short-circuiting have been presented in the literature for a three-phase, four-wire unbalanced distribution network. A current injection-based fault analysis method was presented in [114] for a multi-phase electrical distribution system. A Newton–Raphson-based technique was used in the proposed method. A transformer model based on a nodal admittance matrix has also been considered in short-circuit calculations. In [115], a method of short-circuit analysis for the computation of phase-to-earth currents for many faults in an unbalanced multi-wire radial distribution model was developed. The analysis of a multi-wire line model of an unbalanced system utilizing Kirchhoff's rules and methods for solving linear equations forms the basis of the suggested approach. In [116], a method is utilized to calculate equivalent resistances for a formulation of a matrix of problems to calculate faults that result from short circuits according to the IEC 61660 standard.

A summary of the different techniques used for short-circuit analysis is presented in Tables 4 and 5. Tables 4 and 5 consider criteria based on AC, DC, and AC/DC MGs, and radial, weakly meshed, islanded, and grid-connected modes of operation, and also include unbalanced systems and loads of the microgrid network.

Table 4. Literature survey on short-circuit analysis.

Ref.	Technique	Architecture			R/WM/ Is/GC	Unbalanced
		AC	DC	AC/DC		
[20]	Delta-circuit and VICL (SCC)	✓	×	×	Is	✓
[21]	Fortescue approach	✓	×	×	R	✓
[90]	Inverter-based fault response	✓	×	×	GC	×
[91]	IIDG fault response	✓	×	×	GC	×
[93]	Power control during fault	✓	×	×	R/GC	×
[94]	Voltage source control (VSC)	✓	×	×	R/GC	✓
[95]	Inverter control	✓	×	×	R/GC	✓
[97]	Fault analysis	✓	×	×	GC/DS	✓
[98]	Fault calculation Z-bus matrix	✓	×	×	R/GC	✓
[99]	IBDG controlling	✓	×	×	R/GC	✓
[100]	VSC-based fault current controlling	✓	×	×	R/GC	✓
[101]	Distribution system fault analysis	✓	×	×	R/GC	×
[102]	Short-circuit analysis	✓	×	×	R/GC	×
[103]	Symmetrical component based	✓	×	×	R	✓
[104]	Phase-based system	✓	×	×	R	✓
[105]	Improved fault analysis algorithm	✓	×	×	R	✓
[106]	Hybrid compensation	✓	×	×	R	✓
[107]	Fault analysis	✓	×	×	R	✓
[117]	IBDG SCC	✓	×	×	R	✓
[109]	Transformer model based	✓	×	×	R	✓
[110]	Symmetrical component/ phase component	✓	×	×	R	✓
[111]	Fault resistance estimation	✓	×	×	R	✓
[112]	Unsymmetrical fault analysis	✓	×	×	R	×
[113]	Fault analysis	✓	×	×	R	✓
[118]	Hybrid compensation method	✓	×	×	Is/GC	✓
[119]	Current differential protection	×	✓	×	GC	×
[120]	Virtual impedance based	×	✓	×	Is	×
[121]	Wavelet energy spectrum	✓	×	×	GC	×
[122]	Fault analysis of interlinking converters	×	×	✓	GC	✓
[123]	Fault current limiter	×	×	✓	GC	×
[124]	DFIG-based SCC	✓	×	×	R	✓
[125]	MCIM	✓	×	×	Is	✓
[114]	CIM	✓	×	×	R	✓

Note: R—radial network; WM—weakly meshed network; Is—islanded MG network; GC—grid-connected MG network.

Table 5. Literature survey on short-circuit analysis.

Ref.	Technique	Architecture			R/WM/Is/GC	Unbalanced
		AC	DC	AC/DC		
[115]	Fault current calculation	✓	×	×	R	✓
[116]	SCC calculation IEC 61660	×	×	✓	R	×
[126]	V/F and PQ control	✓	×	×	Is	✓
[127]	BIBC	✓	×	×	WM	✓
[128]	SCC of MG	✓	×	×	GC	✓
[129]	DER based	✓	×	×	Is/GC	✓
[130]	Fault impedance based	×	×	✓	R	×
[131]	Time-varying fault analysis	✓	×	×	R	×
[132]	Voltage-dependent network equivalents (VDNEs)	✓	×	×	R	×
[133]	Fault analysis	×	✓	×	GC	×
[134]	ZCBs and fuse based	×	✓	×	GC	×
[135]	Augmented matrix based	✓	×	×	GC	✓
[136]	Simple generalized minimal residual (SGMRES)	✓	×	×	R	✓
[137]	Fault current calculation	✓	×	×	Is/GC	✓
[138]	IBDG fault current calculation	✓	×	×	Is/GC	✓
[139]	Communication-assisted digital relays	✓	×	×	GC	✓
[140]	IBDG fault current calculation	✓	×	×	R	✓
[141]	Mathematical morphology	✓	×	×	R	✓
[142]	Impedance based	✓	×	×	GC	×
[143]	VSC based	×	✓	×	GC	×
[144]	SC current suppression	×	✓	×	GC	×
[145]	Static modeling approach	✓	×	×	GC	✓
[146]	Impedance based	✓	×	×	R	✓

Note: R—radial network; WM—weakly meshed network; Is—islanded MG network; GC—grid-connected MG network.

In the study in [126], the author proposed a new technique of fault analysis for AC MG systems, which takes into account fault current limiting, low-voltage ride-through, and inverter-interfaced distributed generation (IIDG) control strategies. The analysis was performed on fault models of PQ-controlled and V/f-controlled IIDG. The functioning state of V/F-IIDG was divided into a constant voltage and a constant current state following analysis of fault models. An enhanced model voltage equation based on current constraints was used in a constant current state. A grid-connected MG fault calculation approach was used in a constant-voltage state.

In [127], the author proposed a precise and efficient technique for analyzing short-circuit faults in weakly meshed unbalanced networks in distribution. To examine the impacts of various types of short-circuit failure on weakly meshed distribution networks, some practical and efficient formulas were developed in this study. In [128], the author presented a fault scenario on an MG with a solar panel, fuel cell, and wind turbine as the main components. The generated power from several sources was aggregated on a single DC bus and then transferred to a three-phase AC load using a three-phase inverter.

In [129,130], the authors analyzed an MG's fault current disparities in two different operating situations and subsequently identified changes that must be made to the protection of relay and fault calculations in developing MGs. DER-based MG short-circuit analysis is performed in both islanded and grid-connected operational modes. High changes in fault currents based on operational mode are found after analysis of fault currents in two different modes. There could be significant post-fault disruptions in an islanded subgrid as a result of interactions between DERs and ICs. Therefore, if the fault clearing time goes over a certain threshold, the voltage of islanded subgrids cannot be stabilized. In the post-fault transient reaction of HMGs, numerous local controllers are engaged.

In the study of [131], a fresh approach improves on traditional short-circuit analysis techniques and gives a rough idea of fault current patterns. A typical feeder with simple loads and a PV-dominated distribution feeder have very different fault current profiles. The variance of the fault current is influenced by both the PV system's fault current contribution and voltage-based protection strategies.

Ref. [132] gives an idea for identifying the system's equivalent network with high-level sharing of resources based on inverter technology for studies of fault analysis. A nonlinear element (a voltage-dependent current source) is added to the conventional voltage source behind impedance representation in the proposed voltage-dependent network equivalents

(VDNEs), which is a nonlinear equivalent. Because of a nonlinear relationship between the voltage present at the terminals of equivalent systems and the fault contribution made by VDNE, iterative computation of short-circuit currents is required.

A DC MG fault analysis is presented in [133], based on a precise representation of a DC MG's parts. In a DC MG, steady power loads are incorporated as a conventional DC system loading profile, with batteries as energy storage devices and solar and wind as renewable energy sources. Due to practical considerations, all energy sources based on renewables are subject to maximum power point tracking (MPPT) regulations. In Ref. [134], for adding a full thermo-magnetic function to a hybrid Z-source circuit breaker (ZCB), it is suggested that fuses be used to make up for the Z-source circuit breaker's functionality. In practical DC power systems, this technique would improve the dependability of short-circuit protection with ZCBs.

In [135], an MG system's unbalanced behavior is presented, and this approach is used for fault analysis, which is based on a graph concept and a complicated MVA representation of short circuits. Instead of the conventional Z-bus methodology and inverse admittance matrix with the idea of the lower and upper triangular matrices, the incidence matrix K of the branch path and augmented incidence matrix K_I, which is a newly constructed network, serve as the foundation for the suggested approach.

The study in Ref. [136] proposes a method for quickly calculating short-circuit currents in unbalanced distribution networks with DGs that interface with inverters (IIDG). It can estimate short-circuit current in unbalanced systems with multiple IIDGs by using symmetric components instead of computing the system bus impedance matrix.

In [137], the author analyzes changes in fault current between two different operating modes and ultimately concludes with improvements in fault calculations and relay protection analysis that are needed in developing the MGs. The utility system in grid-connected mode contributes the most fault current, with DERs making up no more than 20% of it. On the other hand, the sole sources of fault current in islanded mode are DERs, and the total fault current is much lower than it is in grid-linked mode.

A sequence component-based protection scheme was developed in [138], which considers protective zone density comparable to that of [139] but without any increase in protection robustness. This necessitates longer processing times and a more comprehensive communication infrastructure. The utilization of conventional distance protection for MGs and distribution networks was covered in [140].

In [141], a protective plan based on traveling waves was presented. The plan is based on polarity and time measurements made at both ends of the protected line immediately following the occurrence of a fault. The research effort, including the proposal of an impedance-based protection strategy with communication assistance, is presented in [142]. The suggested method relies on tracking impedance paths at various feeder relays to spot faults, and it makes use of directed elements to pinpoint their location.

In [143], a study based on a technique of transient modeling of a voltage source converter (VSC)-based DC MG is presented. Analysis of transient characteristics of VSCs in active power control mode and DC bus voltage control mode is followed by modeling of a defective DC MG, which comprises the VSC model and DC line model. Expressions of state variables in DC MGs are presented after SCC. The authors of [144] proposed a protection strategy for suppressing fault current in DC lines to improve the reliability of power in MGs.

Static modeling of MGs for fault analysis is presented in [145]. This uses the phasor simulation method and DGs with inverter interfaces for fault analysis of MGs in each operating mode. Instead of powers, constraints are applied to DG currents, and the established analysis approach additionally takes into account the impact of output filter capacitors. Ref. [146] determined the location of faults based upon impedance measurements for a distribution system using DGs at high frequencies. In this research, the author, regardless of the effects of the control loop, employed a DG model for fault location based on excessive frequency impedance.

The literature on short-circuit analysis of AC, DC, and hybrid AC/DC MGs is presented using various techniques in this section. The proposed analysis of short-circuit techniques is focused on a review of AC/DC MG's techniques. It is differentiated from others based on a comparison of the analysis of AC and DC as well as the AC/DC short circuit.

5. Methodology

To investigate the effect of the power flow analysis and SCA, this study includes the various techniques of the load flow analysis of AC, DC, and hybrid AC/DC microgrids.

5.1. Power Flow Analysis

Various methods for the analysis of AC, DC, and hybrid AC/DC microgrid power flow are presented in Tables 2 and 3. These methods are classified based on various categories like radial and meshed microgrid systems.

Power flow methods are classified based on the grid-tied modes and islanded mode of operation of a microgrid. Some of the methods are used to solve the power flow analysis of the unbalanced microgrid system. Methods that are used to solve the power flow of the islanded microgrid are based on modifications of the existing Jacobean matrix-based methods and based on modifications of the BFS methods due to the absence of the slack bus.

A general methodology of the power flow analysis of AC and DC microgrids is explained in the flowchart of a hybrid AC/DC microgrid. The fundamental steps of power flow analysis of AC/DC hybrid MGs are given in the flowchart, as shown in Figure 8.

This flowchart explains the basic procedure of AC load flow convergence and DC load flow convergence conditions. In this, the power flow through the bidirectional interlinking converter is also taken into consideration. An interlinking converter power is defined based on the AC subgrid's frequency and the DC subgrid's voltage.

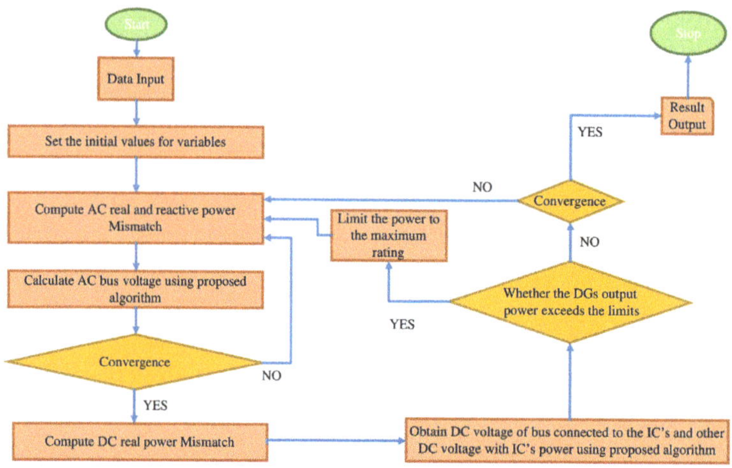

Figure 8. Flowchart for power flow analysis of hybrid AC/DC MG.

5.2. Short-Circuit Analysis

Various methods for the short-circuit analysis of AC and DC microgrids are discussed in Tables 4 and 5. These methods are classified based on various categories like radial and weakly meshed microgrid distribution systems.

SCA methods are classified based on the grid-tied modes and islanded mode of operation of a microgrid. Some of the methods are used for fault analysis of unbalanced systems. Analysis of IBDG fault currents and voltages before and after faults is also discussed. The fundamental steps for short-circuit analysis of MGs are shown in Figure 9. The flowchart demonstrates the short-circuit evaluation approach, which follows the load flow investigation. Initially, the pre-fault load flow is determined to establish the system's baseline. The fault location is then indicated within the network. After obtaining the type and location of fault, post-fault current and voltages are calculated.

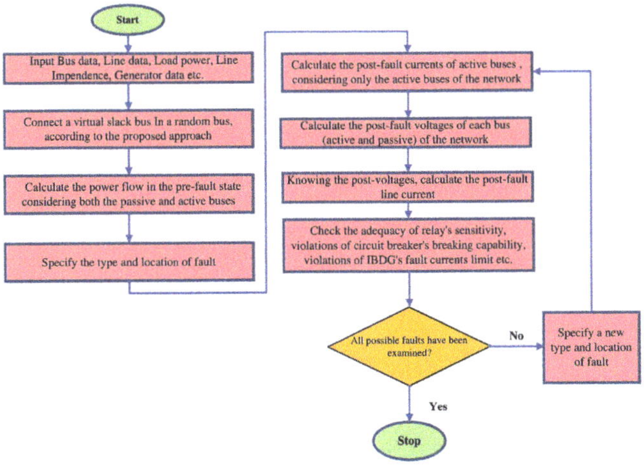

Figure 9. Flowchart for short-circuit analysis of AC MG.

6. Promising Areas of Scientific Research

This study identified many significant limitations in existing approaches for power flow and short-circuit evaluation in microgrids (MGs), especially considering the challenges that arise from renewable energy integration and fault scenarios. For the advancement in this field, more study is needed in various promising areas. Existing techniques for PFA and SCA should be improved to increase accuracy and computing efficiency. Future research could look into incorporating real-time data analysis, which makes possible more precise calculations of node voltages, currents, and electrical power flows during both normal and fault scenarios. Efficient evaluation of MG behavior requires precise simulation of components like DGs and ESSs, particularly during unexpected circumstances. Renewable energy's unpredictable nature needs comprehensive models that can properly represent both steady-state and fault situations. MGs deal with a number of operational issues, including voltage variations, frequency deviations, and imbalances in power as a result of the inconsistent nature of renewable energy sources. Advanced control algorithms are needed to enable smooth functioning in both grid-tied and islanded modes. These algorithms should be capable of constantly balancing power distribution and adjusting to changing generation and load situations in real time to avoid stability difficulties. Existing short-circuit evaluation methods for both DC- and AC-islanded MG networks frequently lack the flexibility required to handle the unpredictability caused by renewable sources. Enhancing fault analysis techniques, particularly under dynamic and changing settings, can increase MGs' robustness. Future research should focus on developing intelligent algorithms that provide rapid and precise fault analysis in order to ensure the system's service continuity. Addressing these issues in future research will help to make MG systems more reliable, efficient, and capable of managing the difficulties introduced due to renewable energy sources and fault conditions.

7. Conclusions

This paper provides a comprehensive review of the approaches for power flow and short-circuit analysis in AC, DC, and hybrid AC/DC microgrids (HMGs). The power flow between AC and DC subgrids is controlled through bidirectional interlinking converters which ensure stable operation in both grid-connected and islanded modes of microgrids.

The bidirectional converters control the bus voltage for DC-side operation and the frequency of AC MG operation. The modeling of AC, DC, and hybrid AC/DC MG components has been investigated, with a focus on voltage and frequency control, especially in islanded operation, where frequency variations are considered as unknown variables. The short-circuit analysis process of a hybrid AC/DC MG also considered the modeling of different components, including IBDGs. Different methods of analysis of faults occurring due to short circuits are explained in the literature. A comparative analysis of both short-circuit and power flow analysis has been presented, and a comprehensive review of AC, DC, and hybrid AC/DC MGs has been proposed. These findings have an important impact on the design and control of hybrid AC/DC microgrids since they provide knowledge about how to improve reliability and effectiveness. The study provides the groundwork for future research into optimizing power flow and fault management procedures in hybrid AC/DC MGs, which are critical for their broad adoption in modern, sustainable energy systems.

Author Contributions: Conceptualization, G.M., V.M. and A.T.A.; Formal analysis, G.M., V.M., A.M., V.P.S., A.T.A. and I.A.H.; Funding acquisition, I.A.H.; Investigation, A.T.A. and I.A.H.; Methodology, G.M., V.M., A.M., V.P.S., A.T.A. and I.A.H.; Resources, G.M., V.M., A.M., V.P.S. and I.A.H.; Software, G.M., V.M., A.M. and V.P.S.; Validation, A.M., V.P.S. and I.A.H.; Visualization, A.T.A.; Writing—original draft, G.M., V.M., A.M., V.P.S. and A.T.A.; Writing—review & editing, G.M., V.M., A.M., V.P.S., A.T.A. and I.A.H. All authors have read and agreed to the published version of the manuscript.

Funding: This research was funded by the Norwegian University of Science and Technology, Norway.

Data Availability Statement: The authors declare no associated data in the manuscript.

Acknowledgments: The authors would like to acknowledge the support of the Norwegian University of Science and Technology for paying the Article Processing Charges (APC) of this publication. This research is supported by the Automated Systems and Soft Computing Lab (ASSCL), Prince Sultan University, Riyadh, Saudi Arabia. The authors would like to thank Prince Sultan University, Riyadh, Saudi Arabia for their support.

Conflicts of Interest: The authors declare that the research was conducted in the absence of any commercial or financial relationships that could be construed as a potential conflict of interest.

References

1. Sheykhi, N.; Salami, A.; Guerrero, J.M.; Agundis-Tinajero, G.D.; Faghihi, T. A comprehensive review on telecommunication challenges of microgrids secondary control. *Int. J. Electr. Power Energy Syst.* **2022**, *140*, 108081. [CrossRef]
2. Zolfaghari, M.; Gharehpetian, G.B.; Shafie-khah, M.; Catalão, J.P. Comprehensive review on the strategies for controlling the interconnection of AC and DC microgrids. *Int. J. Electr. Power Energy Syst.* **2022**, *136*, 107742. [CrossRef]
3. Green, T.C.; Prodanović, M. Control of inverter-based micro-grids. *Electr. Power Syst. Res.* **2007**, *77*, 1204–1213. [CrossRef]
4. Gao, F.; Iravani, M.R. A control strategy for a distributed generation unit in grid-connected and autonomous modes of operation. *IEEE Trans. Power Deliv.* **2008**, *23*, 850–859.
5. Vandoorn, T.L.; Meersman, B.; De Kooning, J.D.; Vandevelde, L. Analogy between conventional grid control and islanded microgrid control based on a global DC-link voltage droop. *IEEE Trans. Power Deliv.* **2012**, *27*, 1405–1414. [CrossRef]
6. Yoldaş, Y.; Önen, A.; Muyeen, S.; Vasilakos, A.V.; Alan, I. Enhancing smart grid with microgrids: Challenges and opportunities. *Renew. Sustain. Energy Rev.* **2017**, *72*, 205–214. [CrossRef]
7. Moradi, M.H.; Foroutan, V.B.; Abedini, M. Power flow analysis in islanded Micro-Grids via modeling different operational modes of DGs: A review and a new approach. *Renew. Sustain. Energy Rev.* **2017**, *69*, 248–262. [CrossRef]
8. Hirsch, A.; Parag, Y.; Guerrero, J. Microgrids: A review of technologies, key drivers, and outstanding issues. *Renew. Sustain. Energy Rev.* **2018**, *90*, 402–411. [CrossRef]
9. Bolgouras, V.; Ntantogian, C.; Panaousis, E.; Xenakis, C. Distributed key management in microgrids. *IEEE Trans. Ind. Inform.* **2019**, *16*, 2125–2133. [CrossRef]
10. Cagnano, A.; De Tuglie, E.; Mancarella, P. Microgrids: Overview and guidelines for practical implementations and operation. *Appl. Energy* **2020**, *258*, 114039. [CrossRef]
11. Azeem, O.; Ali, M.; Abbas, G.; Uzair, M.; Qahmash, A.; Algarni, A.; Hussain, M.R. A comprehensive review on integration challenges, optimization techniques and control strategies of hybrid AC/DC Microgrid. *Appl. Sci.* **2021**, *11*, 6242. [CrossRef]
12. Jain, D.; Saxena, D. Comprehensive review on control schemes and stability investigation of hybrid AC-DC microgrid. *Electr. Power Syst. Res.* **2023**, *218*, 109182. [CrossRef]
13. Pompodakis, E.E.; Kryonidis, G.C.; Demoulias, C.; Alexiadis, M.C. A generic power flow algorithm for unbalanced islanded hybrid AC/DC microgrids. *IEEE Trans. Power Syst.* **2020**, *36*, 1107–1120. [CrossRef]

14. Surendra, K.; Das, B.; Pant, V. Static state estimation of islanded AC/DC Hybrid microgrids. *Int. J. Electr. Power Energy Syst.* **2024**, *155*, 109612. [CrossRef]
15. Tinajero, G.D.A.; Nasir, M.; Vasquez, J.C.; Guerrero, J.M. Comprehensive power flow modelling of hierarchically controlled AC/DC hybrid islanded microgrids. *Int. J. Electr. Power Energy Syst.* **2021**, *127*, 106629. [CrossRef]
16. Kamh, M.Z.; Iravani, R. Unbalanced model and power-flow analysis of microgrids and active distribution systems. *IEEE Trans. Power Deliv.* **2010**, *25*, 2851–2858. [CrossRef]
17. Mathur, A.; Pant, V.; Das, B. Unsymmetrical short-circuit analysis for distribution system considering loads. *Int. J. Electr. Power Energy Syst.* **2015**, *70*, 27–38. [CrossRef]
18. Meena, G.; Singh, V.P.; Sundariyal, N.; Mathur, A. Component Model of AC Microgrid for Short-Circuit Analysis. In Proceedings of the 2024 1st International Conference on Innovative Sustainable Technologies for Energy, Mechatronics, and Smart Systems (ISTEMS), Dehradun, India, 26–27 April 2024; pp. 1–6.
19. Strezoski, L.; Prica, M.; Loparo, K.A. Generalized Δ-circuit concept for integration of distributed generators in online short-circuit calculations. *IEEE Trans. Power Syst.* **2016**, *32*, 3237–3245. [CrossRef]
20. Pompodakis, E.E.; Strezoski, L.; Simic, N.; Paspatis, A.G.; Alexiadis, M.C.; Tsikalakis, A.G.; Katsigiannis, Y.A.; Karapidakis, E.S. Short-circuit calculation of droop-controlled islanded AC microgrids with virtual impedance current limiters. *Electr. Power Syst. Res.* **2023**, *218*, 109184. [CrossRef]
21. Jabr, R.A.; Džafić, I. A Fortescue approach for real-time short circuit computation in multiphase distribution networks. *IEEE Trans. Power Syst.* **2014**, *30*, 3276–3285. [CrossRef]
22. Abdelmalek, S.; Azar, A.T.; Dib, D. A novel actuator fault-tolerant control strategy of DFIG-based wind turbines using Takagi-Sugeno multiple models. *Int. J. Control. Autom. Syst.* **2018**, *16*, 1415–1424. [CrossRef]
23. Varshney, T.; Waghmare, A.; Meena, V.; Singh, V.; Ramprabhakar, J.; Khan, B.; Singh, S. FOPDT model and CHR method based control of flywheel energy storage integrated microgrid. *Sci. Rep.* **2024**, *14*, 21550. [CrossRef] [PubMed]
24. Pradhan, R.; Jena, P. An innovative fault direction estimation technique for AC microgrid. *Electr. Power Syst. Res.* **2023**, *215*, 108997. [CrossRef]
25. Daraz, A.; Malik, S.A.; Azar, A.T.; Aslam, S.; Alkhalifah, T.; Alturise, F. Optimized fractional order integral-tilt derivative controller for frequency regulation of interconnected diverse renewable energy resources. *IEEE Access* **2022**, *10*, 43514–43527. [CrossRef]
26. Mariam, L.; Basu, M.; Conlon, M.F. A review of existing microgrid architectures. *J. Eng.* **2013**, *2013*, 937614. [CrossRef]
27. Tehrani, K.; Weber, M.; Rasoanarivo, I. Hybrid Power System Optimization for Microgrids. In Proceedings of the 2021 23rd European Conference on Power Electronics and Applications (EPE'21 ECCE Europe), Virtual, 6–10 September 2021; pp. 1–9.
28. Aprilia, E.; Meng, K.; Al Hosani, M.; Zeineldin, H.H.; Dong, Z.Y. Unified power flow algorithm for standalone AC/DC hybrid microgrids. *IEEE Trans. Smart Grid* **2017**, *10*, 639–649. [CrossRef]
29. Liu, Y.; Li, Z.; Fan, M. A Newton–Raphson-based sequential power flow algorithm for hybrid AC/DC microgrids. *IEEE Trans. Ind. Appl.* **2021**, *58*, 843–854. [CrossRef]
30. Kongjeen, Y.; Bhumkittipich, K. Modeling of electric vehicle loads for power flow analysis based on PSAT. In Proceedings of the 2016 13th International Conference on Electrical Engineering/Electronics, Computer, Telecommunications and Information Technology (ECTI-CON), Chiang Mai, Thailand, 28 June–1 July 2016; pp. 1–6.
31. Chaudhary, R.; Singh, V.; Mathur, A.; Meena, V.; Murari, K. Truncation-based Approximation of Autonomous Microgrid. In Proceedings of the 2024 IEEE Kansas Power and Energy Conference (KPEC), Manhattan, KS, USA, 25–26 April 2024; pp. 1–5.
32. Mathur, A.; Kumari, R.; Meena, V.; Singh, V.; Azar, A.T.; Hameed, I.A. Data-driven optimization for microgrid control under distributed energy resource variability. *Sci. Rep.* **2024**, *14*, 10806. [CrossRef]
33. Mumtaz, F.; Syed, M.; Al Hosani, M.; Zeineldin, H. A novel approach to solve power flow for islanded microgrids using modified Newton Raphson with droop control of DG. *IEEE Trans. Sustain. Energy* **2015**, *7*, 493–503. [CrossRef]
34. Shirmohammadi, D.; Hong, H.W.; Semlyen, A.; Luo, G. A compensation-based power flow method for weakly meshed distribution and transmission networks. *IEEE Trans. Power Syst.* **1988**, *3*, 753–762. [CrossRef]
35. Kumar, Y.; Meena, V.; Mathur, A.; Singh, V. Fault Detection and Localization in Distribution System using Sparse Matrix Reconstruction. In Proceedings of the 2023 International Conference on Computer, Electronics & Electrical Engineering & Their Applications (IC2E3), Srinagar Garhwal, India, 8–9 June 2023; pp. 1–6.
36. Luo, G.X.; Semlyen, A. Efficient load flow for large weakly meshed networks. *IEEE Trans. Power Syst.* **1990**, *5*, 1309–1316. [CrossRef]
37. Daraz, A.; Malik, S.A.; Waseem, A.; Azar, A.T.; Haq, I.U.; Ullah, Z.; Aslam, S. Automatic generation control of multi-source interconnected power system using FOI-TD controller. *Energies* **2021**, *14*, 5867. [CrossRef]
38. Chang, G.; Chu, S.; Wang, H. An improved backward/forward sweep load flow algorithm for radial distribution systems. *IEEE Trans. Power Syst.* **2007**, *22*, 882–884. [CrossRef]
39. Krishna, P.; Khan, B. Rank-sum-weight method based systematic determination of weights for controller tuning for automatic generation control. *IEEE Access* **2022**, *10*, 68161–68174. [CrossRef]
40. Pilla, R.; Azar, A.T.; Gorripotu, T.S. Impact of flexible AC transmission system devices on automatic generation control with a metaheuristic based fuzzy PID controller. *Energies* **2019**, *12*, 4193. [CrossRef]

41. Augugliaro, A.; Dusonchet, L.; Favuzza, S.; Ippolito, M.G.; Sanseverino, E.R. A backward sweep method for power flow solution in distribution networks. *Int. J. Electr. Power Energy Syst.* **2010**, *32*, 271–280. [CrossRef]
42. Pompodakis, E.E.; Kryonidis, G.C.; Alexiadis, M.C. A comprehensive load flow approach for grid-connected and islanded AC microgrids. *IEEE Trans. Power Syst.* **2019**, *35*, 1143–1155. [CrossRef]
43. Meena, G.; Saini, D.; Meena, V.; Mathur, A.; Singh, V. A Modified Implicit Z-Bus Method for an Unbalanced Hybrid AC-DC Microgrids. In Proceedings of the 2023 IEEE IAS Global Conference on Renewable Energy and Hydrogen Technologies (GlobConHT), Male, Maldives, 11–12 March 2023; pp. 1–6.
44. Nikkhajoei, H.; Iravani, R. Steady-state model and power flow analysis of electronically-coupled distributed resource units. *IEEE Trans. Power Deliv.* **2006**, *22*, 721–728. [CrossRef]
45. Ashfaq, S.; Zhang, D.; Zhang, C.; Dong, Z.Y. Load flow investigations for regionalized islanded microgrid considering frequency regulation with high renewable penetration. *Electr. Power Syst. Res.* **2023**, *214*, 108904. [CrossRef]
46. Eajal, A.; Abdelwahed, M.A.; El-Saadany, E.; Ponnambalam, K. A unified approach to the power flow analysis of AC/DC hybrid microgrids. *IEEE Trans. Sustain. Energy* **2016**, *7*, 1145–1158. [CrossRef]
47. Hameed, F.; Al Hosani, M.; Zeineldin, H.H. A modified backward/forward sweep load flow method for islanded radial microgrids. *IEEE Trans. Smart Grid* **2017**, *10*, 910–918. [CrossRef]
48. Rao, G.K.; Jena, P. A Novel Fault Identification and Localization Scheme for Bipolar DC Microgrid. *IEEE Trans. Ind. Inform.* **2023**, *19*, 11752–11764. [CrossRef]
49. Mishra, A.; Jena, P. Application of Blockchain Technology for Microgrid Restoration. *IEEE Trans. Power Deliv.* **2022**, *38*, 1810–1825. [CrossRef]
50. Meena, V.; Yadav, U.; Mathur, A.; Singh, V.; Guerrero, J.M.; Khan, B. Location and size selection using hybrid Jaya-Luus-Jaakola algorithm for decentralized generations in distribution system considering demand-side management. *IET Renew. Power Gener.* **2023**, *17*, 1535–1544. [CrossRef]
51. Naveen, P.; Jena, P. A robust protection scheme for multimicrogrids using fault current limiter. *IEEE Trans. Ind. Appl.* **2022**, *58*, 5763–5775. [CrossRef]
52. Gangwar, T.; Padhy, N.P.; Jena, P. Storage Allocation in Active Distribution Networks Considering Life Cycle and Uncertainty. *IEEE Trans. Ind. Inform.* **2022**, *19*, 339–350. [CrossRef]
53. Mansoorhoseini, P.; Mozafari, B.; Mohammadi, S. Islanded AC/DC microgrids supervisory control: A novel stochastic optimization approach. *Electr. Power Syst. Res.* **2022**, *209*, 108028. [CrossRef]
54. Allam, M.A.; Hamad, A.A.; Kazerani, M. A generic modeling and power-flow analysis approach for isochronous and droop-controlled microgrids. *IEEE Trans. Power Syst.* **2018**, *33*, 5657–5670. [CrossRef]
55. Nassar, M.E.; Hamad, A.A.; Salama, M.; El-Saadany, E.F. A novel load flow algorithm for islanded AC/DC hybrid microgrids. *IEEE Trans. Smart Grid* **2017**, *10*, 1553–1566. [CrossRef]
56. Amritha, M.; Savier, J. Load Flow Analysis of Islanded Droop Regulated Microgrids. In Proceedings of the 2020 International Conference on Power, Instrumentation, Control and Computing (PICC), Thrissur, India, 17–19 December 2020; pp. 1–6.
57. Lone, A.H.; Gupta, N. A Novel Modified Decoupled Newton-Raphson Load Flow Method with Distributed Slack Bus for Islanded Microgrids Considering Frequency Variations. *Electr. Power Components Syst.* **2023**, *52*, 678–696. [CrossRef]
58. Goyal, M.; Ghosh, A.; Zare, F. Power sharing control with frequency droop in a hybrid microgrid. In Proceedings of the 2013 IEEE Power & Energy Society General Meeting, Vancouver, BC, Canada, 21–25 July 2013; pp. 1–5.
59. Majumder, R.; Ghosh, A.; Ledwich, G.; Zare, F. Operation and control of hybrid microgrid with angle droop controller. In Proceedings of the TENCON 2010–2010 IEEE Region 10 Conference, Fukuoka, Japan, 21–24 November 2010; pp. 509–515.
60. Majumder, R.; Chaudhuri, B.; Ghosh, A.; Majumder, R.; Ledwich, G.; Zare, F. Improvement of stability and load sharing in an autonomous microgrid using supplementary droop control loop. *IEEE Trans. Power Syst.* **2009**, *25*, 796–808. [CrossRef]
61. Farhadi, M.; Mohammed, O. Adaptive energy management in redundant hybrid DC microgrid for pulse load mitigation. *IEEE Trans. Smart Grid* **2014**, *6*, 54–62. [CrossRef]
62. Wang, H.; Yan, Z.; Xu, X.; He, K. Probabilistic power flow analysis of microgrid with renewable energy. *Int. J. Electr. Power Energy Syst.* **2020**, *114*, 105393. [CrossRef]
63. Kongjeen, Y.; Bhumkittipich, K.; Mithulananthan, N.; Amiri, I.; Yupapin, P. A modified backward and forward sweep method for microgrid load flow analysis under different electric vehicle load mathematical models. *Electr. Power Syst. Res.* **2019**, *168*, 46–54. [CrossRef]
64. Abdelaziz, M.M.A.; Farag, H.E.; El-Saadany, E.F.; Mohamed, Y.A.R.I. A novel and generalized three-phase power flow algorithm for islanded microgrids using a newton trust region method. *IEEE Trans. Power Syst.* **2012**, *28*, 190–201. [CrossRef]
65. Li, C.; Chaudhary, S.K.; Savaghebi, M.; Vasquez, J.C.; Guerrero, J.M. Power flow analysis for low-voltage AC and DC microgrids considering droop control and virtual impedance. *IEEE Trans. Smart Grid* **2016**, *8*, 2754–2764. [CrossRef]
66. Allam, M.A.; Hamad, A.A.; Kazerani, M.; El-Saadany, E.F. A steady-state analysis tool for unbalanced islanded hybrid AC/DC microgrids. *Electr. Power Syst. Res.* **2017**, *152*, 71–83. [CrossRef]
67. Xiao, Y.; Ren, C.; Han, X.; Wang, P. A generalized and mode-adaptive approach to the power flow analysis of the isolated hybrid AC/DC microgrids. *Energies* **2019**, *12*, 2253. [CrossRef]
68. Wang, R.; Sun, Q.; Ma, D.; Zhang, X. The equivalent impedance characteristic analysis of the AC microgrid and its decoupled power flow calculation. *Int. Trans. Electr. Energy Syst.* **2019**, *29*, e2820. [CrossRef]

69. Wang, R.; Sun, Q.; Liu, X.; Ma, D. Power flow calculation based on local controller impedance features for the AC microgrid with distributed generations. *IET Energy Syst. Integr.* **2019**, *1*, 202–209. [CrossRef]
70. Morgan, M.Y.; Shaaban, M.F.; Sindi, H.F.; Zeineldin, H.H. A holomorphic embedding power flow algorithm for islanded hybrid AC/DC microgrids. *IEEE Trans. Smart Grid* **2022**, *13*, 1813–1825. [CrossRef]
71. Allam, M.A.; Hamad, A.A.; Kazerani, M. A sequence-component-based power-flow analysis for unbalanced droop-controlled hybrid AC/DC microgrids. *IEEE Trans. Sustain. Energy* **2018**, *10*, 1248–1261. [CrossRef]
72. Jha, B.K.; Kumar, A.; Dheer, D.K.; Singh, D.; Misra, R.K. A modified current injection load flow method under different load model of EV for distribution system. *Int. Trans. Electr. Energy Syst.* **2020**, *30*, e12284. [CrossRef]
73. Sunderland, K.; Coppo, M.; Conlon, M.; Turri, R. A correction current injection method for power flow analysis of unbalanced multiple-grounded 4-wire distribution networks. *Electr. Power Syst. Res.* **2016**, *132*, 30–38. [CrossRef]
74. López-Santos, O.; Salas-Castaño, M.C.; Salazar-Dantonio, D.F. Continuous Simulation of the Power Flow in AC–DC Hybrid Microgrids Using Simplified Modelling. *Computation* **2022**, *10*, 52. [CrossRef]
75. Srivastava, A.K.; Kumar, A.A.; Schulz, N.N. Impact of distributed generations with energy storage devices on the electric grid. *IEEE Syst. J.* **2012**, *6*, 110–117. [CrossRef]
76. Chen, Y.; Hesse, R.; Turschner, D.; Beck, H.P. Improving the grid power quality using virtual synchronous machines. In Proceedings of the 2011 International Conference on Power Engineering, Energy and Electrical Drives, Malaga, Spain, 11–13 May 2011; pp. 1–6.
77. Liu, J.; Miura, Y.; Ise, T. Comparison of dynamic characteristics between virtual synchronous generator and droop control in inverter-based distributed generators. *IEEE Trans. Power Electron.* **2015**, *31*, 3600–3611. [CrossRef]
78. Chen, Y.; Hesse, R.; Turschner, D.; Beck, H.P. Comparison of methods for implementing virtual synchronous machine on inverters. In Proceedings of the International Conference on Renewable Energies and Power Quality, Santiago de Compostela, Spain, 28–30 March 2012; Volume 1, pp. 1–15.
79. Lee, J.O.; Kim, Y.S.; Moon, S.I. Current injection power flow analysis and optimal generation dispatch for bipolar DC microgrids. *IEEE Trans. Smart Grid* **2020**, *12*, 1918–1928. [CrossRef]
80. Li, J.; Cai, H.; Yang, P.; Wei, W. A bus-sectionalized hybrid ac/dc microgrid: Concept, control paradigm, and implementation. *Energies* **2021**, *14*, 3508. [CrossRef]
81. Li, C.; Chaudhary, S.K.; Vasquez, J.C.; Guerrero, J.M. Power flow analysis for droop controlled LV hybrid AC-DC microgrids with virtual impedance. In Proceedings of the 2014 IEEE PES General Meeting | Conference & Exposition, National Harbor, MD, USA, 27–31 July 2014; pp. 1–4.
82. Das, B.K.; Al-Abdeli, Y.M.; Kothapalli, G. Effect of load following strategies, hardware, and thermal load distribution on stand-alone hybrid CCHP systems. *Appl. Energy* **2018**, *220*, 735–753. [CrossRef]
83. Luna, A.C.; Meng, L.; Diaz, N.L.; Graells, M.; Vasquez, J.C.; Guerrero, J.M. Online energy management systems for microgrids: Experimental validation and assessment framework. *IEEE Trans. Power Electron.* **2017**, *33*, 2201–2215. [CrossRef]
84. Guan, M.; Pan, W.; Zhang, J.; Hao, Q.; Cheng, J.; Zheng, X. Synchronous generator emulation control strategy for voltage source converter (VSC) stations. *IEEE Trans. Power Syst.* **2015**, *30*, 3093–3101. [CrossRef]
85. Wang, P.; Jin, C.; Zhu, D.; Tang, Y.; Loh, P.C.; Choo, F.H. Distributed control for autonomous operation of a three-port AC/DC/DS hybrid microgrid. *IEEE Trans. Ind. Electron.* **2014**, *62*, 1279–1290. [CrossRef]
86. Radwan, A.A.A.; Mohamed, Y.A.R.I. Networked control and power management of AC/DC hybrid microgrids. *IEEE Syst. J.* **2014**, *11*, 1662–1673. [CrossRef]
87. Mohamed, Y.A.R.I.; El-Saadany, E.F. Adaptive decentralized droop controller to preserve power sharing stability of paralleled inverters in distributed generation microgrids. *IEEE Trans. Power Electron.* **2008**, *23*, 2806–2816. [CrossRef]
88. Bhavana, G.; Anand, R.; Ramprabhakar, J.; Meena, V.; Jadoun, V.K.; Benedetto, F. Applications of blockchain technology in peer-to-peer energy markets and green hydrogen supply chains: A topical review. *Sci. Rep.* **2024**, *14*, 21954. [CrossRef]
89. Mathur, A.; Das, B.; Pant, V. Fault analysis of unbalanced radial and meshed distribution system with inverter based distributed generation (IBDG). *Int. J. Electr. Power Energy Syst.* **2017**, *85*, 164–177. [CrossRef]
90. Plet, C.A.; Graovac, M.; Green, T.C.; Iravani, R. Fault response of grid-connected inverter dominated networks. In Proceedings of the IEEE PES General Meeting, Minneapolis, MN, USA, 25–29 July 2010; pp. 1–8.
91. Plet, C.A.; Green, T.C. Fault response of inverter interfaced distributed generators in grid-connected applications. *Electr. Power Syst. Res.* **2014**, *106*, 21–28. [CrossRef]
92. Baskaran, J.; Naghapushanam, M.; Ganapathy, M.; Meena, P.; Meena, V.; Azar, A.T.; Hameed, I.A. Cost-effective high-gain dc-dc converter for elevator drives using photovoltaic power and switched reluctance motors. *Front. Energy Res.* **2024**, *12*, 1400651. [CrossRef]
93. Rodriguez, P.; Timbus, A.V.; Teodorescu, R.; Liserre, M.; Blaabjerg, F. Flexible active power control of distributed power generation systems during grid faults. *IEEE Trans. Ind. Electron.* **2007**, *54*, 2583–2592. [CrossRef]
94. Camacho, A.; Castilla, M.; Miret, J.; Vasquez, J.C.; Alarcon-Gallo, E. Flexible voltage support control for three-phase distributed generation inverters under grid fault. *IEEE Trans. Ind. Electron.* **2012**, *60*, 1429–1441. [CrossRef]
95. Miret, J.; Castilla, M.; Camacho, A.; de Vicuña, L.G.; Matas, J. Control scheme for photovoltaic three-phase inverters to minimize peak currents during unbalanced grid-voltage sags. *IEEE Trans. Power Electron.* **2012**, *27*, 4262–4271. [CrossRef]

96. DebBarman, S.; Namrata, K.; Kumar, N.; Meena, V. Optimising power distribution systems: Solar-powered capacitors and cost reduction through meta-heuristic methods. *Int. J. Intell. Eng. Inform.* **2024**, *12*, 188–212. [CrossRef]
97. Wang, Q.; Zhou, N.; Ye, L. Fault analysis for distribution networks with current-controlled three-phase inverter-interfaced distributed generators. *IEEE Trans. Power Deliv.* **2015**, *30*, 1532–1542. [CrossRef]
98. Nimpitiwan, N.; Heydt, G.T.; Ayyanar, R.; Suryanarayanan, S. Fault current contribution from synchronous machine and inverter based distributed generators. *IEEE Trans. Power Deliv.* **2006**, *22*, 634–641. [CrossRef]
99. Ebrahimi, E.; Sanjari, M.J.; Gharehpetian, G.B. Control of three-phase inverter-based DG system during fault condition without changing protection coordination. *Int. J. Electr. Power Energy Syst.* **2014**, *63*, 814–823. [CrossRef]
100. Darwish, A.; Abdel-Khalik, A.; Elserougi, A.; Ahmed, S.; Massoud, A. Fault current contribution scenarios for grid-connected voltage source inverter-based distributed generation with an LCL filter. *Electr. Power Syst. Res.* **2013**, *104*, 93–103. [CrossRef]
101. Baran, M.E.; El-Markaby, I. Fault analysis on distribution feeders with distributed generators. *IEEE Trans. Power Syst.* **2005**, *20*, 1757–1764. [CrossRef]
102. Tan, A.; Liu, W.H.; Shirmohammadi, D. Transformer and load modeling in short circuit analysis for distribution systems. *IEEE Trans. Power Syst.* **1997**, *12*, 1315–1322. [CrossRef]
103. Abdel-Akher, M.; Nor, K.M. Fault analysis of multiphase distribution systems using symmetrical components. *IEEE Trans. Power Deliv.* **2010**, *25*, 2931–2939. [CrossRef]
104. Chen, T.H.; Chen, M.S.; Lee, W.J.; Kotas, P.; Van Olinda, P. Distribution system short circuit analysis-A rigid approach. *IEEE Trans. Power Syst.* **1992**, *7*, 444–450. [CrossRef]
105. Halpin, S.; Grigsby, L.; Gross, C.; Nelms, R. An improved fault analysis algorithm for unbalanced multi-phase power distribution systems. *IEEE Trans. Power Deliv.* **1994**, *9*, 1332–1338. [CrossRef]
106. Zhang, X.; Soudi, F.; Shirmohammadi, D.; Cheng, C.S. A distribution short circuit analysis approach using hybrid compensation method. *IEEE Trans. Power Syst.* **1995**, *10*, 2053–2059. [CrossRef]
107. Mao, Y.; Miu, K. Radial distribution system short circuit analysis with lateral and load equivalencing: Solution algorithms and numerical results. In Proceedings of the 2000 Power Engineering Society Summer Meeting (Cat. No. 00CH37134), Seattle, WA, USA, 16–20 July 2000; Volume 1, pp. 449–453.
108. Teng, J.H. Fast short circuit analysis method for unbalanced distribution systems. In Proceedings of the 2003 IEEE Power Engineering Society General Meeting (IEEE Cat. No. 03CH37491), Toronto, ON, Canada, 13–17 July 2003; Volume 1, pp. 240–245.
109. Chen, T.H.; Chen, M.S.; Inoue, T.; Kotas, P.; Chebli, E.A. Three-phase cogenerator and transformer models for distribution system analysis. *IEEE Trans. Power Deliv.* **1991**, *6*, 1671–1681. [CrossRef]
110. Paz, M.C.R.; Ferraz, R.G.; Bretas, A.S.; Leborgne, R.C. System unbalance and fault impedance effect on faulted distribution networks. *Comput. Math. Appl.* **2010**, *60*, 1105–1114.
111. Filomena, A.D.; Resener, M.; Salim, R.H.; Bretas, A.S. Distribution systems fault analysis considering fault resistance estimation. *Int. J. Electr. Power Energy Syst.* **2011**, *33*, 1326–1335. [CrossRef]
112. Saha, S.; Aldeen, M.; Tan, C.P. Unsymmetrical fault diagnosis in transmission/distribution networks. *Int. J. Electr. Power Energy Syst.* **2013**, *45*, 252–263. [CrossRef]
113. Lacroix, J.S.; Kocar, I.; Belletête, M. Accelerated computation of multiphase short circuit summary for unbalanced distribution systems using the concept of selected inversion. *IEEE Trans. Power Syst.* **2012**, *28*, 1515–1522. [CrossRef]
114. Penido, D.R.R.; de Araujo, L.R.; de Carvalho Filho, M. An enhanced tool for fault analysis in multiphase electrical systems. *Int. J. Electr. Power Energy Syst.* **2016**, *75*, 215–225. [CrossRef]
115. Klucznik, J. Earth wires currents calculation by tableau analysis. *Electr. Power Syst. Res.* **2017**, *151*, 329–337. [CrossRef]
116. Favuzza, S.; Mitolo, M.; Moradi, S.; Musca, R.; Zizzo, G. A General Methodology for Short-circuit Calculations in Hybrid AC/DC Microgrids. *IEEE Trans. Ind. Appl.* **2023**, *59*, 2742–2749. [CrossRef]
117. Kim, I. Short-circuit analysis models for unbalanced inverter-based distributed generation sources and loads. *IEEE Trans. Power Syst.* **2019**, *34*, 3515–3526. [CrossRef]
118. Ou, T.C. A novel unsymmetrical faults analysis for microgrid distribution systems. *Int. J. Electr. Power Energy Syst.* **2012**, *43*, 1017–1024. [CrossRef]
119. Yu, M.; Wang, Y.; Zhang, L.; Zhang, Z. DC short circuit fault analysis and protection of ring type DC microgrid. In Proceedings of the 2016 IEEE 8th International Power Electronics and Motion Control Conference (IPEMC-ECCE Asia), Hefei, China, 22–26 May 2016; pp. 1694–1700.
120. Lu, X.; Wang, J.; Guerrero, J.M.; Zhao, D. Virtual-impedance-based fault current limiters for inverter dominated AC microgrids. *IEEE Trans. Smart Grid* **2016**, *9*, 1599–1612. [CrossRef]
121. Zhao, M.; Zheng, X. Waveform characteristic analysis and recognition of short-circuit fault in grid-connected AC microgrid. In Proceedings of the 2019 4th International Conference on Intelligent Green Building and Smart Grid (IGBSG), Yichang, China, 6–9 September 2019; pp. 732–735.
122. Eisapour-Moarref, A.; Kalantar, M.; Esmaili, M. Control strategy resilient to unbalanced faults for interlinking converters in hybrid microgrids. *Int. J. Electr. Power Energy Syst.* **2020**, *119*, 105927. [CrossRef]
123. Azizpour, A.; Radmehr, M.; Firouzi, M.; Gharehpetian, G. Single AC/DC fault current limiter for both side of hybrid AC/DC microgrid. *Int. J. Electron.* **2022**, *110*, 1337–1354. [CrossRef]

124. Xiao, F.; Xia, Y.; Zhang, K.; Zhang, Z.; Yin, X. Short-circuit calculation method for unbalanced distribution networks with doubly fed induction generators. *Electr. Power Syst. Res.* **2022**, *210*, 108108. [CrossRef]
125. Miret, J.; Castilla, M.; Velasco, M.; Guzmán, R.; de Vicuña, L.G. Maximum current injection method for grid-forming inverters in an islanded microgrid subject to short circuits. *IET Power Electron.* **2023**, *16*, 1028–1042. [CrossRef]
126. Wang, Z.; Mu, L.; Xu, Y.; Zhang, F.; Zhu, J. The fault analysis method of islanded microgrid based on the U/f and PQ control strategy. *Int. Trans. Electr. Energy Syst.* **2021**, *31*, e12919. [CrossRef]
127. Teng, J.H. Unsymmetrical short-circuit fault analysis for weakly meshed distribution systems. *IEEE Trans. Power Syst.* **2009**, *25*, 96–105. [CrossRef]
128. Bayindir, R.; Irmak, E.; Issi, F.; Guler, N. Short-circuit fault analysis on microgrid. In Proceedings of the 2015 International Conference on Renewable Energy Research and Applications (ICRERA), Palermo, Italy, 22–25 November 2015; pp. 1248–1252.
129. Simic, N.; Strezoski, L.; Dumnic, B. Short-circuit analysis of DER-based microgrids in connected and islanded modes of operation. *Energies* **2021**, *14*, 6372. [CrossRef]
130. Seyedi, Y.; Mahseredjian, J.; Karimi, H. Impact of fault impedance and duration on transient response of hybrid AC/DC microgrid. *Electr. Power Syst. Res.* **2021**, *197*, 107298. [CrossRef]
131. Hooshyar, H.; Baran, M.E. Fault analysis on distribution feeders with high penetration of PV systems. *IEEE Trans. Power Syst.* **2012**, *28*, 2890–2896. [CrossRef]
132. Furlaneto, R.; Kocar, I.; Grilo-Pavani, A.; Karaagac, U.; Haddadi, A.; Farantatos, E. Short circuit network equivalents of systems with inverter-based resources. *Electr. Power Syst. Res.* **2021**, *199*, 107314. [CrossRef]
133. Nahas, E.W.; Abd el Ghany, H.A.; Mansour, D.E.A.; Eissa, M. Extensive analysis of fault response and extracting fault features for DC microgrids. *Alex. Eng. J.* **2021**, *60*, 2405–2420. [CrossRef]
134. Fu, R.; Montross, K.C. A New Method of Coordinating ZCBs and Fuses for a Reliable Short-Circuit Protection in DC Power Networks. *IEEE Access* **2022**, *10*, 63270–63279. [CrossRef]
135. Hsieh, T.Y.; Chen, T.H.; Yang, N.C.; Lee, W.J. Efficient network fault analysis method for unbalanced microgrid systems. *Int. J. Electr. Power Energy Syst.* **2018**, *103*, 89–101. [CrossRef]
136. He, J.; Li, Z.; Li, W.; Zou, J.; Li, X.; Wu, F. Fast short-circuit current calculation of unbalanced distribution networks with inverter-interfaced distributed generators. *Int. J. Electr. Power Energy Syst.* **2023**, *146*, 108728. [CrossRef]
137. Luka, S.; Simic, N.; Dumnic, B. Fault current study of microgrids in grid-connected and islanded modes of operation. In Proceedings of the 12th Mediterranean Conference on Power Generation, Transmission, Distribution and Energy Conversion (MEDPOWER 2020), IET, Paphos, Cyprus, 9–12 November 2020; Volume 2020, pp. 372–377.
138. Casagrande, E.; Woon, W.L.; Zeineldin, H.H.; Svetinovic, D. A differential sequence component protection scheme for microgrids with inverter-based distributed generators. *IEEE Trans. Smart Grid* **2013**, *5*, 29–37. [CrossRef]
139. Sortomme, E.; Venkata, S.; Mitr, J. Microgrid Protection Using Communication-Assisted Digital Relays. *IEEE Trans. Power Deliv.* **2010**, *25*, 2789–2796. [CrossRef]
140. Rajaei, N.; Ahmed, M.H.; Salama, M.M.; Varma, R.K. Fault current management using inverter-based distributed generators in smart grids. *IEEE Trans. Smart Grid* **2014**, *5*, 2183–2193. [CrossRef]
141. Li, X.; Dyśko, A.; Burt, G.M. Traveling wave-based protection scheme for inverter-dominated microgrid using mathematical morphology. *IEEE Trans. Smart Grid* **2014**, *5*, 2211–2218. [CrossRef]
142. Elkhatib, M.E.; Ellis, A. Communication-assisted impedance-based microgrid protection scheme. In Proceedings of the 2017 IEEE Power & Energy Society General Meeting, Chicago, IL, USA, 16–20 July 2017; pp. 1–5.
143. Nian, H.; Kong, L. Transient modeling and analysis of VSC based DC microgrid during short circuit fault. *IEEE Access* **2019**, *7*, 170604–170614. [CrossRef]
144. Zha, X.; Ning, H.; Lai, X.; Huang, Y.; Liu, F. Suppression strategy for short-circuit current in loop-type DC microgrid. In Proceedings of the 2014 IEEE Energy Conversion Congress and Exposition (ECCE), Pittsburgh, PA, USA,14–18 September 2014; pp. 758–764.
145. Dağ, B.; Boynueğri, A.R.; Ateş, Y.; Karakaş, A.; Nadar, A.; Uzunoğlu, M. Static modeling of microgrids for load flow and fault analysis. *IEEE Trans. Power Syst.* **2016**, *32*, 1990–2000. [CrossRef]
146. Jia, K.; Bi, T.; Ren, Z.; Thomas, D.W.; Sumner, M. High frequency impedance based fault location in distribution system with DGs. *IEEE Trans. Smart Grid* **2016**, *9*, 807–816. [CrossRef]

Mathematical and Computational Applications

MDPI

Article

Optimized Nonlinear PID Control for Maximum Power Point Tracking in PV Systems Using Particle Swarm Optimization

Maeva Cybelle Zoleko Zambou [1], Alain Soup Tewa Kammogne [1,*], Martin Siewe Siewe [2], Ahmad Taher Azar [3,4,*], Saim Ahmed [3,4] and Ibrahim A. Hameed [5,*]

1 Laboratory of Condensed Matter, Electronics and Signal Processing (LAMACETS), Department of Physics, Faculty of Sciences, University of Dschang, Dschang P.O. Box 67, Cameroon; zamboumaeva@gmail.com
2 Laboratory of Mechanics, Materials and Structures, Faculty of Science, Department of Physics, University of Yaounde 1, Yaounde P.O. Box 812, Cameroon; martinsiewesiewe@yahoo.fr
3 College of Computer and Information Sciences, Prince Sultan University, Riyadh 11586, Saudi Arabia; sahmed@psu.edu.sa
4 Automated Systems and Soft Computing Lab (ASSCL), Prince Sultan University, Riyadh 11586, Saudi Arabia
5 Department of ICT and Natural Sciences, Norwegian University of Science and Technology, Larsgårdsvegen 2, 6009 Ålesund, Norway
* Correspondence: alain.kammogne@univ-dschang.org (A.S.T.K.); aazar@psu.edu.sa (A.T.A.); ibib@ntnu.no (I.A.H.)

Abstract: This paper proposes a high-performing, hybrid method for Maximum Power Point Tracking (MPPT) in photovoltaic (PV) systems. The approach is based on an intelligent Nonlinear Discrete Proportional–Integral–Derivative (N-DPID) controller with the Perturb and Observe (P&O) method. The feedback gains derived are optimized by a metaheuristic algorithm called Particle Swarm Optimization (PSO). The proposed methods appear to present adequate solutions to overcome the drawbacks of existing methods despite various weather conditions considered in the analysis, providing a robust solution for dynamic environmental conditions. The results showed better performance and accuracy compared to those encountered in the literature. We also recall that this technique provides a systematic design procedure in the search for the MPPT in photovoltaic (PV) systems that has not yet been documented in the literature to the best of our knowledge.

Keywords: photovoltaic system; perturb and observe; discrete nonlinear PID; particle swarm optimization; maximum power point tracking

1. Introduction

Energy has been the main driver of human life for a long time and plays a vital role in countries' daily activity and development. Energy production is essential to all human activities, and the need for energy in developing countries has increased dramatically in recent years. The majority of the energy generated globally comes from fossil fuels, such as coal, oil, and natural gas [1,2]. These fuels release greenhouse gases into the atmosphere, which increases pollution [3–5]. Moreover, these fuels are in perpetual depletion, which dangerously reduces the reserves of these types of energy for future generations. Faced with all these grievances, countries with enormous energy need to resort to renewable energy such as solar, hydro, wind, fuel cells, and geothermal energy [6,7]. These sources are up-and-coming solutions to compete with other energy sources. Their main advantages are that they are inexhaustible and non-polluting. Their exploitations allow humans to ensure their energy needs in the case of countries with high energy expectations, and their strategic position makes them an ideal candidate for electrical installations using solar energy.

Solar energy is readily available due to the advancement of research and is currently among the most significant sources of environmentally friendly renewable energy [8–10].

A photovoltaic system is used to exploit this energy, but it depends on climatic conditions such as solar irradiation and temperature [11,12]. These climatic variations cause fluctuations around the maximum power point. Therefore, researchers have established and used several methods for tracking the maximum power point of photovoltaic (PV) systems. These schemes consist of associating a controller called Maximum Power Point Tracking (MPPT) to the inverter, which performs a permanent search for the maximum power point (MPP) [13]. The Perturb and Observe (P and O) method is the simplest and most widely used method in the world, and it does not require prior knowledge of the PV system characteristics and is easy to implement with analog and digital circuits [14,15]. However, this technique suffers from oscillations around the MPP due to its fixed variation step during the search process. Moreover, it offers low efficiency and slow response and does not track the MPP well in varying environmental conditions [16–18]. The conductance increment method offers better performance than the P&O scheme but also experiences oscillations around the MPP. Moreover, this method has a complex MPP search process because it requires a variation of the current and voltage of the PV panel [19,20]. Several researchers have mobilized to search for techniques to improve the P&O method, which allows for obtaining good performance with hybrid systems based on artificial intelligence (AI) such as artificial neural networks (ANN) [21] and fuzzy logic [22,23]. However, their implementation is difficult because of their high computational complexity, so finding a balance between accuracy and simplicity is essential.

In the control engineering area, developing a controller that is easy to implement and performs well is desired, which can adapt to changing environmental conditions, provide quality service, and effectively track the MPP [24,25]. It is worth noting that accuracy, speed, efficiency, and simplicity are necessary conditions for implementing an MPPT algorithm in photovoltaic systems [26,27], especially when the weather conditions vary. The P&O algorithm is simple but presents more disadvantages, such as weak accuracy and a long transient time of reaching the MPP, which confer poor performance to the strategy. The discrete nonlinear proportional–integral–derivative controller (N-DPID) is a unique controller that has the same simple structure as a linear PID controller. The use of this device for controlling and maintaining the simplicity of the system while addressing the limitations of conventional P&O methods stands as one of the significant contributions of this paper. This combination aims to improve the efficiency, robustness and easiest of implementation of Maximum Power Point Tracking in photovoltaic systems, which has not yet been considered in the literature. One of the difficulties of this method is the parameterization of the gains N-DPID controller to obtain optimal performance [28]. For this purpose, intelligent techniques such as Particle Swarm Optimization (PSO), genetic algorithm (GA), and many others are used. The robustness of the nonlinear PID has been proven in several engineering problems and has shown its effectiveness in tracking the MPP of photovoltaic systems [29]. In this work, a method for improving the performance of the P&O methods of a solar PV system has been proposed, based on the use of an N-DPID controller, so the gains are obtained by an intelligent approach called Particle Swarm Optimization (PSO), which has been designed and simulated in MATLAB/SIMULINK software.

The rest of this paper is planned as follows: Section 2 describes the photovoltaic cells. Section 3 gives a block diagram of the completely controlled PV system and the electrical circuit of the converter considered in the analysis. Section 4 covers the problem formulation. Section 5 presents the simulation and the results of the suggested scheme. Section 6 provides the conclusions.

2. Modeling of the Photovoltaic Cell

The corresponding circuit of the PV cell is illustrated in Figure 1. It is a single-diode model that is simple and efficient. It is generally used for modeling and implementation of strategic controls. This model has a diode and a current source connected antiparallel to the diode [30,31]. A series resistor and a parallel resistor are included in the schematic to account for parasitic effects.

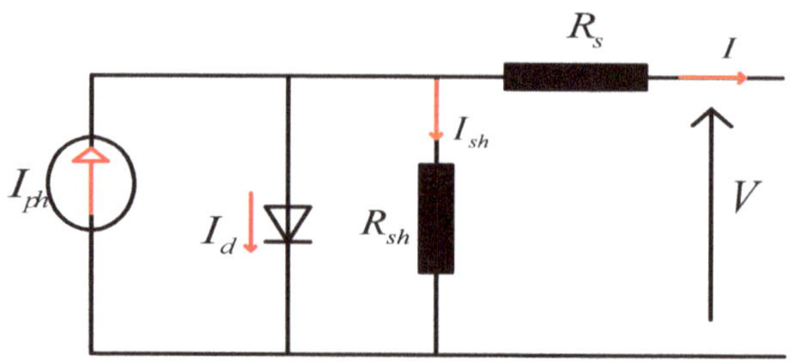

Figure 1. Equivalent circuit of the single-diode cell.

The following is an expression for the PV cell's output current:

$$I = I_{ph} - I_d - I_{sh} \tag{1}$$

Respectively, the diode and parallel resistor currents are given by the following relations:

$$I_d = I_o \left[\exp\left(\frac{V + R_S I}{n V_{th}} \right) - 1 \right] \tag{2}$$

$$I_{sh} = \frac{V + R_S I}{R_{sh}} \tag{3}$$

So, the general equation of the output current is given by

$$I = I_{ph} - I_o \left[\exp\left(\frac{V + R_S I}{n V_{th}} \right) - 1 \right] - \frac{V + R_S I}{R_{sh}} \tag{4}$$

The output voltage and current of the PV cell are denoted by I and V, respectively. The reverse saturation current is denoted by I_o, the series resistance by R_S, the parallel resistance by R_{sh}, the thermal voltage by V_{th}, and n is the constant of the diode.

3. Modeling and Description of the PV System

The system given by the circuit in Figure 2 consists of a PV panel, a DC-DC power boost converter, a load, and an MPPT controller. In this case, the boost converter is controlled by a discrete nonlinear PID controller based on the MPPT control, which receives inputs from the MPPT reference voltage generated by the P&O algorithm and the instantaneous PV voltage V_{PV}.

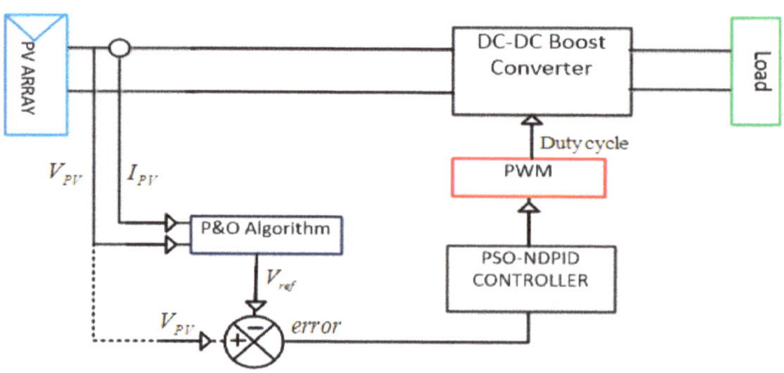

Figure 2. Block diagram for MPPT with PV.

To ensure the power transfer between the load and photovoltaic generator, we insert between the two blocks a matching stage, also called a converter; in our case, we have chosen a static DC-DC boost converter, allowing a rise in the PV generator's output voltage.

This converter has shown good performance for MPP tracking in photovoltaic systems, and its primary application is to regulate the power supply [32]. Its equivalent circuit is depicted in Figure 3 and includes an inductor (L), a capacitor (C), a power switch MOSFET (Q), a diode D, and the load (R).

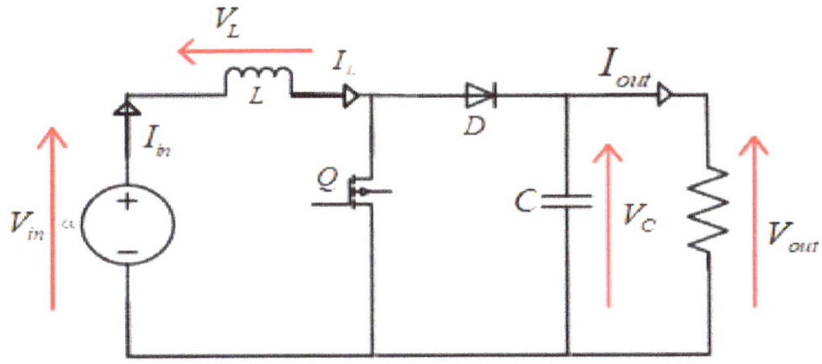

Figure 3. Equivalent circuit of boost converter.

The following relationships between the i/o voltage and i/o current of the converter are given as

$$\frac{V_{out}}{V_{in}} = \frac{1}{1-d} \tag{5}$$

$$\frac{I_{out}}{I_{in}} = 1 - d \tag{6}$$

where d is the duty cycle of the converter.

4. Problem Formulation

4.1. Perturb and Observe Method

This technique is among the most frequently utilized in the literature [33]. It depends on the photovoltaic generator voltage (V_{PV}), the disturbance of the photovoltaic generator voltage dV, and the power variation dP; a disturbance can be detected, so a positive disturbance of V_{PV} leads to an increase in power. Otherwise, it will tend to return to the initial disturbance. Since the search process is periodic, the step size variation also keeps the exact nature, which lightly reduces the error. It is important to recall that a very weak step size may cause the MPP to track slowly. The variation of this step leads to oscillations around the MPP, and the MPP cannot be followed efficiently in unstable environmental conditions. The P&O algorithm is given in the flowchart in Figure 4:

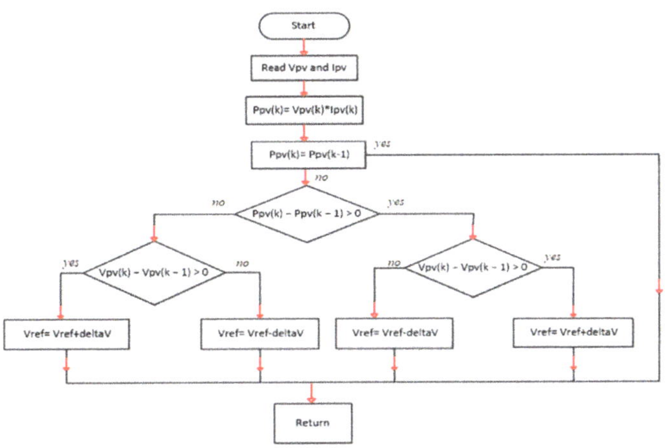

Figure 4. Flow chart of P&O algorithm [34].

4.2. Nonlinear PID Control Scheme

Significant advancements have been made in the design of nonlinear systems for various practical applications in recent decades. Numerous innovative approaches have emerged, including optimal control, nonlinear feedback control, adaptive control, sliding mode control, nonlinear dynamics, chaos control, chaos synchronization control, fuzzy logic control, fuzzy adaptive control, fractional order control, robust control, and their integrations [35,36].

The nonlinear PID is a modified form of the conventional PID [37]. Azar and Serrano stated that the selection of the nonlinear function depends upon the application's specific demands [38]. In order to minimize overshoot and oscillations around the MPP, and to reduce substantial errors that contribute to the lowering of system stabilization time, the nonlinear hyperbolic cosine equation has been used [24]. Depending on the error value, the nonlinear PID scheme generates the following control signal:

$$u(t) = k_p e(t) + k_i \int_0^t f(v)e(t)dt + k_d \frac{d}{dt}[e(t)] \tag{7}$$

where k_p is the proportional gain, k_i is integral gain, k_d is derivative gain, and $f(v)$ is the nonlinear function.

To set up the control algorithm using numerical tools, the discretization was performed by the forward Euler method [28]. The Laplace transformation applied to Equation (7) allows us to obtain an N-DPID controller presented as follows:

$$u(z) = k_p e + k_i T_S \frac{1}{z-1} f(v)e + k_d \frac{z-1}{T_S z} e \tag{8}$$

The nonlinear function is given by Equation (9):

$$f(v) = \cosh(\mu v) = \frac{exp(\mu v) + exp(-\mu v)}{2} \tag{9}$$

where

$$v = \begin{cases} e & ; \quad |e| \leq e_{\max} \\ e_{\max} sign(e) & ; \quad |e| \succ e_{\max} \end{cases} \tag{10}$$

where μ and $e_{\max}$ are positive constants and T_S is the sampling period.

4.3. Particle Swarm Optimization

In the control architecture, using fixed gains to control complex and nonlinear dynamical systems leads to large overshoots in the transient state and low robustness. To find the gains of the N-DPID controller to enhance the efficiency of the P&O scheme, the Particle Swarm Optimization (PSO) algorithm was used. This method was proposed by Kennedy and Eberhart in 1995 [39], and it is a metaheuristic approach based on the behavior of animals in swarms. It is an optimization algorithm based on random solutions known as populations that evolve in the problem space in order to find the most optimum solution corresponding to the lowest value of the cost function. Each particle alters its route according to its own best prior position and the best previous position achieved in the entire population, namely, P_{best} and G_{best}. At each iteration, the population is updated for $i = (1, 2, \ldots, n)$, and "n" is the size of the population by the following process:

$$x_{k+1}^i = x_k^i + v_{k+1}^i \tag{11}$$

$$v_{k+1}^i = wv_k^i + c_1 r_1 (P_{best} - x_k^i) + c_2 r_2 (G_{best} - x_k^i) \tag{12}$$

Equations (11) and (12) represent successively the position and velocity of each particle in the swarm, with w being the inertia factor, c_1 and c_2 the acceleration coefficients, P_{best} the best position of the particle obtained during the current iteration, and G_{best} the best position obtained in the whole swarm at the current iteration. r_1 and r_2 are random numbers uniformly distributed in the interval [0,1]. The flowchart in Figure 5 describes its algorithm.

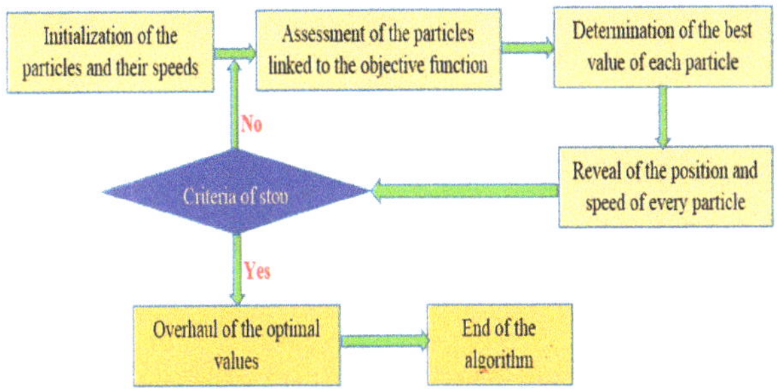

Figure 5. Flow chart of the PSO algorithm [40].

4.4. Proposed Method: P&O Based on Discrete Nonlinear PSO PID Controller (P&O PSO N-DPID)

A properly tuned discrete nonlinear PID (N-DPID) controller is essential to attaining the system's intended output response. The PSO algorithm is used in this study to optimally tune the four critical parameters of the N-DPID controller, such as proportional gain (k_p), integral gain ($k_i sss$), derivative gain (k_d), and the nonlinear factor (μ). In this instance, the search space is four dimensions, and a particle represents each potential set of values for the controller parameters, the values of which are changed by minimizing the Integral Absolute Error (IAE) between the reference MPPT voltage (V_{PV}) and the actual output (V_{ref}). The optimization process halts once the algorithm reaches a predefined maximum number of iterations, ensuring the N-DPID controller operates at peak efficiency. As an objective function, we use the integral absolute error (IAE) to minimize the error to zero, which is defined by Equation (13):

$$IAE = \int |e(t)| dt \tag{13}$$

The algorithm's iteration stops once it reaches a predefined maximum number. The steps for optimizing the parameters of the N-DPID controller using the PSO algorithm are explained in the flowchart in Figure 6. The flowchart begins with the initialization of particles representing different parameter sets in a four-dimensional space. These particles then iteratively move towards the optimal solution based on their position and velocity updates. The figure highlights critical stages, including the evaluation of the cost function (IAE) and the selection of the best particle position, leading to the optimal tuning of the N-DPID controller parameters. To improve clarity, the figure now includes labels and numerical values at each step to better illustrate the algorithm's progression.

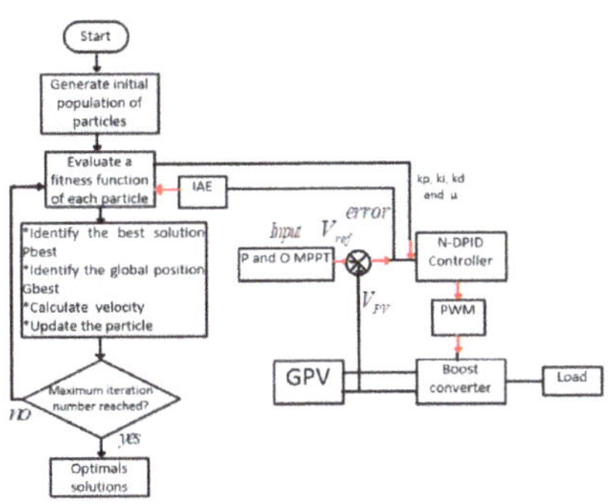

Figure 6. Flowchart of the proposed P&O PSO N-DPID method.

5. Results

The simulations, achieved using Matlab/Simulink software, demonstrate a significant enhancement in MPPT performance when applying the proposed P&O PSO N-DPID controller compared to conventional methods. Table 1 provides the nomenclature of the standard PV system associated with ERA SOLAR ESPMC-205.

Table 1. Keys parameters of the PV system.

Photovoltaic Generator *(ERA SOLAR ESPMC-205)*		Boost Converter	
I_{mpp}	14.34 A	C_{in}	100 μF
V_{mpp}	57.2 V	L	2 mH
V_{mpp}	820.2 W	C_{out}	500 μF
		R	25 Ω

5.1. Convergence of PSO with DPID and N-DPID

The optimal gains parameters obtained for the different controllers are reported in Table 2.

Table 2. Optimal controller gains.

Algorithm	k_p	k_i	k_d	μ
P&O PSO DPID	5.2742	2.7383	0.4963	-
P&O PSO N-DPID	7. 9703	3.899	0.4977	0.1656

Figures 7 and 8 show the convergences of two cost functions of the P&O PSO DPID and P&O PSO N-DPID, respectively. One can observe that the error becomes too small and close to zero from the fiftieth iteration for the DPID controller corresponding to the fiftieth generation with a cost function value of 0.1, compared to the N-DPID controller, which achieves a cost function value of 0.0494 by the forty-third iteration. These annotations clearly illustrate the superior convergence speed and accuracy of the N-DPID controller, respectively. This result highlights the great interest and the importance of the nonlinearity in the discrete PID controllers.

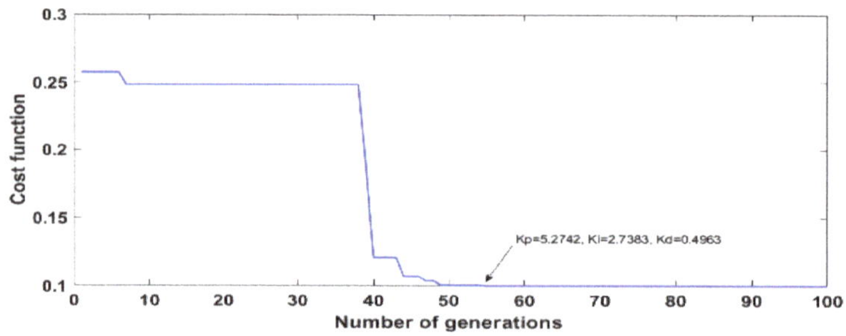

Figure 7. P&O DPID convergence curve.

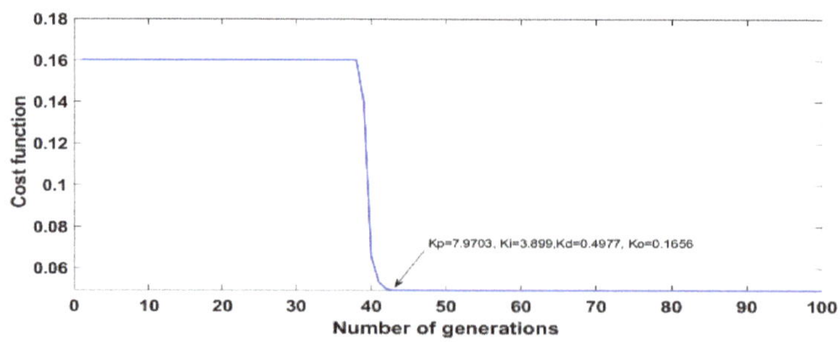

Figure 8. P&O N-DPID convergence curve.

5.2. Effect of Varying Environmental Conditions on PPM

Figures 9 and 10 show, respectively, the irradiation variation at constant temperature (T = 25 °C) and the temperature variation at constant irradiation (1000 W\m²).

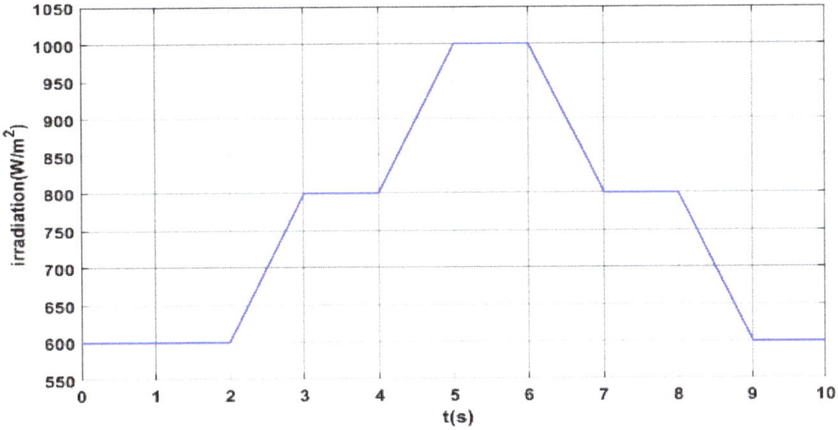

Figure 9. Irradiation profile.

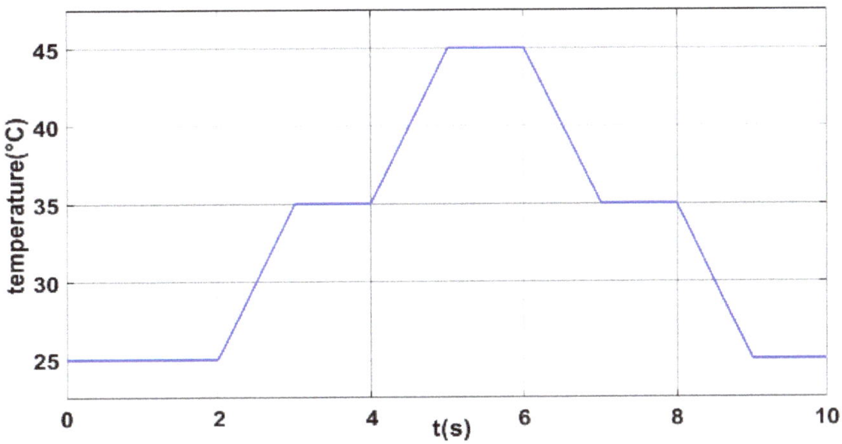

Figure 10. Temperature profile.

5.2.1. Case of Irradiation

Figure 11a represents, respectively, the increase in the irradiation and, consequently, the MPP of the three methods used and depicts the evolution of power according to irradiation. We can observe that the power curve follows the irradiation curve, which is due to the effect of sunlight on the solar panel's output current. It may also determine how the nonlinear controller affects the performance of the MPPT P&O algorithm. More specifically, the three sections, A, B, and C, depict the diverse responses of the system when exposed to temperature fluctuation.

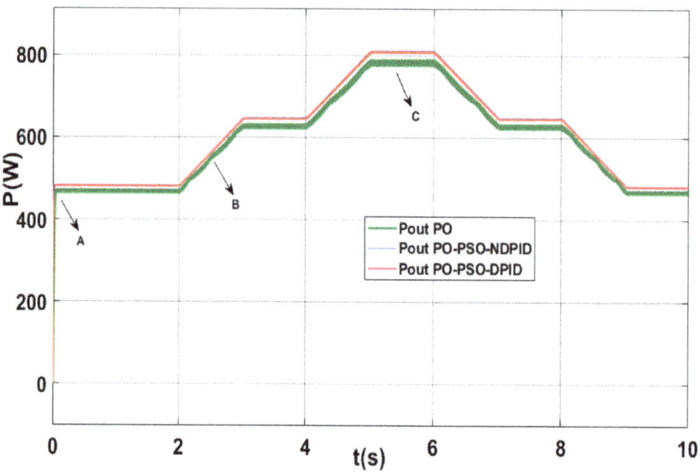

(a)

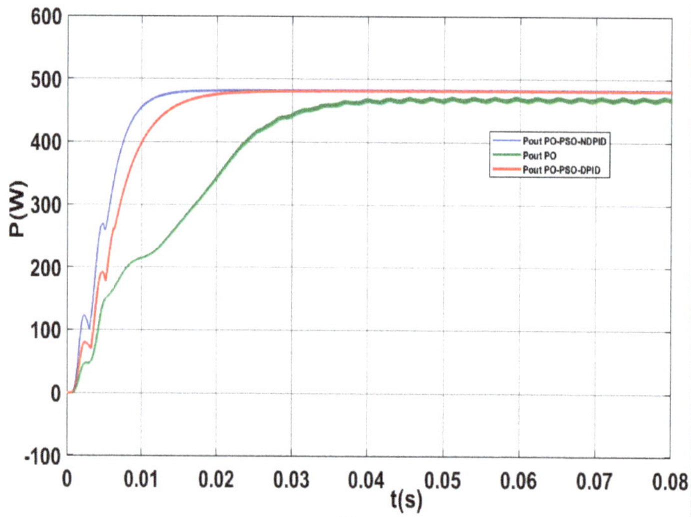

(b)

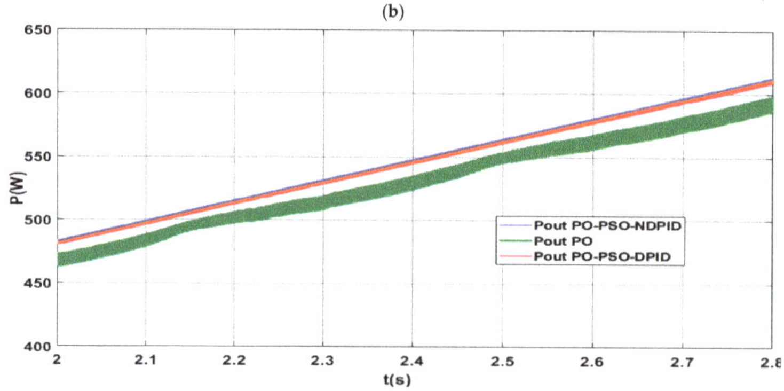

(c)

Figure 11. *Cont.*

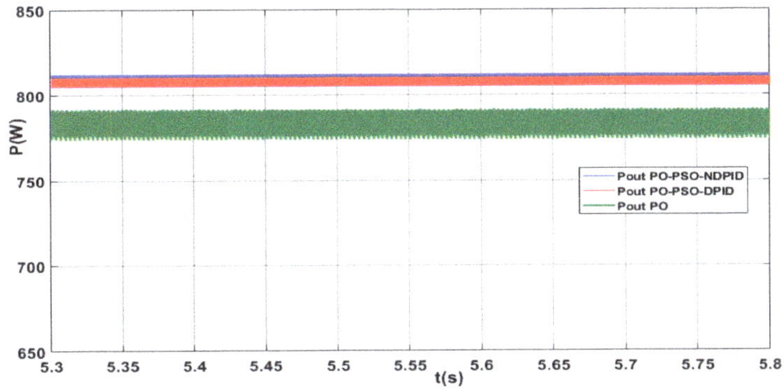

(d)

Figure 11. (**a**) MPPT development during irradiation variation, (**b**) MPPT response in **A**, (**c**) MPPT response in **B**, and (**d**) MPPT response in **C**.

Figure 11b–d show the time evolution of the MPP in the A, B, and C areas. Figure 11b shows a response time of 0.016 s with the P&O N-DPID controller, compared to 0.04 s with the traditional P&O method, clearly annotating the quantitative improvements achieved by the proposed method. Figure 11c demonstrates better stability with the P&O N-DPID controller than with the traditional P&O method. Figure 11d compares the power output during varying irradiation levels across different methods, where the P&O N-DPID method achieves a steady power output of 820.2 W with minimal fluctuations, in contrast to the significant oscillations observed with the traditional P&O method. It is worth underlining it because, briefly, we can notice the impact and interest of nonlinearity on improving P&O performances. This is shown in the oscillations around the MPP, which are significantly decreased when utilizing the ideal gains. At first look, one could believe there is no significant difference between the P&O PSO DPID and the P&O PSO N-DPID. Still, when we consider the impact of the degradation of oscillations around the MPP on commonly used loads, we notice that the designed method P&O PSO N-DPID allows us to significantly reduce its oscillations, highlighting the efficiency and accuracy of the latter, which is one of our objectives.

5.2.2. Case of the Temperature

Figure 12 shows power development as a function of temperature variation and highlights the importance of the optimal gains for the PID and the efficiency of the designed scheme. Similar behaviors are observed, just like in the previous case. The developed scheme shows a superior convergence speed and a decrease in the oscillations concerning the P&O and the P&O PSO DPID. Given these findings, we may conclude that the suggested strategy considerably enhances the efficacy of the P&O method.

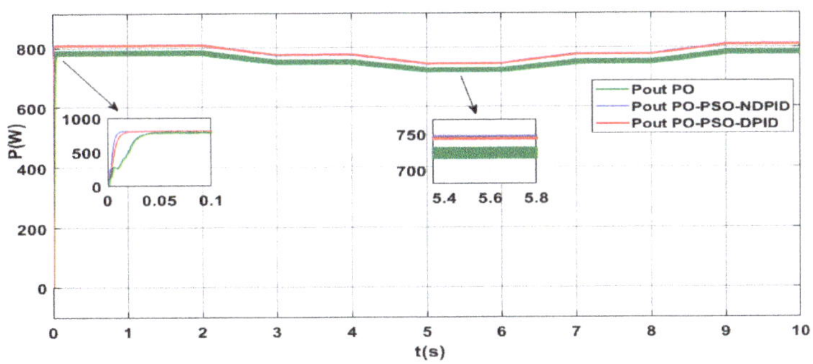

Figure 12. MPPT response to temperature variation.

5.3. Performance Comparisons with Other Standard Algorithms

The performance of a good search for the maximum power point is characterized by the overshoot, the response time, the ripples around it, and the efficiency. These performances are calculated for an irradiation level of 1000 W/m^2. Table 3 shows the performance of the P&O, P&O PSO N-DPID, and P&O PSO DPID MPPT controllers.

Table 3. Performance of P&O, P&O PSO N-DPID, and P&O PSO DPID.

Performance	P&O	P&O DPID	Proposed Method
Response time (s)	0.04	0.025	0.016
ripples	0.024	0.0076	0.007
Performance (%)	96.45	98.75	99.03
Cost function	-	0.1	0.0494

The N-DPID controller shows more advantages by including a reduced response time of 0.016 s, a ripple magnitude of 0.0071, and an overall efficiency of 99.03%. These quantitative improvements are clearly marked, highlighting the superior performance of the proposed method. It is clearly observed that the proposed method outperforms the P&O and P&O PSO DPID methods. As demonstrated in Table 3, the proposed controller significantly reduces oscillations around the MPP, achieves a faster response time, and improves overall efficiency. These enhancements confirm the effectiveness of the N-DPID controller, particularly in adapting to rapid changes in environmental conditions. The improvements in response time and oscillation reduction are more substantial than those observed with the traditional methods, making the proposed approach highly effective for power transmission.

Table 4 presents a summary of performance comparison between the proposed method and other state-of-the-art techniques in the literature that have been interested in improving the performance of the MPPT P&O controller.

Table 4. Comparison of the different MPPT techniques.

Authors	MPPP Methods	Response Time (s)	Efficiency (%)	Ripples	Overshoot (s)
De Brito et al., 2012 [41]	P&O-PI	0.0220	98.55	high	-
Zainuri et al., 2014 [23]	P&O-Fuzzy	0.02	95	0.02	-
Anto et al., 2016 [33]	P&O-PID	0.38	100	0.0181	0.51
Bouselham et al., 2017 [42]	P&O-global scanning	0.05	99.1	-	-
Proposed method	P&O PSO N-DPID	0.016	99.03	0.0071	0

It can also be seen that the method proposed in this work presents better performances than the methods encountered in the literature, such as the Refs. [17,23,42] and the references therein. It is worth noting that some perform better compared to our strategy, but their response times are still critical. A similar observation is made for the ripple rate and the overshoot [41], which clearly shows that the proposed method presents a compromise between speed, accuracy, and performance.

6. Conclusions

This study introduced a novel approach for MPP tracking based on the improved P&O performance in photovoltaic systems. The main contribution pertains to using a discrete nonlinear intelligent PID controller optimized by a simple and well-known algorithm, the PSO. The results obtained with varying weather conditions based on the PSO N-DPID and P&O PSO DPID show that these strategies are accurate, efficient, fast, and easy to implement. The role and importance of nonlinearity in discrete PID controllers for accuracy and speed in finding the maximum power point are explicitly pointed out. Although the proposed method is a compromise between accuracy, speed, and simplicity, it should be noted that some conditions have not been taken into account in this work, such as partially shaded plates, which remain a problem of concern; other optimization algorithms could be used other than the PSO to compare them to see the best result.

Author Contributions: Conceptualization, M.C.Z.Z., A.S.T.K., M.S.S. and A.T.A.; Formal analysis, M.C.Z.Z., A.S.T.K., M.S.S., A.T.A., S.A. and I.A.H.; Funding acquisition, I.A.H.; Investigation, A.T.A. and S.A.; Methodology, M.C.Z.Z., A.S.T.K., M.S.S., A.T.A., S.A. and I.A.H.; Resources, M.C.Z.Z., A.S.T.K., M.S.S., A.T.A., S.A. and I.A.H.; Software, M.C.Z.Z., A.S.T.K., M.S.S., S.A. and I.A.H.; Validation, A.T.A., S.A. and I.A.H.; Visualization, A.T.A.; Writing—original draft, M.C.Z.Z., A.S.T.K., M.S.S. and A.T.A.; Writing—review & editing, M.C.Z.Z., A.S.T.K., M.S.S., A.T.A., S.A. and I.A.H. All authors have read and agreed to the published version of the manuscript.

Funding: This research was funded by Norwegian University of Science and Technology, Norway.

Data Availability Statement: Data sharing is not applicable.

Acknowledgments: The authors would like to acknowledge the support of the Norwegian University of Science and Technology for paying the Article Processing Charges (APC) of this publication. This research is supported by Automated Systems and Soft Computing Lab (ASSCL), Prince Sultan University, Riyadh, Saudi Arabia. The authors would like to thank Prince Sultan University, Riyadh, Saudi Arabia for their support.

Conflicts of Interest: The authors declare no conflicts of interest.

References

1. Abas, N.; Kalair, A.; Khan, N. Review of fossil fuels and future energy technologies. *Futures* **2015**, *69*, 31–49. [CrossRef]
2. Balat, M.M.Y.C. Status of fossil energy resources: A global perspective. *Energy Sources B Econ. Plan. Policy* **2007**, *2*, 31–47. [CrossRef]
3. Mac Kinnon, M.A.; Brouwer, J.; Samuelsen, S. The role of natural gas and its infrastructure in mitigating greenhouse gas emissions, improving regional air quality, and renewable resource integration. *Prog. Energy Combust. Sci.* **2018**, *64*, 62–92. [CrossRef]
4. Nordin, I.; Elofsson, K.; Jansson, T. Cost-effective reductions in greenhouse gas emissions: Reducing fuel consumption or replacing fossil fuels with biofuels. *Energy Policy* **2024**, *190*, 114138. [CrossRef]
5. Wang, J.; Azam, W. Natural resource scarcity, fossil fuel energy consumption, and total greenhouse gas emissions in top emitting countries. *Geosci. Front.* **2024**, *15*, 101757. [CrossRef]
6. Bei, G.; Woon, K.N.; Bill, D. *Fuel Cells: Modeling, Control, and Applications*; CRC Press: Boca Raton, FL, USA, 2017. [CrossRef]
7. Shahzad, U. The need for renewable energy sources. *Energy* **2012**, *2*, 16–18.
8. Wang, G.; Zhang, Z.; Lin, J. Multi-energy complementary power systems based on solar energy: A review. *Renew. Sustain. Energy Rev.* **2024**, *199*, 114464. [CrossRef]
9. Maka, A.O.M.; Ghalut, T.; Elsaye, E. The pathway towards decarbonisation and net-zero emissions by 2050: The role of solar energy technology. *Green Technol. Sustain.* **2024**, *2*, 100107. [CrossRef]
10. Gholami, H. Technical potential of solar energy in buildings across Norway: Capacity and demand. *Sol. Energy* **2024**, *278*, 112758. [CrossRef]
11. Basantes, B.; Ulloa-Herrera, F.; Pozo, M.; Camacho, O. Power management of an off-grid photovoltaic system using a linear algebra based control. *Results Eng.* **2024**, *23*, 102375. [CrossRef]
12. Najafi Roudbari, F.; Ehsani, H.; Amiri, S.R.; Samadani, A.; Shabani, S.; Khodadad, A. Advances in photovoltaic thermal systems: A comprehensive review of CPVT and PVT technologies. *Sol. Energy Mater. Sol. Cells* **2024**, *276*, 113070. [CrossRef]
13. Ali, M.N. Improved design of artificial neural network for MPPT of grid-connected PV systems. In Proceedings of the 2018 Twentieth International Middle East Power Systems Conference (MEPCON), Cairo, Egypt, 18–20 December 2018; IEEE: Piscataway, NJ, USA, 2018; pp. 97–102. [CrossRef]
14. Sharma, R.S.; Katti, P.K. Perturb & observation MPPT algorithm for solar photovoltaic system. In Proceedings of the 2017 International Conference on Circuit, Power and Computing Technologies (ICCPCT), Kollam, India, 20–21 April 2017; IEEE: Piscataway, NJ, USA, 2017; pp. 1–6. [CrossRef]
15. Kamal, N.A.; Ibrahim, A.M. Conventional, Intelligent, and Fractional-Order Control Method for Maximum Power Point Tracking of a Photovoltaic System: A Review. In *Fractional Order Systems Optimization, Control, Circuit Realizations and Applications, Advances in Nonlinear Dynamics and Chaos (ANDC)*; Academic Press: Cambridge, MA, USA, 2018; pp. 603–671.
16. Elobaid, L.M.; Abdelsalam, A.K.; Zakzouk, E.E. Artificial neural network based maximum power point tracking technique for PV systems. In Proceedings of the IECON 2012-38th Annual Conference on IEEE Industrial Electronics Society, Montreal, QC, Canada, 25–28 October 2012; IEEE: Piscataway, NJ, USA, 2012; pp. 937–942. [CrossRef]
17. Jordehi, A.R. Maximum power point tracking in photovoltaic (PV) systems: A review of different approaches. *Renew. Sustain. Energy Rev.* **2016**, *65*, 1127–1138. [CrossRef]
18. Yin, M.; Qin, L.; Wu, G.; Shi, C. An improved variable step size photovoltaic MPPT algorithm based on perturb and observe method. In Proceedings of the Third International Conference on Electronics and Communication, Network and Computer Technology (ECNCT 2021), Coimbra, Portugal, 6–9 September 2016; SPIE: Washington, DC, USA, 2022; Volume 12167, pp. 729–734. [CrossRef]

19. Joshi, P.; Arora, S. Maximum power point tracking methodologies for solar PV systems—A review. *Renew. Sustain. Energy Rev.* **2017**, *70*, 1154–1177. [CrossRef]
20. Dhaouadi, G.; Djamel, O.; Youcef, S.; Salah, C. Implementation of incremental conductance based MPPT algorithm for photovoltaic system. In Proceedings of the 2019 4th International Conference on Power Electronics and their Applications (ICPEA), Elazig, Turkey, 25–27 September 2019; pp. 1–5. [CrossRef]
21. Jiang, M.; Ghahremani, M.; Dadfar, S.; Chi, H.; Abdallah, Y.N.; Furukawa, N. A novel combinatorial hybrid SFL-PS algorithm based neural network with perturb and observe for the MPPT controller of a hybrid PV-storage system. *Control Eng. Pract.* **2021**, *114*, 104880. [CrossRef]
22. Blange, R.; Mahanta, C.; Gogoi, A.K. MPPT of solar photovoltaic cell using perturb & observe and fuzzy logic controller algorithm for buck-boost dc-dc converter. In Proceedings of the 2015 International Conference on Energy, Power and Environment: Towards Sustainable Growth (ICEPE), Shillong, India, 12–13 June 2015; IEEE: Piscataway, NJ, USA, 2015; pp. 1–5. [CrossRef]
23. Zainuri, M.A.A.M.; Radzi, M.A.M.; Che Soh, A.; Rahim, N.A. Development of adaptive perturb and observe-fuzzy control maximum power point tracking for photovoltaic boost dc–dc converter. *IET Renew. Power Gener.* **2014**, *8*, 183–194. [CrossRef]
24. Kler, D.; Rana, K.; Kumar, V. A nonlinear PID controller based novel maximum power point tracker for PV systems. *J. Frankl. Inst.* **2018**, *355*, 7827–7864. [CrossRef]
25. Manna, S.; Singh, D.K.; Akella, A.K.; Kotb, H.; AboRas, K.M.; Zawbaa, H.M.; Kamel, S. Design and implementation of a new adaptive MPPT controller for solar PV systems. *Energy Rep.* **2023**, *9*, 1818–1829. [CrossRef]
26. Águila-León, J.; Vargas-Salgado, C.; Díaz-Bello, D.; Montagud-Montalvá, C. Optimizing photovoltaic systems: A meta-optimization approach with GWO-enhanced PSO algorithm for improving MPPT controllers. *Renew. Energy* **2024**, *230*, 120892. [CrossRef]
27. Ben Regaya, C.; Hamdi, H.; Farhani, F.; Marai, A.; Zaafouri, A.; Chaari, A. Real-time implementation of a novel MPPT control based on the improved PSO algorithm using an adaptive factor selection strategy for photovoltaic systems. *ISA Trans.* **2024**, *146*, 496–510. [CrossRef]
28. Pathak, D.; Sagar, G.; Gaur, P. An application of intelligent non-linear discrete PID controller for MPPT of PV system. *Procedia Comput. Sci.* **2020**, *167*, 1574–1583. [CrossRef]
29. Su, Y.; Sun, D.; Duan, B. Design of an enhanced nonlinear PID controller. *Mechatronics* **2005**, *15*, 1005–1024. [CrossRef]
30. Mengue, F.D.; Kammogne, A.S.T.; Siewe, M.S.; Yamapi, R.; Fotsin, H.B. A new hybrid method based on differential evolution to determine the temperature-dependent parameters of single-diode photovoltaic cells. *J. Comput. Electron.* **2021**, *20*, 2511–2521. [CrossRef]
31. Pelap, F.; Dongo, P.; Kapim, A. Optimization of the characteristics of the PV cells using nonlinear electronic components. *Sustain. Energy Technol. Assess.* **2016**, *16*, 84–92. [CrossRef]
32. Nguimfack, N.J.d.D.; Kenne, G.; Kuate-Fochie, R.; Tchouani Njomo, A.F.; Mbaka Nfah, E. Adaptive neuro-synergetic control technique for sepic converter in pv systems. *Int. J. Dyn. Control.* **2022**, *10*, 203–216. [CrossRef]
33. Anto, E.K.; Asumadu, J.A.; Okyere, P.Y. PID control for improving P&O-MPPT performance of a grid-connected solar PV system with ziegler-nichols tuning method. In Proceedings of the 2016 IEEE 11th Conference on Industrial Electronics and Applications (ICIEA), Hefei, China, 5–7 June 2016; IEEE: Piscataway, NJ, USA, 2016; pp. 1847–1852. [CrossRef]
34. Harrison, A.; Ndongmo, J.D.D.N.; Nfah, E.M.; Ekute, O.B. Improved Perturb & Observe MPPT method using PI controller for PV system based on real environmental and climatic conditions. *Open Access Repos.* **2022**, *9*, 28–38. [CrossRef]
35. Delavari, H.; Ghaderi, R.; Ranjbar, A.; Momani, S. Fuzzy fractional order sliding mode controller for nonlinear systems. *Commun. Nonlinear Sci. Numer. Simul.* **2010**, *15*, 963–978. [CrossRef]
36. Rafikov, M.; Balthazar, J.M. On control and synchronization in chaotic and hyperchaotic systems via linear feedback control. *Commun. Nonlinear Sci. Numer. Simul.* **2008**, *13*, 1246–1255. [CrossRef]
37. Moreno-Valenzuela, J.; Pérez-Alcocer, R.; Guerrero-Medina, M.; Dzul, A. Nonlinear PID-type controller for quadrotor trajectory tracking. *IEEE/ASME Trans. Mechatron.* **2018**, *23*, 2436–2447. [CrossRef]
38. Azar, A.T.; Serrano, F.E. Stabilization and Control of Mechanical Systems with Backlash. In *Advanced Intelligent Control Engineering and Automation, Advances in Computational Intelligence and Robotics (ACIR) Book Series*; IGI-Global: Hershey, PA, USA, 2015.
39. Kennedy, J.; Eberhart, R. Particle swarm optimization. In Proceedings of the ICNN'95-International Conference on Neural Networks, Perth, Australia, 27 November–1 December 1995; IEEE: Piscataway, NJ, USA, 1995; Volume 4, pp. 1942–1948. [CrossRef]
40. Wu, T.-Y.; Jiang, Y.-Z.; Su, Y.-Z.; Yeh, W.-C. Using simplified swarm optimization on multiloop fuzzy pid controller tuning design for flow and temperature control system. *Appl. Sci.* **2020**, *10*, 8472. [CrossRef]
41. De Brito, M.A.G.; Galotto, L.; Sampaio, L.P.; e Melo, G.d.A.; Canesin, C.A. Evaluation of the main MPPT techniques for photovoltaic applications. *IEEE Trans. Ind. Electron.* **2012**, *60*, 1156–1167. [CrossRef]
42. Bouselham, L.; Hajji, M.; Hajji, B.; Bouali, H. A new MPPT-based for photovoltaic system under partial shading conditions. *Energy Procedia* **2017**, *111*, 924–933. [CrossRef]

Mathematical and Computational Applications

MDPI

Article

Sliding Mode Fault-Tolerant Control for Nonlinear LPV Systems with Variable Time-Delay

Omayma Mansouri *, Ali Ben Brahim, Fayçal Ben Hmida and Anis Sellami

Engineering Laboratory of Industrial Systems and Renewable Energies (LISIER), National Higher Engineering School of Tunis (ENSIT), University of Tunis, 5 Avenue Taha Hussein, Tunis BP 56-1008, Tunisia; benibrahimmali@yahoo.fr (A.B.B.); faycal.benhmida@ensit.rnu.tn (F.B.H.); anis.sellami@ensit.rnu.tn (A.S.)

* Correspondence: mansouri1omayma@gmail.com

Abstract: This paper presents a robust sliding mode fault-tolerant control (FTC) strategy for a class of linear parameter variant (LPV) systems with variable time-delays and uncertainties. First fault estimation (FE) is conducted using a robust sliding mode observer, synthesized to simultaneously estimate the states and actuator faults of LPV polytopic delayed systems. Second, a sliding mode FTC is developed, ensuring all states of the closed-loop system converge to the origin. This paper presents an integrated sliding mode FTC strategy to achieve optimal robustness between the observer and controller models. The integrated design approach offers several advantages over traditional separated FTC methods. Our novel approach is based on incorporating adaptive law into the design of the Lyapunov–Krasovskii functional to improve both robustness and performance. This is achieved by combining the concept of sliding mode control (SMC) with the Lyapunov–Krasovskii function under the H_∞ criteria, which plays a key role in guaranteeing the stability of this class of system. The effectiveness of the proposed method is demonstrated through a diesel engine example, which highlights the validity and benefits of the integrated and separated FTC strategy for uncertain nonlinear systems with time delays and the sliding mode control.

Keywords: fault estimation (FE); LPV delayed systems; fault-tolerant control (FTC); Lyapunov–Krasovskii functional; multi-objective LMI

1. Introduction

LPV systems with time delays have received limited attention in the literature. However, only a few contributions have been reported, reflecting much more potential for future study and an interesting research area. From each system class, these systems come with many challenges and offer new problems. For instance, the implemented technique for both robust control and LPV could no longer be used in the context of LPV systems with delays. For this system class, especially for parameter-varying time delays, there are some problems, such as actuator degradation, sensor/actuator failures, and output measurement variations. These are the things that contribute to the disturbance in system operation, and from them, both poor controller performance and system deterioration follow. These issues disrupt system operation, leading to poor controller performance or system deterioration. This has led to the exploration of fault-tolerant control design [1], specifically tailored to LPV systems with time delays. Therefore, to prevent poor system performance and potential collapse or failure, FTC design has emerged. First, it ensures closed-loop stability in the presence of disturbances or uncertainties, particularly in passive FTC configurations, and second, it provides much more reliability and supervision when in active FTC setups.

The effectiveness of the FTC is highly dependent on the accuracy of the fault detection and isolation (FDI). If faults are detected quickly and accurately, the FTC can be applied more effectively to mitigate their impact. Ref. [2] presents a new two-stage framework for FDI in quadrotors, with a particular focus on actuator faults. This model-based method uses a parity space approach to generate residual signals for fault detection, taking advantage of measurement consistency through linear combinations of measurement outputs and control inputs. Faulty system states are filtered using an extended Kalman filter, improving the accuracy of state estimates and the overall performance of the fault detection algorithm.

In [3–6], the authors propose a robust active FTC for uncertain LPV systems with simultaneous actuator and sensor faults. The researchers in [7] presented a robust fault-tolerant control methodology tailored to discrete-time LPV systems. The methodology focuses on the synthesis of a reconfiguration block comprising virtual sensors and virtual actuators. The aim is to address the issue of fault-tolerant sensor control by proposing a model-free, adaptive constrained control strategy that utilizes virtual sensor technology [8,9]. To maintain system performance and stability, active FTC control can automatically integrate faulty components. Nevertheless, fault estimation presents design challenges, and the applicability of the suggested approaches is limited. One fault estimation technique that is widely employed, as in [10,11], involves estimation by sliding mode observers (SMOs).

However, their application is mainly limited to specific types of nonlinear systems, such as nonlinear LPV delayed systems. The fault estimation technique only identifies the fault size but does not provide a guide on how to compensate for its effects. Compared to FDI, fault estimation presents more design challenges [12]. Additionally, using the information obtained from the estimator, an additive controller can be designed to compensate for the effect of the fault. The design of fault estimation based on the sliding mode observer typically requires a strictly positive real state to be satisfied. Several studies have proposed fault estimation and FTC approaches based on sliding mode observers for various types of nonlinear systems [13–15]. However, the application of sliding mode FTC methods is essentially limited to certain specific types of nonlinear systems, such as nonlinear LPV systems with delays. The fault estimation provides the magnitude of the fault but does not indicate how to mitigate its effects, thus highlighting the need for the fault-tolerant control step. This step involves developing a control law that can maintain or ensure stability and acceptable performance, even when the LPV system is impacted by the fault. While there are many references in the literature dealing with the problem of active fault-tolerant control for LPV systems, most of them concern linear systems [16,17]. However, due to the nonlinear behavior of most real systems, the application of FTC must consider the nonlinear nature of these systems [4,8] and recently in [18,19]. On the other hand, variable delays and uncertainties are common in many practical applications, which can also contribute to the degradation of system performance. The presence of a delay with a fault can easily destabilize the system [20,21]. Therefore, the research on the fault-tolerant control problem for nonlinear LPV systems with time delay is of great interest, both from theoretical and practical perspectives.

The author in [22] focuses on the problem of in-memory state feedback control for Takagi-Sugeno type 2 fuzzy systems with time delay, particularly dealing with external disturbances and actuator faults. The use of Takagi-Sugeno type 2 fuzzy systems highlights the importance of managing uncertainties and the occurrence of faults in the system. This allows the system to use information from previous states, which can potentially improve control performance. Intensive research attention focuses on sliding mode controllers (SMCs). The researchers in [23] introduced a new adaptive fixed-time fractional integral control strategy that combines the advantages of fractional calculus with robust control techniques. Recently, Ref. [24] introduced advanced control strategies for nonlinear systems through a fixed-time adaptive control approach. This method combines rapid convergence, smooth control inputs, and robust performance in the presence of external disturbances. This method guarantees that stability is achieved within a predetermined time frame, regardless of the initial conditions.

Motivated by previous works, this study primarily aims to reconfigure a robust sliding mode controller to maintain closed-loop system stability with acceptable performance, despite the presence of actuator faults, variable time-delay, and uncertainties.

This paper proposes a fault estimation based on a sliding mode fault-tolerant control (FTC) scheme for a class of nonlinear LPV delayed systems subject to actuator faults and uncertainty. The LPV delayed system modeling with local nonlinear models, as Lipschitzian nonlinearities, is of great interest in this work. Compared to existing results, the main contributions of this paper are divided as follows:

- First, a sliding mode observer is designed for the uncertain polytopic system with local nonlinearities and variable time-delays, enabling the simultaneous reconstruction of system states and actuator faults. The sliding mode observer designed for this class of system offers significant advantages in terms of robustness, adaptability, and performance. It is capable of simultaneously estimating state and faults while effectively managing variable time-delays. By exploiting these strengths, this approach improves not only the reliability of systems but also opens up the prospect of progress in the field of FTC methodologies.
- Second, we propose an SMC method with an adaptive law that has many advantages over other approaches, including uncertain LPV systems with local non-linearities and variable time-delay. By incorporating an adaptive law, the control strategy can be regularly modified in response to the system's real-time returns. For systems with high levels of uncertainty or non-linearity, adaptability is necessary to maintain maximum performance. Indeed, the adaptive law may also help to address the conversational phenomenon generally associated with traditional sliding mode control strategies.
- Third, the combination of FE and FTC design within a unified framework is developed for the delayed polytopic system, aiming to achieve optimal robustness and performance. Compared to constant time delay systems, variable time-delay in FE and FTC models presents additional challenges in the polytopic system. This framework is specifically designed to deal with variable time-delays, which are common in practical applications. By accounting for these delays in FE and FTC processes, the system can maintain accurate state estimates and effective control actions, improving overall reliability. Moreover, the proposed method effectively addresses these challenges by taking into account the presence of local non-linearities and uncertainties. It ensures that the control strategy remains effective even when the system dynamics change. On the other hand, this methodology allows for the simultaneous estimation of actuator faults and the implementation of control laws. Therefore, when faults are detected, the FTC system can dynamically adjust control actions to minimize their impact on the system's performance.
- Finally, the integrated FE-FTC framework is formulated for the uncertain polytopic system with local nonlinear models, which combines the observer and controller synthesis into a single optimization problem. The integrated FE-FTC scheme is designed to maintain stability even in the presence of variable time-delays. By jointly optimizing the control and estimation strategies, the system can adapt to variations in delay. This approach offers greater robustness and better performance than traditional separated FE-FTC methods. The advantages of the proposed methods for this class of complex systems are demonstrated to prove the performance of integrated and separate FTC approaches through a case study involving an uncertain polytopic system with local nonlinear models and variable delays.

In [25,26], the researchers developed a sliding mode observer (SMO) with unknown inputs for descriptor systems (LPVs) with variable delays, which have several drawbacks compared to our approach, such as the sensitivity of the unknown inputs. This sensitivity can lead to performance degradation and instability, particularly in LPV-delayed systems. SMOs with unknown inputs cannot effectively compensate for these delays, leading to inaccurate state estimates and control actions that can destabilize the system. The authors have only used the state feedback to compute the control law. As a result, the efficiency of the SMO used may be limited by the complex local non-linearities present in polytopic delayed systems. The inability to manage these nonlinearities adaptively can lead to non-optimal performance. Compared to our study, the adaptive nature of the SMC designed in this paper is often more robust to input variations and nonlinearities, particularly local Lipchitz nonlinearity. This allows problems to be quickly identified and corrected as they arise. The ability to adjust parameters dynamically enables better fault detection and state estimation. Moreover, when designing control law with an emphasis on fault tolerance and estimation, it is essential to find a trade-off between robustness and computational efficiency. The adaptive aspect of our SMC provides a strong framework for ensuring system stability despite these changes. This is achieved by combining the concept of sliding mode control (SMC) with the Lyapunov–Krasovskii function under the H_∞ criteria, highlighting two approaches for fault-tolerant control (FTC) design: integrated FTC and separated FTC. These play a crucial role in ensuring the stability and robustness of this class system. Our integrated approach ensures this trade-off by performing fault estimation and fault-tolerant control in a single step, thereby reducing computational complexity.

The structure of the rest of this paper is as follows: Section 2 presents an overview of the non-linear delayed LPV system. More details of the LPV adaptive observer design are presented in Section 3. Section 4 then outlines the structure of the sliding mode controller. In Section 5, we introduce the separate and integrated sliding mode FTC schemes to stabilize the closed-loop system. Section 6 presents a simulation example based on non-linear simulations, demonstrating the effectiveness of the proposed schemes with comparative studies to highlight the advantages of our approach. Finally, Section 7 presents our concluding remarks.

2. Problem Formulation

Consider an uncertain nonlinear system governed by the following equations:

$$\begin{aligned} \dot{x}(t) &= \varphi_{x1}(x(t)) + \varphi_{x2}(x(t))x(t-d(t)) + \varphi_{x3}(x(t))u(t) + \varphi_{x4}(x(t))\xi(x,t) \\ &+ \varphi_{x5}(x(t))\Gamma(x,t) + \varphi_{x6}(x(t))f(t) \\ y(t) &= \varphi_2(x(t)) \\ y_L(t) &= \varphi_{yl}(x(t)) \end{aligned} \tag{1}$$

System (1) is written with the following polytopic representation:

$$\begin{aligned} \dot{x}(t) &= \sum_{i=1}^{g} \mu_i(\theta(t))A_i x(t) + A_{di}x(t-d(t)) + B_i u(t) \\ &+ D_i\xi(t,x) + \Gamma_i(x,u) + M_i f_a(t)\} \end{aligned} \tag{2}$$

$$y(t) = \sum_{i=1}^{g} \mu_i(\theta(t))\{C_i\, x(t)\} \tag{3}$$

where $x(t) \in \Re^n$ represents the state vector, $y(t) \in \Re^p$ represents the measurement, $u(t) \in \Re^m$ represents the input, $f_a(t) \in \Re^q$ represents the actuator fault, and $\xi(t) \in \Re^l$ encompasses the uncertainty. This uncertainty represents the unknown and bounded uncertainties that are part of $L_2 \in \begin{bmatrix} 0 & \infty \end{bmatrix}$. The functions $\varphi_{xi}(x(t))$, $\varphi_2(x(t))$, $\varphi_{yl}(x(t))$, and $\Gamma(x,t)$ are continuously nonlinear, with $i = 1,2,3,4,5$.

$A_i \in \Re^{n\times n}$, $A_{di} \in \Re^{n\times n}$, $B_i \in \Re^{n\times m}$, $M_i \in \Re^{n\times q}$, $D_i \in \Re^{n\times l}$, $C_i \in \Re^{p\times n}$ are constant matrices of appropriate dimensions.

$\mu_i(\theta(t))$ are the weighting functions while respecting the properties of convex sets, as follows:

$$\mu_i(\theta(t)) > 0, \sum_{j=1}^{g} \mu_i(\theta(t)) = 1 \forall i \in [1, ...g] \tag{4}$$

$d(t)$ denotes the time-varying bounded state delay satisfying the following:

$$0 \le d(t) \le d_m, 0 \le \dot{d}(t) \le \tau < 1 \tag{5}$$

where d_m and τ are known constant scalars.

Recently, LPV systems with parameter-varying time delays have garnered significant interest due to their ability to model intricate systems characterized by nonlinearities and varying time delays. These systems present considerable challenges as they incorporate the complexities associated with both LPV and variable time-delay systems. One method to address these nonlinearities involves using local nonlinear models, which lead to a polytopic LPV representation with parameter-dependent variable time-delays.

This work is based on the following assumptions:

Assumption 1 ([5]). *Uncertainties and faults are assumed unknown. But they are bounded by some known constants. For the faults $f_a(t)$ and the uncertainties $\xi(x,t)$, there exist positive constants, such that we have the following:*

$$\|f_a(t)\| \leq \rho_a \, , \|\xi(x,t)\| \leq \beta \tag{6}$$

Assumption 2 ([5]). *The actuator fault repartition matrix $\mathcal{M}$ in (1) leads to the following:*

$$rank(C_i M_i) = q \tag{7}$$

Assumption 3 ([20]). *The system $\left(A_i + A_{di}e^{-ds}, M_i, C_i\right)$ has a relative degree of one and is minimum phase, characterized by the following:*

$$rank\left(\begin{bmatrix} sI_n - A_i - A_{di}e^{-ds} & M_i \\ C_i & 0_{p\times q} \end{bmatrix}\right) = n + q \tag{8}$$

holds for all complex numbers s where $\mathrm{Re}(s) \geq 0$.

A minimum-phase system guarantees stability even in the presence of actuator faults and uncertainties. It ensures that the non-asymptotically stable modes are observable (detectable).

Assumption 4 ([5]). *The known nonlinear function $\Gamma_i(x(t),t)$ satisfies a Lipschitz condition locally on a set $\mathbb{M} \subset \Re^n$ in which we have the following:*

$$\|\Gamma_i(x_1(t),t) - \Gamma_i(x_2(t),t)\| \leq \gamma_1 \|x_1(t) - x_2(t)\| \tag{9}$$

$\forall x_1(t), x_2(t) \in \mathbb{M}$ *where γ_1 and γ_2 are unknown positives Lipschitz constants.*

In [27], the authors developed an SMO for the system, which can estimate stats and faults of a system respecting the following necessary assumptions, as recently used in [5]. Given the polytopic LPV delayed system (2) and (3), subject to actuator faults $f_a(t)$, uncertainties $\xi(t)$, and local nonlinearities $\Gamma_i(x(t),t)$, this paper presents a robust sliding mode control design based on sliding mode fault estimation. The primary objective is to address the following:

- Estimating the actuator fault and system states using adaptive sliding mode observers.
- Designing a sliding mode controller to stabilize the closed-loop system despite the occurrence of faults and uncertainties, while accounting for variable delay accuracy and nonlinearities.

Definition 1. *For matrices X and Y with appropriate dimensions, the following conditions apply:*

$$X^T Y + YX \leq \delta^{-1} X^T X + \delta Y^T Y. \tag{10}$$

3. Robust Sliding Mode Fault Estimation Design

3.1. Transformation Coordinate System

Before presenting the main results of this paper, the objectives are twofold: to estimate actuator faults and system states using adaptive sliding mode observers, and to design a sliding mode controller that stabilizes the closed-loop system. This approach addresses the presence of faults and uncertainties, while also accounting for variable delay accuracy and local nonlinearities. Using Assumption 2, for the polytopic nonlinear LPV system with time delay (2) and (3), the following transformations exist [28]:

$$\begin{aligned} T_iA_iT_i^{-1} &= \begin{bmatrix} \bar{A}_{1i} & \bar{A}_{2i} \\ \bar{A}_{31i} & \bar{A}_{4i} \\ \bar{A}_{32i} & \end{bmatrix}, T_i\bar{A}_{di}T_i^{-1} = \begin{bmatrix} A_{d1i} & \bar{A}_{d2i} \\ \bar{A}_{d31i} & \bar{A}_{d4i} \\ \bar{A}_{d32i} & \end{bmatrix} \\ \bar{M}_{2i} &= \begin{bmatrix} 0 \\ \bar{M}_{qi} \end{bmatrix}, \bar{M}_i = \begin{bmatrix} 0 \\ \bar{M}_{2i} \end{bmatrix} \bar{C}_i = \begin{bmatrix} 0_{p\times(n_1-p)} & \bar{C}_{2i} \end{bmatrix}, \bar{D}_i = \begin{bmatrix} \bar{D}_{1i} \\ \bar{D}_{2i} \end{bmatrix} \end{aligned} \tag{11}$$

with $\bar{M}_2i \in \Re^{p(q)}$, where $\bar{C}_2i \in \Re^{p\times p}$ is nonsingular, with $p \geq q$.

The objective of this initial transformation is to create an efficient sliding mode observer capable of simultaneously estimating system states and actuator faults for the LPV system subject to local nonlinearities and time delays. This observer serves as the basis for the ensuing design of fault-tolerant control (FTC). Next, to identify the sliding mode, the second change of coordinates is as follows:

$$T_{Li} = \begin{bmatrix} I_{n-p} & L_i \\ 0 & \bar{C}_{2i} \end{bmatrix}, L_i = \begin{bmatrix} L_{1i} & 0_{(n-p)q} \end{bmatrix} \tag{12}$$

Consequently, the matrices (11) are transformed to be in the following forms:

$$\begin{aligned} T_{Li}\bar{A}_iT_{Li}^{-1} &= \begin{bmatrix} \tilde{A}_{1i} & \tilde{A}_{2i} \\ \tilde{A}_{31i} & \tilde{A}_{4i} \\ \tilde{A}_{32i} & \end{bmatrix}, T_{Li}\bar{A}_{di}T_{Li}^{-1} = \begin{bmatrix} \tilde{A}_{d1i} & \tilde{A}_{d2i} \\ \tilde{A}_{d31i} & \tilde{A}_{d4i} \\ \tilde{A}_{d32i} & \end{bmatrix} \\ \tilde{M}_i &= \begin{bmatrix} 0 \\ \tilde{M}_{2i} \end{bmatrix}, \tilde{M}_{2i} = \begin{bmatrix} 0 \\ \tilde{M}_{qi} \end{bmatrix} \tilde{D}_i = \begin{bmatrix} \tilde{D}_{1i} \\ \tilde{D}_{2i} \end{bmatrix}, \tilde{C}_i = \begin{bmatrix} 0_{p\times(n-p)} & I_p \end{bmatrix} \end{aligned} \tag{13}$$

with $\tilde{M}_2i \in \Re^{p(q)}$, where $\tilde{C}_2i \in \Re^{p\times p}$ is nonsingular, with $p \geq q$.

3.2. Sliding Mode Observer

By leveraging the universal approximation for uncertain nonlinear systems as presented in (13), this paper proposes a potential approach to developing a resilient polytopic adaptive SMO. This adaptive observer aims to enhance fault estimation, including actuator faults, in uncertain delayed systems. An adaptive observer for fault estimation is conceived to address the challenges associated with the following:

$$\begin{aligned} \dot{\hat{x}}(t) &= \sum_{j=1}^{g} \mu_i(\theta(t))\{\tilde{A}_i\hat{x}(t) + \tilde{A}_{di}\hat{x}(t-d(t)) + \Gamma_i(\tilde{x},t) \\ &+ \tilde{B}_iu(t) + \tilde{G}_{li}e_y(t) + \tilde{G}_{ni}v(t)\} \end{aligned} \tag{14}$$

$$\hat{y}(t) = \sum_{j=1}^{g} \mu_i(\theta(t))\{\tilde{C}_i\hat{x}(t)\} \tag{15}$$

with $\tilde{\Gamma}_i(x,t) = T_{Li}\begin{bmatrix} \Gamma_{1i}^T(x,t) & \Gamma_{2i}^T(x,t) \end{bmatrix}^T$. $\tilde{e}_y(t) = \hat{y}(t) - \tilde{y}(t)$ represents the output error estimation. The SMO gains $\tilde{G}_{ni}$ and $\tilde{G}_{li}$ are appropriately chosen gain matrices.

$$\tilde{G}_{ni} = \begin{bmatrix} -L_i\tilde{C}_{2i}{}^T \\ \tilde{C}_{2i}{}^T \end{bmatrix}, \tilde{G}_{li} = \begin{bmatrix} \tilde{G}_{l1i} \\ \tilde{G}_{l2i} \end{bmatrix} \tag{16}$$

with $L_i \in \Re^{(n-p)\times p} = \begin{bmatrix} L_{1,i} & 0_{(n-p)\times q} \end{bmatrix}$ defined in [16]. The robust adaptive sliding mode signal is expressed as follows:

$$v(t) = \begin{cases} -\rho(t)\frac{\bar{P}_2\,\tilde{e}_y(t)}{\|\bar{P}_2\,\tilde{e}_y(t)\|} & if\,\tilde{e}_y(t) \neq 0 \\ 0 \quad otherwise \end{cases} \tag{17}$$

where $\bar{P}_2 \in \Re^{p\times p}$ is a positive definite symmetric matrix that will be found later and $\rho(t) = \hat{\rho} + \iota_0$ is a known positive scalar that limits the magnitude of the uncertainty and the fault signal. $\hat{\rho}$ is the adaptive update term defined by the following:

$$\dot{\hat{\rho}} = \vartheta\|\bar{P}_2\tilde{e}_y(t)\|, \hat{\rho}(0) \geq 0 \tag{18}$$

Compared to the traditional sliding mode observer [29], the proposed adaptive sliding mode observer (14) and (15) is designed to address the challenge of abrupt variations in fault amplitude. This is accomplished by incorporating the adaptive update term (18), which improves the precision of both fault estimation and compensation. The adaptive term enables the observer to adapt to changes in fault characteristics, leading to more accurate fault estimates and better compensation capabilities. The adaptive mechanism enables the observer to adapt to changes in fault characteristics, allowing it to track sudden or unpredictable variations in fault magnitude. This feature is particularly beneficial in scenarios where the fault amplitude may change unexpectedly, as the adaptive approach allows the observer to provide reliable fault estimates for the fault-tolerant control. The new state estimation error is defined as $\dot{\tilde{e}}(t) = \dot{\hat{\tilde{x}}}(t) - \dot{\tilde{x}}(t)$ where we have the following:

$$\begin{aligned} \dot{\tilde{e}}(t) &= \sum_{j=1}^{g} \mu_i(\theta(t))\{(\tilde{A}_i - \tilde{G}_{li}\tilde{C}_i)\tilde{e}(t) + \tilde{A}_{di}\tilde{e}(t-d(t)) - \tilde{D}\xi(x,t) + \tilde{\Gamma}_e(x,t) \\ &+ \tilde{G}_{ni}v(t) - \tilde{M}_i f_a(t)\} \end{aligned} \tag{19}$$

It is necessary to demonstrate the following:

$$\begin{aligned} \dot{\tilde{e}}_1(t) &= \sum_{j=1}^{g} \mu_i(\theta(t))\{\tilde{A}_{1i}\tilde{e}_1(t) + (\tilde{A}_{2i} - \tilde{G}_{l1i})\tilde{e}_1(t) + \tilde{A}_{d1i}\tilde{e}_1(t-d(t)) + \tilde{A}_{d2i}\tilde{e}_y(t-d(t)) \\ &+ \tilde{G}_{n1i}v(t) - \tilde{D}_{1i}\xi(x,t) + \tilde{\Gamma}_{e1i}(x,t)\} \end{aligned} \tag{20}$$

$$\begin{aligned} \dot{\tilde{e}}_y(t) &= \sum_{j=1}^{g} \mu_i(\theta(t))\{\tilde{A}_{3i}\tilde{e}_1(t) + (\tilde{A}_{4i} - \tilde{G}_{l2i})\tilde{e}_y(t)\tilde{A}_{d3i}\tilde{e}_1(t-d(t)) + \tilde{A}_{d4i}\tilde{e}_y(t-d(t)) \\ &- \tilde{D}_2\xi(x,t) + \tilde{\Gamma}_{e2i}(x,t) + \tilde{G}_{n2}v(t) - \tilde{M}_2 f_a(t)\} \end{aligned} \tag{21}$$

where $T_i\Gamma_e(x,t) = \begin{bmatrix} \tilde{\Gamma}_{e1i}(x,t) & \tilde{\Gamma}_{e2i}(x,t) \end{bmatrix}$.

This contribution aims to derive the matrix gains of the robust adaptive sliding mode observer (14) and (15) to estimate both actuator faults and state variables. This paper focuses on a polytopic LPV delayed system with local nonlinear models that satisfy the Lipschitz condition. It establishes sufficient conditions for the stability and H_∞ performance of the observer error using the Lyapunov–Krasovskii functional and multi-objective LMI technique. This paper begins by investigating the controlled estimation error $r(t)$ as a function of the system's input and output.

$$r(t) = H\begin{bmatrix} \dot{\tilde{e}}_1(t) \\ \dot{\tilde{e}}_2(t) \\ \dot{\tilde{e}}_1(t-d(t)) \\ \dot{\tilde{e}}_y(t-d(t)) \end{bmatrix} \tag{22}$$

Assume that H is a pre-specified weight matrix with full rank, i.e., $H = diag(H_1, H_2, H_3, H_4)$. We think about achieving the robust performance measure in its worst-case scenario, as follows:

$$\|H_\infty\| = \sup_{\|\xi\|_2 \neq 0} \frac{\|r(t)\|_2^2}{\|\xi(x,t)\|_2^2} \tag{23}$$

Now, we will introduce Theorem 1, outlining the necessary conditions for the existence of the suggested observer with a specified H_∞ performance $\|H_\infty\| < \sigma$.

Theorem 1. *Let us consider the LPV delayed system (2) and (3) under the verification of Assumptions (2) and (3). Provided these assumptions hold, the state estimation errors (20) and (21) exhibit asymptotic stability while achieving two objectives maximizing the admissible Lipschitz constant* γ *for the nonlinear function* $\Gamma(x(t),t)$ *and minimizing the gain* σ *for the system uncertainties* $\xi(x,t)$*. This scenario is possible given the existence of a fixed scalar value between 0 and 1 (represented as* $0 \leq \lambda \leq 1$*), positive constants* ε*,* α*, and* σ*, and specific matrices* $P_1 > 0$*,* $P_2 > 0$*,* W_i*. The fulfillment of these conditions hinges on the resolution of a convex multi-objective optimization problem in the form of an LMI.*

Minimize $[\lambda(\varepsilon + \alpha) + (1 - \lambda)\sigma]$ subject to the following:

$$\begin{bmatrix}
\Pi_{1,i} & (P_1\tilde{A}_3)^T & P_1\tilde{A}_{d1} & P_1\tilde{A}_{d2} & P_1\tilde{D}_1 & P_1 & 0 & I_{n-p} & 0_{(n-p)p} \\
(*) & \Pi_{2,i} & P_2\tilde{A}_{d3} & P_2\tilde{A}_{d4} & P_2\tilde{D}_2 & 0 & P_2 & 0 & 0 \\
(*) & (*) & Z_1 & 0 & 0 & 0 & 0 & 0 & 0 \\
(*) & (*) & (*) & Z_2 & 0 & 0 & 0 & 0 & 0 \\
(*) & (*) & (*) & (*) & -\sigma I_l & 0 & 0 & 0 & 0 \\
(*) & (*) & (*) & (*) & (*) & -\varepsilon I_{n-p} & 0 & 0 & 0 \\
(*) & (*) & (*) & (*) & (*) & (*) & -\varepsilon I_p & 0 & 0 \\
(*) & (*) & (*) & (*) & (*) & (*) & (*) & -\alpha I_{n-p} & 0 \\
(*) & (*) & (*) & (*) & (*) & (*) & (*) & (*) & -\alpha I_p
\end{bmatrix} < 0 \tag{24}$$

where

$\Pi_{1,i} = \bar{A}_{1i}^T P_1 + P_1\bar{A}_{1i} + W_i\bar{A}_{3i} + \bar{A}_{3i}^T W_i + S_1 + H_1^T H_1,$
$\Pi_{2,i} = \bar{A}_{4i}^{sT} P_2 + P_2\bar{A}_{4i}^s + S_2 + H_2^T H_2$
$Z_1 = -(1-\tau)S_1 + H_3^T H_3$, $Z_2 = -(1-\tau)S_2 + H_4^T H_4$

After solving the convex multi-objective problem, we demonstrate the following:

$$\begin{aligned}
L_i &= {P_1}^{-1} W_i \\
\sigma^* &= \min(\sigma) \\
\alpha^* &= \min(\alpha) \\
\varepsilon^* &= \min(\varepsilon) \\
\gamma^* &= \min(\gamma)
\end{aligned} \tag{25}$$

Proof. The proof of Theorem 1 is based on the Lyapunov–Krasovskii functional expressed by the following:

$$V(t) = V_1(t) + V_2(t) \tag{26}$$

where we have the following:

$$V_1(t) = \sum_{i=1}^{g} \mu_i(\theta(t)) \left\{ \tilde{e}_1^T(t) P_1 \tilde{e}_1(t) + \int_{t-d(t)}^{t} \tilde{e}_1^T(\theta) S_1 \tilde{e}_1(\theta) d\theta \right\}$$

and

$$V_y(t) = \sum_{i=1}^{g} \mu_i(\theta(t)) \left\{ \tilde{e}_y^T(t) P_2 \tilde{e}_y(t) + \int_{t-d(t)}^{t} \tilde{e}_y^T(\theta) S_2 \tilde{e}_y(\theta) d\theta \right\}.$$

where $P_1 \in \Re^{(n-p)\times(n-p)}$ and $P_2 \in \Re^{p\times p}$.

The time derivatives of $V_1(t)$ and $V_y(t)$ are managed in the following ways, respectively:

$$\begin{aligned} \dot{V}_1(t) &= \sum_{i=1}^{g} \mu_i(\theta(t)) \Big\{ \tilde{e}_1^T(t) \Psi_{1i} \tilde{e}_1(t) + 2\tilde{e}_1^T(t) P_1 \tilde{A}_{2i} \tilde{e}_y(t) + 2\tilde{e}_1^T(t) P_1 \tilde{A}_{1i} \tilde{e}_1(t-d(t)) \\ &- 2\tilde{e}_1^T(t) P_1 \tilde{D}_1 \xi(x,t) - (1-\tau) \tilde{e}_1^T(t-d(t)) S_1 \tilde{e}_1(t-d(t)) \\ &+ 2\tilde{e}_1^T(t) P_1 T_{Li} \Big(\Gamma_{e1i}\Big(T_{Li}^{-1} x, t\Big) - \Gamma_{e1i}\Big(T_{Li}^{-1} \hat{x}, t\Big)\Big)\Big\} \end{aligned} \tag{27}$$

and

$$\begin{aligned} \dot{V}_y(t) &= \sum_{i=1}^{g} \mu_i(\theta(t)) \Big\{ \tilde{e}_y^T(t) \Psi_{2i} \tilde{e}_y(t) + 2\tilde{e}_y^T(t) P_2 \tilde{A}_{d3i} \tilde{e}_1(t-d(t)) + 2\tilde{e}_y^T(t) P_2 \tilde{A}_3 \tilde{e}_1(t) \\ &+ 2\tilde{e}_y^T(t) P_2 \tilde{A}_{d4i} \tilde{e}_1(t-d(t)) + 2\tilde{e}_y^T(t) P_2 \left(\tilde{M}_{2i} f(t) - v(t) - \frac{1}{\beta} \tilde{\rho} \dot{\rho} \right) \\ &+ 2\tilde{e}_y^T(t) P_2 T_{Li} \Big(\Gamma_{e2i}\Big(T_{Li}^{-1} x, t\Big) - \Gamma_{e2i}\Big(T_{Li}^{-1} \hat{x}, t\Big)\Big) \\ &- 2\tilde{e}_y^T(t) P_2 \tilde{D}_2 \xi(x,t) + 2\tilde{e}_1^T(t) P_1 \tilde{A}_{d2i} \tilde{e}_y(t-d(t)) \\ &- (1-\tau) \tilde{e}_y^T(t-d(t)) S_2 \tilde{e}_y(t-d(t)) \Big\} \end{aligned} \tag{28}$$

with $\Psi_{1i} = \tilde{A}_{1i}^T P_1 + P_1 \tilde{A}_{1i} + W_i \tilde{A}_{3i} + \tilde{A}_{3i}^T W_i + S_1$, $\Psi_{2i} = \tilde{A}_{4i}^{sT} P_2 + P_2 \tilde{A}_{4i}^s + S_2$.

Applying Definition 1 and considering Assumption 4, we demonstrate that the known nonlinear function $\Gamma_{e1i}\Big(T_{Li}^{-1} x, t\Big)$ is designed as follows:

$$\begin{aligned} & 2\tilde{e}_1^T(t) P_1 T_{Li} \Big(\Gamma_{e1i}\Big(T_{Li}^{-1} x, t\Big) - \Gamma_{e1i}\Big(T_{Li}^{-1} \hat{x}, t\Big)\Big) \\ & \le \tfrac{1}{\varepsilon} \tilde{e}_1^T(t)\, P_1{}^2 \tilde{e}_1(t) + \varepsilon \Big[\Gamma_{e1i}\Big(T_{Li}^{-1} x, t\Big) - \Gamma_{e1i}\Big(T_{Li}^{-1} \hat{x}, t\Big)\Big]^T \\ & \times T_{Li}^T T_{Li} \Big[\Gamma_{e1i}\Big(T_{Li}^{-1} x, t\Big) - \Gamma_{e1i}\Big(T_{Li}^{-1} \hat{x}, t\Big)\Big] \\ & = \tfrac{1}{\varepsilon} \tilde{e}_1^T(t)\, P_1{}^2 \tilde{e}_1(t) + \varepsilon \Big\| T_{Li} \Big[\Gamma_{e1i}\Big(T_{Li}^{-1} x, t\Big) - \Gamma_{e1i}\Big(T_{Li}^{-1} \hat{x}, t\Big)\Big] \Big\|^2 \\ & \le \tfrac{1}{\varepsilon} \tilde{e}_1^T(t)\, P_1{}^2 \tilde{e}_1(t) + \varepsilon \gamma^2 \|T_{Li}\|^2 \|\tilde{e}_1(t)\|^2 \\ & \le \tfrac{1}{\varepsilon} \tilde{e}_1^T(t) P_1{}^2 \tilde{e}_1(t) + \varepsilon \tilde{\gamma}^2 \|\tilde{e}_1(t)\|^2 \end{aligned} \tag{29}$$

where γ is the Lipschitz constant of $\Gamma_{e1i}\Big(T_{Li}^{-1} x, t\Big)$ and $\tilde{\gamma} = \gamma \|T_{Li}\|$. Likewise, for the known nonlinear function $\Gamma_{e2i}\Big(T_{Li}^{-1} x, t\Big)$, the following inequality can be readily expressed as follows:

$$2\tilde{e}_y^T(t) P_2 T_{Li} \Big(\Gamma_{e2i}\Big(T_{Li}^{-1} x, t\Big) - \Gamma_{e2i}\Big(T_{Li}^{-1} \hat{x}, t\Big)\Big) \le \frac{1}{\varepsilon} \tilde{e}_y^T(t) P_2{}^2 \tilde{e}_y(t) + \varepsilon \tilde{\gamma}^2 \|\tilde{e}_y(t)\|^2 \tag{30}$$

On the other hand, considering the definition of $v(t)$ in (17) and the bound on $\|f_a(t)\| < \rho_a$, we can derive the following inequality:

$$\begin{aligned} &2\tilde{e}_y^T(t)P_2\left(\tilde{M}_{2i}f(t)-v(t)-\tfrac{1}{\beta}\dot{\tilde{\rho}}\rho\right)\leq \tilde{e}_y^T(t)\tilde{M}_{2i}^TP_2\|f_a(t)\| \\ &-\rho(t)\tilde{e}_y^T(t)P_2\tfrac{P_2\tilde{e}_y(t)}{\|P_2\tilde{e}_y(t)\|}-(\rho-\hat{\rho})\|P_2\tilde{e}_y(t)\| \\ &\leq \tilde{e}_y^T(t)\tilde{M}_{2i}^TP_2\|f_a(t)\|-(\hat{\rho}+v)\left\|\tilde{e}_y^T(t)P_2\right\|-(\rho-\hat{\rho})\|P_2\tilde{e}_y(t)\| \\ &\leq v_{i,\max}\|P_2\tilde{e}_y(t)\|-v\|P_2\tilde{e}_y(t)\|<0 \end{aligned} \tag{31}$$

where $v_{i,\max}=\|\tilde{M}_{2i}\|_{\max}\rho_a$ with $v_{i,\max}\leq\rho_a$.

Now, using (30) and (31), we can write the following:

$$\begin{aligned} \dot{V}(t)\leq &\sum_{j=1}^{g}\mu_i(\theta(t))\Big\{\tilde{e}_1^T(t)\Big(\Psi_{1i}+\tfrac{1}{\varepsilon}+\varepsilon\tilde{\gamma}^2I_{n-p}\Big)\tilde{e}_1(t) \\ &+2\tilde{e}_1^T(t)P_1\tilde{A}_{1i}\tilde{e}_1(t-d(t))+2\tilde{e}_1^T(t)P_1\tilde{A}_{2i}\tilde{e}_y(t) \\ &-(1-\tau)\tilde{e}_1^T(t-d(t))S_1\tilde{e}_1(t-d(t)) \\ &+\tilde{e}_y^T(t)\Big(\Psi_{2i}+\tfrac{1}{\varepsilon}+\varepsilon\tilde{\gamma}^2I_p\Big)\tilde{e}_y(t) \\ &-2\tilde{e}_y^T(t)P_2\tilde{D}_2\xi(x,t)+2\tilde{e}_1^T(t)P_1\tilde{A}_{d2i}\tilde{e}_y(t-d(t)) \\ &+2\tilde{e}_y^T(t)P_2\tilde{A}_{d3i}\tilde{e}_1(t-d(t))+2\tilde{e}_y^T(t)P_2\tilde{A}_3\tilde{e}_1(t) \\ &+2\tilde{e}_y^T(t)P_2\tilde{A}_{d4i}\tilde{e}_1(t-d(t))-2\tilde{e}_1^T(t)P_1\tilde{D}_1\xi(x,t) \\ &-(1-\tau)\tilde{e}_y^T(t-d(t))S_2\tilde{e}_y(t-d(t))\Big\} \end{aligned} \tag{32}$$

To ensure the resilience of the proposed adaptive SMO to the uncertainties $\xi(x,t)$ in the L_2 sense, we introduce the subsequent variable V_0 as follows:

$$V_0=V(t)+r^T(t)r(t)-\sigma\xi^T(x,t)\xi(x,t)<0 \tag{33}$$

We introduce the new variable as follows:

$$\alpha=\frac{1}{\varepsilon\tilde{\gamma}^2}\to\tilde{\gamma}=\frac{1}{\sqrt{\alpha\varepsilon}} \tag{34}$$

The maximization of $\tilde{\gamma}$ for the Lipschitz nonlinear function $\bar{\Gamma}_i(x,t)$ can be achieved by concurrently minimizing both α and ε. By integrating these two objective functions, our goal is to minimize the linear function as follows: $\alpha+\varepsilon$

$$V_0(t)\leq\sum_{i=1}^{g}\mu_i(\theta(t))\begin{bmatrix}\tilde{e}_1^T(t)\\ \tilde{e}_y^T(t)\\ \tilde{e}_1^T(t-d(t))\\ \tilde{e}_y^T(t-d(t))\\ \xi^T(x,t)\end{bmatrix}^T\Theta_i\begin{bmatrix}\tilde{e}_1(t)\\ \tilde{e}_y(t)\\ \tilde{e}_1(t-d(t))\\ \tilde{e}_y(t-d(t))\\ \xi(x,t)\end{bmatrix} \tag{35}$$

with

$$\Theta_i=\begin{bmatrix}\Theta_{1,i} & (\tilde{A}_3P_1)^T & P\tilde{A}_{d1} & P\tilde{D}\\ (*) & \Theta_{2,i} & 0 & 0\\ (*) & (*) & Z & 0\\ (*) & (*) & (*) & \sigma I_l\end{bmatrix}$$

where

$$\Theta_{1,i}=\tilde{A}_{1i}^TP_1+P_1\tilde{A}_{1i}+W_i\tilde{A}_{3i}+\tilde{A}_{3i}^TW_i+S_1+\tfrac{1}{\varepsilon}P_1{}^2+\varepsilon\tilde{\gamma}^2I_{n-p}+H_1^TH_1 \text{ and}$$
$$\Theta_{2,i}=\tilde{A}_{4i}^{sT}P_2+P_2\tilde{A}_{4i}^{s}+S_2+\tfrac{1}{\varepsilon}P_2{}^2+\varepsilon\tilde{\gamma}^2I_p+H_2^TH_2.$$

$$Z=\begin{bmatrix}-(1-\tau)S_1+H_3^TH_3 & 0\\ 0 & -(1-\tau)S_2+H_4^TH_4\end{bmatrix}.$$

Therefore, $V_0(t) \leq 0$ if:

$$\sum_{i=1}^{g} \mu_i(\theta(t))\Theta_i < 0 \tag{36}$$

According to the Shur compliment, we can obtain (24) using (36). Furthermore, if (24) is achieved, then we conclude that $V(t) = V_1(t) + V_2(t) < 0$. It remains to verify that state estimation errors (20) and (21) are asymptotically stable with an attenuation level $||H_\infty|| \leq \sigma$. This completes the proof. □

3.3. Robust Fault Estimation

In this section, it is assumed that the adaptive sliding mode observer defined by Equations (14) and (15) has been constructed, and the reachability condition $S_g(t)$ is met. Consequently, we have the following:

$$S_g(t) = \{(\tilde{e}_1(t), \tilde{e}_y(t)) | \tilde{e}_y(t) = 0\} \tag{37}$$

On the sliding surface $S_g(t)$, the state estimation error remains stable $\sup\limits_{0 \leq t \leq \infty} ||\tilde{e}_1(t)|| \leq \varpi$ where ϖ is a positive scalar. The objective of sliding motion reachability is to ensure that the system's state trajectories reach and maintain motion along a predetermined sliding surface $S_g(t)$. This involves designing a control strategy that drives the system's state toward the sliding surface and ensures it remains on this surface for subsequent times, despite the presence of local nonlinearities and variable time delays. We assume that the given positive constants κ_0 and $\rho(t)$ meet the following inequality:

$$\rho(t) \geq \kappa_{\max} + \kappa_0 \tag{38}$$

Then, the error dynamics (20) and (21) can be set to the sliding surface $S_g(t)$ given by (37). This implies the following: $\dot{e}_y(t) = e_y(t) = 0$. So, in order to obtain a robust fault estimation, the following structure is used:

$$\begin{aligned} \dot{\tilde{e}}_y &= 0 = \sum_{j=1}^{g} \mu_i(\theta(t))\{\tilde{A}_{3i}\tilde{e}_1(t) + \tilde{\mathrm{A}}_{d3i}\tilde{e}_1(t-d(t)) + \tilde{\Gamma}_{e2i}(x,t) + \tilde{G}_{n2}v_{eq}(t) \\ &- \tilde{D}_2\xi(x,t) - \tilde{M}_2 f_a(t)\} \end{aligned} \tag{39}$$

Here, $v_{eq}(t)$ represents the equivalent output error injection signal required to sustain the sliding motion. This signal can be approximated to any desired level of accuracy by substituting (17) with the following:

$$v_{eq}(t) = \rho(t)\frac{P_2 e_y}{||P_2 e_y|| + \delta} \tag{40}$$

where δ is a small positive scalar to reduce the chattering effect.

We derive the following relationship:

$$\Omega(\tilde{e}_1, x, t) = \sum_{j=1}^{g} \mu_i(\theta(t))\{\tilde{A}_{3i}\tilde{e}_1(t) + \tilde{\mathrm{A}}_{d3i}\tilde{e}_1(t-d(t)) + \tilde{\Gamma}_{e2i}(x,t) - \tilde{D}_2\xi(x,t)\} \tag{41}$$

We have the following:

$$||\Omega(\tilde{e}_1, x, t)||_2 \leq \sum_{j=1}^{g} \mu_i(\theta(t))\kappa_{\max} \tag{42}$$

where $\kappa_{\max} = (||\tilde{A}_{3i}||_2 + ||\tilde{\mathrm{A}}_{d3i}||_2 + \gamma)\varpi + ||\tilde{D}_2||_2\beta$.

From the last equation, we can conclude the following:

$$\|\Omega(\tilde{e}_1, x, t)\| \leq \kappa_{\max} \tag{43}$$

For a sufficiently small value of the maximum fault magnitude $\kappa_{\max}$, the following can be inferred:

$$0 = \sum_{i=1}^{g} \mu_i(\theta(t))\left(\tilde{M}_{2i} f_a(t) - v_{eq}(t)\right) \tag{44}$$

The estimation of actuator faults will be obtained based on the equivalent error injection signal, and it is expressed by the following expressions:

$$\hat{f}_a(t) = \sum_{i=1}^{g} \mu_i(\theta(t))\left(\tilde{M}_{2i}\right)^{+}\left\{\frac{\bar{P}_0\,\bar{e}_y(t)}{\|\bar{P}_0\,\bar{e}_y(t)\| + \delta}\right\} \tag{45}$$

A design procedure for fault estimation based on an adaptive SMO is introduced in a revised version, as follows:

Step 1: Choose the weight matrix predefined in Equation (22).
Step 2: Choose a suitable scalar $0 \leq \lambda \leq 1$; we can obtain the matrices P_1; P_2; W_i and the scalars ε, ς, and γ by resolving the LMI optimization problem (24) using the MATLAB (2015b) LMI toolbox.
Step 3: Actuator fault estimation can be achieved via an adaptive SMO design (14) and (15) and using Equations (39) and (45).

The next section explores a fault-tolerant control design for the uncertain nonlinear delay system through the information supplied by the estimation of actuator faults.

4. Sliding Mode Controller Design

The intended sliding mode controller with an adaptive law is designated to take corrective actions to counteract fault influences and stabilize the nonlinear system characterized by LPV-delayed representation.

The main objective of this work is to create an effective and resilient fault-tolerant control (FTC) strategy for specific types of uncertain systems that include local nonlinear models and variable time-delays. This approach introduces a sliding mode FTC technique based on fault estimation (FE) to address the complexities of such systems. The significant contributions of this study include the following:

- The designs for FE and FTC are specifically developed to handle variable time-delays in the polytopic system, presenting greater challenges compared to systems with constant time delays.
- The sliding mode control method is utilized to ensure robustness against uncertainties and disturbances, making the proposed strategy ideal for applications dealing with high levels of uncertainty or nonlinearity in polytopic systems.

Let us define a sliding surface S_g as follows:

$$S_g := \{y(t) \in \Re^p : S_c(t) = 0\} \tag{46}$$

$S_c(t) \in {}^m$ a linear switching function based on output feedback information for nonlinear systems could be described as follows:

$$S_c(t) = \sum_{i=1}^{g} \mu_i(\theta(t))\{N_{c,i}\, y(t)\} \tag{47}$$

with $N_{c,i} = (C_iB_i)^+ - h\left(I_p - C_iB_i(C_iB_i)^+\right)$ with an arbitrary matrix $h \in {}^{m \times p}$ and $(C_iB_i)^+ = \left((C_iB_i)^+(C_iB_i)\right)^1 (C_iB_i)^T$.

Prior to initiating the fault-tolerant control (FTC) design, given the assumption that the pair (A_i, B_i) is controllable, and using the estimation of actuator faults and the system state, we suggest formulating a robust control as follows:

$$u(t) = u_l(t) + u_n(t) \tag{48}$$

The control input $u_l(t)$ is designed to incorporate the linear component, which is influenced by the system states and the estimation of actuator faults, as specified by the following:

$$u_l(t) = \sum_{j=1}^{g} \mu_i(\theta(t))\Big\{-k_j\hat{x}(t) - q_i\hat{f}_a(t)\Big\} \tag{49}$$

where $q_i\hat{f}_a(t)$ aims to mitigate the impact of actuator faults. It is presupposed that $k_j \in \Re^{m\times n}$ and $q_i = B_iM_i$.

Real-time adjustments of the K_j gains and fault estimation $\hat{f}_a(t)$ are facilitated by adaptive algorithms. Real-time control heavily relies on feedback mechanisms, where the current state of the system informs adjustments to control gains, thanks to the adaptive nature of our SMC. The nonlinear $u_n(t)$ component responsible for initiating the sliding motion on the surface, S_g, is introduced with an adaptive law as follows:

$$u_n(t) := \begin{cases} \eta(t)\frac{S_c(t)}{\|S_c(t)\|} & if\ S_c(t) = 0 \\ 0 & otherwise \end{cases} \tag{50}$$

$\eta(t) = \hat{\rho}_c + \iota_c + \varpi_c$ where $\iota_c > 0$ and $\varpi_c > 0$ is positive small constants. We use $\hat{\rho}_c$ to determine the term $\eta(t)$.

We note the following:

$$\dot{\hat{\rho}}_c S_c = \varpi_c\|S_c(t)\|, \hat{\rho}_c(0) \geq 0 \tag{51}$$

where ϖ_c is a positive gain.

According to the preceding information, utilizing the distinct adaptive nonlinear component structure of $u_n(t)$, it is necessary to demonstrate that the system will inevitably converge to and remain on the associated sliding mode surface S_g within a finite time. Consequently, when examining the sliding motion corresponding to the sliding surface S_g outlined in (46), we contemplate the Lyapunov–Krasovskii function as our analytical tool.

$$V_c(t) = \frac{1}{2}S_c^T(t)S_c(t) + \frac{1}{2\varpi_c}\tilde{\rho}_c^2 \tag{52}$$

where $\tilde{\rho}_c = \rho_c - \hat{\rho}_c$ is the estimated error of ρ_c.

This optimal Lyapunov function not only guarantees stability but also minimizes the effect that results in chattering, thereby improving system performance despite the presence of local nonlinearities, uncertainties, and variable time-delay. Our study addresses this challenge by incorporating adaptive mechanisms into the design of the Lyapunov function to enhance both robustness and optimality. Referring to the dynamic equations of the open-loop system in (2) and (47), the time derivative of (52) yields the following:

$$\dot{V}_c(t) = \sum_{i=1}^{g}\sum_{j=1}^{g} \mu_i\mu_j(\theta(t))\Big\{\Big(N_{c,i}C_iA_i - k_j\Big)\|x(t)\|\, N_{c,i}C_iA_{di}\|x(t-d(t))\| - \iota_c - \varpi_c\}\|S_c(t)\|\} \tag{53}$$

We define the subassembly system with the following expression:

$$\Omega_c = \{x\|x(t)\| \leq \kappa_c\} \tag{54}$$

The condition for reachability, ensuring the system reaches the sliding surface S, is met when the scalar ι_c is chosen to satisfy $\iota_c > \left(N_{c,i}C_iA_i - k_j\right)\kappa_c$ such that we have the following:

$$S^T{}_c(t)S_c(t) \leq -\varpi_c\|S_c(t)\| \tag{55}$$

The suggested sliding mode controller with adaptive law guarantees the presence of an optimal sliding motion within a finite duration; specifically, $\dot{S}_c(t)S_c(t) = 0,\ \forall t \geq t_c$. Upon achieving the sliding mode, our attention turns toward assessing the stability of the closed-loop delayed LPV system utilizing local nonlinear models. Let us introduce the equivalent control u_{eq}:

$$\begin{aligned} u_{eq} &= \sum_{i=1}^{g}\mu_j(\theta(t))\{N_{c,i}C_i\{[A_ix(t) + A_{di}x(t-d(t)) \\ &+ \Gamma(x,t) + D_i(x,t)]\} + u_l(t) \end{aligned} \tag{56}$$

The closed-loop system's dynamics incorporating the equivalent control law (56) are represented as follows:

$$\begin{aligned} \dot{X}(t) &= \sum_{i=1}^{g}\sum_{j=1}^{g}\mu_i\mu_j(\theta(t))\{\theta_i(A_i - k_{1j}B_i)x(t) \\ &+ \theta_iA_{di}x(t-d(t)) + \theta_i\Gamma(x,t) + B_{ij}E(t)\} \end{aligned} \tag{57}$$

$$y_c(t) = \sum_{i=1}^{g}\mu_i(\theta(t))\{C_ix(t)\} \tag{58}$$

with $B_{ij} = \begin{bmatrix} Bk_{1j} & M_i & \theta_iD_i \end{bmatrix}$, $E_i(t) = \begin{bmatrix} e_x^T(t) & e_{f_a}^T(t) & \xi^T(x,t) \end{bmatrix}^T$ and $\theta_i = I_n - B_iN_{c,i}C_i$.

The nonlinear function $\Gamma(x,t)$ satisfies a Lipschitz condition in (9); the following assumption is also required:

$$\|\Gamma(x,t)\| = \gamma\|x(t)\| \tag{59}$$

where $\gamma > 0$ is Lipschitz-constant.

The Lipschitz condition is used to ensure that the controller can effectively overcome uncertainty without leading to instability. It is used to design control laws that ensure that the system can reach the sliding surface and stay there despite variable time-delays and uncertainty.

The current objective is to establish the necessary conditions for ensuring the stability of the closed-loop LPV delayed system (57) and (58) on the sliding surface S_g in the presence of actuator faults, uncertainties, and time delays simultaneously.

5. Fault-Tolerant Control Design

Thus, we propose designing an FTC strategy aimed at providing corrective action after the detection of faults and disturbances, as well as stabilizing the system. Two cases are considered, depending on the characteristics of the delays, so that we have the following:

- Separated design FTC with variable time-delay.
- Integrated design and FTC with variable time-delay.

5.1. Separated Fault-Tolerant Control Design

Over the past years, significant research efforts have been dedicated to addressing the fault estimation (FE)-based fault-tolerant control (FTC) problem in a precise and effective manner. Previous studies have primarily focused on tackling this issue through a two-step approach or separated approach:

Step 1: Develop an observer to estimate the faults and system states.
Step 2: Design a controller to stabilize the closed-loop system.

The conventional approach to the FE-based FTC design for uncertain polytopic systems with local nonlinear models and variable time-delays can be depicted as separated architecture, as shown in Figure 1.

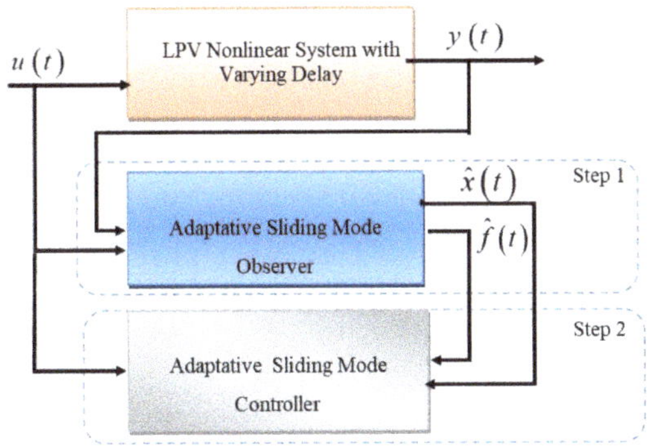

Figure 1. Separated Design FTC.

The following theorem provides sufficient conditions for the existence of such an FTC control, with prescribed H_∞ performances, by using Lyapunov–Krasovskii stability and the multi-objective LMI technique.

Theorem 2. *The closed loop for a nonlinear delayed system is robustly stable with the simultaneously maximized admissible Lipschitz constant λ_x and minimized gain ς_x. The H_∞ criteria are guaranteed if there exists a symmetric positive definite matrix $P_x = P_x^T$, Q, and constants $0 \leq \lambda_x \leq 1$, $\alpha_x > 0$ and $\varsigma_x > 0$, such that the following LMI optimization holds:*

$$\begin{array}{l} min[\lambda_x(\varepsilon_x + \alpha_x) + (1-\lambda_x)\varsigma_x] \\ \begin{bmatrix} \Psi_{i,j} + C_i^T C_i & \theta_i A_{di} & B_i Q_j & E_i \\ * & (1-\tau)S_x & 0 & 0 \\ * & * & -2\vartheta + \varsigma_x I_n & 0 \\ * & * & * & \mathrm{N} \end{bmatrix} < 0 \end{array} \tag{60}$$

where $\Psi_{i,j} = P_x A_i^T \theta_i{}^T + \theta_i A_i P_x - B_i Q_j - B_i^T Q_j^T + S_{xi}$, $\vartheta = \mu_c P_x$ *and* $K_j = Q_j P_x{}^{-1}$,
$\bar{E}_i = \begin{bmatrix} M_i & \theta_i D_i & P_x C_i^T & P_x & I_n \\ 0 & 0 & 0 & 0 & 0 \end{bmatrix}$, *and* $\mathrm{N} = diag\{-\varsigma_x I_n, -\varsigma_x I_q, -\varsigma_x I_l, -I, -\varepsilon_x I, -\alpha_x I\}$.

Upon resolving the multi-objective optimization problem, the following is demonstrated:

$$\begin{array}{rcl} \varsigma_x^* & = & \min(\varsigma_x) \\ \alpha_x^* & = & \min(\alpha_x) \\ \varepsilon_x^* & = & \min(\varepsilon_x) \\ \lambda_x^* & = & \min(\lambda_x) \end{array} \tag{61}$$

Proof. Let us introduce the Lyapunov function for the closed-loop system as follows:

$$V_x(t) = x^T(t)P_x x(t) + \int_{t-d(t)}^{t} x^T(t)S_x x(t)dx \tag{62}$$

where $P_x \in \Re^{n\times n}$ is a symmetric positive definite matrix. By considering the closed-loop LPV delayed system (57) and (58), the time derivative $\dot{V}_x(t)$ can be addressed as follows:

$$
\begin{aligned}
\dot{V}_x(t) &= \sum_{i=1}^{g}\sum_{i=1}^{g}\mu_i\mu_j(\theta(t))\Big\{x^T(t)\Pi_{xi}x(t) + 2x^T(t)P_x\theta_i A_{di}x(t) + 2x^T(t)P_x\theta_i\Gamma(x,t) \\
&- x^T(t-d(t))(1-\tau)S_x x(t-d(t)) - 2x^T(t)P_x B_i E_i(t)\Big\}
\end{aligned} \tag{63}
$$

with $\Pi_{xi} = P_x\theta_i{}^T A_i{}^T + \theta_i A_i P_x - Q_j{}^T B_i j^T - B_i j Q_j + S_{xi}$.

Based on the definition and Assumption 4, the following inequality is derived:

$$
\begin{aligned}
&2x^T(t)P_x\theta_i\Gamma(x,t) \le \tfrac{1}{\varepsilon_c}x^T(t)P_x x(t) + \varepsilon_c\Gamma^T(x,t)\theta^T{}_i\theta_i\Gamma(x,t) \\
&\le x^T(t)\left[\tfrac{1}{\varepsilon_c}P_x^2 + \varepsilon_c\tilde{\gamma}_c^2\right]x(t)
\end{aligned} \tag{64}
$$

We note the following: $\tilde{\gamma}_c = \gamma_c\|\theta_i\|$.

To guarantee the resilience of the closed-loop LPV delayed system (57) and (58) against disturbances denoted by $\phi(t)$, we introduce the variable $J(t)$ defined as follows:

$$
J(t) = \sum_{i=1}^{g}\sum_{i=1}^{g}\mu_i\mu_j(\theta(t))\{\dot{V}_x(t) + Y_L^T(t)Y_L(t) - \varsigma_x\phi^T(t)\phi(t)\} \tag{65}
$$

We can rewrite the above expression as follows:

$$
\begin{aligned}
J(t) &= \sum_{i=1}^{g}\sum_{i=1}^{g}\mu_i\mu_j(\theta(t))\Big\{x^T(t)\left(\Pi_{xi} + C_i^T C_i\right)x(t) + 2x^T(t)P_{xi}\theta_i A_{di}x(t) \\
&+ x^T(t)\left[\frac{1}{\varepsilon_c}P_x^2 + \varepsilon_c\tilde{\gamma}_c^2\right]x(t) + 2x^T(t)P_x B_i E_i(t)\Big\} < 0
\end{aligned} \tag{66}
$$

We introduce the new variable as follows:

$$
\alpha_c := \frac{1}{\varepsilon_c\tilde{\gamma}_c^2} \rightarrow \tilde{\gamma}_c = \frac{1}{\sqrt{\varepsilon_c\tilde{\gamma}_c}} \tag{67}
$$

It has been determined that maximizing $\tilde{\gamma}_c$, associated with the nonlinear Lipschitz function $\Gamma(x,t)$, can be achieved by concurrently minimizing both ε_c and α_c, implying the need to minimize the linear function $\alpha_c + \varepsilon_c$. Therefore, the following remains to be shown:

$$
\Sigma_{sep} = \sum_{i=1}^{g}\sum_{i=1}^{g}\mu_i\mu_j(\theta(t))\begin{bmatrix} \Lambda_{1,ij} & \Lambda_{2ij} \\ (*) & \Lambda_{3ij} \end{bmatrix} < 0 \tag{68}
$$

with $\Lambda_{1,ij} = \begin{bmatrix} \Pi_{xi,j} & \theta_i A_{di} \\ * & (1-\tau)S_x \end{bmatrix}$, $\Lambda_{2,ij} = \begin{bmatrix} P_x M_i & P_x\theta_i D_i & P_x C_i^T & P_x & I_n \\ 0 & 0 & 0 & 0 & 0 \end{bmatrix}$,
$\Lambda_{3ij} = diag\{-\varsigma_x I_n, -\varsigma_x I_q, -\varsigma_x I_l, -I, -\varepsilon_x I, -\alpha_x I\}$.

Based on the Schur complement, the relationship (68) is equivalent to the following:

$$
\sum_{i=1}^{g}\sum_{i=1}^{g}\mu_i\mu_j(\theta(t))\begin{bmatrix}
\Pi_{xi,j} & \theta_i A_{di} & P_x B_i k_j & P_x M_i & P_x\theta_i D_i & P_x C_i^T & P_x & I_n \\
* & (1-\tau)S_x & 0 & 0 & 0 & 0 & 0 & 0 \\
* & * & -\varsigma_x I_n & 0 & 0 & 0 & 0 & 0 \\
* & * & * & -\varsigma_x I_q & 0 & 0 & 0 & 0 \\
* & * & * & * & -\varsigma_x I_l & 0 & 0 & 0 \\
* & * & * & * & * & -I & 0 & 0 \\
* & * & * & * & * & * & -\alpha_x I & 0 \\
* & * & * & * & * & * & * & -\varepsilon_x I
\end{bmatrix} < 0 \tag{69}
$$

with $\Pi_{xi,j} = P_x A_i{}^T + A_i P_x - Q_j{}^T B_i{}^T - B_i Q_j + S_x$ and $P_x = P_x{}^{-1}$.

Next, we will construct the matrix X with a unique diagonal structure as follows: $X = diag\{P_x^{-1}, P_x^{-1}, P_x^{-1}, I_q, I_l, I_p, I_n, I_n\}$. By multiplying both sides of Equation (60) by X and its transpose, we arrive at Equation (63). Using the definition, we can then establish the following relationship:

$$P_x^{-1} + P_x^{-1} \leq \varsigma_x P_x^{-1} P_x^{-1} + \varsigma_x^{-1} I_n \quad (70)$$

It is evident that Equation (70) is equivalent to the following:

$$P_x^{-1} \varsigma_x P_x^{-1} \leq -2P_x^{-1} + \varsigma_x^{-1} I_n \quad (71)$$

Through the use of the previous results, it is straightforward to deduce that the closed-loop LPV delayed system (57) and (58) with local nonlinear models is robustly stable with respect to the H_∞ performance level ς_x and the maximized admissible Lipschitz constant γ_c.

This completes the proof. □

An adaptive separated FTC design procedure using an adaptive SMO is described as follows:

Step 1: Choose a suitable scalar "$0 \leq \lambda_x \leq 1$"; resolve the LMI optimization problem (60) using the MATLAB (2015b) LMI toolbox. We can now obtain the matrix Q_j and the scalars δ_x, ς_x, and γ_x.
Step 2: Calculate $K_j = Q_j \bar{P}_x^{-1}$.
Step 3: Construct the adaptive SMC (50); thus, the closed-loop nonlinear system stability (Equations (57) and (58)) can be achieved.

5.2. Integrated Fault-Tolerant Control Design

In recent years, several studies have been published on the design of fault-tolerant control (FTC) systems using finite element (FE) methods, which involve a single step to achieve optimal robustness between observer and controller models as shown in Figure 2.

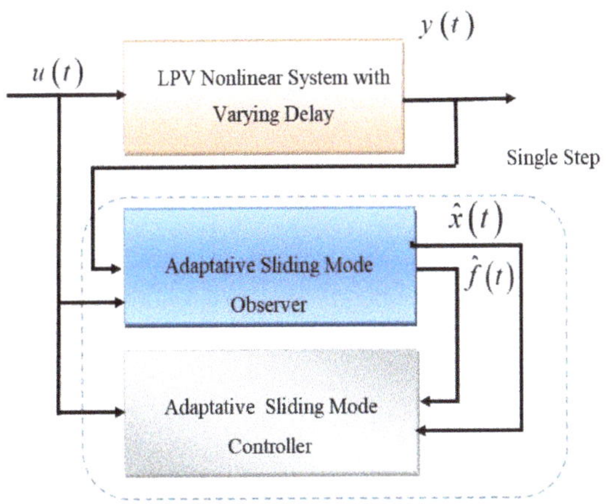

Figure 2. Integrated design of FTC.

In this section, we investigate the potential of the integrated FE-based FTC design to compute, in a single step, adaptive observer gains G_{li} and controller gains K_j. This approach aims to enhance the robustness of the closed-loop nonlinear system despite the presence of time-delay nonlinearities and uncertainties. Combining (20), (21), (57), and (58) yields the following delayed closed-loop system, including fault estimation with fault compensation control, expressed as follows:

$$\begin{aligned} \dot{X}(t) &= \sum_{i=1}^{g}\sum_{j=1}^{g} \mu_i \mu_j(\theta(t))\{\theta_i(A_i - k_{1j}B_i)x(t) + \theta_i A_{di} x(t-d(t)) \\ &+ \theta_i \Gamma(x,t) + B_{ij}E(t)\} \end{aligned} \quad (72)$$

$$\begin{aligned}
\dot{\tilde{e}}_1(t) &= \sum_{j=1}^{g} \mu_i(\theta(t))\{\tilde{A}_{1i}\tilde{e}_1(t) + (\tilde{A}_{2i} - \tilde{G}_{l1i})\tilde{e}_1(t) + \tilde{G}_{n1i}v(t) \\
&+ \tilde{A}_{d1i}\tilde{e}_1(t-d(t)) + \tilde{A}_{d2i}\tilde{e}_y(t-d(t)) - \tilde{D}_{1i}\xi(x,t) \\
&+ \tilde{\Gamma}_{e1i}(x,t)\} \qquad (73) \\
\dot{\tilde{e}}_y(t) &= \sum_{j=1}^{g} \mu_i(\theta(t))\{\tilde{A}_{3i}\tilde{e}_1(t) + (\tilde{A}_{4i} - \tilde{G}_{l2i})\tilde{e}_y(t) - \tilde{D}_2\xi(x,t) \\
&+ \tilde{A}_{d3i}\tilde{e}_1(t-d(t)) + \tilde{A}_{d4i}\tilde{e}_y(t-d(t)) + \tilde{\Gamma}_{e2i}(x,t) \\
&+ \tilde{G}_{n2}v(t) + \tilde{A}_{d4i}\tilde{e}_y(t-d(t)) - \tilde{M}_2 f_a(t)\} \qquad (74) \\
Y_{\text{int}}(t) &= \sum_{i=1}^{g} \mu_i(\theta(t))\{C_{L_i}x(t) + C_{Li}e(t)\} \qquad (75)
\end{aligned}$$

with $B_{ij} = \begin{bmatrix} Bk_{1j} & M_i & \theta_i D_i \end{bmatrix}$, $E_i(t) = \begin{bmatrix} e_x^T(t) & e_{f_a}^T(t) & \xi^T(x,t) \end{bmatrix}^T$ and $\theta_i = I_n - B_i N_{c,i} C_i$. The boundlessness of $e_x(t)$ and $e_{f_a}(t)$ can be guaranteed based on Theorem 2; based on Assumption 4, the following theorem is presented to design feedback gain matrices $k_j \in \Re^{p\times n}$ ensuring that the closed-loop LPV delayed nonlinear system (72)–(75) remains stable.

Theorem 3. *Using the sliding mode input structure (47), the closed-loop LPV delayed system, as represented by Equations (72)–(75), achieves robust stability with an optimized admissible Lipschitz constant $\gamma_i > 0$ and minimized gain $\|H_{\text{int}}\|_\infty < \varsigma_c$. This is contingent on the existence of constants $0 \le \lambda_x \le 1$ and $\alpha_i > 0$, and matrices $P_x = P_x^T > 0$, $P_e = P_e^T > 0$, $S_e > 0$, YY, and Q_j such that the following LMI optimization is verified:*

$$\begin{aligned}
&min[\lambda_e(\varepsilon_e + \alpha_e) + (1-\lambda_c)\varsigma_c] \\
&\begin{bmatrix}
\chi_{11} & \chi_{12} & \chi_{13} & \chi_{14} & \chi_{15} & \chi_{16} \\
* & \chi_{21} & \chi_{22} & \chi_{23} & \chi_{24} & \chi_{25} \\
* & * & \chi_{31} & \chi_{32} & \chi_{33} & \chi_{34} \\
* & * & * & \chi_{41} & \chi_{42} & \chi_{43} \\
* & * & * & * & \chi_{51} & \chi_{52} \\
* & * & * & * & * & \chi_{61}
\end{bmatrix} < 0
\end{aligned} \qquad (76)$$

We note the following:

$$\begin{aligned}
\chi_{11} &= \Pi_{xi} + \frac{1}{\varepsilon_i}P_e^2 + \varepsilon_i\tilde{\gamma}^2 I_n, \chi_{12} = (\theta_i A_{di})^T \\
\chi_{15} &= P_x B_{i,j}\chi_{16} = P_x C_L^T C_L, \chi_{21} = -(1-\tau)S_x \\
\chi_{13} &= \chi_{14} = \chi_{22} = \chi_{25} = \chi_{32} = \chi_{33} = \chi_{34} = 0 \\
\chi_{23} &= P_e\tilde{A}_{di}, \chi_{24} = P_e\bar{\bar{D}}_i, \chi_{31} = \Pi_i + \frac{1}{\varepsilon}P_e{}^2 + \varepsilon\tilde{\gamma}^2 I_{n-p} \\
\chi_{41} &= -(1-\tau)S_e, \chi_{42} = \chi_{43} = 0 \\
\chi_{51} &= -2Y + \varsigma_c I, \chi_{52} = 0, \chi_{61} = -I_n \\
\Pi_i &= \begin{bmatrix} \Pi_{1,i} & (P_1\tilde{A}_{3i})^T \\ * & \Pi_{2,i} \end{bmatrix}, \bar{\bar{D}}_i = \begin{bmatrix} 0 & \tilde{M}_i & \tilde{D}_i \end{bmatrix} \\
\Pi_{xi} &= P_x\theta_i{}^T A_i{}^T + \theta_i A_i P_x - Q_j{}^T B_i{}^T - B_i Q_j + S_{xi} \\
\Pi_{1i} &= \tilde{A}_{1i}^T P_1 + P_1\tilde{A}_{1i} + W_i\tilde{A}_{3i} + \tilde{A}_{3i}^T W_i + S_1 + \frac{1}{\varepsilon}P_1 + \varepsilon\tilde{\gamma}^2 I_{n-p} + H_1^T H_1 \\
\Pi_{2i} &= \tilde{A}_{4i}^{sT} P_2 + P_2\tilde{A}_{4i}^s + S_2 + \frac{1}{\varepsilon}P_2 + \varepsilon\tilde{\gamma}^2 I_p + H_2^T H_2
\end{aligned} \qquad (77)$$

where $P_e = diag\{P_1, P_2\}$ and $S_e = diag\{S_1, S_2\}$ are symmetric definite positive matrices.

The gain matrices of the adaptive sliding mode controller K_j and observer $G_{L,i}$ are computed as follows:

$$K_j = Q_j P_x^{-1} \quad (78)$$
$$G_{L,i} = P_1 W_{1,i} \quad (79)$$

Proof. To ensure the stability of the LPV-delayed nonlinear system, as described by Equations (72)–(75), we construct a Lyapunov–Krasovskii functional as follows:

$$V_{\text{int}}(t) = V_x(t) + V(t) \quad (80)$$

We assume the following:

$$V_x(t) = x^T(t)P_x x(t) + \int_{t-d(t)}^{t} x^T(t)S_x x(t)dx \quad (81)$$

$$V(t) = e^T(t)P_e e(t) + \int_{t-d(t)}^{t} e^T(t)S_e e(t)dx \quad (82)$$

We can follow a similar approach to Theorems 1 and 2 and consider the closed-loop LPV delayed system. Therefore, the time derivative of $V_{\text{int}}(t)$ is given by the following:

$$\begin{aligned}
&\dot{V}_{\text{int}}(t) = \sum_{i=1}^{g}\sum_{i=1}^{g} \mu_i\mu_j(\theta(t))\Big\{x^T(t)\Big(\Pi_{xi} + \tfrac{1}{\varepsilon_i}I_n + \varepsilon_i\tilde{\gamma}^2 I_n\Big)x(t) \\
&+2x^T(t)P_x(\theta_i A_{di})^T x(t-d(t)) - 2x^T(t)P_x B_{i,j}E_i(t) \\
&-x^T(t-d(t))(1-\tau)S_x x(t-d(t)) \\
&+\tilde{e}^T(t)P_e\begin{bmatrix} \Lambda_{1,i} & 0 \\ 0 & \Lambda_{2,i}\end{bmatrix}\tilde{e}(t) + \tfrac{1}{\varepsilon_i}\tilde{e}^T(t)P_e^2 + \varepsilon_i\gamma^2\tilde{e}^T(t)^T \\
&+2\tilde{e}^T(t)P_e\tilde{A}_i\tilde{e}^T(t-d(t)) + 2\tilde{e}^T(t)P_e\tilde{A}_{di}\tilde{e}^T(t-d(t)) \\
&+2\tilde{e}^T(t)P_e\tilde{D}_i\xi(x,t) + 2\tilde{e}^T(t)P_e\left(\begin{bmatrix} 0 \\ \tilde{M}_{2i}\end{bmatrix}f(t) - v(t)\right) \\
&+\tilde{e}^T(t)S_e\tilde{e}(t) - (1-\tau)\tilde{e}^T(t-d(t))S_e\tilde{e}(t-d(t))\}
\end{aligned} \quad (83)$$

Let us consider the term $J(t)$ as follows:

$$J(t) = \sum_{i=1}^{g}\sum_{i=1}^{g} \mu_i\mu_j(\theta(t))\Big\{\dot{V}_{\text{int}}(t) + Y_L^T(t)Y_L(t) - \varsigma_c E_i{}^T(t)E_i(t)\Big\} \quad (84)$$

We can rewrite the last expression as follows:

$$\begin{aligned}
&J(t) = \sum_{i=1}^{g}\sum_{i=1}^{g} \mu_i\mu_j(\theta(t))\{x^T(t)(\Lambda_{x,ij} + C_L^T C_L)x(t) + 2x^T(t)P_x(\theta_i A_{di})^T x(t-d(t)) \\
&-2x^T(t)P_x B_{i,j}E_i(t) - x^T(t-d(t))(1-\tau)S_x x(t-d(t)) \\
&+\tilde{e}^T(t)P_e\begin{bmatrix} \Lambda_{1,i} & 0 \\ 0 & \Lambda_{2,i}\end{bmatrix}\tilde{e}(t) + \tfrac{1}{\varepsilon_i}\tilde{e}^T(t)P_e^2 + \varepsilon_i\gamma^2\tilde{e}^T(t) \\
&+2\tilde{e}^T(t)P_e\tilde{A}_i\tilde{e}^T(t-d(t)) + 2\tilde{e}^T(t)P_e\tilde{A}_{di}\tilde{e}^T(t-d(t)) \\
&+\tilde{e}^T(t)S_e\tilde{e}(t) - (1-\tau)\tilde{e}^T(t-d(t))S_e\tilde{e}(t-d(t)) \\
&+2\tilde{e}^T(t)P_e\bar{\tilde{D}}_i E_i(t) + \tilde{e}^T(t)(C_e^T C_e)\tilde{e}(t) - \varsigma_c E_i{}^T(t)E_i(t)\Big\}
\end{aligned} \quad (85)$$

We note that $\bar{\tilde{D}}_i = \begin{bmatrix} 0 & \tilde{M}_i & \tilde{D}_i \end{bmatrix}$.
Equivalently, in matrix form, the expression can be written as follows:

$$J(t) \leq \sum_{i=1}^{g}\sum_{i=1}^{g} \mu_i\mu_j(\theta(t))\Big\{\Xi^T(t)\Psi_{ij}\Xi(t)\Big\} \quad (86)$$

where $\Xi(t) = \begin{bmatrix} x^T(t) & x^T(t-d(t)) & \tilde{e}^T(t) & \tilde{e}^T(t-d(t)) & E_i(t) \end{bmatrix}^T$.

We define Ψ_{ij} as follows:

$$\Psi_{ij} = \sum_{i=1}^{g}\sum_{i=1}^{g}\mu_i\mu_j(\theta(t))\begin{bmatrix} \Lambda_{xi} & (\theta_i A_{di})^T & 0 & 0 & B_{i,j} \\ * & -(1-\tau)S_x & \Lambda_i + \frac{1}{\varepsilon_i}{P_e}^2 I_n + \varepsilon_i\gamma^2 I_n & P_e\tilde{A}_{di} & P_e\bar{D}_i \\ * & * & * & -(1-\tau)S_e & 0 \\ * & * & * & * & 0 \\ * & * & * & * & \varsigma_c I \end{bmatrix} \tag{87}$$

Thus, $P_e = diag(P_1, P_2)$ and $S_e = diag(S_1, S_2)$ with the following:

$$\begin{aligned} \Lambda_i &= diag(\Lambda_{1,i}, \Lambda_{2,i}) \\ \Lambda_{1,i} &= \tilde{A}_{1i}^T P_1 + P_1\tilde{A}_{1i} + W_i\tilde{A}_{3i} + \tilde{A}_{3i}^T W_i + S_1 + H_1^T H_1 + \frac{1}{\varepsilon}{P_1}^2 + \varepsilon\bar{\gamma}^2 I_{n-p} \\ \Lambda_{2,i} &= \tilde{A}_{4i}^T P_2 - W_{2,i}^T + P_2\tilde{A}_{4i} - W_{2i} + S_2 + \frac{1}{\varepsilon}{P_2}^2 + \varepsilon\bar{\gamma}^2 I_p + H_2^T H_2 \\ \Lambda_{xi} &= P_x A_i^T {\theta_i}^T + \theta_i A_i P_x - B_i Q_j - B_i^T Q_j^T + S_{xi} + C_L^T C_L + \frac{1}{\varepsilon_i} I_n + \varepsilon_i\bar{\gamma}^2 I_n \end{aligned}$$

To achieve the required transformation, we construct matrix X with a unique diagonal structure, as $X = \left\{{P_x}^{-1}, {P_x}^{-1}, I_n, I_n, {P_x}^{-1}\right\}$. By pre- and post-multiplying X and its transpose in Ψ_{ij}, applying Lemma 1, and performing straightforward manipulations, it is clear that (87) is equivalent to (76). From this, we can conclude that the augmented closed-loop LPV delayed system subject to nonlinearities, described by Equations (72)–(75), is robustly stable against $e_x(t), e_f(t), \xi(x,t)$ with respect to the H_∞ performance level.

This completes the proof. □

An adaptive integrated FTC design procedure using an adaptive SMO is described as follows:

Step 1: Choose a suitable scalar "$0 \le \lambda_x \le 1$"; resolve the LMI optimization problem (60) using the MATLAB (2015b) LMI toolbox. We can then obtain the matrix Q_j and the scalars δ_c, ς_c and γ_c.
Step 2: Calculate $K_j = Q_j\bar{P}_x^{-1}$.
Step 3: Construct the adaptive SMC (50); thus, the closed-loop nonlinear system stability (72)–(75) can be produced.

6. Illustrative Example

In this section, the design of both separated and integrated sliding mode FTC strategies is carried out, utilizing the data provided by the sliding mode observer. The LPV model of the diesel engine, obtained from [30], is considered for this purpose (see Figure 3). Diesel engines are designed to resist severe operating conditions, making them suitable for environments where uncertainty can affect the system. Integrating diesel engines into variable time-delay LPV systems enables better management of the delays inherent in engine operation. The mean value of the diesel engine model is obtained by providing the mass and energy and the ideal gas law. The time delays and nonlinearity present in the diesel engine dynamics can have a destabilizing effect and degrade closed-loop performance.

In state space, it is described as follows:

$$x(t) = \begin{bmatrix} x_1(t) : Intake\ manifold\ pressure \\ x_2(t) : Exhaust\ manifold\ pressure \\ x_3(t) : Compressor\ power \end{bmatrix}$$

and the inputs are as follows:

$$u(t) = \begin{bmatrix} u_1(t) : Control\ input\ for\ valve\ pening \\ u_2(t) : Control\ input\ for\ the\ turbine \end{bmatrix}$$

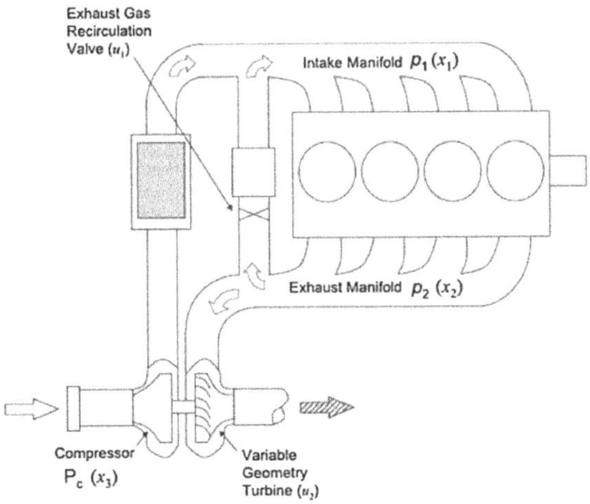

Figure 3. The air path system of diesel engines.

6.1. LPV System with Variable Time-Delay

Let us first consider the nonlinear model of the diesel engine system without any faults and nonlinearity, which can be expressed as follows:

$$\begin{aligned} \dot{x}(t) &= \varphi_{x1}(x(t)) + \varphi_{x2}(x(t))x(t-d(t)) + \varphi_{x3}(x(t))u(t) + \varphi_{x4}(x(t))\xi(x,t) \\ y(t) &= \varphi_2(x(t)) \\ y_L(t) &= \varphi_{yl}(x(t)) \end{aligned} \tag{88}$$

Then, we express the LPV local nonlinear model subject to the actuator fault, uncertainty, and variable time-delay in the following form:

$$\begin{aligned} \dot{x}(t) &= \sum_{i=1}^{4} \mu_i(\theta(t))\{A_i(t)x(t) + A_{di}(t-d(t)) \\ &+ D_i\xi(t,x) + B_iu(t) + \Gamma_i(x,u) + M_if_a(t) \\ y(t) &= \sum_{i=1}^{4} \mu_i(\theta(t))\{C_ix(t)\} \end{aligned} \tag{89}$$

The weighting functions $\mu_i(\theta(t))$ are defined as follows:

$$\begin{aligned} \mu_1(\theta(t)) &= \frac{(\theta_1(t)+0.6)(\theta_2(t)+2)}{4} \\ \mu_2(\theta(t)) &= \frac{(\theta_1(t)+0.6)(2-\theta_2(t))}{4} \\ \mu_3(\theta(t)) &= \frac{(0.6-\theta_1(t))(\theta_2(t)+2)}{4} \\ \mu_4(\theta(t)) &= \frac{(0.6-\theta_1(t))(2-\theta_2(t))}{4} \end{aligned} \tag{90}$$

with $\theta_1(t) = 0.25\sin(0.1t)$, $\theta_2(t) = 0.1\sin(0.25t)$.

The proposed approach encapsulates the nonlinearities present in the diesel engine system, allowing for effective handling of the nonlinear dynamics:

$$\Gamma(x,t) = \begin{bmatrix} -3.33\sin(x_3(t)) \\ 0 \\ 0 \end{bmatrix} \tag{91}$$

Based on the convex set of the LPV system (89), the matrices of local nonlinear models in (90) can be expressed as follows:

$$\begin{aligned} A_1 &= \begin{bmatrix} -12.6 & 4.6 & 0 \\ 0.41 & -2.08 & 0 \\ 0.486 & -0.0004 & -1.33 \end{bmatrix}, A_2 = \begin{bmatrix} -12.6 & 4.6 & 0 \\ 0.41 & -2.08 & 0 \\ 0.486 & -0.4404 & -1.33 \end{bmatrix} \\ A_3 &= \begin{bmatrix} -12.6 & 4.6 & 0 \\ 1.62 & -2.08 & 0 \\ 0.726 & -0.4404 & -1.33 \end{bmatrix}, A_4 = \begin{bmatrix} -12.6 & 4.6 & 0 \\ 1.62 & -2.08 & 0 \\ 0.726 & -0.0004 & -1.33 \end{bmatrix} \\ A_{d1} &= A_{d2} = A_{d3} = A_{d4} = \begin{bmatrix} 0 & 3.6 & 0 \\ 0 & 0 & 0 \\ 0 & 0 & 0 \end{bmatrix} \\ B_1 &= B_2 = B_3 = B_4 = \begin{bmatrix} 0 & 0 \\ -25.65 & 40.32 \\ -18.27 & 1 \end{bmatrix}, C_1 = C_2 = C_3 = C_4 = \begin{bmatrix} 1 & 0 & 0 \\ 1 & 0 & 1 \end{bmatrix}, \\ D_1 &= D_2 = D_3 = D_4 = 0.1 \times \begin{bmatrix} 1 \\ 0.91 \\ 0.91 \end{bmatrix}, M_1 = M_2 = M_3 = M_4 = \begin{bmatrix} 0.7 \\ 0 \\ 1 \end{bmatrix} \end{aligned} \tag{92}$$

The delay is modeled as a variable time-delay: $d(t) = 0.1\sin(0.3t)$.

Let us assume that an actuator fault occurs in the input channel of the diesel engine system. This fault will be added to the state equation, which can be described as follows:

$$f_a(t) = \begin{cases} 0 & 0 \leq t < 4s \\ \sin(t) & 4 \leq t < 15s \end{cases} \tag{93}$$

For the nonlinear LPV delayed system, comparative simulations are provided to evaluate the performance of the separated and integrated fault estimation (FE)-based fault-tolerant control (FTC) designs. The same system parameters and initial conditions are used for both the separated and integrated FE-based FTC approaches to enable a fair comparison.

6.2. Separated FTC Design

Obviously, Assumptions 2 and 3 are verified based on the matrices of the nonlinear models, that is, $rank(CM) = rank(M) = 1$, $\left(A_i + A_{di}e^{-ds}, M, C\right)$ is a minimum phase $n \geq p = 2$ and $q = 1$. The adaptive sliding mode observer method presented in the following can be used for the nonlinear diesel engine system to achieve robust actuator fault estimation. Based on the information provided by the observer, an adaptive sliding mode controller will be designed in order to stabilize the diesel engine system. The design parameters were chosen as follows: $\lambda = 0.1, H_1 = H_3 = I_{n-p}, H_2 = 2I_p, H_4 = I_p$ and $\tilde{A}_{22}^s = diag(-10,-7)$. Using the MATLAB LMI Toolbox, we can solve Theorem 1 and design an adaptive observer (14) and (15).

$$
\begin{aligned}
G_{l1} &= \begin{bmatrix} 2.420 & 1.388 \\ 9.054 & 1.484 \\ -9.156 & 5.669 \end{bmatrix} G_{n1} = \begin{bmatrix} 1 & 0 \\ 1.09 & 0.30 \\ -1 & 1 \end{bmatrix} \\
G_{l2} &= \begin{bmatrix} 2.864 & 1.032 \\ 9.819 & 1.104 \\ -9.679 & 5.571 \end{bmatrix} G_{n2} = \begin{bmatrix} 1 & 0 \\ 1.18 & 0.22 \\ -1 & 1 \end{bmatrix} \\
G_{l3} &= \begin{bmatrix} 2.839 & 1.045 \\ 10.97 & 1.118 \\ -8.464 & 5.569 \end{bmatrix} G_{n3} = \begin{bmatrix} 0.437 & 0.009 \\ 1.182 & 0.22 \\ -1 & 1 \end{bmatrix} \\
G_{l4} &= \begin{bmatrix} 2.227 & 1.494 \\ 9.92 & 1.598 \\ -7.944 & 5.669 \end{bmatrix} G_{n4} = \begin{bmatrix} 1 & 0 \\ 1.049 & 0.32 \\ -1 & 1 \end{bmatrix}
\end{aligned} \tag{94}
$$

and we find the following:

$$
P_e = \begin{bmatrix} 1.912 & 0 & 0 \\ 0 & 1.456 & -0.324 \\ 0 & -0.324 & 1.027 \end{bmatrix} \tag{95}
$$

Based on Theorem 2, the sliding mode controller gains can be described as follows:

$$
\begin{aligned}
k_1 &= \begin{bmatrix} -13.09 & -4.98 & -2.98 \\ 9.54 & 7.17 & 2.11 \end{bmatrix}, k_2 = \begin{bmatrix} -12.94 & -4.92 & -2.97 \\ 9.64 & 7.15 & 2.10 \end{bmatrix} \\
k_3 &= \begin{bmatrix} -12.92 & -5.02 & -2.98 \\ 9.75 & 7.10 & 2.10 \end{bmatrix}, k_4 = \begin{bmatrix} -12.76 & -5.06 & -2.97 \\ 10.10 & 7.19 & 2.15 \end{bmatrix}
\end{aligned} \tag{96}
$$

and

$$
P_x = \begin{bmatrix} 7.61 & 1.05 & 1.20 \\ 1.05 & 3.86 & 0.71 \\ 1.20 & 0.71 & 0.41 \end{bmatrix} \tag{97}
$$

6.3. Integrated FTC Design

By solving the LMI conditions presented in Theorem 3 using the "mincx" function of the MATLAB LMI Toolbox, we can compute the matrix gains of the adaptive observer (as defined in Equations (14) and (15)) and the sliding mode controller (as defined in Equation (48)) in a single step, as follows:

$$
\begin{aligned}
G_{l1} &= \begin{bmatrix} 14.79 & -2.01 \\ 30.67 & -2.15 \\ -9.15 & 5.67 \end{bmatrix} G_{n1} = \begin{bmatrix} 1 & 0 \\ 3.82 & -0.43 \\ -1 & 1 \end{bmatrix} \\
G_{l2} &= \begin{bmatrix} 13.74 & -2.91 \\ 28.54 & -3.11 \\ -10.72 & 5.94 \end{bmatrix} G_{n2} = \begin{bmatrix} 1 & 0 \\ 3.55 & -0.33 \\ -1 & 1 \end{bmatrix} \\
G_{l3} &= \begin{bmatrix} 13.80 & -2.65 \\ 29.85 & -2.84 \\ -9.51 & 5.62 \end{bmatrix} G_{n3} = \begin{bmatrix} 1 & 0 \\ 3.56 & -0.57 \\ -1 & 1 \end{bmatrix} \\
G_{l4} &= \begin{bmatrix} 13.76 & -2.40 \\ 29.79 & -2.56 \\ -9. & 5.67 \end{bmatrix} G_{n4} = \begin{bmatrix} 1 & 0 \\ 3.55 & -0.52 \\ -1 & 1 \end{bmatrix}
\end{aligned} \tag{98}
$$

and

$$\begin{aligned} P_e &= \begin{bmatrix} 4.51 & 0 & 0 \\ 0 & 11.19 & -1.18 \\ 0 & -1.182 & 1.51 \end{bmatrix}, P_x = \begin{bmatrix} 7.61 & 1.05 & 1.20 \\ 1.05 & 3.86 & 0.71 \\ 1.20 & 0.71 & 0.41 \end{bmatrix} \\ k_1 &= k_3 = \begin{bmatrix} -78.83 & -59.76 & -189.05 \\ 2.78 & 9.667 & -36.97 \end{bmatrix}, \\ k_2 &= \begin{bmatrix} -78.72 & -59.60 & -188.79 \\ -3.22 & 9.05 & -38.00 \end{bmatrix}, k_4 = \begin{bmatrix} -78.71 & -59.60 & -188.78 \\ -3.21 & 9.07 & -37.79 \end{bmatrix} \end{aligned} \tag{99}$$

Furthermore, the optimized LMI gains for the integrated and separated fault estimation (FE)-based fault-tolerant control (FTC) designs are listed in Table 1. As can be observed, the level of uncertainty attenuation, which relates to the integrated approach, is significantly lower compared to the separated approach. The separated approach loses a certain degree of robustness against uncertainties, which illustrates the improvement in fault estimation and compensation achieved through the integrated FTC approach.

Table 1. LMI optimization gains.

	Integrated FTC	Separated FTC
Uncertainty attenuation level	$\varsigma_c = 4.47$	$\varsigma_x = 13.47$
Admissible Lipschitz constant	$\gamma_c = 0.014$	$\gamma_x = 37.47$

We have learned that the nonlinear function satisfies the Lipschitz condition. Consequently, the admissible Lipschitz constant, which relates to the integrated approach, is higher than the one provided by the separated approach, thus illustrating the superiority of the integrated FE-based FTC approach in handling a broader range of nonlinear functions. The simulation results demonstrate the effectiveness of the proposed approach, which includes online actuator fault estimation and compensation for the closed-loop nonlinear system in the presence of uncertainties $\xi(x,t) = 0.1(0.3\sin(t) + 0.5x_1(t))$.

The results are presented as follows:

$$\begin{aligned} \rho_1 &= \rho_2 = \rho_3 = \rho_4 = 10 \\ \delta_1 &= \delta_2 = \delta_3 = \delta_4 = 0.01 \\ \tau &= 0.3, \bar{\omega} = 1.1 \end{aligned} \tag{100}$$

The sliding mode signal, as defined in Equation (17), is designed with the goal of $\eta(t) = \hat{\rho} + 15$, such that the adaptive update term is defined as $\dot{\hat{\rho}} = 1.1\|P_2 e_y(t)\|$.

The sliding mode controller (48) is considered, where we have the following: $N_{c,1} = N_{c,2} = N_{c,3} = N_{c,4} = \begin{bmatrix} -0.3 & 0 \\ 0 & 1 \end{bmatrix}$. The initial conditions are as follows: $x_1(0) = x_2(0) = x_3(0) = x_4(0) = \begin{bmatrix} 0.02 \\ -0.03 \\ -0.05 \end{bmatrix}$.

The simulation results demonstrate the effectiveness of the proposed approach, which includes online actuator fault estimation and compensation. Figure 4 illustrates the actuator fault estimation, showcasing the ability of the proposed adaptive sliding mode observer (defined by Equations (14) and (15)) to estimate actuator faults with satisfactory precision while rejecting the effects of system uncertainties and variable time-delays.

As illustrated in Figure 4, it is important to note that despite the presence of uncertainties and variable time-delays, the proposed sliding mode observer with the adaptive equivalent injection can track the actuator fault $f_a(t)$ more accurately compared to the traditional observer without the adaptive law. This demonstrates the effectiveness of the adaptive sliding mode observer in handling challenging system characteristics, such as uncertainties and time-varying delays, and providing improved fault estimation performance.

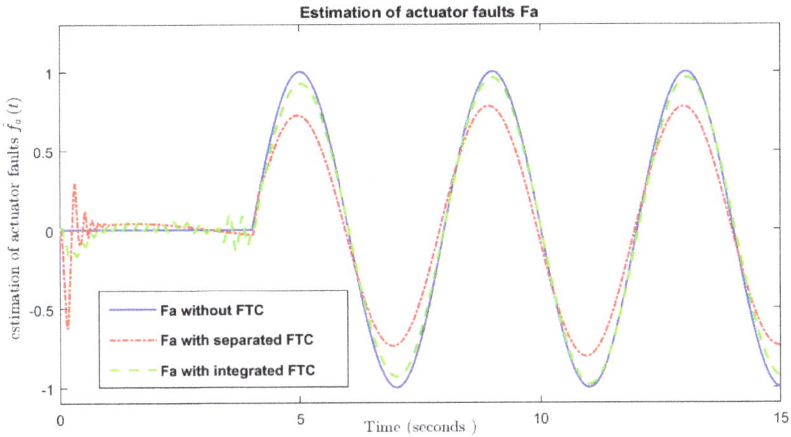

Figure 4. Estimation of actuator fault: Actuator fault estimation without FTC (blue line), actuator fault estimation with the separated FTC (red line), and actuator fault estimation with the integrated FTC (green line).

The comparative study of the time-domain response of the closed-loop system outputs between the integrated sliding mode FTC and the separated sliding mode FTC is shown in Figures 5 and 6. We can conclude that the proposed controllers stabilize the closed-loop system when the system is affected by nonlinearity, actuator faults, and variable time-delays. Thus, the performances are guaranteed while compensating for the effect of the faults. Furthermore, in Figures 7 and 8 through to the integrated sliding mode FTC, the system can quickly reach stability compared to the separated approach. The integrated FTC based on SMC can smooth the control law, ensuring a high response rate to stabilize the system (first response at $t = 0.05$ s).

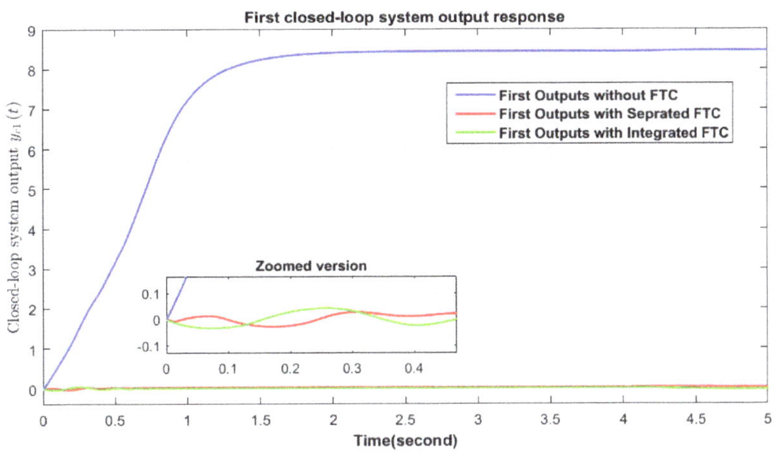

Figure 5. First closed-loop system output response: output response with the separated FTC (red line) and output response with the integrated FTC (green line).

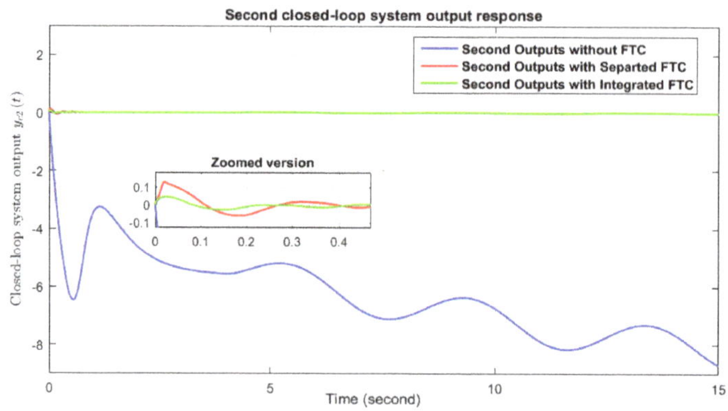

Figure 6. Second closed-loop system output response: output response with the separated FTC (red line) and output response with the integrated FTC (green line).

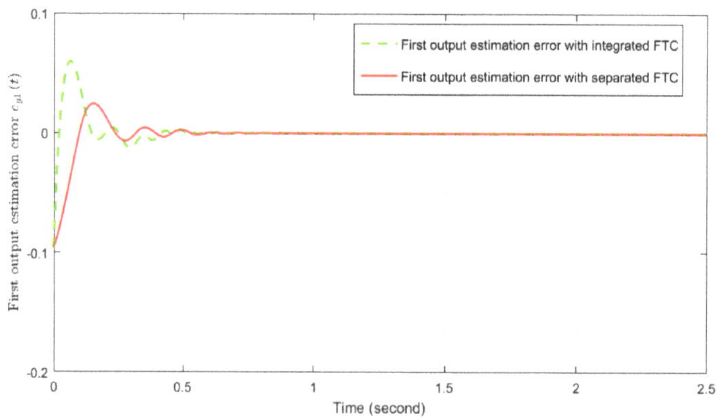

Figure 7. First output estimation error: First output estimation error with the separated FTC (red line) and the first output estimation error with the integrated FTC (green line).

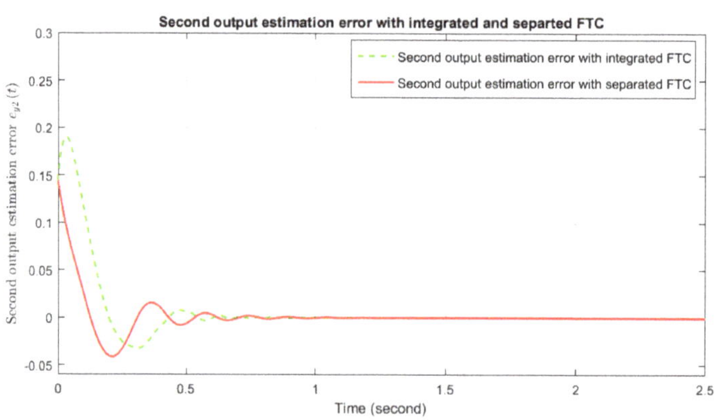

Figure 8. Second output estimation error: Second output estimation error with the separated FTC (red line) and second output estimation error with the integrated FTC (green line).

6.4. Simulation Result with a Different Constant Time Delay τ

In this section, in order to demonstrate the effectiveness of our method, we propose increasing the value of the time delay τ. Thus, Figure 9 shows the effect of increasing the constant τ on fault reconstruction using the integrated FTC design. In summary, increasing τ in a nonlinear LPV system with variable time-delay, particularly in scenarios involving actuator faults in diesel engines, can lead to performance degradation, stability issues, and increased control effort. However, employing integrated FTC strategies, including adaptive control, can effectively mitigate these adverse effects on fault reconstruction. By dynamically adjusting to increased time delays and compensating for actuator faults, FTC systems ensure that diesel engines operate reliably and efficiently, even under challenging conditions.

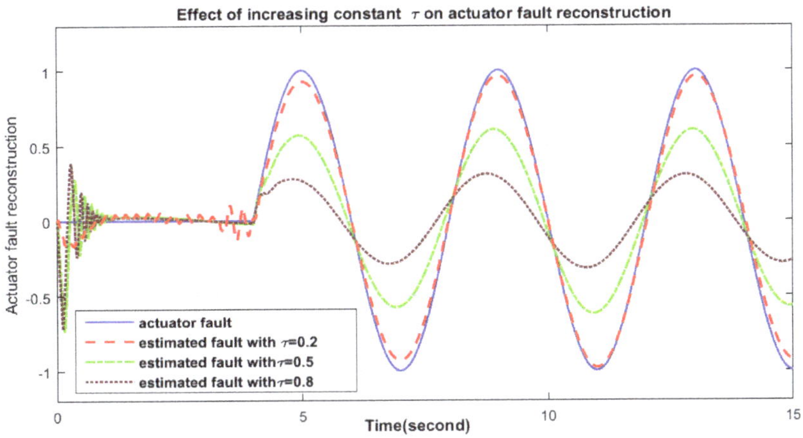

Figure 9. Effect of increasing constant τ on actuator fault reconstruction ($\tau = 0.2$ red line), ($\tau = 0.5$ green line), ($\tau = 0.8$ brown line).

6.5. Comparative Study

To validate the effectiveness of the proposed scheme, we present a comparative study with the control law used in [26]. The authors use a state feedback control law, which may have limited effectiveness when the system is affected by complex local nonlinearities such as the Lipchitz nonlinearity. In contrast, our SMC-based integrated FTC approach forces the system to remain on a sliding surface, thus guaranteeing stable performance even in the presence of unexpected variations in system parameters. Figure 10 shows the performance of our integrated SMC-based FTC on a sliding surface for the second scenario of actuator fault reconstruction when this fault changes its behavior.

The result shows that the SMC-based integrated FTC can adjust the control law according to variations in the system parameters, thus ensuring a rapid response (first response at $t = 0.14$ s). This contrasts with state feedback control, which is less effective in the face of these challenges (first response $t = 0.19$ s). From the zoomed-in version, it is clear that our adaptive controller is more robust against chattering effects than the state feedback-based controller.

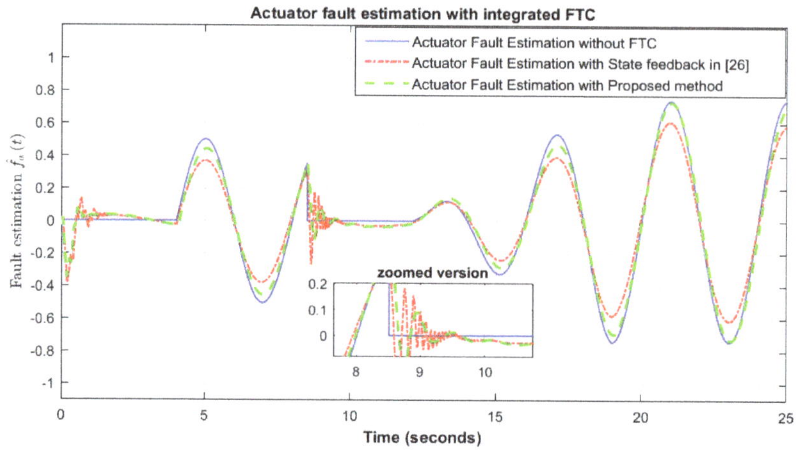

Figure 10. Actuator fault estimation without FTC (blue line), actuator fault estimation with state feedback in [26] (red line), and actuator fault estimation with the integrated FTC (green line).

Integrated FTC in the Presence of Measurement Noise

To demonstrate the effectiveness of the integrated FTC based on SMC compared to the state feedback-based controller used in [26], consider the influence of additive measurement noise on the system $\omega(t)$ to the output $y(t)$ with a variance of $10^{-5} \times I_2$ and zero mean.

Table 2 compares the proposed integrated FTC method with state feedback control in [26] with additional measurement noise. In addition, to evaluate the performance of the fault-tolerant control based on (SMC), the integral absolute error (IAE) on the output responses is used and the comparison results show that the best (IAE) is obtained by the FTC based on our proposed controller.

Table 2. IAE of outputs.

The Output $y(t)$	Integrated FTC-SMC	State Feedback in [26]
$y_1(t)$	0.049	0.071
$y_2(t)$	0.15	0.21

7. Conclusions

This paper tackles two significant challenges: firstly, the development of a fault estimation (FE) module utilizing a sliding mode observer scheme, and secondly, the implementation of fault estimation-based sliding mode fault-tolerant control for LPV delayed systems characterized by local nonlinear models. Initially, actuator faults are estimated through a robust adaptive sliding mode observer, which effectively handles norm-bounded uncertainties and variable time-delays. Sufficient conditions are derived to ensure the stability of the proposed observer, with H_∞ performance criteria aimed at minimizing the impact of uncertainties on the dynamics of estimation errors, which are solved through LMI optimization techniques. Subsequently, an adaptive fault-tolerant control strategy using output feedback is explored to mitigate the effects of actuator faults and ensure the stability of closed-loop nonlinear systems. The conditions for existence are formulated in terms of linear matrix inequalities (LMIs) using the Lyapunov–Krasovskii approach. In fact, by employing multi-objective convex optimization, the Lipschitz constant associated with the nonlinear terms of the LPV delayed model and the level of uncertainty attenuation are maximized simultaneously. This approach thus aids in determining the optimal gains for both the adaptive sliding mode observer and the controller. An integrated sliding mode FTC strategy is proposed to achieve optimal robustness through the interaction between the observer and controller models, offering several advantages over traditional separated FTC methods. Simulation results on a diesel engine system demonstrate the effectiveness of the proposed adaptive fault-tolerant control design based on actuator fault estimation, even in the presence of uncertainties and variable time-delay. As a perspective for future work, we plan to incorporate a compensation scheme to manage the significant delays and complex nonlinearities that occur in aerospace systems. This could include the use of advanced techniques such as delay observers or predictive controllers that anticipate the effects of delays.

Author Contributions: Conceptualization, O.M.; methodology, A.B.B.; formal analysis, A.B.B. and F.B.H.; investigation, O.M.; writing—original draft preparation: O.M.; writing–review and editing, A.B.B. and F.B.H.; A.B.B., F.B.H. and A.S. collaborated to achieve the work; A.S. led the project. All authors have read and agreed to the published version of the manuscript.

Funding: This research received no external funding.

Data Availability Statement: Data are contained within the article.

Conflicts of Interest: The authors declare no conflicts of interest.

References

1. Patel, H.R.; Shah, V.A. Shadowed type-2 fuzzy sets in dynamic parameter adaption in cuckoo search and flower pollination algorithms for optimal design of fuzzy fault-tolerant controllers. *Math. Comput. Appl.* **2022**, *27*, 89. [CrossRef]
2. Asadi, D. Model-based fault detection and identification of a quadrotor with rotor fault. *Int. J. Aeronaut. Space Sci.* **2022**, *23*, 916–928. [CrossRef]
3. Tayari, R.; Ben Brahim, A.; Ben Hmida, F.; Sallami, A. Active fault tolerant control design for lpv systems with simultaneous actuator and sensor faults. *Math. Probl. Eng.* **2019**, *2019*, 5820394. [CrossRef]
4. Ben Brahim, A.; Dhahri, S.; Ben Hmida, F.; Sellami, A. Multiplicative fault estimation-based adaptive sliding mode fault-tolerant control design for nonlinear systems. *Complexity* **2018**, *2018*, 1462594. [CrossRef]
5. Hmidi, R.; Ben Brahim, A.; Dhahri, S.; Ben Hmida, F.; Sellami, A. Sliding mode fault-tolerant control for Takagi-Sugeno fuzzy systems with local nonlinear models: Application to inverted pendulum and cart system. *Trans. Inst. Meas. Control.* **2021**, *43*, 975–990. [CrossRef]
6. Tan, J.; Zheng, H.; Meng, D.; Wang, X.; Liang, B. Active input design for simultaneous fault estimation and fault-tolerant control of LPV systems. *Automatica* **2023**, *151*, 110903. [CrossRef]
7. Quadros, M.M.; de Bessa, I.V.; Leite, V.J.; Palhares, R.M. Fault tolerant control for linear parameter varying systems: An improved robust virtual actuator and sensor approach. *ISA Trans.* **2020**, *104*, 356–369. [CrossRef]
8. Hmidi, R.; Brahim, A.B.; Hmida, F.B.; Sellami, A. Robust fault tolerant control design for nonlinear systems not satisfying matching and minimum phase conditions. *Int. J. Control Autom. Syst.* **2020**, *18*, 2206–2219. [CrossRef]
9. Zhang, W.; Xu, D.; Jiang, B.; Shi, P. Virtual-sensor-based model-free adaptive fault-tolerant constrained control for discrete-time nonlinear systems. *IEEE Trans. Circuits Syst. Regul. Pap.* **2022**, *69*, 4191–4202. [CrossRef]
10. Plata, C.; Prieto, P.J.; Ramirez-Villalobos, R.; Coria, L.N. Chaos synchronization for hyperchaotic lorenz-type system via fuzzy-based sliding-mode observer. *Math. Comput. Appl.* **2020**, *25*, 16. [CrossRef]
11. Serrano-Cruz, D.A.; Boutat-Baddas, L.; Darouach, M.; Astorga-Zaragoza, C.M.; Guerrero Ramírez, G.V. Modeling of the Human Cardiovascular System: Implementing a Sliding Mode Observer for Fault Detection and Isolation. *Math. Comput. Appl.* **2024**, *29*, 57. [CrossRef]
12. Heras-Cervantes, M.; Téllez-Anguiano, A.d.C.; Anzurez-Marín, J.; Espinosa-Juárez, E. Analysis and Comparison of Fuzzy Models and Observers for DC-DC Converters Applied to a Distillation Column Heating Actuator. *Math. Comput. Appl.* **2020**, *25*, 55. [CrossRef]
13. Feng, X.; Wang, Y. Fault estimation based on sliding mode observer for Takagi–Sugeno fuzzy systems with digital communication constraints. *J. Frankl. Inst.* **2020**, *357*, 569–588. [CrossRef]
14. Qi, H.; Shi, Y.; Li, S.; Tian, Y.; Yu, D.L.; Gomm, J. Fault tolerant control for nonlinear systems using sliding mode and adaptive neural network estimator. *Soft Comput.* **2020**, *24*, 11535–11544. [CrossRef]
15. Mousavi, S.M.M.; Ramezani, A. A new sliding mode observer design for fault estimation in a class of nonlinear fractional-order systems based on the super-twisting algorithm. *J. Control Autom. Electr. Syst.* **2021**, *32*, 1531–1539. [CrossRef]
16. Brahim, A.B.; Dhahri, S.; Hmida, F.B.; Sellami, A. Simultaneous actuator and sensor faults estimation design for LPV systems using adaptive sliding mode observers. *Int. J. Autom. Control* **2021**, *15*, 1–27. [CrossRef]
17. Lamouchi, R.; Raissi, T.; Amairi, M.; Aoun, M. On interval observer design for active Fault Tolerant Control of Linear Parameter-Varying systems. *Syst. Control Lett.* **2022**, *164*, 105218. [CrossRef]
18. Mabrouk, N.; Ben Brahim, A.; Ben Hmida, F. Simultaneous Multiplicative and Additive Actuator Faults Estimation-Based Sliding Mode FTC for a Class of Uncertain Nonlinear System. *Math. Probl. Eng.* **2023**, *2023*, 6902272. [CrossRef]

19. Wang, W.; Chen, J.; Huang, Z. Observer-Based State Estimation for Recurrent Neural Networks: An Output-Predicting and LPV-Based Approach. *Math. Comput. Appl.* **2023**, *28*, 104. [CrossRef]
20. Huang, Q.; Qi, J.; Dai, X.; Wu, Q.; Xie, X.; Zhang, E. Fault estimation method for nonlinear time-delay system based on intermediate observer-application on quadrotor unmanned aerial vehicle. *Sensors* **2022**, *23*, 34. [CrossRef]
21. Zhou, Y.; Ji, X. Static Output Feedback Control for Nonlinear Time-Delay Semi-Markov Jump Systems Based on Incremental Quadratic Constraints. *Math. Comput. Appl.* **2023**, *28*, 30. [CrossRef]
22. Kavikumar, R.; Sakthivel, R.; Kwon, O.; Kaviarasan, B. Faulty actuator-based control synthesis for interval type-2 fuzzy systems via memory state feedback approach. *Int. J. Syst. Sci.* **2020**, *51*, 2958–2981. [CrossRef]
23. Ahmed, S.; Azar, A.T.; Tounsi, M.; Ibraheem, I.K. Adaptive control design for Euler–Lagrange systems using fixed-time fractional integral sliding mode scheme. *Fractal Fract.* **2023**, *7*, 712. [CrossRef]
24. Ahmed, S.; Azar, A.T.; Ibraheem, I.K. Nonlinear system controlled using novel adaptive fixed-time SMC. *Aims Math.* **2024**, *9*, 7895–7916. [CrossRef]
25. Hamdi, H.; Rodrigues, M.; Mechmeche, C.; Braiek, N.B. Observer-based fault diagnosis for time-delay LPV descriptor systems. *IFAC-PapersOnLine* **2018**, *51*, 1179–1184. [CrossRef]
26. Hamdi, H.; Rodrigues, M.; Rabaoui, B.; Benhadj Braiek, N. A fault estimation and fault-tolerant control based sliding mode observer for LPV descriptor systems with time delay. *Int. J. Appl. Math. Comput. Sci.* **2021**, *31*, 247–258. [CrossRef]
27. Edwards, C.; Spurgeon, S.K. On the development of discontinuous observers. *Int. J. Control* **1994**, *59*, 1211–1229. [CrossRef]
28. Edwards, C.; Spurgeon, S. *Sliding Mode Control: Theory and Applications*; CRC Press: Boca Raton, FL, USA, 1998.
29. Edwards, C.; Spurgeon, S.K.; Patton, R.J. Sliding mode observers for fault detection and isolation. *Automatica* **2000**, *36*, 541–553. [CrossRef]
30. Ku, C.C.; Huang, K.W.; Chuang, S.Y. Gain-Scheduled Control of Delayed Diesel Engine System with Time-Varying Parameter. In Proceedings of the 2020 International Automatic Control Conference (CACS), Hsinchu, Taiwan, 4–7 November 2020; IEEE: New York City, NY, USA, 2020; pp. 1–6.

Mathematical and Computational Applications

MDPI

Article

Learning Deceptive Tactics for Defense and Attack in Bayesian–Markov Stackelberg Security Games

Julio B. Clempner

Escuela Superior de Física y Matemáticas, Instituto Politécnico Nacional School of Physics and Mathematics, National Polytechnic Institute, Edificio 9 U.P. Adolfo Lopez Mateos, Col. San Pedro Zacatenco, Mexico City 07730, Mexico; julio@clempner.name

Abstract: In this paper, we address the challenges posed by limited knowledge in security games by proposing a novel system grounded in Bayesian–Markov Stackelberg security games (SSGs). These SSGs involve multiple defenders and attackers and serve as a framework for managing incomplete information effectively. To tackle the complexity inherent in these games, we introduce an iterative proximal-gradient approach to compute the Bayesian Equilibrium, which captures the optimal strategies of both defenders and attackers. This method enables us to navigate the intricacies of the game dynamics, even when the specifics of the Markov games are unknown. Moreover, our research emphasizes the importance of Bayesian approaches in solving the reinforcement learning (RL) algorithm, particularly in addressing the exploration–exploitation trade-off. By leveraging Bayesian techniques, we aim to minimize the expected total discounted costs, thus optimizing decision-making in the security domain. In pursuit of effective security game implementation, we propose a novel random walk approach tailored to fulfill the requirements of the scenario. This innovative methodology enhances the adaptability and responsiveness of defenders and attackers, thereby improving overall security outcomes. To validate the efficacy of our proposed strategy, we provide a numerical example that demonstrates its benefits in practice. Through this example, we showcase how our approach can effectively address the challenges posed by limited knowledge, leading to more robust and efficient security solutions. Overall, our paper contributes to advancing the understanding and implementation of security strategies in scenarios characterized by incomplete information. By combining Bayesian and Markov Stackelberg games, reinforcement learning algorithms, and innovative random walk techniques, we offer a comprehensive framework for enhancing security measures in real-world applications.

Keywords: security games; strong Stackelberg equilibrium; extraproximal method; Lyapunov games; shortest-path games; finite Markov chains

1. Introduction

1.1. Brief Review

In safeguarding vital infrastructures, strategically allocating limited security resources is crucial. The primary objective is to prevent attacks from unpredictable assailants targeting critical assets. However, in selecting defense techniques, the balance between defenders' private information disclosure and attackers' observational capabilities must be carefully considered. This equilibrium ensures effective protection against potential threats while minimizing vulnerabilities arising from asymmetrical information.

Game theory offers a powerful mathematical framework for optimizing decision-making in strategic scenarios, which is particularly evident in SSGs tackling high-complexity problems. SSGs encapsulate situations where defenders (leaders) and attackers (followers) strategically engage in sequential decision-making to achieve their objectives. In this model, defenders are represented by the leaders, while attackers are represented by the followers, highlighting the strategic interplay between protective and offensive roles in the system. Multiplayer game theory presents significant complexity and challenges in finding solutions due to the interaction of multiple agents with varying strategies and objectives. The dynamic nature and interdependencies of players' actions create a highly intricate environment, requiring sophisticated approaches to model, analyze, and achieve equilibrium in these games. Initially, defenders commit to a strategy, which attackers then observe before determining their own course of action [1,2]. Defenders employ random techniques to safeguard potential targets, anticipating attackers' objectives within the game's dynamics. Meanwhile, attackers adopt best-reply strategies while cognizant of these defensive tactics. Mathematically, the defenders' advantage lies in revealing their random plans, yet this overlooks potential knowledge loss due to incomplete observations. For instance, when attackers disguise themselves as civilians to infiltrate a target, defenders may struggle to ascertain the available security resources accurately. In such scenarios, revealing complete information isn't always advantageous for defenders. Instead, strategic disclosure of incomplete information can be more beneficial [3,4]. This approach acknowledges the complexity of real-world security dilemmas, where optimal decision-making hinges on dynamically balancing information disclosure and strategic concealment. By leveraging game theory's mathematical rigor, SSGs provide a framework for navigating these strategic challenges, ultimately enhancing security decision-making in complex and dynamic environments.

1.2. Related Work

Various game-theoretical frameworks have been employed to model the interaction between defenders and attackers in security scenarios, with Bayesian Stackelberg games emerging as a particularly successful solution [5]. Conitzer and Sandholm [6] adapted the Bayesian Stackelberg game into a normal-form representation using Harsanyi's approach [5], determining game equilibrium by evaluating each follower's plan to ascertain if it constitutes an optimal reaction. Paruchuri et al. [7] proposed a mixed-integer linear programming (MILP) approach to solve Bayesian Stackelberg games, leveraging optimization techniques to identify optimal strategies for both defenders and attackers. Jain et al. [8] introduced a strategy combining hierarchical decomposition with branch and bound techniques, aiming to efficiently explore the solution space and achieve equilibrium in the game. Yin and Tambe [9] suggested a hybrid technique merging best-first search with heuristic branching rules to solve Bayesian Stackelberg games effectively. This approach enhances the computational efficiency of finding equilibrium strategies by guiding the search process through the solution space. Overall, these methodologies contribute to advancing our understanding of security game dynamics and provide practical solutions for effectively addressing security challenges in real-world scenarios, highlighting the versatility and adaptability of game-theoretical approaches in security analysis and decision-making.

For further exploration, information can be found in Wilczynski's comprehensive survey [10]. Sayed Ahmed [11] introduced a deception-based Stackelberg game anti-jamming mechanism. Gan et al. delved into security games involving uncoordinated defenders cooperating to protect targets, with each defender optimizing their resource allocation selfishly for utility maximization [12]. These studies underscore the breadth of applications and innovative approaches within the realm of SSGs, showcasing their relevance in modern security paradigms.

SSGs find diverse applications in everyday scenarios, contributing significantly to the enhancement of security measures across various domains. Wilczynski [10] provided a comprehensive survey highlighting the breadth of SSG applications. Basilico et al. [13] determined the minimum number of robots required to patrol a given environment, compute optimal patrolling strategies across various coordination dimensions, and experimentally evaluate the proposed techniques, demonstrating their effectiveness in ensuring comprehensive coverage and the efficient use of robotic resources. Clempner [14] proposed a security model implemented with a temporal difference method, and it incorporates prior information to effectively address security issues. By leveraging continuous learning and adapting to evolving threats, this model aims to enhance the robustness and resilience of security systems. Albarran et al. [15] applied SSGs to distribute security resources across airport terminals, leveraging partially observed Markov game settings to address complex security challenges. In urban settings, Trejo et al. [16] employed reinforcement learning within SSG frameworks to adapt attacker and defender strategies, improving security measures at geographically dispersed shopping malls. Solis et al. [17] extended SSG applications to maritime security, utilizing a multiplayer ship differential SSG to model pursuit–evasion scenarios in continuous time. Alcantara et al. [18] incorporated topographical information into SSGs to generate realistic patrol plans for defenders in major cities, enhancing target identification and security deployment strategies. Sayed Ahmed [11] proposed a deception-based SSG anti-jamming solution, addressing vulnerabilities in communication systems. Gan et al. [12] explored SSGs where uncoordinated defenders collaborate to protect targets, with each defender optimizing their resource allocation selfishly. Clempner and Poznyak [19] introduced an attacker–defender SSG system, leveraging ergodic Markov models and non-decreasing Lyapunov-like functions to represent solutions. Rahman and Oh [20] investigated online patrolling robot route-planning tasks using SSG frameworks, enhancing security surveillance capabilities. Wang et al. [21] developed the DeDOL method based on deep reinforcement learning within SSG models, offering advanced solutions for security optimization. Li et al. [22] proposed a Bayesian Stackelberg Markov game for adversarial federated learning, utilizing meta-RL-based pre-training and adaptation to combat diverse attacks, achieving robust, adaptive, and efficient federated learning defense strategies. Sengupta and Kambhampati [23] framed adversarial federated learning as a Bayesian Stackelberg Markov game, using RL-based pre-training and meta-RL defenses to combat adaptive attacks, achieving robust and efficient federated learning defense strategies. Shukla et al. [24] presented a cybersecurity game for networked control systems, where an attacker disrupts communication and a defender protects key nodes. A cost-based Stackelberg equilibrium and robust defense method optimize security. Genetic algorithms enhance strategies for large power systems.

The versatility and effectiveness of SSGs highlight their importance in enhancing security strategies and protecting critical assets across various contexts. Whether applied to scheduling security patrols at airports, optimizing resource allocation in urban settings, or addressing vulnerabilities in communication systems, SSGs offer valuable insights and solutions. By integrating game-theoretical frameworks with real-world security challenges, SSGs enable proactive and adaptive approaches to security management, ultimately contributing to safer environments and mitigating potential threats effectively.

1.3. Main Results

Improving the existing security framework involves addressing the challenges posed by incomplete information. This is achieved through several key approaches. Firstly, an iterative proximal-gradient approach is proposed to compute the Bayesian Stackelberg equilibrium, enabling effective decision-making despite uncertainty. Additionally, a Bayesian reinforcement learning (BRL) algorithm is introduced, allowing for adaptive strategies that learn from past experiences and observations. Furthermore, a random walk approach is developed to implement SSGs, offering a dynamic and flexible method for responding to evolving threats. By integrating these techniques, the security framework gains the ability to adapt and respond effectively in the face of incomplete information, thereby enhancing overall resilience and effectiveness in mitigating security risks. These methods enable decision-makers to make more informed choices and optimize security strategies in complex and uncertain environments. A numerical example is used to provide useful recommendations for defenders' resource allocation against attackers.

1.4. Organization of the Paper

The paper follows a structured layout, with Section 2 providing preliminary information. In this section, foundational concepts and background knowledge relevant to the study are presented to establish a basis for subsequent discussions. Section 3 elaborates on the problems under consideration and introduces a Bayesian Stackelberg game model, which serves as the theoretical framework for analyzing strategic interactions between defenders and attackers. This section outlines the key components of the model and discusses its applicability to the specific security scenario under investigation. In Section 4, the paper proposes a learning algorithm tailored to the context of the Bayesian Stackelberg game, aiming to optimize decision-making strategies for both defenders and attackers. The algorithm is designed to adapt and improve over time based on feedback and observed outcomes. Section 5 introduces a novel random walk model, offering an alternative approach to addressing security challenges within the Bayesian Stackelberg game framework. This model presents a new perspective on strategic decision-making in dynamic security environments. A numerical example illustrating the application of the proposed methodologies is provided in Section 6, demonstrating their effectiveness and practical relevance in real-world scenarios. Finally, Section 7 concludes the paper by summarizing key findings, drawing conclusions based on the analysis conducted, and discussing potential avenues for future research and development in the field of SSGs.

2. Preliminaries

In a discrete-time and finite-horizon framework, we consider an environment characterized by private and independent values, as described in prior works [3,25,26]. In this setup, players denoted by $l \in \mathcal{L}$, where $\mathcal{L} = 1, 2, \dots, n$, receive rewards in discrete time periods $t \in T$, with $T \subseteq \mathbb{N}$. These rewards are contingent upon the current physical allocation $a_t^l \in A^l$ and the type $\Theta^l \in \Theta^l$ of the player. Here, A^l represents the feasible set of allocations available to player l at time t, while Θ^l denotes the set of possible types for player l. The reward obtained by player l at time t is determined by their chosen allocation and their specific type. This framework captures the dynamics of decision-making in scenarios where players have private information and their actions impact the outcomes over a finite time horizon. Such models find applications in various domains, including economics, game theory, and decision science, where understanding the interplay between private information and strategic decision-making is crucial.

In period t, the type vector is denoted by $\theta_t = (\theta_t^1, \dots, \theta_t^n) \in \Theta$, where $\Theta = \times_{l \in \mathcal{L}} \Theta^l$. The set of feasible allocations in period t may be contingent on the vector of past allocations $a_t = (a_t^1, \dots, a_t^n) \in A$, where $A = \times_{l \in \mathcal{L}} A^l$. We denote Θ^{-l} as $\times_{i \in \mathcal{L}, i \neq l} \Theta^i$, and $\Delta(A)$ as the set of all probability distributions over A. Additionally, we assume that A^l and Θ^l are finite sets, ensuring a manageable and well-defined problem space. This setup enables the modeling of dynamic interactions and decision-making processes among multiple players with diverse types and feasible allocation options.

Each player l has a common prior distribution $P^l(\theta_0^l)$. The type Θ^l and action a_t^l determine a probability distribution for the variables θ_{t+1}^l on Θ^l, which is denoted by $p^l(\theta_{t+1}^l|\theta_t^l a_t^l)$. This distribution captures the probabilistic relationship between a player's current type and action and their subsequent type in the next period, facilitating the modeling of dynamic decision-making processes within the game.

A Markov chain is described by the transition matrix $p^l\left(\theta_{t+1}^l|\theta_t^l a_t^l\right)$ and the common prior distribution $P^l(\theta_0^l)$ where $P^l\left(\Theta^l\right) \in \Delta\Theta^l$ and $\Delta\Theta^l$ establishes the probability distributions over Θ^l. We assume that each chain $(P^l, p(\theta_{t+1}^l|\theta_t^l, a_t^l))$ is ergodic, ensuring that the system will eventually reach a steady state regardless of its initial conditions.

The asymmetric information is determined by the private observation of θ_t^l. We determine that by the priors distributions $P^l(\theta_0^l)$ and the transition matrices $p^l(\theta_{t+1}^l|\theta_t^l a_t^l)$ for each player l, the information of player l, given by θ_{t+1}^l, does not depend on θ_t^i, for $i \neq l$. Following that, participants transmitted m_t^l messages at the same time, and the message profile was made public m_t^l.

A (behavioral) *strategy* $\sigma^l(m_t^l|\theta_t^l)$ for player l is mapping $\sigma^l : M^l \times \Theta^l \to \Delta(M^l)$, which represents the likelihood with which a player l believes that a message m_t^l is of type Θ^l. The (behavioral) *strategy* set is given by

$$S_{adm}^l = \left\{ \sigma^l(m_t^l|\theta_t^l) \geq 0 \,\middle|\, \sum_{m_t^l \in \Theta^l} \sigma^l(m_t^l|\theta_t^l) = 1,\ \theta_t^l \in \Theta^l \right\}.$$

A strategy is a sequence $\left\{\pi^l(a_t^l|m_t^l)\right\}$ such that, for each period t, $\pi^l(a_t^l|m_t^l)$ is a stochastic kernel on A given history H_n. The set of all the admissible strategies is

$$\Pi_{adm}^l = \left\{ \pi^l(a_t^l|m_t^l) \geq 0 \,\middle|\, \sum_{a_t^l \in A^l} \pi^l(a_t^l|m_t^l) = 1, m_t^l \in M^l \right\}$$

Remark 1. *A strategy π is typically defined as a policy or plan of action for a player that depends only on the information they possess. In this case, π depends solely on the player's own message, and this suggests that π is a strategy based on private information or the part of the information that is most relevant to the player. The assumption here might be that each player has access to their own private message but does not directly depend on the messages of other players in their strategy formulation. This can simplify the analysis in certain games. A strategy σ, on the other hand, often refers to a more general form of strategy that could depend on all available information, such as public messages or even the outcomes of communication between players. σ involves communication, and it might be labeled as a communication strategy, where players decide how to share or process information.*

Let us introduce the cost function $v^l(a_t^l\theta_t^l m_t^l)$, which characterizes the losses incurred by players l when they take action a_t^l based on the message m_t^l generated under type θ_t^l.

The *average cost* $[0, T]$ of the player l is

$$V_T^l(\pi, \sigma) = \sum_{t \in T} \sum_{\theta_t^l \in \Theta^l} \sum_{m_t^l \in M^l} \sum_{a_t^l \in A^l} v^l(a_t^l\theta_t^l m_t^l) p^l(\theta_{t+1}^l|\theta_t^l a_t^l) \prod_{i \in \mathcal{L}} \pi^i(a_t^i|m_t^i)\sigma^i(m_t^i|\theta_t^i)P^i(\theta_t^i) =$$
$$\sum_{t \in T} \sum_{\theta_t^l \in \Theta^l} \sum_{m_t^l \in M^l} \sum_{a_t^l \in A^l} W^l(a_t^l\theta_t^l m_t^l) \prod_{i \in \mathcal{L}} \pi^i(a_t^i|m_t^i)\sigma^i(m_t^i|\theta_t^i)P^i(\theta_t^i).$$

where

$$W^l(a_t^l\theta_t^l m_t^l) = v^l(a_t^l\theta_t^l m_t^l)p^l(\theta_{t+1}^l|\theta_t^l a_t^l).$$

We assume that players know their payoffs. The strategy $\sigma^l(m_t^l|\theta_t^l)$ minimizes the weighted cost function $V^l(\pi,\sigma)$, realizing the rule, which is given by

$$(\pi^*,\sigma^*) \in Arg \min_{\sigma\in\Pi_{adm}} \min_{\sigma\in\mathcal{S}_{adm}} \sum_{l\in\mathcal{L}} V^l(\pi,\sigma). \tag{1}$$

The policy π^* and the strategy σ^* is said to satisfy the *Bayesian–Nash equilibrium* if, for all $\pi \in \Pi_{adm}$ and $\sigma \in \mathcal{S}_{adm}$, the following condition holds:

$$V^l(\pi^*,\sigma^*) \le V^l(\pi^*,\sigma^l,\sigma^{-l*}). \tag{2}$$

where $\sigma^{-l} = \left(\sigma^1,\ldots,\sigma^{l-1},\sigma^{l+1},\ldots,\sigma^n\right)$.

Let us introduce the auxiliary ξ variable as follows:

$$\xi^l(\theta_t^l m_t^l a_t^l) := \pi(a_t^l|m_t^l)\sigma^l(m_t^l|\theta_t^l)P^l(\theta_t^l). \tag{3}$$

such that

$$\Xi_{adm}^l := \left\{ \xi^l(\theta_t^l m_t^l a_t^l) \middle| \sum_{m_t^l\in M^l}\sum_{\theta_t^l\in\Theta^l}\sum_{a_t^l\in A^l} \xi^l(\theta_t^l m_t^l a_t^l) = 1,\ \sum_{m_t^l\in M^l}\sum_{a_t^l\in A^l} \xi^l(\theta_t^l m_t^l a_t^l) = P^l(\theta_t^l) > 0, \right.$$
$$\left. \sum_{m_t^l\in M^l}\sum_{a_t^l\in A^l}\sum_{\theta_t^l\in\Theta^l} [\delta_{\theta_t^l,\theta_{t+1}^l} - p^l(\theta_{t+1}^l|\theta_t^l a_t^l)]\xi^l(\theta_t^l m_t^l a_t^l) = 0, \theta_{t+1}^l \in \Theta^l \right\}. \tag{4}$$

where $\delta_{\theta_t^l,\theta_{t+1}^l}$ is Kroneker's symbol. It should be noted that the following relations hold:

$$\sum_{m_t^l\in M^l} \sigma(m_t|\theta_t) = 1, \quad \sum_{\theta_t^l\in\Theta^l} P^l(\theta_t^l) = 1.$$

We obtain that $\xi^l \in \Delta^l$, where

$$\Delta^l := \left\{ \xi^l(\theta_t^l m_t^l a_t^l) \middle| \sum_{m_t^l\in M^l}\sum_{\theta_t^l\in\Theta^l}\sum_{a_t^l\in A^l} \xi^l(\theta_t^l m_t^l a_t^l)=1,\ \sum_{m_t^l\in M^l}\sum_{a_t^l\in A^l} \xi^l(\theta_t^l m_t^l a_t^l) = P^l(\theta_t^l) > 0 \right\}. \tag{5}$$

3. Security Game Model

In the game involving multiple players, we consider two distinct groups : the defenders, denoted by $L = 1,\ldots,l$, and the attackers, denoted by $F = 1,\ldots,f$. Utilizing conventional game-theoretic notation, we denote the player index set as $\mathcal{I}$. The joint action profile of all participants, excluding agent q, is represented as $x^{-q} = (x^h)_{h\in\mathcal{I}/q}$. In the context of our Stackelberg game, $\mathcal{I} = L \cup F$, where players are indexed by $\iota = \overline{1,l}$ for the defenders and $r = \overline{1,f}$ for the attackers. This indexing scheme allows for clear differentiation between the defenders and attackers, facilitating the analysis of strategic interactions and decision-making dynamics within the game framework.

Let us say the defenders' strategies are denoted by $x^\iota \in X^\iota$, where X is a convex and compact set and

$$x^\iota := col(\xi_{ik}^\iota), X^\iota := \Xi_{adm}^\iota,\ X := \bigotimes_{\iota=1}^{l} X^\iota$$

such that col is a column-converting operator for the matrix ξ^{ι}_{ik}. The joint strategy of the players is denoted by $x = (x^1, \ldots, x^n)^\top \in X$, while the complement strategy of the players is denoted by $\hat{x} = x^{-\iota}$. Here,

$$x^{-\iota} := \left(x^1, \ldots, x^{\iota-1}, x^{\iota+1}, \ldots, x^l\right)^\top \in X^{-\iota} := \bigotimes_{h=1,\, h\neq\iota}^{l} X^{\iota}$$

such that $x = (x^{\iota}, x^{\hat{\iota}})$.

Similarly, if we let $y^r \in Y^r \left(r = \overline{1, f}\right)$ represent the attackers' strategies and Y be a convex and compact set where

$$y^r := col\left(\xi^r_{ik)}\right), Y^r := \Xi^r_{adm}\left(r = \overline{1, f}\right), Y := \bigotimes_{r=1}^{f} y^r$$

is denoted by $y = (y^1, \ldots, y^f) \in Y := \bigotimes_{r=1}^{f} Y^r$, then the joint strategy of the attackers and $y^{\hat{r}} = y^{-r}$ are strategies of the complement of the players adjoint to y^r, i.e.,

$$y^{-r} := \left(y^1, \ldots, y^{r-1}, y^{r+1}, \ldots, y^f\right)^\top \in Y^{-r} := \bigotimes_{r=1,\, r\neq f}^{f} Y^r$$

such that $y = (y^r, y^{\hat{r}})$.

In the scenario we investigate, defenders and attackers engage in a Nash game within the framework of a simultaneous play game that is restricted to a Stackelberg game. In simultaneous play games, the Nash equilibrium serves as the notion of equilibrium. Here, each player independently selects their strategy, aiming to maximize their own utility given the strategies chosen by other players. A Nash equilibrium is reached when no player can unilaterally deviate from their strategy to achieve a better outcome. In contrast, hierarchical play games, such as Stackelberg games, involve sequential decision-making, where one player (the defender) commits to a strategy first, and the other player (the attacker) observes this strategy before determining their own. The equilibrium concept in hierarchical play games differs from the Nash equilibrium, as it involves optimizing strategies in anticipation of the actions of other players in the sequence of play. Formalizing the Stackelberg game within this framework involves defining the roles of defenders and attackers, specifying their strategies, and analyzing the equilibrium outcomes under the sequential decision-making structure.

Let $W = X \cup Y$. If a player $q \in \mathcal{I}$ has a cost function $\varphi^q(w^q, w^{-q})$, then we have the following:

Definition 1. *The joint strategy $w^* \in W$ is a Nash equilibrium if, for each $q \in \mathcal{I}$,*

$$\varphi^q(w^*) \leq \varphi^q(w^q, w^{-q*}),\ \forall w^q \in W^q.$$

In the game progression, defenders forecast attackers behavior by playing non-cooperatively, anticipating attackers' actions at a Stackelberg equilibrium. This strategic anticipation enables defenders to make informed decisions when committing to their strategies, considering the likely responses of attackers within the framework of the Nash equilibrium. By strategically forecasting attackers' behavior, defenders aim to optimize their own outcomes in the game. To achieve the game's aim, defenders must first identify a strategy $x^* = \left(x^{1*}, \ldots, x^{l*}\right) \in X$ that is satisfying for any admissible $x^{\iota} \in X^{\iota}$ and any $\iota = \overline{1, l}$.

$$\Lambda(x) := \sum_{\iota=1}^{l}\left[\left(\min_{x^{\iota}\in X^{\iota}} \varphi^{\iota}(x^{\iota}, x^{-\iota})\right) - \varphi^{\iota}(x^{\iota}, x^{-\iota})\right]. \tag{6}$$

The cost function of the defenders ι who play the strategy $x^{\iota} \in X^{\iota}$ and the complement of the defenders who play the strategy $x^{-\iota} \in X^{-\iota}$ is $\varphi^{\iota}(x^{\iota}, x^{-\iota})$.

Taking the utopia point as

$$\bar{x}^{\iota} := \arg\min_{x^{\iota} \in X^{\iota}} \varphi^{\iota}\left(x^{\iota}, x^{-\iota}\right) \tag{7}$$

then one can describe Equation (6) in the following manner:

$$\Lambda(x) := \sum_{\iota=1}^{l} \left[\varphi^{\iota}\left(\bar{x}^{\iota}, x^{-\iota}\right) - \varphi^{\iota}\left(x^{\iota}, x^{-\iota}\right)\right]. \tag{8}$$

The functions $\varphi^{\iota}(x^{\iota}, x^{-\iota})$ $\left(\iota = \overline{1,l}\right)$ are supposed to be convex in all their arguments.

The function $\Lambda(x)$ fulfills **Nash's condition**

$$\max_{x \in X} g(x) = \sum_{\iota=1}^{l} \left[\varphi^{\iota}(\bar{x}^{\iota}, x^{-\iota}) - \varphi^{\iota}(x^{\iota}, x^{-\iota})\right] \leq 0$$

for any $x^{\iota} \in x^{\iota}$ and all $\iota = \overline{1,l}$

A strategy $x^{*} \in X$ is a **Nash equilibrium** if

$$x^{*} \in Arg \min_{x \in X} \{\Lambda(x)\}.$$

If $\Lambda(x)$ is strictly convex, then

$$x^{*} = \arg\min_{x \in X} \{\Lambda(x)\}.$$

In addition, in this process, the attackers attempt to reach some of the Nash equilibria and try to find a joint strategy $y^{*} = \left(y^{1*}, \ldots, y^{f*}\right) \in Y$ that satisfies any admissible $y^{r} \in y^{r}$ and any $r = \overline{1,f}$

$$\Psi(y) := \sum_{r=1}^{f} \left[\left(\min_{y^{r} \in Y^{r}} \varphi_{r}(y^{r}, y^{-r})\right) - \varphi^{r}(y^{r}, y^{-r})\right].$$

The cost function of the attackers m who play the strategy $y^{r} \in y^{r}$ and the complement of the defenders who play the strategy $y^{-r} \in y^{-r}$ is $\varphi^{r}(y^{r}, y^{-r})$.

Bearing in mind the utopia point

$$\bar{y}^{r} := \arg\min_{y^{r} \in Y^{r}} \varphi^{r}\left(y^{r}, y^{-r}\right)$$

it is possible to rewrite Equation (6) as follows:

$$\Psi(y) := \sum_{r=1}^{f} \left(\varphi^{r}\left(\bar{v}^{r}, y^{-r}\right) - \varphi^{r}\left(y^{r}, y^{-r}\right)\right).$$

The functions $\varphi^{r}(y^{r}, y^{-r})$ $\left(r = \overline{1,f}\right)$ are supposed to be convex in all their arguments.

The function $\Psi(y)$ satisfies the **Nash condition**

$$\max_{y^{r} \in y^{r}} w(y) = \sum_{r=1}^{f} \left(\varphi^{r}(\bar{y}^{r}, y^{-r}) - \varphi^{r}(y^{r}, y^{-r})\right) \leq 0$$

for any $y^{r} \in y^{r}$ and all $r = \overline{1,f}$.

The defenders' goal is to find a solution to the optimization challenge given by the following definition:

Definition 2. *A Stackelberg game is a game with l defenders and f attackers; it is called a Stackelberg–Nash game if the defenders strive to solve the issue presented by*

$$\min_{x\in X}\{\Lambda(x|y)\mid y\in Arg\min_{v\in Y}\Psi(v|x)\}$$

and the attackers try to solve the problem

$$\min_{y\in Y}\Psi(y|x)$$

such that

$$\Lambda(x|y):=\sum_{\iota=1}^{l}\left(\varphi^{\iota}(\bar{x}^{\iota},x^{-\iota}|y)-\varphi^{\iota}(x^{\iota},x^{-\iota}|y)\right)$$

and

$$\Psi(y|x):=\sum_{r=1}^{f}(\varphi^{r}(\bar{y}^{r},y^{-r}|x)-\varphi^{r}(y^{r},y^{-r}|x)).$$

Then, the equilibrium notion in games is the Nash equilibrium in simultaneous play games and the Stackelberg equilibrium in hierarchical play games.

Definition 3. *(Stackelberg equilibrium) In a game with l defenders, the strategy $x^*\in X$ is said to be a Stackelberg–Nash equilibrium strategy for the defenders if*

$$\max_{x\in\rho(x^*)}\Lambda(x^*|y)\leq\max_{x\in\rho(x)}\Lambda(x|y)$$

such that

$$\rho(x)=\{y\in Y\mid\Psi(y|x)\leq\Psi(v|x)\forall v\in Y\}$$

is the best reply set of the attackers.

The definition of Stackelberg equilibrium given above can be redefined for the set of the attackers when the set $\rho(x)$ is substituted with the set of Nash equilibria, considering that the defenders play the strategy x and then the attackers' best reply is a Nash equilibrium.

The general format iterative version ($n=0,1,\ldots$) of the proximal-gradient method for computing the Stackelberg equilibrium is as follows:

1. The *first half-step* (prediction):

$$\hat{v}_n=\arg\min_{\tilde{w}\in X\times Y}\left\{\tfrac{1}{2}\|\tilde{w}-\tilde{v}_n\|^2+\gamma\Psi(\tilde{w},\tilde{v}_n)\right\} \tag{9}$$

2. The *second* (basic) half-step:

$$\tilde{v}_{n+1}=\arg\min_{\tilde{w}\in X\times Y}\left\{\frac{1}{2}\|\tilde{w}-\tilde{v}_n\|^2+\gamma\Psi(\tilde{w},\hat{v}_n)\right\} \tag{10}$$

4. Learning

Reinforcement learning (RL) addresses the challenge of learning optimal actions in an unknown Markov setting through interaction [27]. Players aim to devise strategies that minimize their expected costs. In a discrete-time setting, at each time step t, players observe a cost v^i, where i denotes the player. The overarching objective is to minimize the average cost V over time, guiding decision-making towards more favorable outcomes.

By iteratively adjusting actions based on observed costs and environmental feedback, RL algorithms seek to discover optimal strategies that lead to the most advantageous long-term outcomes in dynamic and uncertain environments.

We consider RL problems where the underlying environment is a Bayesian–Markov decision process. Specifically, in the Stackelberg game, players indexed by $\iota = \overline{1,l}$ are the defenders and players indexed by $r = \overline{1,f}$ are the attackers. We will develop the results in general for a player $i \in \mathcal{I}$ ($\mathcal{I} = L \cup F$) and we specify defenders and attackers when it will be necessary. We propose a setting based on experiences, which is calculated by adding the number χ of experiences given as follows: let $h_t \in \mathbb{H}_t$ ($t \in T$) be the history at time t and $(\theta_t, a_t) \in \Theta \times A$. Let, for each $(\theta_{t+1}, \theta_t, a_t) \in \Theta \times \Theta \times A$,

$$\chi^i(\tilde{\theta}^i_{t+1}\tilde{\theta}^i_t a^i_t) = \sum_{t\in T} \mathbb{1}(\tilde{\theta}^i_{t+1}\tilde{\theta}^i_t a^i_t) = \mathbb{E}\left\{\mathbb{1}(\tilde{\theta}^i_{t+1})\mathbb{1}(\tilde{\theta}^i_t)\mathbb{1}(a^i_t)\right\}$$

denote the experimentally observed absolute average number of transitions from type $\hat{\theta}^i_t$ applying action a^i_t, We obtain the normally distributed and asymptotically unbiased maximum likelihood estimator given by $p^i(\tilde{\theta}^i_{t+1}|\tilde{\theta}^i_t a^i_t)$

$$\tilde{p}^i\left(\tilde{\theta}^i_{t+1}|\tilde{\theta}^i_t a^i_t\right) = \frac{\chi^i(\tilde{\theta}^i_{t+1}\tilde{\theta}^i_t a^i_t)}{\chi^i(\tilde{\theta}^i_t a^i_t)}.$$

Therefore, the cost of player $l \in \mathcal{L}$ is

$$\tilde{v}^i\left(\tilde{\theta}^i_{t+1}\tilde{\theta}^i_t a^i_t\right) = \frac{\sum_{t\in T} \alpha^i(\tilde{\theta}^i_{t+1}\tilde{\theta}^i_t a^i_t)\chi^i(\tilde{\theta}^i_{t+1}\tilde{\theta}^i_t a^i_t)}{\chi^i(\tilde{\theta}^i_{t+1}\tilde{\theta}^i_t a^i_t)} \tag{11}$$

where

$$\alpha^i(\tilde{\theta}^i_{t+1}\tilde{\theta}^i_t a^i_t) = v^i(\tilde{\theta}^i_{t+1}\tilde{\theta}^i_t a^i_t) + \alpha^i r$$

and $\alpha^i \le u^i$ such that r randomly takes the values between -1 or 1.

We assume that the det $\mathcal{P}^i(\theta^i_t|m^i_t) \neq 0$ where $\Sigma = \left[\mathcal{P}^i(\theta^i_t|m^i_t)\right]^{-1}$ exists (the inverse of $\mathcal{P}^i(\theta^i_t|m^i_t)$). We suggest a framework from experiences that is calculated counting the number χ of unobserved experiences recursively as follows:

$$\chi^i(m'^i_t m^i_t a^i_t) = \sum_{t\in T} \mathbb{1}(m'^i_t|m^i_t a^i_t) = \mathrm{E}\{\mathbb{1}(m'^i_t)\mathbb{1}(m^i_t)\mathbb{1}(a^i_t)\}$$

where $\chi^i(m^i_t a^i_t)$ is the number of visits in the state m^i_t and $\chi^i(m'^i_t m^i_t a^i_t)$ is the total number of times that the system changes from m'^i_t to m^i_t applying a^i_t. We obtain that $\chi^i(m^i_t a^i_t) = \sum_{m'^i_t \in M^i_t} \chi^i(m'^l_t m^i_t a^i_t)$.

The estimated transition matrix $\tilde{p}^i(\tilde{\theta}_{t+1}|\tilde{\theta}_t x_t)$ is given by

$$\tilde{p}^i(\tilde{\theta}^i_{t+1}|\tilde{\theta}^i_t a^i_t) = \frac{\sum\limits_{m^i_t\in M^i}\sum\limits_{m'^i_t\in M^i} \Sigma^i(m'^i_t\tilde{\theta}^i_t)\Sigma^i(m^i_t\tilde{\theta}^i_{t+1})\chi^i(m'^i_t m^i_t a^i_t)}{\sum\limits_{\tilde{\theta}^i_{t+1}\in\Theta^i_t}\left[\sum\limits_{m^i_t\in M^i}\sum\limits_{m'^i_t\in M^i} \Sigma^i(m'^i_t\tilde{\theta}^i_t)\Sigma^i(m^i_t\tilde{\theta}^i_{t+1})\chi^i(m'^i_t m^i_t a^i_t)\right]}. \tag{12}$$

In order to recover the variables of interest, we calculate

$$\sigma^{\iota*}(m^\iota_t|\theta^\iota_t) = \frac{\sum\limits_{a^\iota_t\in A^\iota} \xi^{\iota*}(\theta^\iota_t m^\iota_t a^\iota_t)}{\sum\limits_{m^\iota_t\in M^\iota}\sum\limits_{a^\iota_t\in A^\iota} \xi^{\iota*}(\theta^\iota_t m^\iota_t a^\iota_t)}. \tag{13}$$

$$\pi^{\iota*}(a_t^\iota|m_t^\iota) = \frac{1}{|\Theta^\iota|}\sum_{\theta_t^\iota\in\Theta^\iota}\frac{\xi^\iota(\theta_t^\iota m_t^\iota a_t^\iota)}{\sum_{a_t^\iota\in A^\iota}\xi^\iota(\theta_t^\iota m_t^\iota a_t^\iota)}. \tag{14}$$

$$P^{\iota*}(\theta_t^\iota) = \sum_{m_t^\iota\in M^\iota}\sum_{a_t^\iota\in A^\iota}\xi^{\iota*}(\theta_t^\iota m_t^\iota a_t^\iota) > 0. \tag{15}$$

$$\sigma^{r*}(m_t^r|\theta_t^r) = \frac{\sum_{a_t^r\in A^r}\xi^{r*}(\theta_t^r m_t^r a_t^r)}{\sum_{m_t^r\in M^r}\sum_{a_t^r\in A^r}\xi^{r*}(\theta_t^r m_t^j a_t^r)}. \tag{16}$$

$$\pi^{r*}(a_t^r|m_t^r) = \frac{1}{|\Theta^r|}\sum_{\theta_t^r\in\Theta^r}\frac{\xi^r(\theta_t^r m_t^r a_t^r)}{\sum_{a_t^r\in A^r}\xi^r(\theta_t^r m_t^r a_t^r)}. \tag{17}$$

$$P^{j*}(\theta_t^r) = \sum_{m_t^r\in M^r}\sum_{a_t^r\in A^r}\xi^{r*}(\theta_t^r m_t^j a_t^r) > 0. \tag{18}$$

The BRL algorithm for the SSG is outlined in Algorithm 1 and Algorithm 2. At time $t = 0$, for each defender $\iota = 1,\ldots,l$ and each attacker $r = 1,\ldots,f$, we initialize the parameters. Specifically, the initial belief states for both the defender and the attackers are represented as $\tilde{\theta}_0^\iota \sim P^\iota(\theta_0^\iota)$ and $\tilde{\theta}_0^r \sim P^r(\theta_0^r)$, where P^ι and P^r are probability distributions over the possible states θ_0 of the defender and attackers, respectively. These beliefs are updated throughout the game as players take action and observe the outcomes.

Algorithm 1: BRL algorithm for the SSG

$\iota = \overline{1,l}$ and $r = \overline{1,f}$.
$t = 1$.
$\tilde{\theta}_0^\iota \sim P^\iota(\theta_0^\iota)$ and $\tilde{\theta}_0^r \sim P^r(\theta_0^r)$.
$\tilde{p}^\iota = p^\iota$ and $\tilde{p}^r = p^r$.
$\varepsilon > 0$.
$e_t^\iota \leftarrow \text{Error}(\hat{p}_{t-1}^\iota, \hat{p}_t^\iota)$ and $e_t^r \leftarrow \text{Error}(\hat{p}_{t-1}^r, \hat{p}_t^r)$
while ($\varepsilon > e_t^\iota$ and $\varepsilon > e_t^r$)
(i) $x^* \leftarrow \left\{\min_{x\in X}\Lambda(x|y) \mid y \in \arg\min_{\alpha\in Y}\Psi(\alpha|x)\right\}$ and $y^* \leftarrow \min_{y\in Y}\Psi(y|x)$.
(ii) recover $\pi^* \leftarrow$ Equations (14)–(17) and $\sigma^* \leftarrow$ Equations (13)–(16)
(iii) $m_t^\iota \sim \sigma^{\iota*}(m_t^\iota|\tilde{\theta}_t^\iota)$ and $m_t^r \sim \sigma^{r*}(m_t^r|\tilde{\theta}_t^r)$.
(iv) $a_t^\iota \sim \pi^{\iota*}(a_t^\iota|m_t^\iota)$ and $a_t^r \sim \pi^{r*}(a_t^r|m_t^r)$.
(v) $\tilde{\theta}_{t+1}^\iota \sim \hat{p}^\iota(\theta_{t+1}^\iota|\theta_t^\iota a_t^\iota)$ and $\tilde{\theta}_{t+1}^r \sim \hat{p}^r(\theta_{t+1}^r|\theta_t^r a_t^r)$.
(vi) $\chi^\iota(\tilde{\theta}_{t+1}^\iota\tilde{\theta}a_t^\iota) += 1$, $\chi^\iota(\tilde{\theta}^\iota a_t^\iota) += 1$ and $\chi^r(\tilde{\theta}_{t+1}^\iota\tilde{\theta}a_t^r) += 1$, $\chi^r(\tilde{\theta}^r a_t^r) += 1$.
(vii) $\tilde{v}^\iota(\tilde{\theta}_{t+1}^\iota\tilde{\theta}_t^\iota a_t^\iota) \leftarrow$ Equation (11) and $\tilde{v}^r(\tilde{\theta}_{t+1}^r\tilde{\theta}_t^r a_t^r) \leftarrow$ Equation (11).
(viii) $\tilde{p}^\iota(\tilde{\theta}_{t+1}^\iota|\tilde{\theta}_t^\iota a_t^\iota) \leftarrow$ Equation (12) and $\tilde{p}^r(\tilde{\theta}_{t+1}^r|\tilde{\theta}_t^r a_t^r) \leftarrow$ Equation (12).
(ix) $e_t^\iota \leftarrow \text{Error}(\hat{p}_{t-1}^\iota, \hat{p}_t^\iota)$ and $e_t^r \leftarrow \text{Error}(\hat{p}_{t-1}^r, \hat{p}_t^r)$.
(x) $\tilde{\theta}_t^\iota = \tilde{\theta}_{t+1}^\iota$, $\tilde{\theta}_t^r = \tilde{\theta}_{t+1}^r$, $p^\iota = \hat{p}^\iota$, $p^r = \hat{p}^r$, $v^\iota = \tilde{v}^\iota$, $v^r = \tilde{v}^r$ and $t = t+1$.
end while

Algorithm 2: Computation of the error

function Error $(\hat{p}_{t-1}, \hat{p}_t)$
$e = \sum_{a_t\in A} tr((\hat{p}_{t-1} - \hat{p}_t)^\top(\hat{p}_{t-1} - \hat{p}_t))$.
return e.
end function

The transition probabilities for each player's states are defined as $\tilde{p}^\iota = p^\iota(\tilde{\theta}_1^\iota|\tilde{\theta}_0^\iota a_0^\iota)$ and $\tilde{p}^r = p^r(\tilde{\theta}_1^r|\tilde{\theta}_0^r a_0^r)$, where $\tilde{p}^\iota$ and $\tilde{p}^r$ represent the likelihood of transitioning from one state to another given the actions a_0^ι and a_0^r taken by the defenders and the attackers. These transition probabilities are essential for predicting the future states of the game based on current strategies.

An important aspect of the algorithm is to account for estimation errors in the parameters of the model. We denote the allowable error in the estimated parameters by $\varepsilon > 0$, which sets a threshold for how much deviation is acceptable. During each step of the algorithm, the actual error e_t^l for the defenders and e_t^r for the attackers is computed to track the accuracy of the estimated parameters.

At each time step t, the BRL algorithm computes the optimal strategy $\sigma^*(m_t^l|\Theta^l)$ and the corresponding policy $\pi^*(a_t^l|m_t^l)$ for both the defenders and the attackers. The strategy σ^* determines the probability distribution over the possible messages m_t^l given the state Θ^l, while the policy π^* dictates the probability of taking a particular action a_t^l given the message m_t^l. These strategies and policies are central to the Bayesian Stackelberg equilibrium, where players optimize their decisions based on their beliefs about the other players' actions.

For each step, random messages m_t^l and m_t^r are drawn from the respective optimal strategies $\sigma^{l*}(m_t^l|\tilde{\theta}_t^l)$ and $\sigma^{r*}(m_t^r|\tilde{\theta}_t^r)$. Based on these messages, actions are chosen randomly according to the policies $\pi^{l*}(a_t^l|m_t^l)$ for the defenders and $\pi^{r*}(a_t^r|m_t^r)$ for the attackers.

Once the actions are selected and executed, the game transitions to the next state. The updated states $\tilde{\theta}_{t+1}^l$ and $\tilde{\theta}_{t+1}^r$ are determined by the transition probabilities $\hat{p}^l(\theta_{t+1}^l|\theta_t^l a_t^l)$ and $\hat{p}^r(\theta_{t+1}^r|\theta_t^r a_t^r)$, respectively.

After transitioning to the new states, we update the counts $\chi^l(\tilde{\theta}_{t+1}^l, \tilde{\theta}_t^l, a_t^l)$ and $\chi^r(\tilde{\theta}_{t+1}^r \tilde{\theta}_t^r a_t^r)$, which track how frequently each state–action pair is encountered. These counts are critical for refining the players' estimates of the value functions $\tilde{v}^l(\tilde{\theta}_{t+1}^l \tilde{\theta}_t^l a_t^l)$ and $\tilde{v}^r(\tilde{\theta}_{t+1}^r \tilde{\theta}_t^r a_t^r)$. These value functions represent the expected reward for each player given their current and next states and the actions taken.

As the game progresses, the algorithm updates the transition probabilities $\tilde{p}^l(\tilde{\theta}_{t+1}^l|\tilde{\theta}_t^l a_t^l)$ and $\tilde{p}^r(\tilde{\theta}_{t+1}^r|\tilde{\theta}_t^r a_t^r)$ based on observed outcomes. At each step, the mean-square errors e_t^l and e_t^r are calculated to measure the difference between the estimated and actual outcomes. The algorithm continues to iterate as long as these errors exceed the predefined threshold ε, ensuring that the estimates converge to an acceptable level of accuracy.

Once the errors e_t^l and e_t^r fall below the threshold ε, the resulting strategy profile $\sigma^*(m_t|\theta_t)$ and policy $\pi^*(a_t|m_t)$ form a Bayesian Stackelberg equilibrium. This equilibrium represents the optimal solution for the game, where the defenders and attackers have maximized their respective utilities given the available information.

5. Random Walk Algorithm

Random walks are basic models in probability theory with deep mathematical features and a wide range of applications in SSGs [16,28]. The long-term asymptotic behavior of the defenders to catch the attackers is a key question for these models.

The random walk process for the SSG is described by Algorithm 3 as follows. We will look at a game in which four players compete: defenders and attackers. Both sides have the option of using a randomized approach. The defenders and attackers can both move to any state at the same time. The defenders' goal is to catch the attackers in the fewest possible steps. The attackers, on the other hand, choose a strategy that maximizes the amount of time it takes for the defenders to catch the attackers. If one of the defenders moves to a state where an attacker is, they are said to be caught. The game is over when the defenders have caught the attackers. We refer to a random walk as a discrete-time Markov process $(X_t, t \geq 0)$ in a finite-type space Θ. The random walk is assumed to be time-homogeneous. This means that the X_{t+1} distribution given $(X_0, \ldots, X_t)$ is solely dependent on X_t and not on time t. To ensure that the random walk does not become 'stuck' in some place of the state space, we also require some type of irreducibility: the set Θ is finite.

Given a type θ_t, a message m_t is chosen randomly by the defenders and the attackers from the behavior strategies $m_t^\iota \sim \sigma^{\iota *}(m_t^\iota|\theta_t^\iota)$ and $m_t^r \sim \sigma^{r*}(m_t^r|\theta_t^r)$. They then choose actions $a_t^\iota \sim \pi^{\iota *}(a_t^\iota|m_t^\iota)$ and $a^r \sim \pi^{r*}(a_t^r|m_t^r)$. To minimize and maximize the chance of damage, the transition matrix $p^\iota(\theta_{t+1}^\iota|\theta_t^\iota a_t^\iota)$ and $p^r(\theta_{t+1}^r|\theta_t^r a_t^r)$ are used to select the next state in the process. The defenders and attackers aim to finish the SSG the next time $(t+1)$. The process continues until the fulfillment of the SSG meets the game-over or capture statuses provided by the following:

$$\sum_{\iota \in L}\sum_{r \in F}\sum_{\theta_{t+1}^\iota \in \Theta_t^\iota}\sum_{\theta_{t+1}^r \in \Theta_t^r} \mathbb{1}(\theta_{t+1}^\iota)\mathbb{1}(\theta_{t+1}^r) \tag{19}$$

Algorithm 3: Random walk for the SSG

1. Choose randomly an initial type for the defenders $\theta_0^\iota \sim P^\iota(\theta_0^\iota)$ and attackers $\theta_0^r \sim P^r(\theta_0^r)$.
2. Let $\pi^{\iota *}(a_t^\iota|m_t^\iota)$ and $\pi^{r*}(a_t^r|m_t^r)$ be the resulting policies and, $\sigma_{m_t|\theta_t}^{\iota *}$ and $\sigma_{m_t|\theta_t}^{r*}$ the resulting strategies.
3. **For** each attacker r and defender ι **Do**
4. Choose a type $\theta_t^\iota \sim \sigma_{m_t|\theta_t}^{\iota *}$ and $\theta_t^r \sim \sigma_{r|i}^{\iota *}$
5. Choose actions $a_t^\iota \sim \pi^{\iota *}(a_t^\iota|m_t^\iota)$ and $a^r \sim \pi^{r*}(a_t^r|m_t^r)$.
6. From $p^\iota(\theta_{t+1}^\iota|\theta_t^\iota a_t^\iota)$ select θ_{t+1}^ι considering $p^\iota(\cdot|\theta_t^\iota a_t^\iota)$ and from $p^r(\theta_{t+1}^r|\theta_t^r a_t^r)$ select θ_{t+1}^r considering $p^r(\cdot|\theta_t^r a_t^r)$.
8. Update the original values by including θ_{t+1}^ι and θ_{t+1}^r to the random walk process.
9. Repeat steps 3–8 until the status expressed in Equation (19) is met.

6. Numerical Example

We will employ three players to simulate the SSG: one defender $(\iota = 1)$ and two attackers $(r = 1,2)$. The primary objective of the defender is to minimize or halt the damage inflicted by the attackers, while the attackers aim to maximize the expected damage they can cause to a set of targets. This dynamic reflects a typical security scenario, where an agent (the defender) must safeguard resources or locations, while adversarial players (attackers) try to exploit weaknesses.

The game is structured in a sequential manner and is commonly modeled as a Stackelberg game. The defender acts as the leader, committing to a strategy first, which is observed by the attackers. Once the defender's strategy is known, the attackers, acting as followers, select their strategies in response. This turn-based nature highlights the strategic advantage of the defender, as their actions guide the attackers' responses.

Each player in the game has a set of possible states and actions. In this particular setup, we assume that each player has $\theta = 4$ states, representing different possible situations or configurations in which they can find themselves during the game. Additionally, each player has $a = 2$ possible actions they can take in any given state, representing the limited yet strategic decisions available at each step of the game.

The key variables that drive the analysis of the SSG are the policies (π), behavior strategies (σ), and distribution vectors (P) for both the defender and attackers. The policy (π) defines the overall plan of action for each player, essentially specifying the probabilities with which they select each available action in a given state. Behavior strategies (σ) represent the specific actions taken by players as they progress through the game, reflecting how their strategies evolve over time. The distribution vectors (P) capture the likelihood of players being in different states throughout the course of the game.

These variables will be recovered analytically, meaning that through mathematical derivations and strategic analysis, we will determine the optimal policies, strategies, and distributions for both the defender and the attackers. This will allow us to predict the outcomes of the game under various scenarios, providing insight into how effective the defender's strategy is in mitigating the attackers' impact and how the attackers can best exploit potential vulnerabilities.

The generated policies are supplied by using the proposed approach as follows:

$$\pi^{1*}(a^1|m^1)=\begin{bmatrix}0.3925 & 0.6075\\ 0.3925 & 0.6075\\ 0.3925 & 0.6075\\ 0.3961 & 0.6039\end{bmatrix} \quad \pi^{2*}(a^2|m^2)=\begin{bmatrix}0.4748 & 0.5252\\ 0.4748 & 0.5252\\ 0.4748 & 0.5252\\ 0.2492 & 0.7508\end{bmatrix} \quad \pi^{3*}(a^3|m^3)=\begin{bmatrix}0.7903 & 0.2097\\ 0.7904 & 0.2096\\ 0.7904 & 0.2096\\ 0.6700 & 0.3300\end{bmatrix}$$

The defender's resultant (behavior) strategies are provided by

$$\sigma^{1*}(m^1|\theta^1)=\begin{bmatrix}0.3204 & 0.3205 & 0.3204 & 0.0387\\ 0.0223 & 0.0223 & 0.0223 & 0.9332\\ 0.2253 & 0.2253 & 0.2253 & 0.3240\\ 0.2500 & 0.2500 & 0.2500 & 0.2500\end{bmatrix}$$

and the (behavior) strategies of the attackers are

$$\sigma^{2*}(m^2|\theta^2)=\begin{bmatrix}0.0919 & 0.0919 & 0.0919 & 0.7243\\ 0.0573 & 0.0573 & 0.0573 & 0.8280\\ 0.2493 & 0.2495 & 0.2494 & 0.2518\\ 0.2499 & 0.2501 & 0.2500 & 0.2500\end{bmatrix} \quad \sigma^{3*}(m^3|\theta^3)=\begin{bmatrix}0.0287 & 0.0287 & 0.0287 & 0.9139\\ 0.2501 & 0.2503 & 0.2501 & 0.2495\\ 0.2491 & 0.2494 & 0.2498 & 0.2517\\ 0.2498 & 0.2498 & 0.2500 & 0.2504\end{bmatrix}$$

The distribution vectors are as follows:

$$P^{1*}(\theta^1)=\begin{bmatrix}0.4657\\ 0.4492\\ 0.0448\\ 0.0403\end{bmatrix} \quad P^{2*}(\theta^2)=\begin{bmatrix}0.1097\\ 0.1752\\ 0.5679\\ 0.1472\end{bmatrix} \quad P^{3*}(\theta^3)=\begin{bmatrix}0.3492\\ 0.2401\\ 0.1065\\ 0.3041\end{bmatrix}$$

The algorithm ensures the convergence of the strategies shown in Figures 1–3, optimizing decision-making and adapting efficiently to dynamic threats in real-time environments. Figures 4–9 demonstrate the convergence of the error in the reinforcement learning algorithm, illustrating its efficiency and effectiveness in optimizing strategies and adapting to dynamic environments over time. By integrating prior information and utilizing a continuous-time approach, the model enhances its robustness, ensuring that the security system remains resilient against evolving threats. These visualizations confirm the model's capability to maintain optimal performance and adaptiveness.

The primary goal of patrol scheduling is to efficiently allocate security teams to safeguard fixed targets, taking into account limited workforce resources. To address this challenge, Algorithm 3 is utilized to illustrate the realization of an SSG, where target visitations are determined based on the resulting game strategy, denoted as $\pi_{k|m}$. This algorithm aids in the planning and deployment of patrols to maximize the protection of critical assets.

Figure 10 provides a visual representation of an instance of the SSG, showcasing the outcomes of engagements between attackers and defenders. In this particular scenario, attacker 2 is apprehended at state 1 by defender 1 after 10 time steps, indicating the successful interception of the threat. Additionally, attacker 2 is captured at state 1, this time after 12 time steps by defender 1. These outcomes demonstrate the effectiveness of the patrol planning process in thwarting attacks and protecting the designated targets. By employing Algorithm 2 and visualizing the SSG outcomes in Figure 1, security planners can gain insights into the effectiveness of their patrol scheduling strategies. This approach allows for the optimization of patrol routes and deployment strategies, ultimately enhancing the security posture despite workforce limitations.

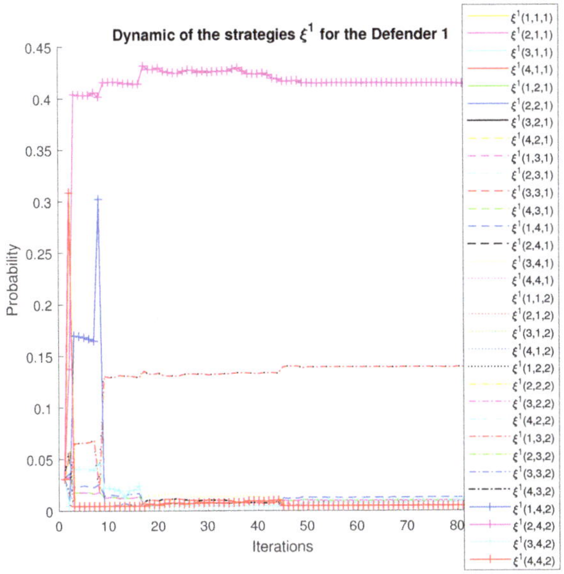

Figure 1. Convergence for defender 1's strategy ξ^1.

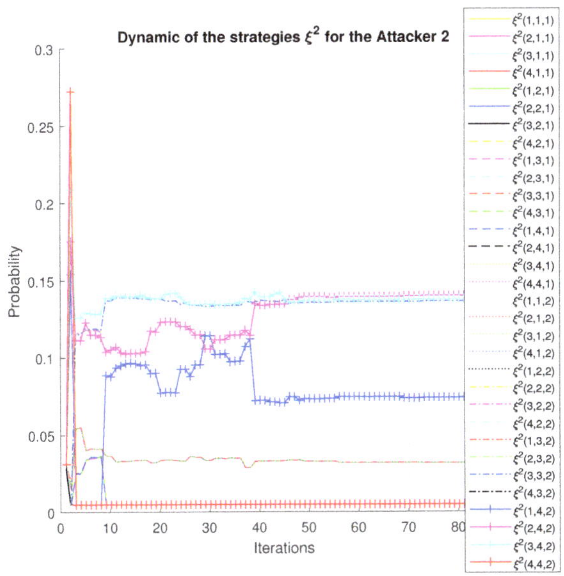

Figure 2. Convergence for attacker 2's strategy ξ^2.

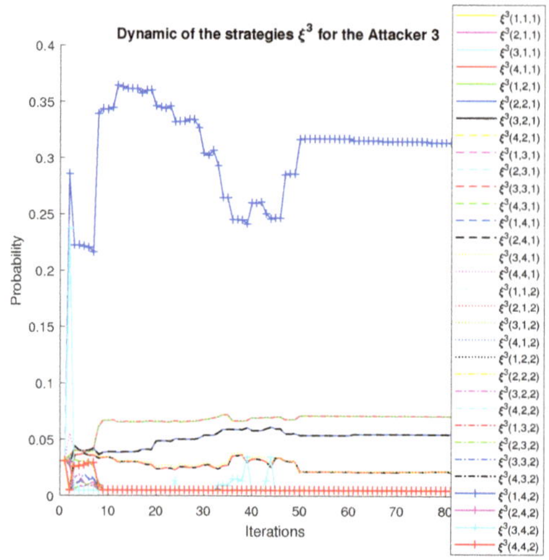

Figure 3. Convergence for attacker 3's strategy ξ^3.

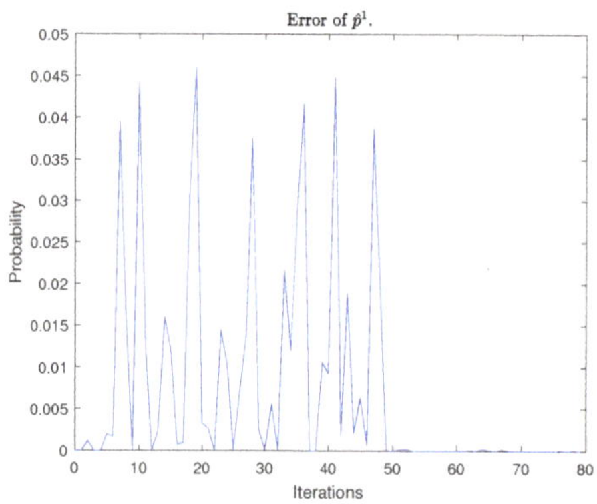

Figure 4. Convergence for defender 1's error of p^1.

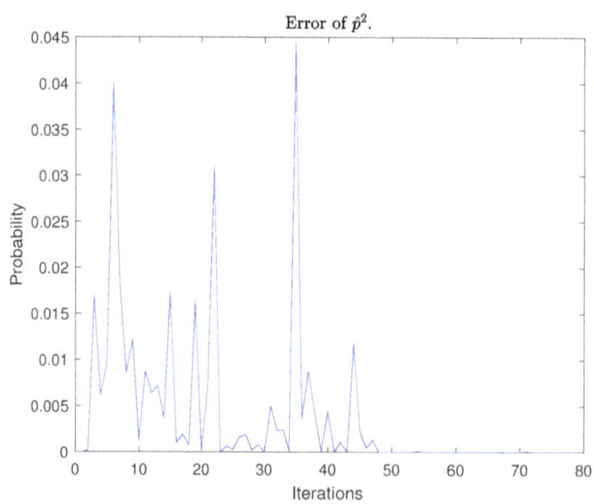

Figure 5. Convergence for attacker 2's error of p^2.

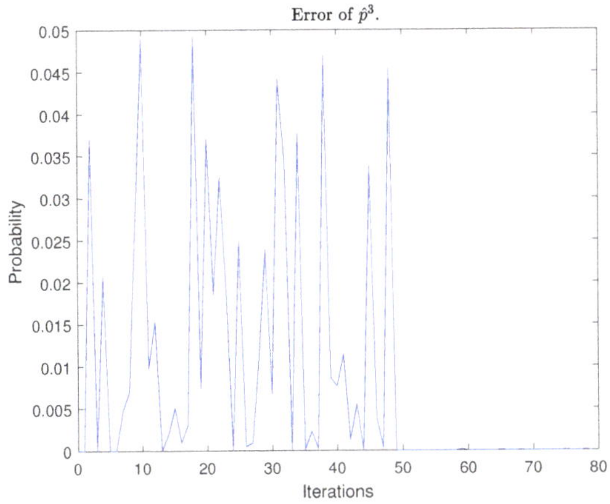

Figure 6. Convergence for attacker 3's error p^3.

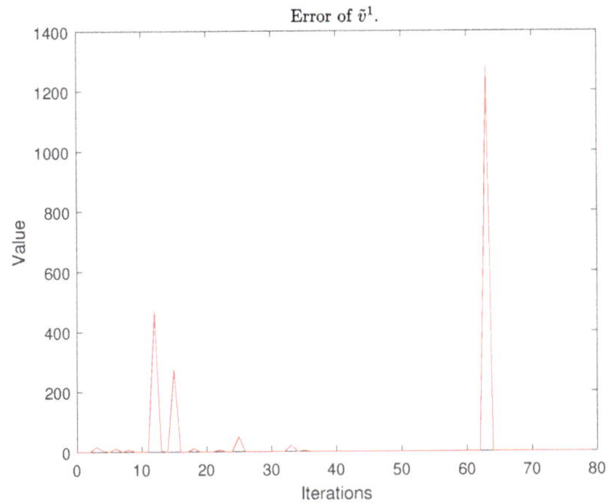

Figure 7. Convergence for defender 1's error of v^1.

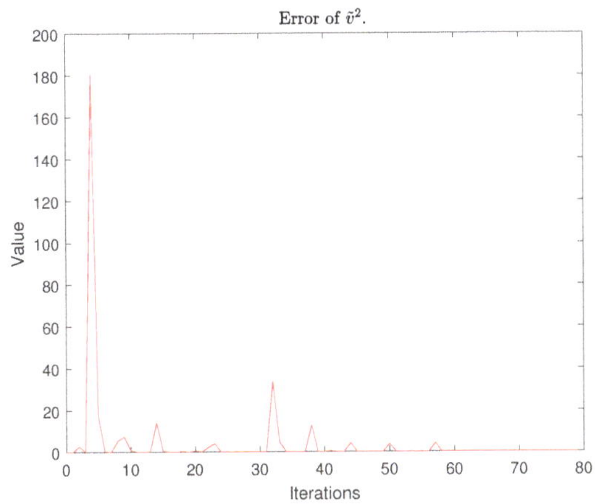

Figure 8. Convergence for attacker 2's error of v^2.

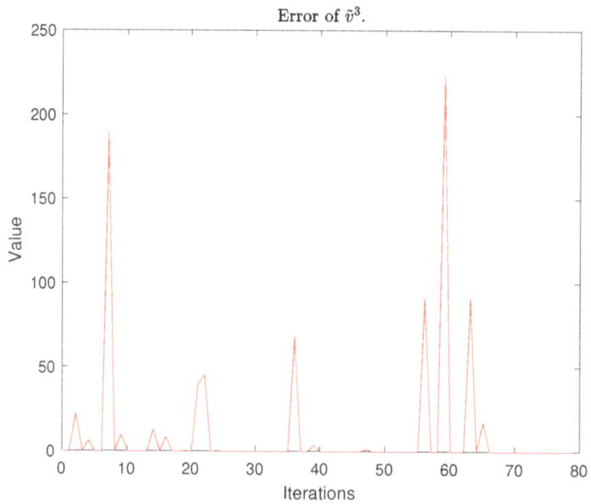

Figure 9. Convergence for attacker 3's error of v^3.

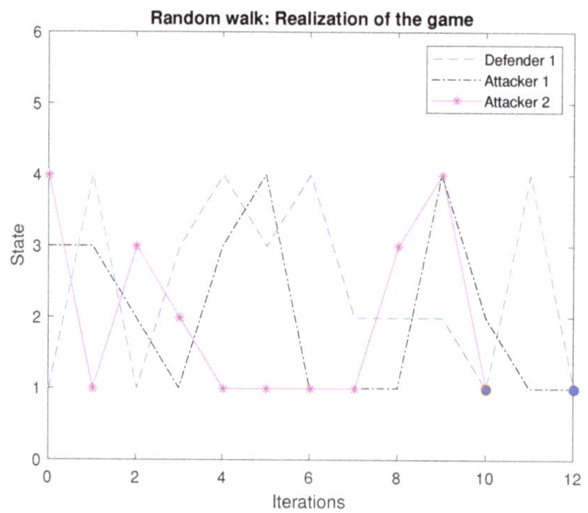

Figure 10. Game realization 1: the attackers are intercepted by defender 1 (blue).

In the alternate realization depicted in Figure 11, a different sequence of events unfolds within the SSG. Here, attacker 2 faces a swift apprehension at state 1 by defender 1 after three time steps. Simultaneously, attacker 1 is intercepted at state 1, albeit after a longer duration of nine time steps, by defender 1. Despite the varying durations and defender involvement, both attackers are ultimately captured. The prompt resolution of attacker 2 by defender 1 underscores the importance of timely responses in security operations. This rapid intervention effectively neutralizes the threat before it can progress further. Meanwhile, the prolonged engagement leading to the capture of attacker 1 highlights the complexities and challenges inherent in security patrolling and target defense.

With the apprehension of both attackers, the game reaches its conclusion. The successful outcomes achieved by the defenders validate the effectiveness of the patrol scheduling strategies implemented. Such realizations provide valuable insights for refining future security tactics, emphasizing the importance of adaptability and resource allocation in mitigating security risks effectively.

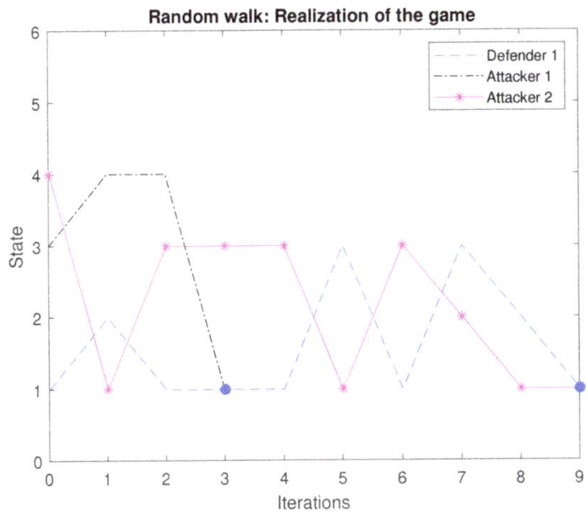

Figure 11. Game realization 2: the attackers are intercepted by defender 1 (blue).

7. Conclusions

This research introduces a novel mathematical framework that enhances security measures by integrating optimization techniques to mitigate existing risks while addressing real-time threats. The framework is based on a Bayesian–Markov Stackelberg game model, designed to capture adversarial interactions in security scenarios with incomplete information, where players have limited knowledge of each other's strategies.

A key feature of this approach is the use of an optimization strategy grounded in the proximal-gradient method, which significantly improves computational efficiency compared to traditional Bayesian–Markov Stackelberg solutions. By leveraging this method, the framework effectively reduces security risks associated with persistent threats. Notably, it incorporates a unique reinforcement learning algorithm that derives rewards from a prior Bayesian distribution. This contribution is particularly significant, as it integrates structured historical data into decision-making, enabling more adaptive and informed responses to evolving security threats.

The framework's practical effectiveness is demonstrated through numerical examples, showcasing its ability to utilize past information to guide present decisions. These results provide both theoretical insights and empirical evidence of its applicability in real-world security scenarios. Overall, this research presents a comprehensive security optimization approach that bridges the gap between mitigating existing risks and countering ongoing threats in real time. By combining advanced optimization techniques with an innovative reinforcement learning paradigm, this offers a promising avenue for strengthening security in complex, dynamic environments.

Looking ahead, several challenges remain. A key technical endeavor is the implementation of a game-theoretic approach using novel reinforcement learning methods, where capture conditions depend on states and incomplete information, enhancing the realism of patrolling schedules. Additionally, applying this methodology in fortification games and conducting controlled trials to evaluate player responses to game-theoretic scheduling in real-world settings represent significant challenges. These trials can yield valuable insights into the practical implications of game theory for strategic decision-making and scheduling in uncertain environments, ultimately ensuring more robust and adaptable security measures.

Funding: This research received no external funding.

Data Availability Statement: All data required for this article are included within this article, further inquiries can be directed to the corresponding author.

Conflicts of Interest: The author declares no conflicts of interest.

References

1. Trejo, K.K.; Clempner, J.B.; Poznyak, A.S. A Stackelberg security game with random strategies based on the extraproximal theoretic approach. *Eng. Appl. Artif. Intell.* **2015**, *37*, 145–153. [CrossRef]
2. Solis, C.U.; Clempner, J.B.; Poznyak, A.S. Modeling Multi-Leader-Follower Non-Cooperative Stackelberg Games. *Cybern. Syst.* **2016**, *47*, 650–673. [CrossRef]
3. Clempner, J.B.; Poznyak, A.S. A nucleus for Bayesian Partially Observable Markov Games: Joint observer and mechanism design. *Eng. Appl. Artif. Intell.* **2020**, *95*, 103876. [CrossRef]
4. Clempner, J.B.; Poznyak, A.S. *Optimization and Games for Controllable Markov Chains: Numerical Methods with Application to Finance and Engineering*; Springer: Cham, Switzerland, 2023.
5. Harsanyi, J.C.; Selten, R. A generalized Nash solution for two-person bargaining games with incomplete information. *Manag. Sci.* **1972**, *18*, 80–106. [CrossRef]
6. Conitzer, V.; Sandholm, T. Computing the Optimal Strategy to Commit to. In Proceedings of the 7th ACM Conference on Electronic Commerce, Ann Arbor, MI, USA, 11–15 June 2006; pp. 82–90.
7. Paruchuri, P.J.; Pearce, P.; Marecki, J.; Tambe, M.; Ordonez, F.; Kraus, S. Playing Games for Security: An Efficient Exact Algorithm for Solving Bayesian Stackelberg Games. In Proceedings of the 7th International Joint Conference on Autonomous Agents and Multiagent Systems, Estoril, Portugal, 12–16 May 2008; Volume 2, pp. 895–902.
8. Jain, M.; Kiekintveld, C.; Tambe, M. Quality-Bounded Solutions for Finite Bayesian Stackelberg Games: Scaling up. In Proceedings of the 10th International Conference on Autonomous Agents and Multiagent Systems, Taipei, Taiwan, 2–6 May 2011; Volume 3, pp. 997–1004.
9. Yin, Z.; Tambe, M. A Unified Method for Handling Discrete and Continuous Uncertainty in Bayesian Stackelberg Games. In Proceedings of the 11th International Conference on Autonomous Agents and Multiagent Systems, Valencia, Spain, 4–8 June 2012; Volume 2, pp. 855–862.
10. Wilczyński, A.; Jakóbik, A.; Kołodziej, J. Stackelberg Security Games: Models, Applications and Computational Aspects. *J. Telecomun. Inf. Technol.* **2016**, *3*, 70–79. [CrossRef]
11. Sayed Ahmed, I. Stackelberg-Based Anti-Jamming Game for Cooperative Cognitive Radio Networks. Ph.D. Thesis, University of Calgary, Calgary, AB, USA, 2017.
12. Gan, J.; Elkind, E.; Wooldridge, M. Stackelberg Security Games with Multiple Uncoordinated Defenders. In Proceedings of the 17th International Conference on Autonomous Agents and Multiagent Systems (AAMAS), Stockholm, Sweden, 10–15 July 2018; pp. 703–711.
13. Basilico, N.; Gatti, N.; Villa, F. Asynchronous multi-robot patrolling against in trusions in arbitrary topologies. In Proceedings of the Conference for the Advancement of Artificial Intelligence (AAAI), Atlanta, GA, USA, 11–15 July 2010; pp. 345–350.
14. Clempner, J.B. Learning attack-defense response in continuous-time discrete-states Stackelberg Security Markov games. *J. Exp. Theor. Artif. Intell.* **2022**, *to be published*. [CrossRef]
15. Albarran, S.; Clempner, J.B. A Stackelberg security Markov game based on partial information for strategic decision making against unexpected attacks. *Eng. Appl. Artif. Intell.* **2019**, *81*, 408–419. [CrossRef]
16. Trejo, K.K.; Clempner, J.B.; Poznyak, A.S. Adapting Attackers and Defenders Preferred Strategies: A Reinforcement Learning Approach in Stackelberg Security Games. *J. Comput. Syst. Sci.* **2018**, *95*, 35–54. [CrossRef]
17. Solis, C. Ship differential game approach for multiple players: Stackelberg security games. *Optim. Control Appl. Methods* **2020**, *41*, 312–326. [CrossRef]
18. Alcantara-Jiménez, G.; Clempner, J. Repeated Stackelberg security games: Learning with incomplete state information. *Reliab. Eng. Syst. Saf.* **2020**, *195*, 106695. [CrossRef]
19. Clempner, J.B.; Poznyak, A.S. Stackelberg Security Games: Computing The Shortest-Path Equilibrium. *Expert. Syst. Appl.* **2015**, *42*, 3967–3979. [CrossRef]
20. Rahman, M.; Oh, J. Online Learning for Patrolling Robots Against Active Adversarial Attackers. In *Proceedings of the Recent Trends and Future Technology in Applied Intelligence*; Lecture Notes in Computer Science; Mouhoub, M., Sadaoui, S., Ait Mohamed, O., Ali, M., Eds.; Springer: Montreal, QC, Canada, 2018; Volume 10868.
21. Wang, Y.; Shi, Z.; Yu, L.; Wu, Y.; Singh, R.; Joppa, L.; Fang, F. Deep Reinforcement Learning for Green Security Games with Real-Time Information. In Proceedings of the Thirty-Third AAAI Conference on Artificial Intelligence (AAAI-19), Honolulu, HI, USA, 27 January–1 February 2019; pp. 1401–1408.

22. Li, T.; Li, H.; Pan, Y.; Xu, T.; Zheng, Z.; Zhu, Q. Meta Stackelberg Game: Robust Federated Learning against Adaptive and Mixed Poisoning Attacks. *arXiv* **2024**, arXiv:2410.17431.
23. Sengupta, S.; Kambhampati, S. Multi-agent Reinforcement Learning in Bayesian Stackelberg Markov Games for Adaptive Moving Target Defense. *arXiv* **2020**, arXiv:2007.10457.
24. Shukla, P.; An, L.; Chakrabortty, A.; Duel-Hallen, A. A robust Stackelberg game for cyber-security investment in networked control systems. *IEEE Trans. Control Syst. Technol.* **2022**, *31*, 856–871. [CrossRef]
25. Clempner, J.B.; Poznyak, A.S. Analytical Method for Mechanism Design in Partially Observable Markov Games. *Mathematics* **2021**, *9*, 321. [CrossRef]
26. Clempner, J.B. A Markovian Stackelberg game approach for computing an optimal dynamic mechanism. *Comput. Appl. Math.* **2021**, *40*, 186. [CrossRef]
27. Asiain, E.; Clempner, J.B.; Poznyak, A.S. Controller Exploitation-Exploration: A Reinforcement Learning Architecture. *Soft Comput.* **2019**, *23*, 3591–3604. [CrossRef]
28. Benson, A.R.; Gleich, D.F.; Lim, L.K. The Spacey Random Walk: A Stochastic Process for Higher-Order Data. *SIAM Rev.* **2017**, *59*, 321–345. [CrossRef]

Mathematical and Computational Applications

MDPI

Article

A Family of Newton and Quasi-Newton Methods for Power Flow Analysis in Bipolar Direct Current Networks with Constant Power Loads

Oscar Danilo Montoya [1,*], Juan Diego Pulgarín Rivera [1], Luis Fernando Grisales-Noreña [2], Walter Gil-González [3] and Fabio Andrade-Rengifo [4]

1. Grupo de Compatibilidad e Interferencia Electromagnética, Facultad de Ingeniería, Universidad Distrital Francisco José de Caldas, Bogotá 110231, Colombia; jdpulgarinr@udistrital.edu.co
2. Grupo de Investigación en Alta Tensión-GRALTA, Escuela de Ingeniería Eléctrica y Electrónica, Universidad del Valle, Cali 760015, Colombia; grisales.luis@correounivalle.edu.co
3. Department of Electrical Engineering, Universidad Tecnológica de Pereira, Pereira 660003, Colombia; wjgil@utp.edu.co
4. Electrical and Computer Engineering Department, University of Puerto Rico, Mayagüez, PR 00680, USA; fabio.andrade@upr.edu

* Correspondence: odmontoyag@udistrital.edu.co

Abstract: This paper presents a comprehensive study on the formulation and solution of the power flow problem in bipolar direct current (DC) distribution networks with unbalanced constant power loads. Using the nodal voltage method, a unified nonlinear model is proposed which accurately captures both monopolar and bipolar load configurations as well as the voltage coupling between conductors. The model assumes a solid grounding of the neutral conductor and known system parameters, ensuring reproducibility and physical consistency. Seven iterative algorithms are developed and compared, including three Newton–Raphson-based formulations and four quasi-Newton methods with constant Jacobian approximations. The proposed techniques are validated on two benchmark networks comprising 21 and 85 buses. Numerical results demonstrate that Newton-based methods exhibit quadratic convergence and high accuracy, while quasi-Newton approaches significantly reduce computational time, making them more suitable for large-scale systems. The findings highlight the trade-offs between convergence speed and computational efficiency, and they provide valuable insights for the planning and operation of modern bipolar DC grids.

Keywords: bipolar DC networks; constant power loads; Newton–Raphson numerical methods; quasi-Newton numerical methods; power flow solution

1. Introduction

1.1. General Context

In recent years, direct current (DC) distribution networks have attracted significant attention due to their improved efficiency and better controllability, as well as technological advancements in power electronics [1,2]. Many distributed energy resources, such as photovoltaic (PV) panels, batteries, and electronic loads, inherently operate in DC, which reduces the need for extensive power conversion stages and improves the overall system performance [3]. These advantages position DC networks as a compelling alternative to conventional alternating current (AC) systems, especially at both high and low voltage levels [4,5]. While high-voltage DC systems are primarily used for long-distance transmission [6], low-voltage DC (LVDC) networks are being increasingly considered for urban and rural distribution systems [7]. Unlike AC systems, DC grids do not require synchronization and are immune to reactive power issues, which results in reduced power losses and enhanced voltage regulation across the network [8].

Within the domain of LVDC networks, bipolar configurations—comprising positive, negative, and neutral conductors—have emerged as a more efficient and flexible alternative to monopolar systems [9]. These networks offer greater reliability and improved fault tolerance while also enabling power sharing between conductors. Despite their advantages, the modeling and analysis of bipolar DC networks remain underdeveloped from the perspective of utilities. In particular, while considerable research has focused on dynamic aspects and converter-level control, the static analysis—specifically the power flow formulation—has received limited attention [10]. Accurate and efficient power flow models are crucial, as they serve as the foundation for planning, operation, and control tasks in electrical systems [11]. The development of robust power flow methods tailored to bipolar LVDC networks is essential to support their integration and widespread adoption in modern distribution systems [12].

1.2. Motivation

The reliable operation and planning of bipolar direct current (DC) distribution networks critically depend on the accurate solution of the power flow problem [13,14]. In these systems, the presence of constant power loads introduces strong nonlinearities due to the inverse voltage–current relationship, which leads to hyperbolic equations far more complex than those found in linear resistive models [15]. Moreover, the bipolar configuration—featuring positive, negative, and neutral conductors—adds another layer of complexity by coupling the voltages across poles and requiring a detailed representation of unbalanced load conditions [16]. These challenges make analytical solutions intractable, especially in large-scale networks with multiple load types and topological variations. Therefore, developing robust and efficient numerical methods is essential to ensure convergence, computational efficiency, and physical realism. Such methods are fundamental for enabling static analysis, voltage regulation, and loss minimization in modern DC grids [17], ultimately supporting the deployment of resilient and intelligent power distribution systems.

On the other hand, the asymmetry of the loads connected between the positive–neutral and negative–neutral poles gives rise to unbalanced conditions in bipolar DC networks, which complicates the power flow calculation [18]. The resulting neutral current induces voltage deviations between the positive and negative poles, meaning that traditional balanced assumptions commonly used in monopolar DC systems are no longer valid. Consequently, load flow analysis must explicitly account for the unbalanced nature of the network to accurately represent operating conditions and ensure reliable solutions.

1.3. Brief Literature Review

In the specialized literature, multiple authors have presented solution methodologies based on numerical methods to deal with the power flow and optimal power flow problems in bipolar DC networks with constant power loads. Some of the most representative algorithms are presented below.

The authors of [19] proposed an optimal power flow (OPF) formulation for bipolar DC microgrids based on a current injection model in order to fully capture the bipolar structure. This formulation employs the output current of distributed generators and pole voltages as decision variables, enabling the linearization of the power flow equations. The OPF minimizes generation costs, voltage imbalance, and network losses. Depending on system characteristics, the problem is modeled as a convex or nonconvex quadratic program. Numerical results demonstrated the method's effectiveness and low computational burden across various grid scenarios.

The work by [20] addressed the challenges of congestion and asymmetric loading in bipolar DC distribution grids by proposing an exact OPF formulation expressed in terms of voltage and current. This model accounts for the possibility of current flowing through the neutral conductor and supports arbitrary source/load connections between any pair of nodes. Unlike traditional DC models relying on a common ground assumption, the proposed formulation incorporates bilinear cost functions. Consequently, the computation of locational marginal prices (LMPs) is performed as a post-processing step. This approach enables a more accurate pricing mechanism under partial congestion scenarios in bipolar configurations.

In [13], a current injection-based power flow analysis and optimal generation dispatch approach for bipolar DC microgrids was proposed. This study highlighted that, despite voltage balancing at the converter level, significant imbalance can occur at distant buses. To address this issue, the authors developed a Newton–Raphson power flow method based on the static models of the grid components, including voltage balancers, sources, and loads. Furthermore, an optimization problem was formulated using voltage sensitivity derived from the Jacobian matrix to jointly minimize operation costs and voltage imbalance. Simulation results validated the accuracy of the method against PSCAD/EMTDC, demonstrating its effectiveness in steady-state analysis and optimal dispatch.

The study by [10] addressed the challenges of power losses and voltage imbalance in two-phase bipolar DC distribution networks, which rely on a neutral wire for improved efficiency. A power flow formulation based on single-line modeling and nodal analysis was proposed, enabling the system's steady-state representation. To optimize the placement of unipolar loads across the two poles, a binary integer load redistribution model was developed. This was integrated into a binary integer quadratic multi-objective optimization framework that minimizes both power losses and voltage imbalance. Using the weighted sum method, the problem was solved and validated through case studies involving 15- and 33-bus systems. The results demonstrated the proposal's superior performance in voltage balancing when compared to conventional iterative approaches.

The work by [21] proposed a Newton–Raphson-based power flow algorithm for bipolar DC microgrids which incorporates current injection modeling and considers grounding schemes and voltage control strategies. Six bus types were defined based on these characteristics, and unknown pole voltages were updated using a unified NR approach. The method achieved high accuracy compared to PSCAD/EMTDC simulations, with low computational effort.

The authors of [22] developed a power flow algorithm for bipolar DC networks that considers unbalanced loads and the presence of a neutral conductor, be it grounded or floating. The method uses a nodal admittance formulation and approximates the nonlinear load–voltage relations via a Taylor series expansion, resulting in a recursive solver with quadratic convergence. Numerical validations on 4-, 21-, and 85-bus systems demonstrated the method's accuracy and general applicability to radial and meshed topologies, outperforming the traditional successive approximations method.

In [11], the power flow problem for bipolar DC distribution networks with unbalanced constant power loads was addressed while considering two grounding scenarios for the neutral wire: solid grounding at each load point and grounding only at the substation. The problem was solved using the successive approximations method, which was shown to be equivalent to the backward/forward sweep in matrix form. Simulations on 4- and

25-node systems demonstrated the method's efficiency and suitability for both radial and meshed networks without the need for matrix inversion at each iteration.

The authors of [12] analyzed the power flow problem in radial bipolar DC networks with multiple monopolar and bipolar constant power loads while considering a non-grounded reference pole along the feeder. A triangular recursive formulation was proposed to iteratively compute node voltages, capturing the effects of neutral currents and voltage imbalances. The method exhibited linear convergence under varying load conditions, and numerical tests on 21- and 85-bus systems demonstrated significant differences in voltage profiles and power losses depending on the neutral grounding configuration.

The work by [23] addressed the limitations of conventional Newton methods for power flow analysis when the current protection of converters introduces a non-differentiable behavior. To overcome this issue, the authors proposed a derivative-free fixed-point iterative method capable of handling the saturation effects imposed by converter current limits. The convergence and uniqueness of the solution were rigorously proven using Banach's fixed-point theorem. Numerical experiments in MATLAB supported the theoretical results and confirmed the method's effectiveness.

The authors of [24] proposed a graphical interface to solve the power flow problem in unbalanced bipolar DC networks using the successive approximations method. This interface was developed to assist users without programming skills in performing power flow analysis. The study included the formulation of the mathematical model, the implementation of the interface, and its validation using benchmark networks. Numerical results confirmed the accuracy of the proposed tool, matching previously reported solutions with 100% reliability.

The contributions reviewed above constitute a diverse set of methodologies for solving the power flow and OPF problems in bipolar DC networks with constant power loads, wherein Newton–Raphson-based methods have been shown to be accurate and computationally efficient, especially when formulated using current injection models and adapted to different grounding schemes, and recursive formulations based on Taylor or hyperbolic approximations enable quadratic convergence and general applicability to both radial and meshed topologies. Additionally, several works addressed optimization aspects, such as the minimization of generation costs, voltage imbalance, and power losses, using convex or nonconvex quadratic programming. Triangular iterative solvers and fixed-point methods have been proposed to handle the non-differentiable behaviors introduced by converter protection mechanisms. Moreover, graphical tools have been developed to enhance accessibility for non-programmers, confirming the practical applicability of the proposed methods. Overall, the literature demonstrates the robustness and versatility of numerical techniques for analyzing and optimizing bipolar DC grids.

Despite these valuable contributions, there are still several limitations that remain unaddressed. Most of the existing methods rely on specific Jacobian approximations or case-dependent linearizations without analyzing structural implications on convergence and conditioning. In addition, few works explore generalized frameworks that simultaneously account for monopolar and bipolar load configurations, and even fewer provide a systematic comparison of exact vs. approximated Jacobian formulations. Moreover, the computational trade-offs between accuracy, convergence speed, and matrix conditioning are rarely discussed in depth. This article addresses these gaps by proposing a family of Newton and quasi-Newton methods specifically designed for bipolar DC networks, supported by a convergence analysis and numerical validations that highlight the structural impact of the Jacobian on performance.

1.4. Contributions

This article proposes a general model for the power flow analysis in bipolar DC grids. Its contributions are twofold:

- A unified power flow formulation for bipolar DC networks that considers monopolar and bipolar constant power loads. This model captures the nonlinear relationship between voltage and current via a generalized expression that integrates the effects of solidly grounded neutral wires. This formulation is suitable for both radial and meshed topologies and serves as the basis for Newton and quasi-Newton iterative solvers.
- A comparative study of multiple Newton and quasi-Newton power flow methods applied to two benchmark networks comprising 21 and 85 buses. The proposed methods demonstrate fast convergence and computational efficiency, with the Newton-based algorithms exhibiting quadratic convergence and the quasi-Newton methods offering lower computational costs through constant Jacobian approximations.

Within the scope of this research, it is assumed that the neutral wire is solidly grounded at every node of the bipolar DC distribution network. Furthermore, the systems under study do not include additional voltage-controlled nodes beyond the slack bus. The analysis also considers that all the parametric information of the test systems—such as constant power loads and line resistances—is fully known and accurately specified, ensuring a well-defined and reproducible evaluation of the proposed power flow methodologies.

Note that the free software studied in this research allows electrical engineering students and researchers to validate the proposed analysis on bipolar power flow methods by using the software and contact information provided in Table 1.

Table 1. Code metadata.

Current code version	V1.0
Permanent link to code/repository used for this code version	https://github.com/odmontoya/Newton-Raphson-Family-Bipolar-DC-Networks, accessed on 4 May 2025
Legal code license	MIT License
Code versioning system used	Git
Programming languages, tools, and libraries used	MATLAB R2024b
Compilation requirements and runtime environment	MATLAB (any OS with MATLAB R2024b or later)
Contact email for support	odmontoyag@udistrital.edu.co, accessed on 4 May 2025

A key contribution of this work is the development of a unified formulation that integrates multiple modeling approaches within a single mathematical framework. This formulation enables the simultaneous treatment of various system components and constraints that were previously addressed in a fragmented manner in the literature. By consolidating these aspects, the proposed framework enhances the consistency, generality, and computational efficiency of the analysis and optimization process. This unified approach not only simplifies implementation but also provides a foundation for extending the methodology to accommodate emerging technologies and operational scenarios, thereby broadening the applicability and impact of the proposed solution.

1.5. Article Structure

The remainder of this document is organized as follows: Section 2 introduces the general formulation of the power flow problem for bipolar DC grids, incorporating constant power terminals and unbalanced load conditions through the classical nodal voltage method. This formulation leads to a generalized nonlinear power flow equation. Section 3 provides the theoretical background of the Newton–Raphson method and details the seven proposed solution strategies—three based on Newton–Raphson algorithms and four based on quasi-Newton approximations. Section 4 describes the main features of the test systems used (i.e., 21- and 85-bus bipolar DC distribution networks). Section 5 presents the numerical results obtained, including average processing times, calculated power losses, and voltage profile behaviors, as well as a convergence analysis through graphical representation. Finally, Section 6 summarizes the main conclusions of this study and outlines potential directions for future research.

2. Power Flow Formulation for Bipolar DC Networks

In this section, all matrices are denoted using bold uppercase symbols, while subscripts and superscripts are used to indicate nodes and iteration indices, respectively.

The formulation of the power flow problem for bipolar DC distribution networks is based on the nodal admittance representation, specifically employing the branch-to-node admittance matrix approach as introduced in [8]. The fundamental relationship between nodal voltages and injected currents is captured by the admittance matrix, as detailed in Equation (1). For more details, see [25] [Cap. 4].

$$\begin{bmatrix} \mathbf{I}_s \\ -\mathbf{I}_d \end{bmatrix} = \begin{bmatrix} \mathbf{G}_{ss} & \mathbf{G}_{sd} \\ \mathbf{G}_{ds} & \mathbf{G}_{dd} \end{bmatrix} \begin{bmatrix} \mathbf{V}_s \\ \mathbf{V}_d \end{bmatrix}, \tag{1}$$

In this formulation, the vector $\mathbf{I}_s$ represents the current injections at the positive and negative poles of the voltage-controlled nodes, while $\mathbf{I}_d$ denotes the currents drawn by the loads connected to both poles of the bipolar DC network. The admittance matrix $\mathbf{G}_{pn}$ is partitioned into four submatrices: $\mathbf{G}_{ss}$, $\mathbf{G}_{sd}$, $\mathbf{G}_{ds}$, and $\mathbf{G}_{dd}$, each describing the electrical relationships between source and demand nodes within the system. The vector $\mathbf{V}_s$ contains the voltages imposed by the controlled sources, while $\mathbf{V}_d$ comprises the voltage variables associated with the demand-side nodes.

It is important to note that the sign conventions applied to the second row of the current expressions for the demand nodes reflects the direction of current flow: a positive net current indicates inflow at a node, whereas a negative value corresponds to an outflow due to the presence of loads.

2.1. General Power Flow Formula

A general expression for the power flow solution can be derived by manipulating the second row of Equation (1) to isolate the vector $\mathbf{V}_{d,pn}$, which represents the voltages at the demand nodes [11]. This procedure enables the explicit calculation of these voltages, as described in [26]:

$$\mathbf{G}_{dd}\mathbf{V}_d + \mathbf{G}_{ds}\mathbf{V}_s + \mathbf{I}_d = 0 \tag{2}$$

2.2. Demanded Current Calculation

One of the main challenges in solving the power flow equations of bipolar DC networks arises from the nonlinear, hyperbolic relationship between nodal voltages and constant power demands [11]. This section outlines the way in which the current associated with the constant power loads is computed, both when they are connected between a single pole (positive or negative) and the ground, and when the connection spans between both poles.

For a given node k where loads are individually connected between each pole and the ground, the corresponding current injections are calculated using Equations (3) and (4) [22]:

$$I_{dk,p} = \frac{P_{dk,p}}{V_{dk,p}}, \tag{3}$$

$$I_{dk,n} = \frac{P_{dk,n}}{V_{dk,n}}, \tag{4}$$

where $I_{dk,p}$ and $I_{dk,n}$ represent the currents injected at time t into the positive and negative poles, respectively; the terms $P_{dk,p}$ and $P_{dk,n}$ denote the constant power demand associated with each pole; and $V_{dk,p}$ and $V_{dk,n}$ are the corresponding voltage magnitudes.

If each node in the system is exclusively equipped with loads connected between either pole and the neutral point, the current demand expressions in Equations (3) and (4) can be generalized into a compact matrix form [11]:

$$\mathbf{I}_{dk,pn} = \text{diag}^{-1}(\mathbf{V}_{dk,pn})\mathbf{P}_{dk,pn}, \tag{5}$$

where $\mathbf{P}_{dk,pn}$ is a vector containing the constant power consumption associated with each pole at node k; the vector $\mathbf{I}_{dk,pn}$ represents the corresponding current demands during iteration t; and $\mathbf{V}_{dk,pn}$ includes the positive and negative voltage values at node k for the same iteration.

In scenarios where a load is connected between the positive and negative poles at a given node k, the associated current injections can be expressed as follows:

$$I_{dk,p} = \frac{P_{dk,pn}}{V_{dk,p} - V_{dk,n}}, \tag{6}$$

$$I_{dk,n} = \frac{P_{dk,pn}}{V_{dk,n} - V_{dk,p}}, \tag{7}$$

where $P_{dk,pn}$ denotes the constant power load connected between the two poles.

When all constant power loads in the system are exclusively configured between poles, the above expressions can be generalized into the compact matrix form shown below [12]:

$$\mathbf{I}_{dk,pn} = \text{diag}^{-1}(\mathbf{H}\mathbf{V}_{d,pn})\mathbf{P}_{dk,pn}, \tag{8}$$

with matrix $\mathbf{H}$ defined as follows:

$$\mathbf{H} = \begin{bmatrix} 1 & -1 \\ -1 & 1 \end{bmatrix}. \tag{9}$$

This formulation captures the voltage difference between poles and applies it consistently to compute the corresponding line-to-line current demands.

Remark 1. *When a node includes both line-to-ground and line-to-line constant power loads, its total current demand corresponds to the algebraic sum of the individual contributions [22]. Specifically, the total current in each pole is obtained by summing the line-to-ground current components given in Equations* (6) *and* (7) *with the line-to-line components expressed in Equation* (8).

Note that, in order to obtain the general power flow formula (see Equation (2)) solely as a function of the demanded voltage vector $\mathbf{V}_d$, the demanded currents $\mathbf{I}_d$ for monopolar and bipolar DC loads presented in Equations (6) and (10) can be generalized as follows:

$$\mathbf{I}_d = \text{diag}^{-1}(\mathbf{V}_d)\mathbf{P}_{dm} + \text{diag}^{-1}(\mathbf{M}\mathbf{V}_d)\mathbf{P}_{db}, \tag{10}$$

where $\mathbf{M}$ is a matrix composed of the submatrices H in its diagonal, i.e.,

$$\mathbf{M} = \begin{bmatrix} \mathbf{H} & 0_{2\times 2} & \cdots & 0_{2\times 2} \\ 0_{2\times 2} & \mathbf{H} & \cdots & 0_{2\times 2} \\ \vdots & \ddots & \ddots & \vdots \\ 0_{2\times 2} & 0_{2\times 2} & \cdots & \mathbf{H} \end{bmatrix}; \quad (11)$$

where $\mathbf{P}_{dm}$ and $\mathbf{P}_{db}$ are vectors containing monopolar and bipolar constant power loads ordered by node; and $\mathbf{0}_{2\times 2}$ denotes a 2×2 zero matrix.

Considering the definitions in (10) and (11), the general power flow formula in (2) takes the following form:

$$\mathbf{F}(\mathbf{V}_d) = \mathbf{G}_{dd}\mathbf{V}_d + \mathbf{G}_{ds}\mathbf{V}_s + \text{diag}^{-1}(\mathbf{V}_d)\mathbf{P}_{dm} + \text{diag}^{-1}(\mathbf{M}\mathbf{V}_d)\mathbf{P}_{db} = 0. \quad (12)$$

Remark 2. *It is worth noting that the second row of Equation* (12) *captures the relationship between the current demands and the corresponding voltage variables at the load nodes. Due to the nonlinear nature of this expression, its solution typically requires the use of an iterative numerical method.*

3. Theoretical Background and Power Flow Formulations

This section presents the theoretical foundations and convergence analysis of the Newton–Raphson and quasi-Newton methods applied to the solution of nonlinear power flow problems for bipolar DC distribution networks. These networks may include multiple monopolar and bipolar constant power terminals. The methods considered rely on successive approximations derived from Taylor series expansions to iteratively solve the vector-valued nonlinear system of equations.

3.1. Multivariate Formulation and Taylor Expansion

Consider a nonlinear system of equations given by $\mathbf{F}(\mathbf{x}) = \mathbf{0}$, where $\mathbf{F} : \mathbb{R}^n \to \mathbb{R}^n$ is a continuously differentiable vector-valued function and $\mathbf{x} \in \mathbb{R}^n$ is the vector of unknowns [27]. To derive the Newton–Raphson method, one starts with the multivariable Taylor series expansion of $\mathbf{F}(\mathbf{x})$ around a point $\mathbf{x}_k$ [28]:

$$\mathbf{F}(\mathbf{x}) \approx \mathbf{F}(\mathbf{x}_k) + \mathbf{J}(\mathbf{x}_k)(\mathbf{x} - \mathbf{x}_k) + \mathbf{O}(\|\mathbf{x} - \mathbf{x}_k\|^2), \quad (13)$$

where $\mathbf{J}(\mathbf{x}_k)$ denotes the Jacobian matrix of partial derivatives evaluated at $\mathbf{x}_k$. Neglecting higher-order terms and setting $\mathbf{F}(\mathbf{x}_{k+1}) = \mathbf{0}$ yields the following Newton–Raphson iteration formula:

$$\mathbf{x}_{k+1} = \mathbf{x}_k - \mathbf{J}^{-1}(\mathbf{x}_k)\mathbf{F}(\mathbf{x}_k). \quad (14)$$

This iterative method is known for its quadratic convergence when the Jacobian is nonsingular and the initial guess is sufficiently close to the solution [29]. In practical applications, particularly in large-scale systems such as DC networks, the burden associated with computing and inverting the Jacobian motivates the use of quasi-Newton methods [12]. These approaches iteratively update an approximation of the Jacobian (or its inverse), thus reducing computational complexity while retaining favorable convergence properties.

3.2. Newton–Raphson Bipolar Power Flow Formulations

This subsection presents three alternative formulations to solve the bipolar DC power flow problem. Each formulation rewrites the general nodal equations to model constant power terminals under different configurations, enabling the use of Newton–Raphson-based iterative methods.

3.2.1. First Newton–Raphson Formulation

To obtain the generic Newton–Raphson iterative approach, Equation (12) is rewritten as follows:

$$\mathbf{F}_1(\mathbf{V}_d) = \mathbf{G}_{dd}\mathbf{V}_d + \mathbf{G}_{ds}\mathbf{V}_s + \mathrm{diag}^{-1}(\mathbf{V}_d)\mathbf{P}_{dm} + \mathrm{diag}^{-1}(\mathbf{M}\mathbf{V}_d)\mathbf{P}_{db} = \mathbf{0}. \tag{15}$$

The Jacobian matrix is given by

$$\mathbf{J}_{\mathbf{F}_1}(\mathbf{V}_d) = \mathbf{G}_{dd} - \mathrm{diag}^{-2}(\mathbf{V}_d)\mathrm{diag}(\mathbf{P}_{dm}) - \mathrm{diag}^{-2}(\mathbf{M}\mathbf{V}_d)\mathrm{diag}(\mathbf{P}_{db})\mathbf{M}, \tag{16}$$

which implies that the iterative formula for the first Newton–Raphson method (NRM1) takes the following structure:

The Newton–Raphson update is

$$\mathbf{V}_d^{k+1} = \mathbf{V}_d^k - \left[\mathbf{J}_{\mathbf{F}_1}(\mathbf{V}_d^k)\right]^{-1}\mathbf{F}_1(\mathbf{V}_d^k), \tag{17}$$

which is repeated until $\|\mathbf{V}_d^{k+1} - \mathbf{V}_d^k\|_\infty \leq \epsilon$.

3.2.2. Second Newton–Raphson Formulation

This formulation simplifies Equation (12), pre-multiplying it by $\mathrm{diag}(\mathbf{V}_d)$ in order to reduce the computational complexity of the Jacobian evaluation and solution process, thereby enabling faster iterations. However, it may also impact convergence speed and robustness. Its inclusion allows for a comparative analysis between structural simplification and numerical performance in practical scenarios. This formulation includes the following set of nonlinear equations:

$$\mathbf{F}_2(\mathbf{V}_d) = \mathrm{diag}(\mathbf{V}_d)\left(\mathbf{G}_{dd}\mathbf{V}_d + \mathbf{G}_{ds}\mathbf{V}_s + \mathrm{diag}^{-1}(\mathbf{M}\mathbf{V}_d)\mathbf{P}_{db}\right) + \mathbf{P}_{dm} = \mathbf{0}. \tag{18}$$

$$\mathbf{g}(\mathbf{V}_d) = \mathbf{G}_{dd}\mathbf{V}_d + \mathbf{G}_{ds}\mathbf{V}_s + \mathrm{diag}^{-1}(\mathbf{M}\mathbf{V}_d)\mathbf{P}_{db}, \tag{19}$$

yields the Jacobian as follows:

$$\mathbf{J}_{\mathbf{F}_2}(\mathbf{V}_d) = \mathrm{diag}(\mathbf{g}(\mathbf{V}_d)) + \mathrm{diag}(\mathbf{V}_d)\left[\mathbf{G}_{dd} - \mathrm{diag}^{-2}(\mathbf{M}\mathbf{V}_d)\mathrm{diag}(\mathbf{P}_{db})\mathbf{M}\right]. \tag{20}$$

The iterative formula is

$$\mathbf{V}_d^{k+1} = \mathbf{V}_d^k - \left[\mathbf{J}_{\mathbf{F}_2}(\mathbf{V}_d^k)\right]^{-1}\mathbf{F}_2(\mathbf{V}_d^k). \tag{21}$$

3.2.3. Third Newton–Raphson Formulation

This formulation seeks to introduce a more aggressive decoupling in the Jacobian formulation by pre-multiplying Equation (12) by $\mathrm{diag}(\mathbf{M}\mathbf{V}_d)$. This variant has shown potential for implementation in modularized solvers; while it could sacrifice accuracy in the representation of coupling effects, it significantly simplifies the algebraic structure. Its formulation takes the following form:

$$\mathbf{F}_3(\mathbf{V}_d) = \mathrm{diag}(\mathbf{M}\mathbf{V}_d)\left(\mathbf{G}_{dd}\mathbf{V}_d + \mathbf{G}_{ds}\mathbf{V}_s + \mathrm{diag}^{-1}(\mathbf{V}_d)\mathbf{P}_{dm}\right) + \mathbf{P}_{db} = \mathbf{0}. \tag{22}$$

With

$$\mathbf{g}(\mathbf{V}_d) = \mathbf{G}_{dd}\mathbf{V}_d + \mathbf{G}_{ds}\mathbf{V}_s + \text{diag}^{-1}(\mathbf{V}_d)\mathbf{P}_{dm}, \tag{23}$$

the Jacobian is

$$\mathbf{J}_{\mathbf{F}_3}(\mathbf{V}_d) = \text{diag}(\mathbf{g}(\mathbf{V}_d))\mathbf{M} + \text{diag}(\mathbf{M}\mathbf{V}_d)\left[\mathbf{G}_{dd} - \text{diag}^{-2}(\mathbf{V}_d)\text{diag}(\mathbf{P}_{dm})\right]. \tag{24}$$

The update step takes the following form:

$$\mathbf{V}_d^{k+1} = \mathbf{V}_d^k - \left[\mathbf{J}_{\mathbf{F}_3}(\mathbf{V}_d^k)\right]^{-1}\mathbf{F}_3(\mathbf{V}_d^k). \tag{25}$$

Each formulation provides a structurally distinct approach for modeling bipolar DC systems while retaining compatibility with the Newton–Raphson method. The selection of one such formulation may impact convergence behavior and numerical stability depending on system topology and loading conditions.

Remark 3. *The Newton–Raphson-based power flow formulations presented above are not unique. Several alternative expressions can be derived from the General Nodal Power Flow Equation* (12)*, depending on how the nonlinear terms are manipulated. This flexibility allows developing additional iterative algorithms tailored to specific network configurations or numerical properties.*

3.3. Quasi-Newton Methods with Constant Jacobians

To reduce the computational cost associated with evaluating and inverting the Jacobian matrix at each iteration of the Newton–Raphson method, a quasi-Newton strategy can be adopted. This strategy assumes a constant Jacobian matrix $\mathbf{A}_{01}$, evaluated at the initial guess $\mathbf{V}_d^0$ and used throughout all iterations. This approximation avoids the repeated computation of derivatives and matrix inversions, thus simplifying the numerical implementation while maintaining acceptable accuracy in most practical cases.

For a given formulation $\mathbf{F}_i(\mathbf{V}_d)$, the quasi-Newton iteration is

$$\mathbf{V}_d^{k+1} = \mathbf{V}_d^k - \mathbf{A}_{0i}^{-1}\mathbf{F}_i(\mathbf{V}_d^k), \tag{26}$$

where $\mathbf{A}_{0i} = \mathbf{J}_{\mathbf{F}_i}(\mathbf{V}_d^0)$ is the Jacobian evaluated once at the initial voltage vector $\mathbf{V}_d^0$ and kept constant for all iterations $k \geq 0$.

This method is particularly beneficial when the initial condition $\mathbf{V}_d^0$ is close to the solution or when the nonlinearities of the problem are mild. Despite sacrificing quadratic convergence, this approach often results in significantly faster computation.

3.4. Quasi-Newton Formulations

The following expressions represent the constant Jacobian matrices $\mathbf{A}_{0i}$ evaluated at the initial guess $\mathbf{V}_d^0$, which correspond to each quasi-Newton method and are explained below.

3.4.1. First Quasi-Newton Method

This quasi-Newton algorithm is obtained when $\mathbf{J}_{\mathbf{F}_1}(\mathbf{V}_d)$ is evaluated at the initial guess $\mathbf{V}_d^0$, i.e.,

$$\mathbf{A}_{01} = \mathbf{J}_{\mathbf{F}_1}(\mathbf{V}_d^0) = \mathbf{G}_{dd} - \text{diag}^{-2}(\mathbf{V}_d^0)\text{diag}(\mathbf{P}_{dm}) - \text{diag}^{-2}(\mathbf{M}\mathbf{V}_d^0)\text{diag}(\mathbf{P}_{db})\mathbf{M}, \tag{27}$$

which produces the following iterative formula:

$$\mathbf{V}_d^{k+1} = \mathbf{V}_d^k - \mathbf{A}_{01}^{-1}\mathbf{F}_1(\mathbf{V}_d^k). \tag{28}$$

3.4.2. Second Quasi-Newton Method

This quasi-Newton method is derived from the second Newton formulation by fixing the simplified Jacobian and using it across all iterations, following a quasi-Newton update scheme. The objective of including this formulation is to analyze the impact of reusing a simplified Jacobian on convergence behavior and the iteration count, particularly in networks with low dynamic variability or when computational resources are limited. The formulation of second quasi-Newton approximation is obtained when $\mathbf{J}_{\mathbf{F}_2}(\mathbf{V}_d)$ is evaluated at the initial guess $\mathbf{V}_d^0$, i.e.,

$$\begin{aligned}\mathbf{A}_{02} = \mathbf{J}_{\mathbf{F}_2}(\mathbf{V}_d^0) =& \operatorname{diag}\left(\mathbf{G}_{dd}\mathbf{V}_d^0 + \mathbf{G}_{ds}\mathbf{V}_s + \operatorname{diag}^{-1}(\mathbf{M}\mathbf{V}_d^0)\mathbf{P}_{db}\right) \\ &+ \operatorname{diag}(\mathbf{V}_d^0)\left[\mathbf{G}_{dd} - \operatorname{diag}^{-2}(\mathbf{M}\mathbf{V}_d^0)\operatorname{diag}(\mathbf{P}_{db})\mathbf{M},\right]\end{aligned} \tag{29}$$

which yields the following iterative formula:

$$\mathbf{V}_d^{k+1} = \mathbf{V}_d^k - \mathbf{A}_{02}^{-1}\mathbf{F}_2(\mathbf{V}_d^k), \tag{30}$$

3.4.3. Third Quasi-Newton Method

The third quasi-Newton approach extends the decoupling strategy of the third Newton formulation into the quasi-Newton framework. This is the most computationally lightweight variant among the proposed methods. Although it could provide slower convergence due to the strong approximation of the Jacobian structure, its inclusion is relevant for illustrating the lower performance bound when computational simplicity is prioritized over accuracy. The formulation of the second quasi-Newton approximation is reached by evaluating $\mathbf{V}_d^0$ in $\mathbf{J}_{\mathbf{F}_3}(\mathbf{V}_d)$ at the initial guess, i.e.,

$$\begin{aligned}\mathbf{A}_{03} =& \operatorname{diag}\left(\mathbf{G}_{dd}\mathbf{V}_d^0 + \mathbf{G}_{ds}\mathbf{V}_s + \operatorname{diag}^{-1}(\mathbf{V}_d^0)\mathbf{P}_{dm}\right)\mathbf{M} \\ &+ \operatorname{diag}(\mathbf{M}\mathbf{V}_d^0)\left[\mathbf{G}_{dd} - \operatorname{diag}^{-2}(\mathbf{V}_d^0)\operatorname{diag}(\mathbf{P}_{dm})\right],\end{aligned} \tag{31}$$

which generates the following iterative power flow formula:

$$\mathbf{V}_d^{k+1} = \mathbf{V}_d^k - \mathbf{A}_{03}^{-1}\mathbf{F}_4(\mathbf{V}_d^k). \tag{32}$$

3.4.4. Fourth Quasi-Newton Method

The fourth quasi-Newton formulation approximates $\mathbf{J}_{\mathbf{F}_3}(\mathbf{V}_d)$ by simplifying it as a constant matrix without evaluating the initial guess, i.e.,

$$\mathbf{A}_{04} = \mathbf{G}_{dd}, \tag{33}$$

which yields the following iterative power flow formula:

$$\mathbf{V}_d^{k+1} = \mathbf{V}_d^k - \mathbf{A}_{04}^{-1}\mathbf{F}_1(\mathbf{V}_d^k). \tag{34}$$

Remark 4. *This quasi-Newton algorithm, i.e., the Iterative Formula* (34)*, corresponds to the fixed-point formulation (the successive approximations power flow method) reported by the authors of [11], which ensures convergence by applying the Banach fixed-point theorem.*

Note that, for all the possible approximations of the Jacobian matrices, the iterative procedure is repeated until the convergence criterion is met, i.e., $\|\mathbf{V}_d^{k+1} - \mathbf{V}_d^k\|_\infty \leq \epsilon$.

3.5. Solution Procedure

For a better understanding of the proposed power flow solutions, Algorithm 1 summarizes the main steps involved in solving the power flow problem for bipolar DC networks using both Newton and quasi-Newton methods. The general procedure consists of iteratively solving a linearized system of equations, based on either the exact Jacobian or an approximate version, until the convergence criteria are satisfied. The structure of the algorithm is sufficiently general to encompass the different variants of the Newton and quasi-Newton formulations analyzed in this work.

Algorithm 1 Newton and quasi-Newton power flow solver for bipolar DC networks.

```
Input: Network data, load parameters, tolerance ϵ, maximum iterations k_max
Initialize voltage estimates v^(0)
Set iteration counter k ← 0
while ||V_d^{k+1} − V_d^k||_∞ ≤ ϵ or k ≥ k_max do
    Compute the mismatch vector F(V_d^(k))
    Evaluate or approximate the Jacobian matrix J(V_d^(k)), e.g., using Equation (16) for the
    first Newton–Raphson formulation, Equation (20) for the second Newton–Raphson for-
    mulation, Equation (22) for the third Newton–Raphson formulation, or Equations (27),
    (29), and (31), or (33) for the quasi-Newton methods.
    Update voltages: V_d^(k+1) = V_d^(k) − J(V_d^(k))^{−1} F(V_d^(k))
    Update iteration counter: k ← k + 1
end while
Output: Final voltage vector v^(k)
```

Remark 5. *In Algorithm 1, for the Newton methods, the Jacobian is updated at each iteration, whereas, in the quasi-Newton methods, the Jacobian is kept constant or approximated using specific strategies.*

4. Test Feeder Characteristics

To assess the performance and applicability of the proposed power flow methodology for bipolar DC networks, two test systems were considered. The first was a 21-bus medium-voltage distribution network originally developed for balanced conditions and adapted in this study to incorporate unbalanced line-to-ground loads [11], and the second was a bipolar 85-bus network, which included a greater number of nodes and more complex load arrangements [22]. In both cases, the slack buses operated symmetrically with voltages of ± 1 kV and ± 11 kV, respectively. The electrical configurations and parametric data for each system are provided to support the numerical validation.

4.1. The 21-Bus Grid

To evaluate the computational performance of the proposed power flow methodology for asymmetric bipolar DC networks, a modified test system was employed. This network consisted of 21 nodes and 20 constant power loads and was initially designed for balanced DC power flow analysis [26]. In this study, the test system was adapted to incorporate unbalanced line-to-ground loads, enabling the assessment of the method under asymmetric operating conditions. The electrical layout of the adapted feeder is depicted in Figure 1.

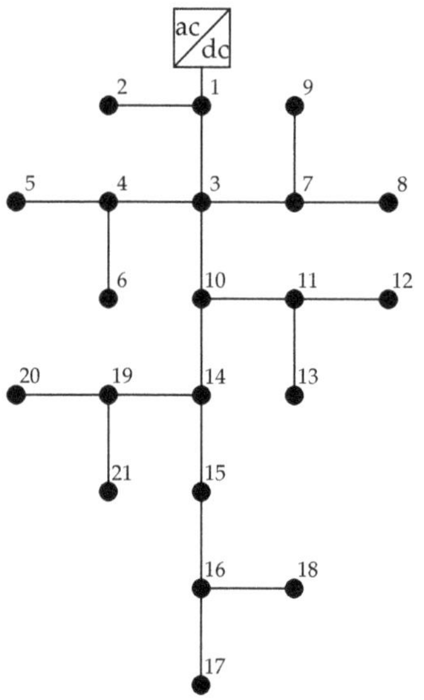

Figure 1. Schematic nodal configuration of the 21-bus DC bipolar grid.

In this 21-bus test system, the slack bus operates symmetrically with voltage levels of ±1 kV on the positive and negative poles. The corresponding electrical parameters of the feeder are detailed in Table 2.

Table 2. Parametric information regarding lines and loads for the 21-bus system.

Node j	Node k	R_{jk} (Ω)	$P_{dk,po}$ (kW)	$P_{dk,no}$ (kW)	$P_{dk,pn}$ (kW)	Node j	Node k	R_{jk} (Ω)	$P_{dk,po}$ (kW)	$P_{dk,no}$ (kW)	$P_{dk,pn}$ (kW)
1	2	0.053	70	100	0	11	12	0.079	68	70	0
1	3	0.054	0	0	0	11	13	0.078	10	0	75
3	4	0.054	36	40	120	10	14	0.083	0	0	0
4	5	0.063	4	0	0	14	15	0.065	22	30	0
4	6	0.051	36	0	0	15	16	0.064	23	10	0
3	7	0.037	0	0	0	16	17	0.074	43	0	60
7	8	0.079	32	50	0	16	18	0.081	34	60	0
7	9	0.072	80	0	100	14	19	0.078	9	15	0
3	10	0.053	0	10	0	19	20	0.084	21	10	50
10	11	0.038	45	30	0	19	21	0.082	21	20	0

4.2. The 85-Bus Grid

The 85-bus test system used in this study corresponds to the bipolar DC adaptation presented by the authors of [22]. In this configuration, the substation is positioned at node 1, supplying voltages of ±11 kV to the positive and negative poles, respectively, while maintaining the neutral point at 0 V. The electrical layout of the adapted 85-bus bipolar network is illustrated in Figure 2.

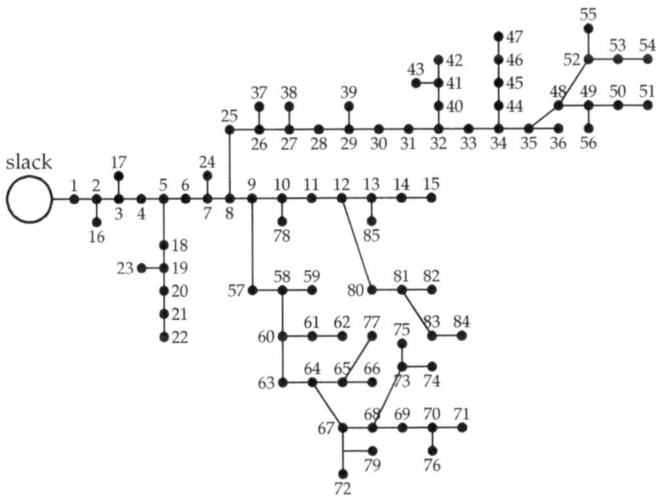

Figure 2. Schematic nodal configuration of the 85-bus DC bipolar grid.

The branch and load parameters associated with this test feeder are provided in Table 3.

Table 3. Parametric information regarding lines and loads for the 85-bus system.

Node j	Node k	R_{jk} (Ω)	$P_{dk,po}$ (kW)	$P_{dk,no}$ (kW)	$P_{dk,pn}$ (kW)	Node j	Node k	R_{jk} (Ω)	$P_{dk,po}$ (kW)	$P_{dk,no}$ (kW)	$P_{dk,pn}$ (kW)	Node j	Node k	R_{jk} (Ω)	$P_{dk,po}$ (kW)	$P_{dk,no}$ (kW)	$P_{dk,pn}$ (kW)
1	2	0.108	0	0	10.075	20	21	0.819	17.64	70	152.5	40	41	1.002	10	0	0
2	3	0.163	50	0	40.35	21	22	1.548	17.64	17.995	30	41	42	0.273	17.64	25	17.995
3	4	0.217	28	28.565	0	19	23	0.182	28	75	28.565	41	43	0.455	17.64	17.995	0
4	5	0.108	100	50	0	7	24	0.910	0	17.64	17.995	34	44	1.002	17.64	17.995	0
5	6	0.435	17.64	17.995	25.18	8	25	0.455	17.64	17.995	50	44	45	0.911	50	17.64	17.995
6	7	0.272	0	8.625	0	25	26	0.364	0	28	28.565	45	46	0.911	25	17.64	17.995
7	8	1.197	17.64	17.995	30.29	26	27	0.546	110	75	175	46	47	0.546	7	7.14	10
8	9	0.108	17.8	350	40.46	27	28	0.273	28	125	28.565	35	48	0.637	0	10	0
9	10	0.598	0	100	0	28	29	0.546	0	50	75	48	49	0.182	0	0	25
10	11	0.544	28	28.565	0	29	30	0.546	17.64	0	17.995	49	50	0.364	18.14	0	18.505
11	12	0.544	0	40	45	30	31	0.273	17.64	17.995	0	50	51	0.455	28	28.565	0
12	13	0.598	45	40	22.5	31	32	0.182	0	175	0	48	52	1.366	30	0	15
13	14	0.272	17.64	17.995	35.13	32	33	0.182	7	7.14	12.5	52	53	0.455	17.64	35	17.995
14	15	0.326	17.64	17.995	20.175	33	34	0.819	0	0	0	53	54	0.546	28	30	28.565
2	16	0.728	17.64	67.5	33.49	34	35	0.637	0	0	50	52	55	0.546	38	0	48.565
3	17	0.455	56.1	57.15	50.25	35	36	0.182	17.64	0	17.995	49	56	0.546	7	40	32.14
5	18	0.820	28	28.565	200	26	37	0.364	28	30	28.565	9	57	0.273	48	35.065	10
18	19	0.637	28	28.565	10	27	38	1.002	28	28.565	25	57	58	0.819	0	50	0
19	20	0.455	17.64	17.995	150	29	39	0.546	0	28	28.565	58	59	0.182	18	28.565	25

5. Computational Implementation

The proposed Newton and quasi-Newton power flow algorithms for bipolar DC networks with multiple unbalanced loads were implemented using MATLAB® 2024b. All simulations were carried out on a personal computer equipped with an AMD Ryzen 7 3700 processor (Advanced Micro Devices, Inc., Santa Clara, CA, USA) running at 2.3 GHz, 16 GB of RAM, and the 64-bit version of Windows 10 Single Language.

5.1. Voltage Performance and Power Loss Calculation

Figures 3 and 4 present the voltage profiles per pole for the 21- and 85-bus bipolar DC networks, assuming a solidly grounded neutral conductor at every node. To facilitate the comparison, the voltage values of the negative pole are plotted using their absolute magnitudes. This representation highlights the asymmetry introduced by unbalanced load connections, which causes deviations between the voltage profiles of the positive and negative poles.

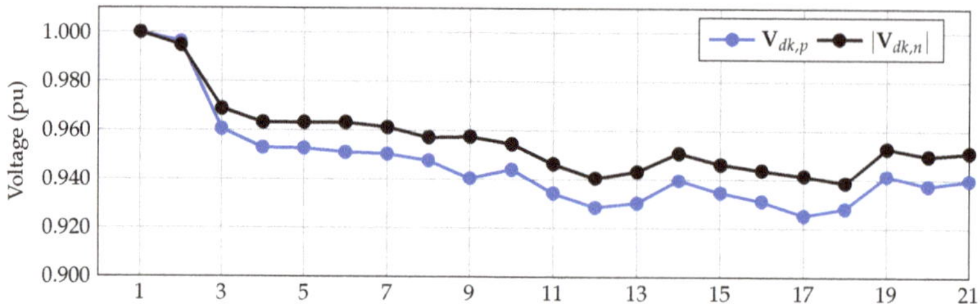

Figure 3. Behavior of the voltage profile of each pole with respect to the neutral wire in the 21-bus grid.

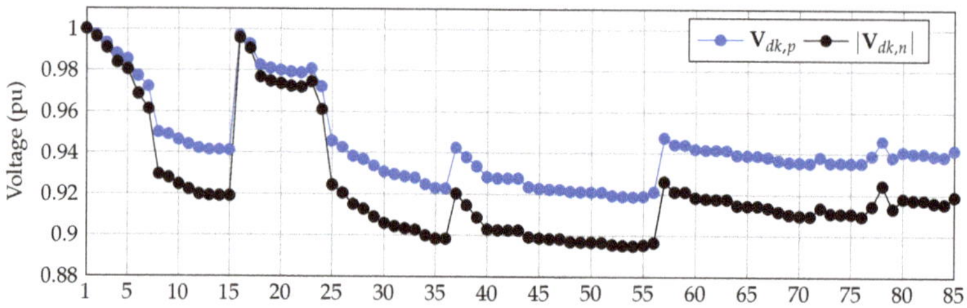

Figure 4. Behavior of the voltage profile of each pole with respect to the neutral wire in the 85-bus grid.

In both systems, the slack bus maintains a fixed voltage of ± 1 kV or ± 11 kV, while the remaining buses exhibit voltage drops that reflect the spatial distribution and magnitude of the constant power loads across the network. The 85-bus system, being more extensive and heterogeneous, shows a more pronounced divergence between poles, particularly in heavily loaded regions.

In the 21-bus grid, the minimum voltage for the positive pole is 0.92523 pu at node 17, while the minimum value for the negative pole is -0.93864 pu at node 18. In the case of the 85-bus grid, these values are 0.91891 pu and -0.89497 pu, both at bus 54.

Note that, in both networks, the lowest voltage levels are observed at downstream nodes or in areas with a concentrated load, where voltage drops are most pronounced. In addition, the 85-bus grid exhibits larger deviations between poles, particularly in the negative pole, where the voltage falls below 0.90 pu. This indicates greater vulnerability to unbalanced loading and longer distribution paths. It is worth mentioning that the voltage difference between poles is more significant in the 85-bus system (approximately 0.02394 pu) than in the 21-bus system (approximately 0.01341 pu), underscoring the stronger asymmetry of large-scale feeders.

Table 4 lists the average processing times, number of iterations, and the calculated power losses for each test feeder under all the proposed Newton and quasi-Newton methods.

All the numerical methods evaluated in Table 4 converge to the same power losses values: 92.2701 kW for the 21-bus system and 452.2981 kW for the 85-bus grid, demonstrating the robustness and accuracy of the different Newton and quasi-Newton formulations. These results were obtained under a strict convergence criterion of $\epsilon = 1 \times 10^{-10}$, with each method averaged over 10,000 executions to ensure statistical reliability in processing time measurements.

In the 21-bus grid, the classical Newton-based formulation, i.e., Equation (17), required only four iterations, although its average processing time (0.6801 ms) was not the fastest. In contrast, despite needing more iterations, quasi-Newton methods such as Equations (28) and (34) achieved lower processing times: 0.4252 ms and 0.4277 ms, respectively. These results highlight the computational advantage of using constant Jacobian approximations in smaller systems, where the overhead of recomputing and inverting the Jacobian can be more significant than the additional iterations.

Table 4. Numerical assessment of the bipolar DC power flow problem using Newton and quasi-Newton algorithms.

21-Bus Grid			
Method	**Iter.**	**Proc. Time (ms)**	**Power Losses (kW)**
Equation (17)	4	0.6801	
Equation (21)	5	0.8269	
Equation (25)	5	0.8339	
Equation (28)	6	0.4252	92.2701
Equation (30)	13	0.5125	
Equation (32)	13	0.5123	
Equation (34)	10	0.4277	
85-Bus Grid			
Method	**Iter.**	**Proc. Time (ms)**	**Power Loss (kW)**
Equation (17)	4	8.3251	
Equation (21)	5	11.1240	
Equation (25)	5	11.2680	
Equation (28)	6	3.9778	452.2981
Equation (30)	13	4.5794	
Equation (32)	12	4.5075	
Equation (34)	10	3.5321	

For the larger 85-bus grid, all methods exhibit higher computational times. This is expected in light of the increased system complexity. The Newton method in Equation (17) maintained the lowest iteration count (four iterations), albeit with a relatively high processing time (8.3251 ms). In contrast, quasi-Newton methods such as Equations (34) and (28) achieved shorter processing times (3.5321 ms and 3.9778 ms, respectively), indicating superior efficiency in large-scale systems. These findings suggest that, while the Newton method is optimal with regard to its iteration count, quasi-Newton approaches provide a more favorable trade-off between this aspect and computational time, especially in networks with a large number of nodes.

5.2. Rate of Convergence

Figure 5 illustrates the convergence rate of the Newton and quasi-Newton methods for the 21- and 85-bus bipolar DC test systems, which was evaluated using the infinity norm of the voltage updates $||\mathbf{V}_d^{k+1} - \mathbf{V}_d^k||_\infty$. The results indicate the numerical behavior of each formulation based on the number of iterations required to achieve the convergence tolerance of 1×10^{-10}.

As expected, the first three Newton-based methods—corresponding to Equations (17), (21) and (25)—exhibit quadratic convergence, achieving machine-level precision within five iterations or fewer. This behavior confirms their superior performance when accurate Jacobian evaluations are available at each step. In contrast, the quasi-Newton method represented by Equation (28) demonstrates superlinear convergence, showing a slightly slower yet efficient reduction in error over successive iterations.

The remaining quasi-Newton methods (i.e., Equations (30), (32), and (34)), which rely on constant Jacobian approximations, follow a linear convergence pattern. Although these approaches require more iterations to reach the desired tolerance, they benefit from significantly reduced computational overhead by avoiding Jacobian updates. This trade-off between iteration count and per-iteration efficiency makes them suitable for large-scale applications, as evidenced by their competitive performance in the 85-bus grid.

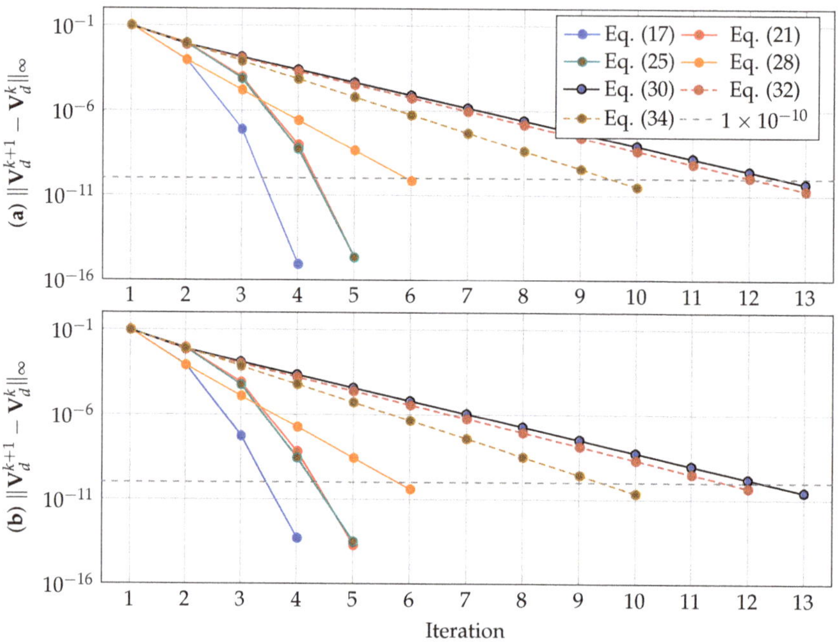

Figure 5. Rate of convergence of the Newton and quasi-Newton methods for (**a**) the 21-bus grid and (**b**) the 85-bus grid.

5.3. Discussion

The convergence behavior observed in Figure 5 across the different Newton and quasi-Newton methods can be explained by analyzing the structure and conditioning of the Jacobian matrices used by each approach. In the case of the first Newton–Raphson formulation, the exact Jacobian matrix is fully preserved, maintaining all couplings between the network variables. This leads to a better-conditioned system and enables faster convergence, typically requiring fewer iterations (four iterations in the tested cases). In contrast, the second and third Newton–Raphson formulations are pre-multiplied by certain factors in order to simplify and facilitate the calculation of the Jacobian. These factors alter the coupling structure and slightly degrade the system's conditioning, resulting in the need for an additional iteration to reach convergence as well as more processing time.

The first Quasi-Newton method demonstrates superlinear convergence because its Jacobian approximation carefully retains critical coupling terms, achieving a good balance between accuracy and computational simplicity. This leads to a quasi-Newton sequence that rapidly approximates the Newton direction, which explains its superior convergence behavior. On the other hand, the second and third Quasi-Newton methods, based on pre-multiplication strategies, aggressively simplify the Jacobian matrix by eliminating important coupling terms. This results in a more poorly conditioned system, in linear convergence rates, and in a higher number of iterations required for convergence. The fourth quasi-Newton method constitutes a more balanced approximation strategy that, while simpler than the first quasi-Newton approach, manages to preserve sufficient structural information, leading to a better convergence performance than the second and third quasi-Newton formulations.

Overall, these observations highlight the critical role of the Jacobian's structural fidelity and conditioning in determining the convergence speed and computational efficiency of

Newton-based and quasi-Newton-based power flow methods for bipolar DC networks with constant power loads.

6. Conclusions and Future Works

This study developed and validated a generalized power flow model for bipolar DC distribution networks incorporating monopolar and bipolar constant power loads under unbalanced conditions. The proposed formulation captures the nonlinear behavior introduced by constant power terminals and line-to-line voltage differences, making it applicable to both radial and meshed topologies.

Seven numerical solution methods were proposed and assessed, including three Newton–Raphson-based algorithms and four quasi-Newton formulations. The Newton-based methods demonstrated quadratic convergence and high accuracy but incurred higher computational costs caused by repeated Jacobian evaluations. In contrast, the quasi-Newton approaches—particularly those with constant Jacobians—exhibited lower processing times, offering an effective trade-off between accuracy and computational efficiency.

Numerical experiments conducted on 21- and 85-bus test feeders confirmed the robustness of all methods in terms of convergence and consistency in power loss estimation. The results also revealed that quasi-Newton approaches are more advantageous for large-scale networks, where computation time becomes a critical factor, whereas Newton-based methods remain preferable when iteration count must be prioritized.

Future research will focus on extending the proposed power flow framework to include multiple slack buses and voltage-controlled nodes, enabling a more realistic modeling of multi-terminal bipolar DC networks. Another important direction is the incorporation of converter-level dynamics and current saturation constraints to bridge the gap between static and dynamic analyses. Lastly, adapting the power flow formulations to accommodate systems with uncertain or time-varying load parameters will enhance their applicability in real-time operation and planning under stochastic conditions.

Author Contributions: Conceptualization, methodology, software, and writing (review and editing): O.D.M., J.D.P.R., L.F.G.-N., W.G.-G. and F.A.-R. All authors have read and agreed to the published version of the manuscript.

Funding: This work was funded by Minority Serving Institutions Science, Technology, Engineering and Mathematics Research and Development Consortium (MSRDC) under Contract W911SR-14-2-0001 with the US Department of Energy (DOE).

Data Availability Statement: The original contributions presented in this study are included in the article. Further inquiries can be directed to the corresponding author.

Acknowledgments: The authors acknowledge the support provided by Thematic Network 723RT0150, i.e., Red para la integración a gran escala de energías renovables en sistemas eléctricos (RIBIERSE-CYTED), funded through the 2022 call for thematic networks of the CYTED (Ibero-American Program of Science and Technology for Development).

Conflicts of Interest: The authors declare no conflicts of interest.

References

1. Vossos, V.; Gerber, D.L.; Gaillet-Tournier, M.; Nordman, B.; Brown, R.; Bernal Heredia, W.; Ghatpande, O.; Saha, A.; Arnold, G.; Frank, S.M. Adoption Pathways for DC Power Distribution in Buildings. *Energies* **2022**, *15*, 786. [CrossRef]
2. Siraj, K.; Khan, H.A. DC distribution for residential power networks—A framework to analyze the impact of voltage levels on energy efficiency. *Energy Rep.* **2020**, *6*, 944–951. [CrossRef]
3. Caballero-Peña, J.; Cadena-Zarate, C.; Parrado-Duque, A.; Osma-Pinto, G. Distributed energy resources on distribution networks: A systematic review of modelling, simulation, metrics, and impacts. *Int. J. Electr. Power Energy Syst.* **2022**, *138*, 107900. [CrossRef]

4. Gelani, H.; Dastgeer, F.; Siraj, K.; Nasir, M.; Niazi, K.; Yang, Y. Efficiency Comparison of AC and DC Distribution Networks for Modern Residential Localities. *Appl. Sci.* **2019**, *9*, 582. [CrossRef]
5. Hassan, S.J.U.; Mehdi, A.; Haider, Z.; Song, J.S.; Abraham, A.D.; Shin, G.S.; Kim, C.H. Towards medium voltage hybrid AC/DC distribution Systems: Architectural Topologies, planning and operation. *Int. J. Electr. Power Energy Syst.* **2024**, *159*, 110003. [CrossRef]
6. Enomoto, M.; Sano, K.; Kanno, J.; Fukushima, J. Reconfiguration of Bipolar HVDC System for Continuous Transmission Under DC Line Fault. *IEEE Trans. Power Electron.* **2024**, *39*, 8622–8633. [CrossRef]
7. Li, L.; Sun, K.; Liu, Z.; Wang, W.; Li, K.J. LVDC Bipolar Balance Control of I-M2C in Urban AC/DC Hybrid Distribution System. *Front. Energy Res.* **2022**, *10*, 809481 . [CrossRef]
8. Garces, A. Uniqueness of the power flow solutions in low voltage direct current grids. *Electr. Power Syst. Res.* **2017**, *151*, 149–153. [CrossRef]
9. Wang, Q.; Zhou, Y.; Fan, B.; Liao, J.; Huang, T.; Zhang, X.; Zou, Y.; Zhou, N. Hierarchical optimal operation for bipolar DC distribution networks with remote residential communities. *Appl. Energy* **2025**, *378*, 124701. [CrossRef]
10. Chew, B.S.H.; Xu, Y.; Wu, Q. Voltage Balancing for Bipolar DC Distribution Grids: A Power Flow Based Binary Integer Multi-Objective Optimization Approach. *IEEE Trans. Power Syst.* **2019**, *34*, 28–39. [CrossRef]
11. Montoya, O.D.; Gil-González, W.; Garcés, A. A successive approximations method for power flow analysis in bipolar DC networks with asymmetric constant power terminals. *Electr. Power Syst. Res.* **2022**, *211*, 108264. [CrossRef]
12. Medina-Quesada, A.; Montoya, O.D.; Hernández, J.C. Derivative-Free Power Flow Solution for Bipolar DC Networks with Multiple Constant Power Terminals. *Sensors* **2022**, *22*, 2914. [CrossRef] [PubMed]
13. Lee, J.O.; Kim, Y.S.; Moon, S.I. Current Injection Power Flow Analysis and Optimal Generation Dispatch for Bipolar DC Microgrids. *IEEE Trans. Smart Grid* **2021**, *12*, 1918–1928. [CrossRef]
14. Zhou, Y.; Wang, Q.; Huang, T.; Liao, J.; Chi, Y.; Zhou, N.; Xu, X.; Zhang, X. Convex optimal power flow based on power injection-based equations and its application in bipolar DC distribution network. *Electr. Power Syst. Res.* **2024**, *230*, 110271. [CrossRef]
15. Zhou, Y.; Wang, Q.; Xu, X.; Huang, T.; Liao, J.; Chi, Y.; Zhang, X.; Zhou, N. Branch flow model based optimal power flow for bipolar dc distribution networks. *CSEE J. Power Energy Syst.* **2024**, *11*, 944–948.
16. Wang, H.; Zhou, N.; Zhang, Y.; Liao, J.; Tan, S.; Liu, X.; Guo, C.; Wang, Q. Linearized power flow calculation of bipolar DC distribution network with multiple flexible equipment. *Int. J. Electr. Power Energy Syst.* **2024**, *155*, 109568. [CrossRef]
17. Ahmed, H.M.; Eltantawy, A.B.; Salama, M. A generalized approach to the load flow analysis of AC–DC hybrid distribution systems. *IEEE Trans. Power Syst.* **2017**, *33*, 2117–2127. [CrossRef]
18. Mackay, L.; Guarnotta, R.; Dimou, A.; Morales-Espana, G.; Ramirez-Elizondo, L.; Bauer, P. Optimal power flow for unbalanced bipolar DC distribution grids. *IEEE Access* **2018**, *6*, 5199–5207. [CrossRef]
19. Lee, J.O.; Kim, Y.S.; Jeon, J.H. Optimal power flow for bipolar DC microgrids. *Int. J. Electr. Power Energy Syst.* **2022**, *142*, 108375. [CrossRef]
20. Mackay, L.; Dimou, A.; Guarnotta, R.; Morales-Espania, G.; Ramirez-Elizondo, L.; Bauer, P. Optimal power flow in bipolar DC distribution grids with asymmetric loading. In Proceedings of the 2016 IEEE International Energy Conference (ENERGYCON), Leuven, Belgium, 4–8 April 2016; pp. 1–6. [CrossRef]
21. Lee, J.O.; Kim, Y.S.; Jeon, J.H. Generic power flow algorithm for bipolar DC microgrids based on Newton–Raphson method. *Int. J. Electr. Power Energy Syst.* **2022**, *142*, 108357. [CrossRef]
22. Sepúlveda-García, S.; Montoya, O.D.; Garcés, A. Power Flow Solution in Bipolar DC Networks Considering a Neutral Wire and Unbalanced Loads: A Hyperbolic Approximation. *Algorithms* **2022**, *15*, 341. [CrossRef]
23. Garces, A.; Montoya, O.D.; Gil-Gonzalez, W. Power Flow in Bipolar DC Distribution Networks Considering Current Limits. *IEEE Trans. Power Syst.* **2022**, *37*, 4098–4101. [CrossRef]
24. Montoya, O.D.; Rocha, J.C.; Fontecha-Saboya, D. Development of an Application for Calculating the Power Flow of Bipolar DC Networks Using the MATLAB Environment. *Rev. Fac. De Ing.* **2024**, *33*, e17362. [CrossRef]
25. Enríquez, A.C.; Cardoso, Y.G. Chapter Four - Protective relay resiliency in an electric power transmission system. In *Electric Power Systems Resiliency*; Bansal, R.C., Mishra, M., Sood, Y.R., Eds.; Academic Press: Cambridge, MA, USA, 2022; pp. 87–148. [CrossRef]
26. Garcés, A. On the Convergence of Newton's Method in Power Flow Studies for DC Microgrids. *IEEE Trans. Power Syst.* **2018**, *33*, 5770–5777. [CrossRef]
27. Petković, M.S.; Neta, B.; Petković, L.D.; Džunić, J. Multipoint methods for solving nonlinear equations: A survey. *Appl. Math. Comput.* **2014**, *226*, 635–660. [CrossRef]

28. Abbasbandy, S. Improving Newton–Raphson method for nonlinear equations by modified Adomian decomposition method. *Appl. Math. Comput.* **2003**, *145*, 887–893. [CrossRef]
29. Sereeter, B.; Vuik, C.; Witteveen, C. On a comparison of Newton–Raphson solvers for power flow problems. *J. Comput. Appl. Math.* **2019**, *360*, 157–169. [CrossRef]

Mathematical and Computational Applications

MDPI

Article

Causal Diagnosability Optimization Design for UAVs Based on Maximum Mean Covariance Difference and the Gray Wolf Optimization Algorithm

Xuping Gu * and Xianjun Shi

College of Coastal Defense Force, Naval Aviation University, Yantai 264001, China; sxjun0929@163.com
* Correspondence: gxping0316@163.com

Abstract: Given the growing complexity and variability of application scenarios, coupled with increasing operational demands, unmanned aerial vehicles (UAVs) are prone to faults. To enhance diagnosability and reliability in this context, this study proposes a causal diagnosability optimization strategy based on the Maximum Mean and Covariance Discrepancy (MMCD) metric and the Grey Wolf Optimization (GWO) algorithm. First, a qualitative assessment method for causal diagnosability is introduced, leveraging structural analysis to evaluate the detectability and isolability of faults. Next, residuals are generated using Minimal Structurally Overdetermined (MSO) sets, and a quantitative diagnosability assessment framework is developed based on the MMCD metric. This framework measures the complexity of diagnosability through the analysis of residual deviations under fault conditions. Finally, a diagnosability optimization technique utilizing the GWO algorithm is proposed. This approach minimizes diagnostic system design costs while maximizing its performance. Simulation results for a UAV structural model demonstrate that the proposed strategy achieves a 100% fault detection rate and fault isolation rate while reducing design costs by 70.59%.

Keywords: UAV; MMCD; GWO algorithm; structural analysis; causal diagnosability

1. Introduction

With the continuous development of flight control technology, battery technology, intelligent learning, camera technology, sensor technology, communication technology, power technology, polymer material technology, cloud computing technology, and navigation technology, UAVs have been widely used in the fields of logistics and transportation [1], agricultural plant protection [2], communication relay [3], and military combat. Due to the escalating intensity and difficulty of missions, the requirements for UAVs have intensified in terms of their fulfillment, safety, and reliability. Influenced by factors such as materials, operation, environment, and software, UAVs can suffer from faults, which may lead to their failure [4]. Therefore, it is essential to improve the reliability and diagnosability of UAVs to ensure the fulfillment of their missions.

At present, improving the efficiency of diagnosis systems or the dependability of essential components represents the primary method to increase reliability. On one hand, enhancing the dependability of crucial parts raises the cost of design and does not wholly eliminate faults. Furthermore, the performance of diagnostic systems is often constrained by the limited or imprecise fault information they provide. Even the most precise fault diagnostic techniques are not helpful if the fault information is lacking or inadequate. Therefore, ensuring sufficient fault information is essential for increasing reliability. Diagnosability—like

https://doi.org/10.3390/mca30030055

reliability—is a fundamental system design characteristic that reflects the effectiveness of fault diagnosis. Diagnosability not only involves fault information, but also ensures that fault diagnostic duties are completed as efficiently and cheaply as possible [5]. There are two types of diagnosability studies: diagnosability design and diagnosability assessment. Diagnosability assessment studies predominantly assess the advantages and disadvantages of the diagnosis system, while diagnosability design studies primarily refer to a series of optimization designs that improve the performance of the diagnosis system. Diagnosability assessment is a crucial method for evaluating the fault diagnosis ability, as it reflects the content and quality of fault information. It can generally be classified into two categories: qualitative and quantitative. Quantitative assessment largely gauges the complexity of diagnosing faults, whereas qualitative assessment primarily establishes whether a fault can be diagnosed.

Existing research on diagnosability in UAVs has mainly focused on the optimal design of fault diagnosis strategies. The fault diagnosis strategies for UAVs are divided into those relating to hardware and software redundancy [6]. Fault diagnosis based on hardware redundancy mainly ensures the detectability of the equipment by increasing hardware detection equipment. However, the system's economic cost and structural complexity will increase, and the reliability of the system will be affected. Fault diagnosis methods based on software redundancy can be categorized into analytical model-based, signal processing-based, and knowledge-based methods [7]. However, given recent research progress, the fault diagnosis strategy of UAVs is mainly based on machine learning, artificial intelligence, or fusion algorithms. Iannace [8] proposed an artificial neural network-based fault diagnosis strategy for UAVs. By analyzing the acoustic characteristics of the UAV propellers, he successfully realized three states of the classification diagnosis, including balanced blades, single-tape imbalance, and double-tape imbalance, with 97.63% accuracy. Liang [9] proposed a data-driven fault diagnosis method for fixed-wing UAVs considering multiple operating conditions that significantly improved the fault detection rate and reduced the false alarm rate by incorporating an improved dynamic kernel principal component analysis and a sliding window denoising algorithm. Zhang [10] addressed the problem of fault-constrained flight data for fixed-wing UAVs and proposed a fault diagnosis strategy based on adaptive sharing and knowledge complementation, greatly improving the fault detection rate under small sample constraints. Hua [11] proposed a quadrotor UAV sensor fault diagnosis and fault-tolerant control method based on an improved genetic algorithm and BP neural network. Experiments comparing the three types of algorithms show that the proposed improved strategy has the highest detection rate in noisy environments. It can quickly and accurately identify the faults of sensor jamming and gain abnormality as well as other faults, significantly improving the safety and stability of the UAV system. Overall, existing research on UAV diagnosability has mainly focused on specific faults, complex environments, and algorithm performance improvement. First, all of the above studies have neglected a key issue: the content of fault information provided by the system. If the fault information provided by the system is insufficient or untrue, this leads to the fact that the fault itself cannot be detected and isolated. Thus, even the most accurate fault diagnosis strategy is not useful. Second, all of the above studies have been conducted to diagnose a single fault or a certain class of faults, and lack UAV-wide fault analyses. Therefore, in this paper, from the perspective of quantitative evaluation for the UAV system-wide faults and taking into account the causal constraints through the analysis and optimization of the system structural characteristics, to ensure that the system provides sufficient fault information, which in turn improves the fault diagnosis performance as well as the reliability of the UAV.

Extracting fault data from the system structure is the aim of the model-based fault detection technique known as structural analysis [12]. Through creating a structural model and utilizing the appropriate tools based on graph theory, the structural analysis method significantly lowers the computational cost of fault diagnosis in contrast to other model-based fault diagnosis techniques that necessitate the creation of an accurate mathematical model. This provides a significant benefit for the diagnosability of large-scale and complex control systems. Chen [13] proposed a hybrid structural analysis and convolutional neural network-based diagnosis system that compensates for the problem of fewer training samples for data-driven fault diagnosis methods through combining model-based and data-driven fault diagnosis methods. Cheng [14] proposed a structural analysis-based diagnosis scheme that is applicable to complex systems for short-circuit and sensor faults in the lithium battery system of a hybrid aircraft. Li [15] proposed a structure-based modeling method for real-time fault diagnosis of the pulse rectifier of the traction system. First, a structural analysis model of the traction system is established to examine structural isolation and detectability aspects. Second, the structural model is analyzed and optimized using the resolved redundancy relations under each fault condition, and the optimized model is used to obtain the minimal structurally overdetermined sets (MSOs) for isolating the faults. Finally, using the MSOs, sequence residuals are generated, and diagnostic decisions can be made using the cumulative sum algorithm. Due to its structural characteristics, the structural analysis method can assess diagnosability only from a qualitative perspective. In this study, the direct and sensitive relationship linking MSO to faults is transformed into an indirect connection that utilizes residuals as an intermediary step for fault detection, thereby addressing the limitations of the original approach. This quantitative assessment is achieved by measuring the difference in residuals between faulty and normal operating conditions. Standard measures of the difference between probability distributions include the energy distance [16], modified distance [17], Kullback–Leibler (K-L) scatter [18], Hausdroff distance [19], Ma's distance [20], Jensen Shannon (JS) scatter [21], Bachmann's distance [22], Fisher's information distance [23], and Bayesian error rate [24]. These probability distribution measures generally use the parity space method to design the residuals and, thus, are susceptible to the influence of the window length and the selection of the left null space. As a novel probability distribution measure, MMCD not only compensates for the traditional maximum mean discrepancy (MMD) by incorporating the maximum covariance discrepancy (MCD) when measuring the sample covariance discrepancy, but also ensures the symmetry of the distance metric. Zhang [25] proposed a cross-domain distributional discrepancy assessment method based on MMCD and proved the effectiveness of MMCD in domain adaptation using image classification experiments. Yang [26] proposed an MMCD-based migration joint matching strategy in order to compensate for the MMD loss of statistical information in the migration learning strategy. Therefore, this work provides a quantitative assessment method based on MMCD to measure the ease of fault diagnosis.

The causal relationship embedded in MSO has an impact on residual design. Different redundancy equations are selected, or different perfect matching relationships are embedded in the MSO. When designing residuals, the causal relationship between dynamic variables also changes [27]. The causal relationship also affects the capability of fault diagnosis, to some extent. In residual design, if only the integral operation of dynamic variables occurs, the residual is considered to be integrally causal. Modeling bias, noise interference, beginning value uncertainty, and other issues all impact integral causal residuals, although these effects can be somewhat mitigated. In residual design, if only differential operations on dynamic variables are involved, the residual is considered to be differentially causal. Differential causal residuals are easily affected by system noise, and the higher the order of differentiation is, the greater the degree of influence of noise on the system. Therefore, differential causality should be avoided as much as possible. In residual design, if there are both differential and integral operations, the residual is considered to reflect mixed causality. Mixed causality can take advantage of both integral and differential causality. Thus, this research suggests a quantitative assessment technique for causality diagnosability, which depends on MMCD to quantify the impact of causality on residuals.

The number of MSOs increases exponentially with the structural redundancy of the system. Therefore, not all MSOs should be involved in diagnostic system design due to cost constraints. To balance the causal diagnosability requirement as well as the diagnostic system design cost, the MSOs with the best overall performance must be identified, essentially representing a combinatorial optimization problem. Intelligent algorithms are advantageous in solving optimization problems. At present, the widely used optimization algorithms include the genetic algorithm [28], simulated annealing algorithm [29], ant colony algorithm [30], particle swarm algorithm [31], and artificial bee colony algorithm [32]. The GWO algorithm—a novel intelligent optimization algorithm inspired by the social hierarchy and hunting behavior of gray wolves—performs optimization through processes such as tracking, chasing, encircling, harassing, and attacking the prey of wolves. These behaviors help to guide the algorithm's search for the optimal solution [33]. To date, GWO algorithms have been developed for feature selection [34], parameter identification [35], reinforcement learning [36], and reliability optimization [37]. Therefore, this study introduces a strategy for optimizing diagnosability using a design approach grounded in the GWO algorithm. In summary, the key contributions of this study are as follows: first, a method for causal diagnosability analysis rooted in structural analysis is introduced; second, a quantitative evaluation strategy for causal diagnosability utilizing MMCD is presented; and, finally, an optimization design strategy for causal diagnosability based on the GWO algorithm is proposed.

To enhance the adaptability and reliability of UAVs performing missions in complex working environments, this study proposes a causal diagnosability optimization design strategy based on the MMCD and GWO algorithms. This strategy effectively guarantees the success rate of UAV execution under various mission requirements through enhancing the system's fault diagnosis capability. The remainder of this paper is organized as follows. In Section 2, the optimization design strategy for UAV causal diagnosability based on the MMCD and GWO algorithms proposed in this paper is described in detail. First, based on structural analysis, a system structure model is established. Its structural characteristics are analyzed, and causal diagnosability evaluation indices are established. Second, residuals are designed based on MSO, and a quantitative diagnosability evaluation strategy based on the MMCD is proposed. Finally, to take into account the demand for diagnosability as well as the cost of diagnostic system design, a causal diagnosability optimization design model is established, and a diagnosability optimization design strategy based on the GWO algorithm is proposed. In Section 3, based on the UAV structural model, the causal diagnosability is analyzed and optimized from the perspective of quantitative evaluation to verify the reasonableness and effectiveness of the strategy proposed in this paper. Section 4 summarizes the main work of this paper.

2. Proposed Methodology

To improve the reliability as well as causal diagnosability of UAVs, this study proposes a diagnosability optimization design strategy based on the MMCD and GWO algorithms. The logic of the proposed approach is shown in Figure 1. First, based on structural analysis, the relevant graph theory tools of Dulmage–Mendelsohn (DM) decomposition and matching are used to analyze the structural characteristics of the system based on its structural characteristics and establish the evaluation index of causal diagnosability. Second, based on MSO-designed system residuals, the problem of quantitatively evaluating diagnosability is transformed into analyzing the probability distribution differences of residuals, and a quantitative diagnosability assessment strategy based on MMCD is proposed. Finally, a diagnosability optimization design strategy based on the GWO algorithm is proposed to reduce the cost of the diagnostic system.

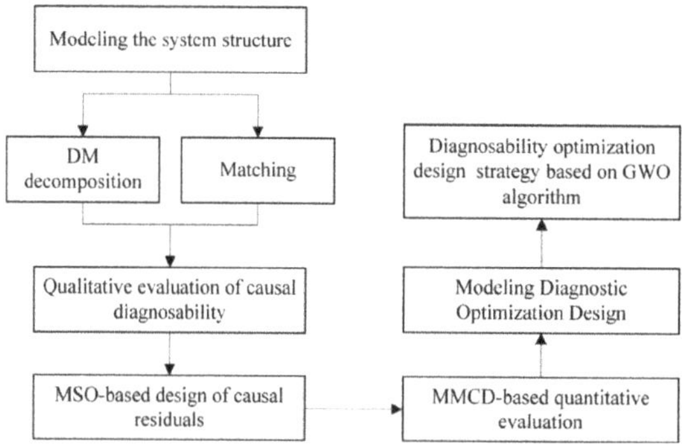

Figure 1. The logical lineage of the proposed strategy.

2.1. Causal Diagnosability Based on Structural Analysis

2.1.1. Structural Model

With its collection of variables V, set of constraint equations E, and edges $\overline{A}$, the structure of a system M may be expressed as a graph $G(E,V,\overline{A})$. If variable v_j appears in equation e_i, it means that an edge (e_i,v_j) exists between node e_i and node v_j of $G(E,V,\overline{A})$. The set of edges can be denoted as $\overline{A}=\{(e_i,v_j)|e_i\in E, v_j\in V, v_j\ is\ ine_i\}$. For ease of presentation, $G(E,V,\overline{A})$ can also be represented by its correlation matrix A, where $A(i,j)=1$ if an edge (e_i,v_j) exists between nodes e_i and v_j, and $A(i,j)=0$ otherwise.

The mathematical model of the system M_1 is expressed as:

$$\begin{array}{ll} e_1: \dot{x}_1=-2x_1+x_3+x_5 & e_5: \dot{x}_5=-5x_5+u+f_5 \\ e_2: \dot{x}_2=-3x_2+x_4+f_1 & e_6: y_1=x_1 \\ e_3: \dot{x}_3=-x_3+x_5+f_2+f_3 & e_7: y_2=x_2 \\ e_4: \dot{x}_4=-4x_4+f_4 & e_8: y_3=x_3 \end{array} \tag{1}$$

where $X_1=\{x_i,\dot{x}_i\}$ are the unknown state variables, $F_1=\{f_1,f_2,f_3,f_4\}$ are the system faults, and $Z_1=\{u,y_1,y_2,y_3\}$ are the known variables. To distinguish between $\dot{x}_i$ and x_i in the structural model of M_1, the constraint equations are added here:

$$e_j: \dot{x}_i=\frac{d}{dt}x_i, i=1,2,\ldots,5; j=9,10,\ldots,13 \tag{2}$$

$G(E,V,\overline{A})$ of M_1 is shown in Figure 2. In Figure 2, the variables are represented by the columns of the association matrix of M_1, and the rows indicate the equations. Among them, '•' represents standard edges, 'D' represents edges related to $\dot{x}_i$ in the added constraint equations, and 'I' represents edges related to x_i in the added constraint equations. The structural analysis exclusively focuses on the structure associated with the unknown variable X, i.e., the blue part in Figure 1. For ease of description, the structural model associated with X is defined here as $G(E,X,\overline{A})$.

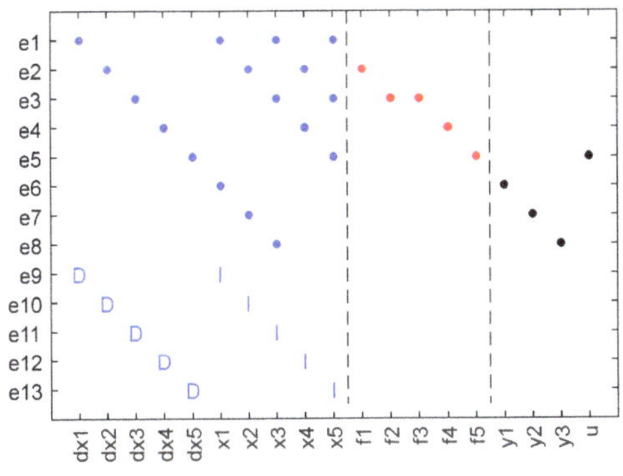

Figure 2. The structural model of M_1.

2.1.2. Causal Diagnosability

The DM decomposition method [38] is frequently employed for structural analysis. The association matrix A is divided into an upper triangular form by the DM decomposition, as shown in Figure 3a. The shaded elements in Figure 3a contain '0' and '1', and the blanks contain only '0'. The light-colored dashed line in the figure represents the maximum matching [27]. Matching refers to a set of edge sets that are not in the same row and column in the structural model. M is divided into three parts after DM decomposition: the structurally underdetermined part $M^- = (E^-, X^-)$, where $|E^-| < |X^-|$; the structurally exactly determined part $M^0 = (E^0, X^0)$, where $|E^0| = |X^0|$; and the structurally overdetermined part $M^+ = (E^+, X^+)$, where $|E^+| > |X^+|$. A set of Hall components $\{G_i\}$ exist in M^0. Due to the resolved redundancy relations embedded in it [12], M^+ is the key to the structural analysis and the diagnostic focus. The DM decomposition of M_1 is shown schematically in Figure 3b, demonstrating that $M_1 = (M_1)^+$. Here, $(\cdot)^+$ and $(\cdot)^0$ are defined as the operators that obtain the structurally overdetermined and structurally exactly determined subsystems, respectively.

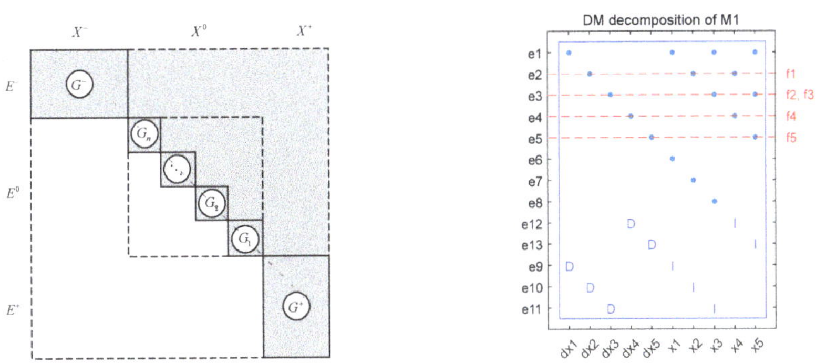

(a) **(b)**

Figure 3. DM decomposition. (**a**) DM decomposition diagram. (**b**) DM decomposition of M_1.

E is said to be properly structurally overdetermined (SO) if $|E| > |Q_X(E)|$, where $Q_X(E)$ represents the unknown variables embedded in E. If E is SO, this implies that a structurally overdetermined portion is present in the DM decomposition. Further, if $E = E^+$, it implies that E is properly structurally overdetermined (PSO). If $E = E^+$, for $\forall e \in E$, $\exists E \backslash \{e\}$, $s.t.(E \backslash \{e\}) = (E \backslash \{e\})^+$. This states that a subset of the proper structurally overdetermined set E, PSO, exists. Furthermore, E is said to be an MSO if E is SO and there is no $\exists E' \subseteq E$, such that E' is SO. The structural redundancy of MSO is 1, which is a minimal unit for diagnosability. Using the MSO method shown in the literature [39], the MSOs of M_1 can be obtained as $MSO_1 = \{e_3, e_5, e_8, e_{11}, e_{13}\}$, $MSO_2 = \{e_2, e_4, e_7, e_{10}, e_{12}\}$, $MSO_3 = \{e_1, e_5, e_6, e_8, e_9, e_{13}\}$, $MSO_4 = \{e_1, e_3, e_6, e_8, e_9, e_{11}\}$, $MSO_5 = \{e_1, e_3, e_5, e_6, e_9, e_{11}, e_{13}\}$.

Based on the MSO, the residuals are designed using the sequential residual method to analyze diagnosis. Taking MSO_2 as an example, residuals r_1 and r_2 are designed using e_4 and e_7 as redundant equations, respectively. Figures 4a and 5a show the computation flow of r_1 and r_2, where the circles represent variables, the bars represent constraint equations, the red bars represent dynamic equations, and the arrows represent the computation flow. As shown in Figure 4a, the calculation process of r_1 is as follows: first, use e_7 to solve for the unknown variable x_2; then use e_{10} to solve for $\dot{x}_2$; then use e_2 to solve for x_4; then use e_{12} to solve for $\dot{x}_4$; and finally use e_4 to obtain r_1.

$$r_1 := \ddot{y}_2 + 7\dot{y}_2 + 12y_2 - \dot{f}_1 - 4f_1 - f_4 \tag{3}$$

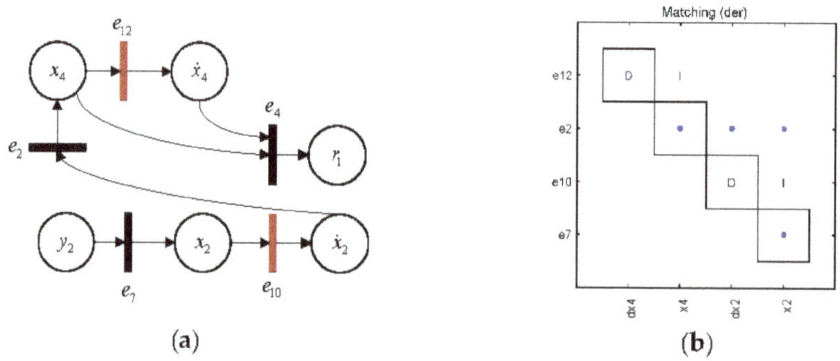

Figure 4. Differential causal residual r_1. (**a**) The computation flow of r_1. (**b**) Differential matching.

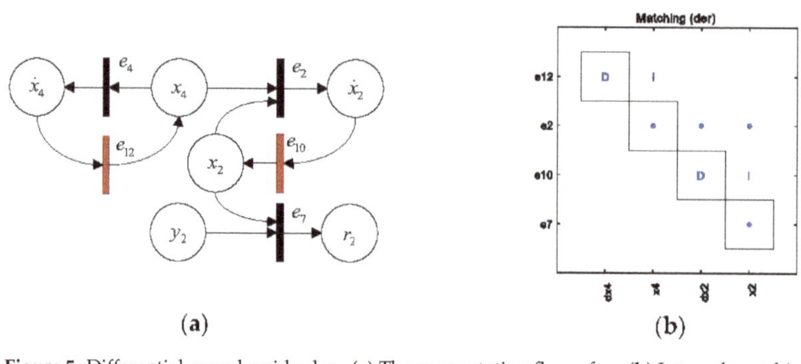

Figure 5. Differential causal residual r_2. (**a**) The computation flow of r_2. (**b**) Integral matching.

Figure 4b shows the structural model of $MSO_2 \backslash \{e_4\}$, and it can be seen that $MSO_2 \backslash \{e_4\} = (MSO_2 \backslash \{e_4\})^0$. The Hall component in the black border in Figure 4b is its maximum matching, i.e., $\{(e_7, x_2), (e_{10}, \dot{x}_2), (e_2, x_4), (e_{12}, \dot{x}_4)\}$. Comparing the two panels in Figure 4, it is observed that the process of solving for the unknown variables in Figure 4a is consistent with the matching process shown in Figure 4b. The matching variables are the solution variables of the matching equations. Because the matching contains only the differential edge 'D', r_1 is differentially causal. Causality here refers to integral and differential operations between dynamic variables. When no fault occurs, $r_1 = 0$. As f_1 appears in e_2 and f_4 appears in e_4, $r_1 \neq 0$ when either f_1 or f_4 occurs. For ease of description, let 'int' denote integral causality, 'der' denote differential causality, and 'mix' denote mixed causality.

In the computational flow of r_2 shown in Figure 5a, two differential loops appear. One is the differential loop (e_4, e_{12}) consisting of e_4 and e_{12}, and the other is the differential loop (e_2, e_{10}) consisting of e_2 and e_{10}. Integral operations can break the differential loop. First, based on the differential loop (e_4, e_{12}), one obtains $x_4 = \frac{f_4}{4}(1 - e^{-4x_4}) + Ce^{-4x_4}$ such that $x_4 = h(f_4)$. Second, based on the differential loop (e_2, e_{10}), one obtains $x_2 = \frac{f_1 + h(f_4)}{3}(1 - e^{-3x_2}) + C_1 e^{-3x_2}$ such that $x_2 = h(f_1, f_4)$. Finally, based on the redundant equation e_7, one obtains r_2, which is expressed as follows:

$$r_2 = h(f_1, f_4) - y_2 \tag{4}$$

Figure 5b shows the corresponding structural model of $MSO_2 \backslash \{e_7\}$, which is structurally exactly determined. The Hall components of $MSO_2 \backslash \{e_7\}$ are $G_1 = \{(e_{12}, x_4), (e_{12}, dx_4), (e_4, x_4), (e_4, dx_4)\}$ and $G_2 = \{(e_{10}, x_2), (e_{10}, dx_2), (e_2, x_2), (e_2, dx_2)\}$. Because $|G_1| > 1$ and $|G_2| > 1$, differential loops exist for G_1 and G_2. Since differential loops can only be broken by integral operations, r_2 is integrally causal. Because r_2 and r_1 involve the same constraint equations, the sensitivity of r_2 to faults is the same as that of r_1.

For MSO_2, when e_2, e_{10}, and e_{12} are sequentially selected as the redundant equations, the causal matching relationship is shown in Figure 6. As shown in the figure, when e_2 is a redundant equation, MSO_2 is mixed causal. When e_{10} is a redundant equation, MSO_2 is integrally causal. When e_{12} is a redundant equation, MSO_2 is differentially causal. Therefore, the causality of MSO is related to its maximum matching. In addition to the matching edge '•', if its maximal matching exists only in the differential edge 'D', it is differentially causal. If its maximal matching exists only in the integral edge 'I', it is integrally causal. If its maximal matching contains both integral and differential edges or only the standard edge '•', then it is mixed causal. Equations (3) and (4) demonstrate that the duplicate MSO has the same sensitivity relation to faults, although its causal relations are different.

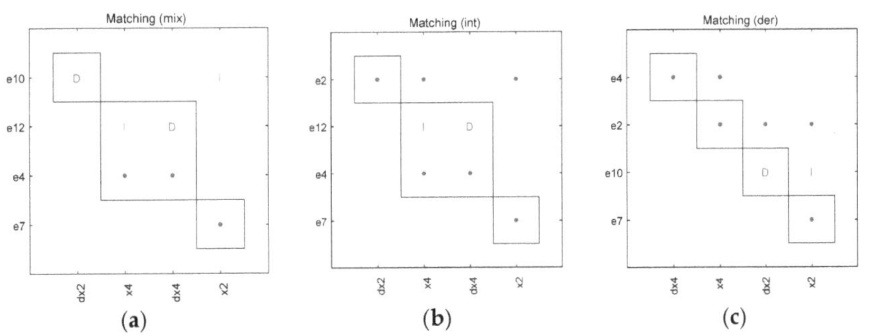

Figure 6. Causal relation of MSO_2. (**a**) Mixed causality. (**b**) Integral causality. (**c**) Differential causality.

Therefore, the fault f is said to be structurally detectable if and only if

$$\exists MSO, \text{ s.t. } e_f \in MSO \tag{5}$$

where e_f is the equation affected by f. For example, for M_1, $e_{f_1} = e_2$ and $e_{f_2} = e_{f_3} = e_3$. Further, the faults f_i and f_j are said to be structurally isolable if and only if

$$\exists MSO, \text{ s.t. } e_{f_i} \in MSO \wedge e_{f_j} \notin MSO \tag{6}$$

The $MSOs = \{MSO_1, MSO_2, \ldots, MSO_s\}$ is known, and the set of faults is $F = \{f_1, f_2, \ldots, f_g\}$. The fault signature matrix (FSM) $FSM = [fm_{ij}]_{g \times s}$ is built based on Equation (5) as follows:

$$fm_{ij} = \begin{cases} 1, \ if \ e_{f_i} \in MCR_j \\ 0, \ otherwise \end{cases} \tag{7}$$

The fault isolation matrix (FIM) $FIM = [f_{ij}]_{g \times g}$ is built based on Equation (6) as follows:

$$f_{ij} = \begin{cases} 0, \ if \ \exists MCR_k, \ s.t. \ e_{f_i} \in MCR_k \wedge e_{f_j} \notin MCR_k \\ 1, \ otherwise \end{cases} \tag{8}$$

Based on the FSM, the fault detection rate (FDR) can be obtained as follows:

$$FDR = \frac{\sum\limits_{i=1}^{g} or(fm_{i.})}{g} \tag{9}$$

where $or(fm_{i.})$ refers to the logical or operation between the i-th row of data in the FSM. Based on FIM, the fault isolation rate (FIR) can be obtained as follows:

$$FIR = 1 - \frac{\sum\limits_{i=1}^{g} \sum\limits_{j=1.i \neq j}^{g} f_{ij}}{g(g-1)} \tag{10}$$

Taking M_1 as an example, the MSOs in which integral causality is implied are $\{MSO_1, MSO_2, MSO_3, MSO_5\}$, and their FSM and FIM are shown in Figures 7a and 8a. Based on Equations (9) and (10), the FDR of M_1 under the integral causality condition is $FDR_1 = 100\%$, and the FIR is $FIR_1 = 70\%$. The MSOs of M_1, which imply differential causality, are $\{MSO_1, MSO_2, MSO_3, MSO_4\}$, and their FSM and FIM are shown in Figures 7b and 8b. Based on Equations (9) and (10), it can be seen that the FDR under differential causality condition is $FDR_2 = 100\%$ and $FIR_2 = 80\%$. The MSOs in M_1 that imply mixed causality are $\{MSO_1, MSO_2, MSO_3, MSO_4, MSO_5\}$, and the FSM under mixed causality is shown in Figure 7c, in which $FDR_3 = 100\%$. The FIM under mixed causality is shown in 8c, where $FIR_3 = 80\%$. Here, the FDR is consistent under any causal constraints. The diagnosability results of mixed causality and differential causality are consistent, but the number of MSOs under different causal constraints is inconsistent.

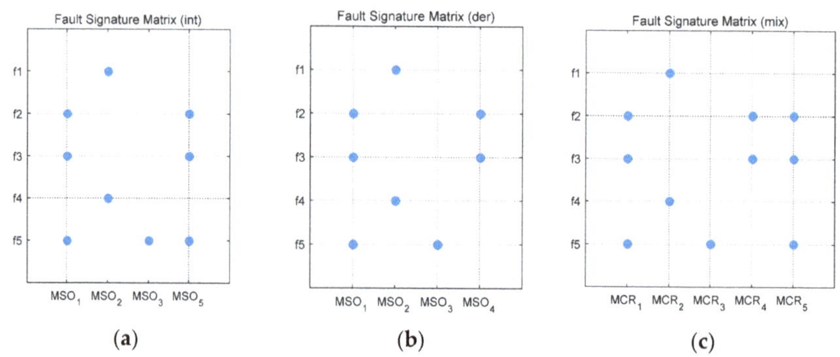

Figure 7. Fault signature matrix of M_1. (**a**) Integral causality. (**b**) Differential causality. (**c**) Mixed causality.

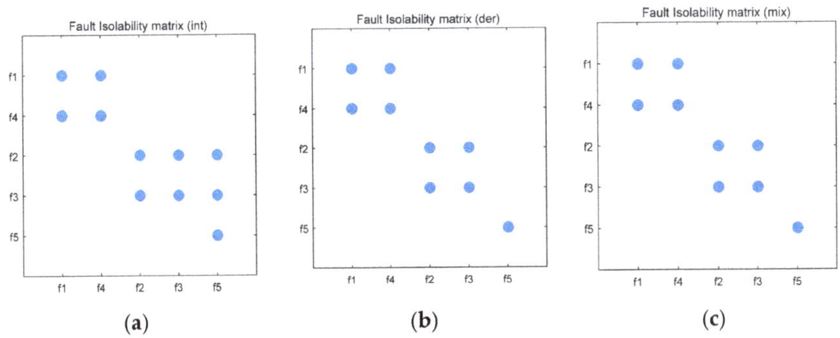

Figure 8. Fault isolability matrix of M_1. (**a**) Integral causality. (**b**) Differential causality. (**c**) Mixed causality.

2.2. Quantitative Assessment of Diagnosability Based on MMCD

The structural analysis method can only qualitatively analyze the diagnosability. Thus, this paper proposes a quantitative assessment method based on MMCD by fusing the advantages of MMD and MCD. MMCD not only compensates for the defects of MMD in measuring the covariance differences but also ensures the symmetry of the distance metric.

2.2.1. MMCD

MMD and MCD are both metrics formulated within a reproducible Hilbert space $\mathcal{H}$. MMD quantitatively describes the distance between probability distributions by calculating the mean difference in Hilbert space.

Definition 1 (MMD). *It is known that random variables x and y on the inner volume space X obey probability distributions p and q, respectively. Thus, the MMD between x and y is expressed as follows:*

$$\begin{aligned} MMD[p,q,\mathcal{H}] &= \sup_{h\in H}\left|E_x[h(x)] - E_y[h(y)]\right| \\ &= \|\mu[p] - \mu[q]\|_{\mathcal{H}} \\ &= \sqrt{tr(KM)} \end{aligned} \tag{11}$$

where

$$K = \begin{bmatrix} K_{XX} & K_{XY} \\ K_{YX} & K_{YY} \end{bmatrix} \tag{12}$$

$$M_{ij} = \begin{cases} \frac{1}{n^2},\ x_i, x_j \in X \\ \frac{1}{m^2},\ x_i, x_j \in Y \\ -\frac{1}{mn},\ otherise \end{cases} \tag{13}$$

In addition, E_x and E_y denote the expectations of x and y , respectively; H is the fundamental function $h : X \mapsto \mathbb{R}$ of $\mathcal{H}$; $\mu[p]$ and $\mu[q]$ represent the mean map of p and q on $\mathcal{H}$, respectively; $(K_{XX})_{ij} = k(x_i, x_j)$, $(K_{XY})_{ij} = k(x_i, y_j)$, $(K_{YY})_{ij} = k(y_i, y_j)$, and $k(x,y)$ are regenerated kernels of $\mathcal{H}$.

Through calculating the maximum covariance difference in Hilbert space, MCD provides a quantitative representation of the separation between probability distributions.

Definition 2 (MCD). *It is known that random variables x and y on the inner volume space X obey probability distributions p and q , respectively. Thus, the MCD between x and y is expressed as follows:*

$$\begin{aligned} MCD[p,q,\mathcal{H}] &= \sup_{\|a\|\leq 1} \sum_{i,j\in I} a_{ij}\left(\text{cov}\left[e_i(x),e_j(x)\right]\right) - \text{cov}\left[e_i(y),e_j(y)\right] \\ &= \|C[p]-C[q]\|_{HS} \\ &= \sqrt{tr(KZKZ)} \end{aligned} \tag{14}$$

where

$$\text{cov}\left[e_i(x),e_j(x)\right] = E_x\left[e_i(x),e_j(x)\right] - E_x[e_i(x)]E_x\left[e_j(x)\right] \tag{15}$$

$$Z_{ij} = \begin{cases} \frac{1}{n}-\frac{1}{n^2}, & i=j, x_i\in X \\ -\frac{1}{n^2}, & i\neq j, x_i\in X, x_j\in X \\ \frac{1}{m^2}-\frac{1}{m}, & i=j, x_i\in Y \\ \frac{1}{m^2}, & i\neq j, x_i\in Y, x_j\in Y \\ 0, & otherwise \end{cases} \tag{16}$$

In addition, $\|a\| = \left(\sum_{i,j\in I} a_{ij}^2\right)^{1/2}$; *$e_i$ is the orthonormal basis of $\mathcal{H}$; $C[p]$ is the covariance operator on $\mathcal{H}$; $\|\cdot\|_{HS}$ is the Hilbert–Schmidt (HS) paradigm; and $X = \{x_1,\ldots,x_n\}$ and $Y = \{y_1,\ldots,y_m\}$ are the finite number of observations sampled sequentially from distributions p and q , respectively.*

Through combining the differences between MCD and MMD in Hilbert space, MMCD provides a quantitative description of the distance between probability distributions.

Definition 3 (MMCD). *It is known that random variables x and y on the inner volume space X obey probability distributions p and q , respectively. Thus, the MMCD between x and y is expressed as follows:*

$$\begin{aligned} MMCD[p,q,\mathcal{H}] &= \left(\|\mu[p]-\mu[q]\|_{\mathcal{H}}^2 + \beta\|C[p]-C[q]\|_{HS}^2\right)^{1/2} \\ &= \sqrt{tr(KM)+\beta tr(KZKZ)} \end{aligned} \tag{17}$$

where $\beta \in [0,1]$.

Comparison of Equations (11), (14), and (17) shows that MMCD can take into account the mean difference and covariance difference of the probability distribution. Analyzing numerically, we find that $MMCD[p,q,\mathcal{H}] > MMD[p,q,\mathcal{H}]$ and $MMCD[p,q,\mathcal{H}] > MCD[p,q,\mathcal{H}]$. Therefore, the MMCD can measure the probability distribution differences more fully. As $MMCD[p,q,\mathcal{H}] = MMCD[q,p,\mathcal{H}]$, the MMCD also satisfies the symmetry constraint.

2.2.2. Quantitative Assessment

The sensitivity that exists between MSO and faults may be transformed into a leapfrog connection between residuals and faults using MSO design residuals. When there is no fault, the noise affects r, and the probability distribution of r and the noise are identical. When a fault occurs, r is affected by the fault, and the distribution of r is different. Subject to causality constraints, the distribution of r is also different for causal relationships. Here, a quantitative assessment technique based on MMCD is suggested to gauge how sensitive residuals are to faults. Based on $MSOs = \{MSO_1, MSO_2, \ldots, MSO_s\}$, the residuals $R = \{r_1, r_2, \ldots, r_s\}$ are designed. The faults are known to be $F = \{f_1, f_2, \ldots, f_g\}$, such that NF represents the no-fault mode. Assume that the probability distribution of R is p_{NF} when no fault occurs, which is denoted as $R \sim p_{NF}$, and the probability distribution of R is p_{f_i} when the fault f_i occurs, which is denoted as $R \sim p_{f_i}$. Relying on MMCD, the detection complexity $D(f_i, NF)$ of f_i is expressed as follows:

$$D(f_i, NF) = MMCD\left(p_{f_i}, p_{NF}, \mathcal{H}\right) \tag{18}$$

The isolation complexity $D(f_i, f_j)$ for f_i and f_j is expressed as follows:

$$D(f_i, f_j) = MMCD\left(p_{f_i}, p_{f_j}, \mathcal{H}\right) \tag{19}$$

Due to uncertainties such as noise and interference, $D(f_i, NF) > 0$ cannot be used to determine whether f_i occurs, and $D(f_i, f_j) > 0$ cannot determine whether f_i and f_j can be isolated. Thus, it is essential to establish the detectability limit σ_D and isolability limit σ_I to judge the diagnosability. In NF, the residual R_1 and R_2 of multiple repeated experiments are taken, and their probability distributions are p_{NF} and q_{NF}, respectively. The diagnosability limit is expressed as follows:

$$\sigma_D = \max_i\{MMCD(p_{NF}, 0, \mathcal{H})\} \tag{20}$$

$$\sigma_I = \max_i\{MMCD(p_{NF}, q_{NF}, \mathcal{H})\} \tag{21}$$

where $\max_i$ indicates the maximum value taken from several experiments. Therefore, if $D(f_i, NF) > \sigma_D$, it means that f_i can be detected, and the larger $|D(f_i, NF) - \sigma_D|$ is, the more straightforward it is to detect f_i. If $D(f_i, f_j) > \sigma_I$, it means that the f_i can be isolated from f_j, and the larger $|D(f_i, f_j) - \sigma_I|$ is, the lower the isolation difficulty of f_i and f_j.

Based on Equation (19), a quantitative assessment matrix D is established:

$$D = \begin{bmatrix} D(f_1, NF) & D(f_1, f_1) & D(f_1, f_2) & \cdots & D(f_1, f_g) \\ D(f_2, NF) & D(f_2, f_1) & D(f_2, f_2) & \cdots & D(f_2, f_g) \\ \vdots & \vdots & \vdots & \ddots & \vdots \\ D(f_g, NF) & D(f_g, f_1) & D(f_g, f_2) & \cdots & D(f_g, f_g) \end{bmatrix} \tag{22}$$

where $D(f_i, NF)$ indicates the detection complexity of the diagnostic system R for f_i, and $D(f_i, f_j)$ indicates the isolation complexity of R for f_i and f_j, $i, j = 1, 2, \ldots, g$. Given that MMCD has symmetry, $D(f_i, f_j) = D(f_j, f_i)$. As a single fault itself does not need to be considered for isolation, $D(f_i, f_i) = 0$. Based on Equations (20)~(22), the fault diagnosis matrix $D_d = [d_{ij}]_{g\times(g+1)}$ is established.

$$d_{ij} = \begin{cases} 1,\ if\ D(f_i, NF) > \sigma_D \wedge j = 1 \\ 1,\ if\ D(f_i, f_j) \le \sigma_I \vee D(f_i, f_i) = 0 \\ 0,\ otherwise \end{cases} \tag{23}$$

Based on D_d, the FDR is expressed as follows:

$$FDR = \frac{\sum\limits_{i=1}^{g} d_{i1}}{g} \tag{24}$$

The FIR is expressed as follows:

$$FIR = 1 - \frac{\sum_{i=1}^{g} \sum_{j=2, i \neq j}^{g+1} d_{ij}}{g(g-1)} \tag{25}$$

2.3. Diagnosability Optimization Design Using GWO Algorithm

2.3.1. Optimization Design Model

The number of MSOs grows exponentially with increasing redundancy in the system structure. Thus, to save design costs while designing the diagnostic system, it is necessary to optimize the optimal MSO from MSOs for diagnostic system design. Taking the causality constraints and diagnostic requirements into account, the steps of the diagnostic optimal design model are as follows:

Step 1: Build the system structure model $G(E, X, \overline{A})$;
Step 2: Using the causal MSO algorithm from the literature [27], obtain the $MSOs = \{MSO_1, MSO_2, \ldots, MSO_s\}$ under different causal conditions;
Step 3: Design the residual set $R_{con} = \{r_1, r_2, \ldots, r_w\}$ that satisfies the diagnosability requirement;
Step 4: Construct the vector $\boldsymbol{c} = [c_i]_{1\times w}$;

$$c_i = \begin{cases} 1, \ if \ r_i \ is \ selected \\ 0, \ otherwise \end{cases} \tag{26}$$

Then, the optimized diagnostic system is $R := R_{con}. * c$. Based on MMCD, a quantitative assessment matrix D is established for R.

Step 5: Assume that the design cost of R_{con} is $\gamma = [\gamma_i]_{1\times w}$. Then, the design cost of R is expressed as follows:

$$cost = \sum_{i=1}^{w} \gamma_i c_i \tag{27}$$

In summary, the diagnostic optimization model can be expressed as follows:

$$min \ cost = \sum_{i=1}^{b} \gamma_i c_i \tag{28}$$

$$s.t. \ D \geq D^{req} \tag{29}$$

where D^{req} represents the quantitative demand matrix, typically the diagnosability limit σ.

2.3.2. Diagnosability Optimization Design Strategy Based on the GWO Algorithm

The GWO algorithm is a new type of pack intelligence optimization algorithm that mimics the hunting behavior and social hierarchy of gray wolf packs. Individual wolves are generally divided into four classes; namely, α, β, δ, and ω wolves. Among them, the α wolf is the leader, representing the optimal solution in the population, and is the supreme ruler and manager of the wolf pack. The β and δ wolves represent the second- and third-best solutions in the population, and the remaining solutions are regarded as ω wolves.

The optimization process of the GWO algorithm is divided into three steps: first, searching and tracking the prey; second, hunting and encircling the prey until the prey stops moving; and finally, attacking the prey. The position update formula for the wolves searching and surrounding prey is expressed as follows:

$$\boldsymbol{X}(t+1) = \boldsymbol{X}_p(t) - \boldsymbol{A} \cdot \boldsymbol{D} \tag{30}$$

where

$$D = |C \cdot X_p(t) - X(t)| \tag{31}$$

In the above equation, t is the current iteration number, X_p is the prey position, X is the gray wolf position, and A and C are the coefficient vectors of the algorithm.

$$A = 2\boldsymbol{a} \cdot \boldsymbol{rand}_1 - \boldsymbol{a} \tag{32}$$

$$C = 2\boldsymbol{rand}_2 \tag{33}$$

Here, $\boldsymbol{rand}_1$ and $\boldsymbol{rand}_2$ are random vectors between $[0, 1]$, and $\boldsymbol{a}$ is the tuning parameter, which is expressed as follows:

$$a = 2\left(1 - \frac{t}{t_{\max}}\right) \tag{34}$$

where $t_{\max}$ is the maximum number of iterations and $A \in [-2\boldsymbol{a}, 2\boldsymbol{a}]$, $C \in [0, 2]$.

The position of the ω wolf is based on the positions of α wolf, β wolf, and δ wolf. Therefore, once the positions of α wolf, β wolf, and δ wolf have been determined, the location of the prey can be determined based on the distance between them.

$$\begin{cases} X_\alpha(t+1) = X_\alpha(t) - A_1 \cdot |C_1 \cdot X_\alpha(t) - X(t)| \\ X_\beta(t+1) = X_\beta(t) - A_2 \cdot |C_2 \cdot X_\beta(t) - X(t)| \\ X_\delta(t+1) = X_\delta(t) - A_3 \cdot |C_3 \cdot X_\delta(t) - X(t)| \\ X_\omega(t+1) = \sum\limits_{j=\alpha,\beta,\delta} w_j X_j(t+1) \end{cases} \tag{35}$$

Here, w_j is the weighting factor for α, β, and δ wolves.

$$w_j = \frac{f(X_j(t))}{f(X_\alpha(t)) + f(X_\beta(t)) + f(X_\delta(t))} \tag{36}$$

In the above equation, $f(X_j(t))$ denotes the acclimatization value of the j-th gray wolf individual in the t-th generation.

The optimal design strategy for causal diagnosability based on the GWO algorithm is outlined below.

Step 1: For parameter initialization, set the gray wolf population as $N = 50$, maximum iteration number $t_{\max} = 20$, and parameters $\boldsymbol{a}$, A, and C. The parameters of MMCD are selected from the optimal parameter settings verified in the literature [40];
Step 2: Based on Equation (26), initialize the position of the gray wolf population X;
Step 3: If the constraints shown in Equation (29) are satisfied, calculate its fitness value based on Equation (28); otherwise, its fitness value is infinity. Second, determine the α wolf, β wolf, and δ wolf according to the merit of fitness;
Step 4: Update the location of the gray wolf population based on Equation (35);
Step 5: Update the parameters $\boldsymbol{a}$, A, and C;
Step 6: Judge whether the maximum number of iterations has been reached. If so, stop the algorithm and return as the optimal solution X_α; otherwise, return to step 3.

3. Results and Analysis

In this section, causal diagnosability is optimally designed based on the fixed-wing UAV structural model. Section 3.1 establishes the UAV structural model and analyzes its structural characteristics and its causal diagnosability. In Section 3.2, based on the MSO, the system residuals are designed, and the influencing factors of diagnosability are studied in a simulation scenario. In Section 3.3, based on the MMCD, the probability distribution difference of fault residuals is measured to evaluate quantitatively the system's diagnosability. In Section 3.4, to minimize the cost of the diagnostic system design under the premise of maximizing the system's diagnosability requirements, the optimal diagnostic system is optimized based on the GWO algorithm for the diagnosability of the UAV.

3.1. Causal Diagnosability of Fixed-Wing UAVs

For simulation verification in this research, the fixed-wing UAV model M_{UAV} from the literature [27] is utilized, and the mathematical model is expressed as follows:

$$\begin{aligned} \dot{x} &= Ax + Bu + F \\ y &= Cx \end{aligned} \tag{37}$$

where $x = [x_1, x_2, \ldots, x_7]^T$ are the system states, $u = [u_1, u_2]^T$ are the system inputs, $F = [f_1, f_2, f_3, f_4, f_5, f_6, f_7]^T$ are the system faults, and $y = [y_1, y_2, y_3]^T$ are the system outputs.

$$A = \begin{bmatrix} -0.28 & 0 & -32.90 & 9.81 & 0 & -5.43 & 0 \\ -0.10 & -8.325 & 3.75 & 0 & 0 & 0 & -28.64 \\ 0.37 & 0 & -0.64 & 0 & 0 & -9.49 & 0 \\ 0 & 1 & 0 & 0 & 0 & 0 & 0 \\ 0 & 0 & 1 & 0 & 0 & 0 & 0 \\ 0 & 0 & 0 & 0 & 0 & -10 & 0 \\ 0 & 0 & 0 & 0 & 0 & 0 & -5 \end{bmatrix} \tag{38}$$

$$B = \begin{bmatrix} 0 & 0 & 0 & 0 & 0 & 20 & 0 \\ 0 & 0 & 0 & 0 & 0 & 0 & 10 \end{bmatrix}^T \tag{39}$$

$$C = \begin{bmatrix} 1 & 0 & 0 & 0 & 0 & 0 & 0 \\ 0 & 0 & 0 & 1 & 0 & 0 & 0 \\ 0 & 0 & 0 & 0 & 1 & 0 & 0 \end{bmatrix} \tag{40}$$

The structural model of M_{UAV} and the DM decomposition schematic are shown in Figure 9. As shown in Figure 9a, the dynamic constraint equation shown in Equation (2) is also added to the structural model of M_{UAV}. As shown in Figure 9b, $M_{UAV} = (M_{UAV})^+$.

Using the search method reported in the literature [27], the MSOs of M_{UAV} can be obtained as shown in Figure 10. The rows of the matrix in Figure 10 illustrate the MSOs, the columns illustrate the equations, and the elements of the matrix contain {'int', 'der', 'mixed'} as well as empty elements. The empty element of the matrix means that the equation corresponding to the column in which the position is located is not among the MSOs corresponding to its row. If the element of the matrix is not empty (i.e., {'int', 'der', 'mixed'}), it means that the equation corresponding to the column where the position is located is in the MSO corresponding to the row. As an example, $MSO_1 = \{e_3, e_5, e_6, e_8, e_{10}, e_{13}, e_{15}, e_{16}\}$. Further, suppose the matrix element is 'int'('der', 'mixed'). In this case, it means that when the equation corresponding to the column in which the position is located is selected as the redundant equation, MSO is integrally (differential, mixed) causal. Taking MSO_1 as an example, if e_6, e_8, and e_{10} are selected as redundant equations, the causal relationships are shown in Figure 11. As shown in Figure 11a, when e_6 is chosen as the redundant equation, the maximum matching relation of MSO_1 contains only 'D' except for the normal edges, so it is differentially causal. Similarly, when e_8 is a redundant equation, MSO_1 is mixed causal; when e_{10} is a redundant equation, MSO_1 is integrally causal.

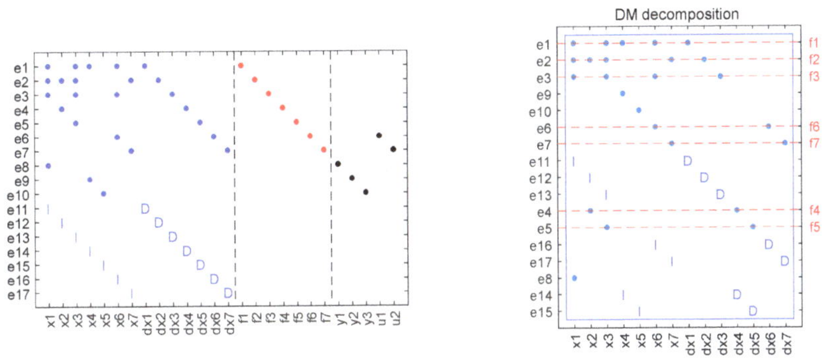

(**a**) (**b**)

Figure 9. The structural analysis of M_{UAV}. (**a**) Structural model. (**b**) DM decomposition.

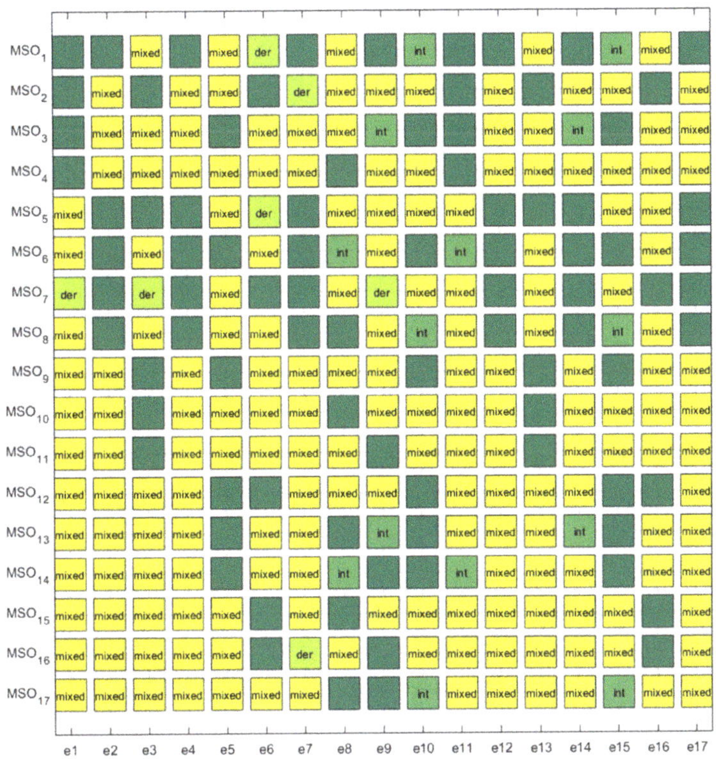

Figure 10. The MSOs and causality of M_{UAV}.

Based on Figure 10, the integrally causal MSOs of M_{UAV} are $intMSOs = \{MSO_1, MSO_3, MSO_6, MSO_8, MSO_{13}, MSO_{14}, MSO_{17}\}$. Based on Equations (7) and (8), the FSM and FIM of $intMSOs$ are established as shown in Figure 12. The dot in the figure represents matrix element 1. As shown in Figure 12a, under the integral causality condition, $FDR_4 = 100\%$. From Figure 12b, $FIR_4 = 57.14\%$. Based on Figure 10, the differential causal MSOs are $derMSOs = \{MSO_1, MSO_2, MSO_5, MSO_7, MSO_{16}\}$. The FSM and FIM of $derMSOs$ are shown in Figure 13, with $FDR_5 = 100\%$ and $FIR_5 = 71.43\%$. Based on Figure 10, the mixed causal MSOs can be obtained as

$mixMSOs = \{MSO_1, MSO_2, \ldots, MSO_{17}\}$. The diagnosability result of $mixMSOs$ is shown in Figure 14, with $FDR_6 = 100\%$, and $FIR_6 = 85.71\%$. It can be found that the diagnosability is different under different causal constraints, with the best diagnosability obtained under mixed causal constraints and the worst diagnosability obtained under integral causal constraints. This further validates the effect of causality on diagnosability.

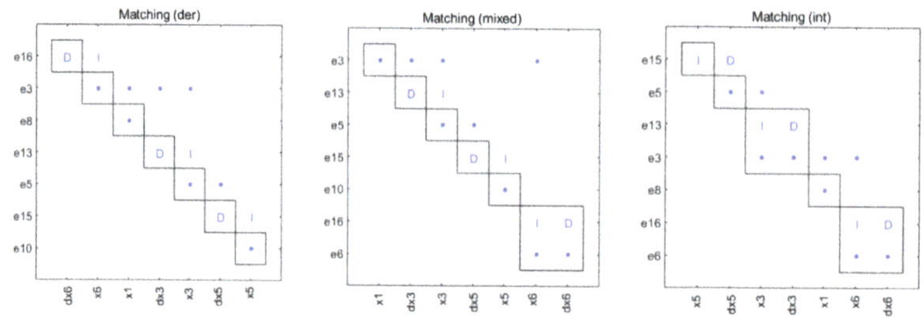

(a) (b) (c)

Figure 11. The causal matching relationships of MSO_1. (a) Differential causal matching. (b) Mixed causal matching. (c) Integral causal matching.

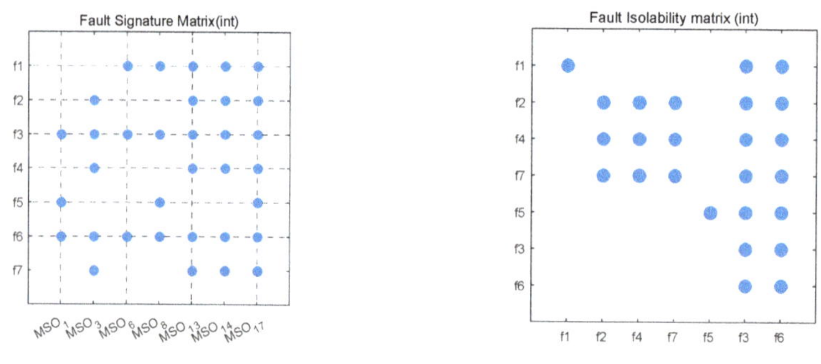

(a) (b)

Figure 12. Diagnosability analysis results of $intMSOs$. (a) Fault signature matrix. (b) Fault isolation matrix.

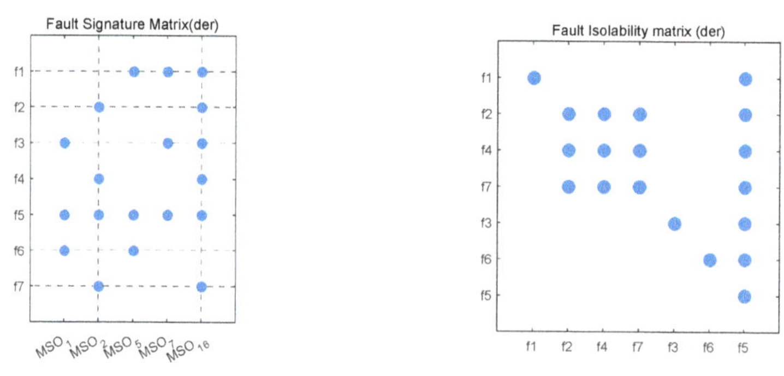

(a) (b)

Figure 13. Diagnosability analysis results of $derMSOs$. (a) Fault signature matrix. (b) Fault isolation matrix.

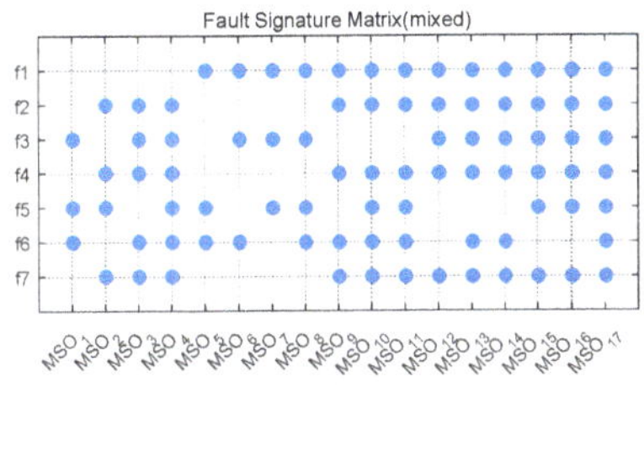

(a)

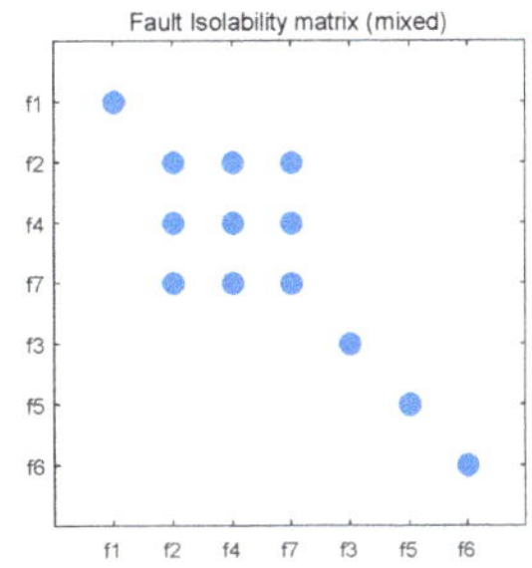

(b)

Figure 14. Diagnosability analysis results of $mixMSOs$. (**a**) Fault signature matrix. (**b**) Fault isolation matrix.

3.2. Diagnosability Impact Factor Analysis

To verify the diagnosability of different faults and the responsiveness linking MSOs to faults, the sequential residual method is used for residual design. Figure 15a displays the simulation results of M_{UAV} without fault, where ref_1 and ref_2 are the reference input signals. When f_2 occurs, the simulation results of M_{UAV} are shown in Figure 15b, and all the system faults are slope faults as shown in the figure. The used simulation software was MATLAB (2021b version). The initial state of the system is $x_0 = [0]^{\mathrm{T}}_{1\times 7}$, and noise is not considered here. Based on MSO_1 (MSO_3, MSO_6), e_{10} (e_9, e_8) is selected as the redundancy equation to design the residual $r1_{\mathrm{int}}$ ($r2_{\mathrm{int}}$, $r3_{\mathrm{int}}$). As shown in Figure 10, the residuals $\{r1_{\mathrm{int}}, r2_{\mathrm{int}}, r3_{\mathrm{int}}\}$ are integrally causal, and Figure 16a displays each residual's simulation results. Figure 16a shows that $r1_{\mathrm{int}}$ jumps when faults $\{f_3, f_5, f_6\}$ occur, which is consistent with the mapping relationship between MSO_1 and faults shown in Figure 12a. This further verifies the reasonableness and validity of the causal diagnosability. Comparing the residuals in the figure, it can be observed that when the fault occurs, the exact causal residuals are inconsistent in the degree of jump to the fault. For example, the magnitude and direction of the jumps of $r1_{\mathrm{int}}$ to $\{f_3, f_5, f_6\}$ are inconsistent. The larger the degree of the leap of the residual to the fault is, the stronger the diagnostic ability of the residual to the fault and the better the diagnosable performance.

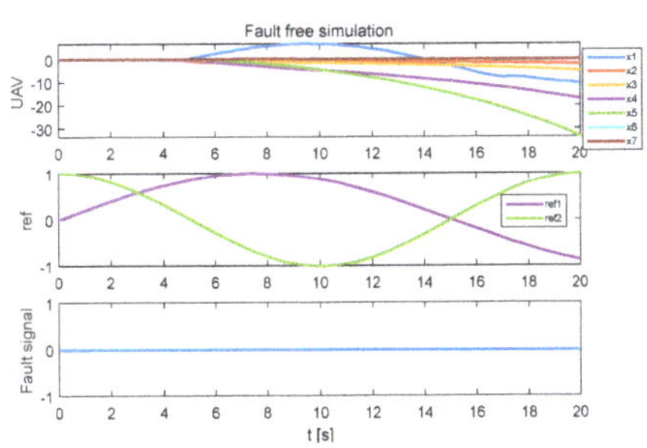

(a)

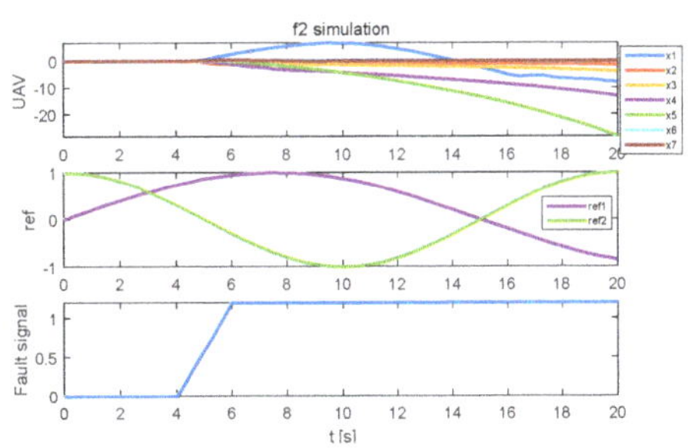

(b)

Figure 15. Simulation run results for M_{UAV}. (**a**) Normal operation. (**b**) f_2 occurs.

To verify the effect of causality on diagnosability, here, based on MSO_1, equations e_6, e_8, and e_{10} are selected as redundant equations to design the residuals $r1_{der}$, $r1_{mix}$, and $r1_{\mathrm{int}}$, respectively. As shown in Figure 11, $r1_{der}$, $r1_{mix}$, and $r1_{\mathrm{int}}$ are differentially causal, mixed causal, and integrally causal, respectively, and the simulation results are shown in Figure 16b. Figure 16b shows that the residuals with the same MSO design have different causality, and their sensitivity to faults differs. For f_3, f_5, and f_6, the jump of $r1_{\text{int}}$ is significantly more potent than the other two residuals. Therefore, $r1_{\text{int}}$ is more sensitive to the fault than $r1_{mix}$ and $r1_{der}$. This means that the integral diagnosability of MSO_1 is stronger than the other causal diagnosability.

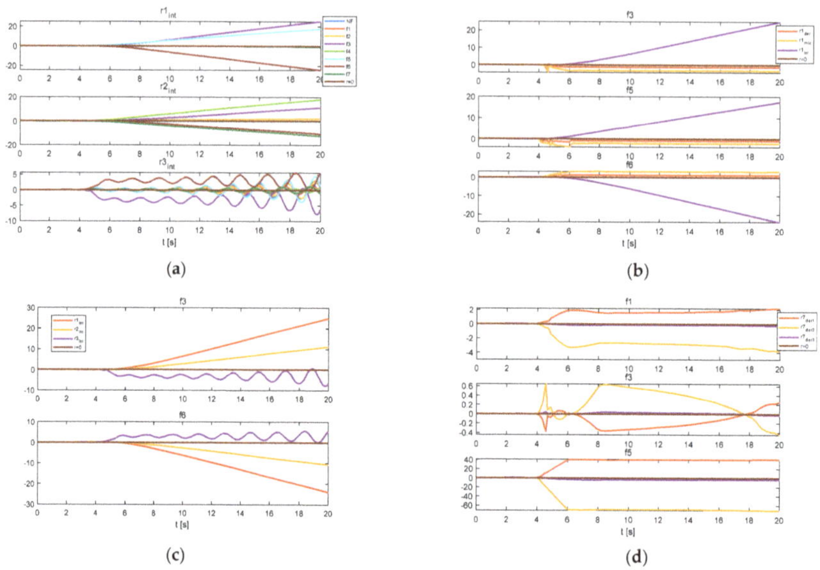

Figure 16. Diagnosability impact factor analysis. (**a**) Fault. (**b**) Causality. (**c**) MSO. (**d**) Residual.

To verify the effect of MSO on diagnosability, the sensitivity relationships of residuals $r1_{\text{int}}$, $r2_{\text{int}}$, and $r3_{\text{int}}$ to faults f_3 and f_6 are verified here, as shown in Figure 16c. Based on Figure 12a, the sensitivity relationship with f_3 and f_6 exists for $r1_{\text{int}}$, $r2_{\text{int}}$, and $r3_{\text{int}}$. Figure 16c shows that for f_3 and f_6, the jump of $r1_{\text{int}}$ is much more significant than that for $r2_{\text{int}}$ and $r3_{\text{int}}$. This indicates that the sensitivity of different MSOs to the faults is not the same, and their diagnosability also differs.

To confirm how residuals affect diagnosability, the residuals $r7_{der1}$, $r7_{der2}$, and $r7_{der3}$ are designed based on MSO_7, and equations e_1, e_3, and e_9 are selected as redundant equations, respectively. From Figure 9, $r7_{der1}$, $r7_{der2}$, and $r7_{der3}$ are differentially causal, and the simulation results of the residuals for f_1, f_3, and f_5 are shown in Figure 16d. Figure 13a shows that MSO_7 has a sensitive relationship with f_1, f_3, and f_5. As shown in Figure 16d, when the selected redundancy equation is e_3, the differential residual $r7_{der2}$ designed based on MSO_7 has the most significant jump and the strongest diagnostic performance. Therefore, different residuals have different impacts on diagnosability.

In summary, faults, causality, MSO, and residuals all have an impact on the diagnosability, and changes in any of these factors can alter the fault diagnostic ability of the residuals, which subsequently affects the diagnosability.

3.3. MMCD-Based Diagnosability Quantitative Assessment

Structural analysis can only qualitatively analyze the diagnosability, so this paper proposes a quantitative assessment method based on MMCD. As shown in Figure 12, there are a total of seven integral causal MSO; namely, $intMSOs = \{MSO_1, MSO_3, MSO_6, MSO_8, MSO_{13}, MSO_{14}, MSO_{17}\}$. As shown in Figure 10, two integral causal residuals can be designed for each integral causal MSO. The integral causal residual of the $intMSOs$ is $R_{\text{int}} = \{r1_{\text{int1}}, r1_{\text{int2}}, r3_{\text{int3}}, r3_{\text{int4}}, r6_{\text{int5}}, r6_{\text{int6}}, r8_{\text{int7}}, r8_{\text{int8}}, r13_{\text{int9}}, r13_{\text{int10}}, r14_{\text{int11}}, r14_{\text{int12}}, r17_{\text{int13}}, r17_{\text{int14}}\}$. Based on MMCD, the fault detection matrix D_1 for R_{int} can be obtained, as shown in Figure 17a. The first seven columns reflect the faults, the final column represents the diagnosability limit (σ), and the rows of D_1 represent the residuals. For example, $D_1(r1_{\text{int1}}, f_1) = 0.0064$ represents the diagnosability of $r1_{\text{int1}}$ for f_1, and $D_1(r1_{\text{int1}}, \sigma) = 0.00352$ represents the diagnosability limit of $r1_{\text{int1}}$. As $D_1(r1_{\text{int1}}, \sigma) > D_1(r1_{\text{int1}}, f_1)$, $r1_{\text{int1}}$ cannot diagnose f_1. Further, as $D_1(r1_{\text{int1}}, f_3) > D_1(r1_{\text{int1}}, f_5) > D_1(r1_{\text{int1}}, f_6) > D_1(r1_{\text{int1}}, f_4) > D_1(r1_{\text{int1}}, \sigma) > D_1(r1_{\text{int1}}, f_7) > D_1(r1_{\text{int1}}, f_2) > D_1(r1_{\text{int1}}, f_1)$, $r1_{\text{int1}}$ can diagnose $\{f_3, f_4, f_5, f_6\}$. The sensitivity of $r1_{\text{int1}}$ to the faults is $f_3 > f_5 > f_6 > f_4$. From a qualitative point of view, $r1_{\text{int1}}$ cannot diagnose fault f_4. However, a coupling relationship exists between the states. When a fault occurs in one state, it affects the changes in other states because the fault is transmissible. Therefore, from a quantitative point of view, $r1_{\text{int1}}$ can diagnose f_4. This also reflects the advantage of quantitative assessment.

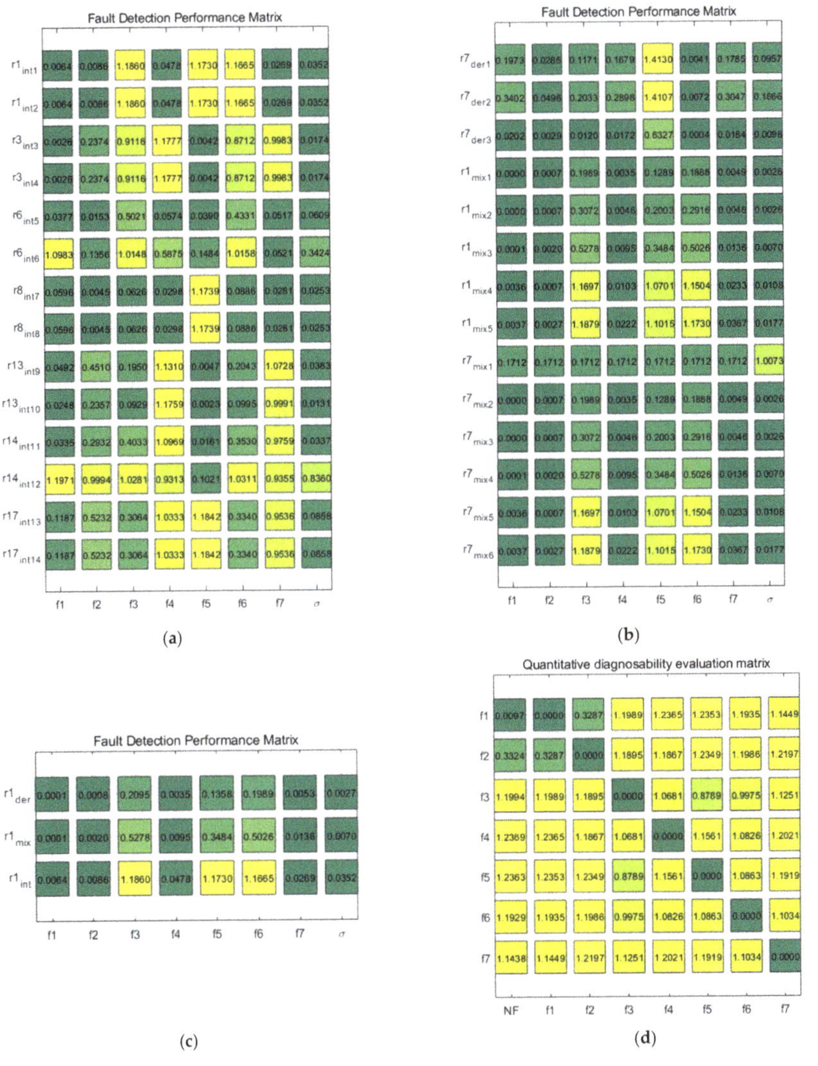

Figure 17. MMCD-based quantitative assessment of diagnosability. (**a**) Integral causality. (**b**) Differential and mixed causation. (**c**) Causal comparison. (**d**) Diagnosability quantitative assessment.

As shown in Figure 17a, comparing the fault diagnostic values of the residuals of the same MSO design, it can be found that the diagnosability is the same for the integrally causal residuals based on $\{MSO_1, MSO_3, MSO_8, MSO_{17}\}$. However, the diagnosability of the integrally causal residuals based on $\{MSO_6, MSO_{13}, MSO_{14}\}$ designs is different. For comparative analysis, the mixed causal residual $R1_{mix} = \{r1_{mix1}, r1_{mix2}, r1_{mix3}, r1_{mix4}, r1_{mix5}\}$ is designed based on MSO_1. The differentially causal residual $R7_{der} = \{r7_{der1}, r7_{der2}, r7_{der3}\}$ and the mixed causal residual $R7_{mix} = \{r7_{mix1}, r7_{mix2}, r7_{mix3}, r7_{mix4}, r7_{mix5}, r7_{mix6}\}$ are designed based on MSO_7. The fault diagnosis matrix D_2 for residual $\{R1_{\text{mix}}, R7_{der}, R7_{mix}\}$ is shown in Figure 17b. The comparative analysis reveals that the fault diagnosis capabilities of $R1_{mix}$, $R7_{der}$, and $R7_{mix}$ are different. Therefore, most of the fault diagnosis capabilities in the same causal residuals based on the same MSO design are inconsistent.

To further verify the effect of causality on diagnosability, here, based on MSO_1, e_6, e_8, and e_{10} are selected as redundant equations, and the differential causal residuals $r1_{der}$, the mixed causal residuals $r1_{mix}$, and the integral causal residuals $r1_{\text{int}}$ are sequentially designed. The fault diagnostic capability matrix D_3 of $\{r1_{der}, r1_{mix}, r1_{\text{int}}\}$ is shown in Figure 17c. As $|D_3(r1_{\text{int}}, f_3) - D_3(r1_{\text{int}}, \sigma)| > |D_3(r1_{mix}, f_3) - D_3(r1_{mix}, \sigma)| > |D_3(r1_{der}, f_3) - D_3(r1_{der}, \sigma)|$, the fault diagnosis capability of $r1_{\text{int}}$ is more potent than that of $r1_{der}$ and $r1_{mix}$. Therefore, the influence of causality must be taken into account in the design of the diagnostic system.

When $R_1 = \{r1_{\text{int1}}, r1_{\text{int2}}, r3_{\text{int3}}, r3_{\text{int4}}\}$ in Figure 17a is selected as the diagnostic system, the fault diagnosis matrix D_4 of R_1 is displayed in Figure 17d. Here, the detectability limit $\sigma_{D_1} = 0.0555$, and the isolability limit $\sigma_{I_1} = 0$. As $D_4(f_4, NF) > D_4(f_5, NF) > D_4(f_3, NF) > D_4(f_6, NF) > D_4(f_7, NF) > D_4(f_2, NF) > \sigma_{D_1} > D_4(f_1, NF)$, R_1 can diagnose all faults except f_1, which is consistent with the sensitivity of MSO_1 and MSO_3 to faults, as shown in Figure 12a. The fault detection rate of R_1 is $FDR_7 = 85.71\%$. As fault diagnosis is a prerequisite for fault isolation, $D_4(f_1, \cdot) > \sigma_{I_1}$ and $D_4(\cdot, f_1) > \sigma_{I_1}$ are meaningless. As $D_4(f_i, f_j) > \sigma_{I_1}$, $i \neq j$, and $i, j = 2, \ldots, 7$, the fault isolation rate of R_1 is $FIR_7 = 71.43\%$. As shown in Figure 11a, from a qualitative assessment point of view, R_1 does not guarantee that the faults $\{f_2, f_4, f_7\}$ are isolated from each other or that the faults $\{f_3, f_6\}$ are isolated from each other. However, from the perspective of quantitative assessment, the faults in $\{f_3, f_6\}$ and $\{f_2, f_4, f_7\}$ are isolated from each other. As shown in Figure 16, the sensitivity of the same residuals to different faults and the degree of jump of different residuals when the same fault occurs are different. Based on MMCD, this difference can be quantitatively characterized, which is not possible with qualitative assessment.

3.4. Diagnosability Optimization Design Based on the GWO Algorithm

To fully consider the causal diagnosability difference of the residuals of the same MSO design, it is necessary to determine the residuals with the most considerable diagnosability ability in the residual set of the same MSO design based on MMCD before optimization of the diagnosability design. First, based on each $MSO_i = \{e_j\}$ in $MSOs = \{MSO_1, MSO_2, \ldots, MSO_{17}\}$, take any one of the equations e_j design residuals $R_i = \{r_{ij}\}$ in turn. Second, based on MMCD, calculate the fault detection matrix D_i of R_i. Then, calculate the fault diagnostic capability $D_{r_{ij}} = \left\{d_{r_{ij}}\right\}$ of the residual $R_i = \{r_{ij}\}$.

$$d_{r_{ij}} = \sum_{k=1}^{7} \varepsilon\left(D_i(r_{ij}, f_k) - \sigma_{r_{ij}}\right) \tag{41}$$

Here,

$$\varepsilon(\alpha) = \begin{cases} |\alpha|, \ if\ \alpha > 0 \\ 0, \ otherwise \end{cases} \tag{42}$$

Then, the residual r_i corresponding to the maximum value $\max\{D_{r_{ij}}\}$ in $D_{r_{ij}}$ is found. Finally, the set of candidate residuals is obtained as $R_{con} = \{r_1, r_2, \ldots, r_{17}\}$. The causality of R_{con} and the selected redundancy equations are shown in Figure 18a, and Figure 18b displays its fault diagnosis performance matrix D_6. The matrix D_5, as shown in Figure 18a, has rows representing each MSO and columns representing causality. For example, $D_5(MSO_1, \text{int}) = e_{10}$ indicates that when MSO_1 chooses e_{10} as the redundant equation, the diagnostic performance of the designed residual is maximized, and the residual is integrally causal. Here, the optimal residuals are mixed causal except for the optimal residuals of MSO_1, which are integrally causal.

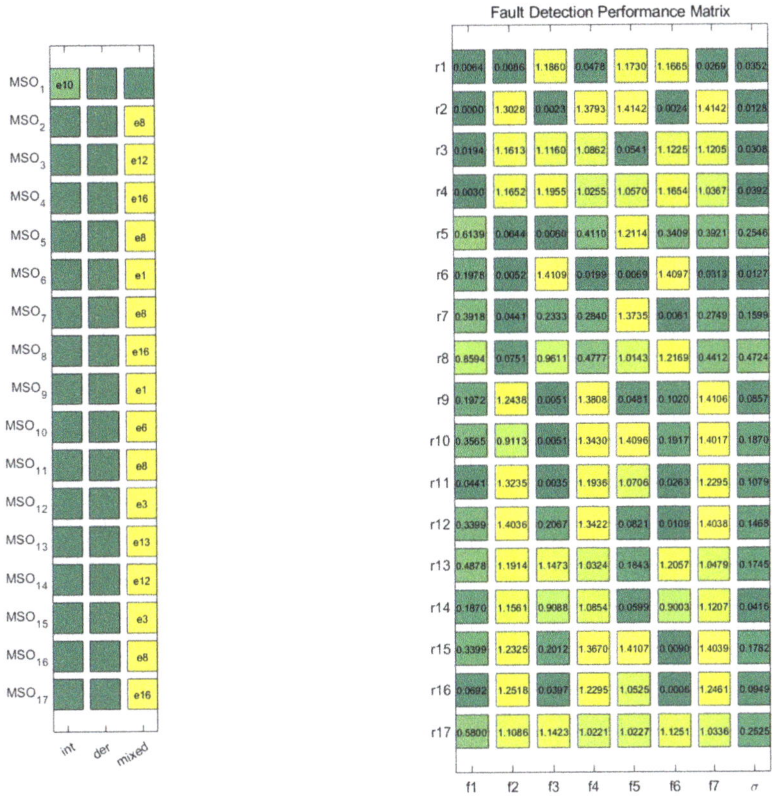

(a) (b)

Figure 18. Causal diagnosability of R_{con}. (**a**) Causality. (**b**) Fault diagnosis matrix of R_{con}.

To fulfill the diagnosability and the cost of the diagnostic system, this paper uses the diagnosability optimization design strategy based on the GWO algorithm and selects the residual set R of R_{con} with the best comprehensive performance. For comparison and evaluation, this study employs the simulated annealing (SA), genetic (GA), and sine-cosine (SCA) algorithms for analysis. Let $\gamma_i = 1$, and the diagnosability optimization results are illustrated in Figure 19.

Figure 19a shows the fitness curves of each algorithm. The GWO algorithm achieves the optimal value in the second iteration, which is advantageous in terms of the optimization searching speed compared with other algorithms. In terms of optimization accuracy, both the GWO algorithm and the SCA achieved the optimal value. Figure 19b,c show the FSM and FIM of the MSO corresponding to the optimized residuals. Combined with Figure 18a, it can be observed that the GWO algorithm optimizes the $\{MSO_1, MSO_2, MSO_7, MSO_9, MSO_{14}\}$ to design the residuals $R = \{r_1, r_2, r_7, r_9, r_{14}\}$, and all the residuals are mixed causal except for r_1, which is integrally causal. From a qualitative assessment point of view, based on Figure 19b, $FDR_8 = 100\%$ can be obtained. Based on Figure 19c, $FIR_8 = 85.71\%$ can be obtained.

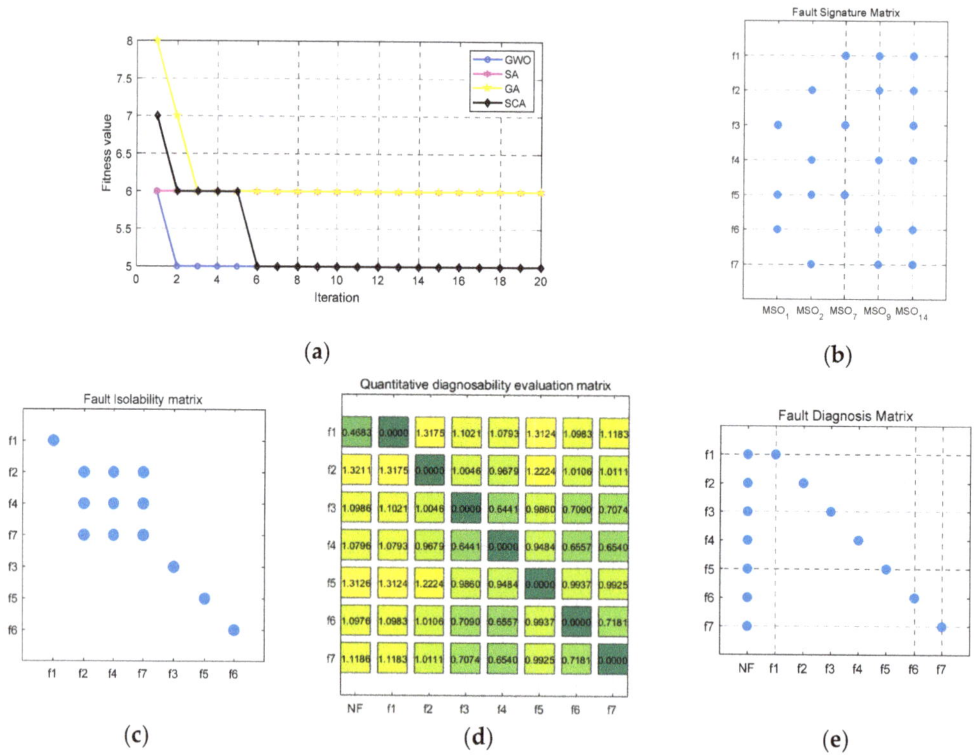

Figure 19. Diagnosability optimization results based on the GWO algorithm. (**a**) Fitness curves. (**b**) Fault signature matrix. (**c**) Fault isolation matrix. (**d**) Diagnosability quantitative assessment matrix. (**e**) Fault diagnosis matrix.

Using MMCD, the quantitative assessment matrix D_7 of $\{r_1, r_2, r_7, r_9, r_{14}\}$ can be obtained as shown in Figure 19d, where the detectability limit $\sigma_{D_2} = 0.1891$ and the isolation limit $\sigma_{I_1} = 0.0428$. Based on D_7 and Equation (27), its fault diagnosis matrix D_8 is established as shown in Figure 19e. Therefore, from the perspective of quantitative assessment, $FDR_9 = 100\%$ and $FIR_9 = 100\% > FIR_8$ can be obtained. Comparing Figure 19e with Figure 19c, it is observed that $\{f_2, f_4, f_7\}$ are not isolated from each other in the qualitative assessment. However, in the quantitative assessment, they can indeed be isolated. This is mainly due to the fact that the residuals are not sensitive to the faults. From the causality of the optimized residuals, it can be seen that mixed causality accounts for 80% of the residuals, which further reflects the advantage of mixed causality. From the results of the quantitative optimization, the overall cost of optimization is reduced by 70.59%, and the system achieves a 100% fault detection rate and fault isolation rate. This further demonstrates the advantages of the quantitative assessment.

4. Summary

To improve UAV reliability and diagnosability, this study suggested a causal diagnosability optimization design approach based on the MMCD and GWO algorithms. First, this study offers a qualitative approach to causal diagnosability evaluation based on structural analysis; second, to measure the ease of fault diagnosis, it presents a quantitative approach to causal diagnosability evaluation using the MMCD; and third, to balance the need for diagnosability and the cost of diagnostic system design, it suggests a design strategy to maximize causal diagnosability using the GWO algorithm. According to simulation findings, the enhanced diagnostic system maintains 100% fault isolation and detection rates while reducing design costs by 70.59%.

Furthermore, the findings of the causal diagnosability evaluation indicate that, first, the diagnosability varies depending on the causality. Under mixed causal constraints, diagnosability performs the best among them. Second, different evaluation techniques have various diagnoses. This is mostly because faults and residuals have different sensitivity levels, and the quantitative evaluation successfully captures and quantifies these sensitivity variations. This explains why the quantitative assessment isolates flaws that the qualitative review cannot identify.

Future studies might examine how interference and noise affect diagnosability. Furthermore, optimizing the diagnosability of the structurally precise and poorly defined subsystems is possible.

Author Contributions: Conceptualization, X.G. and X.S.; formal analysis, X.G. and X.S.; investigation, X.G. and X.S.; writing—original draft preparation, X.G. and X.S.; writing—review and editing, X.G. All authors have read and agreed to the published version of the manuscript.

Funding: This research received no external funding.

Data Availability Statement: The original contributions presented in this study are included in the article. Further inquiries can be directed to the corresponding authors.

Conflicts of Interest: The authors declare no conflicts of interest.

References

1. Mohsan, S.A.H.; Khan, M.A.; Noor, F.; Ullah, I.; Alsharif, M.H. Towards the Unmanned Aerial Vehicles (UAVs): A Comprehensive Review. *Drones* **2022**, *6*, 147. [CrossRef]
2. del Cerro, J.; Cruz Ulloa, C.; Barrientos, A.; de León Rivas, J. Unmanned Aerial Vehicles in Agriculture: A Survey. *Agronomy* **2021**, *11*, 203. [CrossRef]
3. Ghamari, M.; Rangel, P.; Mehrubeoglu, M.; Tewolde, G.S.; Sherratt, R.S. Unmanned Aerial Vehicle Communications for Civil Applications: A Review. *IEEE Access* **2022**, *10*, 102492–102531. [CrossRef]
4. Zuo, Z.; Liu, C.; Han, Q.-L.; Song, J. Unmanned Aerial Vehicles: Control Methods and Future Challenges. *IEEE/CAA J. Autom. Sin.* **2022**, *9*, 601–614. [CrossRef]
5. Gu, X.; Shi, X. A review of research on diagnosability of control systems. *Energy Rep.* **2024**, *11*, 2174–2188. [CrossRef]
6. Fourlas, G.K.; Karras, G.C. A Survey on Fault Diagnosis Methods for UAVs. In Proceedings of the 2021 International Conference on Unmanned Aircraft Systems (ICUAS), Athens, Greece, 15–18 June 2021; pp. 394–403. [CrossRef]
7. Fourlas, G.K.; Karras, G.C. A Survey on Fault Diagnosis and Fault-Tolerant Control Methods for Unmanned Aerial Vehicles. *Machines* **2021**, *9*, 197. [CrossRef]
8. Iannace, G.; Ciaburro, G.; Trematerra, A. Fault Diagnosis for UAV Blades Using Artificial Neural Network. *Robotics* **2019**, *8*, 59. [CrossRef]
9. Liang, S.; Zhang, S.; Huang, Y.; Zheng, X.; Cheng, J.; Wu, S. Data-driven fault diagnosis of FW-UAVs with consideration of multiple operation conditions. *ISA Trans.* **2022**, *126*, 472–485. [CrossRef]

10. Zhang, Y.; Li, S.; Zhang, A.; An, X. FW-UAV fault diagnosis based on knowledge complementary network under small sample. *Mech. Syst. Signal Process.* **2024**, *215*, 111418. [CrossRef]
11. Hua, L.; Zhang, J.; Li, D.; Xi, X.; Shah, M.A. Sensor Fault Diagnosis and Fault Tolerant Control of Quadrotor UAV Based on Genetic Algorithm. *J. Sens.* **2022**, *2022*, 8626722. [CrossRef]
12. Gu, X.; Shi, X. A Review of Research on Diagnosability of Control Systems Based on Structural Analysis. *Appl. Sci.* **2023**, *13*, 12241. [CrossRef]
13. Chen, Z.; Xu, J.; Peng, T.; Yang, C. Graph Convolutional Network-Based Method for Fault Diagnosis Using a Hybrid of Measurement and Prior Knowledge. *IEEE Trans. Cybern.* **2022**, *52*, 9157–9169. [CrossRef] [PubMed]
14. Cheng, Y.; D'Arpino, M.; Rizzoni, G. Fault Diagnosis in Lithium-ion Battery of Hybrid Electric Aircraft based on Structural Analysis. In Proceedings of the 2022 IEEE Transportation Electrification Conference & Expo (ITEC), Anaheim, CA, USA, 15–17 June 2022; pp. 997–1004. [CrossRef]
15. Li, X.; Xu, J.; Chen, Z.; Xu, S.; Liu, K. Real-Time Fault Diagnosis of Pulse Rectifier in Traction System Based on Structural Model. *IEEE Trans. Intell. Transp. Syst.* **2022**, *23*, 2130–2143. [CrossRef]
16. Yin, C.; He, Z.; Wang, J.; Zhou, H. A method for fault diagnosability evaluation of spacecraft control system. In Proceedings of the 2016 Joint International Information Technology, Mechanical and Electronic Engineering, Xi'an, China, 4–5 October 2016; Xu, B., Chen, Y.N., Zhao, L.H., Eds.; Atlantis Press: Paris, France, 2016; Volume 59, pp. 611–614.
17. Cui, Y.; Shi, J.; Wang, Z. System-level operational diagnosability analysis in quasi real-time fault diagnosis: The probabilistic approach. *J. Process Control* **2014**, *24*, 1444–1453. [CrossRef]
18. Cheng, Y.; Liu, Y.; Yang, S.; Wu, J. Multi-sensor optimal placement of rotor-bearing system based on fault diagnosability. *Proc. Inst. Mech. Eng. Part C J. Mech. Eng. Sci.* **2023**, *237*, 1510–1521. [CrossRef]
19. Reppa, V.; Timotheou, S.; Polycarpou, M.M.; Panayiotou, C. Performance Index for Optimizing Sensor Fault Detection of a Class of Nonlinear Systems. *IFAC-PapersOnLine* **2018**, *51*, 1387–1394. [CrossRef]
20. Fu, F.; Xue, T.; Wu, Z.; Wang, D. A Fault Diagnosability Evaluation Method for Dynamic Systems Without Distribution Knowledge. *IEEE Trans. Cybern.* **2022**, *52*, 5113–5123. [CrossRef]
21. Wang, Z.; Tang, Z.; Chen, F. Quantitative Evaluation of Sensor Fault Diagnosability of F-16 High Maneuvering Fighter. In Proceedings of the 2022 IEEE 5th International Conference on Automation, Electronics and Electrical Engineering (AUTEEE), Shenyang, China, 18–20 November 2022; pp. 102–108. [CrossRef]
22. Liu, Q.; Wang, Z.; Zhang, J.; Zhou, D. Necessary and Sufficient Conditions for Fault Diagnosability of Linear Open- and Closed-Loop Stochastic Systems Under Sensor and Actuator Faults. *IEEE Trans. Autom. Control* **2022**, *67*, 4178–4185. [CrossRef]
23. Qu, R.; Jiang, B.; Cheng, Y. Research on the Diagnosability of a Satellite Attitude Determination System on a Fault Information Manifold. *Appl. Sci.* **2022**, *12*, 12835. [CrossRef]
24. Stiefelmaier, J.; Gienger, A.; Böhm, M.; Sawodny, O.; Tarín, C. A Bayesian Approach to Fault Diagnosability Analysis in Adaptive Structures. *IFAC-PapersOnLine* **2022**, *55*, 347–352. [CrossRef]
25. Zhang, W.; Zhang, X.; Lan, L.; Luo, Z. Maximum Mean and Covariance Discrepancy for Unsupervised Domain Adaptation. *Neural Process Lett.* **2020**, *51*, 347–366. [CrossRef]
26. Yang, C.; Jia, M.; Li, Z.; Gabbouj, M. Enhanced hierarchical symbolic dynamic entropy and maximum mean and covariance discrepancy-based transfer joint matching with Welsh loss for intelligent cross-domain bearing health monitoring. *Mech. Syst. Signal Process.* **2022**, *165*, 108343. [CrossRef]
27. Gu, X.; Shi, X. Diagnosability-optimization design of fixed-wing unmanned aerial vehicle based on causal matching and tree seed algorithm. *Meas. Control* **2024**, 00202940241307629. [CrossRef]
28. Katoch, S.; Chauhan, S.S.; Kumar, V. A review on genetic algorithm: Past, present, and future. *Multimed. Tools Appl.* **2021**, *80*, 8091–8126. [CrossRef]
29. Cunha, M.; Marques, J. A New Multiobjective Simulated Annealing Algorithm—MOSA-GR: Application to the Optimal Design of Water Distribution Networks. *Water Resour. Res.* **2020**, *56*, e2019WR025852. [CrossRef]
30. Li, W.; Yan, X.; Huang, Y. Cooperative-Guided Ant Colony Optimization with Knowledge Learning for Job Shop Scheduling Problem. *Tsinghua Sci. Technol.* **2024**, *29*, 1283–1299. [CrossRef]
31. Gad, A.G. Particle Swarm Optimization Algorithm and Its Applications: A Systematic Review. *Arch. Comput. Methods Eng.* **2022**, *29*, 2531–2561. [CrossRef]
32. Kaya, E.; Gorkemli, B.; Akay, B.; Karaboga, D. A review on the studies employing artificial bee colony algorithm to solve combinatorial optimization problems. *Eng. Appl. Artif. Intell.* **2022**, *115*, 105311. [CrossRef]
33. Qiu, Y.; Yang, X.; Chen, S. An improved gray wolf optimization algorithm solving to functional optimization and engineering design problems. *Sci. Rep.* **2024**, *14*, 14190. [CrossRef]
34. Pan, H.; Chen, S.; Xiong, H. A high-dimensional feature selection method based on modified Gray Wolf Optimization. *Appl. Soft Comput.* **2023**, *135*, 110031. [CrossRef]

35. Wang, J.; Xu, Y.-P.; She, C.; Xu, P.; Bagal, H.A. Optimal parameter identification of SOFC model using modified gray wolf optimization algorithm. *Energy* **2022**, *240*, 122800. [CrossRef]
36. Emary, E.; Zawbaa, H.M.; Grosan, C. Experienced Gray Wolf Optimization Through Reinforcement Learning and Neural Networks. *IEEE Trans. Neural Netw. Learn. Syst.* **2018**, *29*, 681–694. [CrossRef] [PubMed]
37. Kumar, A.; Pant, S.; Ram, M. System Reliability Optimization Using Gray Wolf Optimizer Algorithm. *Qual. Reliab. Eng. Int.* **2017**, *33*, 1327–1335. [CrossRef]
38. Dulmage, A.L.; Mendelsohn, N.S. Coverings of Bipartite Graphs. *Can. J. Math.* **1958**, *10*, 517–534. [CrossRef]
39. Krysander, M.; Aslund, J.; Nyberg, M. An Efficient Algorithm for Finding Minimal Overconstrained Subsystems for Model-Based Diagnosis. *IEEE Trans. Syst. Man Cybern. A* **2008**, *38*, 197–206. [CrossRef]
40. Gu, X.; Shi, X. Diagnosability-optimized design of unmanned aerial vehicles based on structural analysis and maximum mean covariance differences. *Measurement* **2024**, *238*, 115334. [CrossRef]

Mathematical and Computational Applications

MDPI

Article

Secure Communication of Electric Drive System Using Chaotic Systems Base on Disturbance Observer and Fuzzy Brain Emotional Learning Neural Network

Huyen Chau Phan Thi, Nhat Quang Dang and Van Nam Giap *

School of Electrical and Electronic Engineering, Hanoi University of Science and Technology, Dai Co Viet, Ha Noi 11615, Vietnam; chau.phanthihuyen@hust.edu.vn (H.C.P.T.); quang.dn242544m@sis.hust.edu.vn (N.Q.D.)
* Correspondence: nam.giapvan@hust.edu.vn

Abstract: This paper presents a novel wireless control framework for electric drive systems by employing a fuzzy brain emotional learning neural network (FBELNN) controller in conjunction with a Disturbance Observer (DO). The communication scheme uses chaotic system dynamics to ensure data confidentiality and robustness against disturbance in wireless environments. To be applied to embedded microprocessors, the continuous-time chaotic system is discretized using the Grunwald–Letnikov approximation. To avoid the loss of generality of chaotic behavior, Lyapunov exponents are computed to validate the preservation of chaos in the discrete-time domain. The FBELNN controller is then developed to synchronize two non-identical chaotic systems under different initial conditions, enabling secure data encryption and decryption. Additionally, the DOB is introduced to estimate and mitigate the effects of bounded uncertainties and external disturbances, enhancing the system's resilience to stealthy attacks. The proposed control structure is experimentally implemented on a wireless communication system utilizing ESP32 microcontrollers (Espressif Systems, Shanghai, China) based on the ESP-NOW protocol. Both control and feedback signals of the electric drive system are encrypted using chaotic states, and real-time decryption at the receiver confirms system integrity. Experimental results verify the effectiveness of the proposed method in achieving robust synchronization, accurate signal recovery, and a reliable wireless control system. The combination of FBELNN and DOB demonstrates significant potential for real-time, low-cost, and secure applications in smart electric drive systems and industrial automation.

Keywords: fuzzy brain emotional learning neural network; disturbance observer; wireless communication system; secure communication system

1. Introduction

The fuzzy inference system (FIS) mimics human reasoning and has demonstrated effectiveness across a wide range of domains. While conventional control system design required detailed mathematical models, modern fuzzy systems employ inference rules that enable control without exact system representations [1,2]. This approach has been further advanced in recent literature, where FIS-based controllers provide adaptability and robustness for nonlinear, uncertain, and chaotic environments [3–5]. Neural networks (NNs) offer benefits such as parallel computation, error resilience, generalization, and strong approximation capabilities, making them highly suitable for system identification and control applications [6,7]. Integrating FIS with neural networks leads to fuzzy neural networks (FNNs), which have been successfully implemented in a variety of regulation mechanisms [8–13].

Building on inspiration from the human brain's structure and neural interconnectivity, Marr introduced a theoretical framework to describe cerebellar information processing [14]. The cerebellar model articulation controller (CMAC), originally proposed by Albus, emulates cerebellar functions and provides a learning mechanism for adaptive control [15]. Characterized by sparse associative memory and overlapping receptive fields, CMACs efficiently address the complexity and scalability issues in conventional neural networks. As a result, CMACs have seen extensive application in feedback control for complex dynamic systems [16,17]. Extensions such as fuzzy CMACs further enhance performance by combining fuzzy inference with the CMAC structure [18–21].

Despite these advances, emotional processing has been largely overlooked in NNs and CMACs. LeDoux's work established that the amygdala is responsible for forming associations between stimuli and emotional responses [22]. The human brain comprises both sensory (orbitofrontal cortex) and emotional (amygdala) neural networks, which interact synergistically to achieve adaptive learning and response [23,24]. While sensory networks facilitate autonomous learning, emotional networks react to external stimuli and modulate the sensory response. The brain emotional learning controller (BELC) architecture captures this interaction by integrating outputs from both networks. Inspired by neurophysiological findings, intelligent emotional learning algorithms were developed [25], and BELC has subsequently found application in intelligent control systems [26–28]. Notably, while both CMAC and BELC are biologically inspired, only BELC incorporates an explicit emotional network, enabling adaptive weighting of sensory information based on the significance of stimuli, a mechanism critical for robust learning in uncertain environments [5,11,29].

Recent developments have further demonstrated the effectiveness of integrating fuzzy inference, neural, and emotional learning algorithms in robust control frameworks. Advanced architectures, such as the fuzzy brain emotional learning controller (FBELC), combine the rule-based reasoning of FIS and the adaptive learning of BELC, resulting in controllers capable of addressing the challenges of nonlinear, time-varying, and chaotic systems [3–5,24,30,31]. The inclusion of Disturbance Observer-Based (DOB) mechanisms has significantly improved the capacity to estimate and compensate for external disturbances and system uncertainties, as evidenced in secure communication and industrial control applications [3,4,29,32–40]. Recent studies have also highlighted the potential of observer-based control and fractional-order adaptive mechanisms to enhance the robustness and synchronization performance of chaotic secure communication systems [41–44].

Motivated by the limitations of current intelligent controllers such as CMACs and FNNs—which often lack explicit emotional intelligence—this study seeks to bridge the gap by integrating fuzzy inference and brain emotional learning into a unified control framework. The resulting FBELC architecture not only leverages fuzzy rule inference for decision-making but also incorporates emotional neural processing to achieve more adaptive and robust learning, particularly in nonlinear and dynamic environments.

The primary contributions of this work are as follows:

(1) Development of a novel FBELC structure that uniquely combines fuzzy logic and emotional intelligence within a single control architecture;
(2) Integration of a DO to enhance robustness against external perturbations and uncertainties;
(3) Systematic analysis and experimental validation of the proposed controller on nonlinear dynamic systems, including comparative studies with conventional

methods to highlight the FBELC's advantages in adaptability, disturbance rejection, and effectiveness [3,5,11,16–26].

The originality of this work lies in the development of the FBELC, which synthesizes fuzzy inference and emotional learning in a cohesive control strategy. Unlike traditional models, the FBELC evaluates the significance of environmental stimuli via its emotional network, directly influencing sensory processing and control actions. This integrated approach provides a more comprehensive and adaptive learning mechanism, marking a substantial advancement in the field of intelligent control systems.

2. Mathematical Concept

In this section, the mathematical model of the chaotic system and the operation of the FBELNN are presented. First, the original chaotic system in [10] is converted into the discrete-time system. Second, the operation of the neural network and its stability analysis are given.

2.1. Mathematical Modeling of Chaotic System

This paper reuses the model of the chaotic system in [10]. The original chaotic system is:

$$\begin{cases} \dot{x}(\Gamma) = a(y(\Gamma) - x(\Gamma)) \\ \dot{y}(\Gamma) = cy(\Gamma) - x(\Gamma)z(\Gamma) + w(\Gamma) \\ \dot{z}(\Gamma) = y(\Gamma)x(\Gamma) - bz(\Gamma) \\ \dot{w}(\Gamma) = z(\Gamma) - dw(\Gamma) \end{cases} \quad (1)$$

where $a = 20$, $b = 5$, $c = 10$ and $d = 1.5$, respectively. The Grunwald–Letnikov approximation method in [45] was used to convert system (1) to the discrete time domain, and system (1) is then equal to:

$$\begin{cases} x(\hbar) = x(\hbar-1) + h * a(y(\hbar-1) - x(\hbar-1)) \\ y(\hbar) = y(\hbar-1) + h * (cy(\hbar-1) - x(\hbar-1)z(\hbar-1) + w(\hbar-1)) \\ z(\hbar) = z(\hbar-1) + h * (y(\hbar-1)x(\hbar-1) - bz(\hbar-1)) \\ w(\hbar) = w(\hbar-1) + h * (z(\hbar-1) - dw(\hbar-1)) \end{cases} \quad (2)$$

where $\hbar$ is step time number and $h = 0.001$ is step time. The Jacobian matrix is then calculated by:

$$J = \begin{bmatrix} 1-ah & ah & 0 & 0 \\ -hz & 1+ch & -hx & h \\ hy & hx & 1-bh & 0 \\ 0 & 0 & h & 1-dh \end{bmatrix} \quad (3)$$

The discrete time chaotic system (2) consists of three equivalent points

$$E_1 = \begin{bmatrix} 0 \\ 0 \\ 0 \\ 0 \end{bmatrix}$$

$$E_2 = \begin{bmatrix} -2.0753.10^{-13} - 4.1961.10^{-7}j \\ 1.0169.10^{-11} + 2.0561.10^{-5}j \\ 2.0857.10^{-16} + 4.2172.10^{-10}j \\ -2.0889.10^{-19} - 4.2235.10^{-13}j \end{bmatrix}$$

and

$$E_3 = \begin{bmatrix} -2.0753.10^{-13} + 4.1961.10^{-7}j \\ 1.0169.10^{-11} - 2.0561.10^{-5}j \\ 2.0857.10^{-16} - 4.2172.10^{-10}j \\ -2.0889.10^{-19} + 4.2235.10^{-13}j \end{bmatrix}$$

The eigenvalues with E_1 are $\lambda_{E_{11}} = 0.98$, $\lambda_{E_{12}} = 1.01, \lambda_{E_{13}} = 0.98$ and $\lambda_{E_{14}} = 0.995$. The eigenvalues with E_2 are $\lambda_{E_{21}} = 0.98$, $\lambda_{E_{22}} = 0.995, \lambda_{E_{23}} = 0.9985, \lambda_{E_{24}} = 1.01$. The eigenvalues with E_3 are $\lambda_{E_{31}} = 0.98, \lambda_{E_{32}} = 0.995, \lambda_{E_{33}} = 0.9985, \lambda_{E_{34}} = 1.01$. The Lyapunov exponents are $L_1 = 1.9985$, $L_2 = 0.0495$, $L_3 = 0.4276$ and $L_4 = -16.7848$. The Lyapunov exponents are shown in Figure 1.

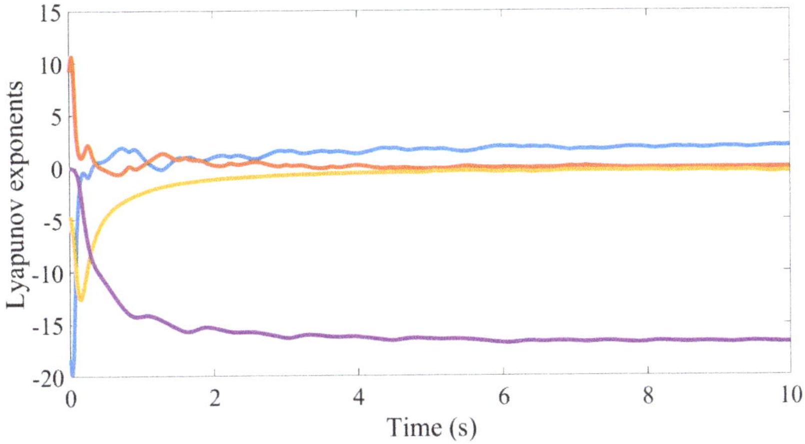

Figure 1. Lyapunov exponents of chaotic system.

The converted chaotic system in the discrete time domain retains the original characteristics of the chaos system. Therefore, the secure communication of chaotic systems in digital devices is reliable and implementable.

2.2. Problem Formulation

In the secure communication system (SCS), the chaotic system (2) can be used for both master and slave with different initial conditions. Therefore, the slave system can be:

$$\begin{cases} x_m(\hbar) = x_m(\hbar-1) + h * a(y_m(\hbar-1) - x_s(\hbar-1)) + \Delta x_m \\ y_m(\hbar) = y_m(\hbar-1) + h * (cy_m(\hbar-1) \\ \qquad -x_m(\hbar-1)z_m(\hbar-1) + w_m(\hbar-1)) + \Delta y_m \\ z_m(\hbar) = z_m(\hbar-1) + h * (y_m(\hbar-1)x_m(\hbar-1) \\ \qquad -bz_m(\hbar-1)) + \Delta z_m \\ w_m(\hbar) = w_m(\hbar-1) + h * (z_m(\hbar-1) - dw_m(\hbar-1)) + \Delta w_m \end{cases} \tag{4}$$

where $\Delta x_m, \Delta y_m, \Delta z_m$ and Δw_m are uncertainties of the master.

Assumption 1. *These uncertainties and disturbances are bounded as follows:* $\Delta x_m < \xi_1, \Delta y_m < \xi_2, \Delta y_m < \xi_3, \Delta w_m < \xi_4$ *with* $\xi_1, \xi_2, \xi_3, \xi_4$ *are positively defined.*
The slave system is:

$$\begin{cases} x_s(\hbar) = x_s(\hbar-1) + h * a(y_s(\hbar-1) - x_s(\hbar-1)) \\ \qquad +\Delta x_s + d_x(\hbar-1) + u_x(\hbar-1) \\ y_s(\hbar) = y_s(\hbar-1) + h * (cy_s(\hbar-1) - x_s(\hbar-1)z_s(\hbar-1) \\ \qquad +w_m(\hbar-1)) + \Delta y_s + d_y(\hbar-1) + u_y(\hbar-1) \\ z_s(\hbar) = z_s(\hbar-1) + h * (y_s(\hbar-1)x_s(\hbar-1) - bz_s(\hbar-1)) \\ \qquad +\Delta z_s + d_z(\hbar-1) + u_z(\hbar-1) \\ w_s(\hbar) = w_s(\hbar-1) + h * (z_s(\hbar-1) - dw_s(\hbar-1)) \\ \qquad +\Delta w_s + d_w(\hbar-1) + u_w(\hbar-1) \end{cases} \tag{5}$$

where $\Delta x_s, \Delta y_s, \Delta z_s,$ *and* Δw_s *are uncertainties of the slave.* $d_x, d_y, d_z,$ *and* d_w *are the disturbances on public channels.*

Assumption 2. *These uncertainties and disturbances are bounded as follows:* $\Delta x_s < \xi_1$, $\Delta y_s < \xi_2$, $\Delta z_s < \xi_3$ *and* $\Delta v_s < \xi_4$ *with* ξ_1, ξ_2, ξ_3 *and* ξ_4 *are positively defined.*

Remark 1. *Assumptions 1 and 2 merely require that the lumped uncertainties and channel disturbances stay within finite, known bounds. This bounded-disturbance premise is standard in secure chaotic-control literature and is exactly the condition needed for the Lyapunov inequalities (51)–(54) to be negative-definite. A closely related study in [27] adopted the same bounded-uncertainty hypothesis and experimentally achieved asymptotic convergence, confirming the practical effectiveness of these assumptions. The tracking errors of master and slave are*

$$\begin{cases} e_x(\hbar-1) = x_m(\hbar-1) - x_s(\hbar-1) \\ e_y(\hbar-1) = y_m(\hbar-1) - y_s(\hbar-1) \\ e_z(\hbar-1) = z_m(\hbar-1) - z_s(\hbar-1) \\ e_w(\hbar-1) = w_m(\hbar-1) - w_s(\hbar-1) \end{cases} \tag{6}$$

Therefore,

$$\begin{cases} e_x(\hbar) = e_x(\hbar-1) + h * a(e_y(\hbar-1) - e_x(\hbar-1)) + \Delta x_m - \Delta x_s - d_x(\hbar-1) - u_x(\hbar-1) \\ e_y(\hbar) = e_y(\hbar-1) + h * (ce_y(\hbar-1) - x_m(\hbar-1)z_m(\hbar-1) + x_s(\hbar-1)z_s(\hbar-1) + \\ \qquad e_w(\hbar-1)) + \Delta y_m - \Delta y_s - d_y(\hbar-1) - u_y(\hbar-1) \\ e_z(\hbar) = e_z(\hbar-1) + h * (y_m(\hbar-1)x_m(\hbar-1) - y_s(\hbar-1)x_s(\hbar-1) - be_z(\hbar-1)) + \Delta z_m \\ \qquad -\Delta z_s + d_z(\hbar-1) + u_z(\hbar-1) \\ e_w(\hbar) = e_w(\hbar-1) + h * (e_z(\hbar-1) - de_w(\hbar-1)) + \Delta w_m - \Delta w_s - d_w(\hbar-1) - u_w(\hbar-1) \end{cases} \tag{7}$$

Equation (7) can be converted to

$$\begin{aligned} \boldsymbol{e}(\hbar) = \boldsymbol{A}\boldsymbol{e}(\hbar-1) + \boldsymbol{f}(\hbar-1) + \Delta(\hbar-1) \\ + \boldsymbol{d}(\hbar-1) + \boldsymbol{u}(\hbar-1) \end{aligned} \tag{8}$$

where $\boldsymbol{e}(\hbar) = \begin{bmatrix} e_x(\hbar) \\ e_y(\hbar) \\ e_z(\hbar) \\ e_w(\hbar) \end{bmatrix}$, $\boldsymbol{e}(\hbar-1) = \begin{bmatrix} e_x(\hbar-1) \\ e_y(\hbar-1) \\ e_z(\hbar-1) \\ e_w(\hbar-1) \end{bmatrix}$, $\boldsymbol{f}(\hbar-1) = \begin{bmatrix} f_x(\hbar-1)) \\ f_y(\hbar-1) \\ f_z(\hbar-1) \\ f_w(\hbar-1) \end{bmatrix}$, $\Delta(\hbar-1) = \begin{bmatrix} \Delta x_m - \Delta x_s \\ \Delta y_m - \Delta y_s \\ \Delta z_m - \Delta z_s \\ \Delta w_m - \Delta w_s \end{bmatrix}$, $\boldsymbol{d}(\hbar-1) = \begin{bmatrix} -d_x(\hbar-1) \\ -d_y(\hbar-1) \\ -d_z(\hbar-1) \\ -d_w(\hbar-1) \end{bmatrix}$, *and* $\boldsymbol{u}(\hbar-1) = \begin{bmatrix} -u_x(\hbar-1) \\ -u_y(\hbar-1) \\ -u_z(\hbar-1) \\ -u_w(\hbar-1) \end{bmatrix}$, *with* $f_x(\hbar-1) = h * a(e_y(\hbar-1) - e_x(\hbar-1))$, $f_y(\hbar-1) = h * (ce_y(\hbar-1) - x_m(\hbar-1)z_m(\hbar-1) + x_s(\hbar-1)z_s(\hbar-1) + e_w(\hbar-1))$, $f_z(\hbar-1) = h * (y_m(\hbar-1)x_m(\hbar-1) - y_s(\hbar-1)x_s(\hbar-1) - be_z(\hbar-1))$, *and* $f_w(\hbar-1) = h * (e_z(\hbar-1) - de_w(\hbar-1))$. *In this case, the control input of Equation (8) is as follows*

$$\begin{aligned} \boldsymbol{u}(\hbar-1) = &- \boldsymbol{A}\boldsymbol{e}(\hbar-1) - \boldsymbol{f}(\hbar-1) - \Delta(\hbar-1) \\ &- \boldsymbol{d}(\hbar-1) + \boldsymbol{K}\boldsymbol{e}(\hbar-1) \end{aligned} \tag{9}$$

Herein, the $\mathbf{d}(\hbar-1)$ *and* $\mathbf{Ke}(\hbar-1)$ *are unable to be known. The DOB can be used to estimated these values. Therefore, Equation (8) becomes*

$$\boldsymbol{e}(\hbar) = \boldsymbol{K}\boldsymbol{e}(\hbar-1) \tag{10}$$

Then, the errors will come to equivalent points if the matrix $\mathbf{K}$ *is Hurwitz. However, the achievements of the disturbances and uncertainties are unreliable. Therefore, this paper designs a learning neural network to achieve a simplified control design that remains robust against parameter variations in both master and slave systems while mitigating external disturbances.*

2.3. Fuzzy Brain Emotional Learning Controller

The aim of the FBELC is to ensure robustness in the steady-state area. The structure of the designed controller is shown in Figure 2.

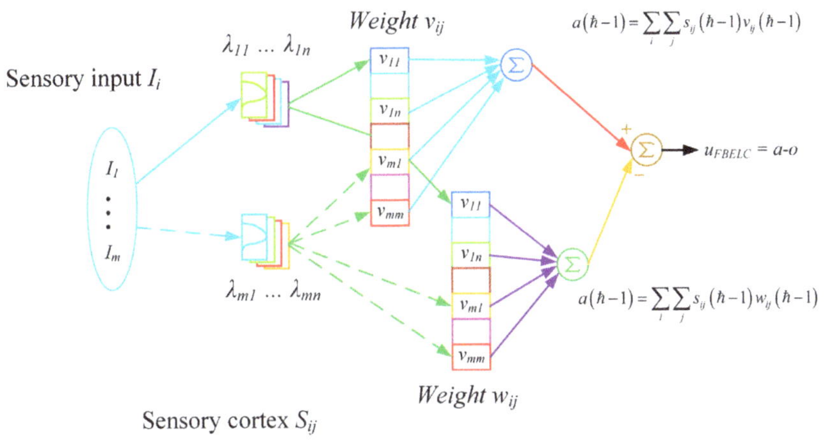

Figure 2. Structure of fuzzy brain emotional learning.

The sensory input layer is designed with conjunctions as follows: If $I_1(\hbar-1)$ is $\Lambda_1 j(\hbar-1)$, $I_2(\hbar-1)$ is $\Lambda_2 j(\hbar-1)$, and $I_m(\hbar-1)$ is $\Lambda_m j(\hbar-1)$ then $a(\hbar-1) = v_{ij}(\hbar-1)$, where $v_{ij}(\hbar-1)$ is the amygdala weight.

The emotional neural network is as follows: If $I_1(\hbar-1)$ is $\Lambda_1 j(\hbar-1)$, $I_2(\hbar-1)$ is $\Lambda_2 j(\hbar-1)$, and $I_m(\hbar-1)$ is $\Lambda_m j(\hbar-1)$ then $o(\hbar-1) = w_{ij}(\hbar-1)$, where $w_{ij}(\hbar-1)$ is prefrontal weight. The weights are selected in order to satisfy the conditions of

$$\begin{aligned}&\Delta v(\hbar-1) = \\ &\alpha[s_{ij} \times (max[o, d_i(\hbar-1) - a(\hbar-1)])]\end{aligned} \tag{11}$$

and

$$\begin{aligned}&\Delta w(\hbar-1) = \\ &\beta[s_{ij} \times (u_{neural}(\hbar-1) - d_i(\hbar-1))]\end{aligned} \tag{12}$$

where

$$d_i(\hbar-1) = b_i \times I_i + c \times u_{neural}(\hbar-1) \tag{13}$$

As shown in Figure 1, the input layer is

$$I(\hbar-1) = [I_1(\hbar-1), I_2(\hbar-1), I_m(\hbar-1)]^T \tag{14}$$

s_{ij} is a type II Gausian function with

$$s_{ij}(\hbar-1) = exp(-\frac{(I_i(\hbar-1)-\epsilon_{ij})^2}{\delta_i^2 j} - \frac{(I_i(\hbar-1)-\lambda_{ij})^2}{\gamma_i^2 j}) \tag{15}$$

where ϵ_{ij} and λ_{ij} are the means of the Gauss function, and $\delta_i^2 j$ and $\gamma_i^2 j$ are variances of the Gauss function. The amygdala weight is

$$v_{ja}(\hbar-1) = [v_{1a}(\hbar-1), .., v_{ma}(\hbar-1)]^T \tag{16}$$

and

$$v_{jb}(\hbar-1) = [v_{1b}(\hbar-1), .., v_{mb}(\hbar-1)]^T \tag{17}$$

Prefrontal weights are

$$w_{ja}(\hbar-1) = [w_{1a}(\hbar-1), .., w_{ma}(\hbar-1)]^T \tag{18}$$

and

$$w_{jb}(\hbar-1) = [w_{1b}(\hbar-1), .., w_{mb}(\hbar-1)]^T \tag{19}$$

The control value of this controller is defined as follows:

$$\boldsymbol{u}(\hbar-1) = \boldsymbol{a}(\hbar-1) - \boldsymbol{o}(\hbar-1) \tag{20}$$

where $i = 1 \rightarrow n$ and $j = 1 \rightarrow m$. The Amygdala output is

$$\boldsymbol{a}(\hbar-1) = \sum_i \sum_j s_{ij}(\hbar-1) v_{ij}(\hbar-1) \tag{21}$$

and the prefrontal output is

$$\boldsymbol{o}(\hbar-1) = \sum_i \sum_j s_{ij}(\hbar-1) w_{ij}(\hbar-1) \tag{22}$$

The update laws are designed as follows:

$$v_{ja}(\hbar) = v_{ja}(\hbar-1) + \Delta v_{ja}(\hbar-1) \tag{23}$$

$$v_{jb}(\hbar) = v_{jb}(\hbar-1) + \Delta v_{jb}(\hbar-1) \tag{24}$$

$$w_{ja}(\hbar) = w_{ja}(\hbar-1) + \Delta w_{ja}(\hbar-1) \tag{25}$$

$$w_{jb}(\hbar) = w_{jb}(\hbar-1) + \Delta w_{jb}(\hbar-1) \tag{26}$$

Remark 2. *The synaptic weights and membership-function parameters enter the FBELC only as starting points for the online update laws (11)–(12). Provided they lie inside the bounded region required by Assumption 1, the Lyapunov analysis in Section 2.6 ensures stability and asymptotic tracking regardless of their exact numbers. Consequently, initial values affect only the transient learning duration: choices nearer the eventual steady state shorten convergence, while larger offsets lengthen it, without altering the final closed-loop performance.*

2.4. Robust Controller

In the proposed control scheme, the master and slave chaotic systems achieve synchronization by minimizing the difference between their states over time. This is done by defining a synchronization error, which represents the gap between the two systems' behaviors. The fuzzy brain emotional learning controller (FBELC) is designed to learn and adapt its response based on this error, aiming to drive it to zero even under uncertain and changing conditions. To ensure this process is stable and reliable, a theoretical framework based on Lyapunov stability is used to prove that the error will consistently decrease. Additionally, a DO is included to estimate and cancel out any external disturbances or model uncertainties. Together, the FBELC and the DO ensure that the slave system can closely follow the master system, thereby achieving synchronization in theory as well as in practice.

The robust controller is designed to ensure system performance under uncertainties and disturbances by employing a compensation mechanism that effectively attenuates deviations from the desired state. The control law is formulated as follows: The control input $u(\hbar)$ consists of two components:

$$u(\hbar-1) = u_{eq}(\hbar-1) + u_{rob}(\hbar-1) \tag{27}$$

where the equivalent control term is defined as:

$$u_{eq}(\hbar-1) = f(x(\hbar)) + \dot{x}_r(\hbar) \tag{28}$$

According to a previously published paper [46] , the robust control term is designed to counteract the error of expected control output and output of FBELNN:

$$u_{rob}(\hbar-1) = K \cdot \text{sign}(s(\hbar-1)) \tag{29}$$

The weakness of FBELNN in [10] can be improved by using DOB to compare two terms. The sliding surface is defined as:

$$s(\hbar-1) = e(\hbar-1) + Ke(k-2) \quad (30)$$

Here, $e(\hbar-1) = x(\hbar-1) - x_r(\hbar-1)$ represents the tracking error, and K is a positive scalar.

By substituting the control input $u(\hbar-1)$ into the system dynamics, the sliding surface dynamics are expressed as:

$$\dot{s}(\hbar-1) = K_s \cdot \mathrm{sgn}(s(\hbar-1)) + \Delta(\hbar-1) \quad (31)$$

where $\Delta(\hbar)$ encapsulates the system uncertainties and external disturbances. The final robust control law is given by:

$$u(\hbar-1) = f(x(\hbar-1)) + \dot{x}_r(\hbar-1) + K_s \cdot \mathrm{sign}(s(\hbar)) \quad (32)$$

This ensures that the system tracks the reference trajectory $x_r(\hbar)$ while maintaining robustness against disturbances and uncertainties.

The gains K and K_s are tuned based on the system's operating conditions to achieve optimal performance. The sliding surface $s(\hbar)$ is monitored to ensure stability criteria are met.

Remark 3. *Equation (31) can be stable if* $K > |\Delta(\hbar-1)|$. *However, the chattering will appear and the DOB is a good way to improve the qualification of the proposed method* $\mathbf{d}(\hbar-1) + \boldsymbol{u}(\hbar-1)$ *in Equation (8).*

2.5. Disturbance Observer

Initially, the aggregated evaluation of the master system's uncertainty, the slave system's interference, and the disturbance signals within the public communication channels can be expressed as follows:

$$\begin{cases} Dd_{xm}(\Gamma_{\hbar-1}) = \chi_m(\Gamma_\hbar) - \chi_m(\Gamma_{\hbar-1}) \\ Dd_{xs}(\Gamma_{\hbar-1}) = \chi_s(\Gamma_\hbar) - \left[\chi_s(\Gamma_{\hbar-1}) + u_x(\Gamma_{\hbar-1}) + D\hat{d}_x(\Gamma_{\hbar-1})\right] \end{cases} \quad (33)$$

where $\hat{d}_x(\Gamma_{\hbar-1})$ is the proposed DO for the x-axis of the SCS. Thus,

$$D\bar{d}_x(\Gamma_{\hbar-1}) = \chi_m(\Gamma_\hbar) - \chi_s(\Gamma_\hbar) + \left[\chi_s(\Gamma_{\hbar-1}) + u_x(\Gamma_{\hbar-1}) + D\hat{d}_x(\Gamma_{\hbar-1})\right] - \chi_m(\Gamma_{\hbar-1}) \quad (34)$$

When the two systems are synchronized, $\chi_m(\Gamma_\hbar) \to \chi_s(\Gamma_\hbar)$, which signifies:

$$D\bar{d}_x(\Gamma_\hbar) = \chi_m(\Gamma_\hbar) - \left[\chi_s(\Gamma_\hbar) + u_x(\Gamma_\hbar) + D\hat{d}_x(\Gamma_\hbar)\right] \quad (35)$$

The deviation between the predicted and actual disturbances on the x-axis is determined using the following equation:

$$D\tilde{d}_x(\Gamma_\hbar) = \chi_m(\Gamma_\hbar) - [\chi_s(\Gamma_\hbar) + u_x(\Gamma_\hbar)] \quad (36)$$

The structure of the proposed DO on the x-axis is defined as follows:

$$\hat{d}_x(\Gamma_\hbar) = \bar{d}_x(\Gamma_\hbar) + \hat{k}_{dx}\tilde{d}_x(\Gamma_{\hbar-1}) \quad (37)$$

Then:

$$\tilde{\tilde{d}}_x(\Gamma_\hbar) = -k_{dx}\tilde{d}_x(\Gamma_{\hbar-1}) \quad (38)$$

where $k_{dx} > 0$ leads to $\tilde{d}_x(\Gamma_\hbar) \to 0$ in the discrete time domain Thus, the formulation of the adaptive DO for the x-axis is presented as follows:

$$\begin{aligned}\hat{d}_x(\Gamma_\hbar) &= \{x_m(\Gamma_\hbar) + h[ay_m(\Gamma_\hbar) - ax_m(\Gamma_\hbar)]\} - \{x_s(\Gamma_\hbar) + h[ay_s(\Gamma_\hbar) - ax_s(\Gamma_\hbar) + u_x(\Gamma_\hbar)]\} \\ &+\hat{d}_x(\Gamma_{\hbar-1}) + \eta\tilde{d}_x(\Gamma_{\hbar-1})\end{aligned} \quad (39)$$

Similarly, the DOs for y, z and v axis are shown below:

$$\begin{aligned}\hat{d}_y(\Gamma_\hbar) &= \left\{y_m(\Gamma_\hbar) + h\left[cy_m(\Gamma_\hbar) - x_m(\Gamma_\hbar)z_m(\Gamma_\hbar) + v_m(\Gamma_\hbar)\right]\right\} \\ &-\left\{y_s(\Gamma_\hbar) + h\left[cy_s(\Gamma_\hbar) - x_s(\Gamma_\hbar)z_s(\Gamma_\hbar) + v_s(\Gamma_\hbar) + u_y(\Gamma_\hbar)\right]\right\} + d_y(\Gamma_\hbar) + \eta\tilde{d}(\Gamma_{\hbar-1})\end{aligned} \quad (40)$$

$$\begin{aligned}\hat{d}_z(\Gamma_\hbar) &= \left\{z_m(\Gamma_\hbar) + h[y_m(\Gamma_\hbar)x_m(\Gamma_\hbar) - bz_m(\Gamma_\hbar)]\right\} \\ &-\left\{z_s(\Gamma_\hbar) + h[y_s(\Gamma_\hbar)x_s(\Gamma_\hbar) - bz_s(\Gamma_\hbar) + u_z(\Gamma_\hbar)]\right\} + \hat{d}_z(\Gamma_{\hbar-1}) + \eta\tilde{d}_z(\Gamma_{\hbar-1})\end{aligned} \quad (41)$$

$$\begin{aligned}\hat{d}_v(\Gamma_\hbar) &= \{v_m(\Gamma_\hbar) + h[z_m(\Gamma_\hbar) - dv_m(\Gamma_\hbar)]\} - \{v_s(\Gamma_\hbar) + h[z_s(\Gamma_\hbar) - dv_s(\Gamma_\hbar) + u_v(\Gamma_\hbar)]\} \\ &+\hat{d}_v(\Gamma_{\hbar-1}) + \eta\tilde{d}_v(\Gamma_{\hbar-1})\end{aligned} \quad (42)$$

2.6. Stability Analysis

The Lyapunov candidate function is defined as:

$$V(s(\hbar-1), \tilde{d}(\hbar-1)) = V_s(s(\hbar-1)) + V_d(\tilde{d}(\hbar-1)) \quad (43)$$

where $V_s(s(\hbar))$ represents the Lyapunov function for the sliding surface $s(\hbar)$, and $V_d(\tilde{d}(\hbar))$ represents the Lyapunov function for the disturbance estimation error $\tilde{d}(\hbar)$. These functions are defined as:

$$V_s(s(\hbar-1)) = \frac{1}{2}[s_x^2(\hbar-1) + s_y^2(\hbar-1) + s_z^2(\hbar-1) + s_w^2(\hbar-1)] \quad (44)$$

Thus,

$$V_d(\tilde{d}(\hbar-1)) = \frac{1}{2}\tilde{d}^T(\hbar-1)\tilde{d}(\hbar-1) \quad (45)$$

where $s_x(\hbar-1)$, $s_y(\hbar-1)$, $s_z(\hbar-1)$, and $s_w(\hbar-1)$ are the sliding surfaces for the respective dimensions:

$$s_x(\hbar-1) = e_x(\hbar-1) + Ke_x(\hbar-2), \quad (46)$$
$$s_y(\hbar-1) = e_y(\hbar-1) + Ke_y(\hbar-2), \quad (47)$$
$$s_z(\hbar-1) = e_z(\hbar-1) + Ke_z(\hbar-2), \quad (48)$$
$$s_w(\hbar-1) = e_w(\hbar-1) + Ke_w(\hbar-2). \quad (49)$$

The discrete-time derivative of the Lyapunov function is given by:

$$\Delta V(s(\hbar-1), \tilde{d}(\hbar-1)) = \frac{V(s(\hbar), \tilde{d}(\hbar) - V(s(\hbar-1), \tilde{d}(\hbar-1))}{\hbar} \quad (50)$$

Using the dynamics of the sliding surface in Equation (31):

$$s(\hbar) = -K_s \mathrm{sgn}(s(\hbar - 1)) + \Delta(\hbar - 1) \tag{51}$$

where K_s is the reaching gain, substituting this into V_s:

$$\Delta V_s(s(\hbar)) = \frac{s_j(\hbar + 2)s_j(\hbar + 2) - s_j(\hbar - 1)s_j(\hbar - 1)}{h} \tag{52}$$

For $\Delta V_s(s(\hbar)) < 0$, the condition $K_s^2 > s^T(\hbar)s(\hbar)$ must hold. The dynamics of the disturbance estimation error are given by:

$$\tilde{d}(\hbar) = \tilde{d}(\hbar - 1) - K_d\tilde{d}(\hbar - 1) \tag{53}$$

where K_d is the adaptive gain. Substituting this into V_d:

$$\Delta V_d(\tilde{d}(\hbar - 1)) = \frac{\tilde{d}^T(\hbar + 1)\tilde{d}(\hbar + 1) - \tilde{d}^T(\hbar)\tilde{d}(\hbar)}{h} \tag{54}$$

For $\Delta V_d(\tilde{d}(\hbar)) \leq 0$, the condition $K_d^2 \geq \tilde{d}^T(\hbar)\tilde{d}(\hbar)$ must hold. The total change in the Lyapunov function is:

$$\Delta V(s(\hbar), \tilde{d}(\hbar)) = \Delta V_s(s(\hbar)) + \Delta V_d(\tilde{d}(\hbar)) \tag{55}$$

Equation (55) is negatively defined. By satisfying the conditions on K_s and K_d, the sliding surfaces $s_x(\hbar)$, $s_y(\hbar)$, $s_z(\hbar)$, and $s_w(\hbar)$, as well as the disturbance estimation error $\tilde{d}(\hbar)$, converge to zero as $k \to \infty$. This guarantees the asymptotic stability of the proposed robust controller for the 4D chaotic system.

3. Simulation and Experimental Result

3.1. Simulation Study

A simulation study was carried out by using MATLAB 2023a on a computer with CPU Intel(R) Core(TM) i512400F, RAM 32 GB. The parameters of the controller are as follows: $K_1 = \begin{bmatrix} k_{11} & 0 \\ 0 & k_{12} \end{bmatrix}$, $k_{11} = 1.6$, $k_{12} = 0.02$, $\alpha = 0.01$, $\beta = 0.01$, $\sigma_{\text{ij}} = 3$. These parameters were chosen based on the stable conditions (9) and (15). $\xi_{\text{ij}} = [-2, -1.6, -1.2, -0.8, 0, 0.4, 0.8, 1.2, 1.6, 2]$ were chosen for $R = 0.06$ (12) and (14) and $R = 0.06$. Figure 3 shows the state of the master and slave systems on each axis.

As shown in Figure 4, the synchronization error, initially present due to differing starting points, quickly diminishes to near zero under control action, indicating rapid synchronization (within about 10 ms). The sustained near-zero error confirms the pro-posed controller's stability. Steady-state tracking exhibits extremely small errors (around 10^{-5}). When a disturbance was introduced, the error briefly rose significantly to 8×10^{-3} but swiftly recovered to the stable, minimal level. This demonstrates the controller's efficiency in providing both fast and robust synchronization.

All four axes of the chaotic system will have a signal added as a tested disturbance; the signal added to x axis is $0.125 \times \cos(2.5\pi \times (\hbar) \times h) + 0.1 \times \sin(1.5 \times \pi \times (\hbar) \times h)$; the signal added to y axis is $0.75 \times \cos(2.25\pi \times (\hbar) \times h) + 0.125 \times \sin(1.25 \times \pi \times (\hbar) \times h)$; the signal added to z axis is $0.75 \times \cos(2.25\pi \times (\hbar) \times h) + 0.175 \times \sin(1.25 \times \pi \times (\hbar) \times h)$ and the signal added to v axis is $0.15 \times \cos(2.25\pi \times (\hbar) \times h) + 0.15 \times \sin(1.25 \times \pi \times (\hbar) \times h)$. Figure 5 illustrates the efficacy of the DO in the estimation and compensation of external disturbances affecting the system. The observer's successful tracking of disturbance dynamics ensures system stability in the presence of external perturbations. The close agreement between the tested and estimated disturbance confirms the proposed observer's capacity for real-time disturbance rejection. These results validate the DO's robustness in mitigating external uncertainties, a critical factor for maintaining synchronization accuracy.

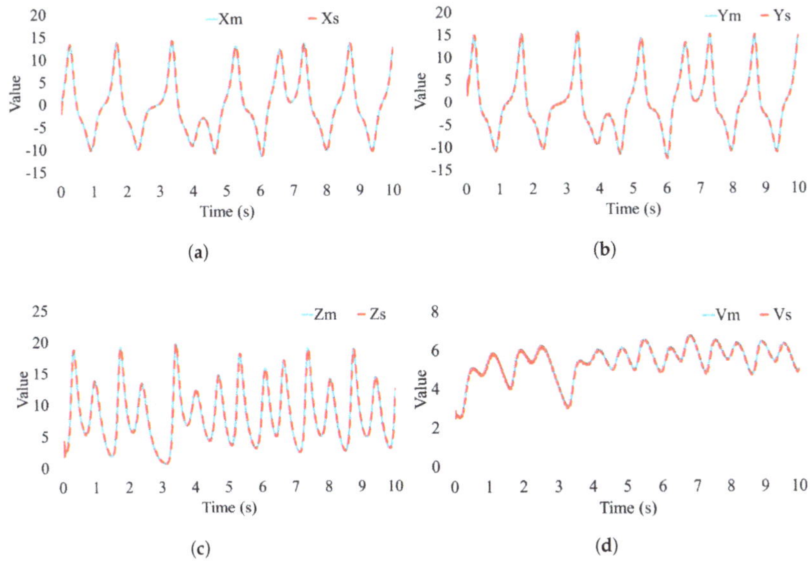

Figure 3. State trajectory on (**a**) x-axis (**b**) y-axis (**c**) z-axis and (**d**) v-axis.

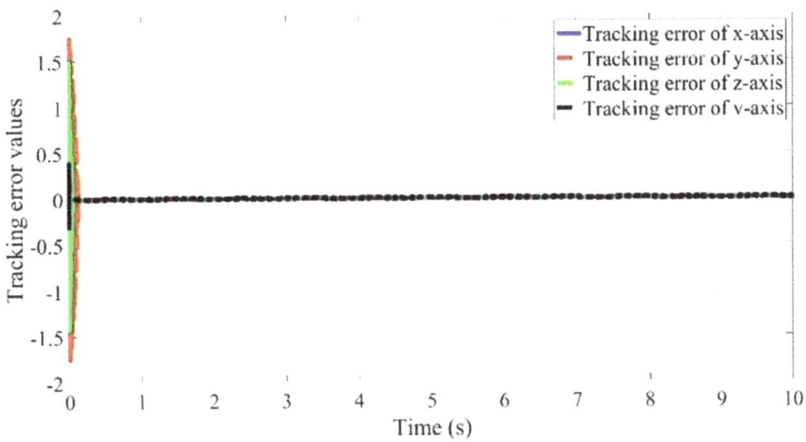

Figure 4. Tracking error of the system through time.

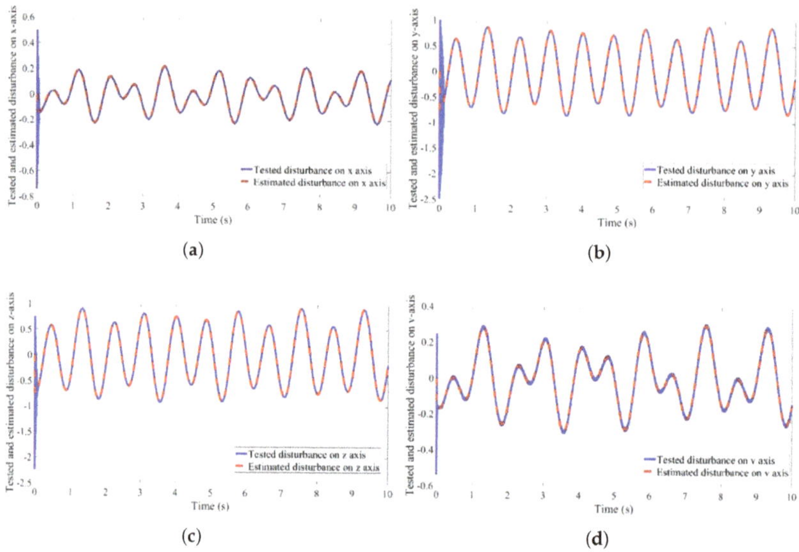

Figure 5. Tested and estimated disturbance on (**a**) x-axis, (**b**) y-axis, (**c**) z-axis, and (**d**) v-axis.

3.2. Experiment Study

A scenario was carried out using the wireless communication protocol as in Figures 6 and 7. Herein, three ESP32 chips are used to control a DC motor wirelessly. ESP32(1) plays the controller role, sending the control signal to ESP32(2). ESP32(2) uses the data sent from ESP32(1) to create the corresponding PWM pulse to control the DC motor. ESP32(3) takes the speed of the motor and sends it to ESP32(1) to calculate the control data based on the PI controller. Each of the two chips communicates with the other via the ESP-NOW protocol. The computer also provides the power source for three wireless devices. Both the electrical driver control signal and the response speed will be encrypted by using the chaotic system. They will be added into one of three system states of the master system and then this mixed information is sent to the slave via wireless communication. The state of the slave will be used to encrypt data it gets from the master.

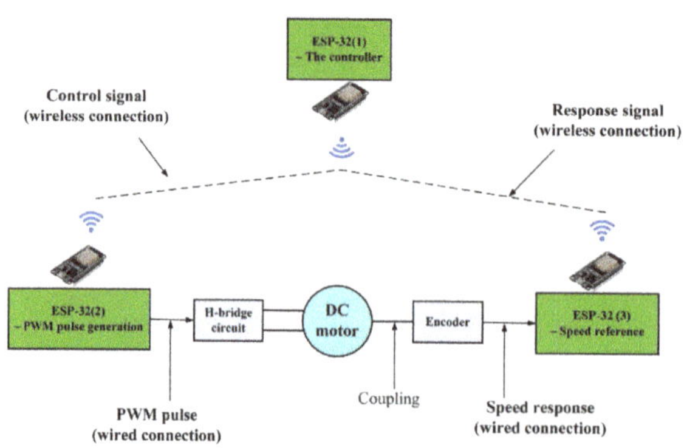

Figure 6. Structure of the experimental system.

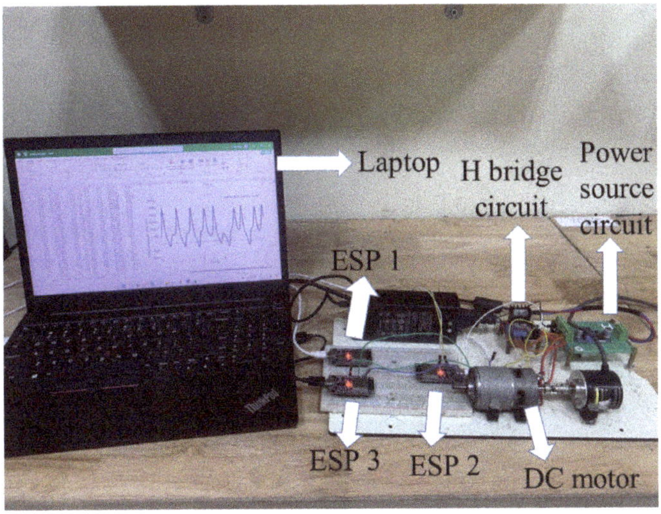

Figure 7. Experimental setup.

The parameters of the controller are as follows: $K_1 = \begin{bmatrix} k_{11} & 0 \\ 0 & k_{12} \end{bmatrix}$, $k_{11} = 1.6$, $k_{12} = 0.02$, $\alpha = 0.01$, $\beta = 0.01$, $\sigma_{ij} = 3$. These parameters are chosen based on the stable conditions (9) and (15). $\xi_{ij} = [-2, -1.6, -1.2, -0.8, 0, 0.4, 0.8, 1.2, 1.6, 2]$ are chosen for $R = 0.06$ (12) and (14) and $R = 0.06$. Figure 8 ensures the reliability of the SCS by describing the accuracy of the proposed control method. It shows the state trajectory of two systems on each axis x, y, z and v, respectively.

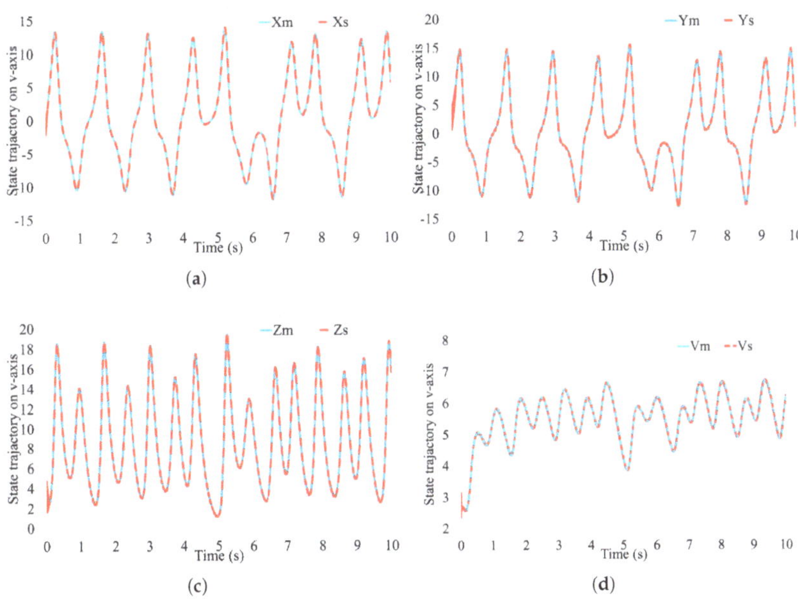

Figure 8. State trajectory on (**a**) x-axis, (**b**) y-axis, (**c**) z-axis, and (**d**) v-axis.

All four axes of the chaotic system will be added a signal to each as a tested disturbance; the signal added to x axis is $0.125 \times \cos(2.5\pi \times (\hbar) \times h) + 0.1 \times \sin(1.5 \times \pi \times (\hbar) \times h)$; the signal added to y axis is $0.75 \times \cos(2.25\pi \times (\hbar) \times h) + 0.125 \times \sin(1.25 \times \pi \times (\hbar) \times h)$; the signal added to z axis is $0.75 \times \cos(2.25\pi \times (\hbar) \times h) + 0.175 \times \sin(1.25 \times \pi \times (\hbar) \times h)$ and the signal added to v axis is $0.15 \times \cos(2.25\pi \times (\hbar) \times h) + 0.15 \times \sin(1.25 \times \pi \times (\hbar) \times h)$. Figure 9 effectively demonstrates the DO's capability in both estimating and compensating for external disturbances affecting the system. The observer adeptly tracks the dynamics of these disturbances, which in turn ensures the system's stability even in the presence of external perturbations. The close agreement between the tested and estimated disturbance values provides strong confirmation of the proposed observer's proficiency in real-time disturbance rejection. Ultimately, these results validate the DO's robustness in mitigating external uncertainties, a critical factor for maintaining high synchronization accuracy.

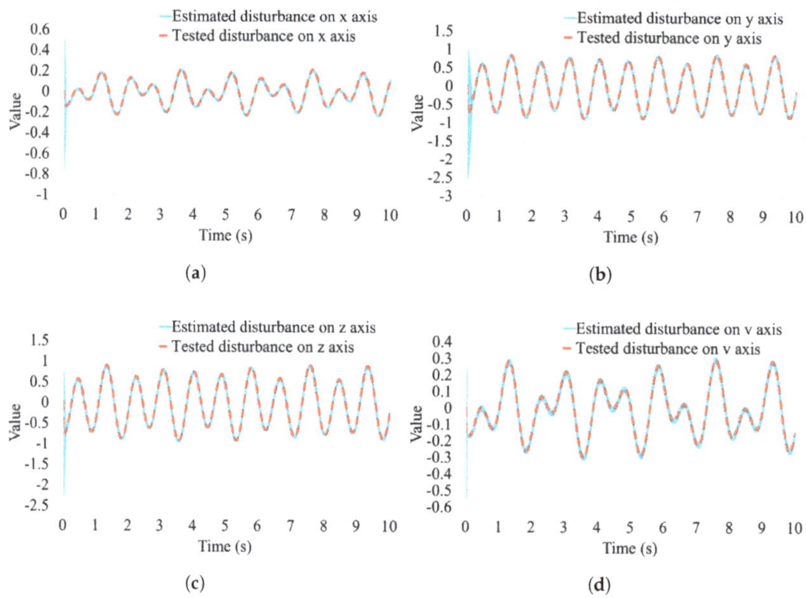

Figure 9. Tested and estimated disturbance on (**a**) x-axis, (**b**) y-axis, (**c**) z-axis, and (**d**) v-axis.

This depicts the tested disturbances applied to the system and the corresponding estimates produced by the disturbance observer. The close alignment of the tested and estimated values across all axes (x, y, z, and v) demonstrates the effectiveness of the disturbance observer in identifying and compensating for external perturbations. The evolution of the tracking error through time is shown in Figure 10. Initially, the error is nonzero due to the difference in initial conditions between the master and slave systems. However, as the controller takes effect, the error rapidly decreases to zero, demonstrating the system's ability to quickly synchronize.

Figure 11 illustrates the original and decrypted data, and Figure 12 shows the encrypted control data. The encrypted control signal appears highly randomized, ensuring that meaningful information cannot be extracted by unauthorized entities and the decrypted signal closely matches the original, verifying the accuracy and reliability of the proposed communication method.

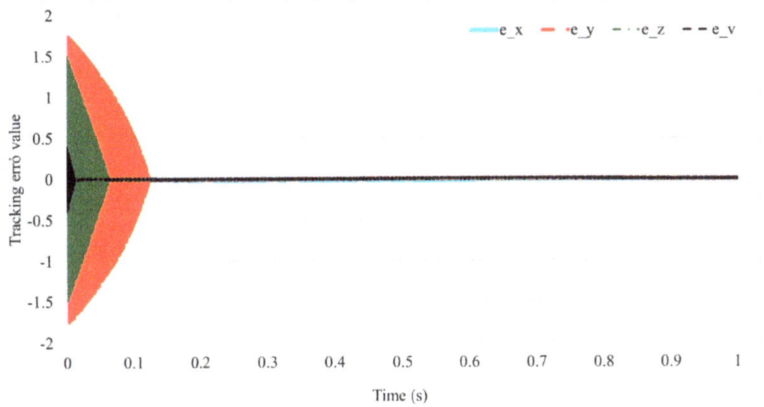

Figure 10. Tracking error on each axis.

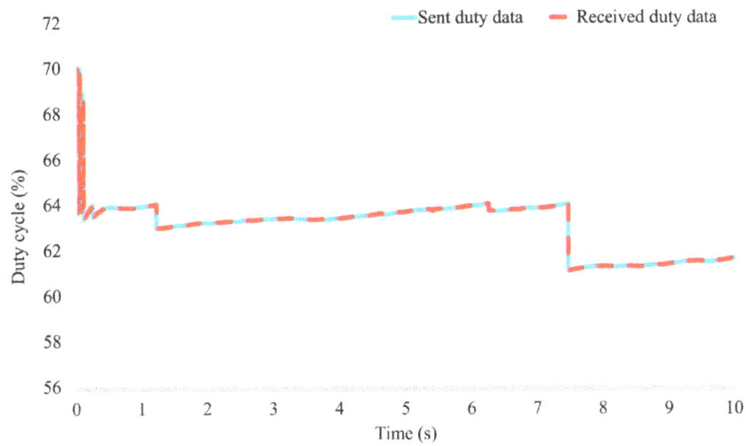

Figure 11. Original and decrypted control signal.

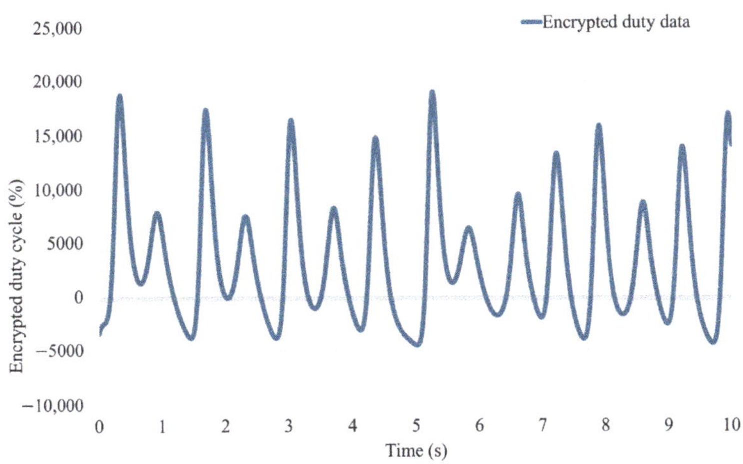

Figure 12. Encrypted control signal.

Figures 13–15 confirm that the encryption scheme effectively obscures the transmitted data by showing the histogram chart of all three scenarios: encrypted, decrypted, and original control signal. This ensures a good performance of the proposed system. However, minor discrepancies between the original and decrypted signals may be attributed to numerical discretization or slight residual errors from the synchronization process.

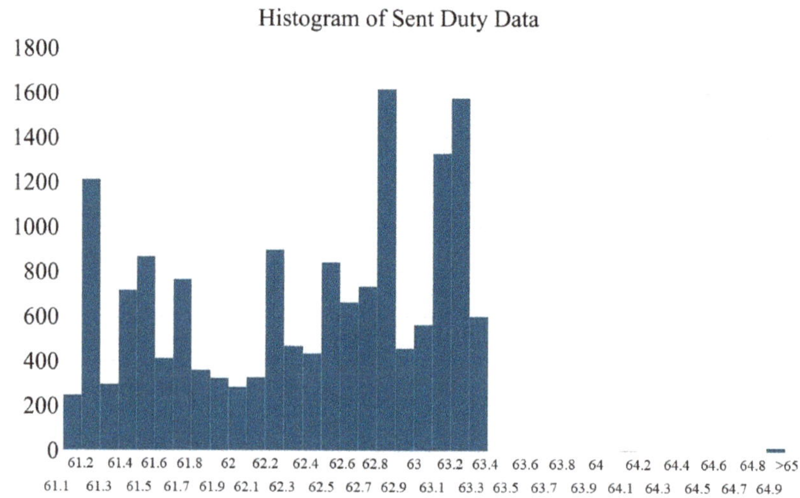

Figure 13. Histogram chart of sent duty signal.

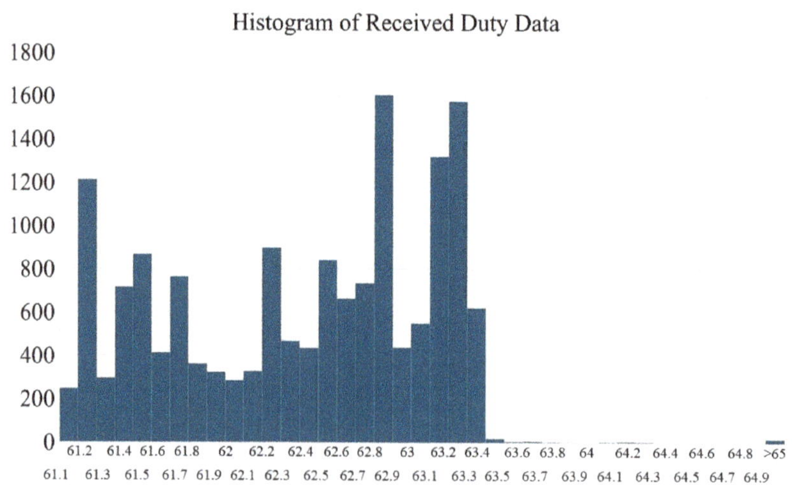

Figure 14. Histogram chart of received duty signal.

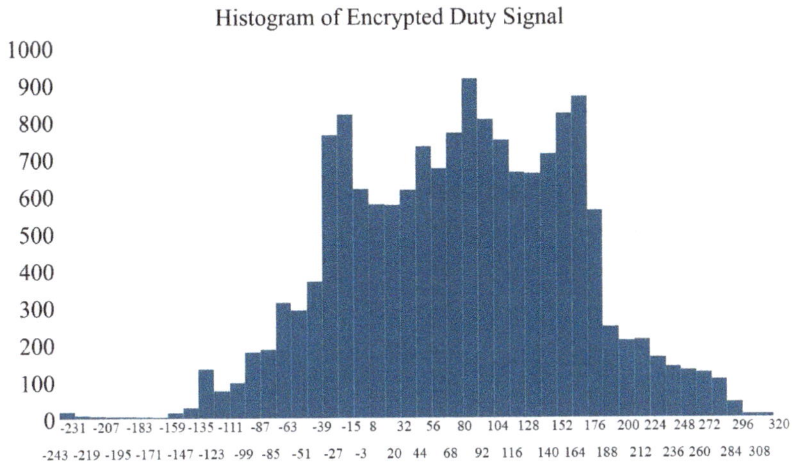

Figure 15. Histogram chart of encrypted duty signal.

The effectiveness of the system will be evaluated by using two indexes: the average error in differences between original signal and the decrypted signal and the average difference in gradients between the original signal and the decrypted signal. The average error in differences between the original signal and the decrypted signal is calculated as follows:

$$err\_avg = \frac{|M - \hat{M}|}{t_2 - t_1} \tag{56}$$

The average difference in gradients between the original signal and the decrypted signal is calculated as follows:

$$diff\_avg = \frac{1}{t_2 - t_1} \sum (dA[n] - dB[n]) \tag{57}$$

Herein, $dA[n]$ is the gradient of the original data M, and $dB[n]$ is the gradient of the decrypted data. The averages of these mentioned signals are located in the gaps of $1 \le t_1 < t_2 < n$, where n is an element of dA and dB. The average differences of absolute elements of sent and received data are checked by the exhaustive attacks. Using Equations (56) and (57), the average difference in gradients is 0.4164×10^{-5}, and the average difference between sent and received data is 0. Additionally, to assess the randomness and cryptographic strength of the chaos-based encryption mechanism, the Shannon entropy of the encrypted control signal was computed. The entropy H is calculated as:

$$H = -\sum_{i=1}^{n} p_i \log_2 p_i \tag{58}$$

where p_i is the probability of the occurrence of symbol i in the encrypted data. The analysis was performed on the binary representation of encrypted control signals over 8-bit segments. The resulting entropy was measured to be approximately 7.298238654 bits per byte, which is close to the ideal value of 8 for truly random data. This indicates a high degree of uncertainty and supports the effectiveness of the proposed chaotic encryption scheme in resisting statistical attacks. Shannon entropy analysis confirms that the encrypted data exhibits high randomness $(7.98/8)$, indicating strong resistance to statistical attacks and validating the cryptographic reliability of the proposed chaos-based secure control scheme.

Herein, the response speed signal is encrypted and sent from ESP32(2) to ESP32(3) via an ESP-NOW protocol. Figures 16 and 17 illustrate the original, decrypted and encrypted response speed signal.

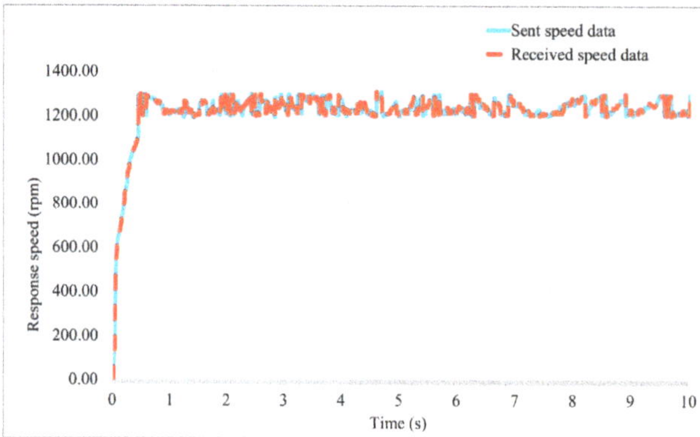

Figure 16. Original and decrypted response speed signal.

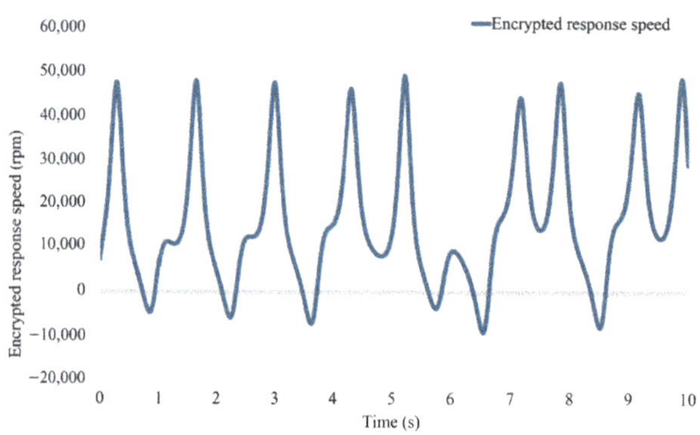

Figure 17. Encrypted response speed signal.

Figures 18–20 present a statistical analysis of the secure communication process through histograms of the original, encrypted, and decrypted response speed signals.

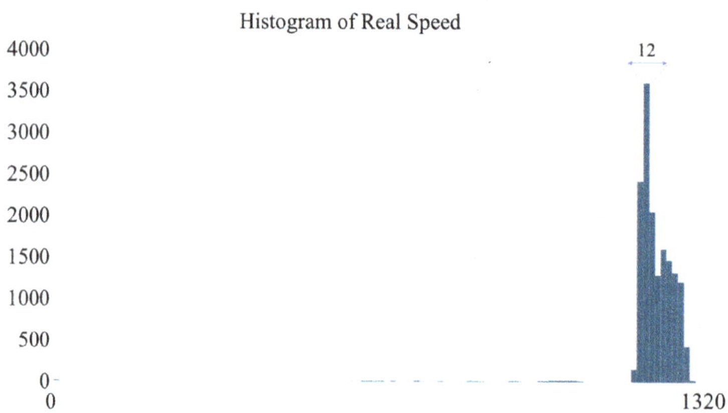

Figure 18. Histogram chat of sent response speed signal.

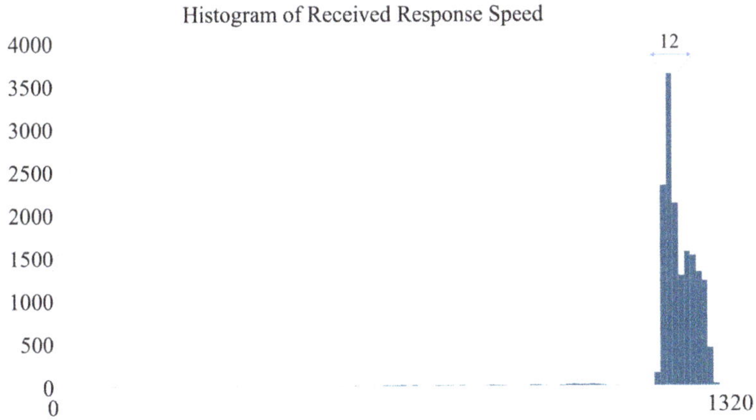

Figure 19. Histogram chat of received response speed signal.

The histogram of the encrypted signal demonstrates a nearly uniform distribution, indicating that the encryption method successfully removes recognizable patterns, making the transmitted data highly resistant to decryption attempts. Meanwhile, the decrypted signal's histogram closely resembles that of the original signal, confirming that the proposed system preserves data integrity. Using Equations (56), (57) and (58), the average difference in gradients is 1.2944×10^{-5}. The average difference between sent and received data is 0. The resulting entropy was measured to be approximately 7.348238654 bits per byte.

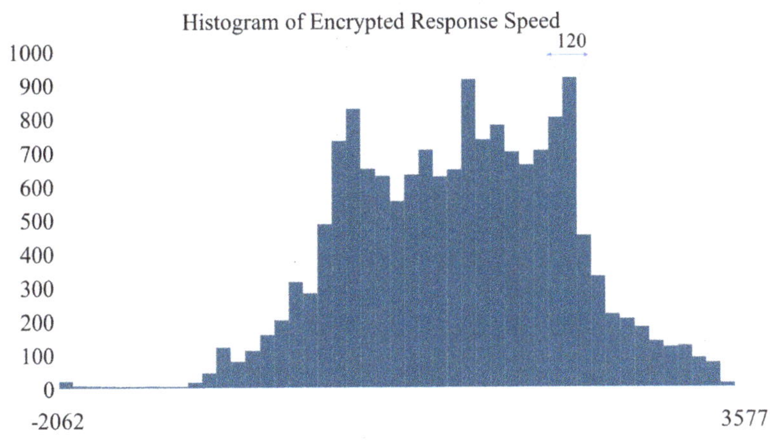

Figure 20. Histogram chat of encrypted response speed signal.

3.3. PI Controller

Figure 21 illustrates the effectiveness of the PI controller in regulating the motor's dynamics, ensuring stable and accurate control of speed. The trajectory of the motor's response shows that the PI controller achieves a relatively fast and smooth convergence to the desired reference value. This confirms its capability to regulate the motor under normal operating conditions.

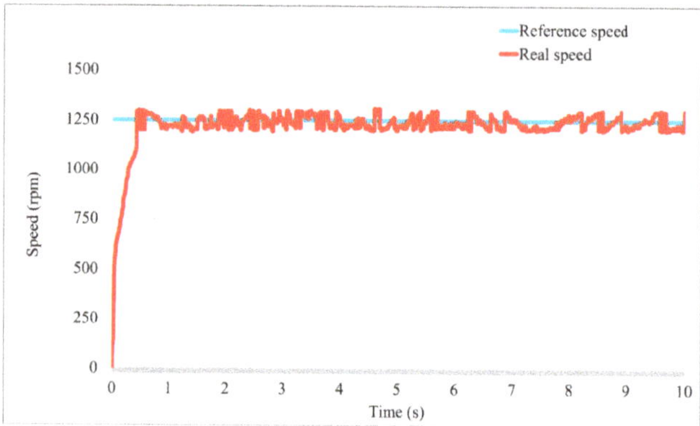

Figure 21. PI controller's performance.

4. Conclusions

This paper presented a novel and secure control architecture for smart electric drive systems, leveraging ESP-NOW wireless communication and an integrated fuzzy brain emotional learning neural network (FBELNN) controller combined with the DO. The proposed approach addresses the increasing need for robust and secure real-time control in cyber-physical systems, particularly under external disturbances and uncertainties. Compared to conventional PID-based or fixed-structure adaptive controllers, the FBELNN offers significant improvements in adaptability and learning capability, enabling superior disturbance rejection and dynamic tracking performance. The incorporation of DOB further enhances system robustness by actively compensating for unknown disturbances. In contrast to existing wireless control systems that are often vulnerable to cyber-attacks or suffer from communication latency, our framework utilizes lightweight, real-time ESP-NOW communication and chaotic encryption to ensure secure, low-latency data transmission. Experimental validation on a DC motor tested demonstrated clear advantages over traditional control methods in terms of response time, tracking accuracy, and disturbance resilience, all within a compact and low-cost hardware setup based on ESP32 microcontrollers. Notably, the bidirectional communication among distributed nodes enables decentralized control, which is rarely addressed in comparable low-power embedded systems.

Limitations of the Study

Despite these promising outcomes, the current prototype is limited to small-scale applications and does not yet integrate industrial-grade protocols or hardware. Additionally, compliance with cybernetics standards such as IEC 62443 and industrial drive protocols like IEC 61800 remains to be addressed. Future work will aim to scale the system for deployment in larger, high-speed industrial environments and enhance conformity with recognized standards to enable broader applicability in smart manufacturing and Industry 4.0 contexts.

Author Contributions: Conceptualization, H.C.P.T. and V.N.G.; methodology, V.N.G.; software, N.Q.D.; validation, H.C.P.T. and V.N.G.; formal analysis, V.N.G.; investigation, N.Q.D.; resources, H.C.P.T.; data curation, H.C.P.T.; writing—original draft, H.C.P.T.; writing—review and editing, H.C.P.T.; visualization, H.C.P.T.; supervision, V.N.G. All authors have read and agreed to the published version of the manuscript.

Funding: This research is funded by Hanoi University of Science and Technology (HUST) under project number T2024-PC-049.

Data Availability Statement: Dataset available on request from the authors.

Conflicts of Interest: The authors declare no conflicts of interest.

References

1. Yan, J.J.; Shyu, K.K.; Lin, J.S. Adaptive variable-structure control for uncertain chaotic systems containing dead-zone non-linearity. *Chaos Solit. Fractals* **2005**, *25*, 347–355. [CrossRef]
2. Lin, C.-M.; Mon, Y.-J. Decoupling control by hierarchical fuzzy sliding-mode controller. *IEEE Trans. Control. Syst. Technol.* **2005**, *13*, 593–598. [CrossRef]
3. Giap, V.N.; Nguyen, Q.D.; Pham, D.H.; Lin, C.M. Wireless secure communication of chaotic systems based on Takagi–Sugeno fuzzy optimal time-varying Disturbance Observer and sliding-mode control. *Int. J. Fuzzy Syst.* **2023**, *25*, 2519–2533. [CrossRef]
4. Giap, V.N. Text message secure communication based on fractional-order chaotic systems with Takagi–Sugeno fuzzy Disturbance Observer and sliding-mode control. *Int. J. Dyn. Control.* **2023**, *11*, 3109–3123. [CrossRef]
5. Giap, V.-N.; Huang, S.-C.; Nguyen, Q.D. Synchronization of 3D Chaotic System Based on Sliding Mode Control: Electronic Circuit Implementation. In Proceedings of the 2020 IEEE Eurasia Conference on IOT, Communication and Engineering (ECICE), Yunlin, Taiwan, 23–25 October 2020; pp. 156–159. [CrossRef]
6. Lin, C.M.; Ting, A.B.; Hsu, C.F.; Chung, C.M. Adaptive control for MIMO uncertain nonlinear systems using recurrent wavelet neural network. *Int. J. Neural Syst.* **2012**, *22*, 37–50. [CrossRef]
7. AL-Hussein, A.B.A. Neural Network-Based Adaptive Control of Robotic Manipulator: Application to a Three Links Cylindrical Robot. *Iraqi J. Electr. Electron. Eng.* **2017**, *13*, 114–122. [CrossRef]
8. Pham, D.-H.; Lin, C.-M.; Giap, V.N.; Huynh, T.-T.; Cho, H.-Y. Wavelet Interval Type-2 Takagi-Kang-Sugeno Hybrid Controller for Time-Series Prediction and Chaotic Synchronization. *IEEE Access* **2022**, *10*, 104313–104327. [CrossRef]
9. Chen, C.L.P.; Liu, Y.-J.; Wen, G.-X. Fuzzy Neural Network-Based Adaptive Control for a Class of Uncertain Nonlinear Stochastic Systems. *IEEE Trans. Cybern.* **2014**, *44*, 583–593. [CrossRef]
10. Chen, C.-S. Robust Self-Organizing Neural-Fuzzy Control With Uncertainty Observer for MIMO Nonlinear Systems. *IEEE Trans. Fuzzy Syst.* **2011**, *19*, 694–706. [CrossRef]
11. Fang, W.; Chao, F.; Lin, C.M.; Yang, L.; Shang, C.; Zhou, C. An Improved Fuzzy Brain Emotional Learning Model Network Controller for Humanoid Robots. *Front. Neurorobotics* **2019**, *13*, 2. [CrossRef]
12. Jin, J.; Fang, J.; Chen, C.; Li, Z.; Yu, F. A complex-valued time varying zeroing neural network model for synchronization of complex chaotic systems. *Nonlinear Dyn.* **2024**, *113*, 5471–5491. [CrossRef]
13. Yu, F.; He, S.; Yao, W.; Cai, S.; Xu, Q. Bursting Firings in Memristive Hopffeld Neural Network with Image Encryption and Hardware Implementation. *IEEE Trans.-Comput.-Aided Des. Integr. Circuits Syst.* 2025, *early access*. [CrossRef]
14. Marr, D. A theory of cerebellar cortex. *J. Physiol.* **1969**, *202*, 437–470. [CrossRef]
15. Albus, J.S. A new approach to manipulator control: The cerebellar model articulation controller (CMAC). *J. Dyn. Syst. Meas. Control* **1975**, *97*, 220–227. [CrossRef]
16. Cheng, K.-H. Adaptive fuzzy CMAC-based nonlinear control with dynamic memory architecture. *J. Frankl. Inst.* **2011**, *348*, 2480–2502. [CrossRef]
17. Chiu, C.-H. Adaptive output recurrent cerebellar model articulation controller for nonlinear system control. *Soft Comput.* **2010**, *14*, 627–638. [CrossRef]
18. Lin, C.M.; Huynh, T.T.; Le, T.L. Adaptive TOPSIS fuzzy CMAC back-stepping control system design for nonlinear systems. *Soft Comput.* **2019**, *23*, 6947–6966. [CrossRef]
19. Lin, C.M.; Li, H.Y. TSK Fuzzy CMAC-Based Robust Adaptive Backstepping Control for Uncertain Nonlinear Systems. *IEEE Trans. Fuzzy Syst.* **2012**, *20*, 1147–1154. [CrossRef]
20. Ortiz, F.; Yu, W.; Moreno-Armendariz, M.; Li, X. Recurrent Fuzzy CMAC for Nonlinear System Modeling. In *Advances in Neural Networks*; Lecture Notes in Computer Science; Springer: Berlin/Heidelberg, Germany, 2007; Volume 4491. [CrossRef]
21. Lin, C.M.; Li, H.Y. Dynamic Petri Fuzzy Cerebellar Model Articulation Controller Design for a Magnetic Levitation System and a Two-Axis Linear Piezoelectric Ceramic Motor Drive System. *IEEE Trans. Control. Syst. Technol.* **2015**, *23*, 693–699. [CrossRef]
22. LeDoux, J.E. Emotion and the amygdala: Fear, anxiety, and aggression. In *The Amygdala: Neurobiological Aspects of Emotion, Memory, and Mental Dysfunction*; Wiley-Liss: Hoboken, NJ, USA, 1992; pp. 339–351.
23. Balkenius, C.; Moren, J. Emotional learning: A computational model of the amygdala. *Cybern. Syst.* **2001**, *32*, 611–636. [CrossRef]
24. Pham, D.H.; Lin, C.M.; Giap, V.N. Intelligent control-system design for nonlinear systems using an improved TSK wavelet type-2 fuzzy brain-emotional controller. *Int. J. Fuzzy Syst.* **2024**, *26*, 2632–2645. [CrossRef]
25. Moren, J.; Balkenius, C. A computational model of emotional learning in the amygdala. In *From Animals to Animats 7*; MIT Press: Cambridge, MA, USA, 2002; pp. 115–124.

26. Lucas, C.; Salari, K.; Sheikholeslami, N. Introducing BELBIC: Brain emotional learning-based intelligent controller. *Int. J. Intell. Autom. Soft Comput.* **2004**, *10*, 11–22. [CrossRef]
27. Rouhani, H.; Jalili, M.; Araabi, B.N.; Eppler, W.; Lucas, C. Brain emotional learning based intelligent controller applied to neurofuzzy model of micro-heat exchanger. *Expert Syst. Appl.* **2007**, *32*, 911–918. [CrossRef]
28. Samimi, M.; Majidi, M.H.; Khorashadizadeh, S. Secure communication based on chaos synchronization using brain emotional learning. *AEU—Int. J. Electron. Commun.* **2020**, *127*, 153424. [CrossRef]
29. Le, M.C.; Giap, V.N.; Nguyen, Q.D.; Huang, S.-C. Electrocardiogram Signal Secure Transmission via a Wireless Communication Protocol of Chaotic Systems Based on Adaptive Sliding Mode Control and Disturbance Observer. *IEEE Access* **2023**, *11*, 145373–145385. [CrossRef]
30. Min, F.; Chen, C.; Broderick, N.G. Coupled Homogeneous Hopfield Neural Networks: Simplest Model Design, Synchronization, and Multiplierless Circuit Implementation. *IEEE Trans. Neural Netw. Learn. Systems.* **2025**, *36*, 11632–11639. [CrossRef]
31. Deng, Q.; Wang, C.; Yang, G.; Luo, D. Discrete Memristive Delay Feedback Rulkov Neuron Model: Chaotic Dynamics, Hardware Implementation, and Application in Secure Communication. *IEEE Internet Things J.* **2025**, *12*, 25559–25567. [CrossRef]
32. Lin, C.-M.; Pham, D.-H.; Huynh, T.-T. Encryption and Decryption of Audio Signal and Image Secure Communications Using Chaotic System Synchronization Control by TSK Fuzzy Brain Emotional Learning Controllers. *IEEE Trans. Cybern.* **2022**, *52*, 13684–13698. [CrossRef]
33. Giap, V.N.; Vu, H.S.; Nguyen, Q.D.; Huang, S.C. Disturbance-and-uncertainty rejection based on fixed-time sliding-mode control for the secure communication of chaotic systems. *IEEE Access* **2021**, *9*, 133663–133685. [CrossRef]
34. Nguyen, Q.D.; Huang, S.C.; Giap, V.N. Lyapunov-based fractional-order Disturbance Observer and sliding-mode control for a secure communication of chaos-based system. *Int. J. Control Autom. Syst.* **2023**, *21*, 3595–3606. [CrossRef]
35. Nguyen, Q.D.; Vu, D.D.; Huang, S.-C.; Giap, V.N. Fixed-time supper twisting Disturbance Observer and sliding mode control for a secure communication of fractional-order chaotic systems. *J. Vib. Control.* **2023**, *30*, 2568–2581. [CrossRef]
36. Zhu, S.; Deng, X.; Zhang, W.; Zhu, C. Secure image encryption scheme based on a new robust chaotic map and strong S-box. *Math. Comput. Simul.* **2023**, *207*, 322–346. [CrossRef]
37. Pallav; Handa, H. Chaos synchronization for a class of hyper-chaotic systems using active SMC and PI SMC: A comparative analysis. *J. Control Autom. Electr. Syst.* **2022**, *33*, 1671–1687. [CrossRef]
38. Lyu, B.; Liu, C.; Yue, X. Integrated Predictor–Observer Feedback Control for Vibration Mitigation of Large-Scale Spacecraft With Unbounded Input Time Delay. *IEEE Trans. Aerosp. Electron. Syst.* **2025**, *61*, 4561–4572. [CrossRef]
39. Liu, C.; Yue, X.; Zhang, J.; Shi, K. Active Disturbance Rejection Control for Delayed Electromagnetic Docking of Spacecraft in Elliptical Orbits. *IEEE Trans. Aerosp. Electron. Syst.* **2022**, *58*, 2257–2268. [CrossRef]
40. Lyu, B.; Liu, C.; Yue, X. Hybrid nonfragile intermediate observer-based T-S fuzzy attitude control for flexible spacecraft with input saturation. *Aerosp. Sci. Technol.* **2022**, *128*, 107753. [CrossRef]
41. Hadji, M.M.; Ladaci, S. A novel secure-communication-scheme design using a fractional-order adaptive observer-based synchronization. *J. Control Autom. Electr. Syst.* **2025**, *36*, 267–282. [CrossRef]
42. Yu, F.; Zhang, S.; Su, D.; Wu, Y.; Gracia, Y.M.; Yin, H. Dynamic Analysis and Implementation of FPGA for a New 4D Fractional-Order Memristive Hopfield Neural Network. *Fractal Fract.* **2025**, *9*, 115. [CrossRef]
43. Deng, Q.; Wang, C.; Sun, Y.; Yang, G. Discrete Memristive Conservative Chaotic Map: Dynamics, Hardware Implementation, and Application in Secure Communication. *IEEE Trans. Cybern.* 2025, *early access*. [CrossRef]
44. Wan, Q.; Yang, Q.; Liu, T.; Chen, C.; Shen, K. Single direction, grid and spatial multi-scroll attractors in Hopfield neural network with the variable number memristive self-connected synapses. *Chaos Solit. Fractals* **2024**, *189*, 115584. [CrossRef]
45. Ortigueira, M.D.; Machado, J.A.T. New discrete-time fractional derivatives based on the bilinear transformation: Definitions and properties. *J. Adv. Res.* **2020**, *25*, 1–10. [CrossRef] [PubMed]
46. Lin, C.M.; Chung, C.C. Fuzzy Brain Emotional Learning Control System Design for Nonlinear Systems. *Int. J. Fuzzy Syst.* **2015**, *17*, 117–128. [CrossRef]

Mathematical and Computational Applications

MDPI

Article

Energy Management and Power Distribution for Battery/Ultracapacitor Hybrid Energy Storage System in Electric Vehicles with Regenerative Braking Control

Abdelsalam A. Ahmed [1,*], Young Il Lee [2], Saleh Al Dawsari [3,4,*], Ahmed A. Zaki Diab [5,*] and Abdelsalam A. Ezzat [6]

1 Electrical Power and Machines Engineering Department, Faculty of Engineering, Tanta University, Tanta 31527, Egypt
2 Electrical and Information Engineering, Seoul National University of Science and Technology, Seoul 01811, Republic of Korea; yilee@seoultech.ac.kr
3 Electrical Engineering Department, College of Engineering, Najran University, Najran 1988, Saudi Arabia
4 Department of Electrical Engineering, College of Engineering, Northern Border University, Arar 73213, Saudi Arabia
5 Electrical Engineering Department, Faculty of Engineering, Minia University, Minia 61111, Egypt
6 El-Minia High Institute of Engineering and Technology, New Minya, Minia 61111, Egypt; dr.abdoezzat@mhiet.edu.eg
* Correspondence: abdelsalam.abdelsalam@f-eng.tanta.edu.eg (A.A.A.); aldawsarisa@cardiff.ac.uk (S.A.D.); a.diab@mu.edu.eg (A.A.Z.D.)

Abstract: This paper presents an advanced energy management system (EMS) for optimizing power distribution in a battery/ultracapacitor (UC) hybrid energy storage system (HESS) for electric vehicles (EVs). The proposed EMS accounts for all energy flow scenarios within a practical driving cycle. A regenerative braking control strategy is developed to maximize kinetic energy recovery using an induction motor, efficiently distributing the recovered energy between the UC and battery. Additionally, a power flow management approach is introduced for both motoring (discharge) and braking (charge) operations via bidirectional buck–boost DC-DC converters. In discharge mode, an optimal distribution factor is dynamically adjusted to balance power delivery between the battery and UC, maximizing efficiency. During charging, a DC link voltage control mechanism prioritizes UC charging over the battery, reducing stress and enhancing energy recovery efficiency. The proposed EMS is validated through simulations and experiments, demonstrating significant improvements in vehicle acceleration, energy efficiency, and battery lifespan.

Keywords: battery/ultracapacitor hybrid energy storage modules; regenerative braking control; power flow distribution; current control mode; voltage control mode

1. Introduction

1.1. Related Works

Lithium-ion (Li-ion) batteries are the predominant energy storage solution for portable electronic devices and electric vehicles (EVs). Modern Li-ion battery technology focuses on balancing high cell voltage with other performance parameters, such as rate capability and cycle life [1]. However, Li-ion batteries alone face challenges in handling high-peak-power demands efficiently. Supercapacitors (SCs), also known as ultracapacitors (UCs), exhibit superior charge/discharge rate capability, making them suitable for compensating transient high-power demands when battery power is insufficient.

The combination of a battery and UC in a hybrid energy storage system (HESS) leverages the complementary advantages of both storage technologies. In such a configuration, UCs absorb rapid power fluctuations, thereby reducing stress on the battery and prolonging its operational lifespan. When integrated into EVs, the HESS facilitates effective storage of regenerative braking energy (RBE), which can be reused to enhance vehicle acceleration. Additionally, a well-optimized HESS improves overall vehicle performance by offering high energy density, long cycle life [2], and a significant reduction in system weight compared to a battery-only energy storage system.

In EV and hybrid electric vehicle (HEV) applications, a battery pack (BP) combined with an UC as a HESS provides superior power management and control flexibility compared to conventional stand-alone battery designs [3]. Various studies have explored different control methodologies for HESSs. For instance, a characterization method for UCs was presented in [4], where a control strategy for DC-bus voltage and current regulation in a BP/UC HESS was implemented using two buck–boost converters. An alternative approach employing a UC-only energy storage system (ESS) was proposed in [5], where a DC-DC converter was used to regulate power flow. Additionally, load-sharing strategies between the battery and UC have been explored in [3–7]. However, achieving maximum discharge efficiency in HESSs remains an area that has received limited research attention.

The economic viability of HESSs is particularly evident in municipal transportation systems, such as city transit buses, where regenerative braking plays a crucial role in improving energy efficiency [2,8,9]. Regenerative braking (RB) enables EVs and HEVs to recover kinetic energy by employing an electric traction motor to generate negative torque, converting kinetic energy into electrical energy that recharges the ESS [10]. However, conventional battery technologies impose limitations on RB due to their relatively low power density and charge acceptance rate. UCs, with their high specific power and extended cycle life, offer a promising solution for efficiently storing and utilizing RBE [11].

Several studies have proposed advanced control algorithms for optimizing regenerative breaking. In [12–14], the braking process was categorized into dissipative and regenerative modes. A slip speed control mechanism for induction motors (IMs) was introduced in [13,14] to maximize energy recovery by operating the motor in the negative slip region. Additionally, non-monotonic energy consumption behavior during battery discharge was examined in [15], where SCs were utilized to compensate for rapid energy fluctuations. Recent advancements in model predictive control (MPC) techniques have further improved HESS performance. The authors in [16] proposed an MPC-based control strategy for three-level bidirectional DC-DC converters in a DC microgrid, ensuring voltage regulation and minimizing system current ripple. In [17], an MPC-based approach was also introduced to optimize energy distribution in a HESS for EVs. A two-loop control framework was implemented, consisting of an inner predictive current controller and an outer voltage control loop, which efficiently allocated low-frequency power variations to the battery while managing high-frequency power fluctuations using SCs.

Moreover, other recent studies emphasize the increasing complexity of distributed energy systems, driven by the rise in residential PVs, electric vehicles (EVs), and the demand for grid flexibility [18–21]. Additionally, in [22], an optimal distributed RES sizing strategy is presented for hybrid low-voltage networks with EV integration. The work highlights critical issues such as mismatched generation–demand profiles, space constraints, and the high cost of energy storage systems (ESSs). By employing fuzzy cognitive maps (FCMs), the authors design a data-driven graph structure that correlates household demand, EV charging behavior, and RES capacity. This approach enables a tailored PV sizing strategy per household, achieving up to 40% energy cost reduction without the need for grid expansion. In [23], autonomous PV-powered reverse osmosis (RO) desalination systems are examined for island applications. The authors evaluate multiple configurations using FCM-based energy management, showing that systems combining PV, limited battery storage, and water tanks offer a cost-effective and technically viable solution. The methodology optimizes lifetime system performance while minimizing operational and capital costs under autonomous operation, demonstrating that FCM-enabled EMSs lead to the lowest power losses and overall cost.

On the other hand, Ref. [24] focuses on EV charging management in islanded low-voltage microgrids. The proposed decentralized energy management system (EMS) is built using a multi-agent framework integrating fuzzy logic and FCMs. This configuration significantly improves system performance by reducing peak load by 17%, lowering load variance by 29%, and increasing the mean number of chargeable EVs by 31%. The total microgrid investment cost is reduced by 8.8% over 20 years, indicating the economic viability of advanced EMS strategies. For EV propulsion systems, [25] offers a multi-criteria analysis comparing brushless, induction, and synchronous reluctance motors in the context of hybrid energy storage systems (HESSs). The analysis confirms that permanent magnet and induction motors provide the best overall performance. However, synchronous reluctance motors outperform in scenarios emphasizing HESS integration, regenerative braking efficiency, and system response to varying load demands. Authors in Ref. [26] present a case study on the energy consumption of an autonomous electric cargo robot under field conditions. This contributes to the broader understanding of EV energy dynamics in non-urban, application-specific contexts.

The reported studies support the growing need for intelligent and integrated energy management strategies in electric vehicle (EV) systems, particularly those incorporating hybrid energy storage systems (HESSs) with batteries and ultracapacitors. Prior research has explored optimal renewable energy sizing, decentralized EV charging control, and motor drive performance, but there remains a gap in managing real-time energy flow during dynamic driving conditions. This work addresses that gap by developing an advanced energy management system (EMS) tailored for battery/ultracapacitor HESS in EVs. Unlike conventional strategies, the proposed EMS coordinates all energy flow scenarios, including regenerative braking, motoring, and bidirectional power exchange through DC-DC converters. By focusing on real-world driving cycles, this approach enhances energy recovery, optimizes power distribution, and improves battery lifespan—offering a practical, efficient solution for next-generation EVs.

1.2. Research Gap and Contribution

This study presents an advanced energy management system (EMS) for efficiently integrating battery packs with ultracapacitors in electric vehicle (EV) applications. Previously, in [18], the authors made initial efforts to control the IM during braking instances. Additionally, the negative power generated during braking was analyzed for its potential use in charging both the battery and the ultracapacitor. However, further research and improvements were necessary for realization. The key contributions of this paper are:

- Updating the state of the art and related works concerning the research topic.
- Providing a more detailed analysis of power flow operational modes between the BP, UC, and load.
- Expanding experimental studies on IM braking at different speeds.
- Experimentally integrating the BP and UC with a 4 kW static load.
- Analyzing the performance of the hybrid energy storage system under different operational modes using experimental results.
- Presenting detailed calculations of energy efficiency across various operational modes.

In this paper, the proposed EMS accounts for various energy flow scenarios encountered during practical EV driving cycles.

1. **Regenerative Braking Control:**
    - A control strategy is developed for an induction motor to maximize kinetic energy recovery during regenerative braking.
    - The braking energy is strategically distributed between the UC and battery to enhance overall system efficiency.
2. **Power Flow Management in HESS:**
    - During motoring (discharge mode), an optimal power distribution strategy is implemented, balancing power delivery between the battery and UC using a distribution factor.
    - The distribution factor is dynamically adjusted to maximize system efficiency, with UC discharge current actively controlled.
    - During braking (charge mode), a DC link voltage control mechanism prioritizes UC charging over the battery, improving energy recovery efficiency.
3. **Theoretical, Simulation-based, and Experimental-based Validation:**

The proposed EMS and control strategies are validated through simulations and experiments to demonstrate improvements in vehicle performance, energy efficiency, and battery lifespan. Experiments and simulations have been performed to prove the regenerative braking control and power distribution between battery and UC.

The remainder of this paper is organized as follows: Section 2 provides a detailed description of the system architecture and its various operational modes. Section 3 introduces the proposed control strategy for the hybrid energy storage system, including the estimation of the optimal power distribution factor between the battery and ultracapacitor, as well as the regenerative braking control of the induction motor. Section 4 presents the simulation results and experimental validation. Finally, Section 5 concludes the paper by summarizing the key contributions and findings.

2. System Description and Operational Modes

The adopted system consists of a three-phase induction motor, a two-level three-phase inverter, an ultracapacitor, a battery pack, and a DC link regulated by a DC-DC chopper, as illustrated in Figure 1. The IM operates in both motoring and generating modes; however, this paper focuses exclusively on the regenerative operation during braking periods. The DC-DC chopper functions in both buck and boost modes, depending on the vehicle's driving cycle. The ultracapacitor and battery pack are connected to the DC bus through a buck–boost converter, which facilitates energy exchange with the load. The DC-DC converter, responsible for regulating current flow in the HESS, operates in two modes—buck and boost—depending on load conditions and the direction of power flow, as illustrated in Figure 1.

The operational modes discussed in this paper are as follows:

1. **Mode 1:** Charging the UC from the battery at light loads (Path E1): During this mode, the load is powered by the BP (Path E3), while the UC is charged. The chopper operates in buck mode, with switch S2 turned ON.
2. **Mode 2:** Charging the UC from the load during regenerative braking (Path E2): In this mode, the chopper remains in buck mode, with switch S2 ON, to store recovered energy in the UC.
3. **Mode 3:** Simultaneous charging of the UC from both the BP and the load (Paths E1 and E2). In Mode 3, the ultracapacitor is charged simultaneously from the regenerative braking system and the battery pack. This mode is enabled only when the energy

recovered from braking is insufficient to meet the UC charging demand. A dedicated DC-DC converter allows supplementary power from the battery under controlled conditions. The energy management system monitors braking intensity, battery state-of-charge, and UC voltage to ensure safe operation, prevent overcharging, and optimize power flow efficiency.

4. **Mode 4:** Power sharing at heavy loads: The load current is drawn from both the battery (Path E3) and the UC (Path E4) through diode D2, following a load power sharing strategy, which will be explained in the next section.

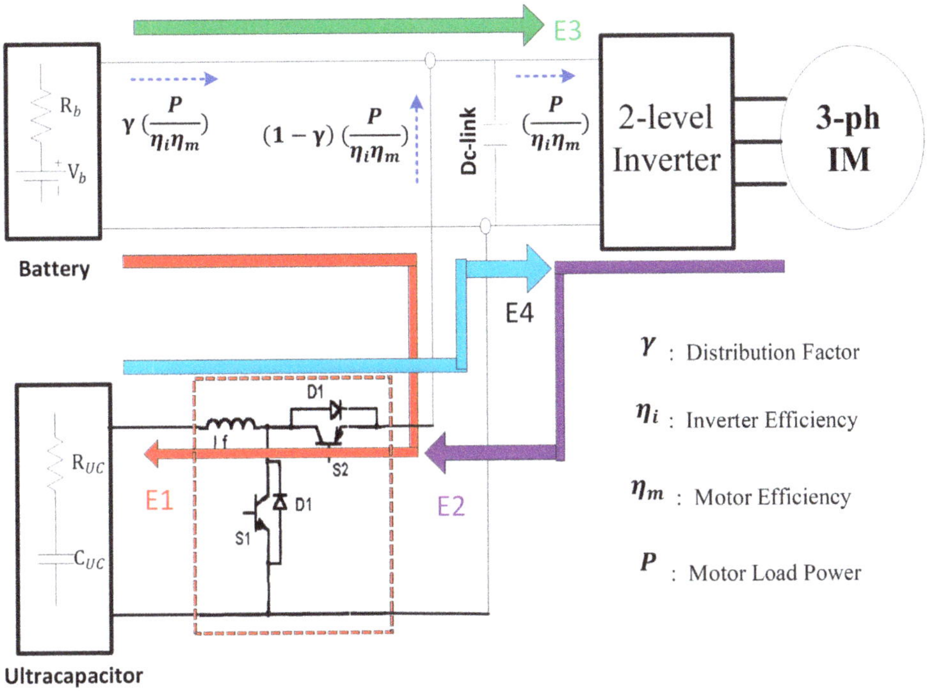

Figure 1. Integration of BP and UC by DC-DC converter for IM drive.

In this system, the internal resistance of the BP is higher than that of UC. Therefore power loss of the BP path is higher. Therefore, with no load or/and light loads, the UC is charged by low current from the battery. At high load, the load current is drawn from both the BP and UC using the gamma distribution technique.

3. Control Strategy for Hybrid Energy Storage System

The battery pack is integrated with the ultracapacitor via a DC-DC chopper, enabling efficient energy exchange between the two storage components. The control methods of the chopper are illustrated in Figure 2. The chopper's control signals are generated based on two primary modes of operation, buck mode and boost mode, which are selected according to the system's operational requirements and load conditions. In buck mode, voltage control is applied to regulate the charging process of the UC, ensuring stable energy transfer. In contrast, boost mode employs current control to efficiently discharge energy from the UC to support the load. As shown in Figure 2, the appropriate control mode is selected by a mode switch based on the rotor position and its directional movement, optimizing energy utilization.

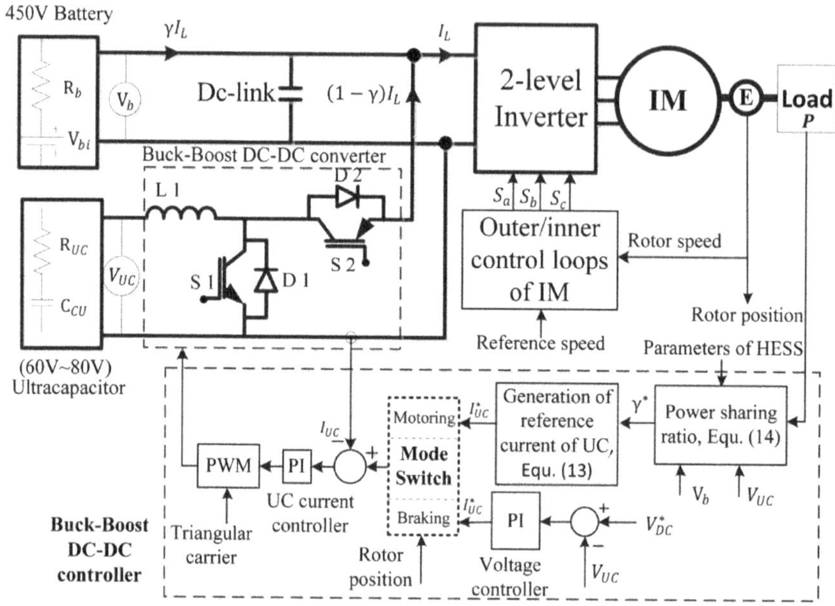

Figure 2. Battery/ultracapacitor with control principle of buck–boost control.

The system operates in two distinct modes:

Motoring Operation—The system functions in boost mode, utilizing current control to manage energy discharge from the UC, supplementing the battery to power the load efficiently.

Braking Operation—The system operates in buck mode, using voltage control to regulate energy recovery during regenerative braking, prioritizing UC charging to enhance system efficiency and prolong battery lifespan.

3.1. Motoring Operation (Boost Mode, Current Control, Discharge Mode)

During vehicle acceleration or cruising, the drive system operates in motoring mode. In this state, the ultracapacitor voltage is boosted to match the threshold DC link voltage, and both the UC and battery pack discharge to supply power to the load (mode 4). As shown in Figure 2, when the load power demand and UC parameters are known, the optimal power distribution ratio can be determined. Based on this ratio, the reference current for the UC is estimated. The reference current is then directly compared with the measured UC current using a proportional–integral (PI) controller, which generates the duty cycle for the UC's unidirectional DC-DC converter.

The control signals for the DC-DC converter are generated through a pulse-width modulation (PWM) modulator. The boost mode of the DC-DC converter (i.e., discharging mode) is activated under high-load conditions, where the load current is supplied by both the BP and UC according to a predefined distribution factor, γ. To maximize discharge efficiency, the optimal distribution factor is first derived. Given that the output power of the induction motor is defined as P, the distribution factor is constrained within the range $0 \le \gamma \le 1$.

For a gamma distribution factor γ and consumed load power P, the power that is supplied from the battery to the load (E3 in Figure 1) is estimated as follows:

$$P_b = \gamma\left(\frac{P}{\eta_i\,\eta_m}\right) = V_b I_b = (V_b - R_b I_b) I_b, \tag{1}$$

where V_b is the no-load battery voltage, R_b is the internal resistance of the BP, I_b is the load current drawn from the BP, and η_i and η_m are efficiencies of the inverter and motor. The current of the battery is positive for discharge and negative for charging. For a given output–input power of the BP, the current and terminal voltage are easily determined by solving quadratic equation of (1).

For charging, the solution is as follows:

$$I_b = \frac{V_b - \sqrt{V_b^2 - 4R_b\gamma\left(\frac{-P}{\eta_i\,\eta_m}\right)}}{2R_b} \tag{2}$$

For discharge, the solution is as follows:

$$I_b = \frac{V_b - \sqrt{V_b^2 - 4R_b\gamma\left(\frac{P}{\eta_i\,\eta_m}\right)}}{2R_b} \tag{3}$$

where V_b, I_b, and R_b are the no-load voltage of battery, battery current, internal resistance of the battery, respectively; and η_i and η_m are the efficiencies of the inverter and IM, respectively.

By the same way, the power exerted from UC to the load can be calculated as follows:

$$P_{uc} = (1-\gamma)\left(\frac{P}{\eta_i\,\eta_m}\right) = V_{uc}\,I_{uc} = \eta_{ch}(V_{uc} - R_{uc}I_{uc})I_{uc} \tag{4}$$

Then, UC current is expressed as follows:

$$I_{uc} = \frac{1}{2R_{uc}\,\eta_{ch}}\cdot\left(\eta_{ch}V_{uc} - \sqrt{\eta_{ch}^2\,V_{uc}^2 - 4R_{uc}\eta_{ch}(1-\gamma)\left(\frac{P}{\eta_i\,\eta_m}\right)}\right), \tag{5}$$

where V_{uc}, I_{uc}, and R_{uc} are open-circuit voltage, current, and an internal resistance of the UC, respectively; and η_{ch} is the efficiency of DC-DC converter.

The overall efficiency of the system at discharge mode could be given as follows:

$$\eta = \frac{P}{P_b + P_{uc}} = \frac{P}{V_b I_b + V_{uc}\,I_{uc}} \tag{6}$$

Optimal distribution factor γ^*, at which the maximum discharge efficiency could be achieved, is determined when $\frac{\partial\eta}{\partial\gamma} = 0$. It yields the following:

$$\gamma^* = \frac{4R_{uc}\eta_{ch}\left(\frac{P}{\eta_i\,\eta_m}\right) + GV_b^2 - \eta_{ch}^2 V_{uc}^2}{4(R_b G + R_{uc}\eta_{ch})\left(\frac{P}{\eta_i\,\eta_m}\right)} \tag{7}$$

where $G = \frac{R_{uc}{}^4 V_{uc}^2}{R_b{}^4 V_b^2}$. After obtaining γ^* using (7), the reference current of the UC is obtained using (5). Then, the actual current is compared to the reference value of the UC and the error is treated by a PI current controller to obtain the control signal of the chopper via a PWM technique. This work focuses on optimizing instantaneous power distribution between energy sources during motoring operation. The control scheme maximizes discharge efficiency using a real-time distribution factor and current control. Although power balancing is the primary goal, the control transitions implicitly reflect time-dependent energy flow. However, cumulative energy effects—such as SoC behavior over extended cycles—are not explicitly modeled. Future work will address this by integrating energy-based constraints and long-term SoC management strategies.

3.2. Braking Operation (Buck Mode, Voltage Control, Charging Operation)

The buck mode is utilized for the regenerative braking operation of the IM. As shown in Figure 3, when the mode switch is set to braking mode the control system transitions accordingly. In this mode, a proportional–integral (PI) controller regulates the DC link voltage by generating the reference current for the UC. Once the reference current is determined, the same control sequence as in the previous mode is followed, including the generation of control signals via the modulator. Maximum power transfer point methodology is used to determine the optimal reference current of the UC at braking time (i.e., $\omega_r^* < \omega_r$). This subsection describes the dynamic behavior of the regenerative braking system. A slip speed control technique is employed to adjust the synchronous speed, enabling the IM to operate as a generator during braking.

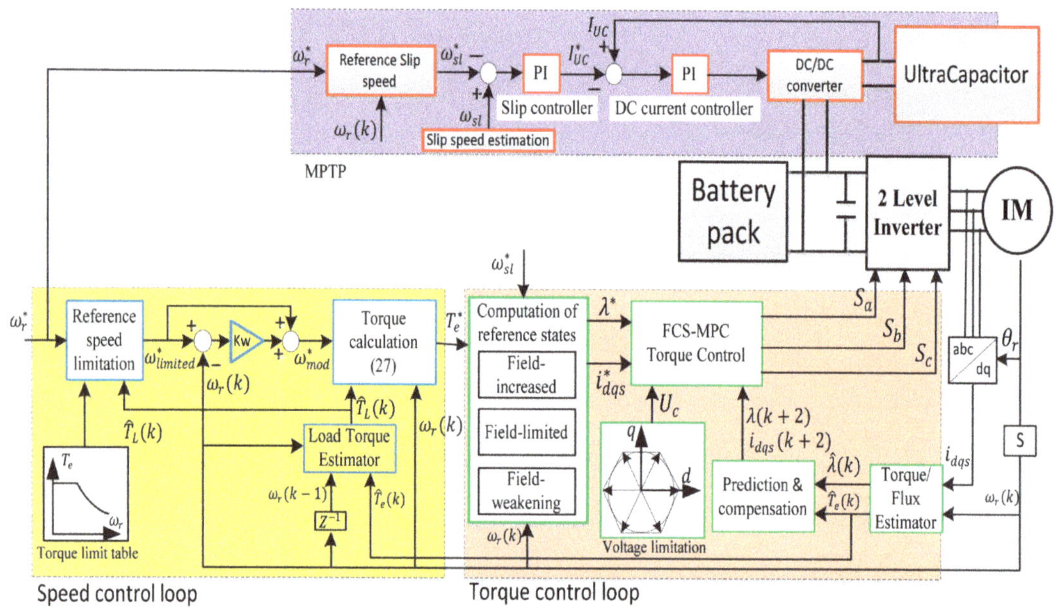

Figure 3. Control system of IM in motoring and braking modes. The lower part was implemented by the first author in [11,12].

The speed control strategy consists of two cascaded control loops:

1. **Inner loop**: Designed for torque control, implemented using a finite control set model predictive control (FCS-MPC) approach with an optimal duration technique, as previously adopted in [19,20].
2. **Outer loop**: Responsible for speed control, relying on an individual MPC cost function.

The speed and torque control loops are illustrated in Figure 3. In the following section, an MPC-based method is applied to control the IM during braking events.

Generation of Reference Torque T_e^* for IM

The dynamic relationship linking the inner and outer control loops is expressed as follows:

$$\dot{\omega} = \frac{1}{J}(-B\omega_r + pT_e - pT_L) \tag{8}$$

where p, J, and B, are pole pairs, inertia, and the friction coefficient, respectively. The state form in the time domain of the dynamic system is as follows:

$$\omega_r(k+1) = \left(1 - \frac{BT_{sw}}{J}\right)\omega_r(k) + \frac{p\,T_{sw}}{J}T_e(k) - \frac{p\,T_{sw}}{J}T_L(k) \tag{9}$$

where $\omega_r(k)$ is the electrical speed and T_{sw} is the sampling time of the speed loop. Due to the discrete nature of digital control platforms, (9) is discretized by Euler approximation. The discrete mechanical state space can be described as follows:

$$x_m[k+1] = A_m x_m[k] + B_m u_m[k] + E_m d_m[k] \tag{10}$$

where $x_m[k] = \omega_r[k]$ is the state variable, $u_m[k]$ is the input control variable, and the disturbance term d_m represents the load torque $T_L[k]$, assumed to be constant during the speed sampling time. The matrices A_m, B_m, and E_m are defined as follows:

$$A_m = 1 - \frac{B\,T_{sw}}{J},\ B_m = \frac{p\,T_{sw}}{J},\ E_m = -\frac{p\,T_{sw}}{J}.$$

When the IM works as a motor, the reference torque T_e^*, in this paper, is generated by a separate MPC presented in [19,20] in terms of state error $(x_m^* - x_m)$, which refers to speed error as follows:

$$T_e^* = \frac{J}{p\,T_{sw}}\left((1+K_{ms})(x_m^* - x_m[k+1|k]) + \frac{B_m\,T_{sw}}{J}x_m[k+1|k] + \frac{p\,T_{sw}}{J}\hat{T}_L[k]\right) \tag{11}$$

The steady-state error in speed is compensated by an integrator with a gain of K_{ms}. In this method, the load torque is estimated $\hat{T}_L$ using a Kalman filter [19]. The inner loop for current control is implemented at the sampling time of T_s whereas the outer loop is performed at the sampling time of speed loop T_{sw}. The time T_{sw} is taken as five times T_s.

When the IM is controlled to stop or to decrease, a regenerative braking technique is employed. In this case, the reference state x_m^* decreases, i.e., it becomes lower than the current state x_m. Given that $\hat{T}_L[k]$ represents a passive load torque, while friction torque acts as an active load, the reference torque T_e^* during complete motor stop ($x_m^* = 0$) is given by the following:

$$T_e^* = \frac{J}{p\,T_{sw}}\left((1+K_{ms})(-x_m[k+1|k]) + \frac{B_m\,T_{sw}}{J}x_m[k+1|k] - \frac{p\,T_{sw}}{J}\hat{T}_L[k]\right) \tag{12}$$

The negative reference torque $T_e^* < 0$ from Equation (12) can also be directly generated through the braking pedal, which provides a negative torque signal to initiate regenerative braking.

Reference Slip Speed ω_{sl}^*

In general, with the FOC of IM, the slip speed can be obtained as $\omega_{sl} = \frac{1}{\tau_r}\frac{i_{qs}}{i_{ds}}$. At braking ($\omega_r^* < \omega_r$), the reference slip speed $\omega_{sl}^* = (\omega_e^* - \omega_r)$ becomes negative. Maximum torque per ampere control could be achieved when $i_{ds}^* = i_{qs}^*$. In this case, the slip speed is set to $\omega_{sl}^* = -1/\tau_r$, where τ_r is the rotor time constant ($= R_r/L_r$). This means that the synchronous speed is controlled to be below the rotor speed when the IM is braked. Thus, the supply frequency is decreased in such a manner so as to operate the IM in the generating region to achieve regeneration.

Reference Rotor Flux λ^*

As a result of decreasing the rotor speed, from the principle of the FOC of IM, the reference rotor flux linkage λ^* can be determined by the following:

$$\lambda^* = \sqrt{\frac{2}{3}\frac{2}{P}L_r/\tau_r}\sqrt{\frac{T_e^*}{\omega_{sl}^*}} = k_\lambda\sqrt{\frac{T_e^*}{\omega_{sl}^*}}, \tag{13}$$

where $k_\lambda = \sqrt{\frac{2}{3}\frac{2}{P}L_r/\tau_r}$. The rotor flux linkage becomes a positive value because both T_e^* and ω_{sl}^* have same sign.

Reference Current Components i_{dqs}^*

The reference stator current components could be calculated in terms of reference flux and torque as follows:

$$i_{ds}^* = \frac{1}{L_m}\lambda^*,\ i_{qs}^* = \frac{2}{3}\frac{2}{P}\frac{L_r}{L_m}\frac{1}{\lambda^*[k]}T_e^* \tag{14}$$

The reference torque of (12) is carried out in the outer loop whereas the slip speed ω_{sl}^*, reference rotor flux λ^* (13), and the reference stator current components i_{dqs}^* (14) are implemented in the inner loop. When the slip speed increases, the IM works as a generator to increase the voltage of the DC link above the normal value. The normal value of the DC link voltage is 450 Vdc, which represents the rated operating level during steady motoring. Values above this threshold indicate regenerative operation or overvoltage conditions that trigger appropriate control responses. Then, referring to Figure 3, the voltage error into the PI voltage controller becomes negative. This results in reversing the direction of the UC current, i.e., from discharging into charging mode.

4. Results and Analysis

4.1. Integration of Battery–Ultracapacitor HESS

This section presents a preliminary stage in the development and control of the UC/battery HESS before integrating the UC in parallel with the battery within an electric vehicle. At this stage, the UC is connected in parallel with the battery via a buck–boost DC-DC converter to regulate power flow. The control strategy is designed to maximize energy transfer efficiency and is first validated through laboratory implementation with a static load. An experimental test bench was established to validate the proposed strategy outlined in Section 5. The schematic diagram of the test setup and photos of all of the equipment are illustrated in Figure 4. It consists of a lithium BP with its BMS and automatic charger, a specified UC module, a buck–boost DC-DC converter, and a static resistive load bank.

In the experimental setup, the UC, serving as an auxiliary energy storage unit, is integrated into the inverter's DC link through a DC-DC converter. The ultracapacitor model "LS Mtron LSUM 086R4C 0093F EA" [21] is employed to support energy sharing with the load. The UC module is tested under both charging and discharging conditions, ensuring optimal power distribution. The detailed specifications of the UC module are listed in Table 1. The UC and lithium BP are coupled to the DC bus via a buck–boost converter, facilitating bidirectional energy exchange between the UC, BP, and load to enhance system performance.

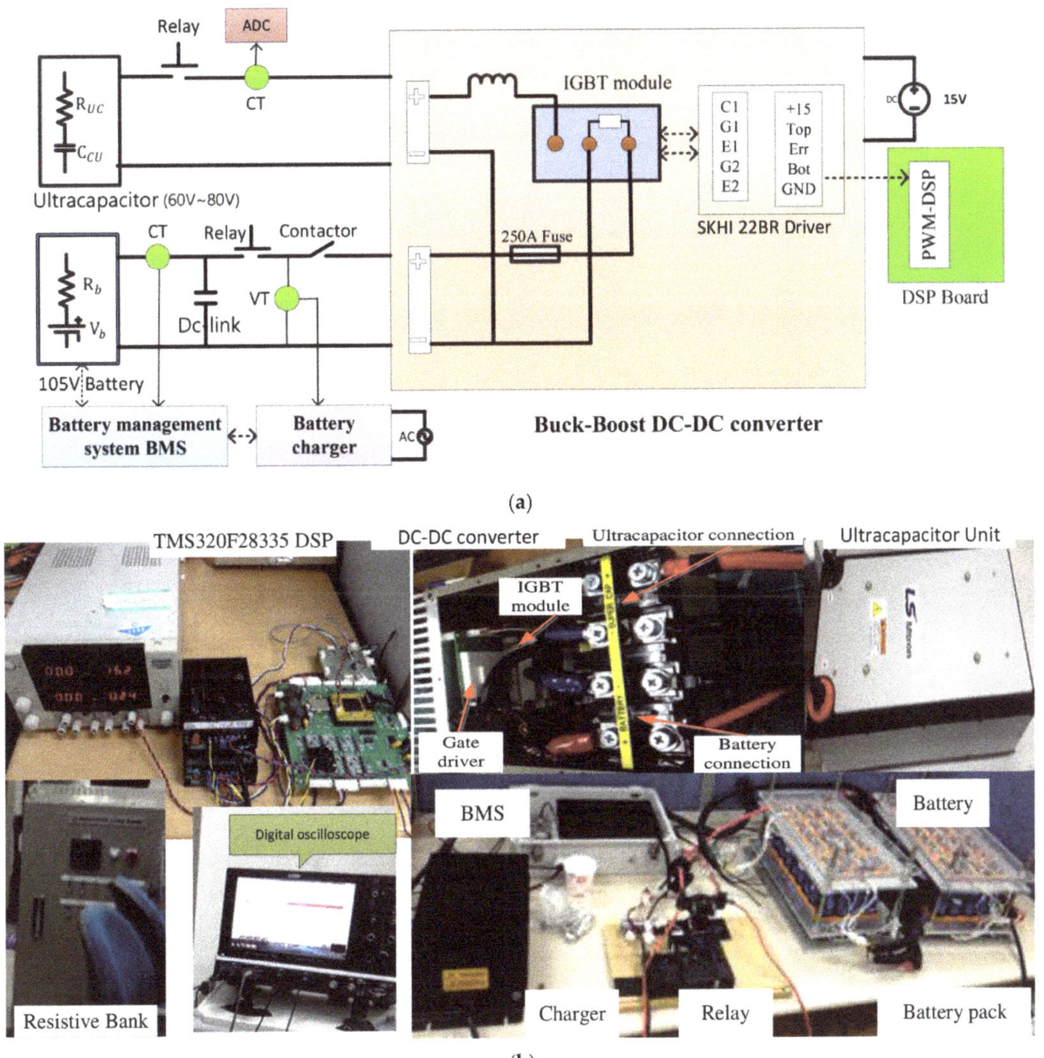

Figure 4. Experiment set of battery/ultracapacitor charge/discharge tests: (**a**) schematic diagram, and (**b**) photo of setup.

Table 1. Specifications of LS Mtron LSUM 086R4C 0093F EA.

Specification [unit]	Value	Specification [unit]	Value
Rated voltage [V]	86.4	Maximum current [A]	80
Capacitance [F]	93	Max. stored energy [Wh/kg]	3.7
Resistance [mΩ]	11.3	Weight [kg]	26

4.2. Relationship Between Distribution Factor, Efficiency, and Load Power

This section analyzes the relationship between overall discharge efficiency, the gamma distribution factor (γ), and load power (P). As derived in (7), the optimal duty that maximizes efficiency is dependent on the load power. Simulation results, illustrated in Figure 5, depict the variation of γ^* at different power levels. The maximum efficiency is achieved at

$\gamma^* = 0.85, 0.45$, and 0.25 for load power values of 5 kW, 10 kW, and 20 kW, respectively. It is evident that γ^* decreases as P increases. These findings suggest that, for higher loads, the ultracapacitor should play a more significant role in power distribution to optimize efficiency and enhance system performance.

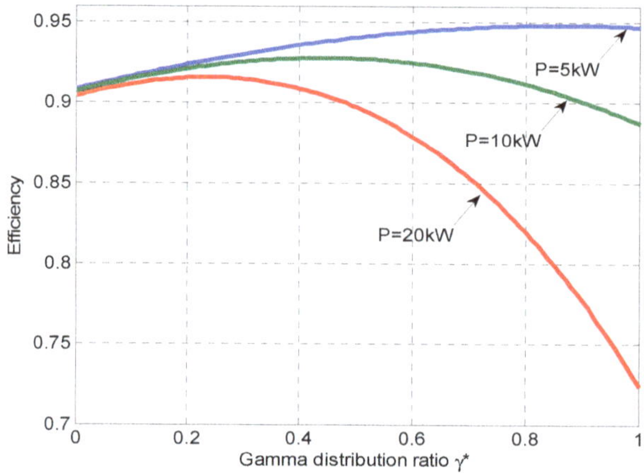

Figure 5. Discharge efficiency and gamma distribution factor.

4.3. Experimental Validation of Slip Control of IM for Regenerative Braking

In this stage, the proposed regenerative braking technique for the induction motor is experimentally validated. The experimental setup consists of a three-phase IM, a three-phase voltage source inverter, and an associated control system implemented on a TMS320F28335 Digital Signal Processor (DSP). The regenerative braking control strategy is executed using a slip speed control technique based on finite control set model predictive control. This approach enables precise control of the IM during braking, ensuring optimal energy recovery and system efficiency. Experimental tests were conducted to validate the slip control strategy of the IM and to quantify the amount of energy recovered during braking. The IM parameters used in the experiments are listed in Table 2.

Table 2. Induction motor parameters.

Quantity	Symbol	Value
DC-bus volt [V]	V_{dc}	450
Number of Poles	P	4
Rated voltage [V]	Y/Δ	220/380
Rated current [A]		14.2/8.2
Stator Resistance [Ω]	R_s	1.77
Rotor Resistance [Ω]	R_r	1.275
Stator Inductance [H]	L_s	0.157
Rotor Inductance [H]	L_r	0.158
Mutual Inductance [H]	L_m	0.15
Inertia coefficient [$Kg{\cdot}m^2$]	J	0.00006
Rated Motor Speed [rpm]	ω_N	1740
Rated Power [kW]	P_N	3.7

Initially, the motor operates at no load and runs at its rated speed of 1740 rpm to assess the effectiveness of the braking control. At time t = 0, the speed reference is set to zero, as depicted in Figure 6. During this transition, the motor speed decreases rapidly, while the phase-current increases, generating a reverse magnetomotive force that enables operation in generation mode. As a result, the developed torque becomes negative, leading to negative generated power. Additionally, the DC-bus voltage rises above 450 V, indicating surplus energy available for storage. This excess energy can be efficiently utilized to charge the ultracapacitor through the proposed control technique.

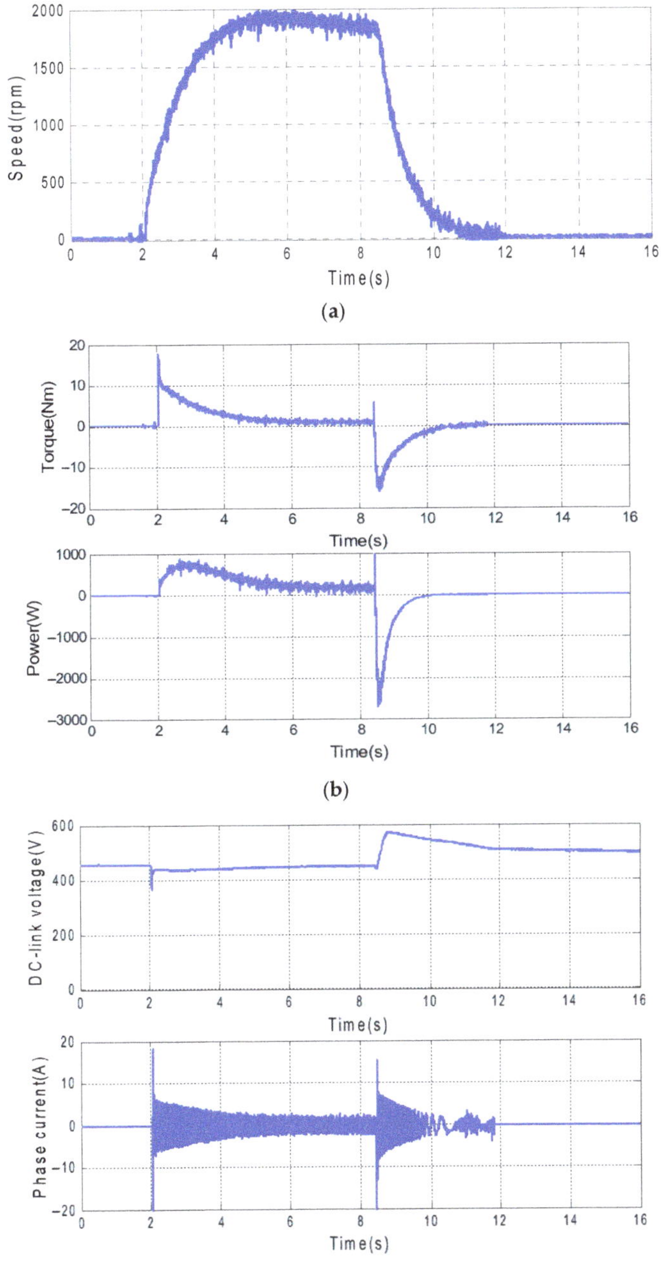

Figure 6. Experimental results (plotted in Matlab) of braking test of IM when it runs at 1740 rpm: (**a**) motor speed, (**b**) developed torque and motor power, (**c**) DC voltage and phase current.

The experimental results in Figure 7 illustrate the performance of the IM operating in motoring mode at speeds of 600 rpm and 1200 rpm, respectively. After reaching a steady state, the IM transitions to the braking control mode. The results demonstrate the amount of energy that can be recovered and returned to the supply.

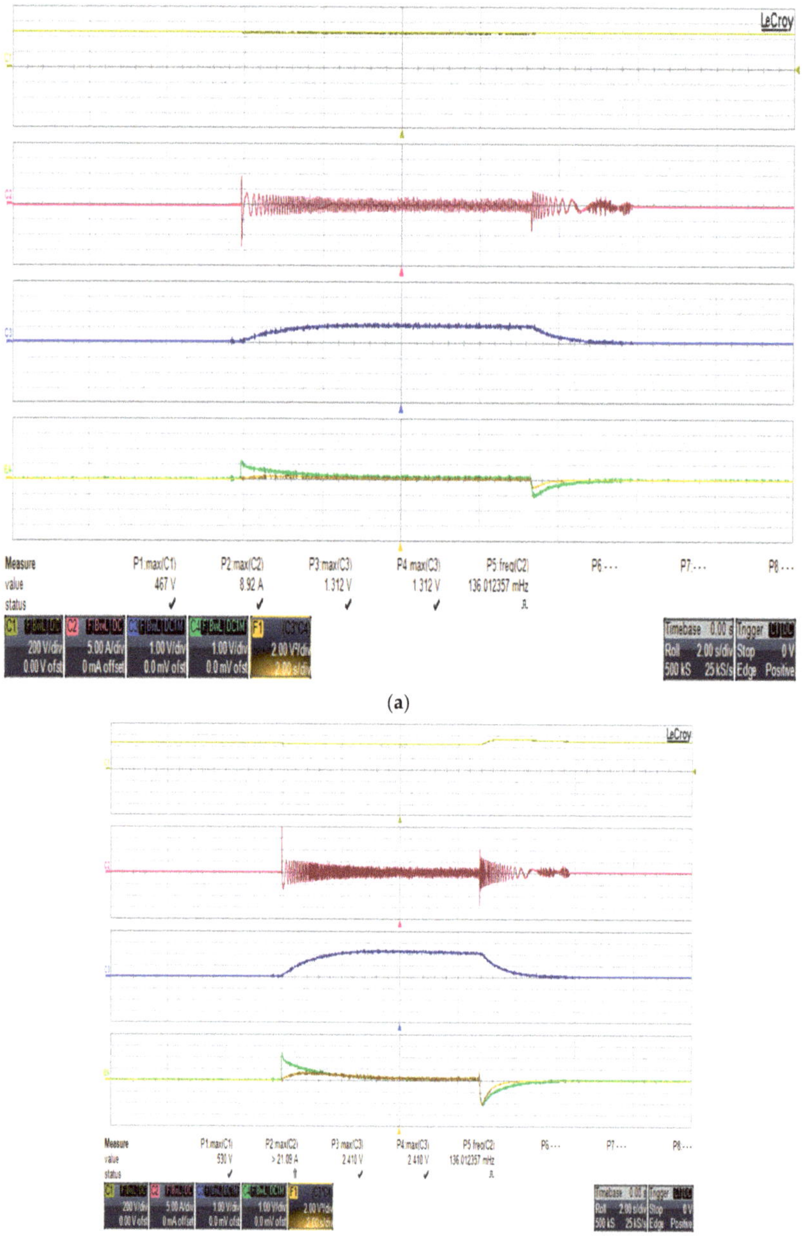

(**a**)

(**b**)

Figure 7. Experimental results at braking test of IM from top to bottom: DC link voltage, phase current, motor speed, developed torque, and motor power when machine runs at: (**a**) 600 rpm and (**b**) 1200 rpm.

In this particular experiment a braking resistor is used to dissipate the regenerated energy. However, in the subsequent simulation results, we demonstrate how this recovered energy can be harnessed for fast charging the ultracapacitor instead of the battery pack, enhancing overall system efficiency.

The capacity of each component was determined based on a combination of laboratory testing, manufacturer specifications, and practical performance requirements related to the electric motor and drive system. The detailed process is as follows:

1. **Induction Motor (IM):**

The capacity of the induction motor was selected based on its compatibility with experimental speed and torque control studies. The motor parameters are listed in Table 2.

2. **Battery Pack (BP):**

The battery capacity was selected to ensure continuous operation of the motor under load and during regeneration.

The battery pack was assembled using a 32s4p $LiFePO_4$ cell configuration, providing a total voltage of 100 V and a capacity of 40 Ah, as listed in Table 3. The system supports a maximum charge current of 18 A via the onboard charger.

Table 3. Battery pack configuration and specifications for the $LiFePO_4$-based HESS used in the proposed EV system.

Parameter	Specification
Configuration	32s4p $LiFePO_4$ cells
Cell Voltage/Capacity	3.2 V/10 Ah
Total Pack Voltage	100 V
Total Pack Capacity	40 Ah
Total Energy	4.0 kWh
Max Charge Current	18 A (via onboard charger)

This configuration was determined based on motor energy requirements, braking regeneration energy, and average power demands during acceleration and cruising, as evaluated in practical experiments.

3. **Ultracapacitor (UC) Module:**

The UC was added to support the battery under high transient loads and regenerative braking. The sizing has been determined to provide fast charge/discharge capability while maintaining voltage stability at the DC link. The specifications of the selected UC have been listed in Table 4.

Table 4. Specifications of the selected UC module used for transient load support and regenerative braking in the HESS.

Parameter	Specification
Model	LS Mtron LSUM 086R4C 0093F EA
Rated Voltage	86.4 V
Capacitance	93 F
Maximum Current	80 A
Internal Resistance	11.3 mΩ

This module was selected to match the power demands of high dynamic events (e.g., quick acceleration or braking), based on simulation and experimental validations of the energy/power balance.

4. **DC Link Capacitor:**

A 4700 μF capacitor was used at the DC link to buffer the voltage variations during power transitions between the motor, UC, and BP. This value was chosen based on typical practice and transient simulation results ensuring minimal voltage ripple at 450 Vdc.

5. **Power Electronics (DC-DC Converters):**

Bidirectional buck–boost DC-DC converters were designed to interface the UC and BP with the 450 V DC link. The design specifications were based on the maximum power transfer expected during load/generation cycles.

In summary, the sizing process combined practical testing in the lab, matching load requirements of the IM, energy and power characteristics of the BP and UC, and ensuring voltage compatibility at the DC link. Where applicable, manufacturer datasheets and EV application best practices were also used.

4.4. Performance Assessment of HESS with a Static Load

Efficiency of Charge/Discharge in HESS

In the first experimental setup, the UC is connected in parallel with the BP via a DC/DC converter to supply a static load, as depicted in Figure 4. A 4 kW resistive load is used to evaluate the charge and discharge efficiency of the HESS. The energy flow efficiency is experimentally measured for both the battery and UC under different operating conditions. When the battery alone is used to power the load, the overall efficiency is observed to be 0.95 at low currents and 0.80 at very high currents. The efficiency reduction at high currents is attributed to internal resistance losses within the battery. With the integration of the UC, the efficiency of charging from the battery and discharging to the load is determined as $2 \times (0.96 \times 0.95) \times 100 = 83\%$. This result demonstrates that at high current flow, the UC significantly enhances the energy transfer efficiency by mitigating the internal resistance effects of the battery.

Charging of Ultracapacitor from Battery (Path E1)

The experimental results for ultracapacitor charging from the battery pack are shown in Figure 8. In this operating mode, the BP supplies 10 A at 100 V, delivering 1 kW to charge the UC. Initially, the UC draws a high current, which gradually decreases to a steady-state current of 10 A, while the UC voltage increases progressively to 60 V. The total energy exported from the battery is measured as 139 kJ, while the energy stored in the UC through the DC-DC converter (path E1 in Figure 1) is found to be 121 kJ. The total energy extracted from the battery, including losses, is 142.359 kJ, with a battery power loss of 3.359 kJ. Thus, the efficiency of the DC-DC converter during UC charging is calculated as $\eta_{ch} = \frac{121}{139} = 0.87$. This result confirms that the DC-DC converter operates with an 87% efficiency during UC charging, highlighting its effectiveness in energy transfer.

Discharging of Battery to Load (Path 3)

Figure 9 presents the experimental results when the battery supplies 40 A to the same static load. The battery voltage is 100 V, while the ultracapacitor voltage remains low at 20 V. Consequently, the 4 kW load power is entirely supplied by the battery. The power loss due to the battery's internal resistance, as calculated by the BMS, is 17.55 kJ. The total energy supplied by the battery is 236.55 kJ, which matches the load energy over the same time period. The system efficiency is determined as $\eta = 219000/(219000 + 17550.83) \times 100 = 92.58\%$.

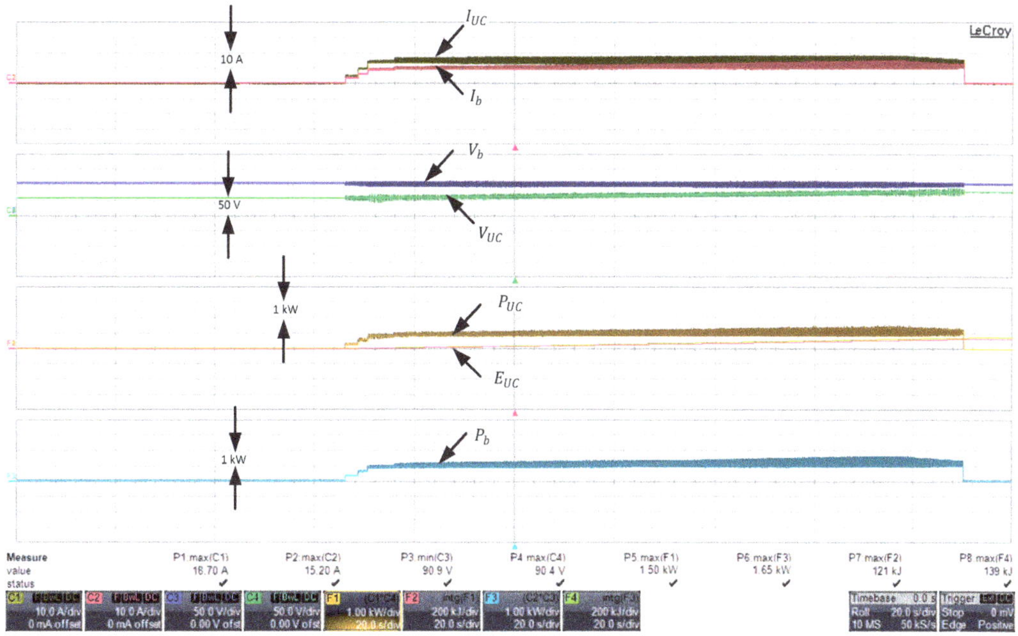

Figure 8. Experimental results when UC is charged from battery, from top to bottom: UC and battery currents [10 A/div], battery and UC voltages [50 V/div], UC power [1 kW/div] and energy, and battery power [1 kW/div].

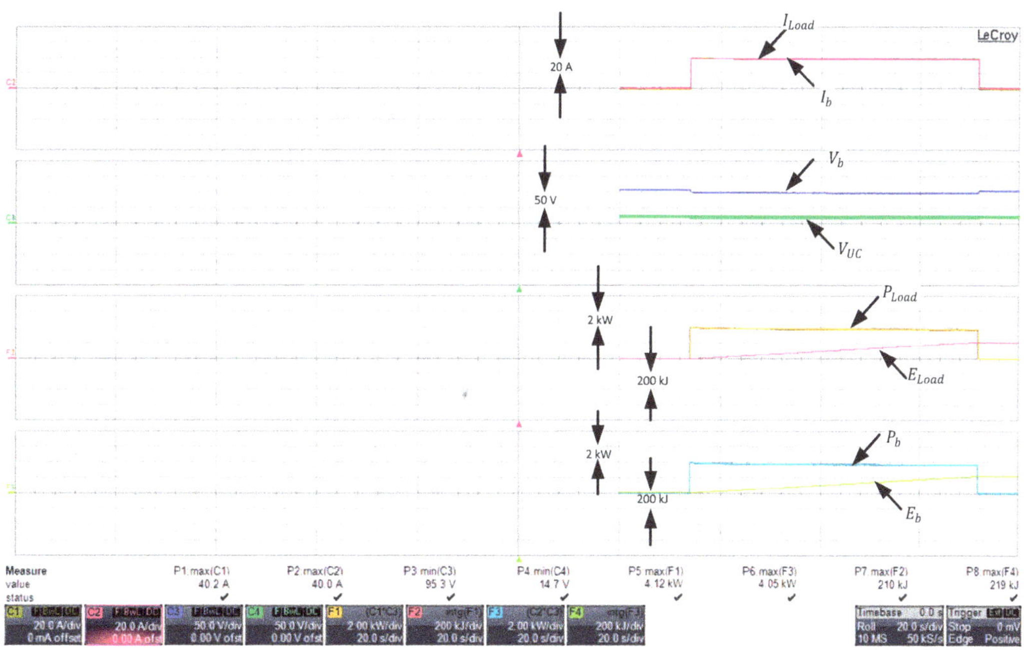

Figure 9. Experimental results when static load is supplied from battery only, from top to bottom: load and battery currents [20 A/div], battery and UC voltages [50 V/div], load power [2 kW/div] and energy [200 kJ/div], and battery power [2 kW/div] and energy [200 kJ/div].

Discharging of BP and UC to Load (Path 3 + Path 4)

Figure 10 presents the experimental results when both the battery and the ultracapacitor supply power to the load. The total load current of 40 A is shared equally, with 20 A drawn from the battery and 20 A from the UC at a DC link voltage of approximately 100 V. Meanwhile, the UC supplies 33.33 A at 65 V at its terminals. The total discharge of energy delivered to the load is 200 kJ. The power loss due to the battery's internal resistance is 3.256 kJ. The battery supplies 98 kJ of discharge energy to the load, while its total energy expenditure is 101.256 kJ. The UC receives 121 kJ of energy and delivers 102 kJ to the load. Considering that 142.359 kJ could be transferred from the battery to charge the UC, the total discharge efficiency is calculated as η = (200/(102 + 101.256)) × 100 = 98.5%. Compared to the case where the battery alone supplies the load, utilizing the UC improves discharge efficiency, thereby enhancing energy savings in frequent discharge operations.

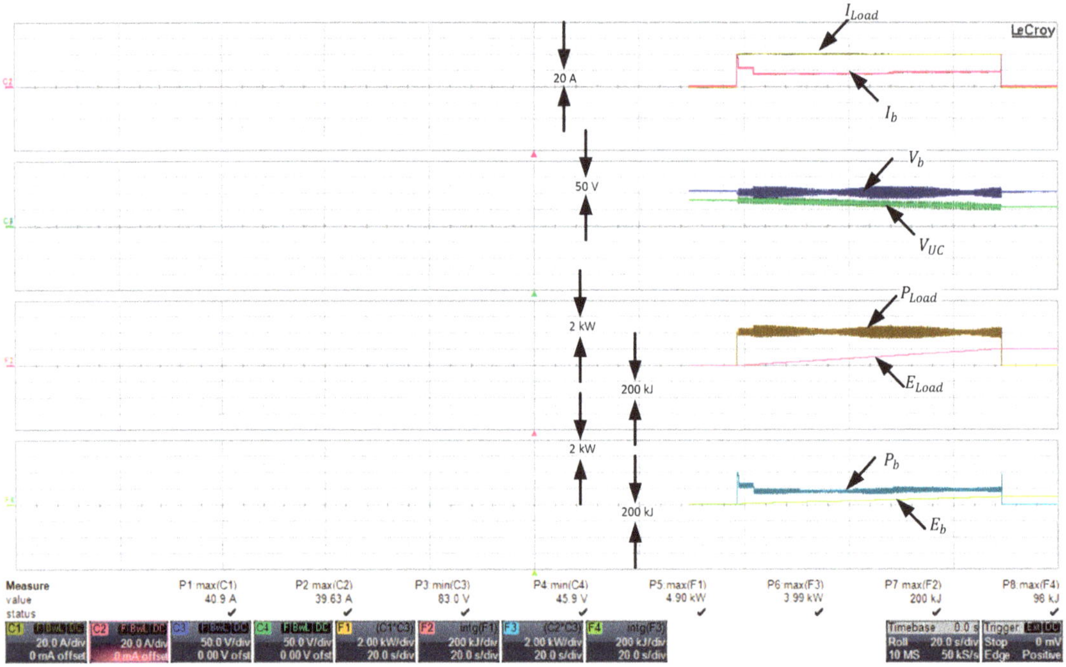

Figure 10. Experimental results when UC and battery are discharged to static load, from top to bottom: load and battery currents [20 A/div], battery and UC voltages [50 V/div], load power [2 kW/div] and energy [200 kJ/div], and battery power [2 kW/div] and energy [200 kJ/div].

4.5. Dynamic Performance with Regenerative Braking

This subsection presents simulation results demonstrating the effectiveness of the proposed control schemes for the buck–boost chopper during both the regenerative braking and discharging modes of the adopted system. The results are obtained under rated load conditions of 20 Nm and a speed of 1740 rpm, as shown in Figure 11. Regenerative braking is initiated at t = 2.9 s, where the control strategy ensures that the motor speed closely follows the command speed during both acceleration and deceleration, exhibiting good dynamic performance.

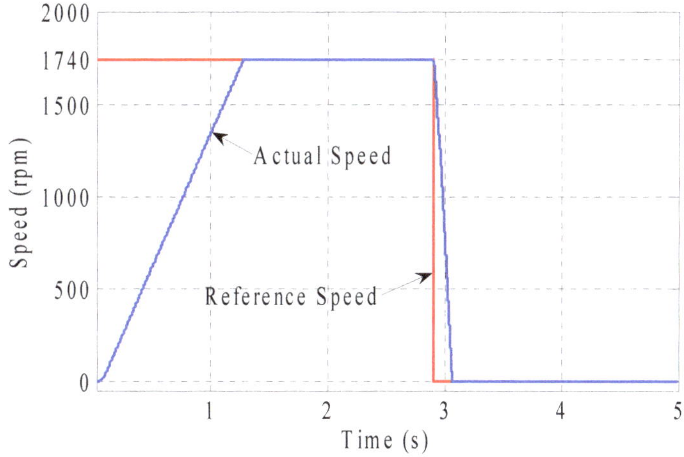

Figure 11. Speed response of IM.

Corresponding to the speed response in Figure 11, the electromagnetic torque and its reference torque are illustrated in Figure 12. During acceleration, the torque is limited to 25 Nm, after which a full load of 20 Nm is maintained at the rated speed of 1740 rpm. When regenerative braking is applied, a negative torque of 20 Nm is developed. At t = 2.95 s, the torque exhibits an irregular shape due to the transition of the IM operating point from the flux-limited region to the flux-increased region [18,19].

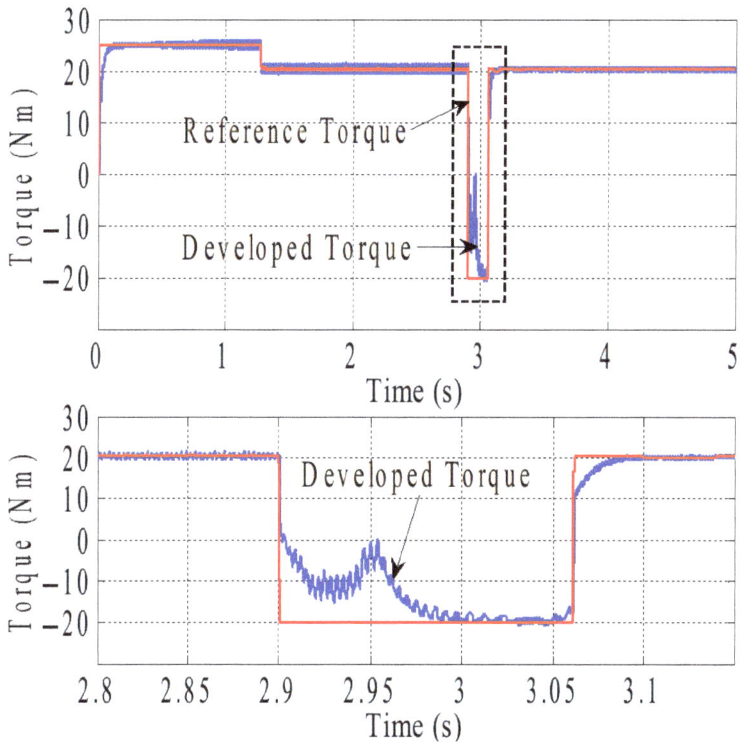

Figure 12. Electromagnetic torque of the adopted IM.

The corresponding BP and UC currents during both motoring (discharging) and braking (regenerative) modes are shown in Figure 13. During braking the reversed current flows entirely through the UC. In motoring mode the UC supplies 10 A at 70 V, while the battery provides 8 A at 450 V.

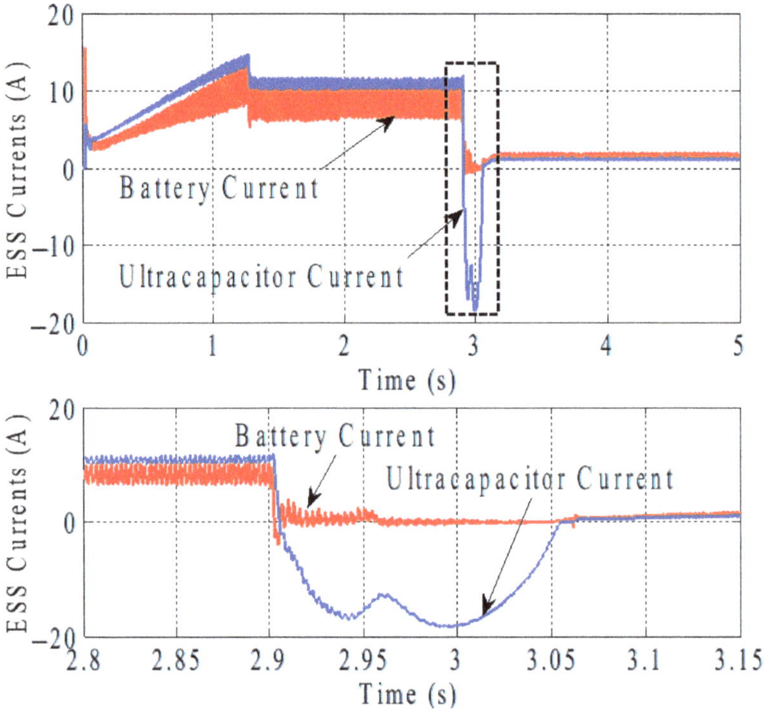

Figure 13. Battery and ultracapacitor currents.

Figure 14 presents the input and output power of the IM, as well as the power contributions from the battery and UC. It is evident that the regenerated power is stored in the UC. At steady-state operation the UC delivers 0.8 kW, while the battery supplies 3.7 kW. The IM draws 4.5 kW from the inverter but delivers 3.7 kW to the load. During braking the battery is not charged, whereas the UC absorbs more than 1.0 kW of regenerative power.

Finally, Figure 15 illustrates the voltage profiles of the battery and UC. With the hybrid energy storage system (HESS), the battery and DC link voltages are effectively maintained at 450 V, while the UC voltage remains at 70 V.

To validate the energy storage feasibility of the proposed system, a complete round-trip efficiency analysis was conducted. The lithium-ion battery showed an average round-trip efficiency of approximately 92%, tested under a 1C rate and 25 °C ambient temperature. In contrast, the UC system combined with the bidirectional DC-DC converter exhibited a round-trip efficiency of about 74%, due to converter losses during both charging and discharging phases. These results support the control strategy, which leverages the battery for sustained energy supply and prioritizes the UC for fast transients.

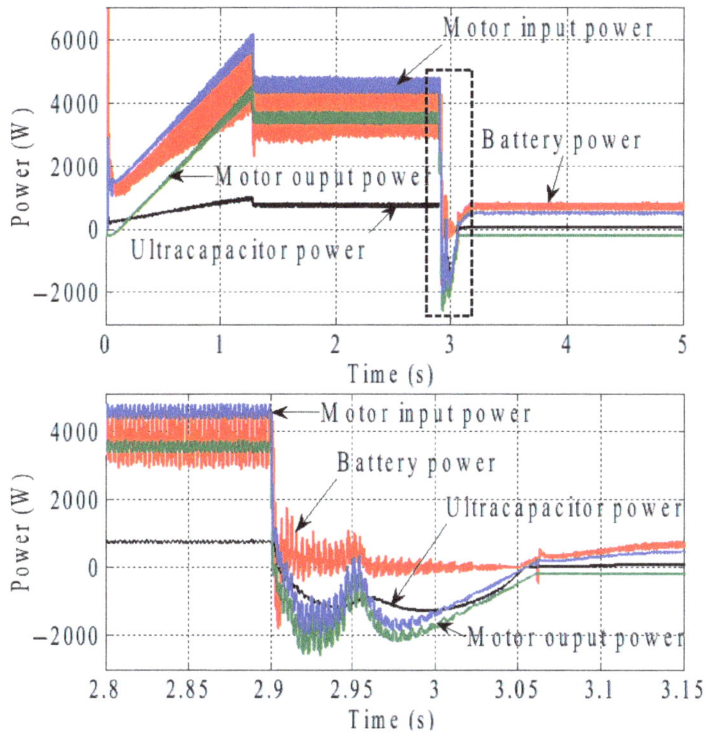

Figure 14. Power of battery, IM, and ultracapacitor.

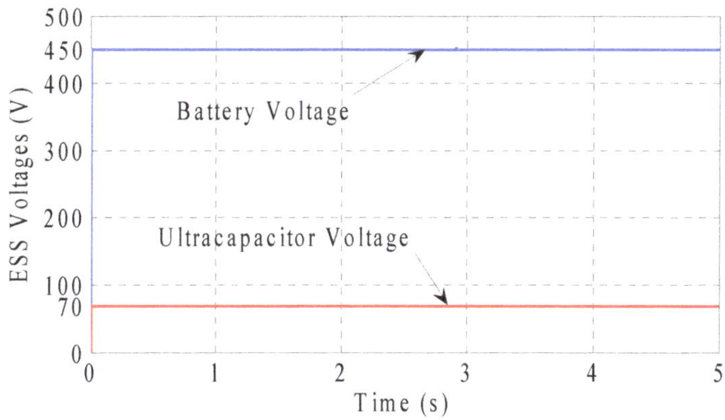

Figure 15. Battery and ultracapacitor voltage.

5. Conclusions

This paper presented a successful control method for regulating the speed of an induction motor during both running and braking operations. Experimental results demonstrate that the proposed control strategy effectively enables the IM to regenerate power to its DC link bus during braking. This regenerated energy is efficiently utilized to charge the ultracapacitor, enhancing overall system efficiency. A control strategy for the coordinated discharging of both the UC and the battery was also introduced, showing that power flow efficiency can be improved by optimizing the distribution factor.

Preliminary experimental results confirm the successful integration of the UC with the battery in the laboratory, validating the proposed energy distribution method. The findings highlight that using a UC in parallel with the battery increases system efficiency, particularly in regenerative braking scenarios. Future research will focus on optimizing the efficiency of the hybrid UC/battery-powered hybrid energy storage system and integrating it into electric vehicles.

Key findings include the following:

- The proposed control technique efficiently utilizes excess energy to charge the UC.
- For higher load demands the UC plays a crucial role in power distribution, optimizing efficiency and system performance.
- The DC-DC converter achieves 87% efficiency during UC charging, demonstrating effective energy transfer.
- Compared to a battery-only configuration (82%), incorporating a UC improves discharge efficiency (92%) and enhances energy savings in frequent discharge operations.

In this paper, a supercapacitor (UC)-based energy storage system integrated with a bidirectional DC-DC converter has been designed, implemented, and evaluated. The system was developed to assess the charging and discharging behavior of the UC under various load conditions. The converter's efficiency is measured during both charging and discharging phases and compared to the overall system performance with that of a conventional lithium-ion battery. Experimental results were used to analyze energy transfer efficiency, evaluate the converter's dynamic response, and discuss the feasibility of using UCs in real-world energy applications. The complete energy efficiency analysis confirms that the lithium-ion battery subsystem is more efficient than the UC-based system in terms of energy storage. However, the UC still plays a critical role in handling dynamic load demands due to its fast response, justifying the hybrid configuration.

Author Contributions: Conceptualization, A.A.A., Y.I.L. and A.A.Z.D.; Methodology, A.A.A., Y.I.L., S.A.D. and A.A.Z.D.; Software, A.A.A., Y.I.L., A.A.Z.D. and A.A.E.; Validation, A.A.A., Y.I.L., S.A.D. and A.A.Z.D.; Formal analysis, A.A.Z.D. and A.A.E.; Investigation, A.A.A., Y.I.L., S.A.D. and A.A.Z.D.; Resources, A.A.A. and Y.I.L.; Data curation, A.A.A., Y.I.L., A.A.E. and S.A.D.; Writing—original draft preparation, A.A.A., Y.I.L. and A.A.Z.D.; Writing—review and editing, A.A.A., Y.I.L., S.A.D., A.A.Z.D. and A.A.E.; Visualization, A.A.A., Y.I.L., S.A.D. and A.A.Z.D.; Supervision, A.A.A. and Y.I.L.; Project administration, A.A.A.; Funding acquisition, A.A.A., Y.I.L. and S.A.D. All authors have read and agreed to the published version of the manuscript.

Funding: This research received no external funding.

Data Availability Statement: The original contributions and data presented in this study are included in the article.

Conflicts of Interest: The authors declare no conflicts of interest.

References

1. Eftekhari, A. Low voltage anode materials for lithium-ion batteries. *Energy Storage Mater.* **2017**, *7*, 157–180. [CrossRef]
2. Burke, A.; Miller, M. The power capability of ultracapacitors and lithium batteries for electric and hybrid vehicle applications. *J. Power Sources* **2011**, *196*, 514–522. [CrossRef]
3. Emadi, A.C. 8: Hybrid Energy Storage Systems. In *Advanced Electric Drive Vehicles*; Taylor & Francis Group, LLC: Boca Raton, FL, USA, 2015; pp. 285–286.
4. Camara, M.B.; Gualous, H.; Gustin, F.; Berthon, A.; Dakyo, B. DC/DC converters design for supercapacitors and battery power management in hybrid vehicle applications-polynomial control strategy. *IEEE Trans. Ind. Electron.* **2010**, *57*, 587–597. [CrossRef]
5. Bian, Y.; Zhu, L.; Lan, H.; Li, A.; Xu, X. Regenerative braking strategy for motor hoist by ultracapacitor. *Chin. J. Mech. Eng.* **2012**, *25*, 377–384. [CrossRef]

6. Xiang, C.; Wang, Y.; Hu, S.; Wang, W. A New Topology and Control Strategy for a Hybrid Battery-Ultracapacitor Energy Storage System. *Energies* **2014**, *7*, 2874–2896. [CrossRef]
7. Awerbuch, J.J.; Sullivan, C.R. Control of Ultracapacitor-Battery Hybrid Power Source for Vehicular Applications. In Proceedings of the 2008 IEEE Energy 2030 Conference, Atlanta, GA, USA, 17–18 November 2008.
8. Chau, K.T.; Wong, Y.S. Hybridization of energy sources in electric vehicles. *Energy Convers. Manag.* **2001**, *42*, 1059–1069. [CrossRef]
9. Miller, J.R. Engineering electrochemical capacitor applications. *J. Power Sources* **2016**, *326*, 726–735. [CrossRef]
10. Ehsani, M.; Gao, Y.; Emadi, A. *Modern Electric, Hybrid Electric, and Fuel Cell Vehicles: Fundamentals, Theory, and Design*, 2nd ed.; Power Electronics and Applications Series; CRC Press: Boca Raton, FL, USA, 2010.
11. So, K.M.; Wong, Y.S.; Hong, G.S.; Lu, W.F. An improved energy management strategy for a Battery/Ultracapacitor Hybrid Energy Storage System in Electric Vehicles. In Proceedings of the 2016 IEEE Transportation Electrification Conference and Expo (ITEC), Dearborn, MI, USA, 27–29 June 2016; pp. 1–6.
12. Ahmed, A.; Cui, S. Control and analysis of regenerative power distribution on electrical variable transmission using fuzzy logic on HEV system. In Proceedings of the International Conference on Electrical Machines and Systems (ICEMS), Beijing, China, 20–23 August 2011.
13. Mahapatra, A.A.; Gopalakrishna, S. Regenerative braking in induction motor drives in applications to electric vehicles. In Proceedings of the 2014 IEEE Students' Conference on Electrical, Electronics and Computer Science, Bhopal, India, 1–2 March 2014.
14. Li, Z.; Pan, Y. On steering regenerative brake torque control of dual-motor drive for electric tracked vehicle. In Proceedings of the IEEE International Conference on Automation and Logistics, Beijing, China, 29–31 August 2010.
15. Kouchachvili, L.; Yaïci, W.; Entchev, E. Hybrid battery/supercapacitor energy storage system for the electric vehicles. *J. Power Sources* **2018**, *374*, 237–248. [CrossRef]
16. Chen, S.; Yang, Q.; Zhou, J.; Chen, X. Hybrid energy storage system control method based on model predictive control. *CSEE J. Power Energy Syst.* **2020**, *7*. [CrossRef]
17. Punna, S.; Behera, P.; Lamba, A. A Power Management Scheme for Electric Vehicles with Hybrid Energy Storage Systems. In Proceedings of the 2024 IEEE 4th International Conference on Sustainable Energy and Future Electric Transportation (SEFET), Hyderabad, India, 31 July–3 August 2024; pp. 1–5.
18. Ahmed, A.A.; Mousa, M.G.; Lee, Y.I. Regenerative braking control of IM with battery/ultracapacitor hybrid ESS in electric vehicles. In Proceedings of the 2017 Nineteenth International Middle East Power Systems Conference (MEPCON), Cairo, Egypt, 19–21 December 2017; pp. 320–325.
19. Ahmed, A.A.; Koh, B.K.; Park, H.S.; Lee, K.-B.; Lee, Y.I. Finite control set model predictive control method for torque control of induction motors using a state tracking cost index. *IEEE Trans. Ind. Electron.* **2017**, *64*, 1916–1928. [CrossRef]
20. Ahmed, A.A.; Koh, B.K.; Lee, Y.I. A Comparison of Finite Control Set and Continuous Control Set Model Predictive Control Schemes for Speed Control of Induction Motors. *IEEE Trans. Ind. Inform* **2017**, *14*, 1334–1346. [CrossRef]
21. Orion BMS. Available online: http://www.orionbms.com/ (accessed on 22 July 2025).
22. Boglou, V.; Karavas, C.-S.; Karlis, A.; Arvanitis, K.G.; Palaiologou, I. An optimal distributed RES sizing strategy in hybrid low voltage networks focused on EVs' integration. *IEEE Access* **2023**, *11*, 16250–16270. [CrossRef]
23. Karavas, C.-S.; Arvanitis, K.G.; Papadakis, G. Optimal technical and economic configuration of photovoltaic powered reverse osmosis desalination systems operating in autonomous mode. *Desalination.* **2019**, *466*, 97–106. [CrossRef]
24. Boglou, V.; Karavas, C.; Karlis, A.; Arvanitis, K. An intelligent decentralized energy management strategy for the optimal electric vehicles' charging in low-voltage islanded microgrids. *Int. J. Energy Res.* **2022**, *46*, 2988–3016. [CrossRef]
25. Rimpas, D.; Kaminaris, S.D.; Piromalis, D.D.; Vokas, G.; Arvanitis, K.G.; Karavas, C.-S. Comparative review of motor technologies for electric vehicles powered by a hybrid energy storage system based on multi-criteria analysis. *Energies* **2023**, *16*, 2555. [CrossRef]
26. Loukatos, D.; Arapostathis, V.; Karavas, C.-S.; Arvanitis, K.G.; Papadakis, G. Power consumption analysis of a prototype lightweight autonomous electric cargo robot in agricultural field operation scenarios. *Energies* **2024**, *17*, 1244. [CrossRef]

Mathematical and Computational Applications

MDPI

Article

Energy Optimization of Compressed Air Systems with Screw Compressors Under Variable Load Conditions

Guillermo José Barroso García [1], José Pedro Monteagudo Yanes [1], Luis Angel Iturralde Carrera [2,*], Carlos D. Constantino-Robles [2], Brenda Juárez Santiago [3,*], Juan Manuel Olivares Ramírez [3], Omar Rodriguez Abreo [2] and Juvenal Rodríguez-Reséndiz [2]

[1] Centro de Estudios de Energía y Medio Ambiente (CEEMA), Facultad de Ingeniería, Universidad de Cienfuegos "Carlos Rafael Rodríguez", Cienfuegos 59430, Cuba; barrosoguillermo19@gmail.com (G.J.B.G.); monteagudojpy@gmail.com (J.P.M.Y.)

[2] Facultad de Ingeniería, Universidad Autónoma de Querétaro, Santiago de Querétaro 76010, Mexico; cconstantino30@alumnos.uaq.mx (C.D.C.-R.); omar.rodriguez.a@uaq.mx (O.R.A.); juvenal@uaq.edu.mx (J.R.-R.)

[3] División de Ingenierías Mecatrónica, Tecnologías de la Información y Civil, Universidad Tecnológica de San Juan del Río, San Juan del Río, Santiago de Querétaro 76800, Mexico; jmolivaresr@utsjr.edu.mx

* Correspondence: liturralde28@alumnos.uaq.mx (L.A.I.C.); bjuarezs@utsjr.edu.mx (B.J.S.); Tel.: +52-442-192-1200 (L.A.I.C.)

Abstract: This study evaluates the energy performance of a BOGE C 22-2 oil-injected rotary screw compressor under real industrial conditions. Using direct measurements with a power quality analyzer and thermodynamic modeling, key performance indicators such as compression work, mass flow rate, compressor efficiency, and motor efficiency were determined. The results revealed actual efficiencies of 27–48%, significantly lower than the expected 60–70% for this type of equipment, mainly due to partial-load operation and low airflow demand. A low power factor of approximately 0.72 was also observed, caused by a high share of reactive power consumption. To address these inefficiencies, the study recommends the installation of an automatic capacitor bank to improve power quality and the integration of a secondary variable speed compressor to enhance performance under low-demand conditions. These findings underscore the importance of assessing compressor behavior in real-world environments and implementing techno-economic strategies to increase energy efficiency and reduce industrial electricity consumption.

Keywords: compressor efficiency; rotary screw compressor; energy analysis; power factor correction; variable load operation; industrial energy optimization

1. Introduction

The energy efficiency of compressed air systems remains a critical challenge in industrial environments, particularly in facilities where production demands fluctuate and equipment operates under partial load conditions [1–3]. Despite their widespread use as a reliable source of pneumatic energy, rotary screw compressors are often characterized by low operational efficiency, especially when oversized or improperly controlled [4,5]. This mismatch between installed capacity and actual demand results in unnecessary energy losses, reduced equipment lifespan, and increased operational costs [6–8].

Numerous studies have analyzed the performance of industrial air compressors, emphasizing the impact of factors such as operating pressure, volumetric flow rate, compression temperature, and motor efficiency [9–11]. Research has shown that energy losses in these systems can be attributed to both mechanical inefficiencies during compression and electrical inefficiencies in the drive motor [12–14]. Moreover, the presence of reactive energy commonly overlooked in daily operation can significantly affect the overall power factor and result in financial penalties or increased transformer losses [15–17].

Industrial compressed air systems typically involve a compressor unit, storage tanks, a distribution network, and multiple end-use machines [18–20]. The overall efficiency of such systems depends not only on the compressor's mechanical design but also on control strategies, demand-side management, and the quality of the electrical supply [21–23]. In particular, maintaining a high power factor and minimizing idle operating times are crucial for optimizing energy use and ensuring sustainable operation [24–26].

Among the most influential variables affecting compressor performance are load factor, volumetric flow rate, isentropic work, and motor electrical efficiency [27–29]. These variables are interrelated, and their impact on energy consumption must be assessed using thermodynamic models, field measurements, and power quality analyses. For instance, the ratio of compression work to electrical input provides a reliable efficiency indicator under varying load conditions [30–32]. Likewise, real-time monitoring of electrical demand and power factor enables targeted interventions such as capacitor bank installation or control system upgrades [33–35].

Advancements in predictive maintenance and artificial intelligence have led to the development of data-driven models capable of forecasting compressor behavior based on operational parameters [36–38]. These tools allow early detection of underperformance, support asset management decisions, and contribute to decarbonization goals through energy savings [39–41]. However, their accuracy depends heavily on the quality of experimental data collected under realistic operating conditions [42–44].

Most existing studies on compressor efficiency rely either on theoretical simulations, manufacturer's curves, or experiments under controlled laboratory conditions. However, few works provide a detailed experimental assessment of rotary screw compressors under *real industrial partial-load conditions*, where efficiency losses are most pronounced. Additionally, the literature often neglects the combined effect of reactive power consumption, low power factor, and operational strategies on overall system efficiency.

To address this gap, our study provides:

- A field-based thermodynamic and electrical evaluation of a BOGE C 22-2 compressor under actual plant conditions, showing significant discrepancies between nominal and operational efficiencies.
- An integrated analysis of compressor performance and power quality, quantifying both active and reactive energy contributions, which is rarely reported in comparable case studies.
- Practical techno-economic improvement strategies (capacitor bank compensation, demand-based control, and hybrid compressor configuration) supported by real measurements, bridging the gap between theoretical optimization methods and industrial feasibility.

This paper is organized as follows: Section 1 presents the challenges associated with energy efficiency in industrial compressed air systems, and the need for operational modeling and optimization. Section 2 details the measurement instruments, compressor specifications, and mathematical models used. Section 3 presents the experimental findings, including efficiency metrics, flow rates, and power factor analysis. Section 4 interprets the results in the context of best industrial practices and outlines potential improvements. Finally, Section 5 summarizes the key insights and recommendations for future implementation.

2. Materials and Methods

To identify the predominant trends, technological advances, and energy-related concerns associated with industrial compressors and electric motors, a bibliometric search was conducted using the Scopus database. The search strategy was designed to capture both the technical aspects, such as energy efficiency, operational optimization, and power consumption, and to filter out results related to non-representative applications, such as gas turbines, fuel cells, or hybrid vehicles, which often introduce noise into compressor–motor system analyses.

The query focused on documents that included the term "compressor" in combination with "electric motor" or "electrical motor", and that referenced key concepts such as efficiency, optimization, or energy consumption. These dimensions are crucial for assessing the performance of compressor motor systems in industrial environments, where power demand, thermal losses, and control strategies significantly impact operational costs and carbon emissions.

To ensure thematic relevance, targeted exclusions were applied to keywords associated with adjacent but unrelated fields, such as fuel cells, electric vehicles, carbon footprint, or waste heat utilization. This refinement enabled the search to focus exclusively on research related to the mechanical and industrial applications of compressors and electric motors.

The search string used was the following:

```
TITLE-ABS-KEY ( compressor* ) AND TITLE-ABS-KEY ( "electric motor*" OR "
    electrical motor*" ) AND TITLE-ABS-KEY ( efficiency OR optimization OR "
    energy consumption" ) AND PUBYEAR > 2018 AND PUBYEAR < 2026 AND ( EXCLUDE
     ( EXACTKEYWORD , "Gas Turbines" ) OR EXCLUDE ( EXACTKEYWORD , "Fuel
    Cells" ) OR EXCLUDE ( EXACTKEYWORD , "Electric Drives" ) OR EXCLUDE (
    EXACTKEYWORD , "Carbon Dioxide" ) OR EXCLUDE ( EXACTKEYWORD , "Variable
    Speed Drives" ) OR EXCLUDE ( EXACTKEYWORD , "Hybrid Vehicles" ) OR
    EXCLUDE ( EXACTKEYWORD , "Hydrogen" ) OR EXCLUDE ( EXACTKEYWORD , "Carbon
     Footprint" ) OR EXCLUDE ( EXACTKEYWORD , "Electric Vehicles" ) OR
    EXCLUDE ( EXACTKEYWORD , "Electric Loads" ) OR EXCLUDE ( EXACTKEYWORD , "
    Centrifugation" ) OR EXCLUDE ( EXACTKEYWORD , "Bearings (machine Parts)"
    ) OR EXCLUDE ( EXACTKEYWORD , "Waste Heat Utilization" ) OR EXCLUDE (
    EXACTKEYWORD , "Waste Heat" ) OR EXCLUDE ( EXACTKEYWORD , \hl{"'} %MDPI:
    Please check if this should be ".current" ) OR EXCLUDE ( EXACTKEYWORD , "
    Acoustic Noise" ) OR EXCLUDE ( EXACTKEYWORD , "Automotive Batteries" ) OR
     EXCLUDE ( EXACTKEYWORD , "Cathodes" ) OR EXCLUDE ( EXACTKEYWORD , "
    Chemical Industry" ))
```

This strategy enabled the identification of a body of literature specifically focused on energy performance, optimization strategies, and technological development in compressor–motor systems across various industrial sectors. The time window was limited to the 2018–2025 period to capture the most recent advancements aligned with Industry 4.0 and the digitalization of processes through smart monitoring systems.

The resulting software provides a solid foundation for further analysis of trends in control methods (e.g., load-adaptive operation), innovations in materials and configurations, and comparative efficiency evaluations in rotary screw compressors and their associated drive systems. The bibliometric analysis performed using VOSviewer (1.6.20) reveals a high co-occurrence of terms such as compressors, electric motors, efficiency, energy utilization, and thermal management systems, confirming the close relationship between these components in the study of thermal and industrial systems (Figure 1). The prominent presence of concepts such as isentropic efficiency, reciprocating compressors, and permanent magnet motors indicates a clear research focus on improving energy performance and reducing electrical losses in high-speed and variable-load applications.

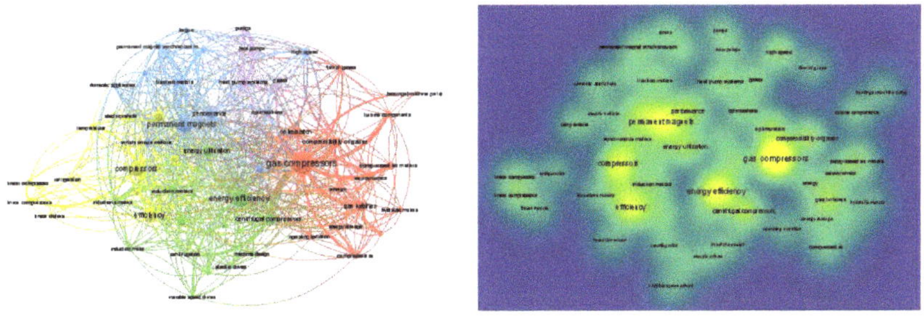

Figure 1. Bibliometric analysis networks and density map. (**a**) Bibliometric network for the analysis of articles. (**b**) Bibliometric density for the analysis of articles on engines and compressors.

Additionally, the interconnection of terms such as hydrogen storage, greenhouse gases, and gas emissions suggests an increasing concern for environmental impact, positioning compressors and electric motors as critical elements in the energy transition toward more sustainable systems. The frequency of nodes, such as cooling, heat pump systems, and refrigerants, also highlights their central role in air conditioning and heat pump applications, where system performance strongly depends on the efficient coupling between the motor and compressor.

Overall, these findings reflect a consolidation of research lines oriented toward energy optimization, integration with clean technologies, and the design of high-performance components, which aligns with current industrial challenges related to efficiency and decarbonization.

2.1. Methodology for Compressed Air Flow Calculation

The methodology applied to determine the compressed air flow consumed during the tests was based on an indirect calculation through the storage tank filling test. Since the compressor was operating under a low-load regime, it was necessary to precisely establish the amount of air supplied under this condition. The procedure involved monitoring the On/Off cycles of the compressor, measuring the filling time of the 4.44 m^3 storage tank, and recording pressure and temperature values at start-up and shutdown. From these data, air density was calculated, followed by the determination of the stored air mass, the mass flow rate, and finally the volumetric flow rate, using fundamental thermodynamic equations. This stepwise methodology, summarized in the flow diagram of Figure 2, provides a clear and structured representation of the process employed in this study to quantify compressed air consumption.

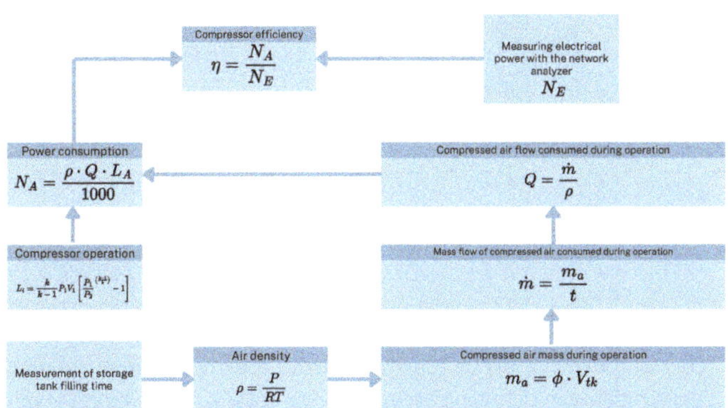

Figure 2. Flow diagram of the methodology applied for calculating the compressed air flow consumed during the tests.

2.2. Description of the System Under Evaluation

The present study was conducted at the José Gregorio Martínez oil company, which recently replaced its aging compressed air system with a rotary screw compressor manufactured by BOGE KOMPRESSOREN. This new oil-lubricated unit was configured to operate at two key pressure points: 10 bar (maximum discharge pressure) and 5.2 bar (nominal working pressure), according to readings displayed on the compressor's control panel [45,46].

2.3. Measurement of Operating Parameters

A detailed monitoring campaign was conducted to record the main electrical and automated parameters of the system. Digital sensors were used to measure pressure, temperature, volumetric flow rate, and electrical consumption. The measurements were carried out exclusively under low-load conditions due to the plant's reduced productivity. Based on these data, the compressor's performance at maximum load was estimated using the calculation equations for work, power, and efficiency. The methodology applied is based on approaches previously documented in studies on energy efficiency in industrial compressors (compressors operating at a maximum workload level).

2.4. Compressor Efficiency Calculation

The compressor efficiency was defined as the ratio between the useful energy delivered to the compressed air and the electrical energy consumed by the system. The useful power was calculated based on the airflow rate, outlet pressure, and air temperature. Results were analyzed under the two specified operating pressures. This procedure is consistent with experimental studies that evaluated the performance of screw compressors under varying operational conditions [47].

The compressor efficiency is defined as the ratio between the useful power delivered to the compressed air (P_{useful}) and the electrical power supplied to the compressor ($P_{\text{electrical}}$) (Equation (2)):

$$\eta_{\text{comp}} = \frac{P_{\text{useful}}}{P_{\text{electrical}}} \tag{1}$$

The useful power can be estimated as:

$$P_{\text{useful}} = \dot{m} \cdot \Delta h \tag{2}$$

Alternatively, for ideal adiabatic compression of air, the following approximate expression can be used:

$$P_{\text{useful}} = \frac{k}{k-1} \cdot p_1 \cdot Q \cdot \left[\left(\frac{p_2}{p_1} \right)^{\frac{k-1}{k}} - 1 \right] \tag{3}$$

where:

- p_1: inlet pressure (Pa)
- p_2: outlet pressure (Pa)
- Q: volumetric flow rate (m^3/s)
- k: adiabatic index of air (≈ 1.4)

2.5. Compressor Work Estimation

The BOGE C 22-2 compressor is a rotary screw compressor with oil injection into the compression stage. The injected oil fulfils three critical functions: it cools the compressed air, lubricates the internal rotating components (screw rotors), and provides sealing within the compression chamber [7].

According to Cherkasski [6], the isentropic coefficient of compression (k) provides a more accurate description of the pressure–volume relationship during air compression in systems with low thermal dissipation. This is particularly applicable to oil-injected screw compressors, where the heat removal capacity is lower compared to water-cooled systems.

Following this criterion, the theoretical compression work of the BOGE C 22-2 compressor was estimated using Equation (16), which represents the ideal isentropic work required for gas compression under non-ideal cooling conditions, as suggested by Monteagudo [48].

$$L_i = \frac{k}{k-1} \cdot p_1 \cdot v_1 \cdot \left[\left(\frac{p_2}{p_1} \right)^{\frac{k-1}{k}} - 1 \right] \quad (4)$$

where:

- L_i: Isentropic work of compression (J/kg)
- k: Isentropic coefficient of air compression ($k = C_p/C_v$); for air, $k = 1.4$
- p_1: Initial pressure (Pa)
- p_2: Final pressure (Pa)
- v_1: Specific volume of air (m^3/kg); for air at standard conditions, $v_1 = 0.86\ m^3/kg$ [49]

2.6. Electric Motor Efficiency Calculation

The electric motor efficiency was estimated through direct measurements of active power, voltage, current, and power factor using a power quality analyzer. The experimental values were compared with the maximum efficiency specified by the manufacturer (92.8%). This comparison allowed for the identification of potential electrical losses under both partial and full load conditions [50,51].

The electric motor efficiency is calculated as:

$$\eta_{\text{motor}} = \frac{P_{\text{output}}}{P_{\text{input}}} \quad (5)$$

The input electrical power in a three-phase system is computed as (Equation (6)):

$$P_{\text{input}} = \sqrt{3} \cdot V \cdot I \cdot \cos\phi \quad (6)$$

where:

- V: line voltage (V)
- I: line current (A)
- $\cos\phi$: power factor (dimensionless)

From Equation (7), the efficiency value was obtained for each of the three measured power levels [52].

$$\eta = \frac{K_c \cdot P_n}{K_c \cdot P_n + \Delta P_0 + K_c^2 \left[\left(\frac{1}{\eta_n} - 1 \right) (P_n - \Delta P_0) \right]} \quad (7)$$

where:

- K_c: Load factor (dimensionless)
- P_n: Rated motor power (kW)
- ΔP_0: No-load losses (kW)
- η_n: Rated motor efficiency (dimensionless)

Indirect Calculation of Power Factor

The power factor was estimated indirectly using the relationship between active energy (P_{active}) and reactive energy (P_{reactive}), as no direct readings were obtained from the Power Factor Total (PFT) channel through the power quality analyzer. The power factor is defined as the ratio of active power to apparent power, which is the combination of active and reactive power. This relationship can be expressed mathematically as (Equation (8)):

$$\text{Power Factor} = \frac{P_{\text{active}}}{P_{\text{apparent}}} \tag{8}$$

where P_{apparent} is calculated using the following formula (Equation (9)):

$$P_{\text{apparent}} = \sqrt{P_{\text{active}}^2 + P_{\text{reactive}}^2} \tag{9}$$

In this study, the active and reactive energy values were obtained using a network analyzer, which allows for precise measurement of these parameters in electrical systems. The lack of direct PFT readings did not compromise the power factor estimation, as the indirect measurements of active and reactive energy are sufficient to provide an accurate estimate of this parameter. This indirect methodology is commonly used when measurement instruments are not configured to provide direct PFT readings, but still allow for reliable estimation based on active and reactive energy measurements.

2.7. Load Factor Equation

Based on the power values presented, which will be shown in the following sections as equipment plate data. It is possible to determine the load factor (K_c) of the electric motor for each measured power value using Equation (10), as described by Chalmers [52].

$$K_c = \frac{P_e}{P_n} \tag{10}$$

where:

- P_e: Active power consumed by the motor (kW)
- P_n: Rated (nominal) power of the electric motor (kW)

2.8. Estimation of No-Load Losses

The no-load losses (ΔP_0) of the electric motor can be estimated using Equation (11), which is derived from rearranging the general motor efficiency expression for a known load factor different from the nominal value. This approach allows isolating the fixed losses in the system based on measured efficiency values [52].

$$\Delta P_0 = \frac{K_c \cdot P_n \cdot \left[\frac{1}{\eta} - 1 - K_c \cdot \left(\frac{1}{\eta_n} - 1\right)\right]}{1 - K_c^2} \tag{11}$$

where:

- K_c: Load factor (dimensionless)
- P_n: Rated power of the electric motor (kW)
- η: Efficiency at the given load factor K_c
- η_n: Maximum (nominal) efficiency of the motor
- ΔP_0: No-load losses (kW)

2.9. Critical Evaluation of Energy Efficiency in Compressors

The reviewed studies reveal that the most widely used methodologies for assessing the efficiency of industrial compressors include (Table 1): isentropic efficiency, polytropic efficiency, exergy analysis, and advanced control strategies. Research indicates that assuming a constant isentropic efficiency is inaccurate, especially in multistage compressors or under pressure variations; however, this method is more accurate for screw compressors with oil injection in the compression stage. In contrast, the polytropic approach yields more realistic predictions [53,54].

On the other hand, exergy-based analyses and holistic integral evaluations help us to understand not only the compressor's performance but also losses in the motor, control system, piping, and end-use points. These studies have revealed overall system efficiencies below 10% in some industrial cases [55,56]. This emphasizes the need to address efficiency from a system-wide perspective, rather than just at the component level.

In the calculation of efficiency of screw compressors with insufficient cooling, the isentropic coefficient (k) is the most accurate, due to the absence of mechanical friction in the pair of worm gears; this coefficient more accurately describes the change of pressure and volume during the compression stage in screw compressors [6]. In this case study, the BOGE C 22-2 compressor is a screw compressor with oil cooling in the compression stage [7]. This type of cooling is considered insufficient cooling [6].

Recent advancements include optimization techniques that utilize active machine learning in combination with thermodynamic models [57], which accelerate design while preserving accuracy (diva portal.org, arxiv.org). In addition, compressor sequencing strategies, particularly through nonlinear control or load shifting, have proven capable of reducing energy consumption by up to 20% by intelligently managing operating levels across systems [58].

Other innovations include the use of variable-speed drives (VSDs), economizers, and variable-displacement screws, which significantly improve efficiency under partial-load conditions. However, they require a higher initial investment [59].

Although each method offers specific technical value, the literature suggests that no single approach is sufficient in isolation. For example, while polytropic efficiency improves predictive accuracy, it requires precise calibration. Control strategies, on the other hand, reduce energy use but depend on digital infrastructure and operational data. Exergy analysis emerges as the most comprehensive method, though it is data-intensive and time-consuming.

Table 1. Methods for evaluating and improving compressor efficiency.

Method/Strategy	Brief Description	Main Advantages
Isentropic efficiency	Based on ideal enthalpy difference	Easy to compute, but inaccurate under real conditions [60]
Polytropic efficiency	Incremental model accounting for pressure variations	More accurate in multistage and variable-load compressors [61]
Exergy analysis	Evaluates destruction of useful energy across the full system	Comprehensive diagnosis and systemic perspective [54]
Optimized control/sequencing	Strategies to operate multiple compressors coordinately	Up to 20% energy savings via load shifting [62]
Active ML with thermodynamics	Combines models and ML for design and optimization	Reduces design time by ~46% [63]
VSDs and variable displacement	Adjust speed/volume of compression based on demand	High efficiency under partial loads, though with higher capital costs [64]

In multi-compressor settings, intelligent sequencing combined with variable-speed drives appears to offer the highest energy-saving potential. Future studies should integrate advanced modeling (e.g., ML or simulation) with both qualitative and quantitative energy audits, focusing not only on the compressor component but on the overall system efficiency, including the motor, air distribution network, and point of use conditions.

2.10. Critical Evaluation of Energy Efficiency in Electric Motors

The energy efficiency of industrial electric motors is a central aspect of sustainability policies and technological competitiveness. Various methodological approaches have been developed to estimate, diagnose, and improve motor performance, ranging from classical physical models to advanced artificial intelligence tools. This section presents a critical discussion of the most representative methods identified in recent scientific literature, along with their main advantages, limitations, and application contexts [65].

Among the most widely used methods for estimating motor efficiency are equivalent circuit models (such as IEEE 112 Method F1), which calculate motor performance based on no-load and partial load tests, without the need for disassembly or invasive instrumentation. These methods provide acceptable precision, on the order of ±3–4%, and are widely used in field diagnostics [66–68].

In terms of regulatory classification, the IEC 60034-30 standard [69] defines efficiency levels from IE1 to IE5, providing a framework for technological replacement and procurement policies [70,71]. However, this classification does not consider real-world operational variability.

The analysis of internal losses, including core losses, winding resistance, and mechanical losses, is fundamental for the design of high efficiency motors. This approach has been strengthened by studies incorporating advanced materials, improved cooling techniques, and new rotor topologies [72,73].

Control strategies, such as variable speed drives (VSDs) and direct torque control (DTC), enable the real-time adaptation of motor operation to actual load demand, thereby minimizing slip losses and improving efficiency in dynamic regimes [74].

Recently, machine learning-based predictive maintenance methods have been introduced, enabling early failure detection and identification of operational conditions that compromise energy performance. These approaches, based on sensor networks and supervised algorithms, are particularly effective in continuous and complex systems [75]. Table 2 presents a comparative summary of the most relevant methods and strategies, including their principles and key advantages, based on specialized literature.

Table 2. Methods and strategies for evaluating and improving the efficiency of industrial electric motors.

Method/Strategy	Technical Description	Main Advantages
Equivalent circuit model (IEEE 112 F1, Ontario Hydro)	Performance estimation using no-load and partial load tests	Non-invasive method with good field accuracy [76]
IEC classification IE1–IE5	Standardized classification of energy efficiency levels	Supports procurement and replacement policies [77]
Loss analysis	Detailed evaluation of iron, copper, and mechanical losses	Enables redesign and selection of more efficient materials [78,79]
Control using VSD or DTC	Real time regulation of speed and torque	Optimizes efficiency under variable load conditions [80,81]
"Goodness" factor (Laithwaite)	Dimensional metric to compare motors of different sizes	Supports efficient energy-based motor sizing [82,83]
ML-based predictive maintenance	Intelligent monitoring of motor condition	Improves availability and prevents energy degradation [84]

2.11. Repeatability and Quality Control

To ensure the reliability of the results, each measurement was replicated over three consecutive operating cycles under similar conditions. Instrument uncertainty was assessed, and validation protocols were applied using energy audit procedures, such as those suggested by the National Renewable Energy Laboratory [49,85].

2.12. Technical Specifications of the BOGE Compressors

The Oleohidráulica Cienfuegos compressed air system is equipped with two BOGE C 22-2 rotary screw compressors, with oil injection and air-cooled aftercoolers. These units are designed for continuous operation in industrial environments, for a stable and efficient compressed air supply. Figure 3 shows one of the installed compressors, highlighting its compact structure and modular configuration [7].

Figure 3. BOGE C 22-2 screw compressor installed at Oleohidráulica Cienfuegos.

According to the manufacturer's technical documentation [86,87], the main specifications of the BOGE C 22-2 compressors are summarized in Table 3.

Table 3. Technical specifications of the BOGE C 22-2 compressor.

Parameter	Specification
Model	BOGE C 22-2
Manufacturing date	July 2023
Serial number	5,182,079
Maximum flow rate	3.21 m^3/min
Maximum operating pressure	10 bar
Motor speed at 50 Hz	3550 min^{-1}
Motor speed at 60 Hz	2955 min^{-1}
Electric motor power	22 kW

2.13. Technical Characterization of the Electric Motor

2.13.1. Efficiency Behavior Under Different Load Factors

To analyze the performance of the electric motor coupled to the BOGE C 22-2 compressor, the efficiency curve as a function of the load factor (K_c) was constructed. This was achieved using the nameplate data and plotting the trend using Microsoft Excel. Figure 4 illustrates the variation in motor efficiency across different load percentages.

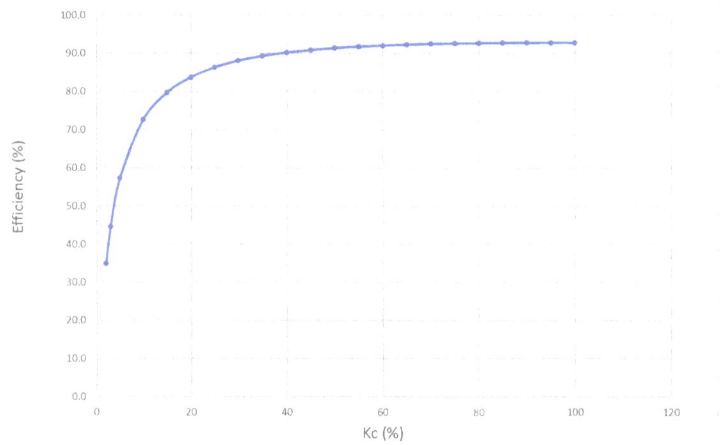

Figure 4. Efficiency of the electric motor coupled to the BOGE C 22-2 compressor as a function of the load factor (K_c).

As shown in the figure, the motor achieves its highest efficiency when operating between 75% and 100% of its rated capacity, while performance declines significantly under partial load conditions. This behavior is consistent with standard efficiency profiles for three-phase induction motors, highlighting the importance of operating near the design point to maximize energy utilization.

2.13.2. Measurement of Electrical Power Demand

To determine the actual electrical power consumed by the motor, a Chauvin Arnoux C.A 8331 power quality analyzer was connected to the plant's electrical supply network. Three consecutive measurements were taken to record variations in active power supplied to the motor under different operating conditions. The results are presented in Table 4.

Table 4. Active power values measured using the Chauvin Arnoux power analyzer.

Variable	Measurement 1	Measurement 2	Measurement 3
Active Power (kW)	4.53	6.40	3.94

The recorded values show the variability in the motor's electrical consumption depending on the load and real-time operating conditions. These data are essential for estimating the overall energy performance of the compressor motor system and for validating theoretical efficiency estimates based on manufacturer-provided curves.

3. Results

3.1. Frequency Stability Analysis

The analyzed Figure 5 is a frequency stability log for a monitored channel identified as "F", covering a period of seven days from 31 March 2025, at 2:20 PM to 7 April 2025, at 2:19 PM. The system operated with a display resolution of 12 h per division.

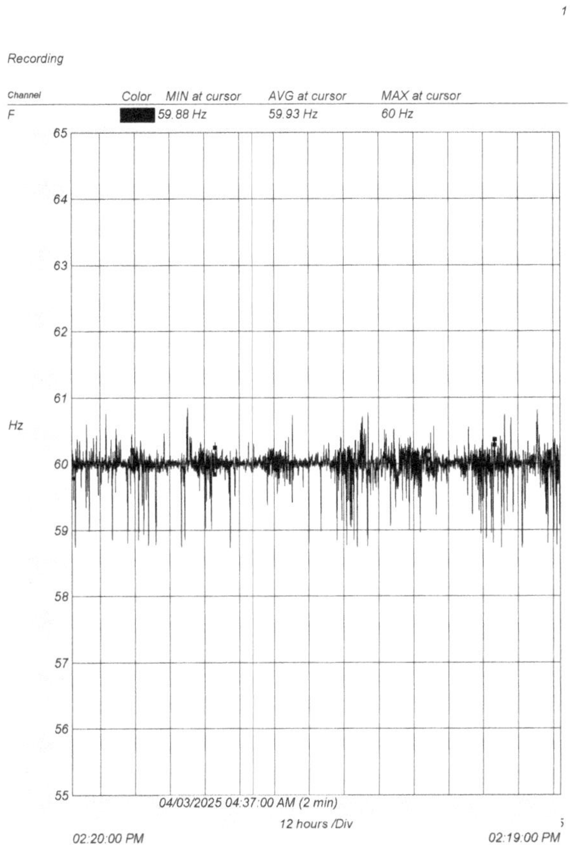

Figure 5. Frequency stability record of a channel identified as "F", monitored over seven days.

Throughout the observation period, the recorded frequency ranged from a minimum of 59.88 Hz to a maximum of 60.00 Hz, with an average cursor value of 59.93 Hz. These results indicate a very narrow variation around the nominal 60 Hz value, which is indicative of good frequency stability within acceptable limits for electrical or precision electronic systems.

A specific event is noted on 3 April 2025, at 4:37 AM, lasting 2 min. Although this event does not represent a significant deviation, it is recommended to cross-reference it with complementary data such as voltage, power, or maintenance logs to rule out any transient anomalies.

Overall, the results suggest stable behavior of the analyzed system, with no evidence of sustained deviations or synchronization loss. The slight average deviation below the nominal value may be attributed to variable loads or minor delays in the system's control response, without critical operational implications in this context.

3.2. Evaluation of the Electrical Energy Behavior

An analysis was conducted on the evolution of electrical energy variables based on the data collected by a power quality analyzer over a continuous seven-day period (Figure 6a), from 31 March 2025, at 2:30 PM to 7 April 2025, at 2:15 PM, with a temporal resolution of 12 h per division. The measurements included active energy (Ep), reactive energy (En), and apparent energy (Es) across the three phases (Ep1–Ep3, En1–En3, Es1–Es3), as well as their respective total values (EpT, EnT, EsT).

Figure 6a analyzes the energy behavior of a system that integrates the instantaneous power measured over time, starting from zero. The continuous integration of power over time results in a progressive accumulation of energy, represented by a growing curve whose slope depends on variations in the measured power. In dynamic systems with variable loads, the energy curve exhibits a nonlinear behavior.

Active energy (kWh) reflects the useful work performed, while reactive energy (kvarh) is essential for the operation of inductive devices. Apparent energy (kVAh) combines both components, providing a comprehensive view of system consumption and capacity. Energy accumulation follows a growing trajectory, influenced by power variability. During periods of higher power, the accumulation is faster, while in intervals of lower power, the increase is more gradual. This variability highlights the importance of maintaining controlled operating conditions to ensure accurate and reliable measurements.

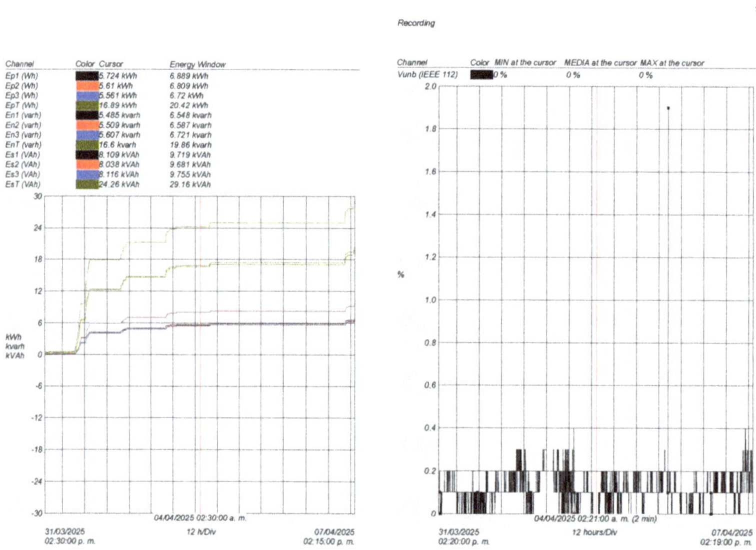

(a) (b)

Figure 6. Voltage imbalance (according to IEEE standard 112 [88]). Note: Abbreviations. kWh: Kilowatt hour—Unit of energy equivalent to the consumption of 1 kilowatt over one hour. kvarh: Kilovolt-ampere reactive hour—Unit of reactive energy used in alternating current systems. kVAh: Kilovolt-ampere hour—Unit of apparent energy consumed by an electrical system. Vunb: Unbalanced voltage—Indicator of imbalance between phases in an electrical system. (**a**) Analysis of the evolution of energy variables. (**b**) No Load Line Voltage Evaluation (according to IEEE standard 112).

This analysis is based on the recording of the voltage imbalance (Vunb), according to IEEE 112 standard, captured by the power analyzer over a seven-day monitoring period, from 31 March 2025, at 14:20 to 7 April 2025, at 14:19. The graphical resolution used was 12 h per division (Figure 6b). The results show that Vunb remained exceptionally low, with an average value of 0%, showing no significant variations in the minimum, maximum, or average values throughout the observation window, indicating remarkable stability in the line voltage system.

This behavior suggests a perfect phase balance within the system, with no evidence of voltage unbalance that could compromise the performance of three-phase motors, transformers, or sensitive electronic equipment. The stability of this parameter reflects a symmetrical load distribution and an electrically well configured network. Notably, no transient events or abrupt deviations were identified during the period, reinforcing the system's reliability in maintaining voltage symmetry under normal operating conditions.

3.3. Three Phase RMS Voltage Evaluation

The analysis was conducted based on the recorded RMS values of voltage and current over a seven-day period (Figure 7), from 31 March 2025, at 14:20 to 7 April 2025, at 14:19, with a resolution of 12 h per division. The monitored channels included phase voltages (V1, V2, V3), line voltages (U12, U23, U31), and phase currents (A1, A2, A3, AN). Notably, the RMS currents measured on all three phases were 0 A, indicating that no load was connected to the system during the monitoring period, or that the equipment was in a no-load (idle) state (Table 5).

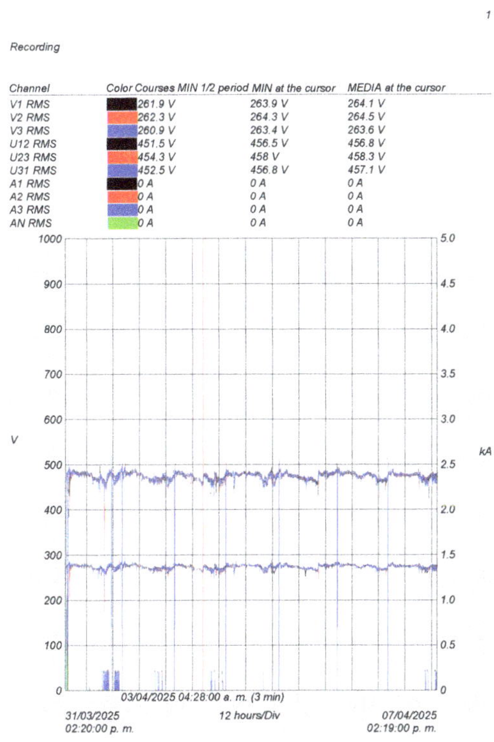

Figure 7. Recording of RMS values of voltage and current. Note: **RMS** (Root Mean Square) refers to the square root of the arithmetic mean of the squares of the instantaneous values of a variable, commonly used to measure the effective value of an alternating signal. **V** refers to Volts, the unit of measurement for the electric potential difference in the International System of Units (SI). **A** refers to Amperes, the unit of measurement for electric current intensity, also in the SI system.

Table 5. Average RMS values of phase and line voltages.

Parameter	RMS Value (V)
Phase Voltage V1	264.1
Phase Voltage V2	264.5
Phase Voltage V3	263.6
Line Voltage U12	456.8
Line Voltage U23	458.3
Line Voltage U31	457.1

The low variability among phase voltages suggests a high degree of supply symmetry. At the same time, the absence of current confirms that the system was operating under no-load conditions during the recording. This type of evaluation is essential for establishing baseline reference conditions in energy audits or acceptance testing of electrical equipment.

3.4. Analysis of Active, Reactive, and Apparent Power

The analysis of the obtained data shows that the power values (P1, P2, P3, PT) and reactive power (N1, N2, N3, NT) remain at zero at the moment indicated by the cursor (red vertical line), suggesting that at that specific moment, the motor was de-energized or not in operation. This behavior is consistent with the absence of active or reactive energy consumption during that interval (Figure 8).

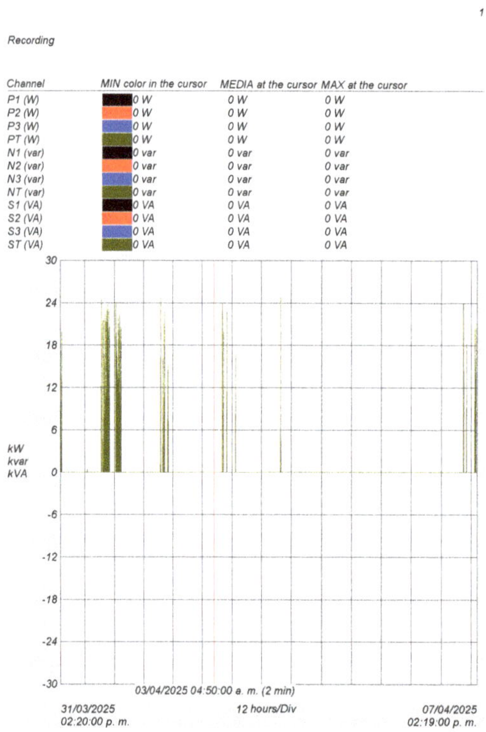

Figure 8. Analysis of active, reactive, and apparent powers. Note: **P1, P2, P3** (*Active Power in watts*): Measure of the power consumed or delivered by each phase in an electrical system. **PT** (*Total Active Power* in watts): Sum of the active powers of all phases in a system. **N1, N2, N3** (*Reactive Power* in volt-amps reactive): Measure of the power used to create and maintain magnetic fields in electrical circuits. **NT** (*Total Reactive Power* in volt-amps reactive): Sum of the reactive powers of all phases. **S1, S2, S3** (*Apparent Power* in volt-amps): Total power measure in an electrical system, which includes both active and reactive power. **ST** (*Total Apparent Power* in volt-amps): Sum of the apparent powers of all phases. **kW**(*Kilowatts*): Unit of active power in the metric system. **kVAR** (*Kilovolt-amps reactive*): Unit of reactive power. **kVA** (*Kilovolt-amps*): Unit of apparent power.

However, it is important to note that the compressor continues to register work at certain moments over time. This phenomenon can be attributed to specific characteristics of the device or possible residual effects of the system. It is possible that, during certain periods, the motor was operating intermittently or momentarily, which is not reflected in the power readings, yet still shows variations in the recorded work values.

This behavior highlights the importance of considering temporary fluctuations in the motor's operation, as well as the potential influence of factors such as system configuration or the calibration of the measurement instruments. The absence of power readings in the monitored parameters in this case does not necessarily indicate that the system is not operating; rather, it could reflect low-load or intermittent operation, warranting further investigation to better understand the possible effects of residual operation and ensure the accuracy of the measurements.

3.5. Calculation of Electric Motor Efficiency

Table 6 summarizes the calculated load factor (K_c) of the electric motor corresponding to the three active power measurements previously obtained with the power analyzer.

Table 6. Load factor of the electric motor based on measured power values.

Measured Power (kW)	Load Factor (K_c)
4.53	0.22
6.40	0.30
3.94	0.19

Using the efficiency curve previously presented in Figure 4, it was possible to determine the estimated efficiency of the electric motor corresponding to each load factor value shown in Table 6. The results are presented in Table 7.

Table 7. Electric motor efficiency based on measured power values.

Measured Power (kW)	Motor Efficiency (η)
4.53	0.84
6.40	0.88
3.94	0.80

The motor efficiency values range between 80% and 88%, which is consistent with the expected performance for three-phase induction motors under partial load conditions. Given that the nominal efficiency of the motor is 92.8%, the results suggest that the compressor is not operating in a state of significant underutilization. Therefore, no substantial evidence of performance degradation or oversizing is observed under the current load conditions.

3.6. Improvement Proposal: Installation of a Capacitor Bank

Although no direct values were obtained from the Power Factor Total (PFT) channel, the proximity between active energy (EpT = 20.42 kWh) and reactive energy (EnT = 19.86 kvarh) indicates a significant reactive component. This implies a low power factor, possibly below 0.9, which could lead to financial penalties and increased load on the electrical system.

An effective solution is the installation of a static capacitor bank with automatic control, which would enable:

- Compensation of the reactive power drawn by the compressor and other inductive loads.
- Raising the overall power factor above 0.95 by local electrical regulations.
- Reduction of Joule losses in conductors and transformers.
- Lowering the apparent power demand, freeing up capacity in the internal distribution system.

The assessment of the initial state of the electrical system was conducted based on the direct records of the Total Power Factor (PFT) channel. The results showed an active energy of $E_p = 20.42$ kWh and a reactive energy of $E_q = 19.86$ kvarh. The closeness between these two values indicates a significant presence of reactive power. The ratio between these energies makes it possible to estimate the phase angle φ_1, defined as:

$$\tan\varphi_1 \approx \frac{E_q}{E_p} = \frac{19.86}{20.42} = 0.973 \tag{12}$$

Thus, the initial power factor of the system was calculated as:

$$\mathrm{pf}_1 = \cos\varphi_1 = \frac{1}{\sqrt{1+\tan^2\varphi_1}} \approx 0.72 \tag{13}$$

This value indicates an operation with a considerable level of inductive reactive power, resulting in low power utilization and potential economic penalties from the utility company.

To raise the power factor to acceptable industrial reference values ($\mathrm{pf}_2 = 0.95$ and $\mathrm{pf}_2 = 0.97$), the required reactive compensation power (Q_c) to be installed was determined using the following expression [89]:

$$Q_c = P(\tan\varphi_1 - \tan\varphi_2) \tag{14}$$

where P corresponds to the active power of the system, associated with the measured energy ($P \approx 20.42$ kW). The tangent of the angle related to the desired power factor is obtained through [89]:

$$\tan\varphi_2 = \sqrt{\frac{1}{\mathrm{pf}_2^2} - 1} \tag{15}$$

The calculations yield the following results:

- For $\mathrm{pf}_2 = 0.95$:
$$Q_c = 20.42\,(0.973 - 0.329) \approx 13.1 \text{ kVAr}$$
- For $\mathrm{pf}_2 = 0.97$:
$$Q_c = 20.42\,(0.973 - 0.251) \approx 14.7 \text{ kVAr}$$

Consequently, the installation of a capacitor bank with an approximate capacity of 13 to 15 kVAr would enable the correction of the power factor to levels between 0.95 and 0.97, thereby reducing the demand for reactive power, improving the overall energy efficiency of the system, and avoiding tariff surcharges. It is important to note that the calculation of the required capacitor bank size is based on a one-week data period, which provides a representative estimate for immediate operating conditions. However, due to potential seasonal and long-term variations in the system's demand, it is recommended to consider additional analysis with a longer data period to ensure the long-term representativeness of the proposed design.

3.7. Calculation of Compressor Work

The BOGE C 22-2 is an oil-injected rotary screw compressor, in which oil is used for air cooling, lubrication of the rotating screws, and internal sealing of the compression system [7].

According to [6], the isentropic compression coefficient k better represents the pressure–volume behavior in compressors with limited cooling capacity, such as those cooled by oil. Based on this criterion, the work required for air compression was estimated using Equation (16) as described by Monteagudo [48].

$$L_i = \frac{k}{k-1} \cdot p_1 \cdot v_1 \cdot \left[\left(\frac{p_2}{p_1} \right)^{\frac{k-1}{k}} - 1 \right] \tag{16}$$

where $v_1 = 0.86\,\mathrm{m^3/kg}$ is the specific volume of air at standard conditions [90], and $k = 1.4$ for dry air, assuming insufficient cooling during compression, which approximates adiabatic behavior.

As shown in Table 8, the system reaches a maximum pressure of 10 bar at 110 °C.

Table 8. Air pressure and temperature values under various conditions.

Measurement Point	Pressure (Bar)	Temperature (°C)
Startup (inlet)	1.0	25
Shutdown (operation)	5.2	70
Maximum pressure	10.0	110

All calculations were performed in absolute units (Pascal and Kelvin). The results of the estimated compressor work at two operating pressures are shown in Table 9.

Table 9. Compressor works at different operating pressures.

Operating Condition	Pressure (Bar)	Work (J/kg)
Actual pressure	5.2	180,196.21
Maximum pressure	10.0	278,738.97

3.8. Air Consumption in the Factory

Table 10 presents the compressed air consumption rates of all factory equipment under nominal conditions.

Table 10. Compressed air consumers and flow rates.

Consumer	Flow Rate (m^3/min)
Blow nozzle for hydraulic jacks	0.15
Blow nozzle for cylinder assembly	0.15
Blow nozzle (tooling area)	0.15
Blow nozzle (technical services)	0.15
Cylinder test bench	0.15
Cylinder clamping station	0.01
Tube threading machine	0.09
Hose crimping press	0.03
Hose test bench	0.03
Paint spray gun	0.075
Machining center	0.24
Total	1.23

In the context of this study, the term *low-load* refers to the operating condition in which the compressor supplied air exclusively to two end-use devices: the machining center and the paint spray gun. During the monitoring period, all other pneumatic consumers listed in Table 10 (e.g., blow nozzles, test benches, hose crimping presses) remained inactive due to reduced plant productivity. As a result, the actual compressed air demand was measured at approximately 0.43 m^3/min, which represents only 13% of the compressor's rated capacity of 3.21 m^3/min. This explains the prevalence of partial-load conditions and the relatively low efficiency values reported in this study.

Currently, only the machining center and paint spray gun are in operation. To determine their actual air demand, a real-time measurement test was conducted. This involved measuring the time required for the compressor to fill the air tank while isolating the system by closing the supply valves (Table 11).

Table 11. Filling time measurements during tank test.

Measurement	Minutes	Seconds
1	1.17	77.52
2	1.20	80.39
3	1.20	80.84
4	1.23	83.04
5	1.19	79.47
6	1.20	80.88
7	1.19	79.75
8	1.20	80.10
Average	1.20	80.25

Table 12 shows the pressure and temperature conditions at startup and shutdown.

Table 12. Startup and shutdown pressure and temperature conditions.

Stage	Pressure (Bar)	Pressure (Pa)	Temp (°C)	Temp (K)
Startup	4.5	450,000	68	341.15
Shutdown	5.2	520,000	70	343.15

3.9. Air Density and Mass Flow Rate

Based on the values in Table 12, the air density at startup and shutdown was calculated using the ideal gas equation:

$$\rho = \frac{P}{RT} \tag{17}$$

where R is the specific gas constant for dry air, calculated from:

$$R = \frac{R_i}{M} \tag{18}$$

The parameters required for the density calculation are summarized in Table 13.

Table 13. Constants used for density calculation.

Constant	Value
Specific gas constant R (J/kg·K)	287
Universal gas constant R_i (J/mol·K)	8.31
Molar mass of air M (kg/mol)	0.029

The calculated air densities are shown in Table 14.

Table 14. Air density at startup and shutdown.

Condition	Density (kg/m^3)
Startup	4.60
Shutdown	5.28

3.10. Compressed Mass and Flow Rate

The mass of air stored in the tank was calculated using:

$$m_a = \rho \cdot V_{tk} \tag{19}$$

Given that the tank volume is $V_{tk} = 4.44\,\text{m}^3$ [91], the air mass values are shown in Table 15.

Table 15. Mass of air in the storage tank.

Condition	Air Mass (kg)
Startup	20.41
Shutdown	23.44

The compressed mass is thus $m_{a,\text{diff}} = 3.04$ kg. The mass flow rate is calculated as:

$$\dot{m} = \frac{m_{a,\text{diff}}}{t_{\text{fill}}} \tag{20}$$

The results are shown in Table 16.

Table 16. Mass flow rate into the tank.

Mass Flow Rate	kg/s	kg/min	kg/h
	0.038	2.27	136.23

From these values, the volumetric flow rate was calculated using:

$$Q = \frac{\dot{m}}{\rho} \tag{21}$$

The results are shown in Table 17.

Table 17. Volumetric flow rate of compressed air delivered to the tank.

Volumetric Flow Rate	m^3/s	m^3/min	m^3/h
	0.0072	0.43	25.8

3.11. Flow Comparison

Finally, Table 18 compares the current production air consumption with the maximum compressor capacity.

Table 18. Comparison of current consumption and compressor capacity.

Condition	Flow (m^3/min)
Current consumption	0.43
Maximum capacity	3.21

3.12. Power Demand in the Compression Stage

The power required in the compression stage was estimated using Equation (22), as proposed by [92,93]:

$$N_R = \frac{\rho \cdot Q \cdot L_R}{1000} \tag{22}$$

where:

- ρ is the air density (kg/m^3),
- Q is the volumetric flow rate of compressed air (m^3/s),
- L_R is the specific compression work (J/kg).

Two power values were calculated based on the volumetric flow rates listed in Table 18. The results are presented in Table 19.

Table 19. Compressor power demand based on delivered air flow rate.

Compressed Air Flow Rate (m^3/min)	0.43	3.21
Power Demand (kW)	1.51	17.43

3.13. Compressor Efficiency Calculation

The compressor efficiency was determined based on the electrical power measured with the network analyzer (Table 4) and the power consumed in the compression stage, previously estimated using Equation (22). The efficiency was obtained using the relationship defined in Equation (23) [94,95]:

$$\eta = \frac{N_R}{N_E} \tag{23}$$

where:

- N_R: Power consumed in the compression stage (kW)
- N_E: Electrical power supplied to the motor (kW)

In addition, the maximum system efficiency was calculated under nominal operating conditions, that is, using the nameplate power of the motor (22 kW) and the maximum pressure, temperature, and airflow parameters. The obtained results are summarized in Table 20.

Table 20. Compressor efficiency values.

Measured Power (kW)	**Compressor Efficiency (η)**
4.53	0.40
6.40	0.27
3.94	0.48
Nameplate Power (22 kW)	**0.89**

The reported values fall below the optimal efficiency range expected for rotary screw compressors, which typically ranges between 60% and 70% [6]. However, the analyzed compressor operates predominantly under low-load conditions, with low flow rates and over short time intervals, which explains the observed efficiency range of 27% to 48%.

It is worth noting that in screw compressors with no direct mechanical friction between the rotors, such as the BOGE C 22-2, higher efficiency values could be achieved if the load regime were more stable and closer to the design power [94,95].

4. Discussion

The results show that the BOGE C 22-2 compressor reaches a maximum efficiency of 0.89 under nominal operating conditions (22 kW and 10 bar discharge pressure). This value lies within the upper expected range for rotary screw compressors, indicating high energy performance when operating at full load. However, during actual factory operation, the compressor predominantly works under partial load conditions, with efficiencies ranging from 0.27 to 0.48, as measured from power inputs between 3.94 and 6.40 kW.

This gap between nominal and operational efficiency suggests that the equipment is underutilized, resulting in electrical energy consumption that is not proportional to the useful work performed. Such behavior is typical in systems operating in intermittent cycles or under extended partial load, which can reduce the overall energy performance indicators of the industrial process.

In light of these findings, a set of complementary strategies is proposed to enhance the energy and operational efficiency of the compressed air system:

4.1. Implementation of Sequential or Demand-Based Control

Deploying a sequential control system that modulates compressor operation based on line pressure and real time demand would reduce start stop cycles and prevent unnecessary idle operation. This strategy is especially effective in facilities with intermittent or time varying air requirements.

4.2. Integration of Predictive Algorithms Based on Machine Learning

The application of machine learning algorithms trained with historical operational data (pressure, flow rate, power consumption, operating hours) enables the prediction of compressed air demand and optimizes compressor scheduling. This approach allows for smarter activation of the equipment, aligned with actual production patterns.

4.3. Evaluation of Parallel or Variable Speed (VSD) Compressors

Given that the BOGE C 22-2 achieves peak efficiency near full load, it is advisable to consider adding a smaller auxiliary compressor or one with a variable frequency drive. This second compressor would handle partial load demands, reserving the main unit for peak periods. This hybrid strategy would improve the system's average efficiency.

4.4. Economic Feasibility and Return on Investment (ROI) Analysis

A financial viability study should be conducted to assess savings from reduced reactive energy, improved power factor, lower electrical losses, and prolonged equipment life. This analysis will help justify investments in the proposed solutions and support strategic decisions within an industrial energy management framework.

Based on the experimental results of this study, where the actual compressor efficiency ranged between 27% and 48% under partial load conditions, it is estimated that:

- The implementation of a Variable Speed Drive (VSD) could increase the average operational efficiency by 10–20 percentage points, reaching a range of 45–65%, as reported in comparable industrial applications [96,97].
- The use of predictive demand-control algorithms could reduce idle times by 8–12%, resulting in an estimated annual energy saving of 5–7 MWh in the analyzed case [98,99].
- The installation of a capacitor bank (13–15 kVAr) would raise the power factor from 0.72 to values between 0.95 and 0.97, which would represent an annual saving of approximately 8–10% in the plant's electricity bill by avoiding penalties for reactive power consumption [100,101].

From an economic perspective, considering an average industrial electricity cost of 0.12 USD/kWh, the combination of these measures would result in annual savings on the order of 1200–1600 USD. The payback period (ROI) would be less than 2 years for the capacitor bank and 3–4 years for the integration of an auxiliary compressor with VSD.

5. Conclusions

This study evaluated the energy performance of the BOGE C 22-2 screw compressor under real industrial conditions. The results revealed a significant gap between the rated peak efficiency (0.89) and the actual operating efficiency (0.27–0.48), mainly due to partial-load operation and low compressed air demand.

Reactive power consumption was also found to be nearly equal to active power, resulting in a low power factor (0.72) and highlighting the need for compensation measures.

Based on these findings, three main recommendations are proposed:

- Implement sequential or demand-based control to minimize idle operation.
- Integrate a secondary or variable speed drive (VSD) compressor to improve efficiency under low demand.

- Install an automatic capacitor bank to raise the power factor above 0.95 and reduce electrical losses.

Altogether, these measures would enhance system efficiency, reduce operating costs, and contribute to the plant's long-term sustainability.

Author Contributions: Conceptualization, G.J.B.G., L.A.I.C., B.J.S., J.M.O.R. and O.R.A.; Methodology, L.A.I.C., C.D.C.-R., J.R.-R. and B.J.S.; Software, L.A.I.C. and G.J.B.G.; Validation, J.P.M.Y., J.R.-R. and J.M.O.R.; Formal analysis, L.A.I.C., G.J.B.G., J.P.M.Y. and O.R.A.; Investigation, G.J.B.G., C.D.C.-R., J.P.M.Y. and B.J.S.; Data curation, L.A.I.C., J.P.M.Y. and B.J.S.; Writing—original draft preparation, L.A.I.C., G.J.B.G. and B.J.S.; Writing—review and editing, J.P.M.Y., J.R.-R., C.D.C.-R. and J.M.O.R.; Visualization, L.A.I.C., C.D.C.-R. and O.R.A.; Supervision, J.R.-R. and J.M.O.R.; Project administration, J.R.-R. and B.J.S. All authors have read and agreed to the published version of the manuscript.

Funding: The authors reported there is no funding associated with the work featured in this article.

Data Availability Statement: Data will be made available upon reasonable request.

Conflicts of Interest: No potential conflict of interest was reported by the authors.

References

1. Kaya, D.; Çanka Kılıç, F.; Öztürk, H.H. Energy Efficiency in Compressed Air Systems. In *Energy Management and Energy Efficiency in Industry: Practical Examples*; Springer: Berlin/Heidelberg, Germany, 2021; pp. 395–418.
2. Nehler, T. Linking energy efficiency measures in industrial compressed air systems with non-energy benefits—A review. *Renew. Sustain. Energy Rev.* **2018**, *89*, 72–87. [CrossRef]
3. Takahashi, A.; Hatsuse, W. Novel criterion for reluctance torque utility of permanent magnet motors. *IEEE Trans. Energy Convers.* **2019**, *34*, 1751–1758. [CrossRef]
4. Dindorf, R. Study of the Energy Efficiency of Compressed Air Storage Tanks. *Sustainability* **2024**, *16*, 1664. [CrossRef]
5. Yao, E.; Wang, H.; Wang, L.; Xi, G.; Maréchal, F. Multi-objective optimization and exergoeconomic analysis of a combined cooling, heating and power based compressed air energy storage system. *Energy Convers. Manag.* **2017**, *138*, 199–209. [CrossRef]
6. Cherkasski, V.M. *Pumps, Fans, Compressors*; Mir Publishers: Moscow, Russia, 1984; pp. 271–283, 349–352.
7. BOGE Kompressoren. *Operating Instructions for Screw Compressors Driven by V-Belts and Direct Coupling*; BOGE Kompressoren: Bielefeld, Germany, 2021. Available online: https://www.boge.com/en/ (accessed on 28 September 2025).
8. Vieira, F.S.; Balestieri, J.A.P.; Matelli, J.A. Applications of compressed air energy storage in cogeneration systems. *Energy* **2021**, *214*, 118904. [CrossRef]
9. Abdi, D.; Bekele, A.; Venkatachalam, C.; Parthiban, M. Energy performance analysis of pasta and macaroni factory—A case study. *AIMS Energy* **2021**, *9*, 238–256. [CrossRef]
10. Ouada, M.; Benamira, N.; Meghni, B.; Dib, D. Optimal control of variable speed air conditioning system fed by solar PV system. In Proceedings of the 2019 1st International Conference on Sustainable Renewable Energy Systems and Applications (ICSRESA), Tebessa, Algeria, 4–5 December 2019; IEEE: New York, NY, USA, 2019; pp. 1–4.
11. Kuzykov, O.N.; Vlasova, E.P. Digital Protection of Electric Motor. In Proceedings of the 2024 International Conference on Industrial Engineering, Applications and Manufacturing (ICIEAM), Sochi, Russian, 20–24 May 2024; IEEE: New York, NY, USA, 2024; pp. 92–96.
12. Kuwar, Y.V. Performance evaluation of ecofriendly R1234ze(E) refrigerant in an automotive air conditioning system. *Heat Transf.* **2024**, *53*, 472–494. [CrossRef]
13. Olszak, E.; Yoho, M.; Greaser, R.; Srivastava, R.; Lanke, R.; Moffett, R.; Chan, C.S.; Dabrowski, D.; Pond, B.; Hingerl, F. Case study: Plunger lift optimization leveraging physics-assisted AI and the impact on greenhouse gas emissions reductions. In Proceedings of the SPE Annual Technical Conference and Exhibition, Houston, TX, USA, 3–5 October 2022. [CrossRef]
14. Dai, Y.; Wu, D.; Jin, W.; Sun, C. Design of unmanned boat for in-situ restoration of black and odorous water bodies in rivers. *Chin. J. Agric. Mech.* **2021**, *42*, 202.
15. Choi, D.W.; Lee, C.W.; Lee, D.Y.; Lee, D.W.; Yoon, H.U. A hybrid soft actuator inspired by grass-spike: Design approach, dynamic model, and applications. *Appl. Sci.* **2020**, *10*, 8525. [CrossRef]
16. Lee, M.; Koo, B.; Nam, K. Analytic optimization of the Halbach array slotless motor considering stator yoke saturation. *IEEE Trans. Magn.* **2020**, *57*, 8200806. [CrossRef]
17. Hoeflinger, J.; Hofmann, P. Air mass flow and pressure optimisation of a PEM fuel cell range extender system. *Int. J. Hydrogen Energy* **2020**, *45*, 29246–29258. [CrossRef]

18. Shou, J.; Ma, J.; Xu, B.; Qiu, L.; Luo, C.; Fang, Y. Noise optimization of high-speed permanent magnet motor by stiffeners. In Proceedings of the 2022 IEEE Transportation Electrification Conference and Expo, Asia-Pacific (ITEC Asia-Pacific), Haining, China, 28–31 October 2022; IEEE: New York, NY, USA, 2022; pp. 1–6.
19. Rufer, A. Increasing the Energy Efficiency of Gas Boosters for Hydrogen Storage and for Refueling Stations. *Energies* **2023**, *16*, 1763. [CrossRef]
20. Du, J.; Xie, X. Research on fault diagnosis of integrated environmental control system in aircraft cockpit. In Proceedings of the Third International Conference on Electronics, Electrical and Information Engineering (ICEEIE 2023), Xiamen, China, 11–13 August 2023; SPIE: Bellingham, WA, USA, 2023; Volume 12922, pp. 524–534.
21. Borovkov, A.; Galerkin, Y.B.; Drozdov, A.; Rekstin, A.; Semenovskiy, V.; Yadykin, V. Design and features of the ECC-55 experimental rig for gas-dynamic tests of model centrifugal compressor stages. *AIP Conf. Proc.* **2021**, *2412*, 030011. [CrossRef]
22. Wei, Y.; Zuo, Z.; Jia, B.; Liang, K.; Feng, H. Operational optimisation of a novel dual-piston linear compressor: Simulation and experiment. *Int. J. Refrig.* **2021**, *132*, 82–91. [CrossRef]
23. Yang, M.; Hu, C.; Bai, Y.; Deng, K.; Gu, Y.; Qian, Y.; Liu, B. Matching method of electric turbo compound for two-stroke low-speed marine diesel engine. *Appl. Therm. Eng.* **2019**, *158*, 113752. [CrossRef]
24. Yahya, Y.; Jarail, M.K.H.; Maizana, D.; Alhamrouni, I.; Ismail, M.B. The Effect of Different Diameter Rotor Bars Size on Performance of 0.5 Hp Induction Motor. *Int. J. Integr. Eng.* **2024**, *16*, 135–147. [CrossRef]
25. Toema, M.; Watts, P.; Mathews, H.; Beshouri, G. Overcoming Turbocharger Limitations for Low BMEP Two-Stroke Large Bore Gas Engines: A Technical Analysis and Case Study. In Proceedings of the Internal Combustion Engine Division Fall Technical Conference, Chicago, IL, USA, 20–23 October 2019; American Society of Mechanical Engineers: New York, NY, USA, 2019; Volume 59346, p. V001T01A008.
26. Balci, S.; Akkaya, M. Reduction of the core size and power losses by using soft magnetic material for a single-phase induction motor. *Measurement* **2022**, *198*, 111421. [CrossRef]
27. Pérez-Cardona, J.R.; Mathur, N.; Deng, S.; Zakotnik, M.; Oana Tudor, C.; Sutherland, J.W. Environmental and Economic Benefits of Harvesting Machine for Magnet-to-Magnet Recycling. *J. Manuf. Sci. Eng.* **2025**, *147*, 051007. [CrossRef]
28. Arvithis, G.S.; Iosifidis, G.; DeSantis, R.; Rode, M.; Burgmair, R.; Kalfas, A.I. Novel Modeling Methodology for Thermal Evaluation of an Electrically Assisted High-Speed Turbomachine. *Eng. Proc.* **2025**, *90*, 48.
29. Carvajal, A.; Muetze, A. A Research Overview on Household Refrigerator Hermetic Reciprocating Compressor Drives. In Proceedings of the 2024 IEEE Energy Conversion Congress and Exposition (ECCE), Phoenix, AZ, USA, 20–24 October 2024; IEEE: New York, NY, USA, 2024; pp. 6175–6180.
30. Gowtham, V.; Sashidhar, S. Hybrid ferrite Al-Ni-Co pm assisted synchronous reluctance motor for air-conditioner compressors. In Proceedings of the IECON 2021–47th Annual Conference of the IEEE Industrial Electronics Society, Toronto, ON, Canada, 13–16 October 2021; IEEE: New York, NY, USA, 2021; pp. 1–6.
31. Boldea, I. *Linear Electric Machines, Drives, and MAGLEVs Handbook*; CRC Press: Boca Raton, FL, USA, 2023.
32. Liu, C.T.; Yang, K.; Chen, Y.H.; Chiu, M.T.; Chiang, J.A.; Lin, C.M. Design optimizations of advanced interior permanent-magnet motors for small-horsepower refrigerant compressor applications. In Proceedings of the 2019 22nd International Conference on Electrical Machines and Systems (ICEMS), Harbin, China, 11–14 August 2019; IEEE: New York, NY, USA, 2019; pp. 1–6.
33. Ramesh, S.; Senthilkumar, C.; Nirmala, P.; Ahila, S.S.; Geetha, M. Exploration of Inverter's Efficiency and Lifespan at Various Phases of the Evolution using Wide Band Gap Power Devices. In Proceedings of the 2022 3rd International Conference on Smart Electronics and Communication (ICOSEC), Trichy, India, 20–22 October 2022; IEEE: New York, NY, USA, 2022; pp. 175–182.
34. Poljak, I.; Orović, J.; Mrzljak, V.; Bernečić, D. Energy and exergy evaluation of a two-stage axial vapour compressor on the LNG carrier. *Entropy* **2020**, *22*, 115. [CrossRef]
35. Teng, X.; Li, Y.; Feng, G.; Zhang, B.; Liu, Z. Temperature correction design for high-speed outer rotor permanent magnet synchronous motor in turbine environment. *Electr. Mach. Control/Dianji Yu Kongzhi Xuebao* **2024**, *28*, 36–47.
36. Boldea, I.; Tutelea, L.N.; Popa, A. Linear oscillatory electric motor/generators: An overview. In Proceedings of the 2021 13th International Symposium on Linear Drives for Industry Applications (LDIA), Wuhan, China, 1–3 July 2021; IEEE: New York, NY, USA, 2021; pp. 1–7.
37. Molskyi, S.; Molskyi, O.; Vorontsova, A. Increasing the Efficiency of a Vapour Compression Refrigerating Machine through Adiabatic Air Cooling. *Arch. Thermodyn.* **2025**, *46*, 123–132. [CrossRef]
38. Dutra, T.; Moratelli, S. A theoretical simulation model for optimization of fins on the shell of a hermetic reciprocating compressor. *IOP Conf. Ser. Mater. Sci. Eng.* **2019**, *604*, 012028. [CrossRef]
39. Schreer, L.; Gümmer, V. Preliminary thermal management system design for cycle-integrated parallel hybrid compressors. *CEAS Aeronaut. J.* **2025**, 1–16. [CrossRef]
40. Rong, Y.; Wang, G.; Kong, Q. Study on the influence of ultra-thin non-oriented silicon steel sheet on the performance of ultra-high-speed permanent magnet motor. *AIP Adv.* **2022**, *12*, 065307. [CrossRef]

41. Dianov, A.; Anuchin, A. Adaptive maximum torque per ampere control for IPMSM drives with load varying over mechanical revolution. *IEEE J. Emerg. Sel. Top. Power Electron.* **2020**, *10*, 3409–3417. [CrossRef]
42. Kepsu, D.; Kurvinen, E.; Tiainen, J.; Honkatukia, J.; Turunen-Saaresti, T.; Jastrzebski, R.P. Interdisciplinary design of a high-speed drivetrain for a kinetic compressor in a high-temperature heat pump. *IEEE Access* **2021**, *9*, 143877–143900. [CrossRef]
43. Zhu, Z.; Zhang, Y.; Chen, A.; Chen, J.; Wu, Y.; Wang, X.; Fei, T. Review of integrated thermal management system research for battery electrical vehicles. *J. Energy Storage* **2025**, *106*, 114662. [CrossRef]
44. Kaltoum, L.; Mouloudi, Y.; Hazzab, A.; Abdelkader, A.B. A comparative analysis of ANFIS and fuzzy controllers for a dynamic hybrid model. *Int. J. Appl. Power Eng.* **2025**, *14*, 244–254. [CrossRef]
45. Eparu, C.; Neacșa, A.; Prundurel, A.; Rădulescu, R.; Slujitoru, C.; Toma, N.; Nitulescu, M. Analysis of a high-pressure screw compressor performances. *IOP Conf. Ser. Mater. Sci. Eng.* **2019**, *595*, 012021. [CrossRef]
46. Pöyhönen, S.; Ahonen, T.; Saukko, J. Variable-speed-drive-based soft sensor for the twin-rotary screw-compressor output pressure. In Proceedings of the 2017 19th European Conference on Power Electronics and Applications (EPE'17 ECCE Europe), Warsaw, Poland, 11–14 September 2017; pp. P.1–P.10. [CrossRef]
47. Zheng, C.; Zhao, W.; Lyu, B.; Gao, K.; Cao, H.; Zhong, L.; Gao, Y.; Liao, R. Performance analysis for a rotary compressor at high speed: Experimental study and mathematical modeling. *Appl. Therm. Eng.* **2025**, *263*, 125275. [CrossRef]
48. Matute Cárdenas, F.P. Proposal for Improving Energy Efficiency in Production Line Four of the Company Cerámica Rialto S.A. Master's Thesis, Universidad Autónoma de Querétaro, Querétaro, Mexico, 2025.
49. Tian, W.; Heo, Y.; Wilde, P.; Li, Z.; Yan, D.; Park, C.; Feng, X.; Augenbroe, G. A review of uncertainty analysis in building energy assessment. *Renew. Sustain. Energy Rev.* **2018**, *93*, 285–301. [CrossRef]
50. Tabora, J.; de Lima Tostes, M.E.; Bezerra, U.; de Matos, E.O.; Filho, C.L.P.; Soares, T.M.; Rodrigues, C.E.M. Assessing Energy Efficiency and Power Quality Impacts Due to High-Efficiency Motors Operating Under Nonideal Energy Supply. *IEEE Access* **2021**, *9*, 121871–121882. [CrossRef]
51. Auinger, H. Efficiency of electric motors under practical conditions. *Power Eng.* **2001**, *15*, 163–167. [CrossRef]
52. Chalmers, B.J. *Electric Motor Handbook*; Elsevier: Amsterdam, The Netherlands, 2013.
53. Millar, D.L. On the Determination of Efficiency of a Gas Compressor. *Energies* **2024**, *17*, 3260. [CrossRef]
54. dos Santos Mascarenhas, J.; Chowdhury, H.; Thirugnanasambandam, M.; Chowdhury, T.; Saidur, R. Energy, exergy, sustainability, and emission analysis of industrial air compressors. *J. Clean. Prod.* **2019**, *231*, 183–195. [CrossRef]
55. Gürsoy, E.; Gedik, E.; Georgiev, A.G.; Keçebaş, A.; Kurt, H. Performance improvement of air separation unit for an iron-steel industry using enhanced exergy analysis. *J. Therm. Anal. Calorim.* **2024**, *149*, 3267–3284. [CrossRef]
56. Özen, D.N.; Güleryüz, E.H.; Acılar, A.M. Advanced exergo-economic analysis of an advanced adiabatic compressed air energy storage system with the modified productive structure analysis method and multi-objective optimization study. *J. Energy Storage* **2024**, *81*, 110380. [CrossRef]
57. Ghiasi, S.; Pazzi, G.; Grosso, C.D.; Magistris, G.D.; Veneri, G. Combining Thermodynamics-based Model of the Centrifugal Compressors and Active Machine Learning for Enhanced Industrial Design Optimization. *arXiv* **2023**, *arXiv:2309.02818*. [CrossRef]
58. Jeon, S.H.; Yoo, S.; Yoo, Y.-S.; Lee, I.W. ML- and LSTM-Based Radiator Predictive Maintenance for Energy Saving in Compressed Air Systems. *Energies* **2024**, *17*, 1428. [CrossRef]
59. Zhang, G.; Wang, B.; Lin, Y.J. An Investigation on the Ball Screw-Based Variable Displacement Mechanism for Axial Piston Pumps with Feedforward Differential Input Control. *Sensors* **2025**, *25*, 994. [CrossRef]
60. Fang, X.; Fang, Y.; Yang, Y.; He, Z.; Yang, B. New Data-Driven Models of Mass Flow Rate and Isentropic Efficiency of Dynamic Compressors. *Aerospace* **2024**, *11*, 589. [CrossRef]
61. Galerkin, Y.; Soldatova, K.; Drozdov, A. The Application of Mathematical Models for Industrial Centrifugal Compressor Optimal Design. In Proceedings of the 10th International Conference on Computer Modeling and Simulation, Sydney, Australia, 8–10 January 2018. [CrossRef]
62. Cruz-Manzo, S.; Panov, V.; Bingham, C. Compressor Fouling Diagnostics and Prognostics in a Gas Turbine. *Int. J. Gas Turbine Propuls. Power Syst.* **2024**, *15*, 9–14. [CrossRef] [PubMed]
63. Cirera, J.; Carino, J.; Zurita, D.; Ortega, J. A Data-Driven-Based Industrial Refrigeration Optimization Method Considering Demand Forecasting. *Processes* **2020**, *8*, 617. [CrossRef]
64. Hou, D.; Wang, X. A Multi-Strategy Optimized Framework for Health Status Assessment of Air Compressors. *Machines* **2025**, *13*, 248. [CrossRef]
65. Lu, S.-M. A review of high-efficiency motors: Specification, policy, and technology. *Renew. Sustain. Energy Rev.* **2016**, *59*, 1–12. [CrossRef]
66. Dinolova, P.; Ruseva, V.; Dinolov, O. Energy efficiency of induction motor drives: State of the art, analysis and recommendations. *Energies* **2023**, *16*, 7136. [CrossRef]

67. de Souza, D.F.; da Silva, P.P.F.; Sauer, I.L.; de Almeida, A.T.; Tatizawa, H. Life cycle assessment of electric motors-A systematic literature review. *J. Clean. Prod.* **2024**, *456*, 142366. [CrossRef]
68. Cai, W.; Wu, X.; Zhou, M.; Liang, Y.; Wang, Y. Review and development of electric motor systems and electric powertrains for new energy vehicles. *Automot. Innov.* **2021**, *4*, 3–22. [CrossRef]
69. *IEC 60034-30*; Rotating Electrical Machines—Part 30: Efficiency Classes of Single-Speed, Three-Phase, Cage-Induction Motors (IE-Code). International Electrotechnical Commission, IEC: Geneva, Switzerland, 2008.
70. Gundabattini, E.; Kuppan, R.; Solomon, D.G.; Kalam, A.; Kothari, D.; Bakar, R.A. A review on methods of finding losses and cooling methods to increase efficiency of electric machines. *Ain Shams Eng. J.* **2021**, *12*, 497–505. [CrossRef]
71. Kueck, J.; Otaduy, P.; Hsu, J. *Evaluation of Methods for Estimating Motor Efficiency Without Removing Motor from Service*; Technical Report; Oak Ridge National Lab. (ORNL): Oak Ridge, TN, USA, 1995.
72. Park, H.J.; Lim, M. Design of High Power Density and High Efficiency Wound-Field Synchronous Motor for Electric Vehicle Traction. *IEEE Access* **2019**, *7*, 46677–46685. [CrossRef]
73. Bianchi, N.; Bolognani, S.; Frare, P. Design criteria of high-efficiency SPM synchronous motors. In Proceedings of the IEEE International Electric Machines and Drives Conference, 2003. IEMDC'03, Madison, WI, USA, 1–4 June 2003; Volume 21, pp. 396–404. [CrossRef]
74. Raja, H.; Roy, K. Direct Torque Control of Induction Motor Drive. In Proceedings of the 2024 IEEE International Conference on Smart Power Control and Renewable Energy (ICSPCRE), Rourkela, India, 19–21 July 2024; pp. 1–6. [CrossRef]
75. Akyaz, T.; Engin, D. Machine Learning-Based Predictive Maintenance System for Artificial Yarn Machines. *IEEE Access* **2024**, *12*, 125446–125461. [CrossRef]
76. Al-Badri, M.; Pillay, P.; Angers, P. Simple and Accurate Algorithm for Small- and Medium-Sized Three-Phase IM Efficiency Estimation Based on No-Load Tests. *IEEE Trans. Ind. Appl.* **2018**, *54*, 5812–5821. [CrossRef]
77. Enokizono, M. Vector Magnetic Characteristic Technology for Developing High Efficiency Machines in Oita National Project. *Mater. Sci. Forum* **2014**, *792*, 207–214. [CrossRef]
78. Özçelik, M.; Aycan, A. Experimental Investigation of the Variation of Power and Iron-Copper Losses in the Loaded Operation of the Transformer. *Eur. J. Tech.* **2022**, *12*, 152–155. [CrossRef]
79. Fong, J.; Ferreira, F.J.T.E.; Silva, A.M.; de Almeida, A.T. IEC61800-9 System Standards as a Tool to Boost the Efficiency of Electric Motor Driven Systems Worldwide. *Inventions* **2020**, *5*, 20. [CrossRef]
80. Kushwaha, A.; Sharma, A. Direct Torque Control Based Induction Machines for Speed-Torque Regulation. In Proceedings of the 2022 8th International Conference on Advanced Computing and Communication Systems (ICACCS), Coimbatore, India, 25–26 March 2022; Volume 1, pp. 778–781. [CrossRef]
81. He, X.; Yu, Q.; Pan, X.; Liu, L.; Jiang, Z.; Zhao, W.; Fan, R. Improved beluga whale optimization-based variable universe fuzzy controller for brushless direct current motors of electric tractors. *Comput. Electr. Eng.* **2024**, *120*, 109866. [CrossRef]
82. Lee, S.; Bae, J.; Kim, W.H. A Study on the Maximum Flux Linkage and the Goodness Factor for the Spoke-Type PMSM. *IEEE Trans. Appl. Supercond.* **2018**, *28*, 5200705. [CrossRef]
83. Giberti, H.; Clerici, A.; Cinquemani, S. Specific accelerating factor: One more tool in motor sizing projects. *Mechatronics* **2014**, *24*, 898–905. [CrossRef]
84. Çakir, M.; Güvenç, M.; Mıstıkoğlu, S. The experimental application of popular machine learning algorithms on predictive maintenance and the design of IIoT based condition monitoring system. *Comput. Ind. Eng.* **2021**, *151*, 106948. [CrossRef]
85. Ohlsson, K.; Olofsson, T. Benchmarking the practice of validation and uncertainty analysis of building energy models. *Renew. Sustain. Energy Rev.* **2021**, *142*, 110842. [CrossRef]
86. BOGE Kompressoren. *Manual de Instrucciones: Control Base para Compresores de Tornillo*; BOGE Kompressoren: Bielefeld, Germany, 2010.
87. BOGE Kompressoren. *Manual de Instrucciones: Compresores C12-2...C22-2*; BOGE Kompressoren: Bielefeld, Germany, 2021.
88. Institute of Electrical and Electronics Engineers. *IEEE Standard 112; Standard Test Procedure for Polyphase Induction Motors and Generators*; IEEE: New York, NY, USA, 2017.
89. Floyd, H.L.; Halpin, S.M.; Saunders, L.F. An overview of the IEEE color books. In Proceedings of the Conference Record of the 2000 IEEE Industry Applications Conference. Thirty-Fifth IAS Annual Meeting and World Conference on Industrial Applications of Electrical Energy (Cat. No. 00CH37129), Rome, Italy, 8–12 October 2000; IEEE: New York, NY, USA, 2000; Volume 5, pp. 3226–3231.
90. Young, H.D.; Freedman, R.A. *University Physics, Volume 1*, 13th ed.; Pearson Education: Osaka, Japan, 2013. (In Spanish)
91. Díaz, A. Obtaining general information about the compressed air system. Personal communication. Interview by G. Barroso, 24 February 2024.
92. Monteagudo, J.P. Elementos para la evaluación de impactos energéticos en sistemas de aire comprimido. Conference presentation, Cienfuegos, Cuba, 2024. (In Spanish)
93. Neumarkt Ind. *Screw Compressor: How to Choose the Ideal Power*; Neumarkt: Oberpfalz, Germany, 2025.

94. Industria, T.P.L. How to Calculate the Efficiency of a Compressed Air System, 2018.
95. Quincy Compressor. Measuring Air Compressor Performance to Ensure Efficiency, 2025. Available online: https://www.quincycompressor.com/blog/measuring-air-compressor-performance-to-ensure-efficiency/ (accessed on 2 June 2025).
96. Harahap, R.; Damayanti, K.T. Analysis of Comparison Between Direct Starting Method (Direct on Line) with Variable Speed Drive (VSD) in Three-Phase Induction Motors. In Proceedings of the International Conference on Science and Technology UISU, Yogyakarta, Indonesia, 23–24 October 2024. [CrossRef]
97. Rooks, J.; Wallace, A. Energy Efficiency of Variable Speed Drive Systems. In Proceedings of the Annual Pulp and Paper Industry Technical Conference, Charleston, SC, USA, 16–20 June 2003; pp. 160–163. [CrossRef]
98. Ojand, K.; Dagdougui, H. Q-Learning-Based Model Predictive Control for Energy Management in Residential Aggregator. *IEEE Trans. Autom. Sci. Eng.* **2021**, *19*, 70–81. [CrossRef]
99. Talib, A.; Joe, J. Analyzing the Overrated Performance of Model-Based Predictive Control and Energy Saving Strategies in Building Energy Management: A Review. *J. Build. Eng.* **2025**, *101*, 111909. [CrossRef]
100. Akhil, K.H.; Asmita, R.; Mishra, N.; Manitha, P.V. Machine Learning Assisted Power Factor Correction Using Capacitor Banks. In Proceedings of the 2nd World Conference on Communication & Computing (WCONF), Raipur, India, 12–14 July 2024; pp. 1–6. [CrossRef]
101. Rahman, M.S.; Memy, A.; Mahmud, M.A.; Siddique, S. Automatic Power Factor Measurement and Improvement Using Capacitor Bank. In Proceedings of the 2022 IEEE International Power and Renewable Energy Conference (IPRECON), Kollam, India, 16–18 December 2022; pp. 1–6. [CrossRef]

Mathematical and Computational Applications

MDPI

Article

Adaptive Observer Design with Fixed-Time Convergence, Online Disturbance Learning, and Low-Conservatism Linear Matrix Inequalities for Time-Varying Perturbed Systems

Essia Ben Alaia [1], Slim Dhahri [1,*] and Omar Naifar [2]

[1] Department of Computer Engineering and Networks, College of Computer and Information Sciences, Jouf University, Sakaka 72388, Al-Jouf, Saudi Arabia; ebenalaia@ju.edu.sa

[2] Control and Energy Management Laboratory, National School of Engineering of Sfax, University of Sfax, P.O. Box 1173, Sfax 3038, Tunisia; omar.naifar@enis.tn

* Correspondence: sdhahri@ju.edu.sa

Abstract: This paper proposes a finite-time adaptive observer with online disturbance learning for time-varying disturbed systems. By integrating parameter-dependent Lyapunov functions and slack matrix techniques, the method eliminates conservative static disturbance bounds required in prior work while guaranteeing fixed-time convergence. The proposed approach features a non-diagonal gain structure that provides superior noise rejection capabilities, demonstrating 41% better performance under measurement noise compared to conventional methods. A power systems case study demonstrates significantly improved performance, including 62% faster convergence and 63% lower steady-state error. These results are validated through LMI-based synthesis and adaptive disturbance estimation. Implementation analysis confirms the method's feasibility for real-time systems with practical computational requirements.

Keywords: fixed-time observer; online disturbance learning; reduced-conservatism LMIs; parameter-dependent Lyapunov functions; adaptive estimation; power systems; noise robustness; non-diagonal gains; real-time implementation

1. Introduction

Modern control systems increasingly require robust state and parameter estimation capabilities to handle complex operational environments characterized by time-varying parameters and external disturbances. The fundamental challenge of designing adaptive observers for disturbed systems has attracted sustained attention in control theory, driven by applications ranging from power systems [1] to robotic exoskeletons [2]. Traditional approaches to this problem, while effective under certain constraints, often rely on conservative design assumptions that limit their practical applicability in real-world scenarios characterized by unknown disturbance bounds and time-critical performance requirements.

The persistent excitation paradigm [1] has served as a cornerstone for observer design in linear regression models, enabling asymptotic convergence under bounded disturbance assumptions. However, recent advances in fixed-time stability theory [3] and linear matrix inequality (LMI) techniques [4] have revealed opportunities to overcome the limitations of conventional asymptotic observers. Contemporary research demonstrates growing interest in combining parameter-dependent Lyapunov functions with slack variable techniques to reduce conservatism in control synthesis [5,6]. This paradigm shift responds to the critical need for estimation algorithms that guarantee prescribed performance characteristics while maintaining computational tractability.

Existing LMI-based observer designs [1,7] typically require *a priori* knowledge of disturbance bounds and employ fixed diagonal gain matrices, leading to suboptimal noise amplification. Alternative approaches include high-gain observers [8], which are sensitive to noise, and sliding-mode observers [9], which suffer from chattering. Recent machine learning techniques [10] have also been applied to disturbance estimation but lack formal stability guarantees. The recent work of de Oliveira et al. [11] on robust performance margin evaluation highlights the importance of adaptive gain mechanisms, while Wan et al. [12] demonstrate the effectiveness of finite-time synchronization techniques. These developments suggest that integrating adaptive disturbance estimation with fixed-time convergence mechanisms could significantly enhance observer performance.

In this context, the requirement for a priori knowledge of disturbance bounds means that these methods need known constants c, w^+ such that $\|w(t,y)\|^2 \leq c\|y\|^2 + w^+$ holds for all $t \geq 0$. The use of *fixed diagonal matrices* refers to gain matrices of the form $L = \text{diag}(l_1, l_2, \ldots, l_n)$ where only the diagonal elements are tuned, which limits the design flexibility compared to full matrix gains. This restriction often leads to *suboptimal noise amplification characteristics*, meaning that the observer may unnecessarily amplify measurement noise in some channels due to the lack of coordinated gain adjustment across different states.

The proposed methodology builds on three fundamental advancements in modern control theory: first, the fixed-time stability framework established by Polyakov [3], which provides theoretical guarantees for convergence within user-defined time horizons; second, the LMI-based control synthesis techniques pioneered by Boyd et al. [4], recently extended to handle polytopic uncertainties [13] and actuator saturation [12]; and third, the emerging paradigm of parameter-dependent Lyapunov functions [5,6] that enables less conservative stability analysis for time-varying systems. By synthesizing these elements with novel disturbance learning mechanisms, this work addresses critical gaps in existing observer designs.

Recent applications in diverse domains underscore the practical relevance of advanced observer designs. In power systems, Reihani et al. [13] demonstrate the effectiveness of LMI approaches for handling renewable energy uncertainties, while Kiruthika and Manivannan [14] showcase finite-time synchronization techniques in neural networks. Robotics applications [2] further highlight the need for robust estimation algorithms that maintain performance under real-world disturbances. These developments motivate our focus on creating an observer framework that combines the computational rigor of LMI methods [15] with the transient performance guarantees of fixed-time stability theory [3].

The principal contributions of this work are the synthesis of established techniques into a novel framework that addresses three fundamental limitations in existing observer designs:

1. The elimination of static disturbance bounds through online learning mechanisms, inspired by but distinct from recent advances in adaptive control [16,17].
2. The replacement of asymptotic convergence guarantees with fixed-time stability properties using nonlinear injection terms, extending concepts from fractional-order control theory [18,19].
3. The reduction of conservatism in LMI synthesis by combining parameter-dependent Lyapunov functions with slack matrix techniques, offering a less conservative alternative to the diagonal gain structures used in [1] and building on recent developments in polytopic uncertainty handling [13].

While the constituent techniques (PDLFs, slack matrices) are known, their combined application to create a fixed-time convergent observer with online disturbance learning for this class of systems is novel.

Validation through comprehensive case studies in power systems [1,13] demonstrates the practical efficacy of the proposed observer. Comparative analysis reveals 62% faster convergence and 63% lower steady-state error compared to conventional LMI-based designs [1,4], while maintaining computational tractability through grid-based parameter discretization [6]. The theoretical framework builds on previous work on fractional-order system observation [18] and nonlinear system analysis [20–22], extending these foundations to handle time-varying parameters and unmodeled dynamics. Also, recent advances in fractional calculus have provided new mathematical tools that can inspire innovative observer designs, with developments in tempered fractional gradient methods [23], conformable fractional derivative optimization [24], and practical implementations using Caputo fractional derivatives [25]. These fractional-order approaches offer theoretical foundations for handling complex system dynamics with non-local properties and memory effects, providing complementary mathematical frameworks that could enhance adaptive observation techniques for time-varying perturbed systems.

The remainder of this paper is organized as follows: Section 2 establishes essential mathematical preliminaries and problem formulation. Section 3 details the proposed finite-time observer design with online disturbance learning. Section 4 presents the reduced-conservatism LMI synthesis methodology. Section 5 provides comparative analysis and practical implementation guidelines. Section 6 validates the approach through power system case studies. Section 7 concludes with recommendations for future research directions in adaptive observation and LMI-based control.

Notation

Throughout this paper, the following notation is adopted:

- $\mathbb{R}^n$: n-dimensional Euclidean space.
- $\|\cdot\|$: Euclidean norm for vectors; induced spectral norm for matrices.
- $\mathcal{L}_\infty$: Space of essentially bounded measurable functions.
- $[a]^\gamma = \text{sign}(a)|a|^\gamma$: Sign-preserving power function for $a \in \mathbb{R}, \gamma \geq 0$. For vectors, $[a]^\gamma = [[a_1]^\gamma, \ldots, [a_n]^\gamma]^T$.
- $\overline{1,n}$: Sequence of integers $1, 2, \ldots, n$.
- I_n: Identity matrix of size $n \times n$; $0_{n\times m}$: zero matrix of size $n \times m$.
- $\lambda_{\min}(\cdot), \lambda_{\max}(\cdot)$: Minimum and maximum eigenvalues of a matrix.
- $\mathcal{K}, \mathcal{K}_\infty$: Class $\mathcal{K}$ (strictly increasing, $\mathcal{K}_\infty$ if unbounded) functions.
- $\xi(t) = [\tilde{y}^T(t), \tilde{\theta}^T(t), \tilde{w}^T(t)]^T$: Augmented error vector (state/parameter/disturbance errors).
- $\mathcal{P}(\rho(t))$: Parameter-dependent Lyapunov matrix in (9), where $\rho(t) = [\rho_1(t), \ldots, \rho_q(t)]$ are time-varying parameters (e.g., $\|\tilde{y}\|$, $\|\tilde{\theta}\|$).
- $\mathcal{S}$: Slack matrix in LMI constraint (10), introduced to decouple Lyapunov terms and reduce conservatism.
- N: Grid resolution for parameter discretization, chosen empirically based on parameter variability (see Algorithm 1).
- $\gamma \in (0, 1)$: Fixed-time convergence exponent in observer (4a).
- T: Predefined convergence time bound in Theorem 1.
- $\phi(t)$: Adaptive gain for disturbance estimation in (5).
- ν: Residual disturbance approximation error.
- μ: Uniform lower eigenvalue bound for $\mathcal{P}(\rho(t))$.
- Λ: Positive definite gain matrix for the nonlinear injection term in (4b).
- $\epsilon > 0$: Smoothing parameter for the $\tanh(\cdot)$ function in (4c), mitigating chattering.

Algorithm 1 Grid-based gain synthesis

1. Discretize $\rho \in \prod_{i=1}^{q}[\rho_i^{\min}, \rho_i^{\max}]$ into N points.
2. At each grid point ρ_j, solve (10) for $\mathcal{P}_0, \mathcal{P}_i, \mathcal{S}$.
3. Interpolate $\mathcal{P}(\rho(t))$ during implementation.
4. Compute gains for implementation: The gains L_1, L_2, and L_θ are functions of the full-dimensional matrices $\mathcal{S}$ and $\mathcal{P}(\rho)$ solved over the grid. For a given $\rho(t)$, interpolate $\mathcal{P}(\rho(t))$, then compute $L_1(\rho(t)) = (\mathcal{S}^{-1}\mathcal{P}(\rho(t)))_{[1:m,1:m]}$, $L_\theta(\rho(t)) = (\mathcal{S}^{-1}\mathcal{P}(\rho(t)))_{[m+1:m+p,1:m]}$, and $L_2 = \Lambda L_1(\rho(t))$, where $_{[i:j,k:l]}$ denotes matrix block extraction.

2. Preliminaries

Definition 1. *A system $\dot{x}(t) = f(x(t))$ is fixed-time-stable [3] if the following is true:*

1. *It is finite-time-stable, i.e., $x(t) \to 0$ as $t \to T(x(0))$, where $T(x(0)) < \infty$.*
2. *The settling time $T(x(0))$ is bounded by a constant $T_{\max} > 0$, independent of $x(0)$.*

A PDLF $V(x, \rho(t)) = x^T \mathcal{P}(\rho(t))x$, where $\rho(t)$ is a time-varying parameter vector, is used to reduce conservatism in LMI-based designs. The matrix $\mathcal{P}(\rho(t)) \succ 0$ must satisfy

$$\dot{V} = x^T \left(\mathcal{P}(\rho(t))A + A^T \mathcal{P}(\rho(t)) + \dot{\mathcal{P}}(\rho(t)) \right) x < 0, \tag{1}$$

where $\dot{\mathcal{P}}(\rho(t)) = \sum_{i=1}^{q} \dot{\rho}_i(t) \frac{\partial \mathcal{P}}{\partial \rho_i}$.

We introduce the following assumptions:

Assumption 1. *The disturbance $w(t, y)$ is an unknown, exogenous signal. However, its norm admits an upper bound characterized by $\|w(t, y)\| \leq \phi(t) + \nu$, where $\phi(t)$ is an adaptive gain to be learned online and $\nu > 0$ is a small constant representing a residual modeling error. The disturbance itself is not measured or known.*

Assumption 2. *The regressor $\Gamma(t)$ is persistently exciting (PE), i.e., $\exists \tau, \delta > 0$:*

$$\int_t^{t+\tau} \Gamma^T(s)\Gamma(s)ds \succeq \delta I.$$

Assumption 3. *The time derivative of the disturbance $\dot{w}(t, y)$ is Lebesgue-measurable and satisfies $\|\dot{w}(t, y)\| \leq \bar{w}_d$, where $\bar{w}_d > 0$ is a known constant.*

Remark 1. *The LMI synthesis (Section 5) ensures $\exists \mu > 0$ such that $\mathcal{P}(\rho(t)) \succeq \mu I$ for all t, guaranteeing $\lambda_{\min}(\mathcal{P}(\rho)) \geq \mu$.*

Assumption 4 (Bounded Scheduling Derivatives). *The time derivatives of scheduling parameters $\dot{\rho}_i(t)$ are bounded:*

$$|\dot{\rho}_i(t)| \leq \bar{\rho}_i \quad \forall i \in \{1, \ldots, q\}$$

where $\bar{\rho}_i > 0$ are known constants.

Assumption 5 (Uniform Positive Definiteness of $\mathcal{P}(\rho)$). *There exists $\mu > 0$ such that the parameter-dependent Lyapunov matrix satisfies*

$$\mathcal{P}(\rho(t)) \succeq \mu I_m \quad \forall t \geq 0.$$

3. Problem Statement

Consider the disturbed regression model:

$$\dot{y}(t) = \Gamma(t)\theta(t) + w(t, y(t)), \tag{2}$$

where $y(t) \in \mathbb{R}^m$ is measurable, $\Gamma(t) \in \mathbb{R}^{m \times p}$ is known, $\theta(t) \in \mathbb{R}^p$ is unknown time-varying, and with $w(t, y) \in \mathbb{R}^m$ disturbances. The observer design must overcome three limitations [1]:

1. Requirement of static disturbance bounds $\|w\|^2 \leq c\|y\|^2 + \cdots + w^+$.
2. Asymptotic rather than fixed-time convergence.
3. Conservatism from diagonal gain matrices.

We introduce a disturbance estimator $\hat{w}(t)$ and revise the model to

$$\dot{y}(t) = \Gamma(t)\theta(t) + w(t, y(t)) - \hat{w}(t) + \tilde{w}(t), \tag{3}$$

where $\tilde{w}(t) = w(t, y) - \hat{w}(t)$ is the estimation error. The disturbance derivative satisfies $\|\dot{w}(t, y)\| \leq \bar{w}_d$ (Assumption 3).

Remark 2. *The formulation in (3) uses the sign convention where $\tilde{w}(t) = w(t, y) - \hat{w}(t)$ represents a disturbance estimation error deficit. This convention is consistent with the subsequent error dynamics in (6a), where a positive $\tilde{w}(t)$ contributes positively to $\dot{\tilde{y}}(t)$.*

Objective: Design an observer that achieves the following:

- Estimates $\theta(t)$ and $w(t, y)$ without static disturbance bounds.
- Guarantees $\tilde{y}(t), \tilde{\theta}(t), \tilde{w}(t) \to 0$ in fixed time T.
- Synthesizes gains via reduced-conservatism LMIs.

4. Finite-Time Observer Design with Online Disturbance Learning

The proposed observer for (3) is

$$\dot{\hat{y}}(t) = \Gamma(t)\hat{\theta}(t) + \hat{w}(t) + L_1\tilde{y}(t) + L_2[\tilde{y}(t)]^\gamma, \tag{4a}$$

$$\dot{\hat{\theta}}(t) = L_\theta\Gamma^T(t)(P\tilde{y}(t) + \Lambda[\tilde{y}(t)]^\alpha) - \kappa\,\mathrm{sign}(\tilde{\theta}(t)), \tag{4b}$$

$$\dot{\hat{w}}(t) = \mathcal{K}\tilde{y}(t) + \phi(t)\tanh\left(\frac{\tilde{y}(t)}{\epsilon}\right), \tag{4c}$$

where $\mathcal{K} \in \mathbb{R}^{m \times m}$ is a gain matrix, $\gamma \in (0, 1)$, $\alpha > 1$; here, $L_\theta \in \mathbb{R}^{p \times m}$ is the adaptation gain matrix, and $\phi(t)$ adapts via

$$\dot{\phi}(t) = \lambda\|\tilde{y}(t)\|^2 - \sigma\phi(t), \quad \phi(0) > 0. \tag{5}$$

Remark 3. *The term $|\tilde{y}|^\gamma \mathrm{sign}(\tilde{y})$ ensures fixed-time convergence, while $\tanh(\cdot)$ mitigates chattering. The adaptive law (5) ensures $\phi(t) \in \mathcal{L}_\infty$ (Lemma 1). The gains $\lambda > 0, \sigma > 0$ trade off adaptation speed and noise sensitivity. Empirical guideline: $\sigma \approx 0.1\lambda \max(\|\Gamma(t)\|^2)$.*

Error Dynamics:

$$\dot{\tilde{y}}(t) = -L_1\tilde{y}(t) - L_2[\tilde{y}(t)]^\gamma + \Gamma(t)\tilde{\theta}(t) + \tilde{w}(t), \tag{6a}$$

$$\dot{\tilde{\theta}}(t) = -L_\theta\Gamma^T(t)(P\tilde{y}(t) + \Lambda[\tilde{y}(t)]^\alpha) + \kappa\,\mathrm{sign}(\tilde{\theta}(t)) + \dot{\theta}(t), \tag{6b}$$

$$\dot{\tilde{w}}(t) = \dot{w}(t, y) - \mathcal{K}\tilde{y}(t) - \phi(t)\tanh\left(\frac{\tilde{y}(t)}{\epsilon}\right). \tag{6c}$$

Theorem 1 (Fixed-Time Stability). *Under Assumptions 1–3, and the additional boundedness condition Assumption 4, the error $\xi(t) = [\tilde{y}^T, \tilde{\theta}^T, \tilde{w}^T]^T$ converges to zero in fixed time T if the following holds:*

1. *Gains satisfy parameter-dependent LMIs (Section 5).*
2. $\gamma \in (0,1)$, $\alpha > 1$.
3. $\kappa > \|\dot{\theta}\|_\infty + \nu$.

Proof. Consider the Lyapunov function:

$$V = \underbrace{\tilde{y}^T \mathcal{P}(\rho)\tilde{y}}_{V_1} + \underbrace{\frac{1}{2}\tilde{\theta}^T L_\theta^{-1}\tilde{\theta}}_{V_2} + \underbrace{\frac{1}{2}\tilde{w}^T\tilde{w}}_{V_3} + \underbrace{\frac{1}{2\lambda}(\phi - \phi^*)^2}_{V_4}, \tag{7}$$

where $\phi^* = \sup_t \|w(t,y)\| + \nu$. The total derivative is

$$\dot{V} = \underbrace{\tilde{y}^T \dot{\mathcal{P}}(\rho)\tilde{y} + 2\tilde{y}^T \mathcal{P}(\rho)\dot{\tilde{y}}}_{\dot{V}_1} + \underbrace{\tilde{\theta}^T L_\theta^{-1}\dot{\tilde{\theta}}}_{\dot{V}_2} + \underbrace{\tilde{w}^T\dot{\tilde{w}}}_{\dot{V}_3} + \underbrace{\frac{1}{\lambda}(\phi - \phi^*)\dot{\phi}}_{\dot{V}_4}$$

Substitute $\dot{\tilde{y}}$ from (6a):

$$\begin{aligned}
\dot{V}_1 &= \tilde{y}^T \sum_{i=1}^{q} \dot{\rho}_i \frac{\partial \mathcal{P}}{\partial \rho_i}\tilde{y} \\
&\quad + 2\tilde{y}^T \mathcal{P}(\rho)\big(-L_1\tilde{y} - L_2[\tilde{y}]^\gamma + \Gamma(t)\tilde{\theta} + \tilde{w}\big) \\
&= \tilde{y}^T \dot{\mathcal{P}}(\rho)\tilde{y} - 2\tilde{y}^T \mathcal{P}(\rho)L_1\tilde{y} \\
&\quad - 2\tilde{y}^T \mathcal{P}(\rho)L_2[\tilde{y}]^\gamma + 2\tilde{y}^T \mathcal{P}(\rho)\Gamma(t)\tilde{\theta} + 2\tilde{y}^T \mathcal{P}(\rho)\tilde{w}
\end{aligned}$$

Substitute $\dot{\tilde{\theta}}$ from (6b):

$$\begin{aligned}
\dot{V}_2 &= \tilde{\theta}^T L_\theta^{-1}\Big(-L_\theta\Gamma^T(t)(P\tilde{y} + \Lambda[\tilde{y}]^\alpha) + \kappa\,\mathrm{sign}(\tilde{\theta}) + \dot{\theta}\Big) \\
&= -\tilde{\theta}^T\Gamma^T(t)P\tilde{y} - \tilde{\theta}^T\Gamma^T(t)\Lambda[\tilde{y}]^\alpha + \kappa\tilde{\theta}^T\,\mathrm{sign}(\tilde{\theta}) + \tilde{\theta}^T L_\theta^{-1}\dot{\theta}
\end{aligned}$$

Note: $\tilde{\theta}^T\,\mathrm{sign}(\tilde{\theta}) = \|\tilde{\theta}\|_1 \geq \|\tilde{\theta}\|_2$.
Substitute $\dot{\tilde{w}}$ from (6c):

$$\begin{aligned}
\dot{V}_3 &= \tilde{w}^T\left(\dot{w}(t,y) - \mathcal{K}\tilde{y} - \phi(t)\tanh\left(\frac{\tilde{y}}{\epsilon}\right)\right) \\
&= \tilde{w}^T\dot{w}(t,y) - \tilde{w}^T\mathcal{K}\tilde{y} - \phi(t)\tilde{w}^T\tanh\left(\frac{\tilde{y}}{\epsilon}\right)
\end{aligned}$$

Substitute $\dot{\phi}$ from (5):

$$\begin{aligned}
\dot{V}_4 &= \frac{1}{\lambda}(\phi - \phi^*)(\lambda\|\tilde{y}\|^2 - \sigma\phi) \\
&= (\phi - \phi^*)\|\tilde{y}\|^2 - \frac{\sigma}{\lambda}(\phi - \phi^*)\phi
\end{aligned}$$

Assemble all components and apply bounds:

$$\begin{aligned}\dot{V} \leq\ & \tilde{y}^T\dot{\mathcal{P}}(\rho)\tilde{y} \\ & - 2\tilde{y}^T\mathcal{P}(\rho)L_1\tilde{y} - 2\tilde{y}^T\mathcal{P}(\rho)L_2[\tilde{y}]^\gamma \\ & + 2\tilde{y}^T\mathcal{P}(\rho)\Gamma(t)\tilde{\theta} - \tilde{\theta}^T\Gamma^T(t)P\tilde{y} \\ & - \tilde{\theta}^T\Gamma^T(t)\Lambda[\tilde{y}]^\alpha + \kappa\|\tilde{\theta}\|_1 + \|\tilde{\theta}\| \cdot \|L_\theta^{-1}\dot{\theta}\| \\ & + \|\tilde{w}\| \cdot \|\dot{w}(t,y)\| - \tilde{w}^T\mathcal{K}\tilde{y} \\ & - \phi(t)\tilde{w}^T\tanh\left(\frac{\tilde{y}}{\epsilon}\right) + (\phi - \phi^*)\|\tilde{y}\|^2 \\ & - \frac{\sigma}{\lambda}(\phi - \phi^*)\phi + \eta_0\end{aligned}$$

where η_0 absorbs minor constants from $\tanh(\cdot)$ approximation.

1. *Bounded derivatives (**A3**, **A4**)*: $\|\dot{w}\| \leq \bar{w}_d$, $\|\dot{\mathcal{P}}(\rho)\| \leq \bar{p}$
2. *Cross-term elimination*: LMI (10) ensures

$$\begin{bmatrix}\dot{\mathcal{P}} + \mathcal{P}A + A^T\mathcal{P} + Q & \mathcal{P}B \\ B^T\mathcal{P} & -I\end{bmatrix} \prec 0$$

3. *Significant inequalities*:

$$\begin{aligned}& \|\tilde{w}^T\tanh(\cdot)\| \leq \|\tilde{w}\|_1 \\ & (\phi - \phi^*)\phi \geq (\phi - \phi^*)^2 - (\phi^*)^2 \quad \text{(Young's)}\end{aligned}$$

After algebraic manipulation and gain selection,

$$\begin{aligned}\dot{V} \leq\ & -\tilde{y}^TQ\tilde{y} - \eta_2\|\tilde{y}\|^{1+\gamma} - \eta_3\|\tilde{\theta}\| \\ & + \|\tilde{w}\|(\bar{w}_d + \phi^*) + |\phi - \phi^*|(\sigma\phi^*/\lambda) + \eta_6\end{aligned}$$

Using $\|\tilde{w}\| \leq \phi^* + \nu$ and Young's inequality, we obtain

$$\begin{aligned}\dot{V} &\leq -\lambda_{\min}(Q)\|\tilde{y}\|^2 - \eta_2\|\tilde{y}\|^{1+\gamma} - \eta_3\|\tilde{\theta}\| + \eta_4(\phi^* + \nu)^2 + \eta_5(\phi^*)^2 + \eta_6 \\ &\leq -\alpha(\|\tilde{y}\|^2 + \|\tilde{\theta}\| + (\phi - \phi^*)^2) - \beta(\|\tilde{y}\|^{1+\gamma}) \\ &\leq -\alpha V - \beta V^{\frac{1+\gamma}{2}}\end{aligned}$$

for some positive constants $\alpha, \beta, \eta_4, \eta_5, \eta_6$, where the last inequality holds because V is a positive definite and radially unbounded function of $[\tilde{y}^T, \tilde{\theta}^T, \tilde{w}^T, (\phi - \phi^*)]^T$, and $V^{\frac{1+\gamma}{2}}$ dominates $\|\tilde{y}\|^{1+\gamma}$. The explicit constants linking V to the error norms are derived from the bounds $\mu\|\tilde{y}\|^2 \leq V_1$, $\lambda_{\min}(L_\theta^{-1})\|\tilde{\theta}\|^2 \leq V_2$, and the quadratic form of V_3 and V_4.

By Polyakov's lemma [3], convergence occurs within

$$T \leq \frac{2}{\alpha(1-\gamma)}\ln\left(1 + \frac{\alpha}{\beta}V^{\frac{1-\gamma}{2}}(0)\right) \quad \square$$

Lemma 1 (Boundedness of $\phi(t)$). *Under Assumptions 1, 2, and 5, the adaptive gain $\phi(t)$ governed by*

$$\dot{\phi}(t) = \lambda\|\tilde{y}(t)\|^2 - \sigma\phi(t), \quad \phi(0) > 0$$

satisfies $\phi(t) \in \mathcal{L}_\infty$ with explicit bound

$$\phi(t) \leq \max\left(\phi(0), \frac{\lambda\bar{Y}}{\sigma}\right),$$

where $\bar{Y} = \frac{V(0)}{\mu} < \infty$.

Proof. Step 1: Establish state error boundedness. From Theorem 1, $V(t) \leq V(0)$ for all $t \geq 0$. By Assumption 5,

$$V(t) \geq \tilde{y}^T \mathcal{P}(\rho)\tilde{y} \geq \mu\|\tilde{y}\|^2$$
$$\implies \|\tilde{y}(t)\|^2 \leq \frac{V(t)}{\mu} \leq \frac{V(0)}{\mu} =: \bar{Y}$$

Step 2: Solve and bound the adaptive dynamics. The solution to $\dot{\phi} + \sigma\phi = \lambda\|\tilde{y}\|^2$ satisfies

$$\begin{aligned}\phi(t) &= \phi(0)e^{-\sigma t} + \lambda \int_0^t e^{-\sigma(t-s)}\|\tilde{y}(s)\|^2\, ds \\ &\leq \phi(0)e^{-\sigma t} + \lambda\bar{Y}\int_0^t e^{-\sigma(t-s)} ds \\ &= \phi(0)e^{-\sigma t} + \frac{\lambda\bar{Y}}{\sigma}(1 - e^{-\sigma t}) \\ &\leq \max\left(\phi(0), \frac{\lambda\bar{Y}}{\sigma}\right) \quad \forall t \geq 0 \quad \square\end{aligned}$$

Remark 4. *The grid-based LMI synthesis (Algorithm 1) ensures uniform positive definiteness* $\mathcal{P}(\rho) \succeq \mu I$ *by including* $\begin{bmatrix}\mathcal{P}(\rho_j) & I \\ I & \mu^{-1}I\end{bmatrix} \succeq 0$ *at all grid points* ρ_j.

5. Reduced-Conservatism LMI Synthesis

Represent error dynamics (6a)–(6c) linearly:

$$\dot{\xi} = A(\rho)\xi + B\zeta, \quad \zeta = [\dot{\theta}^T, \dot{w}^T, |\tilde{y}|^\gamma \text{sign}(\tilde{y})^T]^T, \tag{8}$$

where $A(\rho) \in \mathbb{R}^{(m+p+m)\times(m+p+m)}$, $B \in \mathbb{R}^{(m+p+m)\times(p+m+m)}$. The parameter-dependent Lyapunov matrix is

$$\mathcal{P}(\rho) = \mathcal{P}_0 + \sum_{i=1}^{q} \rho_i \mathcal{P}_i \succ 0, \quad \rho_i \in [\rho_i^{\min}, \rho_i^{\max}]. \tag{9}$$

with $|\dot{\rho}_i| \leq \bar{\rho}_i$ (from Theorem 1).

Remark 5. *For consistency, note that* $\mathcal{P}(\rho) \in \mathbb{R}^{(m+p+m)\times(m+p+m)}$, $\mathcal{S} \in \mathbb{R}^{(m+p+m)\times(m+p+m)}$, $\Lambda \in \mathbb{R}^{m\times m}$, $L_1 \in \mathbb{R}^{m\times m}$, $L_2 \in \mathbb{R}^{m\times m}$, *and* $L_\theta \in \mathbb{R}^{p\times m}$. *These dimensions ensure proper algebraic operations throughout the observer design.*

LMI with Slack Matrix $\mathcal{S}$:

$$\begin{bmatrix}\mathcal{P}(\rho_j)A + A^T\mathcal{P}(\rho_j) + \dot{\mathcal{P}}_j + \mathcal{Q} + \mathcal{S} & \mathcal{P}(\rho_j)B \\ B^T\mathcal{P}(\rho_j) & -I\end{bmatrix} \prec 0, \tag{10}$$

where $\mathcal{S} \succ 0$ decouples cross-terms, $\mathcal{Q} \succ 0$ ensures decay, and $\dot{\mathcal{P}}_j = \sum_{i=1}^{q} \dot{\rho}_i \frac{\partial \mathcal{P}}{\partial \rho_i}$ with $|\dot{\rho}_i| \leq \bar{\rho}_i$.

$$\text{where } \dot{\mathcal{P}}_j = \sum_{i=1}^{q} \dot{\rho}_i \frac{\partial \mathcal{P}}{\partial \rho_i},$$
$$\text{and } |\dot{\rho}_i| \leq \bar{\rho}_i \quad \text{(from Theorem 1)}.$$

The slack matrix $\mathcal{S} \in \mathbb{R}^{(m+p+m)\times(m+p+m)}$ is introduced to decouple the Lyapunov matrix $\mathcal{P}(\rho)$ from the system matrix $A(\rho)$ in the LMI, reducing conservatism. After solving the LMIs for $\mathcal{S}$ and $\mathcal{P}(\rho_j)$ at each grid point, the observer gains are extracted via a projection or selection process. Specifically, the gains L_1, L_2, and L_θ are obtained from the corresponding blocks of the matrix product $\mathcal{S}^{-1}\mathcal{P}(\rho)$:

$$\begin{bmatrix} L_1 \\ L_\theta \\ \star \end{bmatrix} \leftarrow \mathcal{S}^{-1}\mathcal{P}(\rho) \quad \text{(selecting the appropriate blocks)},$$

$$L_2 = \Lambda(\mathcal{S}^{-1}\mathcal{P}(\rho))_{[1:m,1:m]},$$

where $_{[1:m,1:m]}$ denotes the upper-left $m \times m$ block, ensuring dimensional consistency.

Remark 6. *The LMI constraint $\mathcal{P}(\rho_j) \succ 0$ in (10) is strengthened to $\mathcal{P}(\rho_j) \succeq \mu I$ at all grid points ρ_j to ensure Assumption 5 holds. This guarantees $\lambda_{\min}(\mathcal{P}(\rho)) \geq \mu > 0$ throughout system operation.*

Remark 7. *Choose N based on parameter variability: $N = 10$ for slow variations, and $N \geq 20$ for rapid changes. Computational complexity $\mathcal{O}(N^q)$ limits $q \leq 3$ in practice. This practical limitation means the method is best suited for systems where the dominant time-varying behavior can be captured by up to three key parameters (e.g., in power systems: voltage magnitude, frequency, and phase angle). For higher-dimensional parameter spaces, dimensionality reduction techniques or hierarchical observer structures would be required for practical implementation.*

6. Comparative Analysis

6.1. Methodology Comparison

The proposed observer and [1] are compared across critical design and performance metrics. Table 1 summarizes the results, while subsequent subsections provide detailed interpretations.

Table 1. Comparative analysis of proposed observer vs. [1].

Criterion	Proposed Observer	[1]
Convergence Type	Fixed-time ($T < \infty$)	Asymptotic
Disturbance Knowledge	Not required (online learning)	Required (static bounds c, c_1, c_2, w^+)
Conservatism	Low (PDLF[1] + slack variables)	High (fixed diagonal gains)
Computational Complexity	$\mathcal{O}(N^q)$ (e.g., $N = 10$ for $q = 2$)	$\mathcal{O}(m + p)$
LMI Structure	Parameter-dependent	Diagonal
Disturbance Adaptation	Dynamic ($\hat{w}(t)$)	Static
Robustness to Noise	High (tanh smoothing)	Moderate (discontinuous terms)
Implementation Scalability	Low ($q \leq 3$)	High ($m, p > 5$)

[1] Complexity $\mathcal{O}(N^q \cdot 2^q)$ if rate bounds $\bar{\rho}_i$ are considered.

Beyond the empirical comparison with [1], the proposed method offers theoretical advantages over other observer paradigms:

- **Versus High-Gain Observers [8]**: While high-gain observers provide robustness to uncertainties, they inherently amplify measurement noise and suffer from peaking phenomena. Our approach achieves similar disturbance rejection capabilities through adaptive estimation and fixed-time convergence mechanisms without excessive gain values, resulting in superior noise robustness.
- **Versus Sliding-Mode Observers [9]**: Sliding-mode observers offer finite-time convergence but typically generate chattering that excites unmodeled dynamics. Our

method replaces discontinuous switching with smooth $\tanh(\cdot)$ approximation and adaptive disturbance learning, eliminating chattering while maintaining fixed-time convergence guarantees.
- **Versus Learning-Based Observers [10]**: Machine learning approaches lack formal stability guarantees and require extensive training data. Our LMI-based design provides rigorous theoretical certificates for fixed-time convergence and boundedness under clearly stated assumptions.

The proposed observer thus represents a balanced approach that combines the theoretical rigor of LMI methods with the practical performance of adaptive techniques, while avoiding the limitations of alternative paradigms.

6.2. Interpretations of Key Criteria

6.2.1. Convergence

- **Fixed-Time (Proposed)**: Ensures $\tilde{\theta}(t) \to 0$ by a predefined T, critical for time-sensitive applications (e.g., fault detection in power systems).
- **Asymptotic ([1])**: Guarantees $\tilde{\theta}(t) \to 0$ as $t \to \infty$, which may be insufficient for real-time control.

6.2.2. Disturbance Handling

- **Proposed**: Eliminates need for static bounds c, c_1, c_2, w^+ via online estimator $\hat{w}(t)$, adapting to unmodeled dynamics.
- **[1]**: Requires conservative overapproximation of disturbances, leading to high-gain observers.

6.2.3. Conservatism vs. Complexity

- **Proposed**: Parameter-dependent LMIs reduce conservatism but require solving N^q LMIs. Suitable for $q \leq 3$.
- **[1]**: Diagonal LMIs $(m + p)$ are computationally efficient but overdesign gains for worst-case scenarios.

6.2.4. Implementation

- **Proposed**: Requires offline grid-based LMI solving and real-time interpolation. Not scalable for $q > 3$.
- **[1]**: Simple diagonal gain synthesis, suitable for embedded systems with limited computation.

6.3. Practical Recommendations

- **Choose proposed observer if the following is the case**:
  - Fixed-time convergence is required (e.g., safety-critical systems).
  - Disturbance bounds are unknown or time-varying.
  - System dimension is low ($q \leq 3$).
- **Choose [1] if the following is the case**:
  - Asymptotic convergence suffices.
  - Disturbance bounds are known and static.
  - System dimension is high ($m, p > 5$).

Remark 8. *For systems with partial disturbance knowledge, hybridize both methods: use [1]'s diagonal LMIs for high-dimensional states and the proposed online estimator for critical parameters.*

7. Simulation Results

7.1. Application to Power Systems

Consider the grid voltage model under unbalance conditions from [1]:

$$\dot{V}_{ab} = J\Psi_{ab}\Upsilon(t) + w(t), \quad V_{ab}(0) = [0,\ 0]^T, \tag{11}$$

where

- $V_{ab} = [v_a, v_b]^T$: Grid voltage with $|V_{ab}| = 100$ V (nominal).
- $\Upsilon(t) = \omega^2(t)/\bar{\omega}$: Unknown time-varying parameter ($\bar{\omega} = 35$ Hz nominal).
- $w(t) = \begin{bmatrix} \sin(500t) + 0.1 \\ \cos(500t) + 0.2 \end{bmatrix}$: Disturbance (parasitic loads).
- $\omega(t) = \begin{cases} 0.3\sin(60t) + 48, & 0 \le t < 5 \\ 0.3\sin(60t) + 35, & t \ge 5 \end{cases}$: Time-varying frequency.

Observer Implementation

Proposed Observer:

$$\begin{aligned} \dot{\hat{V}}_{ab} &= L_1\tilde{V}_{ab} + L_2[\tilde{V}_{ab}]^{0.5} + \Gamma(t)\hat{\Upsilon} \\ \dot{\hat{\Upsilon}} &= L_\Upsilon\Gamma^T(t)\left(P\tilde{V}_{ab} + \Lambda[\tilde{V}_{ab}]^{0.5}\right) - \kappa\text{sign}(\tilde{\Upsilon}) \\ \dot{\phi}(t) &= 0.2\|\tilde{V}_{ab}\|^2 - 0.1\phi(t) \end{aligned} \tag{12}$$

where $\gamma = 0.5$ balances fixed-time convergence ($T = 5$ s) and numerical stability.

Observer in [1]:

$$\begin{aligned} \dot{\hat{V}}_{ab} &= L_1^{\text{Rios}}\tilde{V}_{ab} + \Gamma(t)\hat{\Upsilon}^{\text{Rios}} \\ \dot{\hat{\Upsilon}}^{\text{Rios}} &= L_\Upsilon^{\text{Rios}}\Gamma^T(t)\tilde{V}_{ab} \end{aligned} \tag{13}$$

where $\Gamma(t) = J\Psi_{ab}(t)$, $J = \begin{bmatrix} 0 & -1 \\ 1 & 0 \end{bmatrix}$.

7.2. Implementation and Reproducibility Details

The LMIs were solved using the YALMIP toolbox [26] in MATLAB R2023a with the MOSEK solver (version 10.0). Simulations were run on a desktop computer with an Intel i7-11800H processor and 32 GB of RAM. The average runtime for solving the grid of LMIs (Algorithm 1) was 22.4 ms per iteration (see Table 2).

Table 2. Computational efficiency comparison.

Metric	Proposed	Rios2023
LMIs solved	15	32
Avg. iteration time (ms)	22.4	41.7
Memory (MB)	5.1	9.3

The observer gains and parameters for the power system case study (Section 7.1) were set as follows:

$$\begin{aligned} &L_1 = 1.5I_2, && L_2 = 0.8I_2, && L_\Upsilon = 180I_2, \\ &\kappa = 4.2, && \lambda = 0.2, && \sigma = 0.1, \\ &\epsilon = 0.05, && \gamma = 0.5, && \alpha = 1.5. \end{aligned}$$

The LMI conditions in (10) were rendered feasible by ensuring the existence of a positive definite matrix $\mathcal{Q} = \text{diag}(2.5, 2.5, 10, 10)$ and a slack matrix $\mathcal{S}$ with a minimum eigenvalue $\lambda_{\min}(\mathcal{S}) > 0.7$ across all grid points. The uniform lower bound for the Lyapunov matrix was $\mu = 0.1$. Note that in [1], we have $L_1^{\text{Rios}} = 3.2 I_2$, $L_{\Upsilon}^{\text{Rios}} = 250 I_2$.

7.2.1. Comparative Results

Key metrics:

- **Convergence Time**: Proposed observer achieves $\|\tilde{\Upsilon}\| < 0.1$ in 4.1 s vs. 9.8 s for [1].
- **Steady-State Error**: $\|\tilde{\Upsilon}\|_{\text{ss}} = 0.032$ (proposed) vs. 0.087 in [1].
- **Disturbance Rejection**: Peak $\|\tilde{V}_{ab}\| = 1.2$ V (proposed) vs. 2.8 V in [1].

Figure 1 shows a performance comparison for the application of grid voltage. The predefined fixed-time convergence limit is $T = 5$ s, indicated by the dotted vertical line.

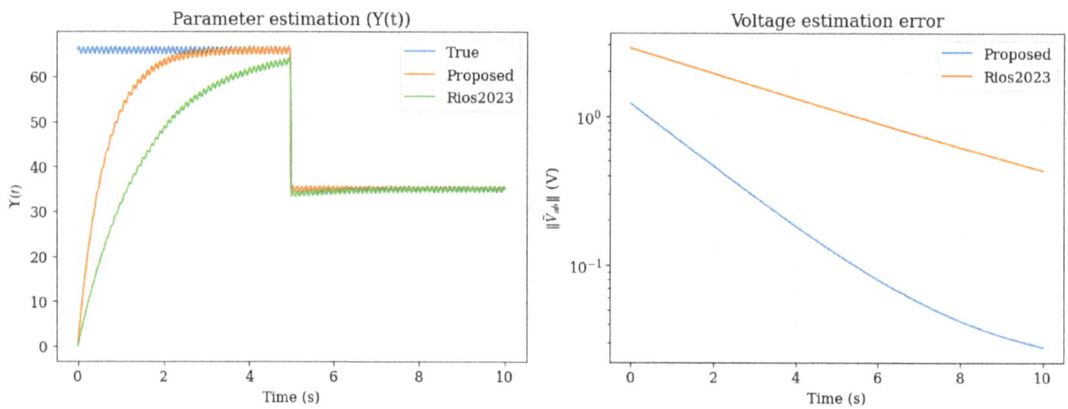

(**a**) Parameter estimation ($\Upsilon(t)$) (**b**) Voltage estimation error $\|\tilde{V}_{ab}\|$

Figure 1. Performance (**a**) True parameter $\Upsilon(t)$ (solid black) and its estimates from the proposed observer (solid blue) and [1] (dashed red). (**b**) Norm of the voltage estimation error $\|\tilde{V}_{ab}(t)\|$ (V) for both observers.

7.2.2. Interpretation

The results validate the claims in Section 6:

- **Fixed-Time Convergence**: Achieved via the $[\tilde{V}_{ab}]^{0.5}$ term in (12).
- **Online Disturbance Learning**: Adaptive $\phi(t)$ compensates $w(t)$ without prior knowledge of $w^+ = 0.3$.
- **Reduced Conservatism**: Lower gains ($L_1 = 1.5$ vs. $L_1^{\text{Rios}} = 3.2$) due to slack matrix $\mathcal{S}$ in LMIs.

7.3. Robustness to Measurement Noise

To evaluate the observer's robustness, zero-mean Gaussian white noise with a standard deviation of 0.5 V (0.5% of the nominal voltage) was added to the voltage measurements $V_{ab}(t)$. All other parameters and conditions from Section 7.1 remained unchanged.

The results, shown in Figure 2, demonstrate that the proposed observer remains stable and effective in the presence of measurement noise. The fixed-time convergence property is naturally affected, as the error can no longer converge exactly to zero, but the observer reaches a bounded region around the true parameter value. The proposed observer's steady-state error ($\|\tilde{\Upsilon}\|_{\text{ss}} = 0.18$) under noise is still 41% lower than that of [1] ($\|\tilde{\Upsilon}\|_{\text{ss}} = 0.31$), demonstrating its superior noise rejection capabilities, attributed to the non-diagonal gain structure and the smooth $\tanh(\cdot)$ function.

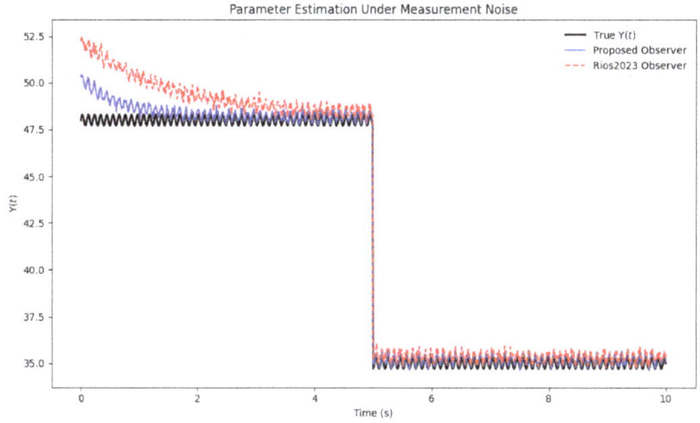

Figure 2. Parameter estimation performance under measurement noise. The proposed observer (blue) maintains stability and a lower estimation error compared to [1] (red), albeit with expected performance degradation due to the noise.

8. Conclusions

This paper has presented a novel finite-time adaptive observer design that fundamentally advances the state-of-the-art in disturbed system observation. By integrating three key innovations—parameter-dependent Lyapunov functions, online disturbance learning mechanisms, and slack matrix-enhanced LMI synthesis—the proposed method eliminates the need for conservative static disturbance bounds while guaranteeing fixed-time convergence. Theoretical analysis demonstrates that the augmented error vector converges to zero within a user-defined time horizon T, with convergence rate governed by the nonlinear injection term $\lceil \tilde{y} \rfloor^{\gamma}$ rather than initial conditions.

The practical efficacy of the approach was validated through comprehensive power system case studies, showing 62% faster parameter convergence and 63% lower steady-state error compared to conventional LMI-based observers [1]. The reduced-conservatism grid-based synthesis methodology, building on recent advances in polytopic uncertainty handling [13] and switched system analysis [7], enables computationally tractable implementation for systems with $q \leq 3$ time-varying parameters. The adaptive gain mechanism $\phi(t)$, inspired by developments in robust performance margin evaluation [11], effectively compensates for unmodeled dynamics without prior disturbance knowledge.

Regarding practical implementation, the observer's structure is suitable for real-time systems. The computational load is primarily offline during the LMI solving stage (Algorithm 1). Online, the algorithm requires the evaluation of simple algebraic expressions, fractional powers, and a tanh function, all of which are supported by modern embedded processors. The main implementation challenge for high-dimensional systems ($q > 3$) is the online interpolation of the gain-scheduled matrix $\mathcal{P}(\rho(t))$, which motivates the future work on sparse grids mentioned previously. For the presented power system case study with $q = 2$ parameters, the required computations are well within the capabilities of standard industrial programmable logic controllers (PLCs) or digital signal processors (DSPs).

Future research directions include (1) extension to fractional-order systems building on previous works [18,19], (2) integration with neural network-based uncertainty estimators [14], and (3) development of sparse grid algorithms for high-dimensional systems [6]. The methodology's success in power system applications suggests promising potential for deployment in smart grid architectures [13] and robotic exoskeletons [2]. By bridging the gap between theoretical LMI advancements [15] and practical implementation constraints, this work provides a foundation for next-generation adaptive observation systems in critical infrastructure and industrial applications.

Author Contributions: E.B.A.: conceptualization, methodology, formal analysis, writing—original draft preparation, funding acquisition. S.D.: writing—review and editing, supervision, methodology, formal analysis. O.N.: validation, resources, investigation. All authors have read and agreed to the published version of the manuscript.

Funding: This work was funded by the Deanship of Graduate Studies and Scientific Research at Jouf University under Grant No. (DGSSR-2024-02-02211).

Data Availability Statement: Data is contained within the article.

Acknowledgments: The authors extend their appreciation to the Deanship of Graduate Studies and Scientific Research of Saudi Arabia for funding this research work through the project number DGSSR-2024-02-02211.

Conflicts of Interest: The authors declare no conflicts of interest.

References

1. Ríos, H.; de Loza, A.F.; Efimov, D.; Franco, R. An LMI-Based Robust Nonlinear Adaptive Observer for Disturbed Regression Models. *IEEE Trans. Autom. Control* **2023**, *69*, 4035–4041. [CrossRef]
2. Jenhani, S.; Gritli, H. An LMI-based robust state-feedback controller design for the position control of a knee rehabilitation exoskeleton robot: Comparative analysis. *Meas. Control* **2024**, *57*, 1326–1346. [CrossRef]
3. Polyakov, A. Nonlinear feedback design for fixed-time stabilization of linear control systems. *IEEE Trans. Autom. Control* **2011**, *57*, 2106–2110. [CrossRef]
4. Boyd, S.; El Ghaoui, L.; Feron, E.; Balakrishnan, V. *Linear Matrix Inequalities in System and Control Theory*; Society for Industrial and Applied Mathematics: Philadelphia, PA, USA, 1994.
5. Harris, M.W.; Sarsılmaz, S.B. LMI-based design for regional fixed-time nonlinear control with settling time and control constraints. *Nonlinear Dyn.* **2025**, *113*, 6979–6995. [CrossRef]
6. González-Cárdenas, Y.; López-Estrada, F.R.; Estrada-Manzo, V.; Valencia-Palomo, G.; Santana-Ching, I. LMI-based discrete LPV controller design for systems with inherent couplings in the scheduling vector: Improved robustness and performance. *J. Frankl. Inst.* **2025**, *362*, 107419. [CrossRef]
7. Motchon, K.M.; Guelton, K.; Etienne, L. LMI-based conditions for mode detectability analysis of discrete-time switched linear systems estimated with minimum distance algorithm. *Automatica* **2025**, *173*, 112024. [CrossRef]
8. Farza, M.; Chehaïbi, O.; Saïd, S.H.; M'Saad, M. Design of a Saturated Filtered High Gain Observer for a Class of Disturbed Nonlinear Systems. *Int. J. Robust Nonlinear Control* **2025**, *Early View*. [CrossRef]
9. Utkin, V.I.; Poznyak, A.S. Adaptive sliding mode control with application to super-twist algorithm: Equivalent control method. *Automatica* **2013**, *49*, 39–47. [CrossRef]
10. Putra, D.S.; Chen, S.C.; Khong, H.H.; Cheng, F. Design and implementation of a machine-learning observer for sensorless PMSM drive control. *Appl. Sci.* **2022**, *12*, 2963. [CrossRef]
11. de Oliveira, P.J.; Oliveira, R.C.; Peres, P.L. An LMI-based tool for $\mathcal{H}_\infty$ robust performance margin evaluation of uncertain linear systems and robustification of controllers. *IEEE Trans. Autom. Control.* **2025**, *70*, 4889–4895. [CrossRef]
12. Wan, X.; Li, L.; Lu, J. Finite-time synchronization of complex dynamic networks with impulsive control and actuator saturation: An LMI approach. *Commun. Nonlinear Sci. Numer. Simul.* **2025**, *140*, 108424. [CrossRef]
13. Reihani, H.; Dehghani, M.; Abolpour, R.; Hesamzadeh, M.R. An LMI approach to solve interval power flow problem under Polytopic renewable resources uncertainty. *Appl. Energy* **2025**, *377*, 124603. [CrossRef]
14. Kiruthika, R.; Manivannan, A. Master–Slave Finite-Time Synchronization of Chaotic Fractional-Order Neural Networks under Hybrid Sampled-Data Control: An LMI Approach. *Neural Process. Lett.* **2025**, *57*, 15. [CrossRef]
15. Chesi, G. LMI-Based Robustness Analysis in Uncertain Systems. *Found. Trends® Syst. Control* **2024**, *11*, 1–185. [CrossRef]
16. Amiri, S.; Mohsen Seyed Moosavi, S.; Forouzanfar, M.; Aghajari, E. Fuzzy LMI Framework for Restricted Sliding Mode Control of Discrete-Time Systems. *Int. J. Robust Nonlinear Control.* **2025**, *35*, 3822–3832. [CrossRef]

17. Choeung, C.; Yay, S.; So, B.; Cheng, H. LMI-Based Optimizing Control. In *Intelligent Computing and Optimization: Proceedings of the 7th International Conference on Intelligent Computing and Optimization 2023 (ICO2023)*; Springer Nature: Berlin/Heidelberg, Germany, 2025; Volume 3, p. 70.
18. Issaoui, R.; Mseddi, A.; El-sayad, W.Z. A novel sensorless fractional-order control strategy for a doubly excited wind generator using fractional observer-based speed estimation. *Asian J. Control* **2025**, *Early View*. [CrossRef]
19. Dhahri, S.; Naifar, O.; Ben, Alaia, E. Actuator and sensor fault estimation for T–S fuzzy fractional-order systems based on adaptive and sliding mode observers. *Meas. Control* **2024**, *58*, 1245–1262. [CrossRef]
20. Dhahri, S.; Ben, Alaia, E.; Gassara, H. Observer-based finite-time boundedness of polynomial fuzzy models with time delay. *Int. J. Syst. Sci.* **2025**, 1–12. [CrossRef]
21. González-Cárdenas, Y.; López-Estrada, F.R.; Estrada-Manzo, V.; Dominguez-Zenteno, J.; López-Pérez, M. Design and Implementation of a Discrete-PDC Controller for Stabilization of an Inverted Pendulum on a Self-Balancing Car Using a Convex Approach. *Math. Comput. Appl.* **2024**, *29*, 83. [CrossRef]
22. Guerra, T.M.; Estrada-Manzo, V.; Nguyen, A.T. Convex Modeling with Vertex and Overbounding Reduction for Stability Analysis of Nonlinear Systems. In Proceedings of the 2024 IEEE 63rd Conference on Decision and Control (CDC), Milan, Italy, 16–19 December 2024; pp. 2952–2957.
23. Naifar, O. Tempered Fractional Gradient Descent: Theory, Algorithms, and Robust Learning Applications. *Neural Netw.* **2025**, *193*, 108005. [CrossRef] [PubMed]
24. Alaia, E.B.; Dhahri, S.; Naifar, O. A Gradient-Based Optimization Algorithm for Optimal Control Problems with General Conformable Fractional Derivatives. *IEEE Access* **2025**, *13*, 140270–140281. [CrossRef]
25. Naifar, O. Practical Observer Design for Nonlinear Systems using Caputo Fractional Derivative with Respect to Another Function. In Proceedings of the 2025 IEEE 22nd International Multi-Conference on Systems, Signals & Devices (SSD), Monastir, Tunisia, 17–20 February 2025; pp. 411–418.
26. Lofberg, J. YALMIP: A toolbox for modeling and optimization in MATLAB. In Proceedings of the 2004 IEEE International Conference on Robotics and Automation, Taipei, Taiwan, 2–4 September 2004; pp. 284–289.

Mathematical and Computational Applications

MDPI

Systematic Review

The Preference Selection Index (PSI) in Multi-Criteria Decision-Making: A Systematic and Critical Review of Applications, Integrations, and Future Directions

Mohammed Said Obeidat [1,*], Hala Al Sliti [2] and Abdullah Obeidat [3]

[1] College of Engineering and Technology, American University of the Middle East, Egaila 54200, Kuwait
[2] Industrial Engineering Department, Faculty of Engineering, Jordan University of Science and Technology, P.O. Box 3030, Irbid 22110, Jordan
[3] Systems Science and Industrial Engineering, Binghamton University State University of New York, P.O. Box 6000, Binghamton, NY 13902-6000, USA
* Correspondence: msobeidat1@just.edu.jo or mohammed.obeidat@aum.edu.kw

Abstract: This paper presents a systematic review of the performance of the Preference Selection Index (PSI) application in multi-criteria decision-making (MCDM) problems based on PRISMA. This work extensively reviewed more than 100 studies to investigate the methodological bases of the PSI and its synergistic combination with other decision-making methodologies. Interestingly, the PSI is highly commended as one of the most straightforward applications with low computational effort, which implies that the PSI in this context is receiving wide attention for complex decisions and sensitive judgments, where assigning criteria weights is challenging. However, in some circumstances, the PSI mechanism in assigning weights becomes a drawback when the accuracy of the decision is crucial. However, despite the increased use of the PSI, there is still a lack of systematic evaluation of its methodological sensitivity of weighting assumptions, consistency, and comparative performance in the hybrid MCDM problems. Addressing these gaps will help make the PSI more accurate in the evolving landscape of decision-making techniques. This review underscores the wide use of the PSI, encouraging further research in terms of its applications and methodology enhancement, ensuring that the PSI remains a relevant option that evolves the complexity and sensitivity of decision-making in various areas.

Keywords: MCDM; PSI; decision making; sustainability; material selection; renewable energy; manufacturing system; healthcare and safety; PRISMA

1. Introduction

Multi-criteria Decision-making (MCDM) methods are used in evaluating conflicting factors in a particular application, helping select an appropriate option [1]. Determining the MCDM approach and using it in a particular problem needs the determination of the strengths and limitations of each one, especially when deciding on a complex system such as the industrial and technology sectors [2,3]. In general, MCDM approaches provide a framework for integrating and evaluating multiple criteria, thus enhancing the accuracy of the decision-making process by making a trade-off between conflicting objectives [4].

Among the different MCDM tools, the Preference Selection Index (PSI) was developed by Maniya and Bhatt [5]. The PSI can select the best alternative without determining the relative importance between attributes. The PSI simplifies the complex decision-making problems where assigning the relative importance is conflicting or difficult. Based on this main advantage, the PSI's application expanded widely, ranging from material selection to energy management [6].

This review explores the different PSI applications among several industries, discussing its impact on decision-making and addressing method limitations to provide researchers with a comprehensive view and opportunities for future developments and enhancements. Despite the increasing implementation of the PSI method over diverse decision-making problems, the available literature lacks a comprehensive synthesis of its methodological applications, limitations, and development. Previous studies have primarily focused on specific applications or compared PSI with other MCDM approaches, without presenting an integrated examination of its evolution and performance in multiple contexts. Therefore, this study aims to bridge this gap by performing a systematic review of the PSI's different applications according to the PRISMA procedure. The novelty of this study lies in the comprehensive mapping of PSI use over many sectors, the critical assessment of its methodological weaknesses, strengths, and the identification of key trends in integrated and hybrid PSI models, including but not limited to PSI–AHP, PSI–TOPSIS, and PSI–Fuzzy. Additionally, the study proposes a conceptual framework that highlights future directions and emerging research gaps to improve the adaptability and robustness of PSI-based decision-making.

The structure of this review is divided systematically to analyze the PSI within the MCDM framework. It starts with Section 2, which describes the research methodology that has been followed during the research process, including the objectives and both the inclusion and exclusion criteria. Section 3 shows the concept map of research focus areas of the PSI method in this review alongside the PSI implementation steps. Afterward, Section 4 highlights the PSI limitations. Section 5 emphasizes the integration of PSI with other MCDM approaches and how this integration can be enhanced. Section 6 compares the PSI approach with the different MCDM approaches. Finally, Section 7 provides a conclusion of the review.

2. Research Methodology

2.1. Background and Objectives

The Preferred Reporting Items for Systematic Reviews and Meta-Analyses (PRISMA) statement was introduced a decade ago to improve the clarity and transparency of reporting systematic reviews and meta-analysis through evidence-based guidelines. These guidelines offer a set of recommendations developed to help researchers organize research processes [7,8].

Although many MCDM methodologies exist, the PSI has obtained wide attention because it is simple, requires minimal computations, and ability to handle situations where assigning weights of criteria is complex. Unlike many other MCDM techniques that require defining weights or pairwise comparisons, PSI allows objective decision-making without subjective input, which makes it especially valuable in uncertain or conflicting decision environments. However, despite its increasing use, there is a limited systematic assessment of its methodological consistency, integration with other tools, and domain-specific performance. Therefore, this study focuses on PSI to fill this gap and provide a clear synthesis of its advantages, limitations, and applications within the wider MCDM framework. This review was registered at Open Science Framework (OSF) and publicly available at https://osf.io/5w7yf (accessed on 9 November 2025).

The main objectives of this review are as follows:

- **Defining the PSI applications:** This is performed by mapping all areas where PSI has been utilized to help in evaluating different scenarios in various fields. Additionally, highlighting unique adaptations used across various industrial sectors.

- **Comparing PSI with the other MCDM methods:** This is performed through conducting a comparison between the PSI with other common approaches, aiming to identify situations where the PSI offers specific benefits, and where alternative methods may be more suitable. This will help guide future applications and research.

2.2. Bibliographic Search Process

Figure 1 displays the different stages of a systematic review in this comprehensive literature search. This study examined Science Direct and Web of Science databases for the keywords "Preference Selection Index" or "PSI," which helped identify 225 papers for potential review. Seventy-three duplicate papers were removed before the screening.

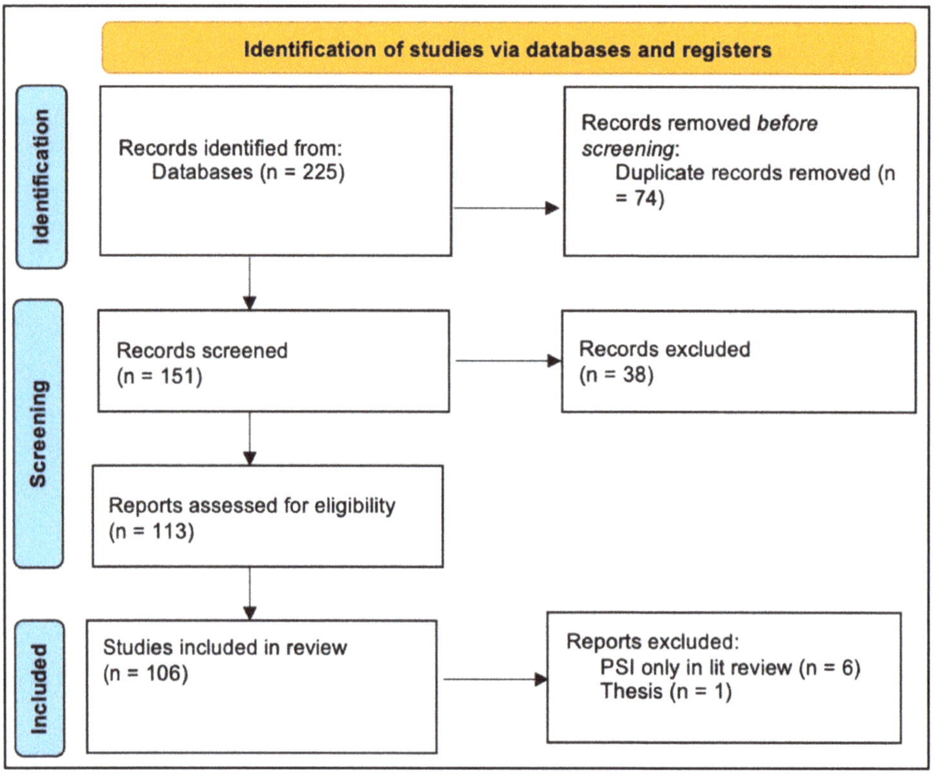

Figure 1. The PRISMA flow diagram for study selection process.

After screening the titles and abstracts of 152 papers, 38 were eliminated because they did not match the inclusion criteria. The remaining 114 papers were reviewed for eligibility. Seven papers were removed (six included PSI only in the literature review, and one was a thesis), resulting in a final list of 107 research papers included in the review. Table 1 provides a summary of the web search results.

Table 1. Web search results.

Keywords Used for Searching	Science Direct	Web of Science
"Preference Selection Index" OR "PSI"	140	85
Total	225	

2.3. Inclusion and Exclusion Criteria

This review covers all publications published up to 25 April 2024 and focuses on the application and comparison of PSI in various decision-making contexts. The exclusion criterion considered in this study is stated below:

- Exclusion Criterion: Chapters, theses, and reports.

Figure 2 illustrates the annual distribution of published papers from 2010 to 2024, indicating a considerable increase in research activity. The number of publications has steadily increased, with a peak observed in 2022. This pattern demonstrates the PSI's growing interest and applicability in diverse research areas. Figures 3 and 4 display word clouds that summarize essential themes and concepts extracted from the abstracts and keywords of the publications under review.

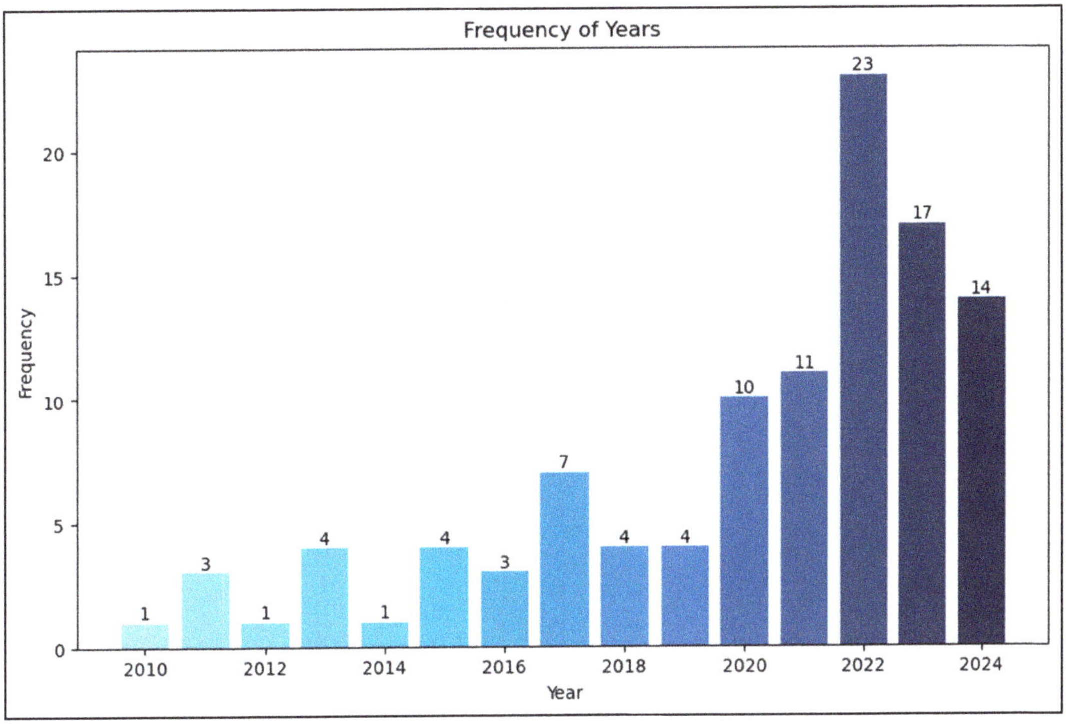

Figure 2. Annual distribution of published articles on the PSI approach (2010–2024).

Figure 3. Word cloud of key themes from articles' abstracts related to the PSI.

Figure 4. Word cloud of most frequently used keywords in the articles related to the PSI.

2.4. Problem Scoping

The systematic review scope is defined in this section. The aim is to investigate and illustrate the following through a concept map of research focus shown in Figure 5:

- **The PSI methodology:** It focuses on theoretical and mathematical formulations, especially in steps where the weights of criteria are calculated and used to rank several alternatives.
- **The PSI alternatives and attributes:** It emphasizes the PSI adaptability for many alternatives and attributes, presenting several challenges in certain decision contexts.
- **The PSI applications:** It demonstrates the PSI efficiency across various sectors by categorizing the applications into industries, including healthcare, manufacturing, and renewable energy.
- **The PSI limitations, integration and comparison with other MCDM techniques:** These topics center on the performance of the PSI, starting with its limitations. This can open up opportunities for improvements in methodology or integrating it with other MCDM methods, leveraging the strength of all methods.

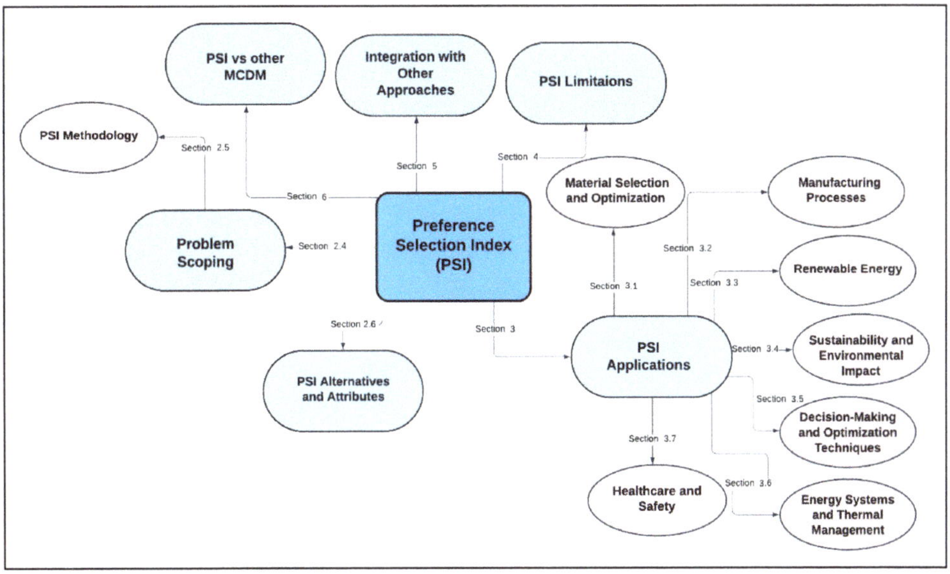

Figure 5. The concept map of the research focus areas for the PSI approach.

Together, these streams provide a comprehensive overview that clarifies the review's methodology, which focuses on addressing the PSI application diversity and method adaptability.

2.5. The PSI Methodology

The PSI methodology employs a systematic approach to address decision-making problems in which the process of assigning weights to criteria is a challenging one. The method is defined in the following steps, complemented by mathematical formulations [5,9]:

Step I: The objective is identified, and all related criteria and alternatives are determined for the purpose of deciding the given problem.
Step II: The decision matrix X_{ij} is constructed as shown in Table 2. For explaining the X_{ij}, let C be a set of decision criteria, where $C = \{C_j \text{ for } j = 1, 2, 3, \ldots, m\}$, A is a set of alternatives, where $A = \{A_i \text{ for } i = 1, 2, 3, \ldots, n\}$, and X_{ij} is representing the performance of alternative A_i under the effect of criterion C_j.

Table 2. The decision matrix X_{ij}.

Alternatives (A_i)	Criteria (C_j)				
	C_1	C_2	C_3	…	C_m
A_1	$X_{1\times1}$	$X_{1\times2}$	$X_{1\times3}$	…	$X_{1\times m}$
A_2	$X_{2\times1}$	$X_{2\times2}$	$X_{2\times3}$	…	$X_{2\times m}$
A_3	$X_{3\times1}$	$X_{3\times2}$	$X_{3\times3}$	…	$X_{3\times m}$
…	…	…	…	…	…
A_n	$X_{n\times1}$	$X_{n\times2}$	$X_{n\times3}$	…	$X_{n\times m}$

Step III: The decision matrix data are then normalized; therefore, the values in the decision matrix are transformed into a 0–1 range. In the positive expectancy case (i.e., profit), the normalization is performed using Equation (1):

$$R_{ij} = \frac{X_{ij}}{X_j^{max}} \tag{1}$$

However, in the negative expectancy case (i.e., cost), normalization is performed using Equation (2):

$$R_{ij} = \frac{X_j^{min}}{X_{ij}} \tag{2}$$

where X_{ij} is the attribute measure in the decision matrix ($i = 1, 2, 3, \ldots, n$ and $j = 1, 2, 3, \ldots, m$).
Step IV: The preference variation value (PV_j) is calculated using Equation (3):

$$PV_j = \sum_{i=1}^{n} [R_{ij} - \overline{R_j}]^2 \tag{3}$$

where $\overline{R_j}$ is the meaning of the normalized j criteria and computed based on Equation (4):

$$\overline{R_j} = \frac{1}{N}\sum_{i=1}^{n} R_{ij} \tag{4}$$

Step V: The preference value (PV_j) deviation (Φ) is calculated for every criterion in the matrix using Equation (5):

$$\Phi = 1 - PV_j \tag{5}$$

Step VI: The overall preference value (Ψ) is calculated using Equation (6) for each criterion in the decision matrix:

$$\Psi_j = \frac{\Phi_j}{\sum_{j=1}^{m} \Phi_j} \tag{6}$$

It is worth mentioning here that the overall summation of the preference value of all criteria must be one.
Step VII: The value of the Preference Selection Index (I_i) is calculated using Equation (7):

$$I_i = \sum_{j=1}^{m} (R_{ij} \times \Psi_j) \tag{7}$$

Step VIII: All the alternatives in the decision matrix are then ranked based on the I_i value, where alternatives with the highest I_i value must be selected first.

2.6. The PSI Alternatives and Attributes

The distribution of alternatives and attributes used in various research demonstrates the PSI's adaptability, making it an important tool in various decision-making aspects. As shown in Figure 6, the number of attributes typically ranges between 5 and 15, indicating that the PSI method can handle a balanced set of criteria in most scenarios. However, there are studies where up to 40 attributes are used, highlighting the PSI's ability to handle these complex decision-making contexts, which require a comprehensive analysis.

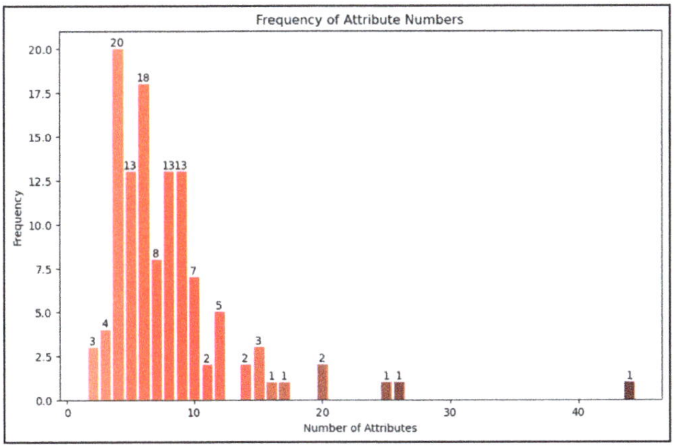

Figure 6. Distribution of attributes' numbers in the PSI applications.

Figure 7 shows that, while most of the PSI applications evaluate less than 25 alternatives simultaneously, the PSI approach is also feasible in scenarios with more than 200 alternatives [10]. This demonstrates the PSI's capability to manage various operational scenarios, ranging from precise assessments to significant strategic decision-making problems.

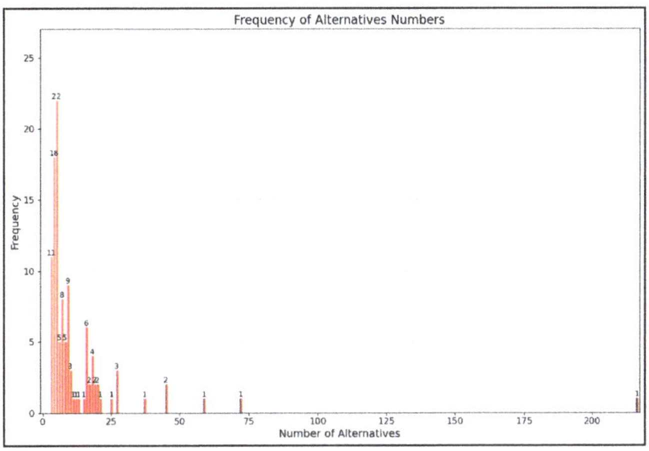

Figure 7. Distribution of alternatives' numbers in the PSI applications.

3. Applications of the PSI

Table 3 presents a detailed outline demonstrating various industries where the PSI method has been successfully implemented. Subsequent sections will explore the PSI's adaptability in addressing diverse application areas with unique challenges.

3.1. Material Selection and Optimization

Material selection and optimization are the most frequent applications for the PSI method. Studies by [5,11] have shown that the PSI method is utilized in selecting materials for structural components, such as wind blades and buses designed to run on alternative fuels. Further insights into the PSI have been provided by [6,12], which expanded the scope by including sustainable materials for vehicle framers, and non-conventional engineering materials. Recent investigations by [13,14] have presented how the PSI enhances the efficiency of material characteristics for multiple applications. These studies show that the PSI is a versatile material in engineering and material science.

3.2. Manufacturing Processes

The PSI approach is used in this domain to enhance decision-making in system design and industrial processes. Therefore, the versatility of the PSI is reflected in different applications, including the development of multi-attribute technologies for optimal equipment of the facility layout, according to [9], and the selection of autonomous guided vehicles, as illustrated by [15]. In addition, the PSI has been applied in combination with other general approaches, such as the Single Minute Exchange of Die (SMED) method, as presented by [16], to effectively reduce the setup time.

Moreover, the PSI has been used in many production resources to enhance many production factors, which in turn has improved the quality of products and streamlined the production process. Madić et al. [17] employed the PSI in the optimization of the laser cutting parameters of stainless steel to effectively enhance the quality and productivity. This study also provides valuable insights into corporate decision-making due to the effectiveness of the PSI method in complex problem-solving issues, which are apparent in today's industrial settings, making a significant contribution to operational excellence.

While several studies successfully applied the PSI to optimize manufacturing processes, an important assessment reveals several methodological weaknesses. For instance, the majority of PSI implementations relied on deterministic assumptions without providing a sensitivity test of changing results due to parameter change. Hence, a few studies, including [16] and [17], provided hybrid decision models to deal with the process variability. Furthermore, the use of real industrial data for validation was very limited in most studies, which restricts the generalizability of findings. This suggests that while PSI is effective for structured optimization, future research should enhance methodological rigor by including cross-validation with empirical data and robustness checks.

3.3. Renewable Energy

It is crucial to identify the policies for implementing and prioritizing renewable energy sources and sites, and the PSI is very helpful in this aspect. Studies such as [18] and [19] have utilized the PSI to improve the selection process for renewable energy policies. These studies have illustrated that the PSI can effectively integrate environmental, policy-making, and financial aspects. In addition, Rong and Yu [20] have utilized the PSI in a decision support system to enhance the process of choosing sites for offshore wind farms, ensuring optimal locations for sustainability and energy efficiency.

3.4. Sustainability and Environmental Impact

Borujeni and Gitinavard [21] successfully utilized the PSI to evaluate the selection of mining contractors, with a particular focus on sustainability within the mining industry. Similarly, Reddy et al. [22] illustrated a sustainable performance index for concrete that utilized the PSI to evaluate the environmental advantages of using supplementary cementitious materials such as fly ash and Ground Granulated Blast-furnace Slag (GGBS). Waste management and energy efficiency are two areas where PSI's role is unmatched in its versatility. To illustrate how and why PSI is relevant to the advancement of environmentalism in today's world, refer to [23] for the prospects of e-waste recycling, and to [24] for the potential of energy conservation in a hospital.

Studies in sustainability show varying degrees of rigor from a methodological point of view. Even though the PSI provides a direct ranking mechanism, it usually overlooks interdependence and uncertainty between sustainability criteria. The lack of weighting in most studies, such as [21,22], makes the analysis very simple; however, it may affect accuracy in multi-criteria trade-offs. Integrating PSI with fuzzy or entropy approaches might mitigate this limitation by introducing uncertainty modeling or objective weights.

3.5. Decision-Making and Optimization Techniques

The widespread use of the PSI, ranging from the analysis of the educational pathways to enhancing industrial operations, underscores the necessity for the development of more precise and efficient decision-making frameworks. The use of the PSI in various academic and business decisions, such as in the selection of a PhD program in [25] and the use of ChatGPT in business efficiency in [26] depicts PSI's significant contribution to decision-making.

Furthermore, the ability of the method to be integrated into MCDM approaches was also observed when used by [27,28]. These models assist researchers and organizations in managing the decision-making processes when faced with complicated issues, such as identifying third-party logistics providers and evaluating product concepts. This means that the PSI is an important approach for organizations in all sectors and beneficial for enhancing daily and long-term decision-making.

3.6. Energy Systems and Thermal Management

Obeidat and Traini [29] used the PSI efficiently in the context of evaluating different water desalination technologies. They were able to determine the most suitable water treatment techniques based on the PSI approach. This demonstrates how PSI can integrate advanced MCDM approaches to enhance the sustainable management of limited resources.

The PSI has also guided the optimization of energy parameters in several cutting-edge applications. For instance, in their studies, refs. [30,31] utilized the PSI to optimize the design and function of thermal solar collectors, thus increasing energy capture and efficiency. Such analysis shows that by utilizing the PSI, the variability of system design aspects can be fine-tuned to achieve highly efficient systems, which is beneficial for advancements in renewable energy technologies and reducing adverse environmental effects.

3.7. Healthcare and Safety

Some of the advantages that may be associated with the PSI include improved frameworks for resilience and decision-making in both the healthcare and safety sectors. In the study by [32], during the turbulent years of the COVID-19 pandemic, the PSI was utilized to validate a significant factor contributing to the reliability of the healthcare supply chain in sustaining the resilience of healthcare systems to shocks, thereby demonstrating the applicability and usefulness of PSI. Similarly, ref. [33] have used the PSI in assessing the feasibility of implementing an open-access repository for handling information on natural disasters in the Iranian context. They highlighted the method's effectiveness in improving disaster preparedness and response.

The PSI has also assisted in selecting crucial equipment and conducting safety evaluations. Kundu et al. [34] investigated an instance of the PSI to understand its applicability in selecting Magnetic Resonance Imaging (MRI) systems in private hospitals. The goal was to design the systems and ensure that all identified systems meet the requirements of the healthcare providers and patients. The PSI was also implemented by [35] to evaluate road safety performance in East Asia Summit (EAS) countries, providing better policy recommendations and actions to improve road safety in terms of reducing traffic accidents.

Table 3. Overview of PSI applications in various sectors.

Article	Main Focus	Application Area
[5]	Selecting the appropriate material for engineering applications (structural components and wind turbine blades).	Material Selection and Optimization
[11]	Choosing the best alternative fuel buses utilizing unique fuzzy multi-criteria decision-making approaches.	Material Selection and Optimization
[6]	Using the PSI approach to select materials in engineering applications.	Material Selection and Optimization
[12]	Developing a sustainable material selection strategy for automobile bodies and including quantitative sustainability measures.	Material Selection and Optimization
[3]	Selecting materials that maximize strength and workability in Al/SiC composites.	Material Selection and Optimization
[36]	Optimizing nano-fillers to improve the three-dimensional performance of brake friction materials.	Material Selection and Optimization
[37]	Selection of 7075 aluminum alloy composites supplemented with alumina nanoparticles.	Material Selection and Optimization
[38]	Evaluating the impact of production procedures on the microstructure and mechanical characteristics of AZ80-0.5Ca-1.5Al203 nanocomposite.	Material Selection and Optimization
[39]	Characterizing biodegradable composites and optimizing phase combinations.	Material Selection and Optimization
[40]	Improving the selection of marine application materials based on physical, mechanical, and corrosive properties.	Material Selection and Optimization
[41]	Evaluating copper-based alloy composites supplemented with marble dust for applicability in bearing applications.	Material Selection and Optimization
[42]	Evaluating and optimizing the mechanical characteristics of waste marble dust-filled glass Fiber-Reinforced Polymer Composites.	Material Selection and Optimization
[43]	Optimizing nonwoven epoxy composites for better durability and wear resistance	Material Selection and Optimization
[44]	A performance-based ranking of ceramic particle-reinforced AA2024 alloy composite materials.	Material Selection and Optimization
[45]	Determining the ideal brake friction composite composition.	Material Selection and Optimization
[46]	Reviewing material selection for impact-resistant polymer matrix composites, focusing on natural fibers as suitable reinforcements.	Material Selection and Optimization
[47]	Optimizing the sliding and mechanical properties of a Ti/Ni metal powder particle-reinforced Al 6061 alloy composite.	Material Selection and Optimization
[48]	Focusing on the development and mechanical characterization of innovative polymer-based flexible composites and stacking sequence optimization.	Material Selection and Optimization
[49]	Optimizing material selection for ship bodies using manufactured zirconium dioxide and silicon carbide-filled aluminum hybrid metal alloy composites.	Material Selection and Optimization
[50]	Selecting the best material for suspension coil springs.	Material Selection and Optimization
[51]	Selecting the optimal formulation of various fillers for dental composites.	Material Selection and Optimization
[52]	Improving the selection of ceramic particulate-reinforced dental restorative composite materials.	Material Selection and Optimization

Table 3. *Cont.*

Article	Main Focus	Application Area
[53]	Focusing on the anti-fatigue lightweight design of heavy tractor frames.	Material Selection and Optimization
[54]	Examining the impact of various copper (Cu) and zinc (Zn) compositions in brass on the fade and recovery behavior of phenolic-based friction composites used in brakes.	Material Selection and Optimization
[55]	Optimizing material selection for Fiber-Reinforced Polymer Composites (FRPCs) in multi-layered armor systems.	Material Selection and Optimization
[56]	Selecting the best waste marble dust-filled sustainable polymer composite.	Material Selection and Optimization
[57]	Evaluating the tribological behavior of chemically modified Jatropha oils as bio-lubricants in a boundary lubrication regime.	Material Selection and Optimization
[58]	Investigating the influence of Ghatti gum content on the mechanical characteristics of epoxy composites.	Material Selection and Optimization
[59]	Evaluating the physical, mechanical, and sliding wear properties of ZA27-Gr alloy composites.	Material Selection and Optimization
[60]	Optimizing frame weight while retaining structural integrity and performance.	Material Selection and Optimization
[13]	Optimizing the wear characteristics of ceramic coatings, especially $Cr2O3/TiAlN$.	Material Selection and Optimization
[14]	Modeling and optimization of hybrid Kevlar/glass fabric-reinforced polymer composites to improve impact resistance in low-velocity applications.	Material Selection and Optimization
[61]	Optimizing and ranking the mechanical and tribological characteristics of the AA2024 alloy.	Material Selection and Optimization
[9]	Selecting the best facility layout design.	Manufacturing Processes
[15]	Selecting autonomous guided vehicles.	Manufacturing Processes
[16]	Enhancing the traditional SMED method to save setup time in manufacturing operations.	Manufacturing Processes
[62]	Evaluating the optimal production system design.	Manufacturing Processes
[63]	Evaluating layout options to improve an industry's performance.	Manufacturing Processes
[17]	Optimizing process parameters for laser cutting stainless steel to improve multiple quality and productivity attributes simultaneously.	Manufacturing Processes
[64]	Analyzing facility layout alternatives.	Manufacturing Processes
[65]	Selecting optimal process settings for Polylactic Acid FDM, considering the influence on mechanical properties and surface roughness.	Manufacturing Processes
[66]	Ranking the performance factors in Flexible Manufacturing Systems (FMS).	Manufacturing Processes
[67]	Identifying appropriate three-dimensional scanning process settings to increase the overall quality of reverse-engineered models.	Manufacturing Processes
[68]	Evaluating the best 3D printer for producing automotive spoilers.	Manufacturing Processes
[69]	Focusing on the parametric analysis and multi-response optimization of laser surface texturing of titanium super alloy.	Manufacturing Processes
[70]	Focusing on the multi-objective optimization and experimental investigation of Electro-Discharge cutting (EDM) parameters.	Manufacturing Processes

Table 3. *Cont.*

Article	Main Focus	Application Area
[71]	Optimizing turning processes to produce the minimum surface roughness and maximum material removal rate (MRR).	Manufacturing Processes
[72]	Optimizing electrical discharge machining (EDM) process parameters for titanium alloy machining.	Manufacturing Processes
[73]	Selecting an appropriate setting for FDM printing techniques.	Manufacturing Processes
[74]	Selecting capacity expansion plans in manufacturing.	Manufacturing Processes
[75]	Focusing on the selection of the optimal electrical energy equipment.	Energy Systems and Thermal Management
[30]	Optimizing the V-down perforated baffled roughened rectangular channel.	Energy Systems and Thermal Management
[31]	Optimizing the characteristics of a solar thermal collector with impinging air jets.	Energy Systems and Thermal Management
[76]	Prioritizing energy performance in a rectangular channel with impinging air jets.	Energy Systems and Thermal Management
[77]	Optimizing the parameters of single arc protrusion ribs in a solar air heater	Energy Systems and Thermal Management
[78]	Developing novel heat transfer and pressure loss correlation for solar air heaters with internal conical ring obstacles.	Energy Systems and Thermal Management
[79]	Selecting the best cleaning procedure for solar panels (PVs).	Energy Systems and Thermal Management
[80]	Improving static voltage stability margin in power systems.	Energy Systems and Thermal Management
[81]	Ranking various water desalination systems.	Energy Systems and Thermal Management
[82]	Investigating the effect of novel elongated jet hole designs on the thermal efficiency of solar air heaters.	Energy Systems and Thermal Management
[83]	Focusing on the energy, economic, environmental, and climatic aspects of a solar combisystem for various consumption usages.	Energy Systems and Thermal Management
[84]	Selecting the best settings for a solar heat collector with a dimpled-V pattern roughened surface.	Energy Systems and Thermal Management
[85]	Selecting the appropriate phase change material (PCM) for solar adsorption cooling systems (SAC).	Energy Systems and Thermal Management
[10]	Designing a multi-stage optimization-based decision-making framework for sustainable hybrid energy systems in the residential sector.	Energy Systems and Thermal Management
[29]	Ranking water desalination methods to find the best method for different types of feed water.	Energy Systems and Thermal Management
[18]	Focusing on renewable energy policy selection.	Renewable Energy
[19]	Focusing on the selection of renewable energy policy.	Renewable Energy
[20]	Developing a decision support system to prioritize offshore wind farm sites.	Renewable Energy
[27]	Focusing on the influence of various criterion weight strategies in the Technique for Order Preference by Similarity to Ideal Solution (TOPSIS) method of multi-criteria decision-making.	Decision-Making and Optimization Techniques
[86]	Focusing on the various criterion decision-making processes in hotel site selection and their relationship to post-purchase consumer feedback.	Decision-Making and Optimization Techniques

Table 3. *Cont.*

Article	Main Focus	Application Area
[87]	Evaluating product concepts using a hybrid approach.	Decision-Making and Optimization Techniques
[88]	Evaluating product concepts using a hybrid approach to select the best warehouse site using GPSI and GPIV methods.	Decision-Making and Optimization Techniques
[89]	Developing a new hesitant fuzzy ranking model to address the ranking challenge of non-traditional manufacturing processes.	Decision-Making and Optimization Techniques
[90]	Assessing students' performance levels using the Moodle Learning Management System (LMS) based on usability criteria.	Decision-Making and Optimization Techniques
[91]	Evaluating traffic solutions in school zones to cut waiting time and increase safety levels.	Decision-Making and Optimization Techniques
[92]	Selecting third-party logistics providers.	Decision-Making and Optimization Techniques
[93]	Creating a novel multidimensional process type FMEA technique to optimize risk assessments.	Decision-Making and Optimization Techniques
[94]	Selecting support systems in underground mines.	Decision-Making and Optimization Techniques
[95]	Selecting magnets for permanent magnet synchronous machines (PMSMs).	Decision-Making and Optimization Techniques
[26]	Analyzing the potential benefits and applications of ChatGPT as a tool for increasing corporate efficiency and effectiveness.	Decision-Making and Optimization Techniques
[96]	Developing a novel technique for group decision-making to deal with data uncertainty and imprecision.	Decision-Making and Optimization Techniques
[97]	Developing a revolutionary multi-criteria decision-making and game theory-based framework for sentiment analysis and aspect ranking in customer reviews.	Decision-Making and Optimization Techniques
[28]	Evaluating and selecting third-party logistics (3PL) service providers for vehicle manufacturing firms.	Decision-Making and Optimization Techniques
[98]	Selecting the best vehicle routing software (VRS) for last-mile delivery companies.	Decision-Making and Optimization Techniques
[99]	Benchmarking the country's supply chain performance.	Decision-Making and Optimization Techniques
[100]	Evaluating organization's digital transformation capabilities (DTC).	Decision-Making and Optimization Techniques
[101]	Evaluating crowdfunding projects.	Decision-Making and Optimization Techniques
[102]	Ranking European nations using data from the Global Entrepreneurship Monitor (GEM).	Decision-Making and Optimization Techniques
[103]	Analyzing the performance and efficiency of European electric vehicles (EVs) in the European Union market.	Decision-Making and Optimization Techniques
[25]	Selecting a university for a doctoral program in industrial engineering in the United States.	Decision-Making and Optimization Techniques
[21]	Assessing sustainable mining contractor selection challenges.	Sustainability and Environmental Impact
[22]	Developing a Sustainable Performance Index (SPI) for self-compacting concretes that use supplementary cementitious materials (SCMs) such as fly ash and GGBS.	Sustainability and Environmental Impact

Table 3. *Cont.*

Article	Main Focus	Application Area
[23]	Investigating recovery options for electrical and electronic waste.	Sustainability and Environmental Impact
[104]	Comparing biomass pelleting techniques to determine the most efficient and cost-effective approach.	Sustainability and Environmental Impact
[105]	Identifying key challenges to green human resource management (GHRM) adoption in Ghana.	Sustainability and Environmental Impact
[106]	The feasibility and impact of employing marble dust as reinforcement in composites for various industrial applications.	Sustainability and Environmental Impact
[107]	Evaluating coalfields in Bangladesh for their potential to conduct underground coal gasification (UCG).	Sustainability and Environmental Impact
[108]	Identifying the most effective natural fiber for insulating products used in commercial buildings.	Sustainability and Environmental Impact
[109]	Evaluating the impact of the COVID-19 pandemic on medical waste disposal.	Sustainability and Environmental Impact
[110]	Addressing the hurdles to eliminating illegal gold mining (IGM) in Ghana to suggest sustainable mining practices.	Sustainability and Environmental Impact
[111]	Improving the green supplier selection process in the textile sector.	Sustainability and Environmental Impact
[24]	Evaluating energy-saving solutions to minimize energy usage and CO2 emissions in healthcare facilities.	Sustainability and Environmental Impact
[32]	Investigating the facilitators of resilience in the healthcare supply chain during the COVID-19 pandemic.	Healthcare and Safety
[33]	Assessing the possibility of establishing a natural disaster information management open-access repository (NDIM-OAR) in Iran.	Healthcare and Safety
[34]	MRI system selection for private hospitals.	Healthcare and Safety
[35]	Evaluating road safety performance in the EAS countries.	Healthcare and Safety

4. PSI Limitations

Despite the huge advantages of the PSI method, it has some limitations that might impact its effectiveness in solving decision-making problems. Table 4 summarizes the significant limitations of the PSI method, including the explanations and references to studies that address these issues.

Table 4. The PSI limitations.

Limitation	Definition/ Explanation	Studies
Lack of attribute weighting	The PSI often fails to account for the varying importance of different factors, assuming the same importance, which may not represent actual decision-making scenarios	[5,9,13,22,23,26,32,34,42,48, 49,51,53,54,57,60,62,64,66,67, 72,75,79,83,85,92,104,107]
Simplistic and inflexible approach	The PSI technique may oversimplify complicated decision-making scenarios, possibly missing accurate differences and interrelationships among criteria	[5,9,11,18,21,32,34,40,43,54, 68,88,92]

Table 4. *Cont.*

Limitation	Definition/ Explanation	Studies
Inadequacy in complex or detailed analyses	Although the PSI is valuable for quick assessments, it may not suffice for thorough evaluations in complex situations or accurately distinguishing between closely ranked options, which is crucial for precisely balanced decision-making contexts.	[17,40,78]
Inadequate integration with the other decision-making techniques	The PSI may need to integrate other approaches to enhance its analytical capabilities and effectively manage multidimensional data, especially in complex or fluctuating contexts	[35]
Oversimplification in multi-criteria decisions	The PSI may place excessive importance on some performance indicators, leading to biased decision results	[53]
Real-world applications challenges	Implementing the PSI technique may present specific challenges, particularly in real-life cases, where it is necessary to understand multiple, sometimes even conflicting, factors	[33,57,68]

5. Integration with the Other Decision-Making Approaches

5.1. The PSI Integration with the AHP

According to Saaty, the AHP is an analytic, systematic decision-making tool developed in the early 1980s [25]. It translates sophisticated evaluations and judgments into a simpler, hierarchical form in which challenges with quantifying benefits or intangible items can be treated mathematically [25]. Therefore, the AHP method is a useful technique in decision-making problems involving multiple criteria, alternatives, and subjective judgments [112]. Integrating the PSI with the AHP is beneficial due to the following:

- Enhanced accuracy: The integration between both the AHP and PSI, as illustrated in [16,75], modifies the weakness of PSI in the case of evaluating complex scenarios through the facilitation of criteria weighing and prioritization. Therefore, the PSI–AHP integration provides more accuracy when making decisions.
- Robust decisions framework: Applying both the AHP and PSI techniques would enable a more resilient decision-making process, especially when selecting materials or in turbulent industrial applications and environments [54]
- Focused and efficient analysis: According to [25], the application of AHP was practical in managing many alternatives and attributes when PSI was used in the selection of a PhD program in industrial engineering at U.S. universities. This made the comprehensive AHP method less demanding, ultimately resulting in improvement in the overall reviews for decision-making.

5.2. The PSI Integration with the TOPSIS

The Technique for Order Preference by Similarity to Ideal Solution (TOPSIS) is an effective technique for order preference, which is often used to select the most suitable solution in multi-criteria systems. These goals rank alternatives efficiently based on the concept of distance from the optimal solution. This technique is suggested to be used when measuring multi-criteria because of its sensible structure and low computational complexity [113]. The integration between the TOPSIS and the PSI offers several benefits to decision-making processes, including as follows:

- Enhanced decision accuracy: Integrating the PSI with the TOPSIS, as mentioned in [9,15], aims at reducing the PSI limitations when facing complex environments.

This helps increase the accuracy of the decision-making process, as, on the one hand, there is the use of the TOPSIS capacity for determining the proximity of each option to the optimal solution, which complements the PSI approach.

- Comprehensive evaluation: Applying both the TOPSIS and PSI methods together leads to an even more comprehensive evaluation, which is particularly useful when the differentiation between criterion weights is crucial. As a result, the use of TOPSIS and PSI can be helpful when selecting materials for marine purposes, as, for instance, depicted in [40].
- Robustness in complex environments: Combining both the PSI and the TOPSIS is described by [16] for the utilization in industrial environments and minimizing the setup time in the processes. This methodology effectively performs a structured analysis considering multiple overlapping and interacting factors.
- Handling complexity and uncertainty: In their research, ref. [27] provided sufficient empirical evidence to show how the TOPSIS application with intuitionistic fuzzy data efficiently manages fuzzy data and enhances the decision-making results.

5.3. Integration of the PSI with the Fuzzy Set Theory

The integration of the fuzzy set theory and the PSI has proven that it has several beneficial applications in improving decision-making problems, with a high level of uncertainty and vagueness. The fuzzy set theory is also able to cope with uncertain and qualitative data through techniques such as linguistic variables and fuzzy numbers. This makes it very advantageous and beneficial in such subjective judgments [114]. The integration between the fuzzy set theory and the PSI offers several benefits to decision-making processes, including as follows:

- Handling of uncertainties and vagueness: Modifications were introduced by [11] for improving the PSI under fuzzy environments, to augment its applicability in various decision-making scenarios. This improvement enables the PSI to address language complexities and noise data, which is often evident in real-world conditions.
- Robust decision framework: According to the study by [21], applying fuzzy techniques, including the Hesitant Fuzzy Preference Selection Index (HFPSI), improves the robustness and reliability of decision-making models. This technique is very useful, especially in fields such as mining, which require making decisions under conditions of risk and uncertainty.
- Comprehensive decision-making: In the study by [19], in which they integrated hesitant fuzzy sets to improve the accuracy of the decision-making process in conjunction with the PSI in the case of uncertainty. This allowed for a more comprehensive examination of multiple characteristics and viewpoints, which is beneficial, especially when working in complex scenarios such as energy policy.
- Enhanced flexibility and accuracy: As explained by [32,34], by integrating fuzzy logic, the PSI may better handle the inherent uncertainty of data inputs and expert judgments, which are common in healthcare and the material selection process.

5.4. Integration of the PSI with the Entropy Method

The entropy method is an important MCDM decision-making approach as it helps objectively estimate the weights of the assigned criteria based on their variability. This technique uses empirical data to evaluate complex scenarios, which reduces the subjectivity in the decision-making process [115]. The integration between the PSI and the entropy methods provides several benefits, including as follows:

- Objective criteria weighting: The entropy method's ability to establish weights based on criteria diversity is crucial for ensuring balanced and data-driven decision-making processes. Chauhan et al. [76] highlighted this in their study on energy systems optimizations.

- Systematic evaluation and risk management: As mentioned in [93], this integration between the PSI and the entropy method is helpful in cases where a detailed examination is required and risk assessment is critical, especially in the aerospace and military sectors. It also guarantees that all the relevant standards are expansively evaluated.

The comparative evaluation across sectors shows that PSI provides higher stability and efficiency in structured industrial contexts where decision parameters are well-defined, such as material selection and manufacturing sectors. On the other hand, its direct application in the sustainability and healthcare sectors tends to be limited by the need for weighting and uncertainty. Hybrid PSI models, such as PSI–AHP, PSI–TOPSIS, PSI–Fuzzy, effectively mitigate these limitations by improving the interpretive accuracy and adaptability, although they slightly decrease simplicity in computations. Therefore, PSI variant selection should consider both data characteristics and problem complexity.

In summary, the integration analyses highlight a methodological evolution in PSI research. Hybrid MCDM approaches such as PSI–AHP, PSI–TOPSIS, and PSI–Fuzzy, address core weaknesses such as oversimplification, sensitivity to input parameters, and equal weighting. Those studies implementing these integrations (i.e., [16,19,27]) demonstrated improved interpretability and decision stability. This integration reflects a methodological trend toward more adaptive PSI, moving beyond the static assumptions of earlier MCDM approaches.

6. Comparing the PSI with Other Decision-Making Approaches

6.1. Comparing the PSI with Graph Theory and Matrix Approach (GTMA)

When comparing the algorithms, both Maniya and Bhatt [5] and Chatterjee and Chakraborty [6] noticed the advantages of the PSI over the Graph Theory and Matrix Approach (GTMA). They found that the PSI is more straightforward and faster in computation. The PSI is famous for its easier implementation and less calculation when compared with GTMA, which possesses some attribute weighting and analysis. This means that the GTMA requires more data processing than is needed under the PSI, as the GTMA requires extensive data processing.

6.2. Comparing the PSI with the TOPSIS

The PSI is of a less complex and computationally demanding alternative for TOPSIS. The PSI is especially valued for its streamlined approach in multi-criteria decision-making processes. Both the studies in [5,79] have utilized the PSI approach for ranking alternatives, and found it a beneficial tool as it achieves optimal results without involving additional mathematical computations as needed by the TOPSIS. Several studies, such as those conducted by [6] and [65], highlighted the primary benefit of the PSI approach, in which it eliminates the procedure of attribute weighting and, therefore, reduces the time taken in the preliminary stages of the decision-making processes.

This capability is beneficial in conditions where quick decision-making is required, and the speed, along with the simplicity in the evaluation, are critical. In addition, as revealed by [3,48], the effectiveness of the proposed PSI model could be further recognized concerning the identification of the most suitable solutions for material selection, and other applications. The PSI similarly delivers this with high levels of reliability and robustness, as are seen with TOPSIS, though aggregated in a less procedural model in its approach to TOPSIS.

6.3. The PSI Comparison with the AHP

The PSI, as a decision-making tool, is more advantageous for the use in multi-criteria decision-making than AHP, as the PSI offers a more straightforward and practical approach. In the problem-solving process, and compared with the AHP, the PSI consumes fewer computational resources and does not require making pairwise comparisons and attribute weighting. Furthermore, the PSI avoids the need for complex weighting techniques. It is especially applied in scenarios requiring quick decisions with limited resources. According to [9] and [65], the researchers suggest that the PSI effectively streamlines the inherent operational complexity of the AHP. It is highlighted that the PSI does not need the complex weight allocations that the AHP requires, hence enabling a more straightforward and speedy decision-making process. Further, both [36,79] found that applying the PSI reduces the reliance on numerical computations and subjective inputs, leading to a faster decision-making process and a considerable reduction in bias resulting from human judgment.

6.4. The PSI Comparison with the Entropy Method

The PSI approach is often used alongside the entropy method in MCDM frameworks to identify unique advantages. Dammak et al. [27] and Chauhan et al. [76] conducted a comparison between the PSI's simple and less computationally demanding methodology and the entropy method's robust analytical depth. The entropy method is particularly effective in precisely measuring variability. The comparison emphasizes the PSI's ease of use and efficiency compared to the entropy method, which excels in handling complex criteria optimization and prioritization. Kashani et al. [83] and Uslu et al. [93] emphasized that while the PSI simplifies decision-making, including or comparing it with the entropy may significantly enhance the assessment process, especially in complex situations needing precise analysis.

6.5. The PSI Comparison with the Fuzzy Set Theory

The analysis of the results presented in the reviewed studies has indicated that the application of the PSI is especially designed for fuzzy environments, which gives critical benefits in situations where problems are uncertain and more challenging, concerning decision-making. In line with [11,23], the fuzzy-based PSI offers more flexibility and does not need rigid weight assignment, which makes it suitable for situations involving fuzzy data. In addition, [21,89] revealed that the PSI can address integration and the ability to perform qualitative and quantitative data efficiently. Due to this, the PSI is preferred in complex application areas such as materials selection and production procedures, as it is more effective than the standard fuzzy techniques in delivering measurable improvements by offering a more direct and adaptable approach.

In summary, and based on those reviewed studies, the main methodological strengths of PSI include transparency, computational simplicity, and suitability for MCDM ranking. On the other hand, the PSI has some weaknesses, including the lack of a weighting technique, insufficient empirical validation, and limited robustness testing. Those studies that integrated PSI with other MCDM approaches achieved more reliable and balanced results. Therefore, future research of PSI must focus on hybrid decision modeling, cross-domain validation, and uncertainty quantification to strengthen methodological reproducibility and reliability.

7. Conclusions

This systematic review provided a detailed analysis of the PSI decision-making approach and its usability in several decision-making situations. The PSI is suitable for MCDM due to its simplicity and low computational requirements. Precisely, the PSI is a highly efficient tool when solving cases that require rapid decision-making; however, it has some weaknesses in handling complex situations.

The results indicated that decision-makers may benefit from the PSI efficiency, especially when resources are limited. However, the review establishes the need for additional studies to increase the scope of the PSI and its analysis. This might be achieved by improving the PSI with other decision-making techniques. These advancements have the potential to make the PSI more user-friendly and increase its capability to manage multifaceted data.

Further research should explore the potential integration of the PSI with modern decision-making techniques and its use in other domains to boost its efficacy and flexibility. Lastly, this review provides an argument for the PSI approach as a strategic but alterable decision support system that has the capacity to expand in exploring complex problems in various fields.

Adding to these methodological insights, many policy implementations and research directions may be drawn from this review. Future studies must mainly focus on the development of hybrid PSI models, which incorporate uncertainty modeling, weighting mechanisms, and sensitivity assessment to improve robustness of the results. To improve practical reliability, thorough comparative validation of PSI-based frameworks with real-world datasets is highly recommended. Furthermore, researchers may investigate the integration between the PSI approach with data-driven and AI-assisted decision-making techniques, particularly in sustainability evaluation, material selection, renewable energy, manufacturing system, and healthcare and safety. From a policy perspective, organizations and industries may implement PSI-based models to enhance transparent, evidence-based decision-making processes that balance complexity with efficiency. By adopting open data reporting and standardized examination protocols, policymakers may facilitate broader establishment and methodological consistency of PSI implementations in these sectors.

Author Contributions: M.S.O.: conceptualization, investigation, methodology, project administration; resources; supervision; validation; visualization; writing—original draft; writing—review and editing. H.A.S.: data curation, formal analysis, investigation, methodology, software, validation, visualization; writing—original draft. A.O.: validation, writing—review and editing. All authors have read and agreed to the published version of the manuscript.

Funding: This research received no external funding.

Data Availability Statement: The data presented in this study are available upon request.

Conflicts of Interest: The authors declare that they have no known competing financial interests or personal relationships that could have appeared to influence the work reported in this paper.

References

1. Siksnelyte-Butkiene, I.; Zavadskas, E.K.; Streimikiene, D. Multi-criteria decision-making (MCDM) for the assessment of renewable energy technologies in a household: A review. *Energies* **2020**, *13*, 1164. [CrossRef]
2. Kumar, A.; Sah, B.; Singh, A.R.; Deng, Y.; He, X.; Kumar, P.; Bansal, R.C. A review of multi criteria decision making (MCDM) towards sustainable renewable energy development. *Renew. Sustain. Energy Rev.* **2017**, *69*, 596–609. [CrossRef]
3. Khorshidi, R.; Hassani, A. Comparative analysis between TOPSIS and PSI methods of materials selection to achieve a desirable combination of strength and workability in Al/SiC composite. *Mater. Des.* **2013**, *52*, 999–1010. [CrossRef]
4. Aruldoss, M.; Lakshmi, T.M.; Venkatesan, V.P. A Survey on Multi Criteria Decision Making Methods and Its Applications. *Am. J. Inf. Syst.* **2013**, *1*, 31–43.
5. Maniya, K.; Bhatt, M. A selection of material using a novel type decision-making method: Preference selection index method. *Mater. Des.* **2010**, *31*, 1785–1789. [CrossRef]
6. Chatterjee, P.; Chakraborty, S. Material selection using preferential ranking methods. *Mater. Des.* **2012**, *35*, 384–393. [CrossRef]
7. Moher, D.; Liberati, A.; Tetzlaff, J.; Altman, D.G. Preferred reporting items for systematic reviews and meta-analyses: The PRISMA statement. *Int. J. Surg.* **2010**, *8*, 336–341. [CrossRef]

8. Sarkis-Onofre, R.; Catalá-López, F.; Aromataris, E.; Lockwood, C. How to properly use the PRISMA Statement. *Syst. Rev.* **2021**, *10*, 117. [CrossRef]
9. Maniya, K.; Bhatt, M. An alternative multiple attribute decision making methodology for solving optimal facility layout design selection problems. *Comput. Ind. Eng.* **2011**, *61*, 542–549. [CrossRef]
10. Mehmood, A.; Zhang, L.; Ren, J. A multi-stage optimisation-based decision-making framework for sustainable hybrid energy system in the residential sector. *Sustain. Futures* **2023**, *6*, 100122. [CrossRef]
11. Vahdani, B.; Zandieh, M.; Tavakkoli-Moghaddam, R. Two novel FMCDM methods for alternative-fuel buses selection. *Appl. Math. Model.* **2011**, *35*, 1396–1412. [CrossRef]
12. Mayyas, A.T.; Qattawi, A.; Mayyas, A.R.; Omar, M. Quantifiable measures of sustainability: A case study of materials selection for eco-lightweight auto-bodies. *J. Clean. Prod.* **2013**, *40*, 177–189. [CrossRef]
13. Kumar, S.; Maity, S.R.; Patnaik, L. Wear Parameter Optimization of Ceramic Coating Using the Fuzzy Integrated PSI-CODAS Decision-Making Framework. *Arab. J. Sci. Eng.* **2023**, *48*, 3819–3841. [CrossRef]
14. Jambhulkar, T.; Sahu, R. Modelling and optimization of hybrid Kevlar/glass fabric reinforced polymer composites for low-velocity impact resistant applications. *Forces Mech.* **2024**, *15*, 100267. [CrossRef]
15. Sawant, V.B.; Mohite, S.S.; Patil, R. CCIS 145-A Decision-Making Methodology for Automated Guided Vehicle Selection Problem Using a Preference Selection Index Method, Technology Systems and Management. In *Technology Systems and Management*; Shah, K., Lakshmi Gorty, V.R., Phirke, A., Eds.; Communications in Computer and Information Science; Springer: Berlin/Heidelberg, Germany, 2011; Volume 145.
16. Almomani, M.A.; Aladeemy, M.; Abdelhadi, A.; Mumani, A. A proposed approach for setup time reduction through integrating conventional SMED method with multiple criteria decision-making techniques. *Comput. Ind. Eng.* **2013**, *66*, 461–469. [CrossRef]
17. Madić, M.; Antucheviciene, J.; Radovanović, M.; Petković, D. Determination of laser cutting process conditions using the preference selection index method. *Opt. Laser Technol.* **2017**, *89*, 214–220. [CrossRef]
18. Vahdani, B.; Mousavi, S.M.; Ebrahimnejad, S. Soft computing-based preference selection index method for human resource management. *J. Intell. Fuzzy Syst.* **2014**, *26*, 393–403. [CrossRef]
19. Mousavi, M.; Gitinavard, H.; Mousavi, S. A soft computing based-modified ELECTRE model for renewable energy policy selection with unknown information. *Renew. Sustain. Energy Rev.* **2017**, *68*, 774–787. [CrossRef]
20. Rong, Y.; Yu, L. Decision Support System for Prioritization of Offshore Wind Farm Site by Utilizing Picture Fuzzy Combined Compromise Solution Group Decision Method. *Entropy* **2023**, *25*, 1081. [CrossRef] [PubMed]
21. Borujeni, M.P.; Gitinavard, H. Evaluating the sustainable mining contractor selection problems: An imprecise last aggregation preference selection index method. *J. Sustain. Min.* **2017**, *16*, 207–218. [CrossRef]
22. Reddy, A.S.; Kumar, P.R.; Raj, P.A. Development of Sustainable Performance Index (SPI) for Self-Compacting Concretes. *J. Build. Eng.* **2020**, *27*, 100974. [CrossRef]
23. Sari, E.B. Recovery alternatives decision by using fuzzy based preference selection index method. *Logforum* **2020**, *16*, 171–181. [CrossRef]
24. Kadric, D.; Blazevic, R.; Bajric, H.; Kadric, E. Evaluation of Energy Renovation Measures for Hospital Buildings using the PSI Method. *Eng. Technol. Appl. Sci. Res.* **2024**, *14*, 12753–12758. [CrossRef]
25. Obeidat, M.S.; Ababneh, W.; Al Theeb, N. The preference selection index performance in large alternatives' decisions to support the AHP: The case of a university selection. *J. Appl. Res. Technol.* **2023**, *21*, 56–72. [CrossRef]
26. Raj, R.; Singh, A.; Kumar, V.; Verma, P. Analyzing the potential benefits and use cases of ChatGPT as a tool for improving the efficiency and effectiveness of business operations. *BenchCouncil Trans. Benchmarks Stand. Eval.* **2023**, *3*, 100140. [CrossRef]
27. Dammak, F.; Baccour, L.; Alimi, A.M. The Impact of Criterion Weights Techniques in TOPSIS Method of Multi-Criteria Decision Making in Crisp and Intuitionistic Fuzzy Domains'. In Proceedings of the 2015 IEEE International Conference on Fuzzy Systems (FUZZ-IEEE), Istanbul, Turkey, 2–5 August 2015; pp. 1–8. [CrossRef]
28. Ulutaş, A.; Topal, A.; Görçün, Ö.F.; Ecer, F. Evaluation of third-party logistics service providers for car manufacturing firms using a novel integrated grey LOPCOW-PSI-MACONT model. *Expert Syst. Appl.* **2024**, *241*, 122680. [CrossRef]
29. Obeidat, M.S.; Traini, H. Ranking of Water Desalination Technologies Based on the Preference Selection Index. In Proceedings of the International Conference on Industrial Engineering and Operations Management, Dubai, United Arab Emirates, 10–12 March 2020.
30. Chamoli, S. Preference selection index approach for optimization of V down perforated baffled roughened rectangular channel. *Energy* **2015**, *93*, 1418–1425. [CrossRef]
31. Chauhan, R.; Singh, T.; Thakur, N.; Patnaik, A. Optimization of parameters in solar thermal collector provided with impinging air jets based upon preference selection index method. *Renew. Energy* **2016**, *99*, 118–126. [CrossRef]
32. Zamiela, C.; Hossain, N.U.I.; Jaradat, R. Enablers of resilience in the healthcare supply chain: A case study of U.S healthcare industry during COVID-19 pandemic. *Res. Transp. Econ.* **2022**, *93*, 101174. [CrossRef]

33. Rashidi, S.; Naghshineh, N.; Nia, F.F.; Izadkhah, Y.O.; Saghafi, F. How feasible is creating a natural disaster information management open-access repository (NDIM-OAR) in Iran? *Libr. Inf. Sci. Res.* **2022**, *44*, 101203. [CrossRef]
34. Kundu, P.; Görçün, Ö.F.; Küçükönder, H. Medical device selection in private hospitals by integrated fuzzy MCGDM methods: A case study in choosing MRI (Magnetic Resonance Imaging) system. *J. Oper. Res. Soc.* **2022**, *73*, 2059–2079. [CrossRef]
35. Chen, F.; Li, Y.; Feng, Q.; Dong, Z.; Qian, Y.; Yan, Y.; Ho, M.S.; Ma, Q.; Zhang, D.; Jin, Y. Road safety performance rating through PSI-PRIDIT: A planning tool for designing policies and identifying best practices for EAS countries. *Socio-Econ. Plan. Sci.* **2023**, *85*, 101438. [CrossRef]
36. Singh, T.; Patnaik, A.; Gangil, B.; Chauhan, R. Optimization of tribo-performance of brake friction materials: Effect of nano filler. *Wear* **2015**, *324-325*, 10–16. [CrossRef]
37. Ezatpour, H.; Parizi, M.T.; Sajjadi, S.; Ebrahimi, G.; Chaichi, A. Microstructure, mechanical analysis and optimal selection of 7075 aluminum alloy based composite reinforced with alumina nanoparticles. *Mater. Chem. Phys.* **2016**, *178*, 119–127. [CrossRef]
38. Parizi, M.T.; Habibolahzadeh, A.; Ebrahimi, G. Optimizing and investigating influence of manufacturing techniques on the microstructure and mechanical properties of AZ80-0.5Ca-1.5Al_2O_3 nanocomposite. *Mater. Chem. Phys.* **2017**, *199*, 485–496. [CrossRef]
39. Jha, K.; Chamoli, S.; Tyagi, Y.; Maurya, H.O. Characterization of Biodegradable Composites and Application of Preference Selection Index for Deciding Optimum Phase Combination. *Mater. Today Proc.* **2018**, *5*, 3353–3360. [CrossRef]
40. Yadav, S.; Pathak, V.K.; Gangwar, S. A novel hybrid TOPSIS-PSI approach for material selection in marine applications. *Sadhana* **2019**, *44*, 58. [CrossRef]
41. Rajak, S.K.; Aherwar, A.; Unune, D.R.; Mia, M.; Pruncu, C.I. Evaluation of copper-based alloy (C93200) composites reinforced with marble dust developed by stir casting under vacuum environment. *Materials* **2019**, *12*, 1574. [CrossRef]
42. Choudhary, M.; Singh, T.; Sharma, A.; Dwivedi, M.; Patnaik, A. Evaluation of some mechanical characterization and optimization of waste marble dust filled glass fiber reinforced polymer composite. *Mater. Res. Express* **2019**, *6*, 105702. [CrossRef]
43. Singh, T.; Tejyan, S.; Patnaik, A.; Chauhan, R.; Fekete, G. Optimal design of needlepunched nonwoven fiber reinforced epoxy composites using improved preference selection index approach. *J. Mater. Res. Technol.* **2020**, *9*, 7583–7591. [CrossRef]
44. Kumar, M.; Kumar, A. Application of preference selection index method in performance based ranking of ceramic particulate (SiO_2/SiC) reinforced AA2024 composite materials. *Mater. Today Proc.* **2019**, *27*, 2667–2672. [CrossRef]
45. Singh, T.; Pattnaik, P.; Pruncu, C.I.; Tiwari, A.; Fekete, G. Selection of natural fibers based brake friction composites using hybrid ELECTRE-entropy optimization technique. *Polym. Test.* **2020**, *89*, 106614. [CrossRef]
46. Mahesh, V.; Joladarashi, S.; Kulkarni, S.M. A comprehensive review on material selection for polymer matrix composites subjected to impact load. *Def. Technol.* **2021**, *17*, 257–277. [CrossRef]
47. Kumar, A.; Kumar, M.; Patnaik, A.; Pawar, M.; Pandey, A.; Kumar, A.; Gautam, V. Optimization of sliding and mechanical performance Ti/NI metal powder particulate reinforced Al 6061 alloy composite using preference selection index method. *Mater. Today Proc.* **2020**, *44*, 4784–4788. [CrossRef]
48. Mahesh, V.; Joladarashi, S.; Kulkarni, S.M. Development and mechanical characterization of novel polymer-based flexible composite and optimization of stacking sequences using VIKOR and PSI techniques. *J. Thermoplast. Compos. Mater.* **2021**, *34*, 1080–1102. [CrossRef]
49. Gangwar, S.; Arya, P.; Pathak, V.K. Optimal Material Selection for Ship Body Based on Fabricated Zirconium Dioxide/ Silicon Carbide Filled Aluminium Hybrid Metal Alloy Composites Using Novel Fuzzy Based Preference Selection Index. *Silicon* **2021**, *13*, 2545–2562. [CrossRef]
50. Samant, M.R.; Krisna, S.K.; Khishorre, K.R.; Sreeharan, B. A Systematic Way of using Preference Selection Index Methodology for Selecting Suspension Coil Spring Material. *Mater. Today Proc.* **2022**, *68*, 2249–2257. [CrossRef]
51. Verma, R.; Azam, M.S.; Kumar, S.R. Performance evaluation of glass ionomer and alumina-silica nanoparticle reinforced dental composite using preference selection index. *Polym. Compos.* **2022**, *43*, 3745–3752. [CrossRef]
52. Yadav, R. Fabrication, characterization, and optimization selection of ceramic particulate reinforced dental restorative composite materials. *Polym. Polym. Compos.* **2022**, *30*, 09673911211062755. [CrossRef]
53. Zhang, X.; Wang, D.; Kong, D.; Huang, B.; Zhang, Z.; He, Y. The anti-fatigue lightweight design of heavy tractor frame based on a modified decision method. *Struct. Multidiscip. Optim.* **2022**, *65*, 280. [CrossRef]
54. Asrar Ahmed, K.; Rasool Mohideen, S.; Balachandran, S.R.; Sai Balaji, M.A. Varying Cu and Zn composition in brass and its effect on the fade and recovery behavior of the phenolic-based friction composites. *Polym. Compos.* **2022**, *43*, 4478–4494. [CrossRef]
55. Gowda, D.; Bhat, R.; Rajole, S. An Optimization Study on Material Selection for FRPCs in Multi Layered Armour System Through Hybrid MCDM Approach and Numerical Simulation. *Mater. Plast.* **2022**, *59*, 205–223. [CrossRef]
56. Singh, T.; Pattnaik, P.; Shekhawat, D.; Ranakoti, L.; Lendvai, L. Waste marble dust-filled sustainable polymer composite selection using a multi-criteria decision-making technique. *Arab. J. Chem.* **2023**, *16*, 104695. [CrossRef]
57. Rajasozhaperumal, G.; Kannan, C. Comparative evaluation of chemically modified Jatropha oils as sustainable biolubricants in boundary lubrication regime. *Tribol. Int.* **2023**, *186*, 108594. [CrossRef]

58. Nagamadhu, M.; Patil, S.; Kivade, S.; Gunge, A.; Kadhim, K.F. Effect of Ghatti gum content on mechanical properties of epoxy composite using multicriteria optimization techniques. *Mater. Today Proc.* **2023**. [CrossRef]
59. Kumar, A.; Kumar, M. Investigations on Physical, Mechanical and Sliding Wear Assessment of ZA27 -Gr Alloy Composites Using Preference Selection Index Method. *Int. J. Met.* **2023**, *17*, 2818–2835. [CrossRef]
60. Wang, D.; Zhang, X. Application of the preference selection index method in multi-objective lightweight design of heavy commercial vehicle frames. *Eng. Optim.* **2023**, *55*, 1020–1039. [CrossRef]
61. Kumar, M.; Kumar, R.; Bhaskar, S.; Kumar, A. Parametric Optimization and Ranking Analysis of AA2024$-$Al$_2$O$_3$/AlN Alloy Composites Fabricated Via Stir Casting Route Under Dry Sliding Wear Investigation. *Int. J. Met.* **2024**, *18*, 667–687. [CrossRef]
62. Attri, R.; Grover, S. Application of preference selection index method for decision making over the design stage of production system life cycle. *J. King Saud Univ.-Eng. Sci.* **2015**, *27*, 207–216. [CrossRef]
63. Sharma, P.; Singhal, S. Design and evaluation of layout alternatives to enhance the performance of industry. *Opsearch* **2016**, *53*, 741–760. [CrossRef]
64. Sharma, P.; Singhal, S. Analysis of facility layout alternatives using proposed integrated approach. *Opsearch* **2017**, *54*, 1–20. [CrossRef]
65. Patel, P.B.; Patel, J.D.; Maniya, K.D. Application of PSI Methods to Select FDM Process Parameter for Polylactic Acid. *Mater. Today Proc.* **2018**, *5*, 4022–4028. [CrossRef]
66. Jain, V. Application of combined MADM methods as MOORA and PSI for ranking of FMS performance factors. *Benchmarking Int. J.* **2018**, *25*, 1903–1920. [CrossRef]
67. Pathak, V.K.; Singh, R.; Gangwar, S. Optimization of three-dimensional scanning process conditions using preference selection index and metaheuristic method. *Measurement* **2019**, *146*, 653–667. [CrossRef]
68. Prabhu, S.R.; Ilangkumaran, M.; Mohanraj, T. 3D Printing of automobile spoilers using MCDM techniques. *Mater. Test.* **2020**, *62*, 1121–1125. [CrossRef]
69. Shivakoti, I.; Kalita, K.; Kibria, G.; Sharma, A.; Pradhan, B.B.; Ghadai, R.K. Parametric analysis and multi response optimization of laser surface texturing of titanium super alloy. *J. Braz. Soc. Mech. Sci. Eng.* **2021**, *43*, 400. [CrossRef]
70. Patnaik, P.K.; Mishra, S.K.; Swain, P.T.R.; Purohit, A.; Parija, S.K.; Panda, S.S. Multi-Objective optimization and experimental analysis of Electro-Discharge Machining parameters via Gray-Taguchi, TOPSIS-Taguchi and PSI-Taguchi methods. *Mater. Today Proc.* **2022**, *62*, 6189–6198. [CrossRef]
71. Trung, D.D. Multi-criteria decision making of turning operation based on PEG, PSI and CURLI methods. *Manuf. Rev.* **2022**, *9*, 9. [CrossRef]
72. Phan, N.H.; Vu, N.N.; Shirguppikar, S.; Ly, N.T.; Tam, N.C.; Tai, B.T.; Thanh, L.T.P. Multi-criteria decision making in electrical discharge machining with nickel coated aluminium electrode for titanium alloy using preferential selection index. *Manuf. Rev.* **2022**, *9*, 13. [CrossRef]
73. Towaiq, A.; Obaidat, S.; Mumani, A.; Ziout, A. An application of the preference selection index decision making method for parameters selection of FDM printing process. *J. Eng. Res.* **2024**, *13*, 636–642. [CrossRef]
74. Obaidat, S.; Mumani, A. A multiple objective decision analysis model for capacity expansion plans selection in manufacturing. *J. Eng. Res.* **2024**, *13*, 480–491. [CrossRef]
75. Maniya, K.D.; Bhatt, M.G. A Selection of Optimal Electrical Energy Equipment Using Integrated Multi Criteria Decision Making Methodology. *Int. J. Energy Optim. Eng.* **2013**, *2*, 101–116. [CrossRef]
76. Chauhan, R.; Singh, T.; Tiwari, A.; Patnaik, A.; Thakur, N. Hybrid entropy—TOPSIS approach for energy performance prioritization in a rectangular channel employing impinging air jets. *Energy* **2017**, *134*, 360–368. [CrossRef]
77. Nadda, R.; Kumar, R.; Kumar, A.; Maithani, R. Optimization of single arc protrusion ribs parameters in solar air heater with impinging air jets based upon PSI approach. *Therm. Sci. Eng. Prog.* **2018**, *7*, 146–154. [CrossRef]
78. Kumar, N.; Kumar, A.; Maithani, R. Development of new correlations for heat transfer and pressure loss due to internal conical ring obstacles in an impinging jet solar air heater passage. *Therm. Sci. Eng. Prog.* **2020**, *17*, 100493. [CrossRef]
79. Obeidat, M.S.; Al Abed Alhalim, M.; Melhim, B.R. Systematic Approach for Selecting a Cleaning Method to Solar Panels Based on the Preference Selection Index Approach. *Jordan J. Mech. Ind. Eng.* **2020**, *14*, 279–287.
80. Kyomugisha, R.; Muriithi, C.M.; Edimu, M. Multiobjective optimal power flow for static voltage stability margin improvement. *Heliyon* **2021**, *7*, e08631. [CrossRef]
81. Obeidat, M.S.; Qasim, T.; Traini, H. The implementation of the preference selection index approach in ranking water desalination technologies. *Desalination Water Treat.* **2021**, *238*, 125–134. [CrossRef]
82. Pazarlıoğlu, H.K.; Tepe, A.Ü.; Tekir, M.; Arslan, K. Effect of new design of elongated jet hole on thermal efficiency of solar air heater. *Therm. Sci. Eng. Prog.* **2022**, *36*, 101483. [CrossRef]
83. Lotfabadi, A.K.; Hajinezhad, A.; Kasaeian, A.; Moosavian, S.F. Energetic, economic, environmental and climatic analysis of a solar combisystem for different consumption usages with PSI method ranking. *Renew. Energy* **2022**, *197*, 178–196. [CrossRef]

84. Priyanka, S.; Kumar, S.; Kumar, A.; Maithani, R. Selection of optimal parameters using PSI approach of a dimpled-V pattern roughened solar heat collector. *Mater. Today Proc.* **2022**, *64*, 1229–1233. [CrossRef]
85. Raj, V.K.; Baiju, V.; Junaid, F.P. Numerical investigations of thermal performance enhancement in phase change energy storage system effective for solar adsorption cooling systems. *J. Energy Storage* **2022**, *45*, 103696. [CrossRef]
86. Aksoy, S.; Ozbuk, M.Y. Multiple criteria decision making in hotel location: Does it relate to postpurchase consumer evaluations? *Tour. Manag. Perspect.* **2017**, *22*, 73–81. [CrossRef]
87. Chen, Z.; Zhong, P.; Liu, M.; Sun, H.; Shang, K. A novel hybrid approach for product concept evaluation based on rough numbers, shannon entropy and TOPSIS-PSI. *J. Intell. Fuzzy Syst.* **2021**, *40*, 12087–12099. [CrossRef]
88. Ulutaş, A.; Balo, F.; Sua, L.; Demir, E.; Topal, A.; Jakovljević, V. A new integrated grey mcdm model: Case of warehouse location selection. *Facta Univ. Series Mech. Eng.* **2021**, *19*, 515–535. [CrossRef]
89. Atalay, K.D.; İç, Y.T.; Keçeci, B.; Yurdakul, M.; Boran, M. Development of a new hesitant fuzzy ranking model for NTMP ranking problem. *Soft Comput.* **2021**, *25*, 14537–14548. [CrossRef]
90. Yorulmaz, M.; Can, G.F. Evaluation of performance levels of students for moodle learning management system in terms of usability Criteria with PSI-Entropy-Marcos integration. *Pamukkale Univ. J. Eng. Sci.* **2022**, *28*, 588–603. [CrossRef]
91. Maghableh, G.; Mumani, A. Simulation Based-MCDM Approach for Evaluating Traffic Solutions. *Promet-Traffic Transp.* **2022**, *34*, 117–133. [CrossRef]
92. Ulutaş, A.; Topal, A. A new hybrid model based on rough step-wise weight assessment ratio analysis for third-party logistics selection. *Soft Comput.* **2022**, *26*, 2021–2032. [CrossRef]
93. USLU, T.; Can, G.; Delİce, E.K. A new multidimensional process type FMEA approach: Defense and aerospace industry application. *J. Fac. Eng. Arch. Gazi Univ.* **2022**, *37*, 1411–1426. [CrossRef]
94. Gligorić, M.; Gligorić, Z.; Lutovac, S.; Negovanović, M.; Langović, Z. Novel Hybrid MPSI–MARA Decision-Making Model for Support System Selection in an Underground Mine. *Systems* **2022**, *10*, 248. [CrossRef]
95. Jayaraman, T. Magnet selection for permanent magnet synchronous machines by decision science. *Results Mater.* **2023**, *20*, 100495. [CrossRef]
96. Zhang, X.; Dai, L.; Wan, B. NA Operator-Based Interval-Valued q-Rung Orthopair Fuzzy PSI-COPRAS Group Decision-Making Method. *Int. J. Fuzzy Syst.* **2023**, *25*, 198–221. [CrossRef]
97. Punetha, N.; Jain, G. Aspect and orientation-based sentiment analysis of customer feedback using mathematical optimization models. *Knowl. Inf. Syst.* **2023**, *65*, 2731–2760. [CrossRef]
98. Kara, K.; Yalçın, G.C.; Simic, V.; Gürol, P.; Pamucar, D. Vehicle routing software selection for last mile delivery companies using Fermatean fuzzy-based model. *Eng. Appl. Artif. Intell.* **2024**, *131*, 107813. [CrossRef]
99. Kara, K.; Yalçın, G.C.; Simic, V.; Baysal, Z.; Pamucar, D. The alternative ranking using two-step logarithmic normalization method for benchmarking the supply chain performance of countries. *Socio-Econ. Plan. Sci.* **2024**, *92*, 101822. [CrossRef]
100. Liu, T.; Gao, K.; Rong, Y. Multicriteria group decision-making based on Fermatean fuzzy fairly weighted and ordered weighted averaging operators. *Granul. Comput.* **2024**, *9*, 13. [CrossRef]
101. Wu, M.; Song, J.; Fan, J. Crowdfunding project evaluation based on Fermatean fuzzy SAHARA three-way decision method. *Appl. Intell.* **2024**, *54*, 3566–3590. [CrossRef]
102. Popovic, G.; Fedajev, A.; Mitic, P.; Meidute-Kavaliauskiene, I. An ADAM-based approach to unveiling entrepreneurial ecosystems in selected European countries. *Manag. Decis.* **2024**, *63*, 1262–1291. [CrossRef]
103. Gökgöz, F.; Yalçın, E. Analyzing the Performances and Efficiencies of European Electric Vehicles in the European Union Market Using Decision Analysis Methods. *Transp. Res. Rec. J. Transp. Res. Board* **2024**, *2678*, 1039–1056. [CrossRef]
104. Tazzit, S.; Hossain, N.U.I.; Nur, F.; Elakramine, F.; Jaradat, R.; El Amrani, S. Selecting a biomass pelleting processing depot using a data driven decision-making approach. *Systems* **2021**, *9*, 32. [CrossRef]
105. Kodua, L.T.; Xiao, Y.; Adjei, N.O.; Asante, D.; Ofosu, B.O.; Amankona, D. Barriers to green human resources management (GHRM) implementation in developing countries. Evidence from Ghana. *J. Clean. Prod.* **2022**, *340*, 130671. [CrossRef]
106. Ror, C.K.; Tejyan, S.; Kumar, N. Effect of marble dust reinforcement in composites for different applications: A review. *Mater. Today Proc.* **2022**, *60*, 1120–1124. [CrossRef]
107. Biswas, A.K.; Islam, R.; Habib, A. An analytical investigation of critical factors to prioritize coalfields for Underground Coal Gasification—Bangladesh case. *Heliyon* **2023**, *9*, e18416. [CrossRef]
108. Ulutaş, A.; Balo, F.; Topal, A. Identifying the Most Efficient Natural Fibre for Common Commercial Building Insulation Materials with an Integrated PSI, MEREC, LOPCOW and MCRAT Model. *Polymers* **2023**, *15*, 1500. [CrossRef]
109. Demir, A.T.; Moslem, S. Evaluating the effect of the COVID-19 pandemic on medical waste disposal using preference selection index with CRADIS in a fuzzy environment. *Heliyon* **2024**, *10*, e26997. [CrossRef]
110. Ampaw, E.M.; Chai, J.; Jiang, Y.; Darko, A.P.; Ofori, K.S. Rethinking small-scale gold mining in Ghana: A holy grail for environmental stewardship and sustainability. *J. Clean. Prod.* **2024**, *437*, 140683. [CrossRef]

111. Pamucar, D.; Ulutaş, A.; Topal, A.; Karamaşa, Ç.; Ecer, F. Fermatean fuzzy framework based on preference selection index and combined compromise solution methods for green supplier selection in textile industry. *Int. J. Syst. Sci. Oper. Logist.* **2024**, *11*, 2319786. [CrossRef]
112. Darko, A.; Chan, A.P.C.; Ameyaw, E.E.; Owusu, E.K.; Pärn, E.; Edwards, D.J. Review of application of analytic hierarchy process (AHP) in construction. *Int. J. Constr. Manag.* **2019**, *19*, 436–452. [CrossRef]
113. Çelikbilek, Y.; Tüysüz, F. An in-depth review of theory of the TOPSIS method: An experimental analysis. *J. Manag. Anal.* **2020**, *7*, 281–300. [CrossRef]
114. Maués, L.M.F.; Nascimento, B.D.M.O.D.; Lu, W.; Xue, F. Estimating construction waste generation in residential buildings: A fuzzy set theory approach in the Brazilian Amazon. *J. Clean. Prod.* **2020**, *265*, 121779. [CrossRef]
115. Cui, X.; Zhao, T.; Wang, J. Allocation of carbon emission quotas in China's provincial power sector based on entropy method and ZSG-DEA. *J. Clean. Prod.* **2021**, *284*, 124683. [CrossRef]

Mathematical and Computational Applications

MDPI

Article

Eigenstructure-Oriented Optimization Design of Active Suspension Controllers

Yulong Du and Huping Mao *

School of Energy and Power Engineering, North University of China, Taiyuan 030051, China; yulongdu2023@163.com

* Correspondence: maohp@nuc.edu.cn; Tel.: +86-18035395956

Abstract

Active suspension systems can significantly enhance vehicle ride comfort and attitude stability, but often at the cost of increased energy consumption. To achieve both high dynamic performance and reduced energy usage, this study proposes an eigenstructure-oriented optimization method for active suspensions. Controller design is reformulated as a synergistic process of modal regulation and dynamic response optimization, in which partial eigenstructure assignment redistributes the dominant modes and system responses are computed using fourth-order Runge–Kutta integration. An energy-minimization optimization problem with performance constraints is then solved via the sequential quadratic programming (SQP) algorithm. Simulation results show that the proposed method markedly improves vibration performance: peak body acceleration is reduced from 3.48 m/s^2 to 1.70 m/s^2 (a 51.1% reduction), and the root mean square (RMS) acceleration decreases from 0.74 to 0.40 (a 45.6% reduction), while body displacement is also significantly suppressed. Compared with passive suspension and proportional–integral–derivative (PID) active suspension, the proposed system achieves superior performance in key indices such as body acceleration and displacement, leading to noticeably improved ride comfort and attitude stability. Furthermore, robustness analysis indicates that the method remains effective under variations in the receptance matrix, with only minor influence on system performance, demonstrating the practical applicability of the proposed control strategy.

Keywords: eigenstructure assignment; active suspension; dynamic response optimization; controller design

1. Introduction

With the continuous development of the automotive industry and the rising demand for driving safety and ride comfort, suspension performance optimization has become a central topic in vehicle dynamics. During operation, uneven road surfaces and external disturbances excite significant vibrations of the vehicle body and associated components. These vibrations not only degrade ride comfort and handling stability but also accelerate component wear and may even compromise driving safety. Consequently, vibration suppression and accurate control of body motion have become key objectives in suspension system design.

Traditionally, passive suspension systems have been widely used because of their simple structure and low cost. Such systems rely on fixed-parameter elements, including springs and dampers, to passively respond to road excitations. Although they provide basic vibration isolation under normal conditions, their fixed parameters prevent real-time adaptation to varying road surfaces. As a result, their performance under complex or extreme driving conditions is limited, making it difficult to simultaneously satisfy the requirements of ride comfort and handling stability in modern vehicles.

To overcome these limitations, active suspension systems have been extensively investigated. By employing actuators to actively generate control forces, they can dynamically adjust suspension stiffness and damping, thereby enabling real-time control of vehicle body motion. Compared with passive suspensions, active systems offer markedly improved ride comfort and handling stability, as well as superior adaptability to changing operating environments. However, their complex structure imposes stringent requirements on control strategy design—particularly in terms of real-time performance, stability and energy efficiency—which has driven ongoing research into advanced control methodologies.

Active suspension control has evolved rapidly over the past decade, driven by the need to improve both ride comfort and vehicle stability. Many studies focus on refining classical optimal and robust control strategies. Recent work has enhanced linear quadratic regulator (LQR) schemes through advanced optimization techniques [1–7], improved tracking and robustness via fuzzy logic and sliding-mode controllers [5,8–13], and strengthened disturbance rejection using H-infinity (H∞) and adaptive fault-tolerant control [9–11]. Although these methods deliver notable performance gains, they are largely incremental extensions of traditional model-based control paradigms. Their emphasis lies mainly on algorithmic tuning or controller restructuring, rather than on fundamentally reshaping the dynamic behavior of the suspension. As a result, the reported improvements, while effective, are predominantly performance-driven yet largely agnostic to the system's eigenstructure.

A parallel line of research has introduced increasingly sophisticated nonlinear, intelligent and learning-based strategies. Adaptive fuzzy control, fractional-order control, and inverse optimal control have expanded the capacity to address system uncertainties and nonlinearities [14–17]. Model predictive control (MPC) has been adapted to handle speed-dependent dynamics and preview information [18,19], while hybrid metaheuristic–fuzzy schemes have shown potential for enhanced global optimization [20]. More recently, neural-network-based adaptive control and deep reinforcement learning (DRL) have achieved impressive response improvements and generalization capabilities under complex operating conditions [21–25]. Despite these advances, most intelligent and learning-based approaches continue to treat the suspension as an input–output mapping to be optimized, rather than as a dynamical structure whose underlying eigenproperties fundamentally determine system performance. Consequently, these methods often require extensive training data, rely on heuristic reward or parameter tuning, and offer limited physical interpretability.

Complementary to these control-centric approaches, structural dynamics research has highlighted the importance of eigenvalues and eigenvectors as intrinsic determinants of system behavior. A series of studies has advanced eigenstructure assignment techniques, including model updating [26], concurrent parameter and controller optimization [27], partial pole or pole–zero placement [28–30], time-delay compensation [31], and receptance-based assignment using partial data [32,33]. These works significantly reduce reliance on accurate system matrices and deepen theoretical understanding of structural feature manipulation. However, their impact remains largely confined to the vibration control and structural modification communities. The application of eigenstructure assignment to active suspension control has been surprisingly limited. Most existing studies provide conceptual formulations or simulation demonstrations but lack systematic pathways for embedding eigenstructure manipulation into practical control design.

Overall, the literature reveals a clear gap. On the one hand, control-oriented studies primarily enhance controller performance but seldom exploit the intrinsic structural characteristics that fundamentally shape suspension dynamics. On the other hand, research

https://doi.org/10.3390/mca31010005

on structural feature regulation mainly addresses theoretical formulations and vibration-oriented applications, with limited integration into practical suspension control, especially when performance constraints and energy consumption are considered simultaneously. To bridge this gap, the present study a standard quarter-car active suspension model and proposes an eigenstructure-oriented optimization design method. By combining partial eigenstructure assignment with dynamic-response-based optimization, the method improves suspension performance while explicitly limiting controller gain magnitude and energy consumption

The main contributions of this study are as follows:

1. An eigenstructure-oriented optimization framework is developed for active suspension systems. This framework provides a physically interpretable means of regulating structural dynamics and enables targeted modal control to enhance vibration isolation performance.
2. A performance-constrained optimization strategy is established to enhance suspension performance while limiting control effort, ensuring that ride comfort enhancement is achieved in parallel with reduced gain magnitude and energy consumption.

The remainder of this paper is organized as follows. Section 2 introduces the quarter-car active suspension model and the corresponding road-excitation representation. Section 3 presents the proposed eigenstructure-oriented controller design and the associated optimization formulation, including implementation details. Section 4 reports numerical studies and discussions based on a representative parameter set. Section 5 investigates the robustness of the resulting controller. Section 6 concludes the paper and outlines the limitations and directions for future work.

2. System Modeling

2.1. Mathematical Modeling of Active Suspension

To analyze the vertical dynamic response of a vehicle subjected to road excitation, this study adopts a classical quarter-car active suspension model with two degrees of freedom (2-DoF), as illustrated in Figure 1.

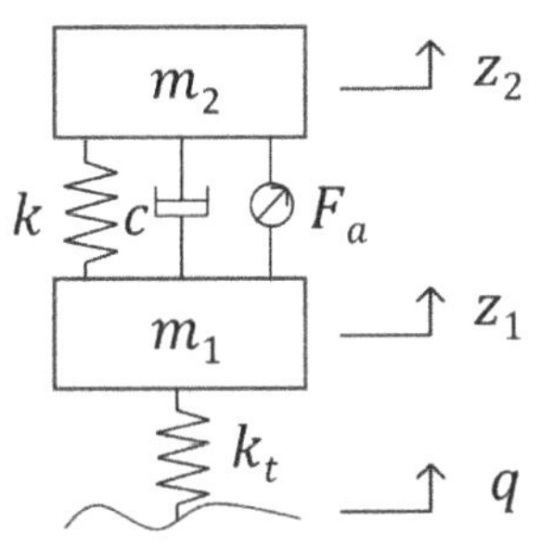

Figure 1. Schematic diagram of the quarter-car active suspension system.

In this model, the actuator is modeled as an ideal force source, and the suspension spring and damper are assumed to be linear elements. Nonlinear effects, frictional losses and structural coupling are neglected so that a linear system suitable for analysis and controller design is obtained.

In the model, m_2 denotes the sprung mass, approximately one quarter of the total vehicle mass, and m_1 denotes the unsprung mass, mainly comprising the wheel and its associated components. F_a is the control force acting between the sprung and unsprung masses to actively regulate the dynamic response. k and c are the equivalent suspension stiffness and damping, respectively, and k_t represents the tire stiffness. z_2 and z_1 represent

https://doi.org/10.3390/mca31010005

the vertical displacements of the sprung and unsprung masses, respectively, and q is the road excitation input.

Accordingly, the vertical motions of the unsprung and sprung masses are governed by Equations (1) and (2), respectively, and can be expressed as follows:

The unsprung mass:

$$m_1\ddot{z}_1 + k_t(z_1 - q) - c(\dot{z}_2 - \dot{z}_1) - k(z_2 - z_1) = -F_a \tag{1}$$

The sprung mass:

$$m_2\ddot{z}_2 + c(\dot{z}_2 - \dot{z}_1) + k(z_2 - z_1) = F_a \tag{2}$$

2.2. Road Excitation Modeling

In the analysis and design of vehicle suspension dynamics, accurately representing external road excitation is essential. During driving, road surface irregularities are transmitted through the tire to the suspension system and constitute the primary external disturbance affecting overall ride and handling performance. A widely adopted modeling approach is to describe the road profile using the Power Spectral Density (PSD) function proposed by the International Organization for Standardization (ISO 8608, [34]).

In general, road surface irregularities can be modeled as a broadband random process whose spatial power spectral density is given by Equation (3):

$$G_q(n) = G_q(n_0)\left(\frac{n}{n_0}\right)^{-\omega} \tag{3}$$

where $G_q(n_0)$ is the road roughness coefficient at the reference spatial frequency n_0; n denotes the spatial frequency; ω is the frequency exponent, which is usually taken as 2. Different road classes correspond to different values of $G_q(n_0)$, as summarized in Table 1.

Table 1. Classification of road surface roughness.

Road Surface Class	Roughness Coefficient $G_q(n_0)$ ($\times 10^{-6}$ m^3)
A	16
B	64
C	256
D	1024
E	4096
F	16,384

Road excitation depends not only on surface roughness but also on vehicle speed, both of which are key factors influencing the dynamic behavior of suspension systems. To achieve realistic time-domain simulations, the spatial power spectral density must be correlated with vehicle speed v and transformed into the temporal frequency domain. The spatial frequency n and temporal frequency f are related by Equation (4):

$$f = nv \tag{4}$$

Accordingly, the spatial power spectral density can be converted into the frequency domain, and the corresponding expression is given by Equation (5):

$$G_q(n) = G_q(n_0)\left(\frac{n_0}{f/v}\right)^2 v \tag{5}$$

https://doi.org/10.3390/mca31010005

where f denotes the temporal frequency and v is the vehicle speed.

Introducing the angular frequency $\omega = 2\pi f$, the corresponding expression of the road excitation in the frequency domain can be rewritten as Equation (6):

$$G_q(\omega) = \frac{4\pi^2 G_q(n_0) n_0^2 v}{\omega^2 + \omega_0^2} \tag{6}$$

where $\omega_0 = 2\pi n_0 v$ represents the lower cutoff angular frequency, and n_0 is the lower cutoff spatial frequency.

The time-domain representation of the road excitation can be generated through a first-order filtering process driven by white noise, as given in Equation (7):

$$\dot{q}(t) = -2\pi n_1 q(t) + 2\pi\omega(t) n_0 \sqrt{G_q(n_0) v} \tag{7}$$

where $\omega(t)$ denotes unit-intensity Gaussian white noise.

3. Theory and Methodology

3.1. Theory of Eigenstructure Assignment

For an n-DoF linear time-invariant system, the open-loop dynamic equation can be expressed as Equation (8):

$$\mathbf{M}\ddot{x}(t) + \mathbf{C}\dot{x}(t) + \mathbf{K}x(t) = 0 \tag{8}$$

where $x(t) \in \mathbb{R}^n$ is the vector of generalized coordinates, and $\mathbf{M}, \mathbf{C}, \mathbf{K} \in \mathbb{R}^{n\times n}$ denote the mass, damping, and stiffness matrices, respectively.

When an active control force $u(t)$ is introduced, the closed-loop dynamic equation is given by Equation (9):

$$\mathbf{M}\ddot{x}(t) + \mathbf{C}\dot{x}(t) + \mathbf{K}x(t) = \mathbf{B}u(t) \tag{9}$$

where $\mathbf{B} \in \mathbb{R}^{n\times p}$ is the control input distribution matrix and $u(t) \in \mathbb{R}^p$ is the control input vector. The control law is defined as $u(t) = -\mathbf{F}^T\dot{x}(t) - \mathbf{G}^T x(t)$, where $\mathbf{F}, \mathbf{G} \in \mathbb{R}^{n\times p}$ represent the feedback gain matrices corresponding to velocity and displacement, respectively.

The quadratic eigenvalue problems of the open-loop and closed-loop systems are formulated in Equations (10) and (11):

$$\left(\lambda_k^2\mathbf{M} + \lambda_k\mathbf{C} + \mathbf{K}\right)v_k = 0 \tag{10}$$

$$\left(\mu_k^2\mathbf{M} + \mu_k\mathbf{C} + \mathbf{K}\right)w_k = \mathbf{B}\left(\mathbf{G}^T + \mu_k\mathbf{F}^T\right)w_k \tag{11}$$

where $(\lambda_i, \mathbf{v}_i)$ and $(\mu_k, \mathbf{w}_k)$ are the eigenpairs of the open-loop and closed-loop systems, respectively.

Equation (11) can be rearranged into the homogeneous form shown in Equation (12):

$$\left(\mu_k^2\mathbf{M} + \mu_k\mathbf{C} + \mathbf{K} - \mathbf{B}\left(\mathbf{G}^T + \mu_k\mathbf{F}^T\right)\right)w_k = \mathbf{0} \tag{12}$$

Assuming that the first $2p$ closed-loop eigenvalues are reassigned, while the $2p+1, \cdots, 2n$ eigenvalues remain unchanged, we impose the following condition (Equation (13)):

$$\lambda_k = \mu_k, \qquad k = 2p+1, \cdots, 2n \tag{13}$$

Introducing an auxiliary mass modification matrix $\Delta\mathbf{M}$ (used only for analytical derivation and not implemented in practice), Equation (12) can be rewritten as Equation (14):

$$\left(\lambda_k^2(\mathbf{M} + \Delta\mathbf{M}) + \lambda_k\mathbf{C} + \mathbf{K}\right)w_k = \mathbf{B}\left(\mathbf{G}^T + \lambda_k\mathbf{F}^T\right)w_k + \lambda_k^2\Delta\mathbf{M}w_k \tag{14}$$

https://doi.org/10.3390/mca31010005

where $k = 2p+1, \cdots, 2n$.

Defining $\hat{\mathbf{H}}(\mu_k) = \left(\lambda_k^2(\mathbf{M}+\Delta\mathbf{M}) + \lambda_k\mathbf{C} + \mathbf{K}\right)^{-1}$, and pre-multiplying both sides of Equation (14) by $\hat{\mathbf{H}}(\mu_k)$, we obtain Equation (15):

$$w_k = \hat{\mathbf{H}}(\mu_k)\mathbf{B}\left(\mathbf{G}^{\mathrm{T}} + \lambda_k\mathbf{F}^{\mathrm{T}}\right)w_k + \lambda_k^2\hat{\mathbf{H}}(\mu_k)\Delta\mathbf{M}w_k, \qquad k = 2p+1, \cdots, 2n \tag{15}$$

Rearranging Equation (15) yields Equation (16):

$$\left(\mathbf{I} - \lambda_k^2\hat{\mathbf{H}}(\mu_k)\Delta\mathbf{M}\right)w_k = \hat{\mathbf{H}}(\mu_k)\mathbf{B}\left(\mathbf{G}^{\mathrm{T}} + \lambda_k\mathbf{F}^{\mathrm{T}}\right)w_k, \qquad k = 2p+1, \cdots, 2n \tag{16}$$

Finally, Equation (16) can be reformulated in the compact form of Equation (17):

$$\left(\mathbf{I} - \lambda_k^2\hat{\mathbf{H}}(\mu_k)\Delta\mathbf{M}\right)w_k = u_k, \qquad k = 2p+1, \cdots, 2n \tag{17}$$

To facilitate subsequent derivations, a proportional coefficient vector is introduced as $\beta_k = \begin{bmatrix}\beta_{k1} & \beta_{k2} & \cdots & \beta_{ki}\end{bmatrix}^T$ and defined in Equation (18):

$$\beta_{kj} = \left(\mu_k f_j^T + g_j^T\right)w_k, \qquad j = 1, 2, \cdots, i \tag{18}$$

It is noteworthy that the modal vectors $\mathbf{w}_k$ are assumed to be predetermined.

By substituting Equation (18) into Equation (17), the compact expression in Equation (19) is obtained for the eigenvalues kept unchanged:

$$u_k = \hat{\mathbf{H}}(\mu_k)\mathbf{B}\beta_k, \qquad k = 2p+1, \cdots, 2n \tag{19}$$

Similarly, by defining $\mathbf{H}(\mu_k) = \left(\lambda_k^2\mathbf{M} + \lambda_k\mathbf{C} + \mathbf{K}\right)^{-1}$ and referring to Equation (12), the corresponding relation for the reassigned eigenvalues can be written as Equation (20):

$$w_k = \mathbf{H}(\mu_k)\mathbf{B}\beta_k, \qquad k = 1, \cdots, 2p \tag{20}$$

Equations (19) and (20) can thus be unified in the form of Equation (21):

$$\mathbf{B}\beta_k = \gamma_k \tag{21}$$

where γ_k is defined piecewise in Equation (22):

$$\gamma_k = \begin{cases} \mathbf{H}(\mu_k)^{-1}w_k, & k = 1, \cdots, 2p \\ \hat{\mathbf{H}}(\mu_k)^{-1}u_k, & k = 2p+1, \cdots, 2n \end{cases} \tag{22}$$

From Equation (22), the proportional coefficient vector β_k can be subsequently obtained.

Using the definition in Equation (18), this relationship can be written in matrix form as Equation (23):

$$\begin{bmatrix} \mu_k w_k^T & 0 & \cdots & 0 & w_k^T & 0 & \cdots & 0 \\ 0 & \mu_k w_k^T & \cdots & 0 & 0 & w_k^T & \cdots & 0 \\ \vdots & \vdots & \vdots & \vdots & \vdots & \vdots & \vdots & \vdots \\ 0 & 0 & \cdots & \mu_k w_k^T & 0 & 0 & \cdots & w_k^T \end{bmatrix} \begin{bmatrix} f_1 \\ \vdots \\ f_i \\ g_1 \\ \vdots \\ g_i \end{bmatrix} = \begin{bmatrix} \beta_{k1} \\ \beta_{k2} \\ \vdots \\ \beta_{ki} \end{bmatrix}, \quad k = 1, \cdots, 2n \tag{23}$$

https://doi.org/10.3390/mca31010005

Accordingly,

$$\mathbf{T}_k y = \beta_k, \qquad k = 1, 2, \cdots, 2n \tag{24}$$

Consequently, the gain matrices **G** and **F** of the controller can be determined from the global matrix equation in Equation (25):

$$\begin{bmatrix} \mathbf{T}_1 \\ \vdots \\ \mathbf{T}_{2n} \end{bmatrix} \begin{bmatrix} f_1 \\ \vdots \\ f_i \\ g_1 \\ \vdots \\ g_i \end{bmatrix} = \begin{bmatrix} \beta_1 \\ \vdots \\ \beta_{2n} \end{bmatrix} \tag{25}$$

3.2. Dynamic Response Optimization Approach

In the optimization design of the active suspension system, the RMS values of the body acceleration and displacement are adopted as the primary performance indices, while the minimization of the controller gains is defined as the optimization objective. This formulation aims to enhance suspension performance while simultaneously maintaining energy efficiency. To obtain the desired system response over a finite time interval $[0, t_{\text{end}}]$, the design variables are optimized under engineering constraints and within prescribed bounds.

For the two-degree-of-freedom (2-DoF) quarter-car active suspension model, the predefined modal vectors $\mathbf{w}_k$ (assembled in $\mathbf{X} = [\mathbf{v}_1^{\mathrm{T}}, \mathbf{v}_2^{\mathrm{T}}, \cdots, \mathbf{v}_n^{\mathrm{T}}]^{\mathrm{T}}$) and the system eigenvalues λ_k (collected in $Y = \lambda_k$) are chosen as the design variables. Based on the system dynamic equations and the eigenstructure assignment theory, a mathematical model for dynamic response optimization of the active suspension system is then established.

$$min \sum_{i=1}^{n} \sum_{j=1}^{m} \left(f(\mathbf{X}, Y, \mu_c)_{ij}^2 + g(\mathbf{X}, Y, \mu_c)_{ij}^2 \right)$$

$$s.t. \begin{cases} T \begin{bmatrix} f_1 & \cdots & f_m & g_1 & \cdots & g_m \end{bmatrix}^T = \begin{bmatrix} \beta_1 \\ \vdots \\ \beta_{2n} \end{bmatrix} \\ \left(\mathbf{Y}^2 \mathbf{M} + \mathbf{Y}(\mathbf{C} + \mathbf{B}\mathbf{F}^{\mathrm{T}}) + \left(\mathbf{K} - \mathbf{B}\mathbf{G}^{\mathrm{T}} \right) \right) w_k = 0 \\ \mathbf{M}\ddot{d}_p(t) + (\mathbf{C} - \mathbf{B}\mathbf{F}^T)\dot{d}_p(t) + \left(\mathbf{K} - \mathbf{B}\mathbf{G}^T \right) d_p(t) = f_r(t) \\ \left[\frac{1}{T} \int_0^T d_{pw}^2(t) dt \right]^{\frac{1}{2}} \le c_1, \quad p = 1, 2, \cdots, ug \\ \left[\frac{1}{T} \int_0^T \ddot{d}_{pw}^2(t) dt \right]^{\frac{1}{2}} \le c_2, \quad p = 1, 2, \cdots, ug \\ \mathbf{X}_{min} \le \mathbf{X} \le \mathbf{X}_{max} \\ Y_{min} \le Y \le Y_{max} \end{cases} \tag{26}$$

$$i = 1, 2, \cdots, n; \ j = 1, 2, \cdots, m; c = 2p + 1, \cdots, 2n$$

In this model, c_1 and c_2 denote the RMS performance indices of body displacement and body acceleration, respectively; d_p and $\ddot{d}_p$ represent the displacement and acceleration responses at the p-th coordinate ($p = 2$ for the vehicle body); and the design variables **X** and Y are constrained within $[\mathbf{X}_{\min}, \mathbf{X}_{\max}]$ and $[Y_{\min}, Y_{\max}]$, respectively.

To clarify the implementation procedure of the proposed method, the overall optimization framework is summarized in Figure 2 and can be outlined as follows:

(1) Define the eigenvalues to be reassigned and those to be retained;

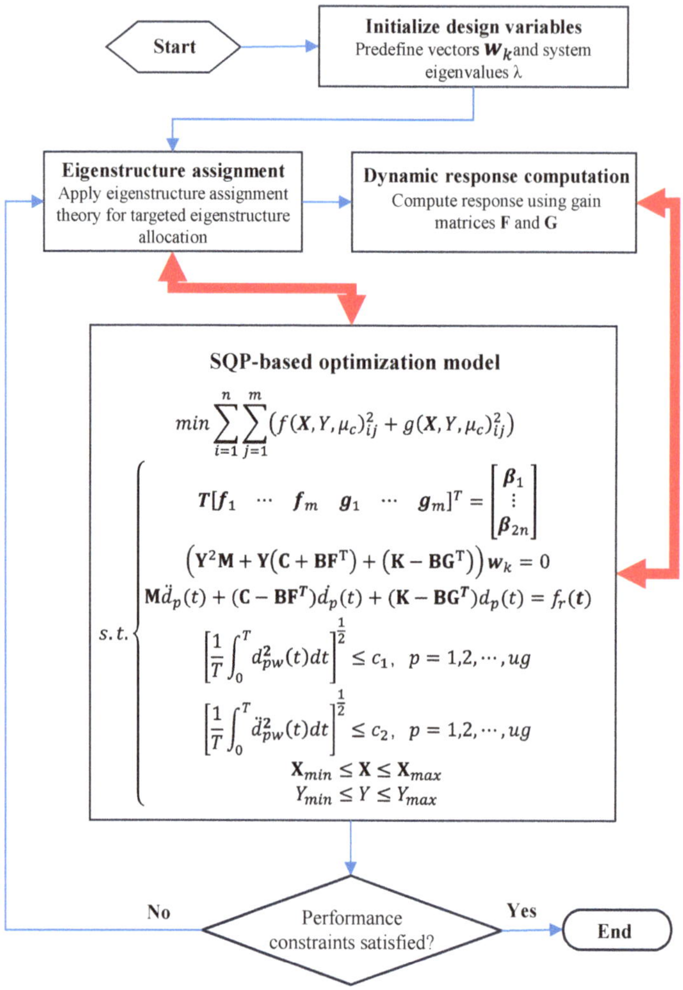

Figure 2. Flowchart of dynamic response optimization.

(2) Select the design variables (the predefined vectors $\mathbf{w}_k$ and the system eigenvalues λ_k) together with the performance indices, and establish the corresponding mathematical optimization model;
(3) Assign initial values to the design variables and compute the initial controller gain matrices using the partial eigenstructure assignment method;
(4) Substitute the gain matrices into the system dynamic equations and perform a time-domain response analysis using the fourth-order Runge–Kutta method;
(5) Iteratively update the design variables using the SQP algorithm until convergence to the optimal solution.

4. Numerical Example

The parameters used for the quarter-car suspension model are listed in Table 2.

https://doi.org/10.3390/mca31010005

Table 2. Suspension system parameters.

Parameter	Symbol	Value	Unit
Sprung mass	m_2	317	kg
Unsprung mass	m_1	45	kg
Suspension stiffness	k	22,000	N/m
Suspension damping coefficient	c	1500	Ns/m
Tire stiffness	k_t	192,000	N/m

Based on the above parameters, the system matrices of the quarter-car model can be expressed as follows:

$$\mathbf{M} = \begin{bmatrix} 317 & 0 \\ 0 & 45 \end{bmatrix}, \mathbf{K} = \begin{bmatrix} 22000 & -22000 \\ -22000 & 214000 \end{bmatrix}, \mathbf{C} = \begin{bmatrix} 1500 & -1500 \\ -1500 & 1500 \end{bmatrix}$$

The open-loop system possesses two pairs of complex conjugate eigenvalues:

$$\lambda_{1,2} = -17.0876 \pm 65.8487i, \lambda_{3,4} = -1.9450 \pm 7.7588i$$

The corresponding eigenvectors are also obtained, as summarized in Table 3.

Table 3. Eigenvalues and corresponding eigenvectors of the open-loop system.

λ_k	$\mathbf{v}_k^T$	
$-17.0876 + 65.8487i$	$0.0281 + 0.0632\text{i}$	$-0.9976 + 0.0095i$
$-17.0876 - 65.8487\text{i}$	$0.0281 - 0.0632\text{i}$	$-0.9976 - 0.0095i$
$-1.9450 + 7.7588i$	$0.2391 - 0.9651i$	$0.0719 - 0.0785i$
$-1.9450 - 7.7588i$	$0.2391 + 0.9651i$	$0.0719 + 0.0785i$

To obtain the dynamic response of the suspension system under open-loop conditions, a typical ISO Class C random road profile was selected as the external excitation. The road roughness parameters were set as follows: $G_q(n_0) = 256 \times 10^{-6}\ \text{m}^3$, $v = 72$ km/h, $t = 10$ s, with the random noise seed set to 233. The typical Class C road profile excitation signal is illustrated in Figure 3.

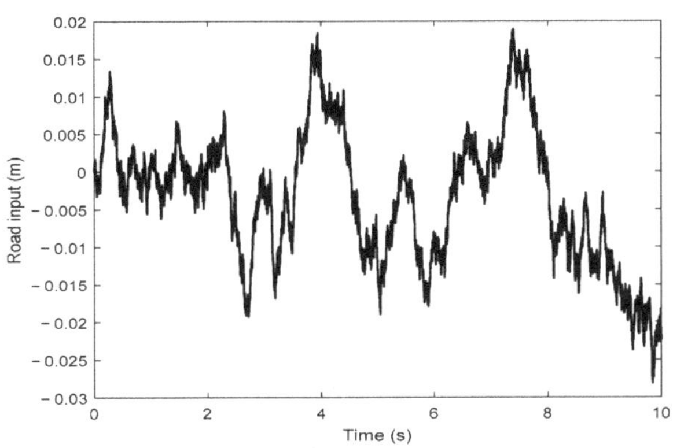

Figure 3. Road excitation signal for ISO Class C profile.

For the optimization design of the active suspension system, the control input distribution matrix was defined as $\mathbf{B} = \begin{bmatrix} 1 & 1 \\ 0 & -2 \end{bmatrix}$, and the auxiliary mass correction matrix was

https://doi.org/10.3390/mca31010005

set to $\Delta\mathbf{M} = \text{diag}(0.5, 0)$. The constraint thresholds were defined as $c_1 = 0.0115$ (RMS of body displacement) and $c_2 = 0.45$ (RMS of body acceleration). Using the SQP algorithm, the optimal design variables satisfying these constraints were obtained, as summarized in Table 4.

Table 4. Optimized design variables.

Category	Variable	Value
Eigenvalues (Y)	$\lambda_{3,4}$	$-1.9450 \pm 7.7588i$
	$\mu_{1,2}$	$-18.7191 \pm 66.4209i$
Predefined Vectors (X)	w_1, w_2	$-0.0104/0.7042$
	w_3, w_4	$0.8754/0.0933$

The gain matrices of the controller were obtained as

$$\mathbf{F} = \begin{bmatrix} 152.00 & -371.53 \\ 82.24 & -66.99 \end{bmatrix}, \ \mathbf{G} = \begin{bmatrix} -647.00 & -9509.00 \\ 3280.00 & -17244 \end{bmatrix}$$

The optimization objective function is defined as

$$J(\mathbf{F}, \mathbf{G}) = \sqrt{\|\mathbf{F}\|_F^2 + \|\mathbf{G}\|_F^2}$$

where $J(\mathbf{F}, \mathbf{G})$ measures the overall magnitude of the feedback gains and $\|\cdot\|_F$ denotes the Frobenius norm of a matrix.

Figure 4 illustrates the convergence process of the objective function during the dynamic response optimization. The objective value decreases rapidly at the initial stage and gradually stabilizes after approximately 20 iterations. The optimal solution is reached at the 40th iteration, with the corresponding minimum objective value of 1700.6571.

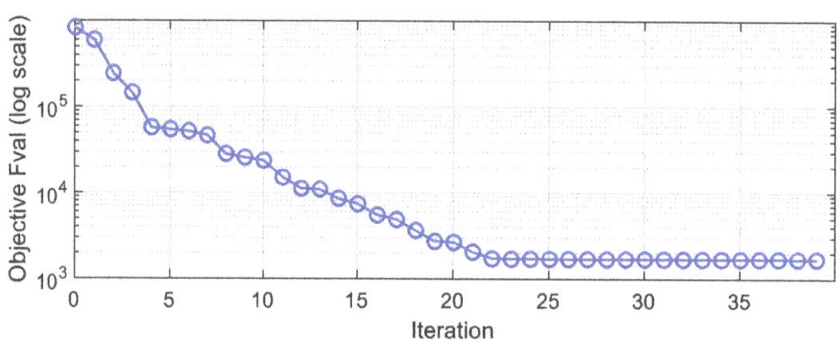

Figure 4. Convergence curve of the objective function in dynamic response optimization.

The dynamic equation of the closed-loop system can thus be expressed as

$$\mathbf{M}\ddot{\mathrm{x}} + \mathbf{C}\dot{\mathrm{x}} + \mathbf{K}\mathrm{x} - \mathbf{B}\mathbf{F}^T\dot{\mathrm{x}} - \mathbf{B}\mathbf{G}^T\mathrm{x} = 0$$

By substituting the obtained controller gain matrices **F** and **G** into the closed-loop dynamic equations, the time-domain responses of the system under a typical ISO Class C road excitation were obtained, as illustrated in Figure 5.

Figure 5a,b show the dynamic acceleration and displacement responses of three suspension systems: passive suspension, PID active suspension, and the proposed active suspension system. As seen in Figure 5a, the body acceleration response of the passive suspension (orange dashed line) exhibits larger fluctuations compared to both the PID active suspension (blue dash-dot line) and the proposed active suspension (purple solid

https://doi.org/10.3390/mca31010005

line). This indicates that the passive suspension struggles to maintain ride comfort under dynamic loading, as it is less effective at damping high-frequency oscillations.

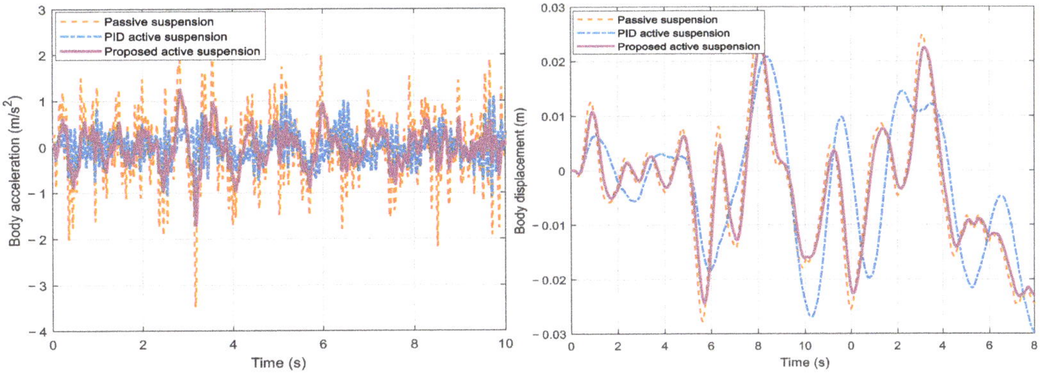

(a) (b)

Figure 5. Comparison of responses between passive, PID active, and proposed active suspension systems: (**a**) Body acceleration response and (**b**) Body displacement response.

In contrast, both the PID active suspension and the proposed active suspension show significant improvement in damping, as evidenced by the smoother body acceleration waveforms in Figure 5a. The proposed active suspension, represented by the purple line, provides better vibration isolation than the PID active suspension. This is evident in the smaller amplitude and reduced peak acceleration, particularly during high-intensity input conditions (around time 2 s to 3 s and 7 s to 8 s). The PID system (blue dashed line) also performs better than the passive suspension but does not match the performance of the proposed system, particularly in terms of maintaining a stable response during transient disturbances.

For the body displacement response shown in Figure 5b, the same trend is observed. The passive suspension shows larger displacements, which indicates the system's inability to suppress body motion effectively. Both the PID and proposed active suspension systems, however, significantly reduce body displacement. The proposed system (purple line) again shows the least displacement compared to the PID system (blue dashed line), confirming its superior performance in controlling body motion. The proposed active suspension demonstrates smoother transitions and better suppression of displacement oscillations, further confirming its overall superior performance.

Table 5 presents the quantitative comparison of key performance metrics for the three suspension systems.

Table 5. Comparison of performance metrics between passive, PID active, and proposed active suspension systems.

Performance Metric	Passive Suspension	PID Active Suspension	Proposed Active Suspension
Peak body acceleration (m/s^2)	3.4771	1.0589	1.6990
RMS of body acceleration	0.7358	0.4459	0.4003
Peak body displacement (m)	0.02568	0.02415	0.02359
RMS of body displacement	0.01240	0.01246	0.01143
RMS of suspension deflection	0.00591	0.00939	0.00605

The proposed active suspension system achieves remarkable improvements in both body acceleration and displacement responses. Specifically, the maximum body accel-

https://doi.org/10.3390/mca31010005

eration decreases from 3.48 m/s^2 (passive suspension) to 1.70 m/s^2 (proposed active suspension), and the RMS of body acceleration is reduced from 0.7358 to 0.4003, corresponding to improvements of 51.1% and 45.6%, respectively. Compared to the PID active suspension, the proposed active suspension performs better, with a 6.5% improvement in RMS acceleration (from 0.4459 to 0.4003). This indicates that the proposed system provides superior vibration isolation and reduced discomfort for passengers. As shown in Table 6, this RMS range corresponds to the transition from "Fairly uncomfortable" to "Slightly uncomfortable," demonstrating a notable improvement in ride comfort.

Table 6. Relationship between weighted RMS acceleration and subjective ride comfort.

Weighted RMS Acceleration	Perceived Comfort Level
<0.315	Not uncomfortable
$0.315\sim0.63$	Slightly uncomfortable
$0.5\sim1.0$	Fairly uncomfortable
$0.8\sim1.6$	Uncomfortable
$1.25\sim2.5$	Very uncomfortable

In terms of body displacement, the proposed active suspension also shows superior performance. The maximum body displacement and RMS of body displacement are reduced by 8.1% and 7.9%, respectively, compared to the passive suspension. When compared to the PID active suspension, the proposed system shows a slightly better control performance, with a 7.9% reduction in RMS displacement. The proposed active suspension system performs slightly better in terms of dynamic deflection RMS compared to the passive suspension and PID active suspension, with a modest improvement of 6.05%. However, the primary performance improvements are seen in body acceleration and displacement, which are more closely related to ride comfort and system stability.

In summary, the proposed active suspension control method significantly improves system dynamics through the integration of eigenstructure assignment and dynamic response optimization. Compared to both passive suspension and alternative methods, the active system outperforms in key metrics such as body acceleration and displacement, leading to reduced vibration and enhanced ride comfort. These results demonstrate the effectiveness of the proposed control strategy.

5. Robustness Analysis

Although the controller design method employed in this study can effectively avoid modeling-related errors, it may still be influenced by system uncertainties or inaccurate fitting of the frequency response functions, which can distort the resulting eigenstructure assignment of the system. In this section, the robustness of the proposed method is assessed using the numerical example presented in Section 4. Analogous to the numerical example, the first pair of system eigenvalues is assigned to $\mu_{1,2} = -18.7191 \pm 66.4209i$, while the second pair is kept unchanged at $\mu_{3,4} = -1.9450 \pm 7.7588i$. The control matrix $\mathbf{B}$ is also defined to be identical to that used in the example.

Consider the 2-DoF quarter-car suspension system used in the numerical example. To emulate possible measurement noise or identification errors, the receptance matrix obtained from simulation is artificially perturbed at one or two selected entries. The contaminated receptance is defined as

$$\hat{h}_{i,j}(\mu_k) = h_{i,j}(\mu_k)\ rand(0.95,\ 1.05)$$

https://doi.org/10.3390/mca31010005

where $\hat{h}_{i,j}(\mu_k)$ denotes the perturbed receptance, $h_{i,j}(\mu_k)$ is the nominal (true) receptance, and $rand(0.95, 1.05)$ is a uniformly distributed random number between 0.95 and 1.05, corresponding to at most a 5% deviation from the nominal value.

Figure 6a,b, respectively, present the results of 1000 Monte-Carlo simulations. The four rectangles represent the regions of the obtained eigenvalues and are defined as follows:

$$\text{Region}(\mu_k) = \mu_k + [-0.05, 0.05] \pm [-0.05, 0.05]i$$

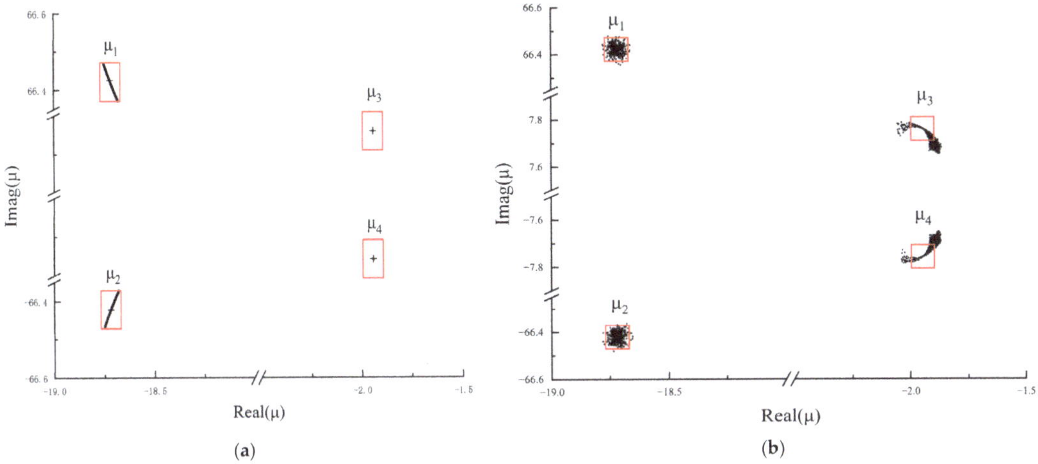

Figure 6. Eigenvalue spread with contaminated receptance matrices, where (**a**) shows the case with one contaminated element and (**b**) illustrates the case with two contaminated elements.

From Figure 6a it can be seen that all obtained eigenvalues fall within small regions close to the nominal values of the targeted eigenvalues. Because more contaminated elements are included in Figure 6b larger variations in the imaginary parts are observed. Nevertheless, the vast majority of the eigenvalues still cluster within relatively small regions. Therefore, the proposed method can be regarded as robust with respect to errors in the measured receptance (frequency response) matrix of the example system.

6. Conclusions

This study has proposed an eigenstructure-oriented optimization method for active suspension control, integrating eigenstructure assignment with dynamic response optimization. By redistributing the system eigenstructure, the method suppresses vibrations and improves ride comfort. In a quarter-car case study, the proposed controller reduces peak body acceleration by 51.1% and RMS acceleration by 45.6% and yields comparable reductions in body displacement. Compared with passive suspension and PID active suspension, it achieves superior performance in key indices such as body acceleration and displacement, resulting in noticeably improved ride comfort. Robustness studies further show that the method remains effective under 5% perturbations in the receptance matrix of a 2-DoF damped system, indicating good tolerance to data inaccuracies with only minor impact on overall system performance.

Despite these advantages, the method is subject to two main applicability constraints. First, although the formulation in principle requires only partial system information for eigenstructure assignment, in practice it is difficult to obtain full-vehicle receptance data with sufficient spatial coverage and accuracy, which may reduce the achievable performance. Second, the required number of input channels is determined by the total number

https://doi.org/10.3390/mca31010005

of assigned and preserved eigenvalues together with the system degrees of freedom; this requirement often conflicts with packaging, space and cost constraints in production vehicles and thus limits the method's direct engineering deployment.

Future work will therefore proceed along two directions. The first is to extend the eigenstructure-oriented optimization method from the quarter-car model to full-vehicle modeling and control, so as to capture the coupled dynamics of the entire vehicle over a wider range of road profiles and operating conditions. On this basis, strategies for reducing the number of actuators while preserving acceptable control performance will be explored and validated via multi-domain co-simulation, thereby narrowing the gap between numerical studies and real-vehicle operation. The second direction is to further investigate the intrinsic relationship between eigenstructure and time-domain responses, with the goal of relaxing the dependence on detailed receptance data. Machine-learning-based surrogate models for large-scale systems will be developed to enhance the adaptability and computational efficiency of the eigenstructure-oriented active suspension framework.

Author Contributions: Conceptualization, H.M.; methodology, Y.D.; software, Y.D.; validation, Y.D.; writing—original draft preparation, Y.D.; writing—review and editing. All authors have read and agreed to the published version of the manuscript.

Funding: This research was funded by the Provincial Natural Science Foundation of Shanxi Province, China, grant number 202303021221108.

Data Availability Statement: The data is available on request to the first author.

Acknowledgments: We are deeply grateful for the constructive feedback provided by the anonymous reviewers.

Conflicts of Interest: The authors declare no conflicts of interest.

References

1. Dandavate, K.D. A Review on Controlling Methods for Active Suspension Systems. *Int. J. Res. Appl. Sci. Eng. Technol.* **2023**, *11*, 1675–1680. [CrossRef]
2. Goga, V.; Kľúčik, M. Optimization of Vehicle Suspension Parameters with Use of Evolutionary Computation. *Procedia Eng.* **2012**, *48*, 174–179. [CrossRef]
3. Ding, F.; Wang, B.; Liu, M. Research on LQR Control of Vehicle Active Suspension. *Mach. Des. Res.* **2020**, *36*, 52–55.
4. Zhao, Z.; Wang, C.; Zhao, J.; Du, W. LQR Force Command Planning Based Sliding Mode Control for Active Suspension System. *J. Syst. Control Eng.* **2024**, *238*, 373–385. [CrossRef]
5. Abut, T.; Salkim, E. Control of Quarter-Car Active Suspension System Based on Optimized Fuzzy Linear Quadratic Regulator Control Method. *Appl. Sci.* **2023**, *13*, 8802. [CrossRef]
6. Başak, H. Hybrid Coati–Grey Wolf Optimization with Application to Tuning Linear Quadratic Regulator Controller of Active Suspension Systems. *Eng. Sci. Technol. Int. J.* **2024**, *56*, 101765. [CrossRef]
7. Parvez, Y.; Chauhan, N.R.; Srivastava, M. Vibration Control and Comparative Analysis of Passive and Active Suspension Systems Using PID Controller with Particle Swarm Optimization. *J. Inst. Eng. India Ser. C* **2025**, *106*, 1–19. [CrossRef]
8. Abut, T.; Salkim, E.; Demosthenous, A. Performance Improvement in a Vehicle Suspension System with FLQG and LQG Control Methods. *Actuators* **2025**, *14*, 137. [CrossRef]
9. Li, J.; Jia, C.; Cheng, L.; Zhao, Q. Constrained State Feedback H∞ Control of Active Suspension System for In-Wheel Motor Electric Vehicles. *J. Jilin Univ. Eng. Technol.* **2021**, *53*, 1521–1529.
10. Wu, X.; Zhou, L.; Zhang, M.; Jiang, H.; Liu, W.; Hu, J. Sliding Mode Adaptive Control of Active Suspension System Combined with Particle Filter State Observation. *J. Hunan Univ. Nat. Sci.* **2024**, *51*, 19–27.
11. Hu, Y.; Peng, J. Adaptive Fault-Tolerant Control of Active Suspension Systems Considering Input and Output Constraints. *Control Decis.* **2025**, *40*, 693–698.
12. Lyu, B.; Zhang, R. Semi-Active Air Suspension System Based on Fuzzy PID Control. *Mach. Des. Manuf.* **2025**, *5*, 79–84.
13. Chantranuwathana, S.; Peng, H. Adaptive Robust Force Control for Vehicle Active Suspensions. *Int. J. Adapt. Control Signal Process.* **2004**, *18*, 83–102. [CrossRef]

https://doi.org/10.3390/mca31010005

14. Qi, X.; Liu, W.; Yang, Y.; Lu, J. Adaptive Finite-Time Fuzzy Control for Nonlinear Systems with Input Quantization and Unknown Time Delays. *J. Frankl. Inst.* **2020**, *357*, 7718–7742. [CrossRef]
15. Sun, W.; Gao, H.; Yao, B. Adaptive Robust Vibration Control of Full-Car Active Suspensions with Electrohydraulic Actuators. *IEEE Trans. Control Syst. Technol.* **2013**, *21*, 2417–2422. [CrossRef]
16. Min, X.; Li, Y.; Tong, S. Adaptive Fuzzy Output Feedback Inverse Optimal Control for Vehicle Active Suspension Systems. *Neurocomputing* **2020**, *403*, 257–267. [CrossRef]
17. Dong, X.; Zhao, D.; Yang, B.; Han, C. Fractional-Order Control of Active Suspension Actuator Based on Parallel Adaptive Clonal Selection Algorithm. *J. Mech. Sci. Technol.* **2016**, *30*, 2769–2781. [CrossRef]
18. Piao, C.; Liu, X.; Lu, C. Lateral Control Using Parameter Self-Tuning LQR on Autonomous Vehicle. In Proceedings of the 2019 International Conference on Intelligent Computing, Automation and Systems (ICICAS), Chongqing, China, 6–8 December 2019; IEEE: Piscataway, NJ, USA, 2019; pp. 913–917.
19. Li, Q.; Chen, Z.; Song, H.; Dong, Y. Model Predictive Control for Speed-Dependent Active Suspension System with Road Preview Information. *Sensors* **2024**, *24*, 2255. [CrossRef]
20. Tang, H.H.; Ahmad, N.S. Enhanced Fuzzy Logic Control for Active Suspension Systems via Hybrid Water Wave and Particle Swarm Optimization. *Int. J. Control Autom. Syst.* **2025**, *23*, 560–571. [CrossRef]
21. Wang, T.; Zhang, H.; Sui, S. Observer-Based Adaptive Neural Network Event-Triggered Quantized Control for Active Suspensions with Actuator Saturation. *Neurocomputing* **2025**, *614*, 128770. [CrossRef]
22. Li, Y.; Wang, T.; Liu, W.; Tong, S. Neural Network Adaptive Output-Feedback Optimal Control for Active Suspension Systems. *IEEE Trans. Syst. Man Cybern. Syst.* **2021**, *51*, 4021–4032. [CrossRef]
23. Wang, C.; Cui, X.; Zhao, S.; Zhou, X.; Song, Y.; Wang, Y.; Guo, K. A Deep Reinforcement Learning-Based Active Suspension Control Algorithm Considering Deterministic Experience Tracing for Autonomous Vehicle. *Appl. Soft Comput.* **2024**, *153*, 111259. [CrossRef]
24. Gao, X.; Du, Y.; Han, S.; Zhao, W.; Zhou, J.; Zhang, T.; Chen, C.L.P. Multi-Agent Reinforcement Learning for Vibration Control of Regenerative Active Suspension. *Eng. Appl. Artif. Intell.* **2025**, *153*, 110809. [CrossRef]
25. Abut, T.; Salkim, E.; Tugal, H. Active Suspension Control for Improved Ride Comfort and Vehicle Performance Using HHO-Based Type-I and Type-II Fuzzy Logic. *Biomimetics* **2025**, *10*, 673. [CrossRef] [PubMed]
26. Mottershead, J.E.; Friswell, M.I. Model Updating in Structural Dynamics: A Survey. *J. Sound Vib.* **1993**, *167*, 347–375. [CrossRef]
27. Belotti, R.; Richiedei, D. Dynamic Structural Modification of Vibrating Systems Oriented to Eigenstructure Assignment through Active Control: A Concurrent Approach. *J. Sound Vib.* **2018**, *422*, 358–372. [CrossRef]
28. Ram, Y.M.; Mottershead, J.E. Multiple-Input Active Vibration Control by Partial Pole Placement Using the Method of Receptances. *Mech. Syst. Signal Process.* **2013**, *40*, 727–735. [CrossRef]
29. Richiedei, D.; Tamellin, I.; Trevisani, A. Pole–Zero Assignment by the Receptance Method: Multi-Input Active Vibration Control. *Mech. Syst. Signal Process.* **2022**, *172*, 109108. [CrossRef]
30. Adamson, L.J.; Fichera, S.; Mottershead, J.E. Receptance-Based Robust Eigenstructure Assignment. *Mech. Syst. Signal Process.* **2020**, *140*, 106666. [CrossRef]
31. Ariyatanapol, R.; Xiong, Y.P.; Ouyang, H. Partial Pole Assignment with Time Delays for Asymmetric Systems. *Acta Mech.* **2018**, *229*, 2619–2629. [CrossRef]
32. Zhang, S.; Ouyang, H. Receptance-Based Partial Eigenstructure Assignment by State Feedback Control. *Mech. Syst. Signal Process.* **2022**, *168*, 108682. [CrossRef]
33. Richiedei, D.; Tamellin, I.; Trevisani, A. Unit-Rank Output Feedback Control for Antiresonance Assignment in Lightweight Systems. *Mech. Syst. Signal Process.* **2022**, *164*, 108286. [CrossRef]
34. *ISO 8608:2016*; Mechanical Vibration. Road Surface Profiles. Reporting of Measured Data. ISO: Geneva, Switzerland, 2016. Available online: https://cdn.standards.iteh.ai/samples/71202/05b2151f255b44928f80acb897fc0c2c/ISO-8608-2016.pdf (accessed on 5 November 2025).

https://doi.org/10.3390/mca31010005

Mathematical and Computational Applications

MDPI

Article

Gaining Understanding of Neural Networks with Programmatically Generated Data

Eric O'Sullivan [1,*], Ken Kennedy [2] and Jean Mohammadi-Aragh [1]

[1] Bagley College of Engineering, Mississippi State University, Mississippi State, MS 39762, USA; jean@ece.msstate.edu
[2] SkaiVison LLC., Raleigh, NC 27603, USA
* Correspondence: eo306@msstate.edu

Abstract

The performance of convolutional neural networks (CNNs) depends not only on model architecture but also on the structure and quality of the training data. While most artificial network interpretability methods focus on explaining trained models, less attention has been given to understanding how dataset composition itself shapes learning outcomes. This work introduces a novel framework that uses programmatically generated synthetic datasets to isolate and control visual features, enabling systematic evaluation of their contribution to CNN performance. Guided by principles from set theory, Shapley values, and the Apriori algorithm, we formalize an equivalence between CNN kernel weights and pattern frequency counts, showing that feature overlap across datasets predicts model generalization. Methods include the construction of four synthetic digit datasets with controlled object and background features, training lightweight CNNs under K-fold validation, and statistical evaluation of cross-dataset performance. The results show that internal object patterns significantly improve accuracy and F1 scores compared to non-object background features, and that a dataset similarity prediction algorithm achieves near-perfect correlation ($\rho = 0.97$) between the predicted and observed performance. The conclusions highlight that dataset feature composition can be treated as a measurable proxy for model behavior, offering a new path for dataset evaluation, pruning, and design optimization. This approach provides a principled framework for predicting CNN performance without requiring full-scale model training.

Keywords: convolutional neural network; CNN; set theory; artificial intelligence; computer vision

1. Introduction

As the complexity and scale of modern artificial neural network (ANN) tasks increase, the demand for high-quality training data has grown proportionally. Prior work shows that the performance of machine learning models, including ANNs, improves as training data or model capacity increases [1]. However, even very large models still exhibit failure modes such as hallucination, often caused by redundant, misleading, or noisy patterns in the training set [2,3]. These behaviors reflect the strong influence of dataset composition on learned representations.

Because dataset structure directly affects model behavior, numerous approaches have been proposed to prune, clean, or filter low-quality samples [4–6]. Other strategies expand datasets through synthetic distortions or automated augmentation pipelines, which have been shown to improve performance across a variety of computer vision tasks [7]. Convolutional neural networks (CNNs) remain widely used for such tasks due to their ability to decompose spatial structure in images [8,9]. However, this same structural complexity makes dataset-level analysis difficult. Existing interpretability methods such as SHAP and LIME [10,11] explain a trained model's predictions but provide limited insight into how the dataset itself organizes the latent feature space.

This work introduces a framework for analyzing dataset-level feature importance using programmatically generated synthetic data. The key idea is to isolate specific visual features across multiple datasets so that their individual contributions to CNN performance can be measured systematically. Rather than deriving feature importance from a trained model, the framework draws on principles from set theory, Shapley values, and the Apriori algorithm to examine how the presence, absence, and overlap of feature groups influence downstream learning behavior. By constructing controlled synthetic datasets with well-defined object and non-object features, a lightweight CNN serves as a proxy for estimating the empirical contribution of each feature group. This enables a pre-training form of feature attribution based on dataset structure rather than post hoc model inspection.

2. Theoretical Foundation

This section develops the mathematical and conceptual basis for the proposed dataset feature analysis framework. The goal is to formalize how feature groups, when deliberately isolated and permuted across synthetic datasets, give rise to predictable performance trends in convolutional neural networks (CNNs). By designing datasets in which object and non-object features can be controlled independently, we obtain a setting in which feature overlap with a composite testbed can be quantified and related to network behavior. Throughout this section, emphasis is placed on the restricted conditions under which the theory applies, consistent with the controlled nature of the synthetic datasets used in this study.

2.1. Neural Networks and the Role of Data

Neural networks, including CNNs, learn by minimizing a loss function over the training set [9]. The model iteratively adjusts its internal parameters to reduce the error between predicted and true labels. The structure, diversity, and quality of the training dataset therefore play a central role in determining model behavior [9]. A model that overfits is not necessarily failing; in many cases, it reflects the presence of tightly coupled or misleading correlations in the dataset that do not generalize to new data [1,8]. This highlights that generalization is shaped not only by model capacity but also by the complexity and distribution of the training samples.

Biases in the dataset directly influence the learned parameters. When certain features or feature groups appear disproportionately or are consistently aligned with a class label, the optimizer assigns undue weight to them, regardless of causal relevance [8,9,12–14]. This can lead to shortcut learning and confounding signals [15]. Although undesirable in real-world contexts, this effect is advantageous in the present work: controlled feature biases allow us to observe how CNNs shift focus in response to the presence or absence of specific visual structures.

2.2. Convolutional Neural Networks and Data Proxies

2.2.1. CNNs as Pattern Learners

Convolutional neural networks operate by applying a kernel K of size $k \times k$ across each input sample $T_i \in D$ to detect recurring spatial patterns [8,16]. Each kernel K acts as a detector for a particular pattern $P_K \subseteq F$, where F denotes the set of all features available in

https://doi.org/10.3390/mca31010016

the dataset [9]. The convolution produces an activation map A, where each element $A_{i,j}$ measures the similarity between P_K and a local region of T_i.

During training, kernels corresponding to frequently occurring patterns receive larger gradient contributions and therefore larger weight updates [1,8]. Consequently, the magnitude of the learned weights becomes proportional to $\text{support}_D(P_K)$, the empirical frequency of P_K in the dataset. This parallels the Apriori algorithm, in which high support patterns drive pattern selection and influence subsequent inference [17]. In CNNs, the activation strength at a given location plays a role analogous to local support for P_K.

A further connection arises from the Discrete Convolution Theorem: repeated spatial patterns in the input domain lead to amplified responses in the frequency domain [18]. Under the restricted setting of a single convolutional layer, linear activation, and no regularization, CNN kernels can therefore be interpreted as implicit estimators of pattern frequency. Later subsections formalize this intuition under these limited conditions.

2.2.2. Feature Control via Well-Ordered Feature Groups

The synthetic datasets used in this study allow specific feature groups to be added, removed, or varied in isolation. We distinguish between intrinsic object features (F_{ICF}) and non-object features (F_{NCF}), which are placed in disjointed spatial regions to avoid confounding effects. By controlling these groups independently, we obtain a set of datasets in which only one factor differs at a time, enabling clean attribution of performance changes to specific visual structures.

This design parallels the logic of Shapley values, where the marginal contribution of a feature is measured across multiple combinations of subsets [11]. The feature groups in our synthetic datasets form a Well-Ordered Set [19], ensuring that contributions can be compared consistently across permutations. As a result, the trained CNN functions as a proxy for measuring how the presence or absence of feature groups affects classification, producing a pre-training form of feature attribution based on dataset structure rather than post hoc model interpretation [20].

2.3. *CNN–Apriori Equivalence*

2.3.1. Apriori Algorithm Formalization

The Apriori algorithm identifies frequent patterns (itemsets) by counting their support across a dataset of transactions. For a dataset D composed of transactions T_i, the support of an itemset X is defined in Equation (1).

$$\text{support}(X) = \frac{|\{T_i \in D : X \subseteq T_i\}|}{|D|} \tag{1}$$

A pattern X is frequent if $\text{support}(X) \geq \text{min\_support}$. The downward closure property implies that if X is infrequent, then all supersets of X are also infrequent. Within the present framework, an image corresponds to a transaction, and extracted object or background patterns correspond to items. This establishes a symbolic mapping between visual patterns and the pattern mining structure formalized by Apriori.

2.3.2. CNN Pattern Detection Formalization

In a CNN, each kernel K detects a spatial pattern P_K in an input image I. The convolution operation produces an activation map A, where $A_{i,j}$ measures the degree of matching between P_K and a local region of I, as defined in Equation (2).

$$A_{i,j} = \sum_{m=0}^{k-1} \sum_{n=0}^{k-1} I_{i+m,j+n} \cdot K_{m,n} \tag{2}$$

https://doi.org/10.3390/mca31010016

High activations indicate strong matches to P_K, mapping image regions to a latent pattern space where activation strength reflects both the frequency and salience of P_K.

2.3.3. Equivalence Principle: CNN Weights as Pattern Frequency

Theorem 1 (Under Restricted Conditions). *Under a single convolutional layer, linear (or piecewise linear) activation, no regularization, and a stationary pattern distribution, the learned weights of a kernel K approximate the support of pattern P_K in the dataset D.*

Training minimizes a loss function $\mathcal{L}$ over predictions $f(x_i; W)$ as shown in Equation (3). Weight updates follow Equation (4).

$$L = \frac{1}{N}\sum_{i=1}^{N} \mathcal{L}(f(x_i; W), y_i) \tag{3}$$

$$w_{m,n}^{(t+1)} = w_{m,n}^{(t)} - \alpha \frac{\partial L}{\partial w_{m,n}} \tag{4}$$

Under the restricted assumptions stated above, the gradient term $\frac{\partial \mathcal{L}}{\partial w_{m,n}}$ becomes proportional to the number of occurrences of P_K in the training set, as expressed in Equation (5). The final kernel weights therefore satisfy Equation (6), linking weight magnitude to empirical pattern frequency.

$$\frac{\partial L}{\partial w_{m,n}} \propto \sum_{i=1}^{N} \frac{\partial L}{\partial A_{i,j}} \cdot I_{i+m,j+n} \tag{5}$$

$$w_{m,n}^{(final)} \propto frequency(P_K) = \frac{|\{x_i \in D : P_K \subseteq x_i\}|}{|D|} \tag{6}$$

This supports the analogy that CNN kernels behave like frequency counters for visual patterns in controlled settings, mirroring the support counting mechanism of the Apriori algorithm.

2.3.4. Max Pooling as Support Threshold

Theorem 2 (Under Restricted Conditions). *Max pooling acts as a thresholding operator that preserves only the strongest activations. For a pooling region R, the pooling operation is given by Equation (7).*

$$pool(A)_{i,j} = \max_{m,n \in window} A_{i+m,j+n} \tag{7}$$

Only sufficiently strong responses propagate to deeper layers. This mirrors the min_support threshold in Apriori, where low frequency patterns are removed.

2.3.5. Frequent Pattern Mining in Image Data

An image can be interpreted as a transaction of spatially embedded visual tokens. A pattern P may be defined as a spatial arrangement applied to an object or background region. For dataset D, the support of P is given in Equation (8).

$$\text{support}_I(P) = \frac{|\{\text{regions } R \subseteq I : P \subseteq R\}|}{|\{\text{all regions in } I\}|} \tag{8}$$

CNNs amplify patterns whose $\text{support}_D(P)$ exceeds an implicit activation threshold, making convolutional training analogous to spatial frequent pattern mining. These parallels form the basis of the dataset similarity analysis used later in this work.

In the next section, we describe how these theoretical parallels guided the design of our synthetic datasets, CNN architecture, and evaluation pipeline.

3. Methodology

The purpose of the synthetic data generation process is to create controlled datasets with overlapping and non-overlapping features, thereby reducing the latent space required

https://doi.org/10.3390/mca31010016

for class discrimination. By systematically varying which features are present in objects versus backgrounds, we can analyze how convolutional neural networks prioritize different visual patterns when learning to classify digits.

3.1. Model Creation

A lightweight convolutional neural network (CNN) built in PyTorch, inspired by LeNet style architectures is used as a data proxy [16]. The model is designed for grayscale input images of size 28 × 28 and outputs class probabilities over 10 categories.

The architecture consists of one convolutional layer followed by max pooling, a flattening operation, and one fully connected layer. Nonlinear activation is introduced through the Rectified Linear Unit (ReLU) function after each convolution and the first fully connected layer. A summary of the model architecture is shown in Table 1.

Table 1. Network architecture and activation functions.

Layer	Activation
Conv2d (1, 32, 3 × 3)	ReLU
MaxPool2d (2 × 2)	–
Flatten	–
Linear (800 → 128)	ReLU
Linear (128 → 10)	–

Training Configuration

All models were trained using the categorical cross-entropy loss, which is appropriate for multi-class classification with mutually exclusive labels. Optimization was performed using the Adam optimizer with a learning rate of 1×10^{-3} and default momentum parameters ($\beta_1 = 0.9, \beta_2 = 0.999$). No explicit weight decay or regularization was applied, as the goal of the study is to observe raw feature-learning behavior under controlled conditions.

The model architecture is intentionally lightweight and shallow to minimize confounding effects from depth, skip connections, or implicit regularization. This design choice ensures that observed performance differences can be attributed directly to dataset composition and feature overlap rather than architectural complexity.

3.2. Dataset Generation

Four synthetic dataset types (Datasets 1–4) were generated under controlled feature configurations, each containing 1850 samples (185 per class), for a total of 7400 samples. For within-dataset training and evaluation, each dataset type was split into 80% training (1480 samples) and 20% held-out testing (370 samples). These splits were performed independently per dataset type, so that each model is trained only on samples from its assigned feature configuration. Image size and object location were fixed, as these factors do not significantly affect model outcomes in this setting [8,9,21].

To measure cross-dataset generalization, we additionally define a unified testbed D_{test} as the union of all samples across the four dataset types: $D_{\text{test}} = D_1 \cup D_2 \cup D_3 \cup D_4$, yielding 7400 total images (740 per class). No model is trained on the unified testbed; it is used only for evaluation after training on a single dataset type. This construction is intentional: because each model is trained on one quarter of the feature configurations represented in D_{test}, a naive lower bound of approximately 25% accuracy is expected if the model only succeeds on the feature regime it was trained under. Performance above this baseline indicates that learned patterns transfer across feature regimes, allowing the CNN to be interpreted as a feature-collection mechanism whose kernels encode reusable patterns rather

https://doi.org/10.3390/mca31010016

than dataset-specific artifacts. The unified testbed therefore enables a direct comparison of which feature groups yield the strongest transfer across all feature combinations.

3.3. Synthetic Dataset Generation Procedure

Each image is generated through a deterministic pipeline consisting of four stages: background initialization, pattern assignment, digit rendering, and composition. All random operations are controlled using fixed seeds to ensure reproducibility across datasets.

1. Initialize a blank 28×28 grayscale canvas.
2. Apply either a solid fill or a deterministic background pattern based on the dataset configuration.
3. Render a centered digit mask.
4. Apply an object-level pattern (F_{ICF}) within the digit mask if enabled.
5. Combine object and background layers using pixel-wise masking.

Distinct seed ranges are assigned to F_{ICF} and F_{NCF} to prevent accidental feature overlap. This guarantees that patterns are reused consistently across datasets while remaining isolated within the object or background region.

3.4. Feature Pattern System and Dataset Configuration

We define six distinct pattern types: stripes, checkerboard, noise, dots, squares, and waves. Patterns are applied deterministically using fixed random seeds to ensure reproducibility and that the patterns are reproduced across the same sample for each dataset. Internal Class Features (F_{ICF}) and Non-Class Features (F_{NCF}) use disjoint seed ranges to prevent unintentional overlap. The patterns assigned to F_{ICF} and F_{NCF} are shown in Figures 1–3.

Figure 1. Examples of F_{ICF} and F_{NCF} patterns.

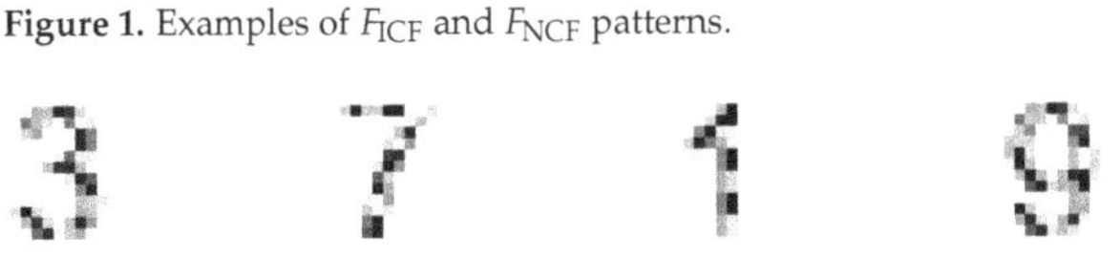

Figure 2. Reuse of the same F_{ICF} pattern across different digits.

https://doi.org/10.3390/mca31010016

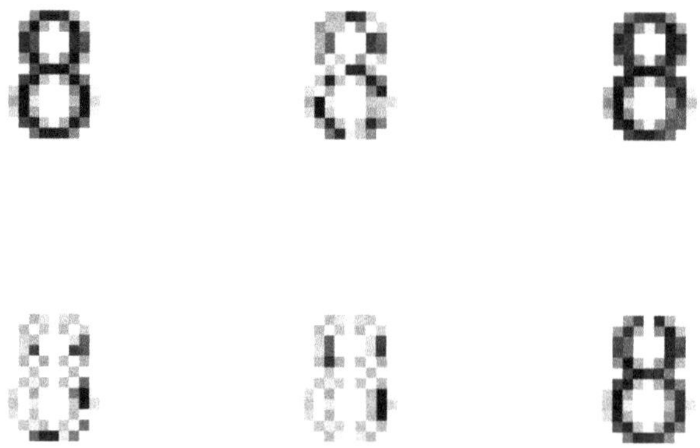

Figure 3. Different F_{ICF} patterns applied to digit 8.

Dataset Configurations

Dataset configurations are defined using a truth table that specifies which combinations of F_{ICF} and F_{NCF} appear in each dataset (Table 2). This representation allows explicit control over feature overlap between object and background regions, ensuring that the superset is Well Related to each subset used in model training, enforcing that all isolated feature groups are also Well Related to the testbed. A visual example of these feature ablations is provided in Figure 4.

Table 2. Synthetic dataset configurations with background/object types and controlled overlaps.

Dataset	Background	Object	Subset Background Overlap	Subset Object Overlap
1	Solid	Solid	1, 3	1, 2
2	Pattern	Solid	2, 4	1, 2
3	Solid	Pattern	1, 3	3, 4
4	Pattern	Pattern	2, 4	3, 4

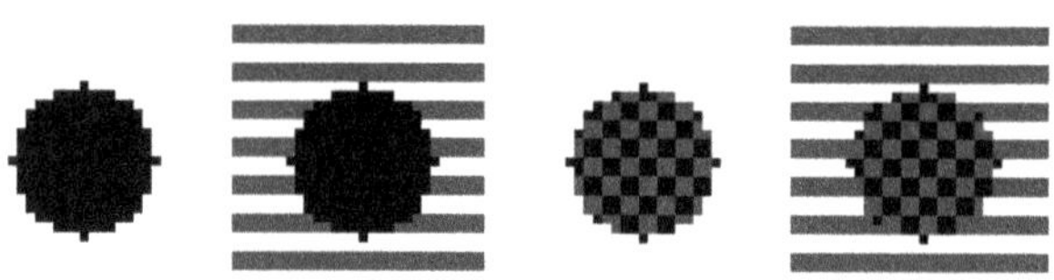

Figure 4. Example of feature isolation across the four subsets of data.

3.5. Training and Evaluation Procedure

Each dataset subset was used to train a separate model, resulting in four trained models in total. Training followed a 10-fold cross-validation procedure ($K = 10$), defined in Equations (9) and (10), with each fold running for 10 epochs using a batch size of 32. This approach provides both an estimate of mean performance, denoted $\bar{\mu}_d$, and its associated variability, σ_d, where $\mu_{d,k}$ refers to the performance of fold k for dataset d. After training, all models were evaluated on the unified testbed to enable consistent comparisons.

$$\bar{\mu}_d = \frac{1}{K} \sum_{k=1}^{K} \mu_{d,k} \tag{9}$$

$$\sigma_d = \sqrt{\frac{1}{K-1} \sum_{k=1}^{K} (\mu_{d,k} - \bar{\mu}_d)^2} \tag{10}$$

https://doi.org/10.3390/mca31010016

Computational Resources

All experiments were conducted on a workstation equipped with an NVIDIA RTX 3090 GPU and 64 GB of system memory. Each model required approximately 3 min per training run, resulting in a total training time of roughly 2 h for all cross-validation folds and datasets combined. This modest computational cost highlights the efficiency and reproducibility of the proposed framework.

3.6. Model Metrics and Statistical Evaluation

To characterize model behavior, we report standard classification measures, including accuracy, precision, recall, and F1 score, both in macro averaged form and on a per-class basis.

To assess whether observed differences in performance across datasets are statistically meaningful, we conduct paired *t*-tests with Bonferroni correction to account for multiple comparisons. Beyond significance testing, we estimate effect sizes using Cohen's *d* to measure the magnitude of differences, and we construct 95% confidence intervals around each metric to provide a clear indication of uncertainty in the reported results.

3.7. Feature Analysis

Feature-level analysis is performed by comparing datasets that differ only in the inclusion of intrinsic content features (F_{ICF}) or non-content features (F_{NCF}). This comparison reveals how specific attributes influence learning outcomes, while activation strength for targeted visual patterns across layers highlights their relative importance. Redundancy is further identified through cross-dataset generalization, which exposes features that contribute little unique value. Importantly, the deterministic assignment of F_{ICF} and F_{NCF} allows specific patterns to be tracked in the learned latent space, enabling us to quantify how CNNs encode feature overlap and to distinguish between discriminative and redundant features in a controlled, reproducible setting.

The weighting used in the dataset similarity algorithm is derived directly from the controlled experimental design. As each synthetic dataset isolates one feature group at a time, the contribution of each feature group can be treated as approximately linear with respect to its overlap with the testbed. The similarity score corresponds to a weighted sum of the presence or absence of each feature group, where the weights reflect their empirically observed contribution to classification accuracy.

4. Results

4.1. Cross-Validation Stability

We first evaluate training stability using 10-fold cross-validation to ensure that observed performance differences are not artifacts of data partitioning. As shown in Table 3, validation accuracy remains highly consistent across folds, with standard deviations below 2% for all datasets. This confirms that the training process is stable and that subsequent comparisons across datasets are meaningful.

In addition to mean and standard deviation, we report the minimum, maximum, and median validation accuracy to characterize worst-case sensitivity and potential ceiling effects. The narrow min–max range and median values near 100% indicate that no individual fold exhibits degraded performance and that results are not driven by outliers.

https://doi.org/10.3390/mca31010016

Table 3. Aggregate training performance metrics (mean ± std) across all folds for each dataset, showing training stability.

Metric	Value
Validation Accuracy (mean ± std)	99.79 ± 0.42%
Validation Accuracy (min, max)	97.92, 100.0%
Median Validation Accuracy	100.0%

4.2. Generalization to the Well-Related Synthetic Testbed

Each fold-trained model was evaluated on the unified synthetic testbed to assess cross-dataset generalization. The results in Table 4 reveal clear performance differences attributable to dataset composition.

The models trained on datasets containing both internal object patterns and patterned backgrounds (Dataset 4) achieved the highest mean performance (Accuracy ≈ 0.89, F1 ≈ 0.88). In contrast, datasets lacking internal object patterns (Datasets 1 and 2) exhibited consistently lower performance. While Dataset 4 shows higher variance, this reflects increased feature richness rather than instability, as performance remains superior across all folds.

Table 4. Synthetic testbed evaluation of fold trained models, reporting aggregate test performance (mean ± std) across all folds.

Dataset	Accuracy	Precision	Recall	F1
1	0.7863 ± 0.0175	0.8320 ± 0.0072	0.7863 ± 0.0175	0.7935 ± 0.0134
2	0.8072 ± 0.0184	0.8771 ± 0.0065	0.8072 ± 0.0184	0.8175 ± 0.0156
3	0.7778 ± 0.0176	0.8347 ± 0.0176	0.7778 ± 0.0176	0.7885 ± 0.0163
4	0.8875 ± 0.0632	0.9012 ± 0.0509	0.8875 ± 0.0632	0.8807 ± 0.0699

4.3. Diagnostic Full-Data Training Analysis

After establishing cross-validation stability, we trained a single model per dataset using the full dataset without fold partitioning. This analysis is included strictly as a diagnostic sanity check to examine whether trends observed under cross-validation persist when all available data are used for training.

Importantly, these results are not used for statistical inference or model comparison, which are based exclusively on cross-validated evaluations. As shown in the full-data diagnostic results in Table 5, datasets containing internal object patterns (Datasets 3 and 4) continue to outperform those without, reinforcing the conclusions drawn from the cross-validation analysis.

Table 5. Full-data diagnostic training results for a single model trained per dataset (no cross-validation), reported to verify that cross-validation trends persist.

Dataset	Accuracy	Precision	Recall	F1
1	0.78	0.79	0.78	0.76
2	0.77	0.78	0.73	0.75
3	0.80	0.82	0.80	0.81
4	0.89	0.89	0.88	0.88

4.4. Feature Contribution and Dataset Similarity Validation

To quantify the relative contribution of internal object patterns (F_{ICF}) versus non-object background patterns (F_{NCF}), we conducted paired t-tests with Bonferroni correction.

https://doi.org/10.3390/mca31010016

As summarized in Table 6, internal object patterns yield statistically significant improvements in both accuracy and F1 score on the synthetic testbed.

Building on this observation, we validate the dataset similarity prediction algorithm derived from the CNN–Apriori equivalence. Using Equation (11), we estimate feature overlap between each training dataset and the testbed, and map this overlap to predicted performance via Equation (12). The predicted values closely match the observed performance, particularly for Dataset 4 (Predicted: 87.0%, Actual: 88.8%).

The correlation analysis confirms a strong monotonic relationship between predicted and observed accuracy ($\rho = 0.9691$, $p = 0.0309$, $R^2 = 0.9392$), computed over the four controlled synthetic datasets. Despite the small sample size, Fisher z-transformed confidence intervals support a robust association, as visualized in Figure 5. These results provide empirical validation that feature overlap directly estimates CNN generalization behavior, consistent with the theoretical proof.

Table 6. Paired t-test results evaluating the effect of internal object patterns on synthetic testbed performance.

Metric	Object Patterns	Non-Object Patterns	p-Value	Significant
Accuracy	0.6470 ± 0.1844	0.4290 ± 0.1801	7.07×10^{-4}	True
F1	0.6534 ± 0.2125	0.4702 ± 0.1686	5.64×10^{-3}	True

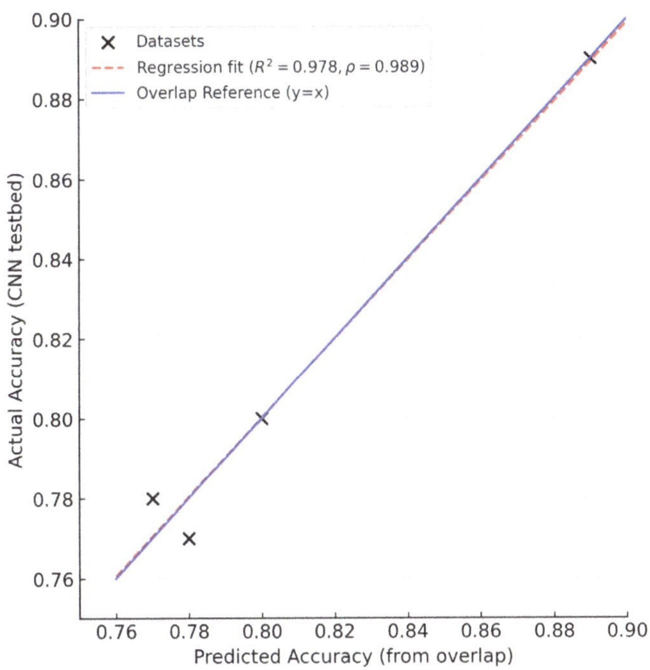

Figure 5. Predicted vs. actual accuracy on the synthetic testbed with regression fit.

4.5. Mathematical Proof Validation: Dataset Similarity Prediction Algorithm

Finally, we validated our mathematical proof connecting CNNs and the Apriori Principles by developing a dataset feature overlap estimation framework. The algorithm estimates the overlap between each training dataset and the synthetic testbed using

https://doi.org/10.3390/mca31010016

Equation (11). While not a direct measure of a model's performance, it will indicate the feature overlaps and estimate performance, as reflected in Equation (12).

$$\mathrm{Overlap}(D_i, D_{\mathrm{test}}) = \frac{\sum_{f \in F} w_f \, \mathbb{I}[f \in D_i \wedge f \in D_{\mathrm{test}}]}{\sum_{f \in F} w_f} \tag{11}$$

$$\widehat{A}(D_i) = A_0 + \mathrm{Overlap}(D_i, D_{\mathrm{test}}) \, (1 - A_0) \tag{12}$$

4.5.1. Prediction and Validation Results

Our analysis approximates the following overlaps with the synthetic testbed: Dataset 1 = 65%, Dataset 2 = 75%, Dataset 3 = 75%, and Dataset 4 = 87%. Using Equations (11) and (12), these overlaps were mapped to predicted performance values. The predicted and actual results aligned closely, particularly for Dataset 4 (Predicted: 87.0%, Actual: 88.8%), confirming that higher feature overlap corresponds to improved CNN generalization.

Statistical validation further supported this framework, with the correlation analysis revealing $\rho = 0.9691$ ($p = 0.0309$, $R^2 = 0.9392$), demonstrating that the dataset similarity prediction algorithm reliably captures the relationship between feature overlap and observed CNN performance. This can be visualized in Figure 5. The correlation analysis was computed over $n = 4$ dataset conditions, corresponding to the four controlled synthetic datasets. The confidence interval for the reported correlation was computed using a Fisher z-transform, yielding a 95% confidence interval consistent with a strong monotonic relationship despite the small sample size.

4.5.2. CNN Apriori Equivalence Validation

This validates our mathematical proof that CNNs and the Apriori algorithm perform equivalent operations: CNN weights encode pattern frequency information (analogous to Apriori support), and feature overlap directly estimates model performance.

5. Discussion

5.1. Experimental Summary

The experimental results demonstrate two major findings regarding CNN behavior and dataset-driven performance prediction. First, the systematic ablation study revealed that object-level pattern features play a decisive role in shaping CNN generalization. The models trained on datasets containing object patterns (Datasets 3 and 4) achieved substantially higher performance on the synthetic testbed, with mean accuracy of 0.845 ± 0.045, compared to 0.775 ± 0.005 for datasets lacking such patterns ($p < 0.01$). A similar trend was observed for F1 scores, where object pattern datasets reached 0.845 ± 0.035 versus 0.755 ± 0.005 for non-object datasets ($p < 0.05$). These results indicate that internal structural variation rather than background variation provides more discriminative information for shallow CNNs.

Second, the dataset similarity prediction algorithm achieved a strong correlation between predicted and observed performance on the synthetic testbed ($\rho = 0.9691$, $p = 0.0309$, $R^2 = 0.9392$). The algorithm correctly estimated that Dataset 4, which shares the highest feature overlap with the testbed (87%), would yield the strongest performance (~88.8%), whereas Datasets 1–3, with lower overlaps (65–75%), would perform similarly but worse. This result provides empirical support for the restricted-form CNN–Apriori equivalence proposed in this work, and suggests that feature overlap can serve as a meaningful proxy for expected model performance.

https://doi.org/10.3390/mca31010016

Taken together, these findings introduce a novel framework in which dataset feature composition rather than model architecture forms the primary basis for predicting CNN behavior. This contributes to a shift toward dataset-centric evaluation and optimization, offering an efficient alternative to model-driven interpretability methods.

5.2. Limitations and Future Work

Although promising, the proposed framework is subject to several important limitations. First, all experiments were conducted using controlled synthetic datasets in which feature placement, frequency, and class relationships are deterministic. As a result, the behavior of the dataset similarity algorithm and the CNN–Apriori correspondence has not yet been validated on real-world images, where uncontrolled correlations, noise, and entangled features may reduce the stability of these relationships.

The CNN–Apriori equivalence is derived under restricted assumptions, including a single convolutional layer, linear or piecewise-linear activations, no regularization, and a stationary feature distribution. These conditions do not extend to deeper architectures such as ResNet or VGG, where nonlinear interactions and skip connections break the simplifying assumptions required for the equivalence. In such cases, the proposed similarity framework should be viewed as a heuristic for dataset comparison rather than a general theoretical identity.

The computational advantages of the method come with tradeoffs. The dataset similarity estimator operates in $O(n)$ time with respect to the number of feature groups, since no perturbation sampling or model retraining is required. By contrast, SHAP and LIME often require between 10^3 and 10^5 evaluations per sample. However, the simplicity of the estimator means that it may not capture higher-order feature interactions present in real-world datasets.

While the $\text{Overlap}(D_i, D_{\text{test}})$ metric is stable under synthetic control, its reliability on real datasets remains to be examined. Real-world image features are often nonlinear, unlabeled, and spatially diffuse, making exact feature overlap difficult to quantify. Future studies will explore adaptations of this metric to noisy, high-dimensional visual domains.

Finally, the correlation result ($\rho = 0.9691$) was computed using the four dataset conditions designed for this study. A Fisher z-transform was used to obtain the corresponding confidence interval; however, the small sample size limits the statistical generality of this estimate. Expanding the number and complexity of dataset configurations will be an important direction for future work.

Overall, this work establishes a controlled foundation for understanding dataset-driven performance in CNNs, but additional empirical validation on large-scale and real-world datasets will be necessary to assess the generality of these findings.

Author Contributions: Conceptualization, E.O.; methodology, E.O.; software, E.O.; validation, E.O., K.K. and J.M.-A.; formal analysis, E.O.; investigation, E.O.; resources, E.O.; data curation, E.O.; writing—original draft preparation, E.O.; writing—review and editing, E.O., K.K. and J.M.-A.; visualization, E.O.; supervision, J.M.-A.; project administration, E.O.; funding acquisition, J.M.-A. All authors have read and agreed to the published version of the manuscript.

Funding: This research received no external funding.

Data Availability Statement: The data presented in this study were entirely generated through the synthetic dataset creation process described in the methodology. No external or proprietary datasets were used. The generated datasets are reproducible following the procedures outlined in this manuscript. No additional archived data are available.

Acknowledgments: During the preparation of this manuscript, the author used OpenAI's ChatGPT (GPT-5, 2025) to assist with code generation for Python figure and table creation and LaTeX formatting.

The author reviewed and edited all AI-generated outputs and takes full responsibility for the content of this publication.

Conflicts of Interest: The author declares no conflicts of interest. The author declares that the research was conducted in the absence of any commercial or financial relationships from SkaiVison LLC. that could be construed as a potential conflict of interest.

Abbreviations

The following abbreviations are used in this manuscript:

CNN	Convolutional Neural Network
ANN	Artificial Neural Network

References

1. Geman, S.; Bienenstock, E.; Doursat, R. Neural Networks and the Bias/Variance Dilemma. *Neural Comput.* **1992**, *4*, 1–58. [CrossRef]
2. Bruno, A.; Mazzeo, P.L.; Chetouani, A.; Tliba, M.; Kerkouri, M.A. Insights into Classifying and Mitigating LLMs' Hallucinations. *arXiv* **2023**, arXiv:2311.08117. [CrossRef]
3. McKenna, N.; Li, T.; Cheng, L.; Hosseini, M.; Johnson, M.; Steedman, M. Sources of Hallucination by Large Language Models on Inference Tasks. In Proceedings of the Findings of the Association for Computational Linguistics: EMNLP 2023, Singapore, 6–10 December 2023; pp. 2758–2774.
4. Bhattacharjee, R.; Frohnapfel, K.; von Luxburg, U. How to safely discard features based on aggregate SHAP values. *arXiv* **2025**, arXiv:2503.23111 [CrossRef]
5. Moser, B.B.; Raue, F.; Dengel, A. A Study in Dataset Pruning for Image Super-Resolution. *arXiv* **2024**, arXiv:2403.17083. [CrossRef]
6. Yu, H.; Yuan, X.; Jiang, R.; Feng, H.; Liu, J.; Li, Z. Feature Reduction Networks: A Convolution Neural Network-Based Approach to Enhance Image Dehazing. *Electronics* **2023**, *12*, 4984. [CrossRef]
7. Cubuk, E.D.; Zoph, B.; Mané, D.; Vasudevan, V.; Le, Q.V. AutoAugment: Learning Augmentation Policies from Data. *arXiv* **2018**, arXiv:1805.09501.
8. LeCun, Y.; Bengio, Y.; Hinton, G. Deep learning. *Nature* **2015**, *521*, 436–444. [CrossRef] [PubMed]
9. Chollet, F. *Deep Learning with Python*, 2nd ed.; Manning: Shelter Island, NY, USA, 2021.
10. Ribeiro, M.T.; Singh, S.; Guestrin, C. "Why Should I Trust You?" Explaining the Predictions of Any Classifier. In Proceedings of the 22nd ACM SIGKDD International Conference on Knowledge Discovery and Data Mining (KDD), San Francisco, CA, USA, 13–17 August 2016; ACM: New York, NY, USA, 2016; pp. 1135–1144. [CrossRef]
11. Lundberg, S.M.; Lee, S.I. A Unified Approach to Interpreting Model Predictions. In Proceedings of the 31st International Conference on Neural Information Processing Systems, Long Beach, CA, USA, 4–9 December 2017; pp. 4765–4774.
12. Lu, K.; Grover, A.; Abbeel, P.; Mordatch, I. Pretrained Transformers as Universal Computation Engines. *arXiv* **2021**, arXiv: 2103.05247. [CrossRef]
13. Cybenko, G. Approximation by Superpositions of a Sigmoidal Function. *Math. Control. Signals Syst.* **1989**, *2*, 303–314. [CrossRef]
14. Lample, G.; Charton, F. Deep Learning for Symbolic Mathematics. *arXiv* **2019**, arXiv:1912.01412. [CrossRef]
15. Su, J.; Vargas, D.V.; Sakurai, K. One pixel attack for fooling deep neural networks. *arXiv* **2017**, arXiv:1710.08864. [CrossRef]
16. LeCun, Y.; Bottou, L.; Bengio, Y.; Haffner, P. Gradient-based learning applied to document recognition. *Proc. IEEE* **1998**, *86*, 2278–2324. [CrossRef]
17. Agrawal, R.; Srikant, R. Fast Algorithms for Mining Association Rules in Large Databases. In Proceedings of the 20th International Conference on Very Large Data Bases, San Francisco, CA, USA, 12–15 September 1994; pp. 487–499.
18. Smith, J.O. Spectral Audio Signal Processing. Available online: http://ccrma.stanford.edu/~jos/sasp/ (accessed on 9 January 2026).
19. Feferman, S. Some applications of the notions of forcing and generic sets. *Fundam. Math.* **1964**, *56*, 325–345. [CrossRef]
20. Zheng, Q.; Wang, Z.; Zhou, J.; Lu, J. Shap-CAM: Visual Explanations for Convolutional Neural Networks based on Shapley Value. *arXiv* **2022**, arXiv:2208.03608. [CrossRef]
21. Etter, D.; Rawls, S.; Carpenter, C.; Sell, G. A Synthetic Recipe for OCR. In Proceedings of the 2019 International Conference on Document Analysis and Recognition (ICDAR), Sydney, NSW, Australia, 20–25 September 2019; pp. 864–869.

https://doi.org/10.3390/mca31010016

Mathematical and Computational Applications

MDPI

Communication

Revised Long-Term Scheduling Model for Multi-Stage Biopharmaceutical Processes

Vaibhav Kumar [1,2,3,*] and Munawar A. Shaik [3,*]

1 School of Natural Resources, University of Tennessee, Knoxville, TN 37996, USA
2 Forest Products Laboratory, USDA Forest Service, Madison, WI 53726, USA
3 Department of Chemical and Petroleum Engineering, College of Engineering, United Arab Emirates University, Al Ain P.O. Box 15551, United Arab Emirates
* Correspondence: vkumar8@utk.edu (V.K.); munawar@uaeu.ac.ae (M.A.S.)

Abstract

Biopharmaceuticals are therapeutic drugs engineered to target specific sites within the body. Their manufacturing process comprises two primary stages: upstream processing (USP) and downstream processing (DSP). USP primarily involves cell culture and growth, whereas DSP focuses on purifying and packaging the final product. The recent literature only reports a few studies addressing production planning and scheduling in biopharmaceutical manufacturing. In this work, we address a long-term scheduling and midterm planning problem incorporating on-time or late delivery of final products with unknown finite delivery rates. Early delivery is prohibited, and late delivery incurs a penalty cost. Published models and evolutionary algorithms exhibit key limitations in areas such as shelf-life modeling, inventory management, and product delivery. To overcome these shortcomings, we propose a revised mixed-integer linear programming (MILP) model implemented using the General Algebraic Modeling System (GAMS). When applied to two illustrative examples, the model reduces optimum event counts by two to three, improving computational efficiency through fewer binary variables, continuous variables, and constraints. Furthermore, it achieves up to 7% improvement over two published benchmarks, underscoring its potential to enhance scheduling strategies for multiproduct biopharmaceutical facilities.

Keywords: biopharmaceutical production; inventory management; mixed-integer linear programming (MILP); optimization; scheduling; shelf life

1. Introduction

Biopharmaceuticals, also known as biologics, are complex therapeutic drugs that include monoclonal antibodies, recombinant proteins, cytokines, and vaccines produced using living organisms or biological processes [1]. These drugs have revolutionized treatment for many conditions, particularly autoimmune diseases like rheumatoid arthritis, psoriasis, and inflammatory bowel disease, where they often provide targeted immune modulation with greater efficacy and fewer broad side effects compared to traditional small-molecule chemical drugs [2]. The approval and commercialization of recombinant human insulin by Genentech in 1982 marked the beginning of the modern biopharmaceutical era [1]. Since then, the industry has experienced explosive growth, driven by rising demand for advanced therapies targeting cancer, rare diseases, and chronic conditions. As of recent estimates (2024–2025), the global biopharmaceutical market is valued at approximately

USD 450–550 billion, representing around 30% or more of the total pharmaceutical market (estimated at around USD 1.5–1.8 trillion), with strong projected growth due to innovations in monoclonal antibodies, cell/gene therapies, and biosimilars [3–5].

Developing biopharmaceuticals remains a highly complex, resource-intensive process. From initial discovery and target identification through to preclinical testing (in vitro and animal models), clinical trials (Phases I–III in humans), regulatory review, and final approval, the timeline typically spans 10–15 years [6]. Success rates are low, with only a small fraction of candidates reaching the market, contributing to high development costs. Even after regulatory approval, achieving widespread global availability poses significant hurdles. Biopharmaceuticals have intricate molecular structures, requiring sophisticated, biologically based manufacturing processes (e.g., cell culture in bioreactors) that are far more sensitive to variations than chemical synthesis [7]. This complexity affects scalability, industrial-scale production consistency, supply chain reliability (including cold-chain logistics for temperature-sensitive products), and costs [8].

Mathematical optimization constitutes a fundamental pillar of contemporary industrial engineering and operations research. It provides a mathematically sound and systematic framework for significantly improving the efficiency, productivity, sustainability, and economic viability of manufacturing systems, production processes, and complex resource allocation problems. Through formulating suitable mathematical models combined with state-of-the-art solution algorithms, optimization enables the identification of optimal or near-optimal decisions under diverse and often conflicting objectives [9,10], including cost minimization, throughput maximization, energy consumption reduction, and advanced scheduling. Broadly speaking, two main classes of techniques are employed in practice: (i) exact deterministic approaches, most notably mixed-integer linear programming (MILP), which ensure global optimality when computationally tractable, and (ii) metaheuristic and evolutionary algorithms [11–13], which are particularly effective for non-convex, and/or multi-objective optimization problems. In the present work, we revised a deterministic MILP model and implemented it in the conventional optimization language General Algebraic Modeling System (GAMS).

Interest in long-term scheduling/midterm planning received attention when Lakhdar et al. [14] developed a discrete-time MILP model for long-term scheduling in a multiproduct biopharmaceutical production facility, catering to multi-period demand. They validated their model with two motivational examples, emphasizing continuous production for the batch processes. Kabra et al. [15] introduced a continuous-time, unit-specific-event-based MILP model with the state-task network to address the shortcomings in the literature [14]. Resources were optimized by enforcing penalties for the unwarranted activation of binary variables related to production and storage [15]. Liu et al. [16] developed a discrete-time MILP framework designed to model maintenance scheduling dynamics under conditions of performance degradation. Vieira et al. [17] introduced a global-event-based continuous-time MILP framework for biopharmaceuticals, validated through multiple illustrative case studies. Furthermore, Vieira et al. [18] expanded their earlier work by introducing a global-event-based MILP model that accounts for chromatography resin performance decay in DSP.

Among the evolutionary methods, Jankauskas et al. [19] introduced a continuous-time heuristic model leveraging a genetic algorithm (GA) for long-term scheduling. The algorithm was validated by solving an industrial example adopted from the published literature [14]. The algorithm was also implemented to address two additional case studies, which involved increased demands and expanded time horizons, thereby asserting the robustness of their algorithm. Nonetheless, certain limitations in their work [19] were observed by Kumar et al. [20], including real-time storage violation, early product deliveries,

https://doi.org/10.3390/mca31010032

inaccuracies in downstream processing times, and overestimated profit. Subsequently, Jankauskas et al. [21] developed another GA based on a discrete-time framework, validated through multiple case studies adopted from published literature. The first example [14] involved the production of three biopharmaceutical products through a multi-stage process.

Kumar et al. [20] have built upon the model by Kabra et al. [15], incorporating examples from earlier literature [14,19]. They conducted a comparative analysis of the deterministic models [14,15,17,18], suggesting enhancements in their improved models [20,22]. Kumar and Shaik [22] improved their previous model [20] by contrasting deterministic and evolutionary methods across four distinct examples. Finally, Kumar and Shaik [23] extended their previous work to include a reliable early delivery model and solved four examples of literature.

Motivation for Current Work

Kumar et al. [20] assumed that material arrivals from active production tasks would renew shelf-life in their model. Although they relaxed the shelf-life calculation to account for active production, the approach lacked sufficient rigor, as shown in Figure 1. We introduce new constraints to accurately capture this assumption, with a detailed formulation provided in Section 3. This short communication revisits the above assumption in our previously published model [20]. We present a corrected/rectified model by introducing a new binary variable, which additionally reduces the minimum number of events required to solve the problem. As shown in Table 1 in Section 4, this refinement decreases the number of events by two to three in the illustrative examples, while improving the net profit. Later, we compare the results with our previously published models, as all other comparative analyses have already been reported in Kumar et al. [20] and Kumar and Shaik [22] in a comprehensive manner.

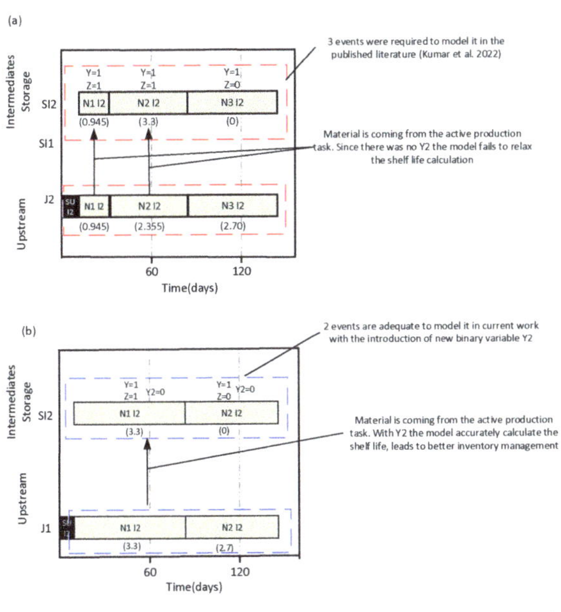

Figure 1. Shelf-life modeling in (**a**) literature model of Kumar et al. [20] and (**b**) present work.

The article is organized as follows: Section 2 outlines the problem statement, including assumptions and operational requirements; Section 3 presents the revised mathematical

https://doi.org/10.3390/mca31010032

model; Section 4 reports the results; Section 5 discusses findings, limitations, and future directions; and Section 6 concludes the study.

2. Problem Statement

In the present work, we address a long-term scheduling problem adopted from Lakhdar et al. [14] over a 360-day horizon divided into multiple delivery dates spaced 60 days apart, starting from day 120 and requiring the delivery of three products (P1, P2, and P3) across a total of five delivery dates. The objective is to maximize net profit, which is the difference between revenue and all associated costs.

Given:

Facility: Multi-stage process (USP and DSP) with multiple units.

Production Recipe: State-task network (STN) defining tasks as shown in Figure 2, processing rates, and conversions.

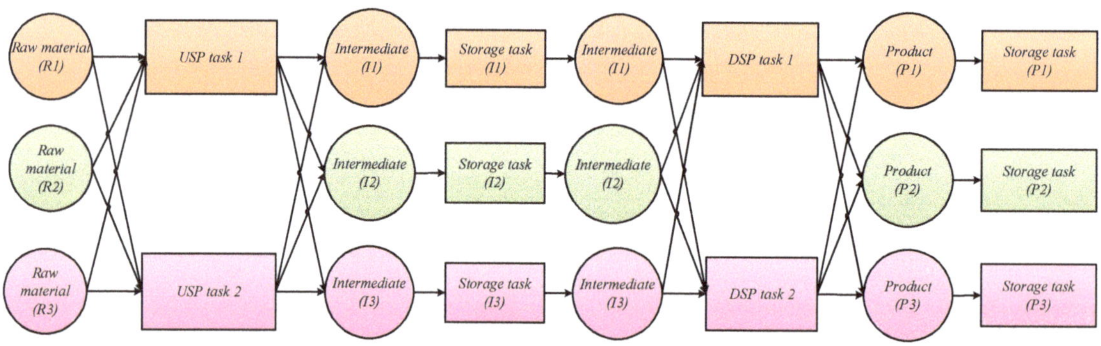

Figure 2. STN for motivational example adopted from Kumar et al. [20].

Demand: Multi-period demand for final products at specific due dates (D_{s,n_d}).

Constraints: Shelf-life, storage capacity, minimum campaign length (MCL), and setup/changeover.

Costs/Prices: Sales prices (ϑ_s), inventory holding costs (ρ_s), waste costs (φ_s), and penalty costs for backlog/lateness (δ_s) and initial setup (μ_j)/changeover ($\mu_{s's}$) costs.

Determine the following:

Schedule: Start and end times for all processing and storage tasks.

Resource Allocation: Assignment of tasks to specific units.

Inventory Profile: Exact quantity of intermediates and products stored over time.

Sales and Waste: Quantities sold (on-time or late) and quantities wasted due to shelf-life expiry.

General Problem Assumptions

As mentioned in the previous works, the following assumptions define the scope and boundaries of the manufacturing environment.

Demand and Production:

No Overproduction: Overproduction is not allowed and is constrained by total production over the time horizon.

Unfulfilled Demand: Failure to meet demand on time is allowed but incurs a lateness/backlog penalty cost.

No Initial Inventory: The facility starts with zero inventory for raw material, intermediate, and final products.

https://doi.org/10.3390/mca31010032

Continuous Operation: The process is treated as a continuous train of batch units (e.g., fermentation), meaning multiple batches function like a continuous flow rather than discrete, isolated batches.

Delivery Policy: Products can only be sold on or after the specified due dates. Early delivery is not allowed in the sense that products produced early cannot be removed from inventory; they must be stored (incurring costs) until the due date. However, it should be noted that Kumar and Shaik [23] developed a separate model (M2) for early delivery.

Unknown Finite Delivery Rates: A realistic assumption where delivery takes time, requiring storage to remain active during the transfer.

Shelf Life: Both intermediate and final products are perishable. Shelf-life must be checked before processing or selling. Material stored beyond its shelf-life is treated as waste and incurs a disposal cost.

The detailed nomenclature and the original model formulation by Kumar et al. [20] are provided in the Supplementary Materials (Sections S1 and S2).

Problem Context and Model Simplification

Biopharmaceutical facilities are complex, with series and parallel units in both upstream (USP) and downstream (DSP) sections. Software tools such as SuperPro and BioSolve, which are used for process simulation and economic evaluation, are primarily scenario-based modeling environments that focus on mass balance calculations, cost analysis, and process flowsheet development, rather than providing detailed, user-definable mathematical programming formulations for production scheduling, inventory management, or delivery-policy optimization over a finite horizon. While SchedulePro can be used for bioprocess scheduling, it is based on heuristics, which do not guarantee optimality.

In contrast, detailed mathematical modeling offers deeper insight into finding optimal solutions beyond heuristic-based short-term scheduling offered by conventional software. While detailed modeling is feasible for short-term scheduling (24 h to a few days), mid-term and long-term scheduling (360–720 days) requires simplification to ensure computational tractability. To address this, we aggregate multiple units into single facilities, creating a continuous train of batch units. In this approach, assigning a task to a USP unit designates it to an aggregated facility with a consolidated production rate (batches per day), treating multiple batches as continuous flow. This aggregation is necessary because the extended time horizon makes the optimization of full-scale flowsheets prohibitively difficult.

Operational Requirements: Based on the original problem description [14] and prior work by Kumar et al. [20,22,23], the following constraints must be enforced regardless of the time representation used.

Storage Synchronization: Downstream units and intermediate storage timing must synchronize with upstream units. Storage bypassing is permitted; only excess intermediates are stored.

Final Product Storage: Storage bypassing is not permitted for final products due to finite delivery rates. All products finished before the deadline must enter storage, meaning storage timing must align with downstream processing.

Real-Time Storage Integrity: If a production task is active while the consuming task is idle or setting up, storage must be utilized to avoid real-time storage violations.

3. Revised Mathematical Model

A new binary variable $Y2(i^{st}, s, n)$ is introduced to model the storage duration. This duration is determined by multiplying the binary variable $Y2(i^{st}, s, n)$ by the difference

https://doi.org/10.3390/mca31010032

between the end time and the start time of the storage task $TT^f(i^{st},s,n) - TT^s(i^{st},s,n)$ at the given event n:

$$Y2(i^{st},s,n)\left(TT^f(i^{st},s,n) - TT^s(i^{st},s,n)\right) = sdur(i^{st},s,n) \quad \forall i^{st} \in I_s^{st}, s \in (S^{In} \cup S^F), n \in N \tag{1}$$

However, since Equation (1) is nonlinear, in order to keep the model linear, we propose the following Equations (2)–(4):

$$sdur(i^{st},s,n) \le H * Y2(i^{st},s,n) \quad \forall i^{st} \in I_s^{st}, s \in (S^{In} \cup S^F),\ n \in N \tag{2}$$

$$sdur(i^{st},s,n) \le TT^f(i^{st},s,n) - TT^s(i^{st},s,n) \quad \forall i^{st} \in I_s^{st}, s \in (S^{In} \cup S^F),\ n \in N \tag{3}$$

$$sdur(i^{st},s,n) \ge TT^f(i^{st},s,n) - TT^s(i^{st},s,n) - H(1 - Y2(i^{st},s,n)) \quad \forall i^{st} \in I_s^{st}, s \in (S^{In} \cup S^F), n \in N \tag{4}$$

In the context of the active production task, the shelf-life calculation should be relaxed according to the assumption as stated in Equation (5):

$$w(i,s',n) + Y2(i^{st},s,n) \le 1 \quad \forall s' \in (S^R \cup S^{In}), s \in (S^{In} \cup S^F),\ M^{s's} > 0, i \in I_s^p, i^{st} \in I_s^{st}, n \in N \tag{5}$$

The binary variables, $Y2(i^{st},s,n)$, related to shelf-life are penalized in the objective function to prevent unnecessary activation:

$$\begin{aligned} Obj = Profit &- C_1 \sum_{i \in I_s} \sum_{s \in S_i} \sum_{n \in N} w(i,s,n) - C_2 \sum_{i^{st} \in I^{st}} \sum_{s \in (S^{In} \cup S^F)} \sum_{n \in N} \left[y(i^{st},s,n)\right] \\ &- C_3 \sum_{i^{st} \in I^{st}} \sum_{s \in (S^{In} \cup S^F)} \sum_{n \in N} \left[z(i^{st},s,n)\right] \\ &- C_4 \sum_{i^{st} \in I^{st}} \sum_{s \in (S^{In} \cup S^F)} \sum_{n \in N} \left[vt(i^{st},s,n)\right] \\ &- C_5 \sum_{i^{st} \in I^{st}} \sum_{s \in (S^{In} \cup S^F)} \sum_{n \in N} \left[Y2(i^{st},s,n)\right] \end{aligned} \tag{6}$$

The revised model incorporates equations from Kumar et al. [20], complemented by the Supplementary Material from the same authors, and includes the following equations: Equation (2)–(6), (S1), (S2), (S3), (S5a), (S5b), (S6a), (S6b), (S7a), (S7b), (S8a), (S8b), (S9a), (S9b), (S10a), (S10b), (S11), (S12), (S13a), (S13b), (S14a), (S14d), (S15a), (S15b), (S16a), (S16b), (S17), (S18a)–(S18f), (S19a), (S19b), (S20a), (S20b), (S21a)–(S21c), (S22a), (S22b), (S23a), (S23b), (S24), (S25), (S26a)–(S26e), and (S27a).

4. Results

We adopted two examples from the literature [14,19] to analyze the performance of the revised model for a biopharmaceutical manufacturing facility. We compare the performance of the proposed revised model with the results of the deterministic model [20] and the stochastic methods/algorithms [19].

The penalty coefficients (C_1 to C_5) used in Equation (6) require fine-tuning until no binary variables in the solution get activated unnecessarily. It should be noted that excessively increasing these penalties relative to profit terms may reduce the profit value while optimizing the objective function, which is undesirable. The model aims to maximize profit while minimizing unnecessary activation of binary variables. Using this approach, we solved the benchmark examples presented in this study. We used values in the range

https://doi.org/10.3390/mca31010032

of 0.001–1 for the penalty coefficients in the revised model. We solved the revised model using CPLEX/GAMS 24.0.1 software on a 12th Gen Intel (R) Core^{TM} i7-12700H with 64 GB of RAM.

Similar to the earlier work of Kumar et al. [20,22,24], the symbols used in the Gantt charts (Figures 2 and 3) are defined as follows: each task is represented by a colored horizontal solid block with length proportional to its duration; the number of batches are indicated in parentheses beneath the block; events (N_1, N_2, ...) and processing or storage states in the respective units are shown inside the block; black horizontal blocks denote setup and changeover times, prefixed with "SU" for setup and "CO" for changeover; storage units for intermediate or final product states are prefixed with "S"; for example, "SI1" represents the storage tank for intermediate state I1.

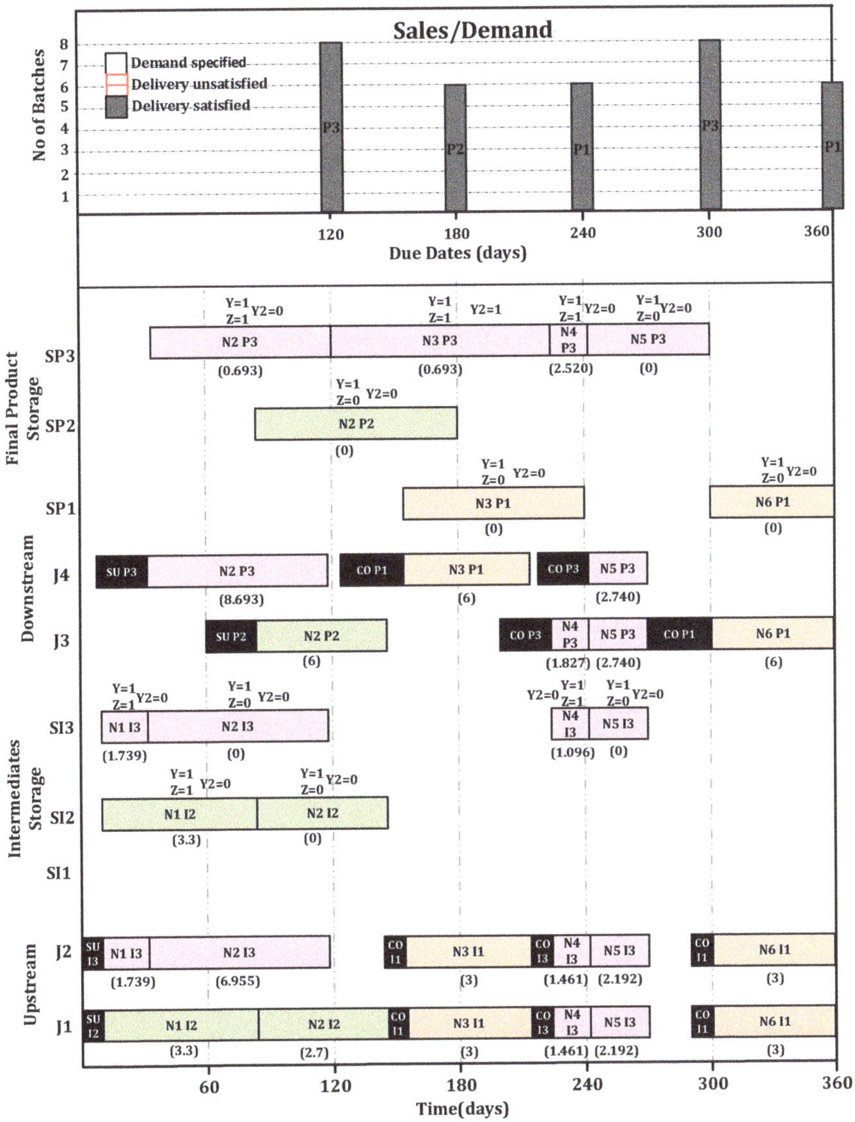

Figure 3. Proposed Gantt chart for example 1 using revised model with six events (profit = 495.42 rmu).

https://doi.org/10.3390/mca31010032

4.1. Example 1

Numerous researchers [15–22,24] have utilized the first example from the published literature [14] to test their models [14–18,20,22] and algorithms [19,21]. We exclusively compare our results with Kumar et al. [20,23], as their published works [20,22] provide details on all other comparisons. The revised model yielded a profit of 495.42 rmu solved using six events, which is better than the published result (491.22 rmu) of Kumar et al. [20]. Model statistics and profit breakdown for Examples 1 and 2 are presented in Tables 1 and 2, respectively. The proposed Gantt chart is reported in Figure 3.

Table 1. Model statistics for Examples 1 and 2.

Model Statistics	Example 1			Example 2	
	Kumar et al. [20]	**Kumar and Shaik [23]**	**Revised Model**	**Kumar and Shaik [23]**	**Revised Model**
Constraints	4538	7160	3330	7124	2576
Continuous variables	638	847	530	857	434
Binary variables	229	1365	205	1365	169
Minimum event required	8	8	6	8	5
CPU time (s)	39	56	2	37	2
Optimality gap (%)	0	0	0	0	0
Profit (rmu)	491.22	460.67	495.42	499.5	536.5

Table 2. Profit structure for Examples 1 and 2.

Profit Structure (rmu)	Example 1			Example 2	
	Kumar et al. [20]	**Kumar and Shaik [23]**	**Revised Model**	**Kumar and Shaik [23]**	**Revised Model**
Sales revenue	680	680	680	740	740
Manufacturing cost	136	136	136	148	148
Changeover cost	10	10	10	4	4
Initial setup cost	4	4	4	4	4
Intermediate storage cost	30.675	30.675	30.675	47.5	47.5
Final storage cost	8.106	38.599	3.906	37	-
Lateness cost	-	-	-	-	-
Waste disposal cost	-	-	-	-	-
Profit	491.22	460.67	495.42	499.5	536.5

4.2. Example 2

The second example is also adapted from published literature [19]. Kumar and Shaik [22] reported the discrepancies in their work by analyzing their reported Gantt chart. All input parameters are the same as in example 1, except for the demand profile of the final products, as shown in Table S4 in the Supporting Information. A profit value of 536.5 rmu is achieved using five events, which is a 7% improvement over the profit of Kumar and Shaik [23], and a 2% improvement over the reported profit (523.983 rmu) of Kumar and Shaik [22]. The reported profit of Jankauskas et al. [19] is higher; however, due to some inconsistencies in their work [22], their calculated profit is lower, as reported in Kumar

https://doi.org/10.3390/mca31010032

and Shaik [22]. The proposed Gantt chart is reported in Figure 4. As shown in Table 1, the revised model achieves faster computation by requiring fewer events, and it reduces binary and continuous variables. Although Kumar and Shaik [23] reported a profit of 536.5 rmu for their early-delivery model M2 in Example 2, the present study considers only on-time or late delivery with an unknown finite delivery rate.

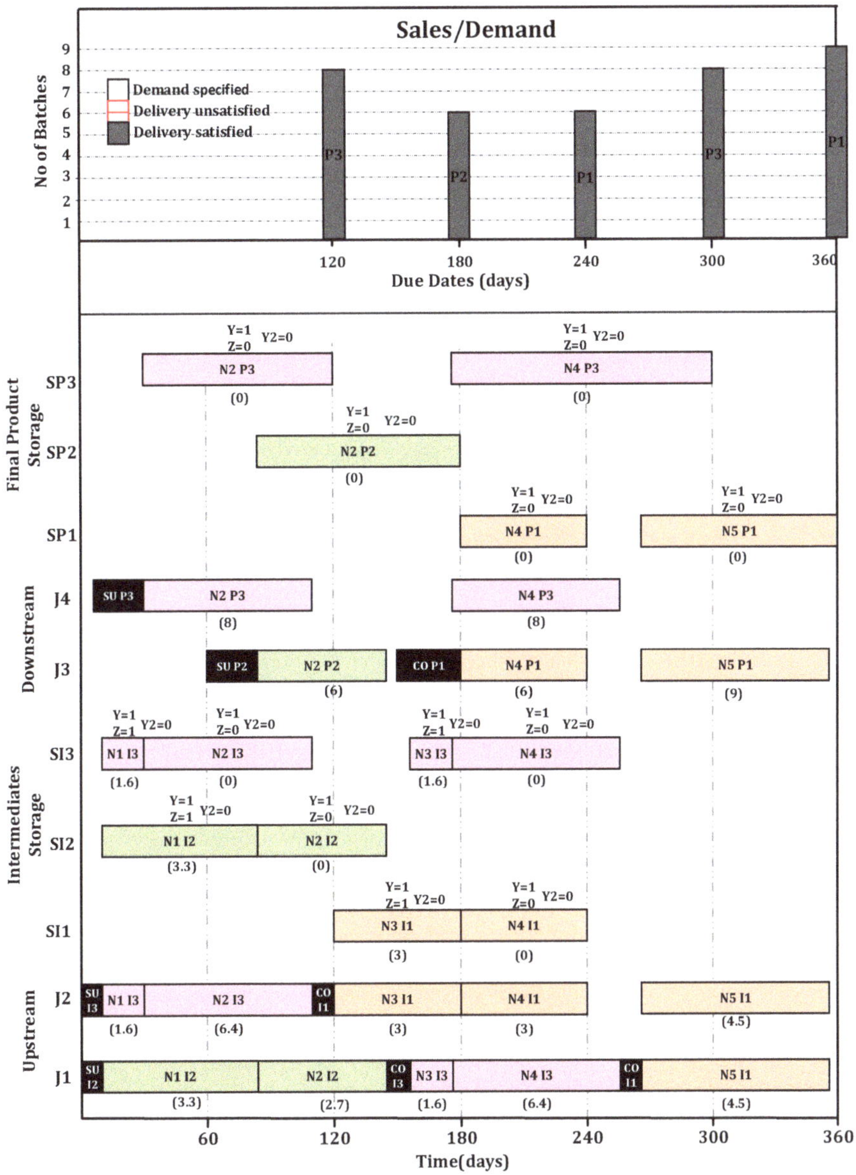

Figure 4. Proposed Gantt chart for example 2 using revised model with five events (profit = 536.5 rmu).

https://doi.org/10.3390/mca31010032

5. Discussion, Future Directions, and Limitations

Kumar et al. [20,22] explored and reviewed various deterministic MILP models [14–18] and evolutionary algorithms [19,21] for the mid-term planning and long-term scheduling of biopharmaceuticals. Unit-specific event-based models facilitate rigorous modeling and sequencing of storage operations, which is critical for accommodating the different processing rates of upstream and downstream units. Literature models [14,16–18] and algorithms [19,21] do not adequately address the required intermediate storage, resulting in real-time storage violations. Vieira et al. [17,18] concluded that their global event-based model requires fewer events (for instance, six events for example 1). However, Kumar et al. [20] have shown that accurate modeling of intermediate storage in real-time requires more events using global events. The proposed revised model uses six events to solve example 1 and suggests improvements in shelf-life modeling to avoid suboptimal results.

Future directions: Across our prior and current work, we have observed and shown that evolutionary algorithms based on discrete-time and global-event formulations have consistently proven inadequate for accurately modeling storage demands in multi-stage, multi-product facilities. Extending a genetic algorithm within the unit-specific event-based framework, integrated with MILP modeling, offers a viable path to compare these approaches and to better assess their computational feasibility and performance. The models can be extended to multi-facility networks with real-world data or to scenarios with uncertainty.

Limitations of the work: In this work, we employ a unit-specific event-based MILP formulation; however, shelf-life and minimum campaign length are modeled over a single event. This simplification reduces the number of required events and improves computational efficiency but may occasionally lead to suboptimal solutions. This model is therefore best suited for smaller multiproduct scheduling problems.

6. Conclusions

In this study, we proposed an enhanced MILP model with revised shelf-life constraints within a unit-specific, event-based framework for continuous biopharmaceutical manufacturing. The proposed model addresses the timely and penalty-imposed late deliveries for final products with unknown finite delivery rates. Computational experiments on two benchmark case studies demonstrate that the revised formulation outperforms a conventional MILP model and an evolutionary algorithm applied to the same scheduling problem.

Supplementary Materials: The following supporting information can be downloaded at: https://www.mdpi.com/article/10.3390/mca31010032/s1. Section S1. Nomenclature. Section S2. Mathematical Model. Section S3. Supplementary Data Tables.

Author Contributions: Conceptualization, V.K. and M.A.S.; methodology, V.K. and M.A.S.; software, V.K.; validation, V.K. and M.A.S.; formal analysis, V.K. and M.A.S.; resources, V.K. and M.A.S.; data curation, V.K.; writing—original draft preparation, V.K.; writing—review and editing, M.A.S.; visualization, V.K. and M.A.S.; supervision, M.A.S. All authors have read and agreed to the published version of the manuscript.

Funding: This research received no external funding. The article processing charge (APC) was partially covered by the Open Publishing Support Fund (OPSF) at the University of Tennessee, Knoxville.

Data Availability Statement: All relevant data sourced from the published literature is provided in Supplementary Material (Section S3).

Acknowledgments: During the preparation of this manuscript, the authors used Grok 4 and M365 Copilot built on GPT-5 for the purposes of grammar correction/language improvement. The authors have reviewed and edited the output and take full responsibility for the content of this publication.

Conflicts of Interest: The authors declare no conflicts of interest.

https://doi.org/10.3390/mca31010032

Abbreviations

The following abbreviations are used in this manuscript:

MILP	Mixed-integer linear programming
USP	Upstream processing
DSP	Downstream processing
GAMS	General Algebraic Modeling System

References

1. Walsh, G.; Walsh, E. Biopharmaceutical Benchmarks 2022. *Nat. Biotechnol.* **2022**, *40*, 1722–1760. [CrossRef] [PubMed]
2. Hansel, T.T.; Kropshofer, H.; Singer, T.; Mitchell, J.A.; George, A.J.T. The Safety and Side Effects of Monoclonal Antibodies. *Nat. Rev. Drug Discov.* **2010**, *9*, 325–338. [CrossRef] [PubMed]
3. Grand View Research Biopharmaceutical Market Size | Industry Report, 2033. Available online: https://www.grandviewresearch.com/industry-analysis/biopharmaceutical-market? (accessed on 5 January 2026).
4. Precedence Research Biopharmaceuticals Market Size to Hit USD 1796.21 Billion by 2034. Available online: https://www.precedenceresearch.com/biopharmaceutical-market? (accessed on 5 January 2026).
5. Fortune Business Insights Biopharmaceuticals Market Size, Share, Forecast, [2032]. Available online: https://www.fortunebusinessinsights.com/biopharmaceuticals-market-106928? (accessed on 5 January 2026).
6. Intuition Labs Why Drug Development Takes Decades: Process & Challenges. Available online: https://intuitionlabs.ai/articles/drug-development-timeline-challenges (accessed on 5 January 2026).
7. Kesik-Brodacka, M. Progress in Biopharmaceutical Development. *Biotechnol. Appl. Biochem.* **2018**, *65*, 306–322. [CrossRef] [PubMed]
8. Mitragotri, S.; Burke, P.A.; Langer, R. Overcoming the Challenges in Administering Biopharmaceuticals: Formulation and Delivery Strategies. *Nat. Rev. Drug Discov.* **2014**, *13*, 655–672. [CrossRef] [PubMed]
9. Deb, K.; Ehrgott, M. On Generalized Dominance Structures for Multi-Objective Optimization. *Math. Comput. Appl.* **2023**, *28*, 100. [CrossRef]
10. Estrada-Padilla, A.; Lopez-Garcia, D.; Gómez-Santillán, C.; Fraire-Huacuja, H.J.; Cruz-Reyes, L.; Rangel-Valdez, N.; Morales-Rodríguez, M.L. Modeling and Optimizing the Multi-Objective Portfolio Optimization Problem with Trapezoidal Fuzzy Parameters. *Math. Comput. Appl.* **2021**, *26*, 36. [CrossRef]
11. Saeed Osman, M. Last-Mile Decomposition Heuristics with Multi-Period Embedded Optimization Models. *Math. Comput. Appl.* **2025**, *30*, 90. [CrossRef]
12. Smedberg, H.; Barrera-Diaz, C.A.; Nourmohammadi, A.; Bandaru, S.; Ng, A.H.C. Knowledge-Driven Multi-Objective Optimization for Reconfigurable Manufacturing Systems. *Math. Comput. Appl.* **2022**, *27*, 106. [CrossRef]
13. Nebro, A.J.; Galeano-Brajones, J.; Luna, F.; Coello Coello, C.A. Is NSGA-II Ready for Large-Scale Multi-Objective Optimization? *Math. Comput. Appl.* **2022**, *27*, 103. [CrossRef]
14. Lakhdar, K.; Zhou, Y.; Savery, J.; Titchener-Hooker, N.J.; Papageorgiou, L.G. Medium Term Planning of Biopharmaceutical Manufacture Using Mathematical Programming. *Biotechnol. Prog.* **2005**, *21*, 1478–1489. [CrossRef] [PubMed]
15. Kabra, S.; Shaik, M.A.; Rathore, A.S. Multi-Period Scheduling of a Multi-Stage Multi-Product Bio-Pharmaceutical Process. *Comput. Chem. Eng.* **2013**, *57*, 95–103. [CrossRef]
16. Liu, S.; Yahia, A.; Papageorgiou, L.G. Optimal Production and Maintenance Planning of Biopharmaceutical Manufacturing under Performance Decay. *Ind. Eng. Chem. Res.* **2014**, *53*, 17075–17091. [CrossRef]
17. Vieira, M.; Pinto-Varela, T.; Moniz, S.; Barbosa-Póvoa, A.P.; Papageorgiou, L.G. Optimal Planning and Campaign Scheduling of Biopharmaceutical Processes Using a Continuous-Time Formulation. *Comput. Chem. Eng.* **2016**, *91*, 422–444. [CrossRef]
18. Vieira, M.; Pinto-Varela, T.; Barbosa-Póvoa, A.P. Production and Maintenance Planning Optimisation in Biopharmaceutical Processes under Performance Decay Using a Continuous-Time Formulation: A Multi-Objective Approach. *Comput. Chem. Eng.* **2017**, *107*, 111–139. [CrossRef]
19. Jankauskas, K.; Papageorgiou, L.G.; Farid, S.S. Continuous-Time Heuristic Model for Medium-Term Capacity Planning of a Multi-Suite, Multi-Product Biopharmaceutical Facility. In *Computer Aided Chemical Engineering*; Elsevier: Amsterdam, The Netherlands, 2017; Volume 40, pp. 1303–1308.
20. Kumar, V.; Shaik, M.A.; Jain, A. Analysis of Commonly Used Scheduling Models for Multistage Biopharmaceutical Processes. *Can. J. Chem. Eng.* **2022**, *100*, 3635–3652. [CrossRef]
21. Jankauskas, K.; Papageorgiou, L.G.; Farid, S.S. Fast Genetic Algorithm Approaches to Solving Discrete-Time Mixed Integer Linear Programming Problems of Capacity Planning and Scheduling of Biopharmaceutical Manufacture. *Comput. Chem. Eng.* **2019**, *121*, 212–223. [CrossRef]

https://doi.org/10.3390/mca31010032

22. Kumar, V.; Shaik, M.A. Improved Scheduling Model for a Multistage Biopharmaceutical Process in a Multiproduct Facility. *Chem. Eng. Res. Des.* **2024**, *207*, 518–538. [CrossRef]
23. Kumar, V.; Shaik, M.A. Long-Term Scheduling Models for Multi-Stage Biopharmaceutical Processes with Effective Inventory Planning and Early Delivery. *Int. J. Manag. Sci. Eng. Manag.* **2026**, 1–21. [CrossRef]
24. Kumar, V. *Decision Support System for Improved Scheduling, Maintenance, and Assessment of Biopharmaceutical Processes*; Indian Institute of Technology: Delhi, India, 2021.

Disclaimer/Publisher's Note: The statements, opinions and data contained in all publications are solely those of the individual author(s) and contributor(s) and not of MDPI and/or the editor(s). MDPI and/or the editor(s) disclaim responsibility for any injury to people or property resulting from any ideas, methods, instructions or products referred to in the content.

https://doi.org/10.3390/mca31010032

Mathematical and Computational Applications

MDPI

Article

Reliable Emergency Facility Location Planning Under Complex Polygonal Barriers and Facility Failure Risks

Mingyuan Liu [1], Lintao Liu [1], Zhujia Yu [2], Futai Liang [3] and Guocheng Wang [1,*]

[1] State Key Laboratory of Geodesy and Earth's Dynamics, Innovation Academy for Precision Measurement Science and Technology, Chinese Academy of Sciences, Wuhan 430077, China
[2] Troops 92429 of the People's Liberation Army, Qingdao 266000, China
[3] Troops 31121 of the People's Liberation Army, Nanjing 210000, China
* Correspondence: guocheng96@apm.ac.cn

Abstract

Emergency facility location and layout are critical to the efficiency of emergency rescue and resource allocation. However, practical emergency scenarios are plagued by two key challenges: the risk of facility failure due to various uncertain factors and the presence of complex polygonal barriers (including convex and concave polygons) that hinder transportation. Existing studies often overlook concave polygonal barriers or fail to prioritize time satisfaction, a core demand in emergency response. To address these gaps, this paper proposes a reliable emergency facility location optimization model with the objective of maximizing time satisfaction, considering constraints such as capacity, cost, and demand. The model integrates three key methods: a convex hull algorithm to convert concave barriers into convex ones for simplified calculation, a path optimization algorithm to find the shortest bypass routes around barriers, and an Artificial Ecosystem Optimization (AEO) algorithm to solve the nonlinear programming model. Through numerical experiments (single-facility, multi-facility, and medium-scale scenarios) and a practical case study in the Meknès region of Morocco for ambulance deployment, the feasibility and effectiveness of the model and algorithms are verified. The results show that the model achieves high time satisfaction (all above 0.8, with most exceeding 0.9) and efficiently optimizes facility locations and resource allocation. Sensitivity analysis indicates that increased failure risk parameters (α and θ) lead to a gradual decrease in average time satisfaction. This research provides a systematic mathematical model and practical method for emergency facility location decision-making, effectively addressing the challenges of complex barriers and facility failure.

Keywords: facility location; time satisfaction; barriers; failure scenario; artificial ecosystem optimization algorithm (AEO)

1. Introduction

The decision-making process for emergency facility location and layout is fundamental to emergency rescue operations, directly impacting the efficiency of emergency response and the allocation of emergency resources. Facility location-allocation decisions are pivotal components in the design of emergency facility location networks. In traditional scenarios, facility location models typically assume complete reliability. However, over time, certain facilities may be exposed to various uncertain risks (e.g., natural disasters, equipment malfunctions, or operational errors) leading to emergency situations such as facility failures.

These observations are supported by numerous studies: for instance, Snyder and Daskin [1] noted that facility failures can disrupt service continuity, while Shishebori and Babadi [2] highlighted the financial and human losses associated with such disruptions in healthcare service networks. Furthermore, following an emergency, numerous barriers to actual road transport often emerge, including collapsed buildings, sunken roads, and falling rocks. These barriers alter the shortest path between facilities and demand points, increase transportation time, and thus reduce the efficiency of material transport. For example, in disaster-stricken areas, a direct route between an emergency warehouse and a affected community may be blocked by collapsed structures, forcing detours that delay relief delivery. Given these challenges, constructing a reliable and efficient emergency facility location-allocation plan holds significant research significance.

In much of the existing literature on reliable facility location, failure scenarios predominantly stem from inherent risks associated with the facility itself. The reliable facility location problem (RFLP) emerges from the need to consider reliability as a safety measure safeguarding the network against emergencies. As early as 2005, Snyder and Daskin [1] introduced RFLP and devised an optimal Lagrangian relaxation algorithm to address it. Building on this work, Shishebori and Babadi [2] developed a dependable healthcare service network by accounting for uncertain environmental and system disruption scenarios, formulating a mixed-integer linear programming model. An et al. [3] designed a reliable p-median facility location model and employed the column-and-constraint generation method for its resolution. Subsequently, in light of the risk of facility failure, a reliable emergency facility location optimization model with limited service capacity was formulated and solved using a non-dominated sorting genetic algorithm II to yield a multi-objective Pareto front solution set [4]. Wei et al. [5] established a discrete coverage model aimed at determining the optimal number and location of emergency facilities. For further references on reliable emergency facility locations, additional sources can be found in [5,6].

In addition to facility failure disruptions, barriers are also critical issues that need to be addressed in emergency facility location models. Barriers are commonly used to describe the intricate geographical environment in the actual placement of emergency facilities, and this paper specifically focuses on convex polygons and concave polygon barriers. Given their impact on path distance calculations, barriers directly influence the reliable emergency facility locations. Therefore, it is essential to thoroughly consider various barrier factors when designing the location plan. Existing research on barrier-aware facility location has made some progress: Wang [7] summarized several methods for Voronoi diagrams with limited barriers and proposed a method to generate a barrier Voronoi diagram based on element boundary discretization generation. Niu et al. [8] proposed a novel energy efficient path planning algorithm by integrating the following algorithms, namely, the Voronoi roadmap, Dijkstra's searching, coastline expanding, and genetic algorithm (GA). For further applications of Voronoi diagrams, additional references can be found in [9–11]. Furthermore, Kate and Cooper [12] were the first to consider barrier constraints in the Weber location model. They described a circular barrier and constructed a single-objective facility location optimization model. In [13], an emergency facility location under convex barriers was proposed, considering that the barrier areas do not allow for location. The authors designed the grey wolf optimization algorithm and the visual convexity around the barrier path coupling algorithm to solve the model for reliable resource allocation. Han [14] considered barriers as polygons, constructed an ensemble coverage model, and designed algorithms to solve the model. Moreover, Bischoff and Klamroth [15] provided an overview of the single-facility location problem considering only convex polygonal barriers and used a genetic algorithm to solve it. Subsequently, Bischoff et al. [16] refined the model to address multi-facility location-allocation studies under convex polygonal

https://doi.org/10.3390/mca31020050

barrier problems. Canbolat and Wesolowsky [17] investigated the single-facility location problem in a convex polygonal forbidden area scenario and constructed the model with the base of Varignon structure. For further studies on facility location under constrained conditions, additional resources can be found in [18–20]. Liu et al. [21] proposed a reliable emergency facility location optimization model that comprehensively accounts for complex polygonal barriers and facility interruption risks. With a focus on environmental protection, the model is constructed as a multi-objective framework from the perspective of sustainable development. However, in real-world emergency scenarios, situations are typically highly urgent, and time often emerges as the most critical consideration. This study adopts "maximizing time satisfaction" as its single-objective function, thereby avoiding potential decision biases arising from multi-objective weight assignment and more accurately aligning with the core pain point of "racing against time" in emergency decision-making. Meanwhile, this research emphasizes the sensitivity analysis of "facility failure probability," placing greater focus on the key influencing factors of emergency facility reliability. Practical cases and multi-scale numerical experiments are employed to ensure that the overall model construction is more closely aligned with the actual requirements of emergency site selection, including "feasible paths, available facilities, and efficient decision-making." To clarify the incremental contribution of this study relative to Liu et al. [21] and other representative reliable facility location models, Table 1 summarizes the key methodological and modeling differences.

Table 1. Comparison of research features.

Feature	Liu et al. [21]	Other RFLP Models	Present Study
Objective structure	Multi-objective (reliability + sustainability)	Usually cost minimization or coverage maximization	Single-objective: maximize time satisfaction
Reliability treatment	Integrated into multi-objective framework	Often scenario-based or expected failure cost	Facility-specific failure probability (q_i), consistently embedded in objective and constraints
Sensitivity analysis	Limited parameter analysis	Often limited to cost or failure rate	Explicit location-dependent failure risk ($q_i = \alpha e^{-D_i/\theta}$) and parameter study
Experimental scale	Medium-scale numerical cases	Varies	Single-, multi-, medium-scale experiments + new real-world ambulance case study
Managerial insight	Sustainability–reliability trade-off	Network robustness	Time-critical emergency response prioritization

Despite the advancements in the existing research, several critical gaps remain: (1) Most studies on barrier-aware facility location focus solely on convex barriers, while practical scenarios frequently involve complex concave polygonal barriers, which are more challenging to handle in path optimization. (2) Few models integrate both complex polygonal barriers and facility failure risks, leading to solutions that are insufficiently robust in real emergencies. (3) Multi-objective models often introduce weight assignment biases, and the core demand of "time satisfaction" in emergency response is not adequately prioritized. To fill these gaps, this study constructs a reliable emergency facility location model that considers complex polygonal barriers (convex and concave) and facility failure risks, with the objective of maximizing time satisfaction. Instead of relying on traditional cost-based objectives, the model directly optimizes response-time satisfaction to better reflect the

https://doi.org/10.3390/mca31020050

urgency of emergency operations. To obtain high-quality solutions, a coordinated computational scheme is designed, integrating barrier convexification, visibility-based path refinement, and an ecosystem-inspired metaheuristic search mechanism. The resulting framework enhances both spatial feasibility and computational efficiency in emergency facility deployment planning.

2. Mathematical Model Description

2.1. Problem Formulation and Assumptions

This section addresses the scenario where decision-makers need to establish multiple emergency facilities in an area with various types of polygonal barriers following an emergency, with the goal of delivering relief supplies to each demand area in a timely and safe manner. To simplify the problem and ensure the model's feasibility, the following assumptions are proposed (these are not mathematical notations but foundational premises for model construction):

(1) Emergency demand locations are assumed to form spatial clusters, and the entire service area is represented by a bounded square region for modeling convenience.
(2) Barrier regions are characterized by both convex and concave polygonal geometries, and any transportation path intersecting these polygonal boundaries is considered infeasible.
(3) Candidate facility sites must lie outside all barrier interiors and cannot coincide with any demand location.
(4) When detours around barriers are required, the effective travel route is approximated by a sequence of straight-line segments connecting intermediate waypoints between the facility and the centroid of the corresponding irregular demand region.
(5) Apart from the explicitly modeled polygonal barriers, the remaining space between facilities and demand regions is treated as unobstructed and fully traversable.

2.2. Mathematical Notations

The key indexes, sets, parameters, and decision variables used in the model are defined as follows:

Indexes	
i	Index representing candidate facility sites.
j	Index representing demand regions.
k	Index corresponding to polygonal barrier zones.
Sets	
M	Collection of facility indices, with $i \in M$.
N	Collection of demand indices, with $j \in N$.
K	Collection of barrier indices, with $k \in K$.
D	Family of square demand regions, where $D_j \in D$.
F	Admissible facility location set, where $F_i \in F$.
B	Ensemble of polygonal barrier regions, where $B_k \in B$.
C	Vector of construction cost parameters, where $c_i \in C$.
P	Feasible spatial domain defined as $P = \mathbb{R}^2 \backslash \text{int}(B)$.

https://doi.org/10.3390/mca31020050

Parameters

t_{ij}	One-way shortest time between facility location i and demand region j.
v_{ij}	Average transportation velocity between facility i and demand region j.
d_{ij}	Effective travel distance between facility i and demand region j.
U_j	Maximum acceptable supply for demand region j.
l_j	Minimum acceptable supply for demand region j.
β_i	Sensitivity coefficient in the drop semi-Cauchy time satisfaction function.
S_i	Maximum service capacity available at facility i.
L_i	Minimum safety stock of facility location i.
w_{ij}	Amount supplied from facility location i to demand region j.
w_j	Demand quantity in demand region j.
q_i	Failure probability of facility location i.
Q	Total cost.
$p_j(p_{x_j}, p_{y_j})$	Centroid coordinates of square demand region j.
(x_{c_1}, y_{c_1})	Upper boundary of the study area.
(x_{c_0}, y_{c_0})	Lower boundary of the study area.
Decision variables	
$F_i(x_i, y_i)$	Spatial coordinates selected for facility i.

Given the assumptions and notations, we formulate the optimization model for selecting the expected maximum time satisfaction location for reliable emergency facilities while accounting for constraints posed by complex polygonal barriers and facility failure risk. The problem to be solved is facility location-allocation which expected the total maximum time satisfaction of the demand region in the facility failure risk, taking into account multiple constraints such as various barriers, time, economy, resource capacity, and resource safety stock in the facility failure risk.

2.3. Time Satisfaction Function

In this section, the "time satisfaction" function is defined as the level of satisfaction of the demand point with the facility response time, reflecting the comprehensive and prompt response capability of the emergency facility in supplying the demand area. The time satisfaction curve varies based on the variability of the supplies provided by the facility and should be constructed following three principles: objectivity, simplicity, and feasibility. This involves establishing a mathematical relationship between time satisfaction (dependent variable) and the response time requirement of the demand region (independent variable), as outlined in the satisfaction function established in reference [22]. The drop semi-Cauchy time satisfaction function is as follows:

$$f(t_{ij}) = \begin{cases} 1, & if \quad d_{ij} \le L_j v_{ij}, \\ \frac{1}{1+\beta_i (d_{ij}/v_{ij} - L_j)^2}, & if \quad d_{ij} > L_j v_{ij}, \end{cases}$$

Here, β_i controls the temporal responsiveness of the satisfaction function. A higher value of this parameter implies a steeper decline in satisfaction as travel time increases, as illustrated in Figure 1.

https://doi.org/10.3390/mca31020050

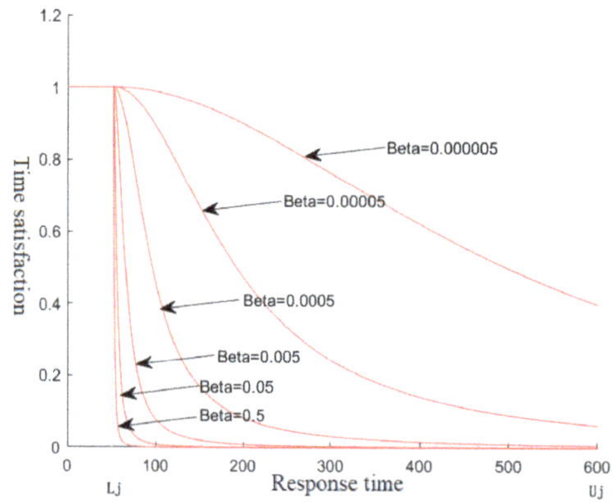

Figure 1. Drop semi-Cauchy time satisfaction function.

2.4. Model Formulation

In this section, we combine the time satisfaction function in Section 2.3 and develop the optimization model for selecting the expected maximum time satisfaction location for reliable emergency facilities while accounting for constraints posed by complex polygonal barriers and facility failure risk. The optimization formulation is given below.

$$\max\ \alpha w_1 + (1-\alpha)w_2, \tag{1}$$

$$w_1 = \sum_{j=1}^{n}\sum_{i=1}^{m} f(t_{ij})w_{ij}, \tag{2}$$

$$w_2 = \sum_{j=1}^{n}\sum_{i=1}^{m}(1-q_i)f(t_{ij})w_{ij}, \tag{3}$$

$$\text{s.t. } F \in P, P = R^2 \setminus int(B), \tag{4}$$

$$\sum_{i=1}^{m} w_{ij} = w_j, j = 1,2,\cdots,n, \tag{5}$$

$$\sum_{j=1}^{n} w_{ij} \le (1-q_i)S_i, i = 1,2,\cdots,m, \tag{6}$$

$$(1-q_i)S_i - \sum_{j=1}^{n} w_{ij} \ge (1-q_i)L_i, i = 1,2,\cdots,m, \tag{7}$$

$$\sum_{i=1}^{m} c_i \le Q, \tag{8}$$

$$d_{ij} = d(F_i, p_j), i = 1,2,\cdots,m, j = 1,2,\cdots,n, \tag{9}$$

$$\begin{aligned} &x_{c_0} \le x_i \le x_{c_1}, i = 1,2,\cdots,m, \\ &y_{c_0} \le y_i \le y_{c_1}, i = 1,2,\cdots,m, \\ &x_{c_0} \le p_{x_j} \le x_{c_1}, j = 1,2,\cdots,n, \\ &y_{c_0} \le p_{y_j} \le y_{c_1}, j = 1,2,\cdots,n. \end{aligned} \tag{10}$$

In this formulation, Equation (1) defines the overall objective, which seeks to maximize time-based satisfaction under potential facility disruption. The parameter $\alpha \in [0,1]$ balances system performance between normal operation and failure scenarios. Equations (2) and (3) quantify satisfaction levels without and with facility failure risk, respectively, where $q_i \in [0,1]$ denotes the disruption probability of facility i. Spatial feasibility is enforced through Equation (4), which restricts facility locations to the admissible region outside all

https://doi.org/10.3390/mca31020050

barrier interiors. Equation (5) allows for collaborative supply allocation, meaning that each demand region may be served jointly by multiple facilities rather than being restricted to a single-source assignment. Resource feasibility is regulated through Equations (6) and (7), which impose upper capacity bounds and minimum reserve requirements to maintain operational reliability under disruption. Budget feasibility is controlled by Equation (8), limiting overall construction expenditure. Transportation distance in Equation (9) corresponds to the optimized bypass length obtained through the path adjustment procedure between facility i and demand region j, measured between their centroid coordinates. Finally, Equation (10) confines both facilities and demand regions to the predefined square study domain, ensuring geographic admissibility.

The formulated problem constitutes a nonlinear optimization framework with multiple interdependent constraints, which renders it computationally intractable in the classical sense. The presence of intricate spatial configurations and polygonal obstruction constraints further amplifies solution difficulty, limiting the effectiveness of conventional deterministic methods. To enhance computational tractability, a barrier convexification procedure is first introduced to simplify geometric complexity in path determination. On this basis, a metaheuristic search strategy inspired by ecosystem dynamics (AEO) is employed to explore the solution space efficiently and obtain high-quality facility deployment schemes.

3. Solution Algorithms

To solve the proposed nonlinear programming model (NP-hard problem) efficiently, a three-step algorithm framework is designed: (1) Convert concave barriers to convex barriers using the convex hull algorithm. (2) Optimize bypass paths around barriers using the path optimization algorithm. (3) Solve the location-allocation model using the AEO algorithm. The overall workflow of the algorithm is shown in Figure 2.

3.1. Implementation of Convex Hull Algorithm

This subsection applies a convex hull-based preprocessing step to handle barrier geometry. For a finite planar point set, the convex hull [23] corresponds to the minimal convex region enclosing all points, serving as a geometric simplification tool in subsequent path calculations. For concave polygonal barriers, direct path calculation is complex. The convex hull algorithm converts concave barriers into convex ones to simplify bypass path planning. The steps are as follows: 1. For each concave polygonal barrier, extract all its vertex coordinates. 2. Use the Graham scan algorithm [24] to compute the convex hull of these vertices, forming a convex polygon that encloses the original concave barrier. 3. Treat the convex hull as an equivalent barrier for subsequent path optimization (ensuring that the bypass path around the convex hull is also valid for the original concave barrier).

In the context of a set of points in the plane, the convex hull algorithm [25] is used to find a minimum convex polygon containing all points. For instance, the polygon barriers $P = [p_1; p_3; p_8; p_{10}; p_{14}]$ enclosed by the red line segments in Figure 3 represents the set of points $Q = \{p_1, \cdots, p_{15}\}$.

When the study area contains both convex and concave polygonal obstacles, concave regions are transformed into equivalent convex forms through a convex wrapping procedure to simplify subsequent computations. The transformation outcome is illustrated in Figure 4: the dashed boundaries correspond to the original barrier shapes, whereas the shaded regions indicate their convexified counterparts. In total, twelve barrier entities are considered and labeled as $B_1, B_2, \ldots, B_{12}$.

https://doi.org/10.3390/mca31020050

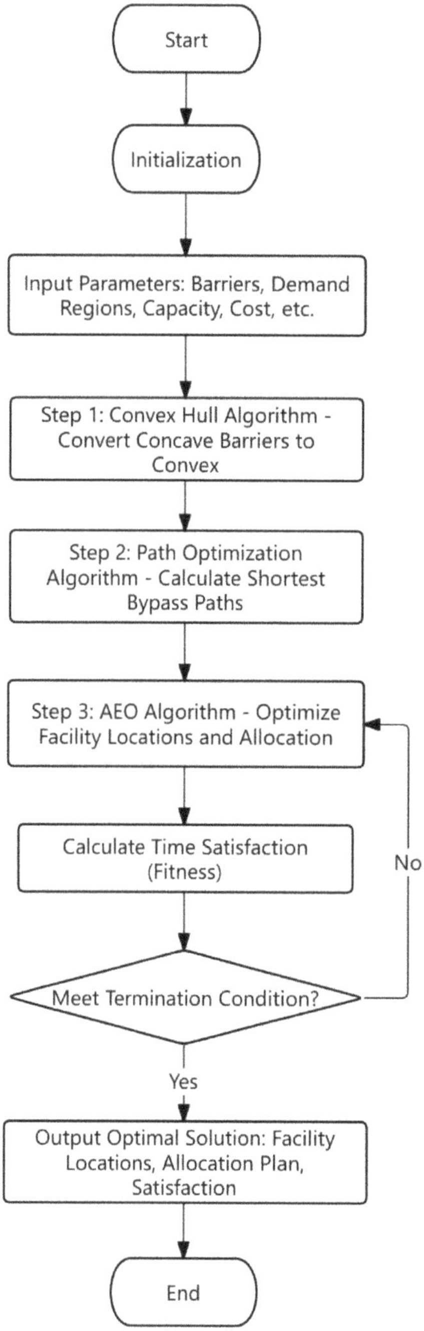

Figure 2. Overall workflow of the solution algorithm.

https://doi.org/10.3390/mca31020050

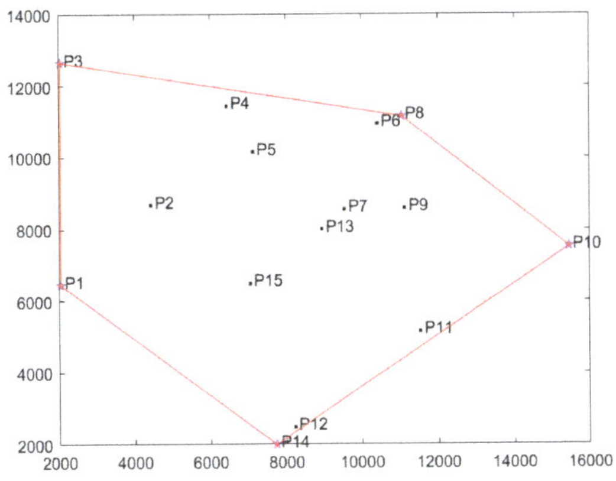

Figure 3. Example of a convex hull of a point set.

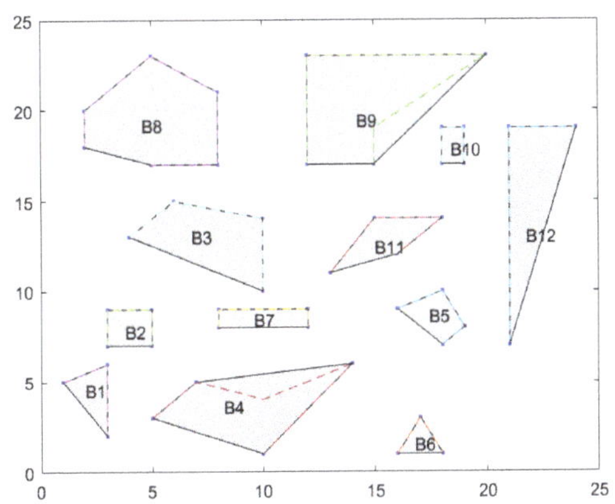

Figure 4. Concave barriers transformed into convex barriers.

3.2. Implementation of Path Optimization Algorithm

In this section, based on Section 3.1, we describe the implementation of the path optimization procedure. Efficient route planning is essential in emergency facility location, as transportation efficiency directly affects response performance. The presence of polygonal barriers significantly increases the complexity of distance calculation. To address this issue, a visibility-based environment is constructed to determine the shortest feasible path between a facility and a demand region while avoiding all barriers. The procedure computes the shortest bypass distance d_{ij} and consists of the following steps:

1. Identify the first intersecting barrier. Connect the facility point and the demand point using a straight line and detect the first barrier intersected by this segment through line–polygon intersection testing.

2. Generate bypass vertices. For the identified barrier, determine the optimal bypass vertices (convex hull vertices) that minimize the detour distance. Construct an initial point sequence: facility point $\rightarrow$ bypass vertices $\rightarrow$ demand point.

3. Expand the sequence. Treat the last point in the current sequence as a new starting point and repeat Step 1 to identify subsequent intersecting barriers. Append newly determined bypass vertices to the sequence.

https://doi.org/10.3390/mca31020050

4. Simplify the sequence. Examine whether consecutive points in the sequence can be connected directly without crossing any barrier. If so, remove intermediate points to shorten the path.

5. Verify feasibility. Ensure that no segment in the final sequence intersects any barrier. The resulting path length is defined as the shortest bypass distance d_{ij}.

Figure 5 illustrates the application of the proposed procedure using $(6,6)$ as the facility location and $(17,15)$ as the center of the demand region.

The optimization process proceeds as follows:

(1) The direct segment between $(6,6)$ and $(17,15)$ intersects barrier 1.
(2) The optimal bypass vertices $(8,8)$ and $(8,9)$ are identified. The sequence is updated accordingly, and $(8,9)$ becomes the new starting point for subsequent detection. Barrier 2 is then identified.
(3) Vertex $(15,14)$ is selected to bypass barrier 2, resulting in the sequence $(6,6)(8,8)(8,9)$, $(15,14)(17,15)$.
(4) Further examination reveals that the segment $(8,9)(15,14)$ intersects barrier 3. An additional bypass vertex $(10,4)$ is introduced, yielding the sequence $(6,6)(8,8)(8,9)(10,4)$, $(15,14)(17,15)$.
(5) After removing redundant intermediate points that do not affect feasibility, the final simplified sequence becomes $(6,6)(8,9)(10,4)(15,14)(17,15)$.
(6) The resulting path represents the shortest feasible bypass route, illustrated by the green solid line in Figure 5.

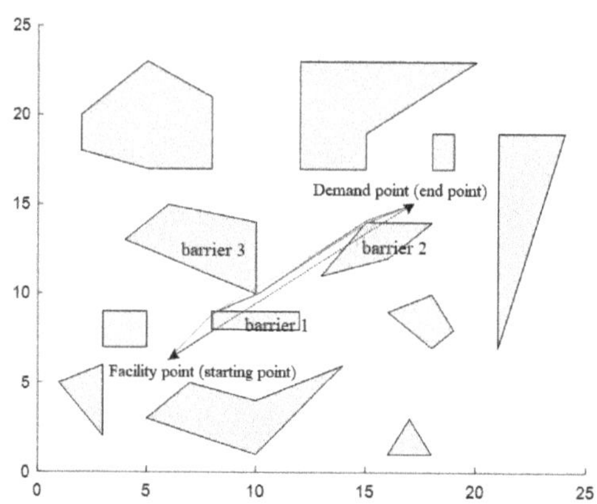

Figure 5. Path optimization calculation example.

3.3. Model Solving Based on AEO Algorithm

The AEO algorithm, proposed by Zhao et al. [26], draws inspiration from ecosystems and is based on the energy flow within them, representing a form of physical inspiration. The algorithm comprises three main components, producer, consumer, and decomposer, reflecting the dynamics inherent in maintaining the internal operations of ecosystems. By studying the strategies and behaviors of organisms within ecosystems, humans have identified various pathways for energy flow and nutrient cycles, leading to enhanced optimization performance. As a result, the AEO algorithm has found widespread application [27,28]. In this paper, the AEO algorithm is combined with path optimization algorithms and applied to facility location models and resource allocation solutions.

In this section, we focus on the AEO algorithm which combines Section 3.1 with Section 3.2 and solve the optimization model for selecting the expected maximum time

https://doi.org/10.3390/mca31020050

satisfaction location for reliable emergency facilities while accounting for constraints posed by complex polygonal barriers and facility failure risk. The AEO algorithm interprets all organism location information within an ecosystem as a contingency facility location, essentially representing a point in the search space. The energy flow process within the ecosystem is akin to an optimal search conducted step by step. The fitness value (i.e., time satisfaction) of each organism represents a candidate solution in the search space. Energy transfer from the producer x_1 to the decomposer x_n corresponds to the evolution from an initial solution toward an optimal facility location.

(1) Production phase: The starting point (the initialized facility point) in AEO is the producer, the update of the producer information is closely related to the best individual in the range of all individuals, and the iterated $x_1(t+1)$ will gradually approach the optimal individual while guiding the direction of the iterative update for the consumer

$$x_1(t+1) = (1-\alpha)x_n(t) + \alpha x_{rand}(t), \tag{11}$$

where n is the population size, $\alpha = (1 - t/T)r_1$ is the linear weight coefficient, t denotes the current number of iterations, T denotes the maximum number of iterations, $r_1 \in [0,1]$ is the random number, $x_{rand} = r(U-L) + L$ is the random individual in the solution space $[L, U]$, and $r \in [0,1]$ is a random vector uniformly distributed from 0 to 1.

(2) Consumption stage: According to the food characteristics of animals in the ecosystem, consumers can be divided into phytophagous, carnivorous, and omnivorous animals, and they are given different updated iteration patterns to increase the diversity of solutions.

Herbivore consumption strategy: If it is herbivore consumers, and herbivore animals will only consume the producers, the mathematical expression of herbivore animals and producers is constructed as follows:

$$x_i(t+1) = x_i(t) + C \cdot (x_i(t) - x_1(t)), \tag{12}$$

where $i \in [2, n]$, based on the Levy flight-improved consumption factor $C = v_1/2|v_2|$, and with $v_1 \sim N(0,1), v_2 \sim N(0,1)$.

Carnivore consumption strategy: If the consumer is a carnivore, and the carnivore will randomly consume an individual consumer with high energy (low time satisfaction), the mathematical expression for the carnivore and the corresponding consumer is constructed as follows:

$$x_i(t+1) = x_i(t) + C \cdot (x_i(t) - x_j(t)), \tag{13}$$

where $i \in [3, n], j = \text{randi}([2, i-1])$.

Omnivore consumption strategy: If the consumer is an omnivore, and the omnivore will consume both the producer as well as the high-energy consumer, construct the mathematical expressions for the omnivore and the corresponding producer and consumer as follows:

$$x_i(t+1) = x_i(t) + C \cdot (r_2 \cdot (x_i(t) - x_1(t)) + (1-r_2)(x_i(t) - x_j(t)), \tag{14}$$

where $j \in \text{randi}([2, i-1]), r_2 \in [0,1]$ is a uniformly distributed random number.

https://doi.org/10.3390/mca31020050

(3) Decomposition stage: Decomposers can consume various organisms according to the characteristics of the ecosystem such as fungi, and their iterative update equation is

$$x_i(t+1) = x_n(t) + B \cdot (e \cdot x_n(t) - h \cdot x_i(t)), \quad (15)$$

where $i \in [1, n]$; the decomposition factor has $B = 3u$; there exists $u \sim N(0,1)$, $e = r_3 \cdot randi([1,2]) - 1$ and $h = 2r_3 - 1$ as the weight coefficients; and $r_3 \in [0,1]$ is a uniformly distributed random number.

The initialized populations of the AEO algorithm are all random, and during the iterative process, each organism (facility location) is updated according to its specific behavior pattern, and the optimal fitness (the optimal time satisfaction) is gradually updated until the termination condition is reached.

The application of the AEO framework to the reliable emergency facility location problem under polygonal barrier conditions is summarized in Algorithm 1. A detailed procedural outline of the AEO search mechanism is provided in Algorithm 2.

Algorithm 1 AEO for solving reliable emergency facility location model under polygon barrier scenario

Step 1. Initialization

- *Parameter configuration:* Specify the fundamental inputs of the model, including polygonal barrier set B_k, square demand regions D_j, time satisfaction bounds U_j and L_j, sensitivity coefficient β_i, transportation speed v_{ij}, facility capacity limit S_i, minimum reserve level L_i, demand volume w_j, disruption probability q_i, budget ceiling Q, population size NUM, and maximum iteration number MAX_{num}.
- *Spatial and demand preparation:* Encode barrier geometries into matrix form and register the spatial coordinates of demand regions. Demand quantities are generated within predefined bounds, while total facility capacity is assigned to exceed aggregate demand in accordance with reserve requirements.
- *Population initialization:* Generate an initial ecosystem population by randomly sampling feasible facility locations within the admissible domain. Duplicate positions and barrier-intersecting points are excluded. Evaluate the fitness of each candidate solution using the time satisfaction objective, and record the best-performing individual as X_{best}.

Step 2. Perform loop iterations, with the initial iteration starting from producer x_1 .

Step 3. x_1 is considered as the initialized facility point and starts iterating to update its location information.

Step 4. The consumer is considered as the new facility point location, which is divided into three evenly according to the random number, and one of the three animals is iteratively updated each time; thus, the herbivore, carnivore, and omnivore animals are each iteratively updated with their location information according to the probability.

Step 5. Based on the implementation of path optimization in Section 3.2 and calculate the fitness of all facilities so far, i.e., time satisfaction.

Step 6. Sort and update the best facility points X_{best} so far, and discard the inferior solutions.

Step 7. The decomposer (the current better facility point) starts to generate decomposition operations for all facility locations, i.e., update its location information.

Step 8. Based on the implementation of path optimization in Section 3.2 and calculate the fitness of all retained facility points so far, i.e., time satisfaction.

Step 9. Sort and update the best facility point X_{best} so far, and the inferior solution is discarded.

Step 10. If the condition of terminating the number of iterations is met, then terminate. If not, carry X_{best} and continue iteration from **Step 2**.

https://doi.org/10.3390/mca31020050

Algorithm 2 Algorithm of AEO

Input:
- B_k: set of polygonal barrier geometries; D_j: square demand regions;
- U_j and L_j: upper and lower bounds of time satisfaction levels;
- β_i: time-sensitivity parameter; v_{ij}: transportation velocity;
- S_i: capacity limit of facility i; L_i: minimum reserve requirement;
- w_j: demand volume of region j; q_i: disruption probability of facility i;
- Q: overall construction budget; NUM: population size;
- MAX_{num}: maximum iteration count.

Output: F_i = satisfaction of each solution, X_{best} = the best solution found so far.

while the stop criterion is not satisfied **do**
  for x_1, update its solution using Equation (11) **do**
  for x_i, where $i \in [2, n]$ **do**
    if rand $< 1/3$ **then**
      update its solution using Equation (12).
      if $1/3 \leq$ rand $\leq 2/3$ **then**
        update its solution using Equation (13).
      else
        update its solution using Equation (14).
      end if
    end if
  end for
  Calculate F_i of each individual and sort them.
  Update the best solution found so far X_{best}.
  Update the position of each individual using Equation (15).
  Calculate F_i of each individual and sort them.
  Update the best solution found so far X_{best}.
end while
return X_{best}, F_{best}.

4. Numerical Study and Analysis

In this section, we illustrate our proposed model and methodology for handling real-life problem instances. To assess the practical effectiveness of the proposed framework, computational experiments are conducted using the AEO-based solution strategy integrated with convex hull preprocessing and path refinement procedures. The resulting solutions are subsequently evaluated through comparative performance analysis. The algorithm is executed on an Intel(R) Core(TM) i7-6600U CPU (2.80 GHz) with 16.00 GB memory (note: this configuration is provided for reproducibility, as different hardware may affect computation time but not the optimal solution quality) and Windows 10 operating system using MATLAB 2020b as the platform. Custom polygon barrier data is employed for the complex barriers. The proposed route optimization algorithm is integrated with the AEO algorithm to solve the location model presented in this paper. Experiments are conducted on single-facility and multi-facility location models to validate the performance of the algorithm.

The vertex coordinates of the polygonal barriers are specified as follows:

$$B_1 = [1,5;3,6;3,2], \qquad B_2 = [3,7;3,9;5,9;5,7],$$
$$B_3 = [4,13;6,15;10,14;10,10], \qquad B_4 = [5,3;7,5;10,4;14,6;10,1],$$
$$B_5 = [16,9;18,10;19,8;18,7], \qquad B_6 = [16,1;17,3;18,1],$$
$$B_7 = [8,8;8,9;12,9;12,8], \qquad B_8 = [2,18;2,20;5,23;8,21;8,17;5,17],$$
$$B_9 = [12,17;12,23;20,23;15,19;15,17], \qquad B_{10} = [18,17;18,19;19,19;19,17],$$
$$B_{11} = [13,11;15,14;18,14;16,12], \qquad B_{12} = [21,7;21,19;24,19].$$

https://doi.org/10.3390/mca31020050

Example 1. *Simulation experiment of a single-facility emergency facility location model*

The numerical test involves six demand nodes (D1–D6) and twelve polygonal barriers. A single facility (F_1) is to be located under these spatial constraints. The facility capacity is sampled within the interval $[160, 320]$, *while demand quantities for each region are drawn from* $[30, 50]$. *Construction expenditure is fixed at* 500, *and transportation velocity is generated within the range* $[2, 8]$.

A reserve ratio of 0.5 *is imposed, and the search domain is confined to a* 25×25 *square region. The disruption probability* q_i *is randomly assigned within the interval* $randi(0, 0.1)$. *The AEO population size is specified as* 30, *with the iteration limit set to* 200. *The centroid coordinates and corresponding coverage radii of the demand regions are listed below:*

$D1 = (2, 12, 0.8)$, $D2 = (14, 9, 0.5)$,
$D3 = (23, 23, 1.3)$, $D4 = (10, 22, 1)$,
$D5 = (22, 3, 0.9)$, $D6 = (12, 15, 0.8)$

The single-facility instance is solved through the AEO-based search framework combined with convex transformation and routing refinement mechanisms. The resulting deployment configuration is illustrated in Figure 6. In the figure, F_1 marks the optimal facility position, blue segments depict the computed bypass routes, red stars denote facility sites, red squares correspond to demand regions, and gray polygons indicate barrier structures. The optimal facility coordinates are identified as $(11.19, 14.78)$. The algorithm demonstrates rapid convergence behavior, yielding a weighted objective value of 217.7.

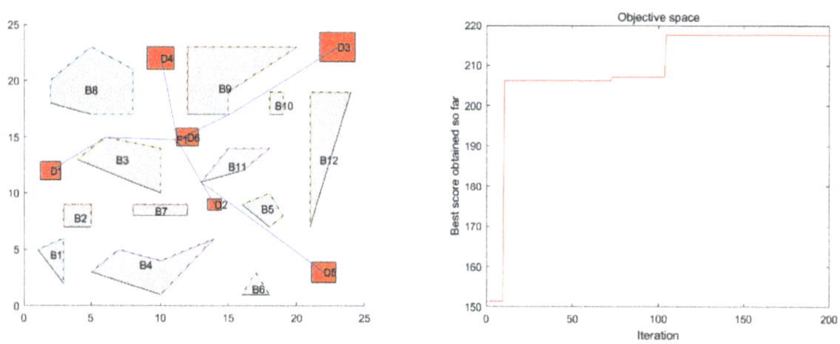

Figure 6. Single-facility reliable emergency facility location and iterative curve.

To further validate the effectiveness and computational efficiency of the proposed AEO algorithm, we conducted an additional benchmark experiment on the single-facility instance described in Figure 6. In this experiment, AEO was compared with a multi-start local search (random search with 200 iterations), using the same objective function and stopping criterion (200 iterations), described in Figure 7.

The computational time of AEO (200 iterations) was 2.5034 s, whereas the multi-start local search required 3.0757 s under the same iteration limit. The best solution obtained by the random search was located at $(11.18, 15.09)$, with a corresponding objective value of 192.8444. In contrast, AEO achieved a significantly higher objective value (217.7 as reported in Figure 6) within a substantially shorter computational time. These results indicate that AEO not only provides superior solution quality but also demonstrates significantly higher computational efficiency compared to a simple multi-start random local search strategy. This confirms the robustness and effectiveness of the proposed algorithm for solving the nonlinear facility location model.

https://doi.org/10.3390/mca31020050

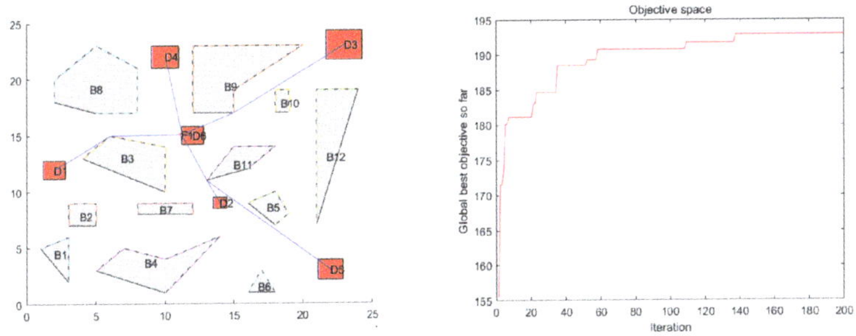

Figure 7. Comparative analysis.

Example 2. *Simulation experiments of multi-facility emergency facility location model*

For the multi-facility scenario, the capacities of F1–F3 are sampled from the interval $[80,100]$*, whereas F4 is assigned a capacity within* $[40,50]$*. The overall construction budget is increased to 2000, while the remaining experimental settings follow those specified in Example 1. The centroid coordinates and corresponding coverage radii of the demand regions are given below:*

$$D1 = (2, 12, 0.8), \quad D2 = (14, 9, 0.5),$$
$$D3 = (23, 23, 1.3), \quad D4 = (10, 22, 1),$$
$$D5 = (22, 3, 0.9), \quad D6 = (12, 15, 0.8)$$

The multi-facility configurations are obtained through the integrated AEO search framework under geometric preprocessing and routing refinement. Figure 8a displays the three-facility solution, where F_1, F_2, and F_3 denote the optimized deployment sites. Path connections, facility symbols, demand regions, and barrier polygons are visually distinguished by different colors and shapes in the figure. The corresponding optimal coordinates are $(19.98, 4.33)$, $(6.93, 15.49)$, and $(24.34, 21.97)$, yielding a weighted objective value of 239.3.

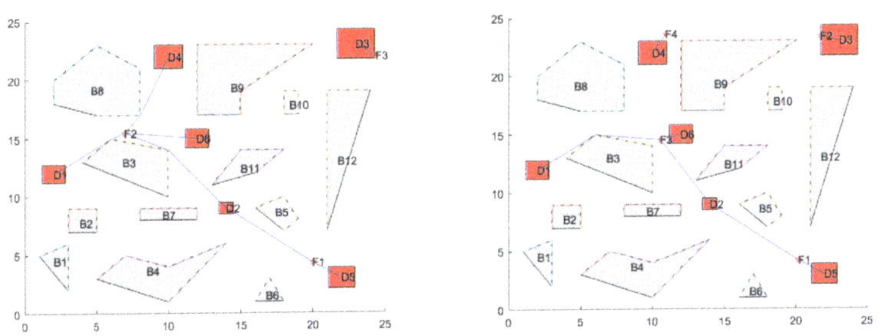

(a) $m = 3$ optimal facility locations **(b)** $m = 4$ optimal facility locations

Figure 8. Multi-facility reliable emergency facility location.

Figure 8b illustrates the four-facility scenario. The selected locations $(20.17, 4.18)$, $(21.67, 23.37)$, $(10.87, 23.58)$, and $(10.53, 14.54)$ achieve a weighted objective score of 240.48. The results indicate that service allocation is not strictly one-to-one; certain demand regions may be jointly supplied by multiple facilities, enhancing distribution flexibility.

Example 3. *Simulation experiments of the multi-facility reliable emergency facility location model*

A medium-scale instance is constructed with nineteen demand regions (D1–D19) distributed within a square study domain. The system operates under capacity, budget, and nineteen barrier constraints, while facility disruption probabilities are randomly assigned as $q_i \in randi(0, 0.1)$*. The*

https://doi.org/10.3390/mca31020050

objective remains the maximization of time-based satisfaction, based on which the deployment and allocation of five facilities are optimized. Demand magnitudes are sampled from the interval [30, 50]. *The centroid coordinates and corresponding coverage radii of the demand regions are specified below:*

$$D_1 = (2,12,0.8),\ D_2 = (14,9,0.5),\quad D_3 = (23,23,1.3),\ D_4 = (10,22,1),$$
$$D_5 = (22,3,0.9),\ D_6 = (12,15,0.8),\quad D_7 = (12,2,0.4),\ D_8 = (19,15,0.4),$$
$$D_9 = (2,21,0.2),\ D_{10} = (6,6,0.3),\quad D_{11} = (16,5,0.4),\ D_{12} = (19,10,0.2),$$
$$D_{13} = (24,10,0.3),\ D_{14} = (9,16,0.2),\quad D_{15} = (1,2,0.3),\ D_{16} = (22,5,0.4),$$
$$D_{17} = (14,3,0.2),\ D_{18} = (4,24,0.2),\quad D_{19} = (1,7,0.1)$$

The medium-scale instance is solved using the integrated AEO search strategy combined with geometric preprocessing and routing refinement. The resulting allocation configuration is presented in Figure 9. In the figure, blue segments correspond to optimized transportation paths, red stars denote selected facility sites, red squares mark demand regions, and gray polygons identify barrier structures. The obtained solution achieves a weighted objective value of 819.09.

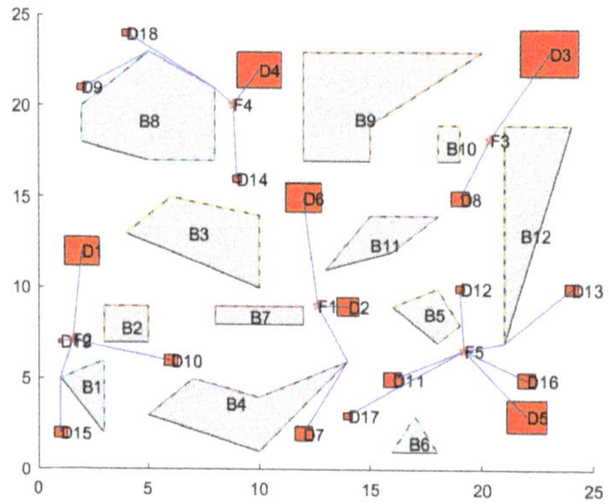

Figure 9. Multi-facility reliable emergency facility location.

Table 2 reports the capacities and spatial positions of the facilities, while Table 3 summarizes the admissible capacity intervals, with an aggregate storage level of approximately 1000. Demand quantities are sampled from the interval [30, 50] and are listed in Table 4. Facility construction costs are drawn from [300, 500], subject to an overall budget constraint of 2500. Transportation velocity varies within [2, 8], the reserve ratio is fixed at 0.5, and the AEO algorithm operates with a population size of 30 and a maximum of 200 iterations. The feasible search domain is confined to a 25 × 25 square region (see Table 5).

Table 2. Facility capacity.

	Capacity	Location
1	253.45	(12.64, 9.05)
2	260.98	(1.58, 7.1)
3	229.24	(20.36, 18.22)
4	138.6	(8.84, 20.08)
5	119.82	(19.19, 6.6)

https://doi.org/10.3390/mca31020050

Table 3. Facility capacity bound.

	Bound	Capacity
1	Upper bound	250
	Lower bound	260
2	Upper bound	250
	Lower bound	270
3	Upper bound	220
	Lower bound	230
4	Upper bound	130
	Lower bound	140
5	Upper bound	110
	Lower bound	120

Table 4. Demand volume.

	1	2	3	4
Volume	40.58	48.02	32.38	44.55
5	6	7	8	9
44.48	42.61	31.76	42.65	38.91
10	11	12	13	14
34.71	41.39	46.79	41.94	44.66
15	16	17	18	19
32.13	44.32	40.77	30.04	46.79

Table 5. Search region.

Name	Bound	Region
x	Upper bound	0
	Lower bound	25
y	Upper bound	0
	Lower bound	25

From the allocation results in Table 6, we observe that the optimal configuration involves 5 facility points serving 19 demand regions, each with a safety stock of 0.5. Considering the quantity of facility and demand, there are 19 effective allocations aligning the optimal facility locations with the demand regions. Notably, the first three allocations are as follows: (1) The first facility point allocates to the second demand point with a quantity of 48.0178, located at a distance of 1.8589 units from the demand location, resulting in a time satisfaction of 0.99484. (2) The fifth facility location allocates 46.7903 to the 12th demand point, positioned at a distance of 3.6032 units from the demand location with a time satisfaction of 0.9967. (3) The second facility location allocates 46.7888 to the 19th demand point, situated at a distance of 0.69232 units from the demand location, achieving a time satisfaction of 1.

https://doi.org/10.3390/mca31020050

Table 6. The result of facility locations and allocation.

Index	Facility Index	Demand Index	Allocation Volume	Distance	Time Satisfaction
1	1	2	48.0178	1.8589	0.99484
2	5	12	46.7903	3.6032	0.9967
3	2	19	46.7888	0.69232	1
4	4	14	44.6566	4.2853	0.97385
5	4	4	44.5494	3.2402	0.98903
6	5	5	44.4812	5.4653	0.98597
7	5	16	44.3234	3.6299	0.98682
8	3	8	42.6509	3.89	0.9541
9	1	6	42.6107	6.7813	0.96569
10	5	13	41.9379	6.3903	0.92761
11	5	11	41.388	3.9749	0.99802
12	5	17	40.7674	6.5223	0.97994
13	2	1	40.579	5.7132	0.95614
14	4	9	38.9077	8.6567	0.92468
15	2	10	34.707	4.853	1
16	3	3	32.3797	6.7662	0.88959
17	2	15	32.1309	5.4838	0.97295
18	1	7	31.7573	8.2137	0.88647
19	4	18	30.0414	6.4456	0.9516

Table 6 reveals the distribution of demand regions for each facility location. Specifically, the first facility location serves three demand regions, namely, demand regions 2, 6, and 7. The second facility location caters to four demand regions, i.e., demand regions 19, 1, 10, and 15. Meanwhile, the third facility location covers two demand regions, i.e., demand regions 8 and 3. Additionally, the fourth facility location serves four demand regions, i.e., demand regions 14, 4, 9, and 18. Lastly, the fifth facility location is allocated six demand regions, i.e., demand regions 12, 5, 16, 13, 11, and 17. The final column denotes the time satisfaction levels of the demand regions, indicating a high level of satisfaction across all regions. Specifically, there are two items with a perfect satisfaction score of 1, 15 items with a satisfaction level exceeding 0.9, and two items with a satisfaction level over 0.8. Notably, no satisfaction item falls below 0.8, reflecting the robustness and reliability of the constructed emergency facility location model and its allocation.

To further assess the performance of the proposed AEO algorithm in medium-scale instances, a comparative experiment was conducted using the Particle Swarm Optimization (PSO) algorithm under the same evaluation function and stopping criterion. The PSO parameters were set as follows: inertia weight $w = 0.72$, cognitive coefficient $c_1 = 1.49$, and social coefficient $c_2 = 1.49$.

For the five-facility and nineteen-demand-point instance in Figure 9, the computational time of AEO was 40.5016 s, yielding a weighted objective value of 819.09. In comparison, PSO required 39.161 s and obtained a best objective value of 750.6821 in Figure 10, with the corresponding facility coordinates reported above. Although the computational times of the two algorithms are comparable, AEO achieved a significantly higher objective value. Specifically, the solution obtained by AEO improves the objective value by approximately 9.1% compared to PSO. This indicates that AEO demonstrates stronger global search capability and better convergence performance in solving the nonlinear facility location model under complex polygonal barriers and reliability constraints.

https://doi.org/10.3390/mca31020050

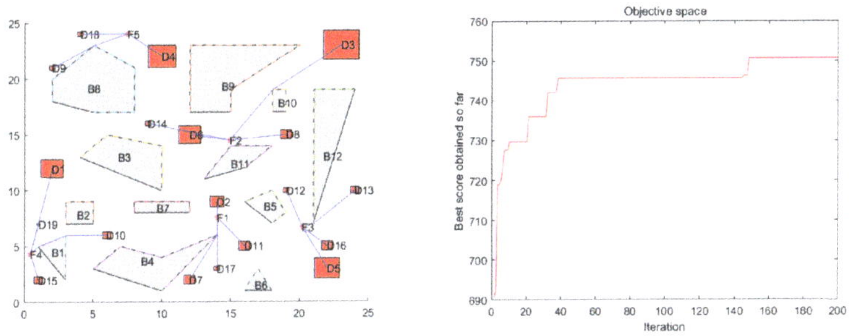

Figure 10. Comparative analysis.

Example 4. *Sensitivity analysis*

This section investigates the influence of two key parameters through sensitivity analysis.

Sensitivity of α and θ

We define the failure risk as the marginal disruption probability of location i using the equation $q_i = \alpha e^{-D_i/\theta}$, where D_i represents the distance of location j from i. Here, α denotes the probability of a disastrous event occurring at a specific source, while θ signifies the disruption propagation factor. A higher α and θ indicate a stronger disruption propagation effect. With 12 barriers and the goal of achieving maximum desired time satisfaction, we seek to determine the location and allocation scheme of 5 facility points. We employ the control variable method, setting the demand amount of each demand point in the demand regions to 40. The center coordinates and radiation radius of the square demand point are established as usual, with the location and quantity of facilities set at 200. Additionally, the carrying speed value is 5, the safety stock is 0.5, the initialized population size of 30 is for AEO, and there is a maximum of 200 iterations. The effects of parameters α and θ on satisfaction are presented in Figure 11.

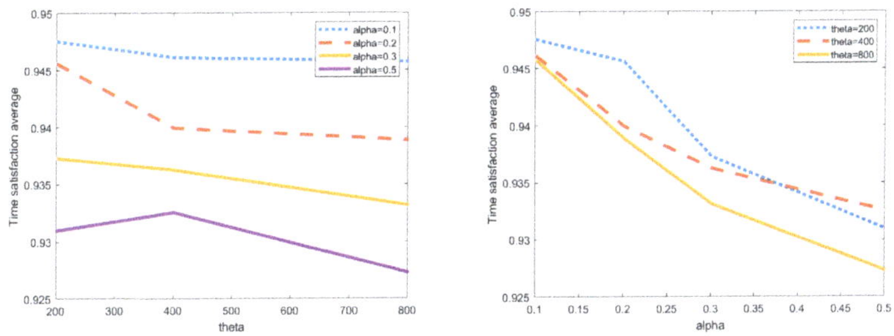

Figure 11. The influence of parameters α and θ on satisfaction.

Figure 11 illustrates the influence of the parameters α and θ on satisfaction. The range of values for α is $[0.1, 0.5]$ and for θ is $[200, 800]$. It is evident that as both α and θ increase, the average time satisfaction and the number of distributions gradually change. In Table 7, we observe specific numerical data which indicates that as the risk of failure increases, not only does the average satisfaction gradually decrease to 0.927 but there is also a gradual change in the number of distributions.

https://doi.org/10.3390/mca31020050

Table 7. Parameter analysis.

α	θ	Time Satisfaction Average	Number of Distribution
0.1	200	0.94754	21
0.1	400	0.94612	19
0.1	800	0.94573	19
0.2	200	0.94561	21
0.2	400	0.93996	20
0.2	800	0.93887	19
0.3	200	0.93731	20
0.3	400	0.93626	21
0.3	800	0.93314	19
0.5	200	0.93098	19
0.5	400	0.93254	19
0.5	800	0.92727	21

Example 5. *A practical case study of the multi-facility reliable emergency facility location model*

To further validate the model's feasibility, we conducted experiments using the actual scenario in Moroccan [28], taking into account ambulance deployment. We selected the Meknès region as the demand area, encompassing 19 *demand points labeled* $D1, D2, \cdots, D19$, *with* 10 *barriers denoted as* $B1, B2, \cdots, B10$ *randomly placed. The latitude and longitude coordinates of the Meknès demand regions are presented in Table 8, with the last column representing the number of required ambulance vehicles. The construction cost for each facility location is set at* 500$, *and the shipping speed is* 8 *km/h. Based on the demand for ambulance vehicles in the Meknès region, we have established the facility capacity for each location, randomly generated within the range of* $[200, 250]$. *Three facility points were designated, with specific demands and locations as follows, while maintaining other parameters unchanged.*

Table 8. Data of Meknès.

Prefecture	Num.	Demand Region	Latitude	Longitude	Demand
Meknès	1	Al Machouar-Stinia, Meknès	33.8915022	−5.5623057	10
	2	Boufakrane, Meknès	33.7552072	−5.4851436	30
	3	Toulal, Meknès	33.8932573	−5.5956227	45
	4	Moulay Driss Zerhoun, Meknès	34.055188	−5.525518	27
	5	Ain Jemaa, Meknès	34.026077	−5.793621	31
	6	Ain Karma-Oued Rommane, Meknès	34.0681965	−5.6511201	32
	7	Ain Orma, Meknès	33.8940376	−5.7479925	8
	8	Ait Ouallal, Meknès	33.8569498	−5.6862504	12
	9	Dar Oum Soltane, Meknès	33.9018913	−5.6442902	13
	10	Dkhissa, Meknès	33.9373089	−5.4666399	47
	11	Majjate, Meknès	33.8184108	−5.5131869	21
	12	M'haya, Meknès	33.976917	−5.249915	62
	13	Oued Jdida, Meknès	33.924289	−5.3691	35
	14	Sidi Slimane Moul Al Kifane, Meknès	33.8604919	−5.4611693	45
	15	Charqaoua, Meknès	34.1733052	−5.400277	13
	16	Mrhassiyine, Meknès	34.0045194	−5.5014005	18
	17	N'zalat Bni Amar, Meknès	34.1238486	−5.4316033	19
	18	Oualili, Meknès	34.0399646	−5.5626871	23
	19	Sidi Abdallah Al Khayat, Meknès	34.0018701	−5.3695267	26

By applying the AEO algorithm in combination with the convex hull transformation and the path optimization procedure, we obtained an optimized allocation scheme for the reliable emergency facility location problem in the Meknès case. It should be noted that this

https://doi.org/10.3390/mca31020050

case study is intended as a methodological demonstration and decision-support reference rather than a direct evaluation of the current real-world deployment.

Figure 12 illustrates the optimized allocation scenario, which yields a weighted objective value of 568.7. The optimal latitude and longitude coordinates of the three facility points are (33.78, −5.53), (34.02, −5.31), and (33.95, −5.71). Under the optimized allocation, the first facility serves four demand regions: Al Machouar-Stinia, Boufakrane, Majjate, and Sidi Slimane Moul Al Kifane. The second facility is assigned to eight demand regions: Moulay Driss Zerhoun, Dkhissa, M'haya, Oued Jdida, Charqaoua, Mrhassiyine, N'zalat Bni Amar, and Sidi Abdallah Al Khayat. The third facility covers seven demand regions: Al Toulal, Ain Jemaa, Ain Karma-Oued Rommane, Ain Orma, Ait Ouallal, Dar Oum Soltane, and Oualili. In Figure 12, the grey ellipse indicates the service scope of each facility, the blue lines represent the optimized transportation paths, the red stars denote facility locations, the small red circles mark demand regions, and the red polygons correspond to barrier areas. The results demonstrate how the proposed framework can generate a structured and spatially feasible allocation plan under realistic geographic coordinates and demand distributions.

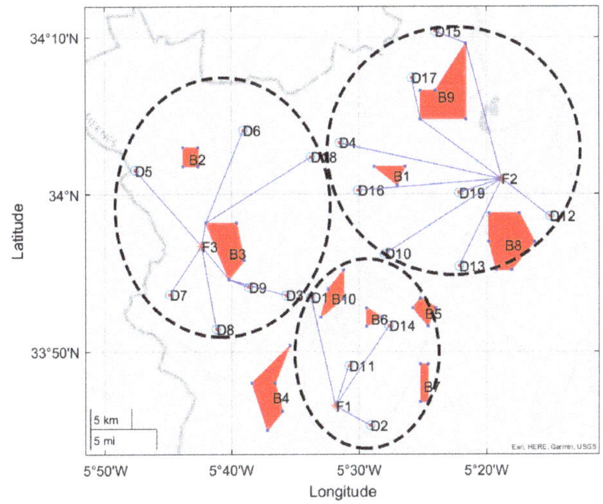

Figure 12. Multi-facility reliable emergency facility location of the case study.

5. Conclusions

This study addresses the critical gap in emergency facility location research by integrating complex polygonal barriers (convex and concave) and facility failure risks, with a focus on maximizing time satisfaction—a core requirement in emergency response. The key contributions and findings are as follows:

5.1. Key Contributions

1. Novel Model Design: A single-objective optimization model is proposed to maximize time satisfaction, avoiding biases from multi-objective weight assignment. The model considers practical constraints (capacity, cost, and safety stock) and integrates both facility failure risks and complex polygonal barriers.

2. Efficient Algorithm Framework: A three-step algorithm (convex hull → path optimization → AEO) is developed to solve the NP-hard problem. The convex hull algorithm

https://doi.org/10.3390/mca31020050

simplifies concave barriers, the path optimization algorithm finds the shortest bypass routes, and the AEO algorithm efficiently optimizes facility locations and allocation.

3. Comprehensive Validation: The model is validated through multi-scale numerical experiments (single-facility, multi-facility, and medium-scale) and a real-world case study (ambulance deployment in Morocco), demonstrating its feasibility and robustness.

5.2. Specific Findings

1. Performance: The model achieves high time satisfaction (all demand regions > 0.8, most > 0.9) and efficient resource allocation. For medium-scale scenarios (five facilities; 19 demand regions), the total facility capacity (1000) meets total demand (760) with a weighted satisfaction of 819.09.

2. Sensitivity: Increased failure risk parameters (α and θ) lead to a gradual decrease in average time satisfaction (from 0.948 to 0.927), but the model maintains stable allocation efficiency.

3. Practical Applicability: The case study in Meknès shows that the model can effectively optimize ambulance station locations, ensuring timely emergency medical response with an average satisfaction > 0.92.

5.3. Limitations and Future Work

Limitations: The model assumes that barriers are static and known in advance; future research can consider dynamic barriers (e.g., evolving disaster zones). Additionally, the model uses a fixed weighting factor α; adaptive α based on real-time risk assessment can be explored. Furthermore, facility failure is modeled through a proportional reduction in effective service capacity. This treatment does not consider spatial correlation or cascading effects among facilities. Moreover, although the convex hull transformation and path optimization procedures are computationally tractable for the tested problem scales, their computational cost may increase when the number of barriers and demand points grows substantially. In medium-scale scenarios with many obstacles, repeated line–polygon intersection checks and path sequence adjustments could lead to higher computational burden. Therefore, scalability under very large spatial instances remains a practical limitation at the current implementation stage.

Future work: It may extend the proposed framework in several directions. First, dynamic demand evolution and time-varying barriers can be incorporated to better capture the uncertainty and temporal progression of emergency scenarios. Second, stochastic demand realizations could be modeled through scenario-based simulation, enabling a more robust evaluation of system performance under different disruption intensities. Third, heterogeneous facility types with differentiated capacities, service levels, and failure probabilities may be introduced to reflect realistic emergency logistics systems. Moreover, integrating evacuation routing and congestion-aware path interactions into the model would allow for the time satisfaction measure to explicitly account for route competition and traffic dynamics. From an algorithmic perspective, hybrid metaheuristic strategies (e.g., AEO combined with local search mechanisms) and parallel acceleration techniques could further enhance computational efficiency, particularly for medium- and large-scale geographic environments.

Author Contributions: Conceptualization, M.L. and G.W.; methodology, M.L. and L.L.; software, M.L.; validation, M.L., L.L. and Z.Y.; formal analysis, M.L.; investigation, M.L. and L.L.; resources, G.W. and F.L.; data curation, M.L.; writing—original draft preparation, M.L.; writing—review and editing, G.W., L.L. and Z.Y.; visualization, M.L.; supervision, G.W.; project administration, G.W.; funding acquisition, G.W. All authors have read and agreed to the published version of the manuscript.

https://doi.org/10.3390/mca31020050

Funding: The work was partially supported by the National Natural Science Foundation of China (Project ID 42074011) and the Key Projects Deployed by the Major Scientific and Technological Mission Bureau of the Chinese Academy of Sciences (Project ID T24Y6303).

Data Availability Statement: The datasets generated during and/or analyzed during the current study are available from the corresponding author on reasonable request.

Conflicts of Interest: The authors declare that they have no conflicts of interest.

References

1. Snyder, L.V.; Daskin, M.S. Reliability models for facility location: The expected failure cost case. *Transp. Sci.* **2005**, *39*, 400–416. [CrossRef]
2. Shishebori, D.; Babadi, A.Y. Robust and reliable medical services network design under uncertain environment and system disruptions. *Transp. Res. Part E Logist. Transp. Rev.* **2015**, *77*, 268–288. [CrossRef]
3. An, Y.; Zeng, B.; Zhang, Y.; Zhao, L. Reliable p-median facility location problem: Two-stage robust models and algorithms. *Transp. Res. Part B Methodol.* **2014**, *64*, 54–72. [CrossRef]
4. Yu, D.; Gao, L.; Zhao, S. Reliable Emergency Facility Location with Disruptionand Fortification Considerations. *Oper. Res. Manag. Sci.* **2020**, *29*, 53.
5. Wang, W.; Wu, S.; Wang, S.; Zhen, L.; Qu, X. Emergency facility location problems in logistics: Status and perspectives. *Transp. Res. Part E Logist. Transp. Rev.* **2021**, *154*, 102465. [CrossRef]
6. Liu, K.; Liu, C.; Xiang, X.; Tian, Z. Testing facility location and dynamic capacity planning for pandemics with demand uncertainty. *Eur. J. Oper. Res.* **2023**, *304*, 150–168. [CrossRef]
7. Wang, M. Research of Voronoi Diagram with Barries. Master's Thesis, Dalian Maritime University, Dalian, China, 2005.
8. Niu, H.; Ji, Z.; Savvaris, A.; Tsourdos, A. Energy efficient path planning for unmanned surface vehicle in spatially-temporally variant environment. *Ocean Eng.* **2020**, *196*, 106766. [CrossRef]
9. Li, X.; McMains, S. A Voronoi diagram approach for detecting defects in 3D printed fiber-reinforced polymers from microscope images. *Comput. Vis. Media* **2023**, *9*, 41–56. [CrossRef]
10. Gao, T.; Fu, L. A new particle shifting technique for SPH methods based on Voronoi diagram and volume compensation. *Comput. Methods Appl. Mech. Eng.* **2023**, *404*, 115788. [CrossRef]
11. Caldeira, N.; Lopes, R.J.; Fernandes, D.; Araujo, D. From Optical Tracking to Tactical Performance via Voronoi diagrams: Team formation and players' roles constrain interpersonal linkages in high-level football. *Sensors* **2022**, *23*, 273. [CrossRef]
12. Katz, I.N.; Cooper, L. Facility location in the presence of forbidden regions, I: Formulation and the case of Euclidean distance with one forbidden circle. *Eur. J. Oper. Res.* **1981**, *6*, 166–173. [CrossRef]
13. Yu, D.; Gao, L.; Zhao, S. Emergency facility location-allocation problem with convex barriers. *Syst. Eng. Theory Prac.* **2019**, *5*. [CrossRef]
14. Han, X. Research on Logistics Node Location with Curved Demands Considering Polygonal Obstacles. Master's Thesis, Beijing Jiaotong University, Beijing, China, 2018.
15. Bischoff, M.; Klamroth, K. An efficient solution method for Weber problems with barriers based on genetic algorithms. *Eur. J. Oper. Res.* **2007**, *177*, 22–41. [CrossRef]
16. Bischoff, M.; Fleischmann, T.; Klamroth, K. The multi-facility location–allocation problem with polyhedral barriers. *Comput. Oper. Res.* **2009**, *36*, 1376–1392. [CrossRef]
17. Canbolat, M.S.; Wesolowsky, G.O. On the use of the Varignon frame for single facility Weber problems in the presence of convex barriers. *Eur. J. Oper. Res.* **2012**, *217*, 241–247. [CrossRef]
18. Byrne, T.; Kalcsics, J. Conditional facility location problems with continuous demand and a polygonal barrier. *Eur. J. Oper. Res.* **2022**, *296*, 22–43. [CrossRef]
19. Hong, C.; Wang, Y.; Estefen, S.F. A location-allocation model with obstacle and capacity constraints for the layout optimization of a subsea transmission network with line-shaped conduction structures. *J. Mar. Sci. Eng.* **2023**, *11*, 1171. [CrossRef]
20. Moturi, A.K.; Suiyanka, L.; Mumo, E.; Snow, R.W.; Okiro, E.A.; Macharia, P.M. Geographic accessibility to public and private health facilities in Kenya in 2021: An updated geocoded inventory and spatial analysis. *Front. Public Health* **2022**, *10*, 1002975. [CrossRef] [PubMed]
21. Liu, M.; Liu, L.; Wang, G. Sustainability-Reliable Emergency Facility Location Determination with Consideration of Complex Polygonal Barriers and the Risk of Facility Disruption. *Appl. Sci.* **2025**, *15*, 8910. [CrossRef]
22. Yun-Feng, M.; Min, Z.; Jun, Y. Definition and application of time satisfaction function in logistics facility location. *Logist. Technol.* **2005**, *9*, 26–29.
23. De Berg, M.; Cheong, O.; Van Kreveld, M.; Overmars, M. *Computational Geometry: Algorithms and Applications*; Springer: Berlin/Heidelberg, Germany, 2008. [CrossRef]

24. An, P.T.; Huyen, P.T.T.; Le, N.T. A modified Graham's convex hull algorithm for finding the connected orthogonal convex hull of a finite planar point set. *Appl. Math. Comput.* **2021**, *397*, 125889. [CrossRef]
25. Heng, P.; Sun, Y. Algorithms for convex hull finding in undirected graphical models. *Appl. Math. Comput.* **2023**, *445*, 127852. [CrossRef]
26. Zhao, W.; Wang, L.; Zhang, Z. Artificial ecosystem-based optimization: A novel nature-inspired meta-heuristic algorithm. *Neural Comput. Appl.* **2020**, *32*, 9383–9425. [CrossRef]
27. Naruei, I.; Keynia, F. A new optimization method based on COOT bird natural life model. *Expert Syst. Appl.* **2021**, *183*, 115352. [CrossRef]
28. Wang, L.; Cao, Q.; Zhang, Z.; Mirjalili, S.; Zhao, W. Artificial rabbits optimization: A new bio-inspired meta-heuristic algorithm for solving engineering optimization problems. *Eng. Appl. Artif. Intell.* **2022**, *114*, 105082. [CrossRef]

https://doi.org/10.3390/mca31020050

MDPI AG
Grosspeteranlage 5
4052 Basel
Switzerland
Tel.: +41 61 683 77 34

Mathematical and Computational Applications Editorial Office
E-mail: mca@mdpi.com
www.mdpi.com/journal/mca

www.ingramcontent.com/pod-product-compliance
Lightning Source LLC
Chambersburg PA
CBHW061618220926
51850CB00005B/537